Economic Analysis of Markets and Games

Economic Analysis of Markets and Games

Essays in Honor of Frank Hahn

edited by
Partha Dasgupta
Douglas Gale
Oliver Hart
and
Eric Maskin

The MIT Press
Cambridge, Massachusetts
London, England

Set in Times Roman by Asco Trade Typesetting Ltd., Hong Kong.
Printed and bound in the United States of America.

Library of Congress Cataloging-in-Publication Data

Economic analysis of markets and games : essays in honor of Frank Hahn
edited by Partha Dasgupta ... [et al.].
p. cm.
Includes bibliographical references and index.
ISBN 0-262-04127-8
1. Economics. I. Hahn, Frank. II. Dasgupta, Partha.
HB31.E25 1992
330—dc20 91-26107
CIP

Contents

Preface

Frank Hahn has had a long and varied career, and it is not over yet. His first publication dates from 1948, so one could say that his career has intersected six decades of economics. That is a long time by anyone's reckoning, but it was an exceptionally lively period for economic theory. Hahn was active in many of the most exciting episodes. His research interests are broad, and he has made contributions to a variety of fields: monetary theory, macroeconomics, general-equilibrium theory, the economics of information, economic dynamics, and capital theory. For all these reasons, a collection of essays that attempts to honor Hahn's work and interests will necessarily be wide-ranging.

There is another reason, however, why this collection should cover such a wide range of topics. Frank Hahn has always had a keen interest in the work of other economists, especially younger theorists. A number of the contributors were encouraged by Hahn early in their careers and their contributions reflect the breadth of his interests.

The contributors to this volume include old friends, colleagues, and young theorists whom Hahn has encouraged in recent years. Twenty-four of the contributions are grouped into three parts titled Microeconomic Foundations of Macroeconomics, Information and the Theory of Games, and Optimality and Equilibrium with Missing Markets. In each of these broad areas, the contributions represent the diversity of research on the frontier of economic theory, as well as the diversity of Frank Hahn's research and interests. The fourth part of the volume, comprising papers by Terence Gorman, Paul Samuelson, and Partha Dasgupta, is titled Miscellany.

Microeconomic Foundations of Macroeconomics

At the beginning of his career, Hahn was mainly concerned with macroeconomics. His Ph.D. dissertation (published in 1972) developed a macroeconomic theory of output and employment. It was remarkable for giving a central role to the distribution of income (in this, it anticipates the Kaldor-Passinetti theory of distribution) and for incorporating a number of recent theoretical advances, such as expected-utility theory, that were quite novel at that time in the mainstream of macroeconomic theory. Bob Solow reviews this theory in his essay "Hahn on the Share of Wages in National Income." Hahn maintained his early interest throughout the rest of his career; it is exemplified by his later work on conjectural equilibrium (1978), an attempt to put Keynesian economics on a sound general-equilibrium footing (a typically Hahnian enterprise). He also found time to comment rather negatively on other schools of macroeconomic thought.

The first part of the volume also includes Walt Heller's "Underemployment as a Coordination Problem with Savings and Inceasing Returns," which is closely related to Hahn's work on conjectural equilibrium. This paper, which is very much in the general-equilibrium tradition of which Hahn approved, deals with multiple, Pareto-ranked equilibria (a favorite Hahn theme of recent years). At the other extreme we have the information-based model of Oliver Hart and Eric Maskin in "Production Fluctuations and Fiscal Policy in an Economy with Aggregate and Idiosyncratic Shocks." Others write on savings (Starrett), unemployment (Atkinson), and wage setting (Bliss). Each of the essays has a firm microeconomic underpinning.

Information and the Theory of Games

Hahn has not yet to my knowledge published a paper on game theory, but it is neither inappropriate nor accidental that so many of the contributions to this volume deal with games, incentives, mechanism design, and the like. Hahn has been following the burgeoning game-theory literature (and commenting on it in typical Hahnian fashion) for years, and the contributors who have written on these topics are well acquainted with his views.

In the early 1960s Hahn began spending his summers in Stanford at the now-famous Institute for Mathematical Studies in the Social Sciences (IMSSS). Together with Bob Aumann and Ken Arrow, he led a series of workshops and seminars that included many of the most eminent theorists over a period of almost three decades. The IMSSS was notable for attracting the brightest young theorists, many of them just out of graduate school. (Spotting future leaders of the profession appears to have been a favorite pastime among the older members of the IMSSS.) Many of the contributors to this volume passed through that rather grueling "finishing school."

At the IMSSS, Hahn followed developments in game theory and the theory of incentives and mechanism design with interest. In the late 1970s he established his own version of the IMSSS at Cambridge University, with the help of David Newbery and Oliver Hart and with funding from the Social Science Research Council (SSRC). Among other things, the

SSRC project supported visitors to Cambridge and some young theorists who ended up staying there. Over the next ten years, David Kreps, Eric Maskin, Louis Makowski, John Geanakoplos, Heraklis Polemarchakis, Tim Kehoe, Hamid Sabourian, and Adam Brandenburger worked in Cambridge thanks to this project. Most of these contributors would have participated in another Hahnian innovation: the informal seminar dubbed the "Quaker Meeting," so called because the participants were expected to "speak when the spirit moved them." The extemporaneous debate that characterized this forum was exactly the sort of rough-and-tumble that Hahn loved. Some of the ideas contained in the essays in this part of the volume may well have been discussed, in embryonic form, in the Quaker Meeting.

Optimality and Equilibrium in Missing Markets

Hahn was always a practitioner and exponent of general-equilibrium theory. He made important contributions to pure general-equilibrium theory, notably his work on the stability of competitive equilibrium. But although he appreciated the esthetic and intellectual achievement of the Arrow-Debreu-McKenzie model, he was never satisfied with it. In particular, he could not accept the assumption of a complete set of contingent markets; he always strove to get beyond it in his own work.

In the late 1960s and the early 1970s, Hahn began to work on the problem of "missing markets." This was a natural extension of his earlier studies in monetary economics. From the first, however, he realized that the issue of missing markets had a broader significance, and he sometimes seemed to regard it as the key to understanding macroeconomics. His major contribution was his analysis of transaction costs and the study of the welfare properties of equilibria when markets are incomplete. He argued convincingly (1971a, 1973) that the welfare properties of the Arrow-Debreu-McKenzie model are lost when markets are incomplete. Subsequent work by Grossman, Hart, and others confirmed his position.

Several of the essays in the third part of this volume deal with welfare issues. Peter Hammond writes on "The Impossibility of Perfect Capital Markets." The paper by Tim Kehoe, David Levine, and Mike Woodford, "The Optimum Quantity of Money Revisited," recalls Hahn's famous review of Friedman's *Optimum Quantity of Money* (Hahn 1971b). Diamond and Mirrlees write on optimal taxation with incomplete markets.

Hahn is known above all for his contributions to monetary theory. As he never tired of saying, there is no role for money in the Arrow-Debreu model. Later research suggests this may have been an overstatement, but Hahn was substantially correct, and his own work on existence of monetary equilibrium (1965) was a theoretical milestone. Pradeep Dubey and John Geanakoplos explore a related question in their essay, "The Value of Money in a Finite-Horizon Economy: A Role for Banks."

Several of the papers treat issues of indeterminacy of equilibrium. Hahn was a pioneer in this area. His work on growth models with heterogeneous capital goods (1968) established the indeterminacy of dynamic equilibrium long before it became a fashionable topic. In recent years, he has enjoyed pointing out that simple policy prescriptions based on looking at a single equilibrium are useless if there are many equilibria. The essay by Pierre-André Chiappori and Roger Guesnerie, "The Lucas Equation, Indeterminacy, and Non-Neutrality: An Example," should be a favorite of Hahn for this reason. Another essay in this category is Andreu Mas-Colell's "Three Observations on Sunspots and Asset Redundancy."

Sometimes Hahn has gone so far as to suggest that indeterminacy provides a role for government. This is something many economists would find debatable.

The Uses of Economic Theory

The papers in parts I–III reflect Hahn's influence as an active researcher and as a "patron" of the young. But there is another important respect in which these essays reflect his influence. Hahn is a believer in the practical value of economic theory. From my days as a graduate student I remember him stressing "the difference between thinking about a problem and not thinking about it." That has always seemed to me a good justification of economic theory. But this is not a defense of ivory-tower thinking. In the last part of the book, for example, Dasgupta stresses the instrumental (practical) virtues of freedom and Gorman discusses the education of civil servants. What distinguishes Hahn's work and many of the essays in this book is that, even in the most abstract pieces, the motivation often comes from practical concerns about unemployment, savings and investment, the stability of markets, poverty, and so forth. Rigorous thinking need not be irrelevant.

Douglas Gale

References

Hahn, F. 1965. "On some problems of proving the existence of an equilibrium in a monetary economy." in *The Theory of Interest Rates*, ed. F. Hahn and F. Brechling. Macmillan.

Hahn, F. 1968. "On warranted growth paths." *Review of Economic Studies* 35: 175–184.

Hahn, F. 1971a. "Equilibrium with transaction costs." *Econometrica* 39: 417–439.

Hahn, F. 1971b. "Professor Friedman's views on money." *Economica* 38: 61–80.

Hahn, F. 1972. *The Share of Wages in National Income: An Enquiry into the Theory of Distribution.* Weidenfeld & Nicholson.

Hahn, F. 1973. "On transaction costs, inessential sequence economies and money." *Review of Economic Studies* 40: 449–461.

Hahn, F. 1978. "On non-Walrasian equilibria." *Review of Economic Studies* 45: 1–18.

I MICROECONOMIC FOUNDATIONS OF MACROECONOMICS

Hahn on the Share of Wages in National Income

Robert M. Solow

Frank Hahn materialized for me in the fall of 1956, when he and Dorothy arrived from Birmingham to spend the year at MIT. I cannot remember if it was literally a case of love at first sight. By the end of that year, however, a lifelong friendship had come into being. (I am entitled to a *little* extrapolation.) By 1956 Hahn was already recognizably the economic theorist the world knows now. When we worked together or talked economics seriously, the subject was usually general-equilibrium theory, especially multimarket dynamics. It may therefore come as a surprise to many of his friends and admirers that Hahn has an excellent claim to be the originator of the "macroeconomic theory of distribution," to have been—dare I say it?—a sort of proto-Kaldor. It came as something of an embarrassment to him too. Let us see.

The scene of the crime is the London School of Economics, where Hahn was awarded a Ph.D. in 1951; his thesis was entitled "The Share of Wages in the National Income." He recorded later that Nicholas Kaldor was his supervisor for the first three months of research, to be followed by Lionel Robbins for the rest. Hahn reports that Kaldor recalled (presumably in 1971 or 1972) having suggested to his student in 1947 that "the best approach to distribution theory is macroeconomic." It is not clear to me that so vague a statement has any cash value. Nor is it clear from our hero's reporting whether he is generously sharing priority with Kaldor or fastidiously blaming the thought on someone else. I will come back to Hahn's second thoughts later.

The only immediate publication to come out of the thesis was a mere 11-page article in *Oxford Economic Papers* in 1951 with the same title as the whole thesis. The article is essentially a reproduction of chapter 3 of the thesis, called "A Simple Model" in the original.

Chapter 1, let it be said, is a critical account of the discussion that began with Hicks's *Theory of Wages* in 1932 and ended with his "Distribution and Economic Progress: A Revised Version" in 1936, and which involved most of the important names in English-speaking economics (except for Keynes) in between.[1] The young Hahn was not very much amused by this literature. He thought that the vital transition from the partial-equilibrium analysis of a single industry facing a given demand to the general-equilibrium analysis of the income distribution produced by an interrelated system of (perhaps imperfectly competitive) markets had been fudged, except perhaps in certain special cases of dubious interest.

Chapter 2 was a discussion of Kalecki's model that makes the division of income between wages and profits primarily a matter of the "degree of monopoly" or excess of price over prime cost (or, more accurately, of the elasticity of demand for the representative firm).[2] Hahn does not care for this story at all; indeed, he takes it apart rather unsparingly for its looseness of definition and its elision of essential assumptions.

Having made his bow—if that is the word—to the literature, Hahn turns to his own entirely original contribution. I propose to devote the whole of this essay to a commentary on the model of Hahn's chapter 3 and on his discussion of it some 20 years later.

My purpose is not particularly doctrine-historical. It would not be very enlightening to trace the literature that may have influenced Hahn. My purpose is celebratory and—in a loose way—methodological. My own belief is that economics, as an applied science, is about approximations, not about theorems. So I have a deep interest in the aggregative use of microeconomic ideas. I wish everyone had. To look back at this early effort by Hahn, especially Hahn, seems therefore intrinsically interesting.

A Simple Model

The description in the thesis is considerably less explicit in laying out assumptions and deriving conclusions than the style of middle-period or late-period Hahn would lead one to expect. So I shall begin by reproducing the model, including details that its author omitted (perhaps in a gesture to the expository style of the time).

The "simple model" contains three novelties. To begin with, it is a macroeconomic model—a one-sector general-equilibrium model—whose market form is straightforward imperfect competition. Nowadays the fashion[3] is to start one turtle further down, if you remember the joke, with n symetrically producible goods and a utility function that makes them imperfectly but symmetrically substitutable for each other, and then to deduce the typical firm's perceived demand curve. Hahn cannot know about that finesse. He just postulates a common demand curve whose shifts are assumed to preserve the elasticity at each price. Thus $x = AD(\pi)$ in his notation, where π is the nominal price of goods, x is output or sales, and A

is a shift parameter. (I say this a little more confidently than I ought, because the thesis does not always say whether it means "real" or "nominal.")

When I describe this as a novelty I mean only that Hahn's procedure makes a break with the immediately preceding literature on the functional distribution of income. Imperfect competition was more discussed then than it was later, but usually in a partial-equilibrium way, not as a feature of a complete model.

The second novelty is more novel. The representative firm maximizes something more complicated than profit. Hahn has in mind an entrepreneurial utility function that is increasing in profit and decreasing in the scale of output. Almost at once he assumes (with the usual apology) that the marginal utility of (profit) income is constant, so that the firm is actual-maximizing $P - V(x)$, where P is profit and $V(x)$ is an increasing convex function. To motivate this departure from routine, Hahn describes V itself as a "general disutility of production." He seems to have in mind that larger real output entails a larger beginning-of-period commitment of funds to the firm and thus a larger exposure to the risk of loss or bankruptcy. (There is a kinship to Kalecki's principle of increasing risk."[4] This idea may have been in the air around the London School of Economics at the time.) One could imagine a more explicit deduction from the maximization of expected (quadratic) utility, which case the objective would be, say

$$P - aP^2 - aV(x),$$

where now P is the mean value of profit and V, its variance, is assumed to increase with x. The refinement does not seem to be worth very much, so I shall keep to Hahn's assumption with the the addition of a parameter to measure the importance of this risk-aversion factor; thus, the firm maximizes $P - \lambda V(x)$.

The third novelty, the proto-Kaldorian novelty, is the explicit assumption that aggregate saving depends on the division of aggregate income between wages and profits. These are the only two sources of income considered, and the natural presumption is maintained: aggregate saving from any given aggregate income is less the greater the wage share. This effect is taken to be definite, though small; it diminishes as the wage share rises.

The last building block of the model is the demand for investment. This is discussed with some richness of detail, for a 12-page chapter, so I shall describe it accurately. Let the firm's current output, a near-normal output for its current stock of capital, be x_0. Investment is assumed—rather casually—to be insensitive to the interest rate. Most economists would have agreed *circa* 1950; I guess that Hahn would be less casual today, even for short-run purposes. As x increases from x_0, investment increases more than proportionally. Thus, for $x > x_0$ we can say $I = xi(x)$ with $i(\cdot)$ an increasing function. This superproportionality is meant as a sort of static moral equivalent to the acceleration principle. For $x < x_0$, on the other hand, only replacement and autonomous investment occur, and these may be treated as more or less independent of current output. Thus, $I = x_0 i(x_0)$ for $x < x_0$.

There is neither taxation nor public expenditure in this model, so that equilibrium in the goods market requires that Saving = Investment. Hahn's description of consumption-saving behavior would naturally be formalized to say that $S = s(w)x$, where w is the share of the wage bill in the value of output. (He suggests that the marginal propensity to consume is approximately invariant to income as a matter of fact, and that the marginal-and-average propensity to consume is an increasing concave function of w. Thus, $s(w)$ is decreasing and convex.) The equation of Saving and Investment yields $s(w) = i(x)$ for $x > x_0$ and $s(w)x$ = constant for $x > x_0$. When plotted in the (x,w) plane as an aggregate demand curve (not the conventional one, of course, but a locus of (x,w) pairs that make $C + I = x$), this has a peculiar shape. For $x > x_0$, $dx/dw < 0$; for $x < x_0$, $dx/dw > 0$. In the first case, higher output means a higher ratio of investment to output and requires a higher ratio of saving to output, and thus a lower wage share. In the second case, higher output leaves aggregate investment unchanged and requires unchanged saving; thus, a higher wage share is needed to offset the higher saving from higher output itself. This second phase seems a little farfetched; nor does one observe a shrinking wage share as income falls below normal in the business cycle. Hahn does not actually make much of the rising branch of the aggregate demand curve, anyway.

I have laid out the "Kaldorian" part of the model first. Now I return to the supply side of the model, which is distinctly non-Kaldorian. As already suggested, the typical firm is engaged in imperfect competition. Hahn has been careful to assume that the typical firm's demand curve undergoes only isoelastic shifts, i.e., $\pi = d(x/A)$, where d is D^{-1}. He postulates constant nominal wages and thus constant costs ($= cx$, say) as well. The firm's profit is $P(x) = xd(x/A) - cx$, but it maximizes $P(x) - \lambda V(x)$. Thus,

$$d(x/A) + d'(X/A)X/A = c + \lambda V'(x).$$

From this condition it follows easily that the comparative-static derivative $dx/dA > 0$. (Imagine the condition satisfied, and insert a larger value of A. The LHS is just marginal revenue, a decreasing function of its argument, so it is now larger than the RHS. If x were to decrease, the RHS would be smaller and the LHS would be larger still. So x must increase to preserve equality, though x/A must fall.)

Moreover, $P(x)/x$, the profit margin per unit of output, is equal to $d(x/A) - c$. We have just seen that x/A decreases when x increases. So $P(x)/x$ increases when A increases. Thus, P/x and x increase and decrease together when aggregate demand shifts, as parametrized by A.

The share of profits in output is

$$\frac{P}{x\pi} = 1 - \frac{c}{\pi},$$

so the wage share is

$$w = \frac{c}{\pi} = \frac{c}{d(x/A)}.$$

Thus, w falls and rises as A rises and falls. An equivalent statement is that w and x move inversely under demand shocks. This is Hahn's "aggregate supply curve." It is not the conventional one at all, but it is entitled to the name. It derives entirely—well, almost entirely—from the supply side of the economy. Under these assumptions, which could obviously be relaxed a little, firms will produce more output the higher the profit margin, and only when the profit margin is higher. Notice that this is not an aggregation of individual supply curves; these firms are imperfect competitors and do not have supply curves. The correspondence between P/x (or w) and x is parametric in character. The point is that firms will produce x only when they can sell x; and sales of exactly x require that the share of wages be exactly w, higher x requiring smaller w.

Figure 1, copied from Hahn, brings the aggregate supply and demand curves together. Their intersection generates a pair of values x and w that satisfy both demand and supply conditions: when the share of wages is w, consumption and investment add up to x; when the profit share is $1 - w$, firms are just prepared to produce x.

Hahn gives an informal argument to show that an intersection like that in Figure 1 is stable. In effect it goes like this: at a higher value of w, firms would wish to produce the corresponding output along AS; since this com-

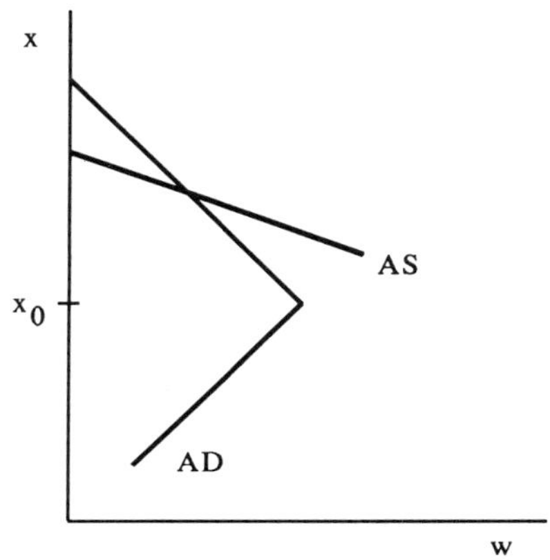

Figure 1
Aggregate demand and aggregate supply in the Hahn model.

bination lies to the right of *AD*, there will be excess demand for goods and the price level will rise. Since the nominal wage is fixed, the real wage and with it *w* will fall. Similarly for downward displacements of *w*.

This is not only informal but pretty special too. As so often happens, the dynamic story sharpens certain queries about the underlying model. To give only two examples in this context:

(a) The stability argument brings to the surface the previously more or less submerged constancy of the nominal wage, which looks less innocuous as soon as the price of goods starts to move.

(b) If, as is certainly plausible, investment were also a function of the profit margin (i.e., of *w*), then the behavior of aggregate demand would be more delicate.

A Closer Look

The thesis does a certain amount of comparative statics with this model by informally shifting the *AS* and *AD* demand curves. I want to be more nearly exhaustive, so I shall begin by formulating the model more explicitly. In this I am surely doing what the mature Hahn would do.

Since I am not going to pursue business-cycle topics, I shall forget the upward-sloping portion of the *AD* curve. Thus, the first equation of the model is just

$$s(w) = i(x) + e. \tag{1}$$

This differs from what I wrote before only in the addition of a parameter, e, to represent exogenous shocks to investment (or saving, for that matter). It should be noticed that in this form e is a shock to the investment *quota*, the ratio of investment to output; this is of no importance given the use I shall make of the model.

Next I want to make a minor change in Hahn's original specification of the entrepreneurial utility function. In the expression $P - \lambda V(x)$, V is supposed to represent uncertainty or the "general disutility of production" and has to do with the unwillingness to commit funds to production. In that case the argument of V is more properly total cost, cx, rather than output, x. This is an empty distinction for the thesis, since it does not ask about the consequences of variations in c. I want to do so, so I shall write $V(cx)$. Then the typical firm's utility maximization leads to

$$d(x/A) + d'(X/A)x/A = c(1 + \lambda V'(cx)).$$

The LHS is of course the marginal-revenue function, which I shall naturally take to be downward-sloping. So it has an inverse function, to be designated $r(\cdot)$. In the notation already established, $x/A = D(\pi)$ and $\pi = c/w$. The second equation of the model can therefore be written as

$$D(c/w) = r[c(1 + \lambda V'(cx))]. \tag{2}$$

Equations (1) and (2), taken as determining w and x as functions of e, c, and λ, form precisely the simple model illustrated in figure 1 above. One can proceed to do comparative statics with each of the parameters. Total differentiation leads to the equations of variation

$$\begin{bmatrix} S' & -i' \\ -D'c/w^2 & -\lambda c^2 r' V'' \end{bmatrix} \begin{pmatrix} dw \\ dx \end{pmatrix} = \begin{pmatrix} de \\ cr'V'\,d\lambda + \left[r'(1 + \lambda V' + cx\lambda V'') - \frac{1}{w} D' \right] dc \end{pmatrix}.$$

The sign pattern of the determinant Δ is

$$\begin{pmatrix} - & - \\ + & + \end{pmatrix},$$

but it can easily be checked that the "stable" configuration of the diagram, with AS flatter than AD, is equivalent to the determinant being negative. Under that assumption, straightforward calculation gives the following comparative-static derivatives:

$$\frac{\partial w}{\partial e} = \Delta^{-1} \begin{vmatrix} 1 & -i' \\ 0 & -\lambda c^2 r' V'' \end{vmatrix} < 0, \tag{3a}$$

$$\frac{\partial x}{\partial e} = \Delta^{-1} \begin{vmatrix} s' & 1 \\ -D'c/w^2 & 0 \end{vmatrix} > 0, \tag{3b}$$

$$\frac{\partial w}{\partial \lambda} = \Delta^{-1} \begin{vmatrix} 0 & -i' \\ cr'V' & -\lambda c^2 r' V'' \end{vmatrix} > 0, \tag{3c}$$

$$\frac{\partial x}{\partial \lambda} = \Delta^{-1} \begin{vmatrix} s' & 0 \\ -D'c/w^2 & cr'V' \end{vmatrix} < 0. \tag{3d}$$

These derivatives are worth a comment. Inside (3b) is hidden a multiplier formula; it says that an exogenous increment to investment causes output to increase by a multiple equal to (essentially) the reciprocal of the marginal propensity to save minus the marginal propensity to invest. The qualification arises only because s is given as a function of w and has to be translated into the proper dimension. The same increment to investment-demand must lead to a lower wage share in order to elicit the additional saving. It is intuitive that a greater "general disutility of production" should reduce equilibrium production. In turn, this reduces investment, and the wage share must rise to choke off the unneeded saving.

The cost parameter c requires a word of explanation. If labor were the only input to production, c would be equal to Wn, where W is the nominal wage and n is the constant labor requirement per unit of output. Units could be chosen so that $n = 1$, and then c would be just the nominal wage. In that literal interpretation, however, "investment" makes no practical sense. If capital and labor were both required for production, but with labor the only variable input in the short run, constant returns to scale would imply increasing short-run unit cost, so c would be an increasing function of x. The interpetation that was pretty clearly in Hahn's mind is that there are fixed proportions in the short run. Then as long as output falls short of "capacity" (which must exceed x_0) and user costs are negligible, the labor-only version is effectively valid. Varying c is like varying W. That seems to be the correct spirit.

There remains a gray area, however. The coefficient of dc in the RHS of the equations of variation is the difference between two negative quantities; thus, it is ambiguous in sign. This, in turn, reflects the fact that both sides of (2) are decreasing in c. Without resolving the ambiguity, one does not know which way AS shifts when c varies. The direction in which this cookie crumbles is determined in part by the curvature of the demand curve. I observe that, for any constant-elasticity demand curve, AS shifts down when c increases. If we take that for the "normal" case, then

$$dx/dc < 0, \tag{3e}$$

$$dw/dc > 0; \tag{3f}$$

however, it should be remembered that these could go the other way under reasonable assumptions. In the thesis, Hahn notes the ambiguity. His very brief discussion invokes the elasticity of substitution of an unspecified production function. This would surely matter in a more detailed model, as the later Hahn would insist.

The economics of this difficulty calls attention to a weakness in this sort of model. Think of c as standing for the nominal wage. We are accustomed to the notion that a change in c might push the share of wages in either direction. (Hence Hahn's reference to the elasticity of substitution.) If the wage share is to rise, however, the saving rate will fall and the necessary cutback in the investment quota requires a fall in output. The case that the wage share falls is analogous. Most of us—including, I suspect, the later Hahn—think of distributive shares as the resultant of a number of more fundamental events, and thus as a poor candidate to be the central concept of a theory. The point is reinforced by (3c): one is not too happy with the thought that changes in the weight of entrepreneurial risk aversion have direct and unambiguous consequences for relative shares. But that is proto-Kaldorism for you.

In this context it is natural to ask what effect a change in the degree of monopoly (i.e., in the elasticity of demand) would have. Hahn gives the answer: a lower elasticity of demand goes with lower output and a higher wage share. He does not comment on the apparent paradox here: an event that would normally be understood to strengthen the firm's hand actually reduces the share of profits. The reason, once again, is that the lower output reduces the investment quota and the higher wage share is required to induce the necessary fall in the saving rate. There might even be a mechanism for this: investment down, induced "recession," accompanying fall in profit share. But that lies outside this model, as Hahn would be the first to insist. Perhaps if we really believed that aggregate demand is highly sensitive to distributive shares we would find this story less odd-sounding. All this points up the truth and importance of a point Hahn makes very forcefully in his 1972 preface to the published thesis: factor shares may be sociologically salient facts, but that does not make them natural players on the stage of an economic model.

Commentary I

I now want to stand back and make a few general comments on this particular model. (The later Hahn will have his chance in a later section of this paper.)

The first thing to say is that it is genuinely a determinate general-equilibrium model. (But see a qualification below.) It determines w and x, aggregate output and its distribution between wages and profits, as well as the price of goods. It will be remembered that Kaldor's own paper on this subject[5] is less complete, less "Keynesian" one might say. It reduces, in effect, to equation (1) alone, and adds the bald assertion that there is a unique level of output such that at higher levels prices rise faster than wages and the wage share falls, whereas at lower levels wages fall more slowly (or rise faster) than prices and the wage share rises. Since the demand for goods rises and falls with the wage share, this level of output is an attractor. (Is it the "natural" level of output?) The Hahn model has a theory of output determination, and an imperfectly competitive one at that.

This theory of output rests on a rigid nominal wage. Indeed, if $s(w)$ is assumed to be independent of w and if the perceived elasticity of demand goes to infinity, the model boils down to something very like the 45°-line Keynesian cross supplemented by the usual elementary supply side. The only difference is that rising short-run marginal cost stems from entrepreneurial risk aversion and not from diminishing returns to labor.

It is also a real theory. There is no monetary mechanism at all. None is urgently needed, because the nominal wage is given and because the interest rate is assumed to have a negligible effect on investment. This characteristic extends to the whole thesis, of which I am discussing only a tiny fraction. The spirit of the time holds sway.

Notice one peculiarity. The absence of the demand-shift parameter A from (1) and (2) implies that the equilibrium level of output is independent of the position of the typical firm's perceived demand curve. That is not quite the right way to put it, however. Since $x = AD(c/w)$, A is actually determined by the model. It cannot be arbitrary, because it is pinned down by an adding-up condition. If a parameter like A is to be allowed to move the demand curve isoelastically, then it must be allowed to affect something else in the model. One-good general-equilibrium models have to be formulated with some care.

This point is worth elucidating. The model of the household is not derived from explicit utility maximization. If it were, then of course all income would have to be accounted for; what households do not spend, they save. Any parameter, like A, that changes x for given w must also generate an offsetting change in s, given w. We would all get this straight automatically now; indeed, Hahn and I use a similar but more elaborate construction—but not focused on factor shares—in our current joint work. The model of 1951 ignores this point, but the algebra compensates by "determining" A.

As things stand, the investment quota $i(x)$ depends only on the level of output. Thus, any event that leads to a lower equilibrium price π and thus to higher output must generate increased investment regardless of profitability. That suggests making investment an increasing function of A itself; favorable shifts of demand ought to work themselves out in higher investment, higher output, and a higher price. So write $I = i(x,A)x$. Then a higher value of A shifts the AD curve to the left: at any given x, higher investment will require additional savings and thus a lower wage share. (I am pretending that A can be varied independently, which is not so, to give the flavor of a monetary model in which it could be.) It can be seen from the figure that this amendment to the model produces the desired result. Higher A generates higher x and lower w, therefore higher $\pi = c/w$.

I have emphasized, in praise of this analysis, that it is a complete short-run macro-model. It determines the level of output and therefore, if implicitly, the level of employment. For instance, we could, as was noted above, treat the wage bill as the only prime cost and assume the labor requirement per unit of output to be the constant n, so that employment is nx and c is simply Wn. All the model has to say about the labor market is that W is constant. There was a time when that assumption would have been replaced by some sort of Phillips curve in real or nominal wages. One would hardly contemplate that amendment without introducing a rudimentary monetary sector. Anyway, nowadays the preferred treatment of the labor market would be different.

One simple way of patching the model, more or less consistent with efficiency-wage theory or any of several insider-outsider models, would be to make W (or $W/\pi = w/n$) an increasing function of employment or just of x itself. Suppose $Wn = g(x)$, for example. Then (2) becomes

$$D(g(x)/w) = r[g(x)(1 + V(xg(x))]. \tag{2'}$$

It is straightforward to check that (2′) defines a downward- sloping curve, as in (2), only steeper. Along the AS curve, an increment to x will correspond to a higher MC because the nominal wage, as well as the normal risk premium, will be higher. Thus, the increment to x will generate a larger increment to π than it would have if the wage were rigid, and thus a larger fall in w. This extra lift to aggregate demand makes the model less stable. Otherwise the structure of the model is much as it was, only a bit more contemporary.

With the few changes I have suggested, we have a working model with reasonable properties. Its distinguishing feature is that it accommodates fluctuations of investment, as Hahn says, by "explicitly postulat[ing] that the burden of adjustment will fall on the share of wages and not the rate of interest." The later Hahn might not wish to do just that, but he can look back and say that if it were to be done, this was an intelligent way to do it.

Second Thoughts

The whole thesis was published,[6] essentially unchanged, in 1972—more than 20 years after it was written—with a new preface by the middle-period Hahn. What does he think of his handiwork?

It is striking that he pays no attention to the details of his thesis. There is much more of it than I have mentioned here, much of it still fresh and interesting. But Hahn gives the impression that he cannot be bothered. Not that he dislikes it. To the contrary, although there are some things he would wish to do differently, on the whole he approves of the earlier work. This is not surprising, partly because it is a good thesis and partly because star economic theorists usually like what they see when they read what they wrote. Self-doubt is not much to be found among the successful.

The preface is really about something altogether different. In the intervening years, some of Hahn's most eminent colleagues at Cambridge had come to regard social-class differences in savings propensities as a central stylized fact and to believe that they could somehow use it as a stick with which to beat "neo-classical" economic theory. The form in which the beating was to be administered was the development of a theory of interest or profit that was entirely independent of technology. (The motive for this was presumably the belief that the linking of capitalists' income with the marginal productivity of something or other could be taken as the major step in an apologia for the distribution of income in a capitalist economy. Hahn is quite properly scornful of every link in this argument.) So here is the author of what may be the first decent theory of distribution built explicitly on saving-rate differences, who happens also to be (a) an eminent but never naive neo-classical economist, within the meaning of the act, (b) a person who neither admires the distribution of income in developed capitalist economies nor believes that anything in neo-classical economics provides the slightest ethical justification for it, and (c) a professor at Cambridge. He knows, indeed he has shown by example, that there is no conflict between paying attention to differences in savings propensities and paying attention to productivity considerations.

The preface dismisses this claptrap (Hahn's word) forthrightly. Hahn points out that rigorous theory does not usually classify agents according to social class or make much of the distinction if it does. This may be a serious deficiency in practice, if social class matters for supply or demand, but it has nothing to do with the logic of economic theory. He then describes succinctly what it means to find an equilibrium vector of input prices and quantities, emphasizing the ahistorical character of the construction. The only problem for a reader today is to imagine that this once needed to be said to famous economists in one of the world's centers of learning.

About his youthful effort, Hahn insists that his main concern in 1950 had been with disequilibrium anyway. There is truth in that. The bulk of the thesis, after the first few chapters, is given over to sequence analysis. But I leave it aside because I have wanted to emphasize the basic macromodel, and that is a piece of temporary equilibrium theory. The middle-period Hahn wishes that he had been less aggregative: "... there is too much in the book which relies on the 'representative firm' and occasionally on aggregate production functions. I now believe this to be a vital flaw.

It may well be that it is an illusion to hold the view that there are any macroeconomic shortcuts." Carried to its logical end, this would probably entail abandoning the very idea of a theory of distributive shares. Building that quantity up from its constituents is not a serious practical pursuit for the theorist. Assumptions that would make it so would probably also make rigorous macroeconomics possible. Absent those assumptions, Hahn seems to hold out only the prospect of an austere theory that does not speak directly to the national income and product accounts. I find no fault with his analysis; but I hold to a different aesthetic.

Commentary II

I have left that last sentence standing so that I can now point out that it is a dodge. The doctrine that there is no point arguing about tastes provides a temptation to classify differences of opinion as aesthetic because one is relieved of the necessity to defend one's own views seriously. (I once said to Ronald Dworkin that I found gross income differences "unaesthetic." He asked if I didn't mean "immoral." I gulped.) The truth is that I resist the 1972 Hahn's rejection of loosely aggregative economics, and I would defend the approach of the younger Hahn even against his maturer self.

The later Hahn says: "On purely theoretical grounds there is nothing to be said [in favor of an aggregative version of neo-classical models]. The view that nonetheless it 'may work in practice' sounds a little bogus and in any case the onus of proof is on those who maintain this. I am glad to see that I did not believe this argument in 1951 and sorry to see that I nonetheless every so often slipped into the aggregative version of the neo-classical model."

That is certainly a legitimate stance. I do not think it is the only legitimate stance. I try out the following alternative on my beloved and admired friend. A model is a logically consistent representation of a possible economy (or part of an economy). Apart from purely technical amusement, which is not to be sneezed at, a model becomes interesting if it can defensibly be said to be an adequate representation of some real economy. "Adequate" does not mean perfect or nearly perfect; standards of adequacy are discussable, and a model may be adequate for some purposes and not for others. This means, I suspect, that it is not at all "bogus" to say of a model that it works pretty well in practice even if in some or many ways it is transparently "unrealistic" or theoretically lacking. It is a risky defense because its use suggests that one does not have any good idea of the circumstances in which it works, or whether any particular test of its working is stacked in the model's favor. But that is not bogus.

There are two ways in which it can be checked if a model "works reasonably well." One is to see if the elementary assumptions of the model correspond approximately to the facts. They may still be combined in fruitless ways. (That is, some nonelementary assumptions—e.g., "all markets clear" or "there is excess supply of labor"—may be inappropriate.) But it is surely better that the building blocks be realistic than not. The other and more interesting way is to take seriously the point long emphasized by Paul Samuelson. The main empirical implication of a model is its comparative-static properties—in this case, the inequalities (3a)–(3f). That is the sort of "prediction" a laboratory science finds it easier to check than we ever can. The model "works reasonably well" to the extent that those inequalities seem to hold in data, to the extent that the relative size of the comparative-static derivatives matches up with what we can guess about the basic parameters, and to the extent that the basic parameters enter in an empirically plausible way.

We now know, as the young Hahn did not, how to construct a representative-firm model of imperfect competition as a "true" aggregation of an economy with n imperfectly but symmetrically substitutable goods. Hahn and I have used that device in our joint work. I suppose that lends a little additional interest to the model of chapter 3 of the 1951 thesis. But only a little, I would say. In my view it would be much more compelling to be able to produce evidence that all or most of the comparative-static properties of (3) hold for five- or ten-year averages of the modern British economy.

Of course there may be other inoffensive but different models that iead to the qualitative results of (3). Then reasonable people can continue the argument. They can find places where the alternative models have different implications and consider the weight of the evidence. They can debate the factual plausibility of assumptions. They can, in short, do all the things that Frank Hahn does superbly well in addition to the one thing he likes to pretend to emphasize.

Notes

1. Hicks' famous book was published by Macmillan. The article appeared in *Review of Economic Studies* 4 (1936): 1–12, and was republished with the second edition of *Theory of*

Wages in 1963. Articles by Friedman, Hicks, Kahn, Lerner, Machlup, Meade, Robinson, Sweezy, and Tarshis appeared in *Review of Economic Studies* in the years 1933–1936.

2. Kalecki's article "The Determinants of Distribution of the National Income" appeared in *Econometrica* 6 (1938): 97–112, and was reprinted in *Essays in the Theory of Economic Fluctuations* (Allen & Unwin, 1939).

3. The origin is A. K. Dixit and J. E. Stiglitz, "Monopolistic Competition and Optimum Product Diversity," *American Economic Review* 67 (1977): 297–308.

4. See "The Principle of Increasing Risk," *Economica* N.S. 4 (1937): 440–447, reprinted in the volume cited in note 2.

5. "Alternative Theories of Distribution," *Review of Economic Studies* 23 (1955–56).

6. *The Share of Wages in the National Income* (Weidenfeld and Nicolson, 1972).

Nominal-Wage Setting and the Theory of Games

Christopher Bliss

Keynes believed that the fact that "wage bargains" (as he put it) are fixed in nominal terms makes an essential and critical difference to the behavior of a monetary economy. The point was taken up by Joan Robinson, who often invoked the idea, and formed the basis of the Friedman-Phelps supply function of labor (Phelps 1970) and, with staggered wage contracts, of the efficacy of monetary policy for stabilization in the models of Fischer (1977) and Taylor (1979).

Thus Keynes' idea that money-wage setting makes an essential difference is echoed in contemporary macroeconomic theory. The lines along which the argument proceeds, however, have developed radically. In current macroeconomic models the coordination problem of wage setting, which worried Keynes, plays no central role. Workers may set the wages at which they are willing to work in imperfect knowledge of the price level, but they do not need to consider what other workers will ask for. Indeed, the joint wage setting of different groups of workers will be ideally coordinated if they all have rational expectations about prices.

The trend of the theory has also been toward modeling real-wage setting. Among the many possibilities are: trade-union-based models (Macdonald and Solow 1981) and insider-outsider models (Lindbeck and Snower 1986). These latter models, however, take the argument away from nominal-wage setting and reinforce a consensus according to which Keynes' original idea is valid only for transitory periods during which nominal wages are adjusted to take new information into account.

Outside the mainstream of the literature, the coordination problem has enjoyed a certain revival. Blanchard and Fircher (1989, p. 373) note that "this problem of coordination among price-setters and thus of *nominal rigidities* is an old, though often vague, theme in the Keynesian literature; recent work has shown more precisely its structure as well as its limitations." The work in question typically involves the modeling of wage and price setting in imperfect competition, which makes the agents large enough for their actions to have macroeconomic effects. Such models also break out of the extreme aggregation of labor and output markets characteristic of models designed to illuminate particular macroeconomic ideas but less suitable for these questions. Examples of the imperfect-competition approach include Blanchard and Kiyotaki 1987 (which is exposited in section 8.1 of Blanchard and Fischer 1989) and Hart 1982.

To say that the coordination problem as envisioned by Keynes is important is not to claim that going back to Keynes is a fruitful way of sorting it out. Even if one agrees with Frank Hahn when he writes "... Keynes had no real grasp of formal economic theorizing (and also disliked it), and he consequently left many gaping holes in his theory. I nonetheless hold that his insights were several orders more profound and realistic than those of his recent critics." (1982, pp. x–xi), it remains the case that Keynes' treatment of wage setting is incomplete and far from clear.

In Keynes' discussion, issues having to do exclusively with real-wage setting are included in the discussion of money-wage settlement. Workers apparently care about their relative success in the wage-fixing process, but why is not well explained. It is even suggested that wage bargaining may be influenced by workers' intuitive comprehension of the futility of trying to increase the real money supply by an all-round cutting of nominal wages. Basic game theory teaches us that a demonstration that a scramble for employment via cut-throat wage-reducing competition would be collectively futile, even if correct, is not the same as the implication that it will not occur.

The present paper will proceed in a different direction, to see how far game theory can elucidate these issues. One point made by Keynes does seem compelling, however, and it explains why game theory may be an appropriate tool with which to analyze wage setting.

Keynes was skeptical about how far nominal-wage cutting would help solve the problem of unemployment. This is mainly because he believed that a general fall in prices would accompany a wage-cutting episode and that this would greatly moderate the employment-expanding effects. If that might only imply that nominal wages need to fall greatly to have the desired effect, Keynes noted what in modern terminology would be called a coordination problem: Workers may be unwilling to cut their wage demands, even when there is unemployment, for fear that other workers will not do the same.

One advantage of using game theory to attack this problem is that we can set aside the issue of whether rational expectations concerning future values of the model variables resolve it. If they do it will be because rational expectations must be common expectations and their communality will automatically coordinate individual decisions. Should this define the key that unlocks the door, which I think it does not, then our game theory will arrive at the same conclusion.

1 Wage Setting by Perfectly Substitutable Workers

Suppose that all workers provide essentially the same labor service, so that the work of one may be perfectly substituted for the work of another. I relax that assumption later. Imagine that individual workers, or groups of workers, advertise or post the wage rate at which they are willing to accept employment. Production is carried out by one large firm, which, however, acts competitively. The firm offers work to all or some of the workers.

One can imagine a labor market that operates with such efficiency that employment will go first to workers asking for lower wages. Suppose further that these workers will be paid the low wages they have demanded. This specification of how the labor market operates is not realistic. Usually all workers who get employed are employed at the same wage rate. Trade unions partly account for the absence of wage discrimination between workers according to the level of wage demanded. One could interpret wage differentials as differential net advantages, as would apply were various workers employed at the same wage rate to negotiate different detailed terms. On that interpretation, the application of the model would be severely limited.

Perhaps the firm is not really one productive unit but rather is an aggregate of the economy's production. Then it would be more natural to allow employers in aggregate to discriminate between workers according to the different wages demanded. Even so, it is not realistic to suppose that each firm employs only one worker and that for some reason more productive firms are allowed to take their pick of the labor on offer first. How much the unreality matters can be assessed only when we see what kind of equilibrium will emerge and whether a wide dispersion of wage rates among the employed will be a typical outcome. Later I consider a different specification in which the work of different groups of workers are partly complements for the work of other groups, rather than perfect substitutes as here.

Let there be N workers, who each set a nominal wage τ at which they are willing to accept employment up to their maximum supply, one unit for each worker. The firm treats its cost of labor as the maximum wage at which it buys labor. In other words, provided that the firm is buying labor from all workers with a wage demand not greater than $\tau^{\max}$, then $\tau^{\max}$ becomes the firm's cost of labor, and the fact that it pays less than $\tau^{\max}$ to most of its workers gives it intra-marginal rent.

Let the firm employ labor Λ in total and produce $\omega = f(\Lambda,\sigma)$, where σ is a random variable showing the effects of supply shocks. Total product is equal to aggregate demand:

$$\omega = d(\omega,\pi,\rho,\delta), \tag{1}$$

where π is the nominal price of output, ρ is the rate of interest, and δ is a random variable incorporating demand shocks. The presence of π as an argument of $d(\ )$ shows that something like a real balance effect operates.

The formulation (1) ignores the influence of income distribution on demand, but this is only for the sake of simplicity. If all workers demanding a wage lower than $\tau^{\max}$ lower their wage demands, slightly, there will be a shift from wage income to profit income, with no effect on the demand for labor and no effect on aggregate demand. This is not realistic, but a simple model serves my present purpose.

As the firm acts competitively, employment Λ satisfies

$$\pi \cdot f_1(\Lambda,\sigma) = \tau^{\max}, \tag{2}$$

where the subscript 1 denotes the marginal product of the first argument of $F(\ )$, labor. Because the amount of labor that the firm can buy is implicitly a function of the highest wage actually paid, Λ is implicitly a function of $\tau^{\max}$. The competitive assumption is not realistic, but again it is relaxed later. Now Λ, and hence $\tau^{\max}$, can be solved for from

$$f(\Lambda,\sigma) = d\left[f(\Lambda,\sigma), \frac{\tau^{\max}}{f_1(\Lambda,\sigma)}, \rho, \delta\right]. \tag{3}$$

Some relation like this is essential to the argument. The IS/LM model, in the Keynes-Hicks version with competition and unrationed producers, provides it straightforwardly, when (3) is essentially the IS curve. Particular features of the IS/LM model are not required. Any assumptions that relate employment negatively to the price level, which in turn is related positively to the maximum nominal wage at which employment is obtained, will do.

To close the model we need to determine the rate of interest. Money-market equilibrium provides the extra functional relation that will do that. So add a money-market equilibrium condition (an LM curve or its equivalent),

$$M\left[\frac{\tau^{\max}}{f_1(\Lambda,\sigma)}\cdot f(\Lambda,\sigma),\rho\right] = 0, \tag{4}$$

and the system is closed given the wage demands set by all workers.

As $\tau^{\max}$ is the highest wage actually paid, and effectively the cost of labor to the firm, the higher is $\tau^{\max}$ the lower is demand and equilibrium output for given values of δ and σ. This is because an increase in $\tau^{\max}$ pushes up the price level and thereby contracts output through its effect on demand (the real balance effect) and also by forcing up the rate of interest (the Keynes effect), both working in the same direction.

It is usual to argue that where there is no uncertainty nominal-wage setting is equivalent to real-wage setting, since one value can be translated to the other. This is true in the present case with the proviso that the certainty must extend to the wage demands of all other workers. When those are known, however, and all parties know the model in detail, it is the case that nominal-wage and real-wage setting are the same.

When the stochastic variables δ and σ are added, the case is significantly altered. The total demand for labor will be a stochastic function of the workers' choices of their nominal-wage demands, denoted $(\tau_1, \tau_2, \ldots, \tau_n)$. For a given realization of the stochastic variables δ and σ, the demand will depend on the distribution of the τ's.

With uncertainty built into the model, there is no strict dichotomy between labor supply dependent on the real wage and labor supply dependent on the money wage. When a worker announces that he is available for work at wage τ_i, the real value of this wage will be τ_i/π, and the latter value will be known only when δ and σ have revealed themselves and the price level has emerged from the equations of the model. A worker does not know what real wage he will receive if he is employed, or even whether a specific demand for a nominal wage will see him employed.

Whereas demand may be inferred from $\tau^{\max}$, $\tau^{\max}$ itself is the outcome of an equilibriating process in which $\tau^{\max}$ will satisfy

$$H[\tau^{\max}] = \Lambda, \tag{5}$$

where $H[\tau]$ is the cumulative frequency distribution of nominal-wage demands. Thus, $H[\tau]$ is the number of workers demanding a wage no higher than τ, where, by an obvious convention, any value down to the next lowest integer may be assigned to $H[\cdot]$. For example, if 25 workers demand a wage of 100 or less, then $H[100] = 24.3$ may be used, if necessary, to satisfy (5).

Keynes stressed the noncooperative nature of wage setting to argue that workers cannot engineer an all-round cut in nominal wages to boost aggregate demand through the operation of the Keynes effect. This argument seems to be quite wrongheaded. A noncooperative Nash specification, for instance, should greatly promote competitive wage cutting because workers will suppose that they can obtain a competitive edge by cutting while others stick.

Let a Nash equilibrium with rational expectations concerning the stochastic mapping from nominal-wage demands to individual income levels be a *Renash* (rational-expectations Nash) equilibrium. The mapping comes from the solution to a model like the one already detailed. Given the τ_i values, and δ and σ, a solution for π emerges and hence a global demand for labor, and with it an allocation of employment to individuals. Suppose, for example, that all that matters to individuals is their real income levels, and let these be denoted $\iota_1, \iota_2, \ldots, \iota_n$. The mapping may be represented as

$$\begin{bmatrix} \tau_1 \\ \tau_2 \\ \vdots \\ \tau_n \end{bmatrix} \xrightarrow[\delta,\sigma]{} \begin{bmatrix} \iota_1 \\ \iota_2 \\ \vdots \\ \iota_n \end{bmatrix}. \tag{6}$$

I refer to (6) as the *NOWRIM* (nominal-wage-to-real-income mapping). The NOWRIM is a stochastic mapping. The ι values depend uniquely on the τ values only when δ and σ are given. It is the existence of a mapping like (6) regardless of how it is derived that is basic to the argument.

As is well known, we would get a different result if workers were to set their wage demands in terms of real purchasing power. In the IS/LM model, for example, both the random variables δ and σ (that is, both demand and supply shocks) contribute to fluctuations in output. In the classical model with real-wage setting, however, only supply shocks cause fluctuations. Real-wage setting replaces (2) by

$$f_1(\Lambda,\sigma) = \tau_{\mathrm{r}}^{\max}, \tag{7}$$

where $\tau_{\mathrm{r}}^{\max}$ is the maximum real wage of a worker gaining employment. Now Λ follows from (7) given σ and $\tau_{\mathrm{r}}^{\max}$, and a demand shock cannot affect the level of output but only the rate of interest, the price level, and possibly, in a disaggregated model, the composition of output.

It is no surprise to obtain starkly classical conclusions from a model that makes the strong classical assumption that wages are set in real terms. However, the model helps to clarify the nature of labor-market equilibrium in a Keynesian setting. With classical real-wage setting, σ has no effect, all shocks are on the demand side, and equilibrium reigns with the wage at the equilibrium level of τ_r^{max}. All unemployment is voluntary.

In the NOWRIM game, on the other hand, workers cannot pinpoint the market-clearing real wage and cannot know exactly how their nominal-wage demands will translate to real-wage levels. The labor market has become a less certain and less attractive environment in which to operate, and this uncertainty affects the labor supply and should do on standard welfare economic grounds.

2 A Model with a Wage Distribution

To pursue the consequences of nominal-wage setting, assume that σ has no effect, and that all shocks are on the demand side. Further, assume that workers are risk neutral. As long as the demand for labor does not exceed the supply—for which case see below—the equations of the complete model will be the following:

$$\omega = f(\Lambda), \tag{8}$$

$$\pi \cdot f_1(\Lambda) = \tau^{max}, \tag{9}$$

$$f(\Lambda,\sigma) = d\left[f(\Lambda,\sigma), \frac{\tau^{max}}{f_1(\Lambda,\sigma)}, \rho, \delta\right], \tag{10}$$

$$M\left[\frac{\tau^{max}}{f_1(\Lambda,\sigma)} \cdot f(\Lambda,\sigma), \rho\right] = 0, \tag{11}$$

$$H[\tau^{max}] = \Lambda. \tag{12}$$

Noting that the maximum wage depends on Λ according to the inverse of the cumulative density function $H(\tau^{max})$, denoted $H^{-1}(\Lambda)$, we may simplify equations (8)–(12) to obtain a simple model involving Λ and ρ. The model will be as follows:

$$f(\Lambda,\sigma) = d\left[f(\Lambda,\sigma), \frac{H^{-1}(\Lambda)}{f_1(\Lambda)}, \rho, \delta\right], \tag{13}$$

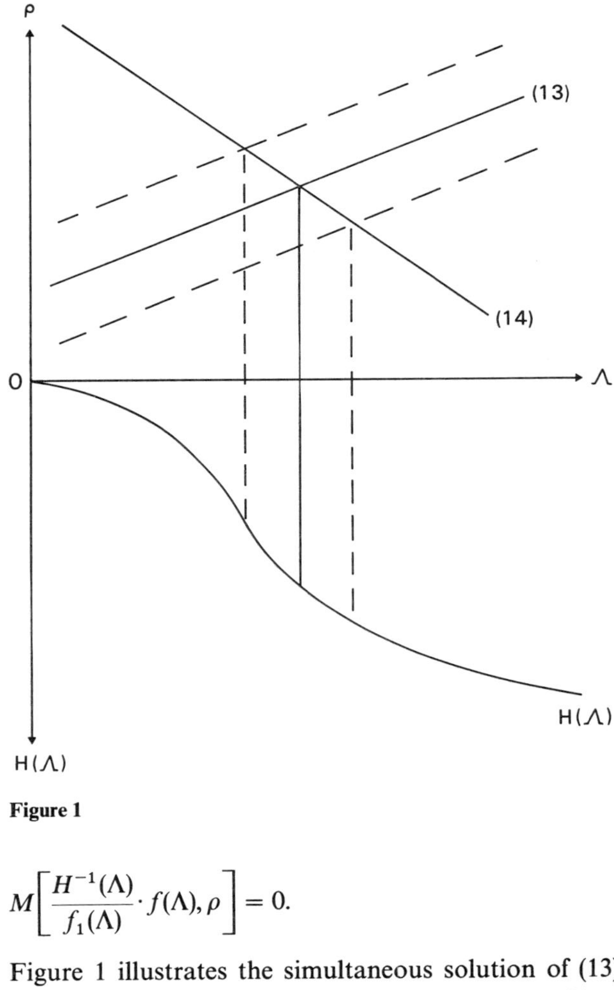

Figure 1

$$M\left[\frac{H^{-1}(\Lambda)}{f_1(\Lambda)}\cdot f(\Lambda), \rho\right] = 0. \tag{14}$$

Figure 1 illustrates the simultaneous solution of (13) and (14), with the curves drawn linear for convenience. It has a familiar IS/LM appearance. However, the effects of price-level movements are already included in the curves as drawn, because the price level is a function of employment through

$$\pi = \frac{H^{-1}(\Lambda)}{f_1(\Lambda)}. \tag{15}$$

The "IS curve" (13) is stochastic, as it is influenced by the shocks transmitted by δ. The "LM curve" (14) does not shift about. Figure 1 illustrates how the solution to the model varies as changes in δ shift the IS curve up and down. The lower quadrant shows how the maximum wage will vary if the distribution of nominal-wage demands leads to a smooth cumulative density function. Note that the real value of $\tau^{\max}$ varies inversely with total employment, although $\tau^{\max}$ itself will increase with employment.

If there is no variation in δ, and/or no risk aversion, it is not reasonable to suppose an $H(\Lambda)$ function as drawn. Why should any workers ask for relatively low nominal wages when they know that they will almost certainly be employed, and would almost certainly be employed at even higher wages than those that they demand? This point does not matter for the conclusion at which we shall soon arrive. To keep the argument simple, imagine that we start with the curve (13) lying only at its central value, drawn bold in figure 1. In that case the model should collapse to the classical real-wage-setting model. Then the $H(\Lambda)$ curve as drawn really will not do, for all workers who want to work at the now-constant real wage which the model can provide will ask for the nominal wage that leads to that real wage. Workers who wish to "sit out" employment this round will signal that intention by asking for any higher nominal wage.

Now let the fixed curve (13) be replaced by a mean-preserving spread (MPS) in which δ takes a high or a low value with equal probabilities such that $d(\cdot,\cdot)$ is moved up for a high δ, or down for a low δ, for any given value of ρ, by the same distance in each direction. Inspection of figure 1 confirms the following conclusions:

- An MPS of the IS curve necessarily leads to an MPS of the solution for Λ only if the LM curve is linear.
- If the fluctuations affect a region within which the cumulative density function is concave, as in figure 1, there is a fall in the average solution value for Λ.
- To maintain expected income, an individual worker may have to lower his wage demand. If it is held at the value appropriate to the no-uncertainty case, he will be unemployed part of the time, and this may more than offset the fact that the average real value of the wage demanded will have risen.

We have touched on the question of whether an assumed pattern of wage demands is reasonable or not. To get to the bottom of that question, we have to apply explicit game-theoretic solution concepts to the problem. This is the subject of the next section.

3 Equilibrium Configurations of Wage Demands with Perfectly Substitutable Workers

Figure 1 does not depict a Renash equilibrium. Take the case where the IS curve takes a high or a low position with equal probability. Recall that workers are not risk averse, let them all be the same, and let all care only about expected income. No disutility attaches to work. What would a Renash look like for that simple case?

Competition between different workers is extreme in a Nash solution. Define a symmetrical Nash equilibrium to be a Nash equilibrium in which all workers ask for the same nominal wage. In a symmetrical Nash equilibrium, no worker prefers employment to unemployment for states of positive measure in which there will be some unemployment.

The no-disliked-unemployment result above is rather trivial. Suppose it to be false. Let worker i prefer to be employed rather than unemployed for the given common nominal wage level and for specific values δ and σ of positive measure. Now suppose that worker i reduces his nominal wage demand by a tiny amount, denoted ε. His expected earnings from employment decline for every state in which he might be employed, but almost negligibly, as ε is arbitrarily small. However, his probability of employment jumps up to 1 for all unemployment states, as he has undercut his fellow workers. So he must gain, and therefore he was not initially in Nash equilibrium, contrary to assumption.

The simplicity of the demonstration of the last result makes its force clear. However, it needs the assumptions, explicit and implicit, which are employed to prove it. In particular, it needs symmetry, for symmetry ensures that the smallest cut in the wage demanded will be associated with a discontinuous jump in employment experience. Also, it needs the assumption that a cut in the nominal wage demanded can be arbitrarily small. It was because ε could be as small as desired that the loss in welfare associated with existing employment was essentially a second-order effect when compared with the relatively unbounded gain in the benefit from desired employment. In the next two sections I provide examples of equilibrium unemployment based on the violation of (respectively), symmetry and boundedness below of the absolute size of changes in wage demands.

4 Spaced-Out Wage Demand

We might have an asymmetrical Nash solution with identical players. I cannot see anything to rule that out. However, more important is the diversified Nash equilibrium that will emerge when workers differ in their constraints or in their tastes (including differences in degree of risk aversion). In those circumstances, the workers will spread out their wage demands and put distance between themselves and their unlike fellows.

EXAMPLE 1 The demand for labor is unbounded at a variable nominal wage, denoted τ^*. The price level is constant. A worker of type i has a nominal reservation wage of $10/i$. The variable τ^* is uniformly distributed on [0, 10]. Workers maximize their expected nominal incomes. A worker of type i solves

$$\operatorname*{Max}_{\tau_i} \left[\frac{10}{i}\right] \cdot \tau_i + (10 - \gamma_i) \cdot \tau_i. \tag{16}$$

The solution is

$$\tau_i = 5 \cdot \left[\frac{i+1}{i}\right]; \tag{17}$$

and the wage demands are spaced out, as required. It is immediate that the solution values given in (17) define a Nash equilibrium, because with the price level constant there is no interaction between the decisions of workers of different types. However, given the Nash assumption and spaced-out demands, the interaction is never strong. A worker who takes other wage demands as given sees himself as influencing the general level of prices only over a restricted range of τ^* values where those with values of i higher than his are employed and he is still unemployed. This range apart, the price level depends on τ^*, as if mechanically, and the problem could be adapted to a real-wage formulation without making any essential difference. Certainly the wage demands will always be spread out, and some workers will prefer employment by the firm to their reservation employment position for values of τ^* with positive measure.

The reader will notice that the example is not a case of the macroeconomic model. The reason is simple. Solving for true solutions for joint maximizations of the type of (16) is horribly complicated. I will not say that it cannot be done, for fear that some smart graduate student will immediately do it, but it is certainly not easy. In any case, the conclusion is robust. If workers' equilibrium wage demands are spaced out, the frantic competitive wage cutting which one may think of as constraining symmetrical Nash-equilibrium solutions no longer applies.

So far the argument seems to say that Keynes was mainly wrong. A lack of coordination in wage setting seems more likely to result in cutthroat-competitive wage cutting than in stickiness of wages.

5 Wage Demands on a Course Grid

What underlies the impossibility of combining unwelcome unemployment with a symmetrical Nash equilibrium is not wage cutting as such. It is what might be called competitive wage shaving. The worker who dislikes an unemployment outcome in a particular state of the world just shaves ε off his wage demand and ducks under the demands of his fellow workers.

In the next example wage shaving is excluded. Wage demands have to be selected from a discrete range of values. Indeed, for simplicity we assume that only two nominal-wage demands are allowable: \$1 per week and \$2 per week. Now we no longer need asymmetry, and the workers will be assumed to be the same.

EXAMPLE 2 Let there be two workers, who each set a nominal wage at which they are willing to accept employment up to their maximum supply, taken to be 1 week per week for each worker. Each worker sets one of two nominal-wage rates: either \$1 per week or \$2 per week. Employment goes first to the cheapest worker up to a maximum of 1 week. If both workers ask the same wage rate ($\tau_1 = \tau_2$) then employment is divided between them equally, again up to their maximum. We look at a case in which both workers are the same. We also adopt a very simple IS model.

Let the production function be

$$\omega = \Lambda^{0 \cdot 8}, \tag{18}$$

where Λ is the total employment measured in weeks. As long as no excess demand for labor arises, the real wage per week of a worker receiving $\tau^{\max}$ per week will be

$$\text{pw} = 0.8 \cdot \Lambda^{-0 \cdot 2}, \tag{19}$$

where the abbreviation pw stands for "product wage." Notice that if one worker asks for \$1 per week while the other worker asks for \$2 per week, and if demand is sufficiently high to generate employment for the high-wage worker, then the low-wage worker will earn only half of pw per week. It is the risk of this outcome, in which a worker suffers from asking for a low wage while the higher nominal demand of another worker inflates the price level, that accounts for the possible downward stickiness of nominal wages in a Nash equilibrium. If $\tau^{\max}$ denotes the highest wage paid, then π will be given by

$$\pi = \frac{\tau^{\max} \cdot \Lambda^{0 \cdot 2}}{0.8}. \tag{20}$$

Demand is obtained by solving

$$\omega = 5.744 \cdot \delta - 4 \cdot \pi + 1.74, \tag{21}$$

where π is the nominal price level and δ is distributed as follows:

$$\begin{aligned} &\delta = 1 \text{ with probability } 0.2, \\ &\delta = 2 \text{ with probability } 0.8. \end{aligned} \tag{22}$$

Suppose that both workers ask for a low wage, \$1, and that $\delta = 2$. If the workers were to obtain 2 weeks' employment and earn the real wage corresponding to the real marginal product of 2 weeks' employment, π would take the value 1.436 and ω would take the value 7.485, which would imply $\Lambda = 12.38$. The firm would like to employ more labor time than is available In that case the firm would be rationed as a buyer of labor, π would be higher, and workers would earn less than their full-employment real wage in the 80%-likely outcome of a boom.

That danger would prohibit setting the nominal-wage demand low. There is no doubt a lesson there, but as I want to illustrate a coordination problem I shall cheat a bit and impose another solution on the model. I simply assume that the real value of the wage received by the highest-paid worker will always be the real marginal product of labor, even when both workers ask for \$1 and $\delta = 2$. It is not what the strict logic of the model dictates, yet it hardly affects the force of the example.

There are three possible patterns of wage demands, expressed as pairs of required weekly payments: (1,1), (2,2) and (1,2). Another possibility is (2,1), but it is essentially the same as (1,2). Each of the three cases leads to differ-

Table 1
Employment rates for the two workers, expressed as proportions of one week.

	Wage demands		
	(1,1)	(1,2)	(2,2)
$\delta = 1$	(1,1)	(·2,0)	(·1,·1)
$\delta = 2$	(1,1)	(1,1)	(1,1)

Table 2
Real earnings for the two workers.

	Wage demands		
	(1,1)	(1,2)	(2,2)
$\delta = 1$	(·7,·7)	(1 · 2,0)	(·6,·6)
$\delta = 2$	(·7,·7)	(·35,·7)	(·7,·7)

Table 3
Payoffs in the game with discrete choices.

		Worker I	
		$w = \$1$	$w = \$2$
Worker II	$w = \$1$	·7 ·7	·56 ·52
	$w = \$2$	·52 ·56	·68 ·68

ent specific consequences according to the value taken by δ. The solution values for the number of weeks' work obtained by the respective worker types are shown in table 1. Table 2 shows the real earnings of the respective workers according to the outcome that is realized. From these data the expected payoffs of the two-person game shown in table 3 can be computed.

What table 3 shows us is a nice example of a two-person coordination game. A coordination game may be defined as a game in which there is a Nash equilibrium Pareto dominated by another Nash equilibrium. We see this feature in table 3: if the players play (2,2) the result is a Nash equilibrium, although if they played (1,1) a Nash equilibrium would again result and they would both be better off.

The game shown in table 3 is rather evocative of Keynes' imprecise argument. The two workers can get stuck in a high-nominal-wage demand trap. They would both like the level of nominal wages to be lower, but they have to worry about relativities. The worker who cuts his wage demand while his fellow worker stays high picks up full employment in a recession. However, in a boom his \$1 buys only a miserable standard of living, as the price level is inflated by the \$2 rate being paid to his fellow. So he cannot risk a cut, and neither can the other worker. An expansion in the money supply, however, could make a \$2 demand equivalent to an old \$1 demand and shove the workers to a preferable Nash equilibrium.

The conclusion is plain, although the particular example is fabricated and the details are fudged. If wage demands have to be selected from a lumpy range of values, there must exist coordination games of the type indicated. One needs only a joint benefit to moving together—getting the general level of wages down, for example—and serious costs to moving out of step to arrive at the possibility of a Nash equilibrium that is inefficient even among Nash equilibria.

6 Focal Points and the Coordination of Wage Demands

Example 2 is likely to bring two questions to the mind of the game theorist. First, the story has been told as if there is a natural reference point (high nominal wage) from which the players may or may not shift to a Pareto-superior point with both demanding lower nominal wages. History would seem to provide a possible justification for viewing the game that way. Perhaps wages were high last period, for whatever reason, with the consequence that the (high,high) point is a natural focal point.

Focal points do play an essential role in selecting among multiple Nash equilibria. Even so, inserting a prior history that plays no role in the actual game in order to pick out a particular focal point, especially an inferior one, does amount to a suspect procedure. The game theorist is likely to insist that focal points should emerge from the unadorned game, and that if history really is material its influence should be incorporated explicitly. Otherwise, the argument would run, the overwhelmingly natural focal point will be the Pareto-efficient Nash equilibrium point—(low,low) in the example.

The second question that is likely to occur to the game theorist concerns how the inefficient equilibrium would be affected if the allowable steps in nominal-wage demands were to be gradually decreased. It is clear that as long as wage demands are confined to a course grid there will always be a possibility of an inefficient Nash equilibrium. Equally plainly, if very small changes become admissible we eventually approach the earlier result according to which wage shaving in a symmetrical equilibrium will provide no more desired employment.

The last conclusion leaves open the question of what will happen if we start from a situation in which for some reason a (high,high) point does have some claim to be a focal point. Suppose that (high,high) is history and each worker worries that the other worker may not act rationally and join him in a jump to the Pareto-efficient (low,low) Nash point. Each will start to shave his wage demands and will eventually discover that the other is doing likewise, and in due course the process will accelerate and arrive at the Pareto-efficient Nash point. This process, however, could take some time.

If we rule out uncertainty as to the rationality of the other player, a common-knowledge assumption will exclude a tentative and creeping approach to the optimum. If one player decides that a 5% cut in the wage demanded is the best strategy for himself, he should believe that it will be the best strategy for his partner. Then, however, a cut of more than 5% is a better strategy for the player and hence for his partner, and so on. The only consistent calculations will take both players straight to the optimum Nash point.

As serious coarseness of allowable wage-demand values does not appear to be a reasonable specification, it might seem that example 2 does not illustrate an important possibility. On the other hand, common knowledge is a very powerful assumption, and it is doubtful whether it describes the wage-demand-coordination games of real economies. Without it, groups of workers may get stuck at inefficient Nash points, away from which they will drift sluggishly as they learn more about the game and about each other.

The reference to groups of workers reminds us that the present model treats workers as essentially alike but as setting their wage demands independently. This is not very natural. In the model of the next section, the labor of different workers may be imperfect substitutes for each other.

7 The Wage Demands of Imperfectly Substitutable Type of Labor

For convenience, consider a model with just two labor types. The results, however, are all general. The production function is

$$\omega = F(\lambda_1, \lambda_2) \ldots, \tag{23}$$

where ω is real product and λ_1 and λ_2 are the inputs of the two types of labor. The unit cost function is

$$c(\tau_1, \tau_2, \omega), \tag{24}$$

where τ_1 and τ_2 are nominal wage demands. Demand functions for labor may be derived from the the cost function as

$$\lambda_i = \frac{\partial c}{\partial \tau_i} \cdot \omega. \tag{25}$$

These demand functions will be denoted

$$\lambda_i = \lambda_i(\tau_1, \tau_2, \omega). \tag{26}$$

In place of the competitive model of the previous sections I now introduce markup pricing. There is no logical connection between the new specification of the labor market and the new pricing model. In fact, all the results of the paper can be obtained with either specification. Markup pricing, however, is a convenient assumption to work with in the present case. Therefore, let the price level be given by

$$\pi = (1 + \alpha) \cdot c(\tau_1, \tau_2, \omega). \tag{27}$$

The markup α may be set to zero without changing the results. The price level and output must also be consistent with a reduced-form macroeconomic model so that

$$\omega = S(\pi), \tag{28}$$

where ω is a declining function of π. The ith type of labor chooses τ_i, taking the other value of τ as given, so as to maximize an objective function:

$$V^i \left[\frac{\tau_i}{\pi}, \lambda_i \right], \tag{29}$$

where V^i is an increasing function of its first argument. With regard to its second argument, its partial derivative is positive if $\lambda_i > \lambda_i^0$, where λ_i^0 is the employment target of labor type i. Similarly, the partial derivative is negative if $\lambda_i > \lambda_i^0$ and employment exceeds the target level. Substituting from (27), (28), and (29), we may express the problem of maximizing the value of the objective function as a constrained maximization involving the variables τ and ω as follows.

Maximize by choice of τ_i:

$$V^i\left[\frac{\tau_i}{(1+\alpha)\cdot C(\tau_1,\tau_2)}, \lambda_i(\tau_1,\tau_2,\omega)\right], \tag{30}$$

subject to

$$S[(1+\alpha)\cdot C(\tau_1,\tau_2,\omega)] - \omega \geq 0. \tag{31}$$

Let the multiplier attaching to the constraint be ζ. Then the first-order conditions for a maximum are

$$V_1^1\cdot\left[\frac{1}{1+\alpha}\cdot\frac{C(\tau_1,\tau_2)-\tau_1\cdot\lambda_1}{C(\tau_1,\tau_2)^2}\right] + V_2^1\cdot\frac{\partial\lambda_1}{\partial\tau_1} + \zeta\cdot S_1\cdot(1+\alpha)\cdot\lambda_1 = 0, \tag{32}$$

$$V_2^1\cdot\frac{\partial\lambda_1}{\partial\omega} + \zeta\cdot\left[S_1\cdot(1+\alpha)\cdot\frac{\partial C}{\partial\omega} - 1\right] = 0, \tag{33}$$

where subscripts denote either differentiation or partial differentiation, as appropriate.

The main points that I want to make about the noncooperative Nash equilibrium of the game in which the two players independently set their nominal-wage demands (τ_1,τ_2) are most conveniently demonstrated in diagrams (figures 2 and 3). First note that there is a fundamental ambiguity about what one would feel as a player of this game concerning the choice of a wage demand by his partner. *Partner* is a better term than *opponent*, because it is not a zero-sum game, although there will be conflicts of interest.

Put yourself mentally in the position of player 1. The higher is τ_2, the higher will be π, the lower will be ω and the lower will be demand for your labor on that account—the aggregate-demand effect, or income effect for short. However, the higher is τ_2, the higher will be the demand for your labor, given ω—the substitution effect for short. It is not clear how these effects will balance out. Indeed, in general it could go either way.

The extreme cases make the point clear. If labor of type 2 is a very close substitute for labor of type 1, you will typically want τ_2 to be high. Then producers will substitute in favor of your labor, and the influence of a high τ_2 on the general price level will be moderated. On the other hand, if type 1 and type 2 labor are employed in fixed proportions, τ_2 is like a tax on your

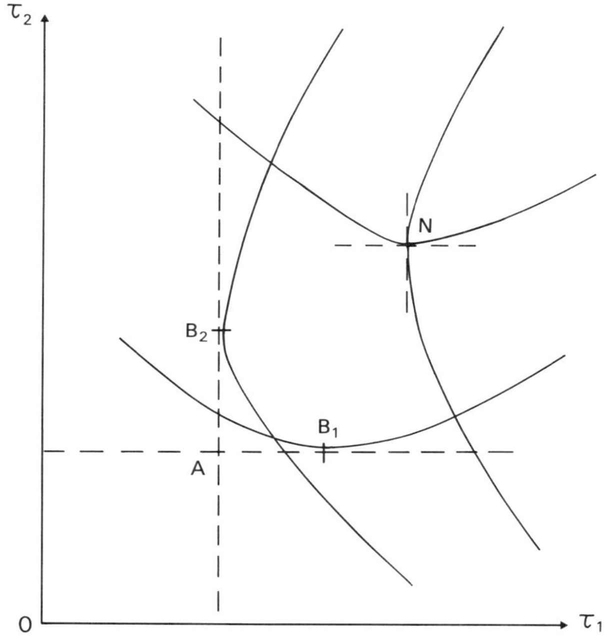

Figure 2

wages. In choosing τ_1 you are choosing $\tau_1 + \tau_2$, and hence π. It is as if you alone set the wage but did not receive all the wage. Rather, you receive what you ask less τ_2, so the lower τ_2 the better.

In both figures, A is the competitive point to which wages would converge if both τ values rose whenever $V_2^i > 0$ and fell when $V_2^i < 0$. As both players are indifferent to small changes in employment level at that point but would like higher real wages, they would both opt for a higher value of τ than applies at A if they were to take the other value of τ as fixed. The best points that they would choose in that case are respectively B_1 and B_2, again in both figures. The Nash equilibrium is at N, and as usual (see, e.g., Hamada 1979) it is inefficient. Both wage setters would benefit from a coordinated cut in wage demands.

It is important to understand the nature of this conclusion, and not to confuse it with an earlier case or with arguments that were advanced by Keynes. The Nash equilibrium N is inefficient because uncoordinated Nash equilibrium is typically inefficient. There is no ranking of Nash equi-

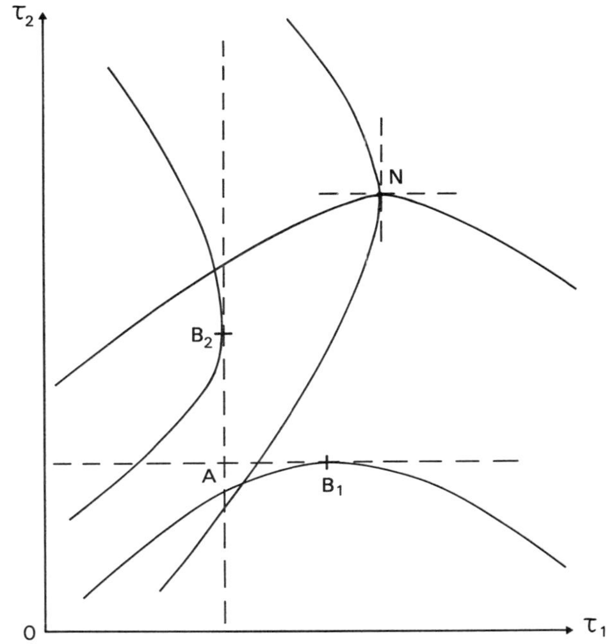

Figure 3

libria here; this is not a coordination game. To underline the point, what takes the players to *N* is not that they are unable to coordinate a joint move away from *N*. What takes the players to *N* is that *N* is the unique and natural equilibrium. To get away from *N* the players have to change the game to a cooperative game.

The conclusion of the last model seems to be the most evocative of Keynes. Unemployment emerges in equilibrium. A coordinated cut in nominal wages would be in the interest of all workers. For precisely this reason it is important to emphasize the differences. The fact that the conclusions happened to be derived in a markup model is not important. The same type of conclusion would emerge from a competitive IS/LM model of the Keynes/Hicks type.

The labor market in the last model is not and could not be competitive, however, and this accounts entirely for the equilibrium unemployment. The imperfection of competition in the labor market arises because wage setters are large in the economy. This is not the same as the model of Hart (1982) in which workers are large in local markets but small in the economy. Here workers calculate the macroeconomic effects of what they do.

The most important difference from Keynes emerges when policy is considered. For Keynes, nominal-wage flexibility was a substitute for changes in the money supply. If the authorities would increase the money supply sufficiently, there would be no need for nominal-wage flexibility. The last model is quite different. There is no wage stickiness as such. Nominal-wage levels are set optimally and freely by the players. They are pushed above the full-employment level because wage setters are large. They are pushed too far above the full-employment level from the point of view of the players' interests because they are playing a noncooperative game.

Contrary to a true Keynesian model, alterations in the quantity of money alter the real outcome of (in this case noncooperative) wage setting only if they change the relationship between suitably renumbered settings of the τ levers and real outcomes in the wage game. As there is no uncertainty in the present model, the argument would reach the same conclusion if the players made real-money wage demands. If the demand for money wages is for real-money wages, there is no reason why money-supply changes will achieve anything that flexible, if uncoordinated, wages could not achieve. Above I mentioned the possibility that a change in the money supply might jolt the economy from an unfavorable to a more favorable Nash equilibrium. Under common knowledge, however, the unfavorable Nash equilibrium was a doubtful case. Without common knowledge, on the other hand, all kinds of possibilities have to be taken seriously, and active monetary policy would be powerful in theory, even if impractical to apply.

8 Employers and the Government as Players

Our nominal-wage games have been played by active workers setting wage demands. Nature has been random shocks operating on an economy in which employers mechanically carry out production routines, minimizing cost, meeting demands, and marking up unit costs but not becoming active players in the game. This is unrealistic and makes no sense in terms of the logic of the game. If the employers are large, it is in their interests to try to influence the outcome of the game by entering into direct bargaining with workers or by changing demands for labor away from the simple mechanically determined values.

Governments too have an interest in the outcome of wage setting. In particular, they would not like the inflationary bias implicit in some of our models. If so, and in general, they can influence tendencies to inflation by running a tight policy, refusing to monetize inflation or to spend to increase demand.

The usual problems of credibility are soon encountered and may be illustrated by some of the models in the paper. Take the (high,high) outcome of example 2. This was seen to be a dubious case in its own right. The workers should be able to see the merits of a (low, low) outcome and move to it. Suppose, however, that there are some costs to cutting the wage rate. Workers would prefer the government to increase the money supply and underwrite the (high,high) outcome. There are costs to the government to doing this. Imagine real costs of inflation.

Enough has been said to make it clear that this could be analyzed as a three-player game. Moreover, the two-player wage-setting game embedded in the three-player game is qualitatively different from the simple two-player game. It is far from clear, for instance, that (low,low) is a natural focal point. It will be if the government has made a credible commitment not to intervene if the workers opt for inflation by playing (high, high). However, could such a commitment be credible?

Concluding Remarks

Setting wage demands in nominal terms makes a big difference. The structure of the game played by wage setters is changed. The question of which shocks to the model matter for the outcome is affected, and the supply of labor may be influenced. These conclusions follow in a model with uncertainty, in which the real value of a given nominal-wage demand cannot be calculated in advance. Requiring expectations to be rational makes the calculations simpler but does not negate the conclusions.

Game theory does appear to be a useful tool for analyzing wage setting in a macroeconomic context. However, the resulting models are quite complicated to solve. A seductive simplifying assumption, symmetrical Nash equilibrium, can lead to a conclusion that wage setting will be blindly and extremely competitive. This conclusion, however, is sensitive to the specification of the model. If workers spread out their wage demands for any of a variety of reasons, we see that a particular type of worker enjoys a natural local monopoly of his own wage level and involuntary unemployment will occur in some states of the world.

It was Keynes' coordination problem that originally suggested the application of game theory. It is easy to model the coordination problem in a game where wage levels are chosen from a discrete set of values. However, it is hard to see the assumption as realistic. If workers can vary their demands continuously, then a high-nominal-wage trap would tend to get eroded by small wage cuts. Just the knowledge that it would be so would then take the players quickly to a Nash equilibrium Pareto optimal among Nash equilibria. That is the natural focal point under common knowledge.

When different types of labor are imperfect substitutes but the wage demanded by each type is chosen by all workers of that type cooperatively, different types of workers are imperfect competitors. As a higher wage demand by one type causes an external diseconomy to other types by raising the general price level and deflating aggregate demand, uncoordinated wage setting is jointly inefficient. However, the outcome that improves on uncoordinated wage setting is not a Nash equilibrium. This last case seems to be the only one in which Keynes' conclusions are replicated. Even there coordinated wage cutting and monetary expansion do not have equivalent effects.

Employers of labor and the government should be modeled as active participants in the game. When the government is modeled as an active player, standard issues of credibility and time consistency are encountered.

References

Blanchard, O. J., and S. Fischer. 1989. *Lectures on Macroeconomics.* MIT Press.

Blanchard, O. J., and N. Kiyotaki. 1987. "Monopolistic competition and the effects of aggregate demand." *American Economic Review* 77: 647–666.

Fischer, S. 1977. "Long-term contracts, rational expectations and the optimal money supply rule." *Journal of Political Economy* 85: 163–190.

Hahn, F. H. 1982. *Money and Inflation.* Blackwell.

Hamada, K. 1979. "Macroeconomic strategy and coordination under alternative exchange rates." In *International Economic Policy*, ed. R. Dornbusch and J. A. Frenkel. Johns Hopkins University Press.

Hart, O. D. 1982. "A model of imperfect competition with Keynesian features." *Quarterly Journal of Economics* 97: 109–138.

Keynes, J. M. 1936. *The General Theory of Employment Money and Interest.* Macmillan.

Lindbeck, A., and D. Snower. 1986. "Wage setting, unemployment and insider-outsider relations." *American Economic Review* 76: 235–239.

Macdonald, I. M., and R. M. Solow. 1981. "Wage bargaining and employment." *American Economic Review* 71: 896–908.

Phelps, E. S. 1970. *Microeconomic Foundations of Employment and Inflation Theory*. Norton.

Taylor, J. 1979. "Staggered price setting in a macro model." *American Economic Review* 69: 108–113.

Underemployment as Coordination Problem with Savings and Increasing Returns

Walter P. Heller

Are temporary shocks sufficient to cause permanent underemployment in a dynamic model? That is the question being addressed here. A temporary equilibrium model with oligopolized output markets is analyzed. There are two types of agents: type 1 produces only goods that type 2 likes, while type 2 produces goods that only type 1 likes. The main result is that there are Pareto-ranked multiple equilibria, all with low levels of employment by comparison with competitive equilibrium. The model displays "comovements" in equilibrium output and employment. Across equilibria, lower economic activity gives rise to lower economic welfare, if the degree of increasing returns is small. The multiple equilibria exhibit coordination failure: At a low-level equilibrium, a government should send a market signal that guides agents to behavior corresponding to the Pareto-best equilibrium. An announced increase in government spending is shown to be such a signal.

There is a dynamic disequilibrium adjustment story for the framework given below. The economy is subject to random exogenous shocks that push it away from, say, a highlevel equilibrium and into the basin of attraction of a low-level equilibrium. The shock is only temporary, but the adjustment process converges to a low-level equilibrium. A policy shock is now necessary to shift the economy back to a Pareto-superior equilibrium. This is in contrast to the real business cycle view in which shocks move the system from one Pareto-efficient equilibrium to another. Policy has no role in these models.

There are two oligopolized industries, one for each type of output. Workers in industry 1 care only for output of industry 2. Workers in industry 2 care only for output of industry 1. There is a potential for strategic complementarity across industries, because it may not be profitable for firms in one industry to produce at high levels unless firms in the other industry are also at high levels of production.[1]

This simple two-industry economy can be readily extended to a multi-industr economy, so long as one preserves the same structure of workers in one industry desiring only goods produced by another industry. In this case, there is a closed chain of linked markets. All the results below obtain in this more general case.

Hahn (1978) pointed out that a persuasive model of persistent disequilibrium ought to allow price flexibility. In addition, he argued that agents should have rational conjectures about market quantity responses to individual price experimentation. Hart's (1982) work on imperfect competition was one such model, but it had a unique equilibrium. The "coordination failure" property was found in the context of a search model by Diamond (1982). Search models, however, operate with price rigidities, i.e., they do not permit maximizing agents to respond to disequilibrium with price adjustments. Under conditions of perfect price flexibility and rational market demand perceptions, Heller (1986) presented a static general equilibrium model with multiple equilibria. For a good survey and synthesis of the coordination failure literature through 1988, see Cooper and John 1988.

The model here is dynamic in that there is a consumer saving decision under uncertainty. Kiyotaki (1988) obtained similar results in a two-period capital goods model with specific functional forms for utility and production. However, equilibrium multiplicity occurs here even in the absence of increasing returns. Durlauf (1990) presents a model without price flexibility, but with a Markov process in which externalities among neighboring agents give rise to high- or low-level equilibria, depending on parameters.

The research reported here shows that coordination failure can occur in a temporary equilibrium model with imperfect competition even without the investment decision. Increasing returns to scale is also allowed. The extra complication is worthwhile, since it is now possible to account for recession and simultaneous decreases in labor productivity (cf. Hall 1988a,b).

In addition to Keynesian policy remedies, one can demonstrate Keynesian-style comparative statics: if preferences shift toward more saving, the result is lower economic activity. For a related result, see Bryant 1987.

1 The Model

There are two consumption goods, each produced by a different industry and consumed by different consumers. Consumers live many periods, wish to consume in all periods, and possess different kinds of labor skills. A worker with type 1 labor can produce only type 2 goods; similarly for type 2. Firms live in Cournot industries. In keeping with the temporary equilibrium method of Grandmont (1986), attention is focused entirely on equilibria in the present period.

There are n consumers of each type and N firms of each type. Generally, subscripts will denote time periods and superscripts will denote types of commodities and agents.

Firms

There are two Cournot-like industries. Firms are identical in each industry. A firm in industry j uses type j labor (L^j) to produce type j goods (y^j) under an increasing/decreasing returns technology: $y^j = f(L^j)$. The product function f is the same across firms, and the functional form is the same across industries. Assume that f has continuous third partial derivatives, and that it satisfies the Inada conditions $f'(0) = \infty$ and $f'(\infty) = 0$. Firms have no intertemporal decisions to make. The labor market is competitive. Let g be the input requirements function, i.e., the inverse of the production function f. The cost function for any firm is then $wg(y)$.

Consumers

Consumers of type i ($i = 1,2$) are identical multi-period competitive households. The types differ in the kind of consumption they desire and in the type of labor skill they are endowed with, but their utility functions have the same functional form. For the moment, the type of consumer will be suppressed in the notation. Consumers value both consumption and leisure at each date. The initial stock of saving is s_0. The only possible assets in the model are the stock of fiat money and storage of output.

Income in period 1 consists of wages earned on current labor, $w_1 L_1$, interest earned on past saving, $r_1 s_0$, and other income, I_1. Other income includes dividends paid on past and present profits, as well as government net transfer payments. Below, we will examine specific examples—e.g., when other income consists solely of current profits, or when it includes government monetary and fiscal policy.

The price of consumption goods in the present is taken as given by the consumer. Suppose current prices and incomes are known to the consumer and defined as $a_1 \equiv (w_1, r_1, p_1, i_1)$. The period 1 budget constraint is then

$$p_1 c_1 + s_1 = (1 + r_1)s_0 + w_1 L_1 + I_1. \tag{1.1}$$

For simplicity of argument here, suppose that the only store of wealth in this model is a liquid paper asset such as fiat money. I will now present a dynamic programming style of argument that saving enters a one-period utility function. (Readers already familiar with this may want to skip to expressions (1.8).) Suppose that future prices, wages, interest rates, and dividends are unknown, but the consumer has subjective beliefs about them. The subjective probability distribution over any future state at $a_t \equiv (w_t, r_t, p_t, I_t)$ is not affected by current realization a_1.[2]

The period t budget constraint is

$$p_t c_t + s_t = (1 + r_t)s_{t-1} + w_t L_t + I_t \quad (t = 1, 2, \dots, T). \tag{1.2}$$

Let q_t be the present value price of either nominal income or consumption expenditure at time t, so that

$$q_t = [(1 + r_1)(1 + r_2)\cdots(1 + r_t)]^{-1}.$$

The consumer must expect to die with no debts:

$$q_T s_T = 0. \tag{1.3}$$

Given an expected lifetime work plan $(L_1, L_2, \dots, L_T)$ and wage stream $(w_1, w_2, \dots, w_T)$, the expected present value of the income stream after period 1 is

$$\mathrm{PV} \equiv \sum_{t=2}^{T} q_t [w_t L_t + I_t]. \tag{1.4}$$

As is well known, (1.2) and (1.3) can be written as a present value T-period budget constrainted:

$$\sum_{t=1}^{T} q_t p_t c_t = s_0 + q_1 [w_1 L_1 + I_0] + \mathrm{PV}. \tag{1.5}$$

Alternatively, from (1.1),

$$q_1 s_1 = \sum_{t=2}^{T} q_t p_t c_t - \mathrm{PV}. \tag{1.6}$$

Constraint (1.6) says that the period 1 pospective gap between future expected income and planned consumption can be filled only by the level of saving chosen for that period.

The lifetime utility function is $W(c_1, L_1, \dots, c_T, L_T)$. Let W exhibit strict quasiconcavity and monotonicity. Let V be the maximum utility for the period 1 consumption-leisure-saving triple (c_1', L_1', s_1'), given all future prices and incomes:

$$V(c_1', L_1', s_1' \mid p_2, w_2, r_2, I_2, \dots, p_T, w_T, r_T, I_T)$$
$$\equiv \max_{(c_2, L_2, \dots, c_T, L_T)} [W(c_1', L_1', c_2, L_2, \dots, c_T, L_T) \mid \text{constraint (1.6)}]. \tag{1.7}$$

For the sake of notational simplicity, drop the subscripts for period 1 variables. Let U denote the expected value of V:

$$U(c,L,s) \equiv \mathrm{E}V(c,L,s\,|\,(p_2,w_2,r_2,I_2),\ldots,(p_T,w_T,r_T,I_T)), \tag{1.8b}$$

where the expectation is taken over future wages, prices, interest rates, and incomes. Even though the current interest rate r_1 enters only as an income effect, tomorrow's interest rate r_2 does affect the margin between the present and the future, because the function U depends on it implicitly via equation (1.8a).

In what follows, we shall drop the subscripts for period 1 quantities and prices. Preference for period 1 saving is partly a proxy for desires for future consumption; a shift toward a preference for s may come about as the result of a decrease in the discount rate implicit in W. However, such a shift may also come about because PV is lower in expected value or more uncertain than before.

The focus will be now be on this derived utility function over today's consumption, labor, and saving, given subjective beliefs about prices and incomes in the future. Consumers are endowed with one unit of labor in the first period and face a known wage. A consumer of type 1 has labor skills of type 1, but wishes to Consume only type 2 goods. A similar statement holds for type 1. Therefore, a consumer cannot work in the industry that produces a good that is desirable to him. To summarize, the tastes and labor endowments are the following:

$$U(c^2,L^1,s^1) \text{ with 1 unit of type 1 labor (type 1 consumer)}, \tag{1.8b}$$

$$U(c^1,L^2,s^2) \text{ with 1 unit of type 2 labor (type 2 consumer)}. \tag{1.8c}$$

Note in particular that the functional forms of U are the same for both types. The total labor endowment of each type is n units.

Let us see how U is related to the familiar recursive dynamic problem. Suppose for a moment that W is additively separable across time, and that prices, wages, interest rates, and other income are known and independent of time:

$$W = \sum \beta^t u(c_t,L_t); \qquad p_t = p, \quad w_t = w, \quad r_t = r, \quad I_t = I. \tag{1.9}$$

Let the value function be denoted $T(s)$. Then the Bellman functional equation is

$$T(s) = \operatorname*{Max}_{(c,\,L)} \{U(c,L,s')\,|\,pc + s' = (1+r)s + wL + I\}, \tag{1.10}$$

where

$$U(c, L, s') = u(c,L) + \beta T(s'). \tag{1.11}$$

The following neoclassical assumptions on U are made.

Assumption U

(1) The function U is thrice continuously differentiable and strictly quasi-concave.

(2) Consumption and leisure are normal goods.

(3) (Inada conditions) For all (L,s), there is some survival level of consumption $\underline{c} \geq 0$ such that $U_c(\underline{c},L,s) = \infty$ and $U_c(\infty,L,s) = 0$. For all (c,s), $U_L(c,0,s) = 0$ and $U_L(c,1,s) = -\infty$. For all (c,L), $U_s(c,L,0) = \infty$ and $U_s(c,L,\infty) = 0$.

In the standard recursive case (1.9), it is easily seen that these properties are inherited from similar properties placed on the return function $u(\cdot)$.

Without loss of generality, $w^1 = w^2 = w$, since industry technologies and labor supplies are essentially identical. Assume that a consumer of type i owns shares only in industry i ($i = 1,2$). Furthermore, each consumer has s_0 units of wealth at birth. Now drop the time subscripts in (1.1) and insert superscripts to indicate consumer and commodity types. So, budget constraints can be written as follows:

$$p^2c^2 + s^1 = wL^1 + I^1 + (1 + r_1)s_0 \text{ and } L^1 \leq 1 \text{ (type 1)}, \tag{1.12a}$$

$$p^1c^1 + s^2 = wL^2 + I^2 + (1 + r_1)s_0 \text{ and } L^2 \leq 1 \text{ (type 2)}. \tag{1.12b}$$

Each consumer type maximizes (1.8) subject to (1.12). The outcomes of consumer maximization are the demand and supply functions $c^j(p^j,w,I^i)$, $L^i(p^j,w,I^i)$, and $s^i(p^j,w,I^i)$, where $i \neq j$ and $i, j = 1, 2$. It is suppressed in the notation that these functions depend upon today's known interest rate r_1 and on expectations for all future interest rates, prices, and incomes.

Industrial Organization

Each industry consists of N identical firms; each firm knows today's objective market demand function and maximizes one-period profits under the Cournot hypothesis.

The objective market demand function for industry 1 is an aggregate over all consumers of type 2:

$$C^1(p^1,w,I^2) \equiv nc^1(p^1,w,I^2).$$

Each firm takes as given the wage rate and makes a forecast of other income I. Profits for firm k in industry 1 are

$$\Pi_k^1 = p^1[C^1(p^1,w,I^2) - Y_k^1] - wg(C^1(p^1,w,I^2) - Y_k^1),$$

where Y_k^1 is the output of the rest of the industry. Similarly for industry 2.

Symmetry (i.e., that firms and households are functionally identical across types) allows us to drop the distinction between goods 1 and 2 in any subsequent mathematics and therefore drop all the superscripts (e.g., $p^1 = p^2 = p$, etc.).

2 Necessary Conditions

Let U_c, U_L, and U_s be the partials of U. Recall in equation (2.1) that C is a function $C(p, w, I)$, and let the price elasticity of demand ε also be the function

$$\varepsilon = \varepsilon(p,w,I) = \frac{-p}{C}\frac{\partial C(p,w,I)}{\partial p}.$$

Then the standard first-order conditions for the maximizing agents in this model are as follows: The *symmetric industry equilibrium*[3] is

$$p[1 - (N\varepsilon(p,w,I))^{-1}] = wg'(C/N), \tag{2.1}$$

and the *consumer maximization*[4] is give by

$$\frac{U_c}{U_s}(c,L,s) = p,$$

$$\frac{U_L}{U_s}(c,L,s) = -w, \tag{2.2}$$

$$pc + s = wL + I + (1 + r_1)s_0.$$

Equation (2.1) is the standard Cournot first-order condition for a profit maximization at an equilibrium of a symmetric oligopoly. The left-hand side is of course marginal revenue; the right-hand side is marginal cost.

Alternatively, the first-order condition in the nonsymmetric case can be written as

$$\Pi_p = pC_p\left[\frac{C - Y^1}{pC_p} + 1 - \frac{wg'}{p}\right] = 0. \qquad (2.1')$$

Under the Inada conditions assumed above, solutions to producer and consumer maximization are always interior, so equations (2.1) and (2.2) are necessary conditions. In the appendix, there are given conditions (* and **) under which (2.1) and (2.2) are sufficient. From the work of Roberts and Sonnenschein (1976), it is readily seen that there is always an industry equilibrium.

3 General Cournot Equilibrium

Recall that the labor market is competitive. Also, define the aggregate labor supply to be $L^S(p, w, I) \equiv nL(p, w, I)$. Because of condition (3.1), there can be no involuntary unemployment in equilibrium:

$$Ng(N^{-1}C(p,w,I)) \leq L^S(p,w,I) \text{ and } w = 0 \text{ if strict inequality.} \qquad (3.1)$$

This labor market equilibrium condition is sometimes omitted in the unemployment literature (e.g., Weitzman 1982). It is important to build in the notion that excess supply with a positive real wage cannot be an equilibrium rest point of a competitive labor market. Without more complicated labor contracts than those above, an involuntarily unemployed worker would revise his plans away from the competitive ones. Hart (1982) handles this problem by positing that labor markets are cleared by labor syndicates. In the present case, it has been assumed that leisure has value and that labor markets are competitively cleared. In both models, there is underemployment in equilibrium in the sense that economic activity is less than optimal. Here, there is also a more troublesome kind of underemployment.

To illustrate the difference, simplify for a moment to the case where leisure has no value to the consumer. Consider those equilibria for which $C < Nf(n/N)$ and $w = 0$. This can be a competitive equilibrium in the labor market, since free goods may be in excess supply. By definition, there is no involuntary unemployment, but there is underemployment in the sense that there are wasted human resources. As in Hart 1982, this occurs because monopoly power in the output markets or monopsony power in the labor market restricts production below the economy's potential.

However, even when there is demand for leisure, one can prove the existence of additional, Pareto-inferior equilibria in the present case. These low-level equilibria also generate lower degrees of econornic activity in general, and so they smack unambiguously of underemployment.

The asset market is described as follows. With identical households, there can be no debt contracts written in equilibrium, and there is no capital. The only possible stores of wealth are therefore either goods or a liquid paper asset such as fiat money. If goods are durable to some extent, the interest rate r_1 represents the rate of depreciation and storage costs. Period 1 saving is, from the budget constraint,

$$s_1 = wL + I_1 + (1 + r_1)s_0 - pc.$$

Unfortunately, if s_1 is dependent on output prices or wage rates, the method of equilibrium analysis used below does not work. There is a fairly realistic case in which s_1 is independent of p and w: Suppose that I_1 consists solely of dividends from current profits, so in equilibrium other income is

$$I_1 = \pi = N\Pi/n = pc - wL.$$

Then

$$s_1 = (1 - r_1)s_0,$$

and the level of saving does not differ across equilibrium states.

Alternatively, goods are not at all durable and there is a supply of fiat money that is fixed at some level m_1.[5] Then $s_1 = m_1$ is an additional equilibrium condition. The level of saving cannot be endogenous; rather, it is determined by the policymaker. Monetary policy can be used to combat underemployment. As is shown below, the levels of output and consumption differ across equilibria, even though the level of saving does not.

A *general Cournot equilibrium* is a price-wage pair (p^j, w^j) for each industry such that (a) consumers maximize U subject to the above budget constraints; (b) producers maximize profits with complete knowledge about the objective market demand functions, with realized forecasts of household income; (c) the output market is in Cournot equilibrium; (d) the labor market is in competitive equilibrium, satisfying (3.1); and (e) the asset market is in competitive equilibrium. We say that the equilibrium is *symmetric* if $(p^j, w^j) = (p, w)$ and $y^j = C/N$ for all j. It is *nontrivial* if $y^j > 0$, for some j.

4 Equilibrium Multiplicity

The theorem of this section establishes that the equilibrium rates of employment, consumption, and output are all below Walrasian levels. This is to be expected when there is some market power. However, there are multiple equilibria, and some of the equilibria involve lower employment and welfare than others. Furthermore, the equilibria are Pareto-ranked. Refer to figure 1.

The agents have identical functional forms for their utility and production functions, so it is no surprise that multiple symmetric equilibria can be Pareto-ranked. The equilibria cannot always be Pareto-ranked by output levels when there are increasing returns, as is shown in figure 2.

Equations (2.1), (2.2), and (3.1) can be shown to be sufficient for equilibrium. If local second-order conditions always hold at values of (p, w, I) satisfying first-order conditions, then there can be only one critical point, and it is the maximizer. Lemma 1 in the appendix formalizes this argument; lemma 2 establishes conditions on the utility and production functions that yield the desired properties of the profit function.

Let the total output of each good be C, and define per capita consumption to be $c \equiv C/n$. If C is given, feasibility dictates per capita labor requirements to be

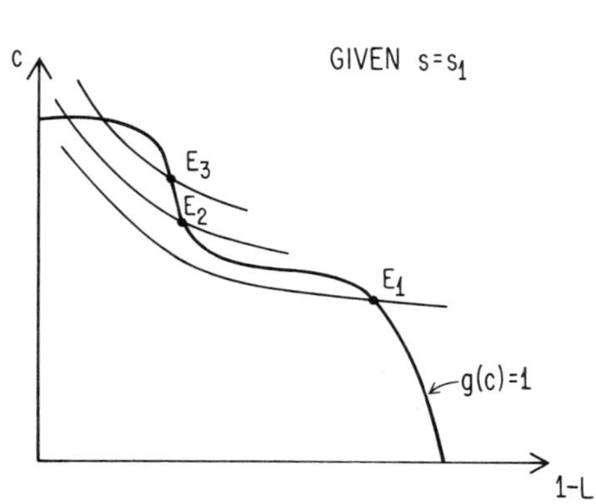

Figure 1

$$L(C) \equiv n^{-1}Ng(N^{-1}C).$$

Let the associated marginal rate of substitution between the present and the future be denoted

$$p(C,s_1) \equiv U_c(c,L(C),s_1)/U_s(c,L(C),s_1).$$

Similarly, define the associated wage rate to be

$$w(C,s_1) \equiv -U_L(c,L(C),s_1)/U_s(c,L(C),s_1).$$

Also, let the associated per capita profit share be defined as

$$\pi(C,s_1) = p(C,s_1)c - w(C,s_1)L(C).$$

Define $I \equiv I(C,s_1)$ to be autonomous income I' plus any portion of other income dependent on C, such as current profits, $\pi(C,s_1)$. Finally, let

$$\varepsilon(C,s_1) \equiv \varepsilon[p(C,s_1), w(C,s_1), I(C,s_1)]$$

and

$$\eta(C,s_1) \equiv 1/\varepsilon(C,s_1).$$

It is not hard to show that if U is separable in L,[6] then

$$\eta(C,s_1) = -\frac{cU_{cc}}{U_c} + \frac{cU_{sc}}{U_s}$$

$$= \text{Elasticity of } U_c - \text{Elasticity of } U_s. \qquad (4.1)$$

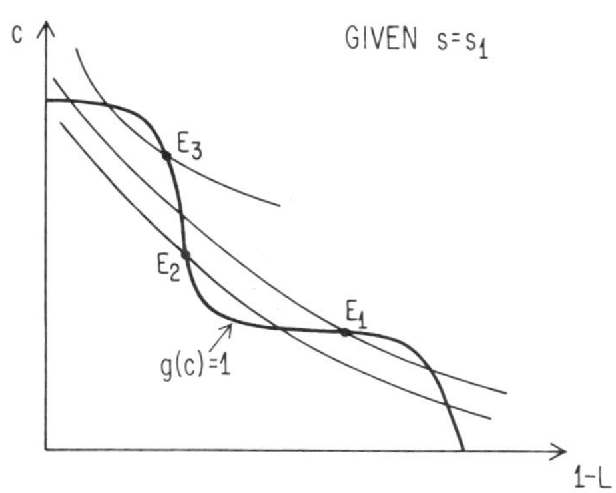

Figure 2

A similar, but more complicated expression would result in the nonseparable case. Thus, we can relate consumer demand elasticity to familiar elasticity parameters of the underlying utility function. Indeed, if the standard recursive preferences (1.9) were the case, we would have $U_{sc} \equiv \partial T/\partial c \equiv 0$ from (1.11). In that case, we would have

$$\eta(C,s_1) = -\frac{cu_{cc}}{u_c}. \tag{4.1'}$$

For the sake of the analysis, it is convenient to rewrite all the functions in (2.1) as functions of C and rearrange terms:

$$\eta(C,s_1) = N\left[1 - \frac{w(C,s_1)g'(C/N)}{p(C,s_1)}\right]. \tag{4.2}$$

Recall that s_1 is fixed either by a monetary authority or by the condition that profits are paid out contemporaneously as dividends. For fixed s_1, (4.2) is an equation in the single unknown, C; as such, it determines a set of equilibrium values of C. It is clear from (4.1) and (4.2) that $\eta(C,s_1)$ can be made to wander on either side of the curve defined by the right-hand side of (4.2), so multiple equilibria are possible (see figure 3). However, it is of greater interest to specify conditions that are sufficient for multiplicity, so that any given realization may be tested in principle for multiple equilibria.

It is established in the appendix that the following two curvature restrictions on preferences vis-à-vis production guarantee that the necessary

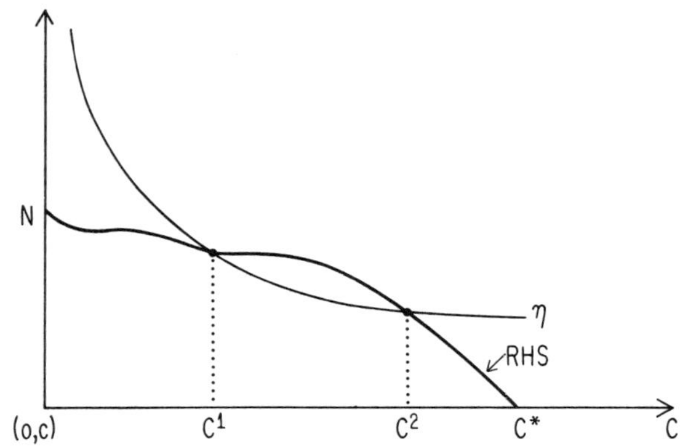

Figure 3

conditions are also sufficient:

(*) There is a $\xi < 1$ such that for all equilibria (p,w), $wg'(0)/p > \xi$.

(**) $\dfrac{EC_p}{Ep} < \dfrac{2}{1-\xi} + \dfrac{\xi\kappa}{(1-\xi)^2}$ at all critical points of $\Pi(\cdot)$.

Because of the presence of increasing returns, a further assumption is needed to ensure that there is a competitive equilibrium; this is necessary for our construction of equilibrium multiplicity.

Assumption C There is a competitive equilibrium, (c^*,L^*).

With figure 1 in mind, this means that the tangent line at (c^*,L^*) never intersects the production frontier, so that profits are non-negative.

The next assumption ensures that firms can make positive profits at some level of production below the Walrasian level. It simply says that at some feasible allocation, there is enough productivity so that marginal profit, $\Pi' = p(1 - N^{-1}\eta) - wg'$, is positive.

Assumption P Let there be a consumption level C', less than the Walrasian level C^*, such that marginal profit is positive, i.e.,

$\eta(C',s_1) < N[1 - w(C',s_1)g'(C'/N)/p(C',s_1)]).$

Let $\underline{c}$ be the lowest (survival) level of consumption for the individual, i.e., the level such that $U'(\underline{c},L,s) = \infty$. By Assumption (U(3)), such a $\underline{c}$ exists. Let $\underline{C} = n\underline{c}$.

THEOREM Under assumptions (C), (P), (U), (*), and (**): (a) Suppose that U is such that the demand elasticity $\varepsilon(\underline{C},s_1)$ at the survival level $\underline{C}$ is less than $1/N$, where N is the number of firms. Then, generically,[7] there exist an even number of nontrivial symmetric general Cournot equilibria, all but one of which is an underemployment equilibrium. (b) The equilibria are Pareto-ranked. If there are no increasing returns, the equilibria with higher levels of underemployment are Pareto-dominated by those with lower levels. (c) If $\eta(\underline{C},s_1) = \infty$, then there is an underemployment equilibrium regardless of the number of firms, N.

Remarks

The condition in (a) above says that demand becomes highly inelastic as consumption nears survival levels. As can be seen from (4.1), this will occur if the own elasticity of marginal utility of consumption in (4.1) becomes sufficiently large as c becomes small. The same kind of reasoning tells us that η will become large when c is small if the cross-elasticity of the marginal utility of saving becomes negative and large in absolute value. An example that meets all the restrictions is given in section 5.

The conditions in (b) are standard neoclassical assumptions, of course. Simple diagrams show that more activity is better if the degree of increasing returns is not too large, but there can be reversals otherwise. See figure 2. The intuition is that a lower level of consumption may be accompanied by a greatly lower level of labor requirements in the locale of a nonconvexity. Still, welfare losses and gains can occur because of coordination failure. Moreover, switches between equilibria may resemble business cycles.

Low-level equilibria are related to Nash equilibria caused by the failure of agents to coordinate their strategies so as to attain the best equilibrium. The only strategic behavior in this model is that of managers of firms. However, there is no incentive for profit-maximizing managers to coordinate their output strategies on low-profit but Pareto-superior equilibria. E.g., if demand is income-inelastic, high-output equilibria could offer lower profits.

In any case, low-level equilibria are *constrained Pareto-inefficient* in the sense that agents could move to better equilibria without changing market institutions.

(c) If consumption demand becomes perfectly inelastic at survival consumption, then the condition is met. The example in section 5 satisfies this property.

Proof (a) Since U is thrice continuously differentiable and by (4.1), there is continuity of η, so the intermediate value theorem applies. Near $\underline{c}$, $w/p = -U_L/U_c$ is near 0, so the RHS of (4.2) is near N. Thus, η is bigger than the RHS of (4.2) near low levels of c. By assumption, η is smaller than the RHS for some values of C below C^*. An intersection of η with the RHS must occur at $C^1 < C^*$, since both of the conditions $\eta > N$ and $\eta < N$ occur for values of C below C^*. At C^*, the RHS is 0 since price equals marginal cost at C^*, i.e., $p = wg'$. Thus, η is larger than the RHS at points just to the left of C^*. Thus, there is at least one other intersection between η and the RHS at a value C^2 between C^1 and C^*. Thus, C^1 is an underemployment equilibrium. It is clear from figure 3 that, generically, there are an even number of nontrivial equilibria. (b) It is clear that the equilibria may be Pareto-ranked, since there is only one representative consumer. To see that without increasing returns the lower-employment equilibrium is always worse, argue as follows: Let L_1 and L_2 correspond to two equilibria such that $L_1 < L_2 < L^*$, and let $C^j = Nf(N^{-1}nL^j)$; thus, $C_1 < C_2 < C^*$. What must be shown is that $U(c_1,L_1 s_1) < U(c_2,L_2,s_1)$, where $c = C/n$. Let $\lambda \in (0,1)$ be such that $c_2 = \lambda c_1 + (1-\lambda)c^*$. Define $\theta = N/n$. By convexity of g,

$$\begin{aligned} L_2 &= \theta g(C_2/N) \\ &= \theta g[\lambda C_1/N + (1-\lambda)C^*/N] \\ &\leq \lambda\theta g(C_1) + (1-\lambda)\theta g(C^*/N) \\ &= \lambda L_1 + (1-\lambda)L^*. \end{aligned} \tag{4.3}$$

By (4.3) and monotonicity in labor,

$$U(c_2,L_2,s_1) > U(c_2,\lambda L_1 + (1-\lambda)L^*,s_1).$$

But, by strict quasi-concavity of U,

$$\begin{aligned} U(c_2,\lambda L_1 + (1-\lambda)L^*,s_1) &= U(\lambda c_1 + (1-\lambda)c^*,\lambda L_1 + (1-\lambda)L^*) \\ &> U(c_1,L_1,s_1). \end{aligned}$$

(c) For any N, one can find a $C > \underline{C}$ such that $\eta(C,s_1) > N$, and so increasing the number of firms cannot remove all the low-level equilibria when $\eta(\underline{C},s_1) = \infty$. ■

The economic reasons for the multiplicity here have partly to do with strategic complementarity as analyzed, say, by Cooper and John (1988) or Milgrom and Roberts (1990). High incomes give rise to high demands, which in turn lead to large-output strategy choices. These, in turn, generate higher incomes.

The link between high demand and high outputs deserves elaboration. Let $(w',I') > (w,I)$; then $c(p,w',I') > c(p,w,I)$. If c_p is not much changed, then elasticity $\varepsilon' < \varepsilon$ at given p. From the markup formula (2.1), this means that output must increase[8] to bring about equality between marginal revenue and marginal cost. The economic intuition for the necessity of the assumption of high demand inelasticity at low levels of output now becomes clear: It is only then that low levels of output can be profit-maximizing. Regardless, there is always some level of output somewhat near the competitive level that is profit-maximizing.

Now look at the causes of multiplicity from a more mathematical point of view. Figure 3 exemplifies the well-known fact that any nonlinear system of equations will generally have multiple solutions. For the case of recursive preferences, (4.1′) makes it clear that greater curvature in utility leads to greater nonlinearities in the equations expressing the equilibrium conditions, (4.2). Also clear from (4.2) is that the nonlinearities will tend to vanish locally at a given level of C, if N is large.

There remains the curious fact that the number of nontrivial equilibria is even. But, there is a trivial equilibrium when one removes the numeraire property from fiat money. If assets have a price of 0, the wage rate is 0, and forecasted profits and other income is 0, then the demand is 0. So the profit-maximizing output is 0. Thus, the total number of equilibria is odd. However, what if inverse elasticity η is strictly bounded above by N? Then there is a unique nontrivial equilibrium, in addition to the trivial one, so the total is even.

5 Policy Remedies and Comparative Statics

What is a policy remedy? If the economy is at one of the low-level equilibria, then an announcement of a deficit-financed tax cut (or subsidy increase) could work. By setting wages and other income equal to that prevailing at a high-level equilibrium, the government effectively raises consumption demand to the level that would induce firms to choose prices and output corresponding to the high-level equilibrium. The increase in the budget deficit only need be temporary, since the increase in production is sufficient to generate the high-level equilibrium employment and income levels. This is Keynesian pump-priming.

As was mentioned in section 4, monetary policy in this model can operate through changes in fiat money, which in turn affects the level of saving, $s_1 = m_1$ and which also can affect s_1 through changes in the interest rate r_1. This is possible because r_1 is not endogenous in the temporary equilibrium conditions. It is apparent from (4.2) that changes in s_1 will change the associated equilibrium set but will not resolve the coordination problem among equilibria.

Thus, a curiosity here is that monetary policy has real effects but cannot compete with fiscal policy in correcting a coordination failure.

Now let us turn to the paradox of thrift. Holding all other aspects of preferences fixed, consider a shift in preferences toward future goods (i.e., an increase in the propensity to save). This could occur either because of a shift in time preference or because of a shift in expectations about the future (for example, consumers could expect lower prices in the future). Model this by a change from the function U to the function $\tilde{U}$ where everywhere $U_s/U_c < \tilde{U}_s/\tilde{U}_c$, i.e., where for all c, $p(C,s_1) > \tilde{p}(C,s_1)$. Let $\tilde{U}$ have the additional property that along the direction given by $s = s_1$ and $L = L(C)$ the rate at which p changes with C, dp/dc, is the same for U as for $\tilde{U}$ at each c. Then $\tilde{\eta}(C,s_1) > \eta(C,s_1)$ for all C.

Finally, suppose that the marginal rate of substitution between leisure and consumption, $w(C,s_1)/p(C,s_1)$, is unaffected. Thus, at every level of C, the RHS of equation (4.3) is unaffected, while the LHS is shifted up. As figure 4 shows, a shift in preference toward more saving and less consumption today can lead to a paradoxical increase in today's consumption at the low-level equilibrium. At the high-level equilibrium, the reverse is true: a shift in favor of future consumption in fact reduces today's consumption.

The following utility and (inverse) production functions serve as an alternative example: Let c be per capita consumption. Then

$$U = \frac{\alpha(c - \underline{c})^{-\sigma}}{1 - \sigma} + \frac{\beta(1 - L - \underline{L})^{1-\tau}}{1 - \tau} + \frac{\gamma(s - \underline{s})^{1-\omega}}{1 - \omega},$$

where

$$L = \delta C^{\mu}.$$

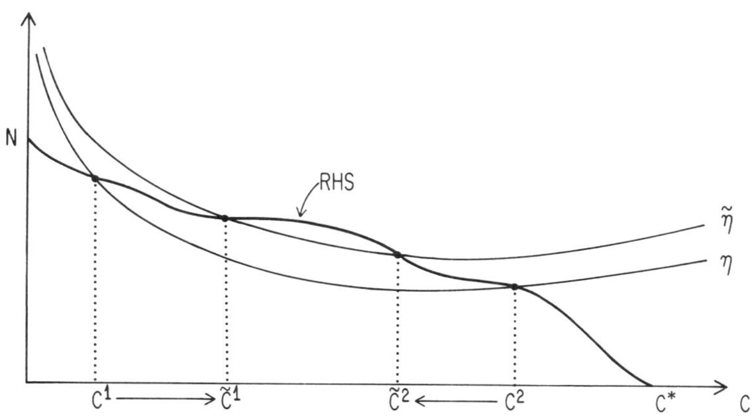

Figure 4

It can be shown that

$$p = \frac{\alpha(c - \underline{c})^{-\sigma}}{\gamma(s_0 - \underline{s})^{-\omega}}$$

and

$$\eta = \frac{\sigma c}{c - \underline{c}},$$

while (if $\mu = 1$) the RHS of (4.3) is

$$\frac{\beta\delta(L - \underline{L} - \delta c)^{-\tau}}{\alpha(c - \underline{c})^{-\sigma}}.$$

This example possesses multiple equilibria if δ is small enough relative to the other parameters. For example, if

$$U = \alpha \log(c - 1) + \beta \log(1 - L - \underline{L}) + \frac{(s - \underline{s})^{1-\omega}}{1 - \omega}$$

and

$$\delta = 0.05,$$

then multiple equilibria exist for all $N \geq 1$ by the same kinds of arguments used in the proof of part a of the theorem. Lowering $\underline{c}$ reduces p and η while raising the RHS of (4.3). This reverses the result of the previous example: a decrease in preference for current consumption increases equilibrium current consumption in the high-level equilibrium and decreases in the low-level one.

As is so often true with comparative statics analysis, it can go either way, depending on utility functions. However, the main point is upheld regardless of the particular utility functions: The actual response of consumption to a shift in saving propensities depends on which one of the many equilibria is the current state of the world.[9]

Conclusion

It has been shown if this model of this paper has any equilibria, it has multiple Pareto-ranked equilibria. The extra assumptions of significance are that utility is sufficiently quasi-concave to offset increasing returns and that consumption demand becomes quite inelastic as consumption nears survival levels.

Under reasonable conditions on the nature of preference shifts toward future consumption, it turns out that a kind of paradox of thrift occurs at the some of the equilibria but not at others.

A standard Keynesian fiscal policy remedy was developed to solve the coordination problem. Monetary policy has real effects but does not handle coordination failures.

Technical Appendix

LEMMA 1 Let assumption U hold. Let (C', L') be any point on the production possibility frontier defined by (3.1) which also satisfies the industry first-order condition (2.1) and the consumer choice first-order condition (2.2). Suppose also that the profit function π for each firm satisfies the local second-order condition for maximization ($\pi_{pp} < 0$) at all the critical points where it satisfies the first-order condition (2.1′); i.e., the profit function is quasi-concave in p. Then (C', L') is a general Cournot equilibrium.

Proof Let p' satisfy condition (2.1) given w' and π'. Let

$$\Pi(p,w',I',Y') \equiv p[C(p,w',I') - ((N-1)/N)Y'],$$

where $Y' \equiv C(p',w',I')$. By (2.1), $\Pi'_p = 0$. It will first be shown that p' is a global maximum. If not, there exists a $\hat{p}$ such that $\Pi(\cdot,w',I',Y')$ is maximized at $\hat{p}$. Suppose $\hat{p} > p'$ (the other case is similar). Then, by the second-order conditions, $\Pi_p < 0$ in a neighborhood to the right of p', whereas $\Pi_p > 0$ in a neighborhood to the left of $\hat{p}$. By continuity of derivatives, there exists a point p'' between p' and $\hat{p}$ such that $\Pi''_p = 0$ and $\Pi''_{pp} > 0$. But this contradicts the hypothesis that the second-order conditions for a maximum are satisfied at every critical point. Thus, p' is the global maximum, and so p' is a Cournot equilibrium for w', I'. By construction, each firm is producing the same level of output at p', so p' is a symmetric Cournot equilibrium. The labor market clears since (3.1) holds. Because of (3.2) and the budget constraint, forecast income is realized. ■

The conditions on profit functions in lemma 1 need to be derived from conditions on the primitives. Lemma 2 does this by giving conditions on the curvatures of the utility and production functions. Define the elasticity operator for any function $y = F(x,z)$:

$$\frac{Ey}{Ex} \equiv -\frac{x\partial F}{y\partial x}.$$

Thus, for

$$p \equiv U_c(c,L,s)/U_s(c,L,s),$$

with

$$s = wL + I + (1 + r_1)s_0 - pc,$$

we have

$$\psi \equiv \frac{Ep}{Ec};$$

i.e., $\psi \equiv \psi(c,L,w,I)$ is the inverse of the price elasticity of demand, ε. ψ equals $\eta(C,s)$ at equilibrium values of w and L.

Graphically, ψ is a measure of the speed with which the marginal rate of substitution between consumption and saving changes per increment of c as one moves up the offer curve determined by w and I. The greater ψ, the less the willingness to consume more as price decreases. From the definition, it is easy to see that ψ can be expressed in terms of the second partial derivatives of the utility function. Conditions on the rate of change of ψ, which amount to another curvature condition on the utility function, are given below.

It can be shown that

$$\frac{E\varepsilon}{Ep} = \frac{EC_p}{Ep} - \varepsilon - 1$$

and that

$$\frac{E\psi}{Ec} = \frac{1}{\varepsilon}\frac{E\varepsilon}{Ep}.$$

It follows that

$$\frac{EC_p}{Ep} = 1 + \varepsilon + \frac{E\varepsilon}{Ep}$$

$$= 1 + \frac{1}{\psi} + \frac{1}{\psi}\frac{E\psi}{Ec}. \qquad \text{(A.1)}$$

Define $\kappa \equiv yg''/g'$ to be the elasticity of the marginal labor requirements function. This is a measure of the returns to scale of the production function. If $\kappa > 0$ we have decreasing returns; $\kappa < 0$ is the case of increasing returns. There will be limits (given in (**) below) put on the degree of increasing returns in order to rule out troublesome convexities in the profit function. If there are no increasing returns, then (**) always holds.

LEMMA 2 Let the utility and production functions satisfy the following conditions:

(*) There is a $\xi < 1$ such that, for all equilibria (p,w), $wg'(0)/p < \xi$.

(**) $\dfrac{EC_p}{Ep} < \dfrac{2}{1-\xi} + \dfrac{\xi\kappa}{(1-\xi)^2}$ at all critical points of $\Pi(\cdot)$.

Then at all critical points, $\Pi_{pp} < 0$.

Remarks Condition (*) places a bound on the marginal rate of substitution between consumption and leisure in equilibrium. Essentially, the condition guarantees that each firm will produce a positive amount in any equilibrium. It can be derived from conditions on the utility function. Condition (**) places an upper bound on $E\psi/Ec$ by equation (A.1). In essence, there must be enough curvature in the utility function to offset the degree of increasing returns.

Proof Define

$$\Pi(p,w,I,Y') \equiv p(C(p,w,I) - Y') - wg(C(p,w,I) - Y').$$

Then

$$\Pi_p = C - Y' + (p - wg')C_p,$$

where the subscript denotes partial derivative with respect to price p. The first-order condition is

$$\Pi_p = pC_p\left[\frac{C - Y'}{pC_p} + 1 - \frac{wg'}{p}\right] = 0, \tag{2.1'}$$

or

$$\frac{C - Y'}{-pC_p} = \frac{y}{C\varepsilon} = 1 - \frac{wg'}{p} > 1 - \xi > 0, \tag{A.2}$$

by (*). The last term on the RHS of (2.1′) represents marginal cost, whereas the previous terms together are marginal revenue. This expression yields (2.1) if all firms produce at the same level: $y \equiv C - Y' = C/N$.

The seond partial of Π is

$$\Pi_{pp} = 2C_p + pC_{pp} - wg'C_{pp} - wC_p^2 g''$$
$$= C_p\left[2 - \frac{EC_p}{Ep} + \frac{wg'}{p}\frac{EC_p}{Ep} - wC_p g''\right]. \tag{A.3}$$

The slope of marginal revenue is contained in the first two terms of (A.3) and is

$$C_p(2 - EC_p/Ep). \tag{A.4}$$

The sum of the last two terms in (A.3) is the slope of marginal cost, which can be written

$$-C_p\left[wC_p g'' - \frac{wg'}{p}\frac{EC_p}{Ep}\right]. \tag{A.5}$$

The term in the brackets in (A.5) is equal to

$$\frac{wg'}{p}\left[\frac{pC_p g''}{g'} - \frac{EC_p}{Ep}\right] = \frac{wg'}{p}\left[-\frac{C}{y}\frac{pC_p}{C}\frac{yg''}{g'} - \frac{EC_p}{Ep}\right]$$
$$= \frac{wg'}{p}\left[-\frac{C}{y}\varepsilon\kappa - \frac{EC_p}{Ep}\right]. \tag{A.6}$$

Using (A.6), (A.3) becomes

$$\Pi_{pp} = C_p\left[2 - \frac{EC_p}{Ep} - \frac{wg'}{p}\left[-\frac{C}{y}\varepsilon\kappa - \frac{EC_p}{Ep}\right]\right]$$
$$= C_p\left[2 + \frac{wg'}{p}\frac{C}{y}\varepsilon\kappa - \left(1 - \frac{wg'}{p}\right)\frac{EC_p}{Ep}\right]. \tag{A.7}$$

By (*), wg'/p has an upper bound of $\xi < 1$. Therefore, by (A.2), $\varepsilon C/y$ has an upper bound of $(1 - \xi)^{-1}$. The second term in (A.7) has a lower bound of $\xi\kappa/(1 - \xi)$. It follows that the expression in brackets in (A.7) is greater than

$$2 + \frac{\xi\kappa}{1 - \xi} - (1 - \xi)\frac{EC_p}{Ep} > 0$$

by (**). Thus, $\Pi_{pp} < 0$, since $C_p < 0$.

Acknowledgments

Thanks are due to Russell Cooper, Douglas Gale, Louis-Andre Gerard-Varet, Karl Shell, and Joaquim Silvestre for helpful comments. I am also grateful to the NSF for partial support.

Notes

1. Although the latter occurs under "Keynesian" conditions wherein high production levels are associated with high worker incomes and demand, the opposite happens if demand is inelastic. In this case, higher incomes can be associated with lower output. This happens because the firms can be very profitable through charging high prices. In this case, high profits occur when output is low. Managers in these conditions will oppose a policy movement to a high-output equilibrium.

2. To have past realizations affect current expectations would create major difficulties for the simple methods used below to establish multiple equilibria. Otherwise, degree theory methods would have to be substituted.

3. The Cournot conjecture of constant output by other firms is maintained, albeit that price rather than quantity is the decision variable. The proof of lemma 2 below contains a derivation of (2.1).

4. Even though the current interest rate r_1 enters only as an income effect, tomorrow's interest rate r_2 does affect the margin between the present and the future, because the function U depends on it implicitly via equations (1.8)

5. If both cases hold, then $s_1 = (1 + r_1)s_0 = m_1$ and $s_0 = m_0$. Thus, r_1 is the rate of growth of the money stock.

6. I.e., $U(c,L,s) = u(c,s) + \varphi(L)$. Differentiating $p(c) = U_c(c,s)/U_s(c,s)$ yields the result.

7. It is possible that there are an odd number if the curves are just tangent at a point.

8. I.e., price must decrease and marginal cost must increase.

9. This model could be extended to provide a rigorous account of the famous passage from Keynes to the effect that a decision by consumers to temporarily postpone today's buying can lead to a permanent contraction in economic activity tomorrow instead of the increase that was intended by consumers. This can be illustrated by considering the case of many equilibria. The temporary shift in today's consumption demand can mislead producers into thinking that they are now at one of the lower-level equilibria. They shift their output and hiring strategies accordingly, which leads to a low-level income for consumers, who have returned to their old buying behaviors, but the lower level of income leads to less consumption. If the shifts are exactly right, the prophecy by producers that they are at a new, lower-level equilibrium is self-fulfilling. If the shifts are not exactly right, one must go into some detail to establish the local stability of the adjustment dynamics out of equilibrium. Short of a situation with a continuum of equilibria, this kind of analysis could be exemplary of Keynes' paradigm. It is also clear that a futures market could prevent the pernicious dynamics possible with missing markets.

References

Bryant, John. 1987. "The paradox of thrift, liquidity preference, and animal spirits." *Econometrica* 55: 1231–1235.

Cooper, Russell, and Andrew John. 1988. "Coordinating coordination failures in Keynesian models." *Quarterly Journal of Economics* 103: 441–463.

Diamond, Peter. 1982. "Aggregate demand management in search equilibrium." *Journal of Political Economy* 90: 881–894.

Durlauf, Steven. 1990. Locally Interacting Systems, Coordination Failure, and the Behavior of Economic Activity. NBER working paper.

Grandmont, Jean-Michel. 1986. *Money and Value*. Cambridge University Press.

Hahn, Frank. 1978. "On non-Walrasian equilibria." *Review of Economic Studies* 45: 1–18.

Hall, Robert. 1988a. "The relation between price and marginal cost in U.S. industry." *Journal of Political Economy* 96: 921–947.

Hall, Robert. 1988b. Increasing Returns: Theory and Measurement Using Industry Data. Mimeo, Stanford University.

Hart, Oliver. 1982. "A model of imperfect competition with Keynesian features." *Quarterly Journal of Economics* 98: 109–138.

Heller, Walter P. 1986. "Coordination failure in complete markets with applications to effective demand." In *Equilibrium Analysis: Essays in Honor of Kenneth J. Arrow*, volume 2, ed. W. P. Heller et al. Cambridge University Press.

Kiyotaki, Nobu. 1988. "Multiple expectational equilibria under monopolistic competition." *Quarterly Journal of Economics* 103: 695–713.

Milgrom, Paul, and John Roberts. (1990). "Rationalizability, learning, and equilibrium in games with strategic complementarities." *Econometrica* 58: 1255–1275.

Roberts, John, and Hugo Sonnenschein. 1976. "On the existence of Cournot equilibrium without concave profit functions." *Journal of Economic Theory* 13: 112–117.

Weitzman, Martin. 1982. "Increasing returns and the foundations of unemployment theory." *Economic Journal* 92: 787–804.

Properties of Aggregate Saving in Overlapping-Generations Models

David A. Starrett

One of the most important features of life-cycle models is the fact that (in the absence of credit restrictions) consumption profiles depend only on lifetime wealth and not on the particular income profile.[1] A natural corollary of this proposition is that saving behavior will respond in a quite predictable way to changes in this income profile. For example, if the change occurs in such a way as to leave wealth invariant, consumption will be invariant and private saving will simply "undo" the income change. Here we will exploit this structure to analyze the long-run behavior of aggregate-savings functions derived from an overlapping-generations model. First, we analyze the effects on private saving of transfer programs such as "pay as you go" social security. Later, we look at target saving for big-ticket items.[2]

Almost all practical questions concerning the responsiveness of saving to changes in prices and income are complicated by issues of uncertainty and expectations. If the interest rate changes today, people's behavior will be quite different if they believe the change is permanent than if they think it is temporary. Indeed, the short-run saving function cannot be defined without reference to some explicit expectations assumption. However, it is possible to talk about a long-run savings function without any such reference. This is done by evaluating steady-state responses to permanent shifts in underlying parameters of the income profile or the price structure. This paper is confined to studying such long-run responses.[3]

In principle, long-run saving responses can be computed from aggregate data as follows. With B_t standing for aggregate net saving balances at date t, the aggregate budget constraint may be written as

$$S_t = \frac{\partial B_t}{\partial t} = rB_t + W_t - C_t, \tag{1}$$

where W_t stands for the value of aggregate market resources at date t and C_t stands for the corresponding value of aggregate consumption. In a long-run steady state, B must grow at the natural rate of growth of the economy (m). Consequently, we have the steady-state relationship

$$B = \frac{C - W}{r - m}, \tag{2}$$

where capital letters without time subscript stand for steady-state levels as of date 0.

Assuming that resources are supplied exogenously, aggregate saving responses can be computed from knowledge of an aggregate long-run consumption function; for example, the pure interest-rate response is calculated as

$$\eta^{s} = \frac{C}{C - W}\eta^{c} - \frac{r}{r - m}, \tag{3}$$

where η^{s} stands for the long-run interest elasticity of saving and η^{c} stands for the corresponding elasticity of consumption. Note that nothing is assumed about structure in this formulation except the presence of a perfect capital market. Note further that changes in income profile that do not affect the wealth of individual households would affect aggregate saving only through their impact on aggregate resources (W).[4]

1 Responses of Saving to Exogenous Changes in Income

One important implication of our perfect-capital-markets formulation is that all the information about behavior we need to compute long-run saving responses to changes in income is captured in a single number. We can see this as follows: Suppose we want to calculate the impact on saving of a particular "permanent" change in the resource profile. (The change is permanent in that it is the same for all future generations.) We start with an arbitrary status-quo resource profile $w(\cdot)$, where $w(v)$ stands for the resources that will accrue at age v to the generation born today. Then, under the constant-growth assumption (with a T-period life span), today's aggregate resources are measured as

$$W^{m} = \int_{v=0}^{T} w(v)e^{-mv}dv. \tag{4}$$

This profile is to be changed in some direction defined by relative shares $a(v)$. If we let λ parametrize the magnitude of the change, then the new resource profile ($w_{\lambda}(v)$) becomes

$$w_{\lambda}(v) = w(v) + \lambda a(v). \tag{5}$$

We focus on evaluating the responses in saving to a change in λ for an arbitrary profile $a(\cdot)$. Here, we use the key feature of the life-cycle model with perfect capital markets: consumption depends on resources only through their present value (W^r); in particular,

$$\frac{\partial c(v)}{\partial \lambda} = \frac{\partial c(v)}{\partial W^r} a(v). \tag{6}$$

Consequently, when we differentiate with respect to λ in (2) we obtain

$$\frac{\partial B}{\partial \lambda} = \frac{1}{r - m}\left[\frac{\partial C^m}{\partial W^r} A^r - A^m\right], \tag{7}$$

where A^x stands for the discounted value of $a(\cdot)$ using discount rate x. Thus we see that all relevant information about individual behavior is contained in the single number $M = \partial C^m/\partial W^r$. As we will see momentarily, the magnitude of M is related to the rate at which compound interest accumulates relative to the size of the economy.

Although the magnitude of M must depend in some ways on the nature of preferences, we can argue that it will be greater than 1 assuming only that the interest rate exceeds the growth rate and that consumption at each date is a normal good. To see this, note that the budget constraint implies $\partial C^r/\partial W^r = 1$ and

$$M - 1 = \frac{\partial(C^m - C^r)}{\partial W^r} = \int_0^T \frac{\partial c(v)}{\partial W^r}(e^{-mv} - e^{-rv})dv. \tag{8}$$

Since maintained assumptions imply that all terms in the integrand are positive, M must exceed 1. Further, M is an increasing function of the gap between the interest rate and the growth rate in the sense that, for a given interest rate, M decreases in the growth rate.

A sharper lower bound can be placed on M if we are willing to make some assumptions about the form of preferences. For example, if we knew that preferences were homothetic, we would know that a proportional increase in all resources would lead to a proportional increase in saving. Consequently, the right side of (7) will be non-negative when $a(v) = w(v)$, which implies

$$M > W^m/W^r. \tag{9}$$

(Indeed, referring to (7), we see that (9) must hold as long as saving does not fall when resources are increased proportionally.) To get some flavor for the orders of magnitude involved here, suppose that resources grow at a constant rate g within a cohort lifetime up to the retirement age J. Then we can compute the closed-form formula:

$$\frac{W^m}{W^r} = \frac{g - r}{g - m} \frac{e^{(g-r)J} - 1}{e^{(g-m)J} - 1}. \tag{10}$$

With a working lifetime of $J = 40$, the lower bound on M depends primarily on the gap between r and m, regardless of the absolute values of growth parameters. When this gap is 0.01 the lower bound is approximately 1.2. With a gap of 0.02 the lower bound rises to 1.5, and with a gap of 0.03 to 1.8.

Further intuition for the magnitude of M can be gained by computing its value for commonly used functional forms. Such computations for an additive separable Stone-Geary functional form showed that, even though this form is not homothetic, values computed for M were still roughly consistent with the bounds found above. (See appendix A for details of the functional form simulated.)

2 The Effect on Private Saving of Intergenerational Transfers

We now consider the effects of "forced-saving" programs (such as social security). In the absence of private transfer links among generations, we expect that a government "forced-saving" program will lower private saving. Indeed, our model implies that if the government institutes a forced-saving program paying the rate of interest and consumers face no borrowing constraints, then private saving falls by exactly the same amount by which government saving increases. (Neutrality always holds for present-value transfers within a family.) When the government instead institutes pay-as-you-go transfers from young to old, there is no government saving, but there will still be a reduction in private saving.[5] Here, we will assume that the market interest rate exceeds the growth rate, so that participation in the government program will not be voluntary.[6]

It is commonly believed that the private response will be less than one-for-one in the sense that households will reduce their private saving by less than the government "attempts" to increase it. There are two reasons for this belief: first, empirical studies appear to confirm it; second, it has to be true in the two-period Fisherian (1936) model of saving as long as consumption is a normal good in both periods. However, both of these arguments are misleading in the present context. Indeed, I will show that a magnification in the steady-state saving response is at least theoretically possible.

We will examine the empirical evidence later. However, to get some intuition for where the magnification effect may come from, it is useful to start with the Fisherian argument. Suppose the government institutes a transfer program from young to old in a two-period context and that consumers reduce their saving balances by an exactly compensating amount. Here this means they reduce private saving when young by exactly the amount of the "social security tax," which implies that they do not change their planned consumption during the "saving" period of the program. As long as the interest rate exceeds the growth rate, this plan will require that they reduce consumption during "retirement" over what it otherwise would have been. (Wealth is reduced by the "unfair" forced-saving program.) Given normality of consumption demand in each period, the consumer can improve on this plan by reducing consumption some in the early period also, thus reducing saving by less than the amount of the tax.

Why does this logic not carry over to the general continuous-time model? The reason has to do with the accumulation of interest within the saving period. Suppose households reduced their contributions to private saving plans *in each period* by exactly the amount by which taxes increased. Then the reduction in steady-state private saving balances would *already* be larger than the (paper) saving balances attributable to the pay-as-you-go plan, because of the forgone interest that otherwise would have accumulated in private accounts. Now, the Fisherian logic still implies that private saving will be reduced somewhat less than taxes increase, but the net effect clearly is ambiguous.

To sort out these effects rigorously, we must first develop a measure for the size of a forced-saving program. Suppose we consider the long-run effect on saving of a forced change in cohort consumption plans of the form

$$\Delta c(v) = a(v); \tag{11}$$

saving is "forced" in that we insist here that changes in the income stream translate directly into corresponding changes in the consumption stream. Suppose further that this program pays an implicit rate of return ρ so that

$$\int_{v=0}^{T} a(v)e^{-\rho v}dv = 0. \tag{12}$$

Assuming that this program is completely isolated from other decisions (so that it is not undone by consumer reactions), the same reasoning used above implies that steady-state balances attributable to this program (ΔB^{ρ}) will be measured by

$$\Delta B^{\rho} = \frac{1}{\rho - m} \int_{v=0}^{T} a(v) e^{-mv} dv. \tag{13}$$

When the interest rate happens to equal the growth rate (as with pay-as-you-go social security) the quotient above is indeterminate, and we use L'Hospital's rule to compute

$$\Delta B^{m} = \int_{v=0}^{T} v a(v) e^{-mv} dv. \tag{14}$$

In order to compare pay-as-you-go plans to forced-saving programs paying other rates of return, it is useful to express ΔB^{ρ} as a Taylor expansion in $\rho - m$:

$$\Delta B^{\rho} = \int_{v=0}^{T} v a(v) e^{-mv} dv - \frac{\rho - m}{2} \int_{v=0}^{T} v^2 a(v) e^{-mv} dv + \text{higher-order terms}. \tag{15}$$

Given these measures for the size of an exogenously imposed saving program, we ask how the private economy will respond to the imposition of such a program when cohorts have the opportunity to alter their behavior as they choose. That is, we think of the government program as augmenting private resources by amount $\lambda a(v)$ at age v, and we seek to measure the effect on private saving balances *after* consumption decisions are adjusted in an optimal way.

If the government program is fair (pays the market rate of interest r), the change in private resource profile will have no effect on private wealth ($A^r = 0$) and therefore no effect on the consumption plan. Consequently, our general expression (7) implies

$$\left.\frac{\partial B}{\partial \lambda}\right|_{\lambda=1} = -\frac{1}{\rho - m} \int_{v=0}^{T} a(v) e^{-mv} dv. \tag{16}$$

Thus, comparing with (13), we see that private saving goes down by exactly the same amount by which public forced saving goes up. This verifies the observation made above.

Now, suppose the public program we contemplate is pay-as-you-go so that it satisfies the normalization

$$A^m = \int_{v=0}^{T} a(v)e^{-mv}dv = 0. \tag{17}$$

What will be the saving response now? Since aggregate resources are uneffected, all the effects must be realized through the impact of changes in the present value of wealth on aggregate consumption. Thus,

$$\left.\frac{\partial B}{\partial \lambda}\right|_{\lambda=1} = M\frac{1}{r-m}\int_{v=0}^{T} a(v)e^{-rv}dv. \tag{18}$$

Representing the decrease in present value as a Taylor approximation in $r - m$, to facilitate comparison, yields

$$\left.\frac{\partial B}{\partial \lambda}\right|_{\lambda=1} \approx M\left[-\int_{v=0}^{T} va(v)e^{-mv}dv + \frac{r-m}{2}\int_{v=0}^{T} v^2 a(v)e^{-mv}dv\right]. \tag{19}$$

Expression (19) seems to capture the two effects discussed above. The first term represents a magnification (at rate M) of the saving response that will result from the compounding of interest if consumers choose their new saving stream "as if" there was no wealth effect; the second term provides a correction for further adjustments to this plan. The resolution of this "conflict" depends on specific features of the saving profile and other parameters.

To get some feel for the relative importance of these influences, the model was simulated with a Stone-Geary cohort preference function. (See appendix A for the precise specification.) Unfortunately, as has been found before in work with this type of model, results are quite sensitive to specification, so no definitive conclusions are possible without some difficult empirical work. However, it does seem that the intertemporal elasticity of substitution has to be relatively high before a more than one-for-one reduction in private saving can be observed. For example, when the single period felicity functional form

$$U[c_v] = \frac{[c_v - \bar{c}_v^s]^\gamma}{\gamma}$$

is used, it is found that with γ less than about -1, private saving always responds less than one-for-one to social security. On the other hand, with

$\gamma = 0$ (the logarithmic form) saving goes down by as much as 120% of the size of the social security program.

Most empirical studies to date have appeared to show a less than one-for-one response of private saving to social security saving.[7] However, these studies are not definitive for our purposes, since they look at flow rates of saving rather than saving balances and are not based on steady-state comparisons. Indeed, most of the data on which empirical estimates are based involve a period of time when the older generation's wealth was increased by an initial social security windfall. In such a period, the presence of social security has a positive wealth effect and consequently may reduce private saving less than one- for-one.

3 Target Saving

We now use the simple analytics of steady-state overlapping-generation saving to analyze the commonly held view that target saving has a negative influence on saving elasticities. It is widely believed that the income effect due to an increase in interest rates has a significant negative impact on saving.[8] The starkest examples of this effect come from models of target saving in which a consumer saves for the purpose of buying an item of fixed size (so that there is no substitution effect). Clearly, the higher the interest rate in this situation, the less money must be committed for a fixed period of time (or, alternatively, the shorter the length of time a fixed amount of money need be committed) in order to purchase this item, so that saving will fall as the interest rate rises.

This negative influence is easily quantified in a two-period model. If Γ represents the fixed purchase size and S stands for the amount saved in the initial period, then $S(1 + r) = \Gamma$, where r stands for the interest rate. Differentiating with respect to r and rearranging somewhat, we find

$$\frac{1 + r}{S}\frac{dS}{dr} = -1; \tag{20}$$

that is, the elasticity of saving with respect to its return factor is -1.

However, there are again reasons to believe that a two-period model is misleading; in particular, it generally will overstate the importance of income effects in saving. For example, in a world with additively separable logarithmic preferences (and no big-ticket items), income effects exactly cancel substitution effects of interest-rate changes on savings in the two-period model, whereas they are less important in multiple-period alternatives.[9] And regardless of the merits or deficiencies of a two-period model for studying general saving issues, it obviously cannot be appropriate for addressing issues of timing. This is unfortunate, since timing issues are likely to be important for many target saving items (houses, vacations, etc.).

Naturally, when timing changes, the saving profile for any given household changes with it. Therefore, to study the systematic effects on aggregate saving, we need to aggregate over cohorts in an overlapping-generations context. Also, to avoid time-interval effects, we employ a continuous-time formulation. Below, we develop a simple framework for studying timing effects associated with target purchases and ask whether or not they generate negative elasticities.

Target saving associated with big-ticket items raises many interesting questions with respect to short-run (or transition) saving behavior. For example, if increases in the interest rate induce the new generation to plan for earlier purchase, then there is likely to be a transition period in which that generation and previous generations are purchasing concurrently. Such a "hump" in purchases will reduce short-run savings. While this and related issues are important, they are difficult to formalize analytically and will not concern us here. Rather, we will focus on long-run steady states, as in the previous section, and ask how changes in the steady-state interest rate would affect saving associated with target purchases.

4 Big-Ticket Items and Target Saving

Here we isolate those elements of consumption that are associated with big-ticket purchases, and further assume that the size of these purchases is fixed so the associated saving will be "target" in character. Ways in which our model can be imbedded in a broader context will be discussed later.

It turns out that the timing choice need not have much effect on saving response functions as long as the growth rate is "close" to the interest rate. Intuitively, the reason is as follows: If people are induced to purchase earlier in life, then each of them will indeed be saving less. However, the saving they do occurs earlier in life, so there is "more" of it relative to the (fixed) size of the economy. These two effects will tend to cancel. Of course, if people are induced to purchase later in life, these considerations work in reverse and any positive effect on saving is correspondingly muted.

To explore this tradeoff, we assume that a fixed resource stream is used to finance the purchase of the target big-ticket item. The item is purchased as soon as it can be afforded using these resources. Since perfect capital markets are assumed, we may expect to see some borrowing at the date of purchase (so some resources are committed after the date of purchase to repay debt). However, we do want to assume that the big ticket is large enough relative to the bundle of resources committed to it so that positive saving on balance (more saving beforehand than borrowing after) will be required for feasibility. This requirement always can be achieved with a sufficiently large "ticket"; for example, if big-ticket cost is set equal to end-of-life saving balances achievable with committed resources, there will be no borrowing period at all.

A typical consumer commits the exogenous income stream $w(v)$ at age v. This income is used to purchase a single big-ticket item at fixed cost Γ at age v^*. Given a constant interest rate r, the budget constraint faced

$$\Gamma e^{-rv^*} = \int_{v=0}^{T} w(v)e^{-rv}dv. \tag{21}$$

To avoid boundary problems, we further assume that the range of parameter values is such that v^* is strictly interior in the interval $[0, T]$. Under maintained assumptions, aggregate consumption of big-ticket items at date t will be measured as $\Gamma e^{m(t-v^*)}$. (Note that aggregate consumption is measured as a flow: stock purchase times density of purchasers per unit time.) Now we use (2) to obtain the following formula for steady-state savings balances:

$$B = \frac{1}{r-m}\left[\Gamma e^{-mv^*} - \int_{v=0}^{T} w(v)e^{-mv}dv\right]. \tag{22}$$

To analyze the impact of interest-rate changes, we differentiate, obtaining after substitution

$$\frac{dB}{dr} = \frac{-B}{r-m} - \frac{m\Gamma}{r-m}\frac{dv^*}{dr}e^{-mv^*}. \tag{23}$$

We see that there are two influences, one proportional to the net saving balance (B), which we may think of as the pure target effect, and the other proportional to the growth rate (m), which we may think of as the pure timing effect.

It is convenient to adopt the following shorthand:

$$F(y) = \int_{v=0}^{T} w(v)e^{-y(v-v^*)}dv. \tag{24}$$

Then we can write the budget constraint as

$$\Gamma = F(r) \tag{25}$$

and the saving balance as

$$B = e^{-mv^*}\frac{F(r) - F(m)}{r - m}. \tag{26}$$

Recall that we have chosen relative magnitudes to ensure that B will be positive; as is shown in appendix B, this implies $F'(r) > 0$. With Γ fixed, the tradeoff between timing and interest rate can be computed from the budget constraint as

$$\left.\frac{dv^*}{dr}\right|_{\Gamma} = -\frac{F'(r)}{rF(r)} < 0. \tag{27}$$

Thus, an increase in the interest rate will cause people to purchase earlier, as we would expect under maintained assumptions. Combining (23) and (27) and substituting from (25) and (26), we obtain the following expression for interest elasticity:

$$\left.\frac{r\,dB}{B\,dr}\right|_{\Gamma} = m\frac{F'(r)}{F(r) - F(m)} - \frac{r}{r - m}. \tag{28}$$

Notice first that we get the pure-target-saving result (elasticity $= -1$) when the growth rate equals 0. However, with positive growth there is a positive contribution deriving from the fact that aggregate spending per person increases with an earlier acquisition date. Indeed, it can be proved that the elasticity is always larger than -1 whenever the growth rate is positive (see appendix B), and computations show that the elasticities rise rapidly in m. Consider the following example, which utilizes a growth rate of $m = 0.035$, a working life of $T = 40$, a resource growth rate within lifetime of $h = 0.02$, and a status-quo purchase date of $v^* = 19$:[10]

interest rate:	0.04	0.05	0.06	0.07
saving rate:	0.05	0.07	0.09	0.12
interest elasticity:	0.76	0.19	−0.09	−0.25

We see that the elasticity is positive until the interest rate reaches a level roughly twice the growth rate. Although it is difficult to know exactly what relationship is empirically reasonable since we have not dealt with uncertainty and associated risk premiums, these and similar calculations suggest that relevant elasticities will be well away from −1, if not actually positive.

Of course, the model considered here is very stark, and there are many reasons why the presence of big-ticket items might affect saving in other ways. For example, if the decision of whether or not to purchase becomes endogenous to the model, we might expect interest-rate increases to stimulate saving by inducing more people to engage in big-ticket purchases. Moreover, even if we assume that everyone buys, the particular assumptions we made to isolate target saving from the overall consumer choice problem are quite restrictive. Unfortunately, if we try to imbed the big-ticket choice into a general life-cycle problem it is difficult to say much analytically about resulting properties. However, the preceding analysis suggests that, regardless of whether interest-rate changes induce earlier or later purchase dates, the effect on elasticities will be less than might have been predicted on the basis of naive reasoning. Indeed, we have simulated a model incorporating both big-ticket purchases and standard flow consumption (see appendix A for the precise formulation) and found that the timing response of the big-ticket purchase had a quite minor effect on corresponding savings elasticities (see Starrett 1988).

Appendix A

In the additively separable Stone-Geary formulation, the cohort born at date s solves a lifetime problem of the form

$$\text{Max} \int_{v=0}^{T} \frac{[c_v - \bar{c}_v^s]^\gamma}{\gamma} e^{-\delta v} dv \tag{A.1}$$

subject to

$$\int_{v=0}^{T} c_v e^{-rv} dv = \int_{v=0}^{T} w_v^s e^{-rv} dv - \Gamma^s e^{-rv*},$$

where, apart from standard variables, $\bar{c}_v^s$ stands for the consumption base, Γ^s for the amount of a big-ticket purchase, and v^* for the age at which this purchase is made. Of course, γ represents the elasticity of "felicity" with respect to consumption and serves to index the intertemporal elasticity of substitution (σ). Indeed, $\sigma = 1/(1-\gamma)$.

Problem (A.1) is easily solved in closed form and yields the consumption functions

$$c_v^s = \bar{c}_v^s + (N^s - \Gamma^s e^{-rv^*})\left[\frac{x}{e^{xT}-1}\right] e^{(r-\delta)/(1-\tau)^v}, \tag{A.2}$$

where

$$x = \frac{\gamma r - \delta}{1-\gamma}, \quad N^s = \int_{v=0}^{T} [w_v^s - \bar{c}_v^s] e^{-rv} dv.$$

In simulating this model, we made the following assumptions. Cohorts grow at the constant rate n per unit time. Within lifetimes, incomes grow at the constant rate h up to the date of retirement $\hat{T}$, while the consumption base grows at constant rate k. Economy-wide productivity grows at the rate g over time, so that initial wages of cohort s can be measured as e^{gs}. Further, we suppose that both the initial consumption base and the big-ticket purchase grow at this same rate, g. Although these latter assumptions are required if we are to have steady states, we think they are reasonable in their own right because of the so-called ratchet effect. The perception of "necessities" is relative, so each generation perceives such spending as a constant percentage of the general standard of living. This percentage is parametrized by α, measured as the initial consumption base as a fraction of initial income. Under these assumptions,

$$\bar{c}_v^s = \alpha e^{gs} e^{kv}, \quad \Gamma^s = \Gamma e^{gs}, \tag{A.3}$$

and

$$N^s = \left[\frac{1-e^{-(r-h)\hat{T}}}{r-h} - \alpha\frac{1-e^{-(r-k)T}}{r-k}\right] e^{gs}. \tag{A.4}$$

Aggregate consumption is computed by substituting (A.3) and (A.4) into (A.2) and integrating over cohorts. Aggregate resources are similarly obtained by integrating over cohorts and savings balances computed using (1). For further details and computational formulas, see Starrett 1983.

Appendix B

Here we examine properties of the function $F(\cdot)$. Given that $r > m$ and savings balances are assumed positive, (26) implies $F(r) > F(m)$. Furthermore, differentiating (24) twice yields

$$F''(y) = \int_{v=0}^{T} (v - v^*)^2 w(v) e^{-y(v-v^*)} dv > 0. \tag{B.1}$$

It follows that $F'(r) > 0$, since otherwise F' would have to be nonpositive everywhere in the interval $[m,r]$, contradicting $F(r) > F(m)$.

Equation (B.1) also implies that F is a convex function and must lie everwhere above its supporting hyperplane at r. Consequently,

$$F'(r)(r - m) > F(r) - F(m), \quad \text{or} \quad \frac{F'(r)}{F(r) - F(m)} > \frac{1}{r - m}. \tag{B.2}$$

Substituting this inequality into (28), we find that as long as $m > 0$,

$$\left.\frac{r\,dB}{B\,dr}\right|_{\Gamma} > \frac{m}{r - m} - \frac{r}{r - m} = -1. \tag{B.3}$$

Acknowledgments

I would like to thank Frank Hahn for helpful comments on an earlier version of this paper.

Notes

1. See Ando and Modigliani 1963 for an early discussion of these models.

2. It is assumed here that the reader is familiar with many of the standard issues that arise concerning saving in life-cycle models. See, for example, Auerbach and Kotlikoff 1983a, King 1985, and Kotlikoff 1984.

3. Naturally, short run response functions can be estimated once appropriate expectations assumptions are made; see King 1985 for a survey.

4. For discussions of interest elasticities in this context, see Summers 1981 and Starrett 1983, 1988.

5. These arguments were put forth by Feldstein (1974) and have been discussed and tested by many others since; for example, see Kotlikoff 1979.

6. If the interest rate is less than the growth rate, the economy is dynamically inefficient, and a pay-as-you-go plan dominates private saving; the government can (and should) eliminate this inefficiency by freely offering pay-as-you-go options so as to establish the growth rate as a floor on equilibrium interest rates.

7. See, for example, Kotlikoff 1979 and Auerbach and Kotlikoff 1983b.

8. This belief is due largely to the fact that income effects are commensurate in size and opposite in sign with substitution effects in the two-period saving model of Fisher (1936) when consumption in both periods is a normal good.

9. That the two-period model of saving puts a misleading emphasis on the income effect has been argued by Hall (1979) and Summers (1981).

10. The saving rate is measured here as saving relative to aggregate exogenous resources. Consequently, the numbers are smaller than we would get if we measured saving relative to total income.

References

Ando, A., and F. Modigliani. 1963. "The 'life-cycle' hypothesis of saving: Aggregate implications and tests." *America Economic Review* 53: 55–84.

Auerbach, A., and L. Kotlikoff. 1983a. "National savings, economic welfare, and the structure of taxation." In *Behavioral Simulation Methods in Tax Policy Analysis*, ed. M. Feldstein. University of Chicago Press.

Auerbach, A., and L. Kotlikoff. 1983b. "An examination of empirical tests of social security and savings." In *Social Policy Evaluation: An Economic Perspective*, ed. E. Helpman et al. Academic Press.

Feldstein, M. 1974. "Social security, induced retirement and aggregate capital accumulation." *Journal of Political Economy* 82: 905–926.

Fisher, I. 1936. *The Theory of Interest*. Macmillan.

Hall, R. 1979. "Stochastic implications of the life-cycle-permanent-income hypothesis: Theory and evidence." *Journal of Political Economy* 86: 971–987.

King, M. 1985. "The economics of saving: A survey of recent contributions." In *Frontiers of Economics*, ed. K. Arrow and S. Honka-pohja. Blackwell.

Kotlikoff, L. 1979. "Testing the theory of social security and life cycle accumulation." *American Economic Review* 69: 396–410.

Kotlikoff, L. 1984. "Taxation and savings: A neoclassical perspective." *JEL* 22: 1576–1629.

Starrett, D. 1983. Long Run Savings Elasticities in the Life Cycle Model. Mimeo, Stanford.

Starrett, D. 1988. "Effects of taxes on savings." In *Uneasy Compromise: Problems of a Hybrid Income-Consumption Tax*, ed. H. Aaron et al. Brookings Institute.

Summers, L. 1981. "Capital taxation and capital accumulation in a life cycle growth model." *American Economic Review* 71: 553–544.

Institutional Features of Unemployment Insurance and the Working of the Labor Market

Anthony Barnes Atkinson

The subject of unemployment and the labor market is one which has engaged the attention of Frank Hahn in recent years, and to which he has contributed in a characteristically incisive manner.

My interest in the subject originates from the side of social security and from my concern with the way in which unemployment insurance is treated in economic analyses of the labor market. The principal theme of this paper is that much of the theoretical literature dealing with the relationship between benefits and unemployment fails to capture the essential institutional features of unemployment insurance. The literature—with some notable exceptions—has ignored important aspects of how benefits actually operate in the real world. As a result, the conclusions reached may be misleading. It is not adequate to treat unemployment insurance as simply wages received when not in work. One has to consider the conditions under which benefits are paid, their link to labor-market decisions, the contributory basis of unemployment insurance, and the limited duration of insurance benefit.

Section 1 describes certain key institutional features of unemployment insurance, distinguishing it from unemployment assistance and from general welfare benefits. Among the most important aspects are that claimants may be disqualified from unemployment insurance if they have quit voluntarily or been dismissed for industrial misconduct, that entitlement to benefit depends on the past record of insured employment, and that there is a limited duration of benefit. These features are illustrated by reference to the social security systems of the United States and the United Kingdom. Section 2 considers the extent to which these institutional features have been modeled in a selection of contributions to the theoretical literature on unemployment benefits and the labor market. Section 3 concentrates on a model of a dual labor market with efficiency wages related to the need to induce workers to apply effort, with imperfect matching of unemployed workers and vacancies, and with queue unemployment. This model, used in Atkinson 1988, has evident limitations, but it serves to illustrate some of the key features of unemployment insurance. These features are the subject of section 4. Among the most important of them is that the existence of unemployment insurance does not directly affect the incentive of workers to supply effort, in contrast to what has been assumed in earlier literature, if in the case of dismissal for shirking they are disqualified from benefit. At the same time, unemployment insurance affects the level of wages, since it increases the attractiveness of employment in a sector in which there is an external risk of job termination. The main conclusions are summarized at the end of the paper.

1 Institutional Features of Unemployment Insurance

In much of the literature on unemployment benefit, it is assumed that the benefit operates just like a wage for the unemployed: for example, "the wage when working is w, and is b when not working" (Oswald 1986, p. 369). Probing more deeply, one finds that it is assumed, as far as the recipient is concerned, that

(a) the benefit is paid irrespective of the reasons for entry into unemployment,
(b) there are no contribution conditions related to past employment,
(c) the benefit is not related to past earnings in employment, and is usually assumed to be a constant flat-rate amount,
(d) payment of the benefit is independent of the recipient's efforts to search for new work, or of his availability for work, and
(e) the benefit is paid for an unlimited duration.

On this basis, all of those out of work are assumed to be in receipt of unemployment compensation. Yet in reality this is not the case, because real-world benefits do not satisfy these assumptions.

Unemployment insurance (UI), the principal focus of this paper, is better described as follows:

(a*) the benefit is refused, or there is a period of disqualification, where the claimant has quit employment voluntarily or has been dismissed for industrial misconduct,
(b*) entitlement to UI depends on the past record of insured employment, typically requiring a minimum earnings level for eligibility and a minimum contribution period,
(c*) the UI benefit may be a flat-rate amount, but is more typically related to past earnings,
(d*) continued receipt of benefit is conditional on making demonstrable efforts to search for new employment, on being available for employment, and on accepting suitable job offers, and

(e*) there is a limited duration of entitlement, after which UI benefit ceases to be paid.

As a result of these conditions, there may be a sizeable portion of the unemployed who do not receive UI benefit. There are those who have been refused benefit, or disqualified for a period, on grounds of voluntary quitting or dismissal for industrial misconduct, failing to search for work, or refusing suitable job offers. There are those who do not satisfy the contribution conditions: for example, new entrants to the labor force may not be eligible. There are those who have received UI earlier in their unemployment spell but whose entitlement is now exhausted.

In listing these features, I have referred explicitly to unemployment insurance. It is important to distinguish this from *unemployment assistance* (UA). In some countries, UA is closer to the hypothetical "wage when not working" in that there may be no contribution conditions (condition b) and that it may be paid for an unlimited duration (condition e). However, assumptions a and d are not typically valid. People may be disqualified from UA on grounds of voluntary quitting or dismissal for industrial misconduct; and benefit may be withdrawn if they are not considered to be actively seeking employment or if they refuse suitable job offers.

In what follows, I concentrate on unemployment insurance. Much of the literature has referred to UI, doubtless because in the United States this is the principal social security scheme for the unemployed. In the US there is no specific unemployment-assistance scheme, and the role played by general assistance is limited. The US unemployment-insurance system is a state program, and therefore varies from state to state, but it typically has features similar to those listed under a*–e*. The method of job separation may disqualify an applicant from UI: "The purpose of such qualifications is to restrict benefits to those who become unemployed through no fault of their own; that is, it is generally held that an employee who 'voluntarily' leaves his job should take the consequences. The series of disqualifying reasons includes voluntary separation from work, discharge for misconduct, refusal of suitable work, and unemployment due to a labor dispute." (Williams, Turnbull, and Cheit 1982, p. 394) Eligibility for UI depends on the applicant's having earned qualifying wages in covered employment during the "base year" (for example, the first four of the last five calendar quarters completed prior to filing a claim), generally requiring wages to have been earned in more than one quarter of that year. The benefit formula takes the form in many states of a fraction (for example, 1/26) of the wages in the quarter for which wages were the highest, subject to a minimum and a maximum. Applicants must demonstrate continuing attachment to the labor force by registering for work at an employment office, and are subject to disqualification if they refuse suitable work. Some states pay benefits up to the end of a stated period, but most limit the total dollar payments to a fraction (usually one-third) of the base-year wages. In periods of "high unemployment," the maximum duration may be extended. The benefits are financed by employer contributions, with experience rating of employers (the contribution rate is related to the history of claims). There are some private unemployment-insurance plans, negotiated between unions and employers, known as *supplementary unemployment benefits*, but the coverage of these plans is largely restricted to manufacturing (Oswald 1986). (Private unemployment insurance is discussed in Barr 1988.)

The American UI system therefore departs in significant ways from the hypothetical "wage when not working." The same is true of National Insurance (NI) unemployment benefit in the United Kingdom. Where a claimant left his previous job voluntarily, he may be disqualified from benefit unless there was good cause for leaving. Disqualification may also ensue in the case of dismissal for industrial misconduct, which "can cover a wide range of disruptive behaviour and bad work, which is causally connected with the loss of employment, and where there is evidence of fault" (Fenn 1980, p. 243). There are complex contribution conditions for NI benefit, which were significantly tightened in 1988 (Atkinson and Micklewright 1989). They require that the person should (in effect) have been in the labor force for the two tax years preceding the start of the benefit year, and that contributions should have been paid of at least 25 times the lower limit for weekly earnings in at least one of those years. Contributions are paid by both employers and employees as part of the general National Insurance system, which covers retirement pensions, invalidity benefits, widows' benefits, and other contingencies apart from unemployment (there is no earmarking within the scheme). The UK now has a flat-rate unemployment-insurance benefit (it is the only European Community country not to have an earnings-related system), but an earnings-related supplement was in force from 1966 to 1982. Benefit may be withdrawn if a claimant fails to make use of a reasonable opportunity of suitable employment, refuses to apply for a vacancy, or fails to follow advice intended to assist the claimant in finding a job. National Insurance unemployment benefit is paid for a maximum of one year in any spell of interruption of employment, and two periods of unemployment separated by less than 8 weeks constitute a single spell. Once benefit is exhausted, the person must work at least 13 weeks before any further eligibility is possible (in addition to satisfying the contribution conditions).

In the UK the unemployed may also receive assistance. Historically, this has been quite separate. Unemployment insurance was introduced in Britain by Lloyd George in the National Insurance Act of 1911, which drew on the German social insurance system initiated by Bismarck and on the existing trade-union schemes for insurance against unemployment. Unemployment assistance, on the other hand, had its origins in the Poor Law and now forms part of the general means-tested system of Income Support.

2 Treatment of Unemployment Compensation in the Theoretical Literature: A Selective Review

It is commonly believed that an increase in unemployment benefit leads to a rise in equilibrium unemployment, either directly or else indirectly via an increase in wages. The theoretical literature provides grounds for this belief. (The empirical literature is not considered here, for a recent survey see Atkinson and Micklewright 1989a.)

The *Handbook of Labor Economics* seems an appropriate place to commence this selective review of the theoretical writing on unemployment benefit. In their chapter entitled "The Natural Rate of Unemployment: Explanation and Policy," Johnson and Layard (1986, p. 923) summarize the findings from their first supply-and-demand model: "The model yields some immediate policy insights. It shows, for example, that, if the market clears, unemployment insurance will increase unemployment, as in all our models." In this model, individuals may choose a fraction of the year to be unemployed; in the words of Johnson and Layard, "unemployment is the annual holiday." During this period they receive a benefit, b, in place of wages, so that annual consumption is given by

$$c = (1 - u)w + ub, \tag{1}$$

where u is the fraction of the year spent unemployed. The individual's utility depends on c and leisure (u), and it is assumed that leisure is a normal good. For those choosing an interior value of u, a rise in b reduces the effective labor supply at any given wage on account of both income and substitution effects. If the rise in b is assumed to be financed by a tax on wages in work, then there is purely a substitution effect. The supply curve shifts upward, and there is an increase in "voluntary" unemployment.

The other models considered by Johnson and Layard include those where the firms set wages and those where wages are set by trade unions. In the former case, they consider versions of the efficiency wage model. Suppose that firm i is concerned about the rate at which workers quit—this depending on the variable x which is the ratio of the wage offered by firm i, w_i, to the expected income on quitting, given by the right-hand side of (1), where w is the average wage paid in the rest of the economy. In other words, the quit rate faced by firm i is assumed to be $q(x)$, where

$$x = w_i/[(1 - u)w + ub]. \tag{2}$$

There is a cost-minimizing level of quitting, and hence x, denoted by $x^{\cdot}$. It follows that

$$w_i/w = x^{\cdot}[(1 - u) + u\rho], \tag{3}$$

where ρ is the replacement rate, b/w. In equilibrium all firms pay the same wage, so (3) determines the equilibrium relationship between the replacement rate and the level of unemployment: "If the replacement rate is higher, quitting becomes more attractive and, to offset this, unemployment has to be higher" (Johnson and Layard 1986, p. 961). Johnson and Layard then consider a model of "matching," with frictions in matching workers to jobs and with a cost of unfilled vacancies. The probability of filling a vacancy depends on the proportion of the unemployed who search, and this latter proportion is assumed to be a declining function of the replacement rate; leading again to a positive relationship between benefits and unemployment.

In the union wage-setting model, it is assumed in the simplest version that workers are either employed at the union wage or unemployed and receiving b. The conclusion is straightforward: "... the higher the replacement ratio the less union members will suffer if the union pushes up wages and reduces employment. Thus a higher replacement ratio will lead to lower employment." (Johnson and Layard 1986, p. 974)

In a more realistic dual-labor-market model, with a unionized sector and a non-unionized (competitive) sector, Johnson and Layard assume that there is a queue of unemployed people waiting for union jobs, there being no direct recruitment from the non-unionized sector. There is a union wage differential; people in the unionized sector earn $(1 + \mu)$ times the competitive wage. From the condition that the expected present value of waiting should equal that of working in the competitive sector, Johnson and Layard derive an equilibrium relationship for the unemployment rate (u) and the replacement rate (ρ, defined relative to the competitive wage), the rate of interest (r), the rate of job termination in the union sector (δ), the proportion of employment in the union sector (v), and the union markup (μ):

$$1/u = 1 + r(1 - \rho)/[\delta\mu v]. \tag{4}$$

(See Johnson and Layard 1986, pp. 976–977, where they assume that the present value of a union job is not affected by the probability of termination.) Once more a rise in the benefit rate is associated with a rise in the equilibrium unemployment rate.

In this range of models, therefore, it appears to be the case that a rise in unemployment benefit leads to a rise in equilibrium unemployment. However, it is also clear that the specification of the benefit corresponds to our hypothetical "wage when not working" rather than to the institutional features of UI identified in the previous section. The model of quitting was based on the assumption that benefit would be received, but we have seen that UI in principle disqualifies claimants who have entered unemployment voluntarily. No role is played in any of these models by contribution conditions. All of the unemployed are assumed to receive benefit. No distinction is made between those who have entered unemployment after losing their jobs and those who are new entrants to the labor force (and have no rights to UI). In the model of matching the unemployed person is assumed to be able to choose whether or not to search for a vacancy, whereas UI legislation embodies job-search requirements and in the UK considerable administrative resources are devoted to enforcing this condition. The benefit is assumed in the theoretical models to be of unlimited duration, so that none of the unemployed have exhausted their entitlements. Thus, whatever conclusions may be drawn from these models, they cannot be assumed without further analysis to apply to unemployment insurance with the institutional features identified in section 1.

If we turn to other reviews of the theoretical literature, then the findings are in some cases different. For example, Stiglitz (1986, p. 188) has argued that the policy conclusions drawn may vary in efficiency-wage models:

> The policy consequences may differ markedly depending on the explanation of the dependence of productivity on wages. Consider, for instance, an increase in the unemployment compensation. In the "shirking" version of the efficiency wage model, this results in firms having to raise their wages in order to induce workers not to shirk (the penalty for being caught is smaller at any fixed wage and unemployed level). This in turn results in a higher equilibrium unemployment rate and a higher real wage.... on the other hand, in the quality-efficiency wage model, an increase in unemployment compensation may have a differential effect on the search intensities of individuals of different abilities and thus shift the wage-productivity curve facing different firms. If low productivity workers' search is reduced relative to the high productivity workers, then the applicant productivity-wage curve may shift up ... with a consequent change in the wage (which may either increase or decrease) and increase in the demand for labor.

But despite the different conclusions, the treatment of unemployment compensation is again of the "wage when not working" variety. In the shirking model of Shapiro and Stiglitz (1984), the central feature is the choice between supplying the required level of effort and "shirking" (in which case there is a probability that the worker will be caught and fired by his employer). It is assumed that workers who are fired receive unemployment compensation. Yet we have seen that UI legislation specifically excludes those who are discharged for misconduct (and the same applies to UA). In the real world the condition may not be fully enforced, but the worker has to allow for the possibility that benefit would be denied. The same objection applies to the dual labor market model of Bulow and Summers (1986).

The real-world features of UI have not been totally neglected in the theoretical literature. As was noted above, there are notable exceptions to the criticism made in this paper. Mortensen (1977) and Burdett (1979) have examined the implications of the fact that UI is paid for a limited duration and that entitlement depends on the past earnings record. Burdett and Mortensen (1980) have analyzed the consequences of the fact that UI benefits are paid only to laid-off workers and not to new entrants. The fact that benefits are related to past earnings is the focus of the model of Hey and Mavromaras (1981). Lippman and McCall (1980) have considered the differences between UI and welfare assistance. Hamermesh (1979) has drawn attention to the fact that the possibility of qualifying for UI may induce people to supply more labor. (For further references to the theoretical literature, see Atkinson and Micklewright 1989a.)

From these articles, it is clear that the effects of UI may be rather different from those of a benefit paid simply as a "wage when not working." But this warning has not been heeded, and much of the literature on unemployment continues to treat UI in a oversimplified way. The aim of this paper is to show the effect of introducing into an equilibrium model of unemployment the five features of UI identified in section 1. The representation is necessarily stylized, but it goes beyond earlier research in attempting to introduce all the features rather than just some of them.

The final point to be noted from this brief review of earlier work is that the comparative-static analysis of unemployment compensation has in part treated a rise in benefits with no change in taxes or contributions and in part considered a balanced-budget change, with both benefits and contributions being increased. The latter is illustrated by the first model of Johnson and Layard, where the cost of the benefit is assumed to be met out of a tax on wages in work, but their discussion of the quitting and wage-setting models considers only a rise in benefits with no change in taxes. Shapiro and Stiglitz (1984, p. 439) refer to both benefit and contribution sides of the budget, arguing that the two effects reinforce each other: "Increases in unemployment benefits have the same impact on the No-Shirking Condition [the wage has to rise at any level of employment], but they also reduce labor demand as workers become more expensive [on account of increased contributions], so they cause unemployment to rise for two reasons."

In the analysis of unemployment insurance in section 4 below, both comparative-static exercises are considered. It seems interesting both to ask how the unemployment compensation system as a whole affects the working of the labor market and to examine the impact of changes in benefit levels with no change in contributions (it being assumed that the deficit on the UI scheme is met by lump-sum taxes). The latter is (for example) the relevant question when one is considering policy changes in the UK over the past decade, since benefits have been cut with no corresponding adjustment in contributions.

3 A Dual-Labor-Market Model

The model described in this section draws on a number of sources. The matching of workers and vacancies in a search framework builds on the work of Diamond (1981, 1982), Mortensen (1988), and Pissarides (1979, 1984, 1985). The shirking version of the efficiency wage is discussed by, among others, Bowles (1985), Calvo and Wellisz (1979), Foster and Wan

(1984), and Shapiro and Stiglitz (1984). The dual-labor-market formulation is influenced by Doeringer and Piore (1971), Bulow and Summers (1986), McDonald and Solow (1985), and van de Klundert (1988). As in a number of these articles, the model is dynamic (in continuous time), but the analysis is simplified by concentrating on a stationary state.

The economy is assumed to consist of a primary sector, in which L_p workers are employed each earning a wage w_p, and a less-favored secondary sector, in which L_s workers are employed each earning a wage w_s. The features distinguishing the two sectors are described below. The total labor force is fixed at N, and the level of unemployment is U:

$$U = N - L_p - L_s. \tag{5}$$

In the primary sector, firms are unable to monitor effort precisely and, as in the model of Shapiro and Stiglitz (1984), a worker can choose between supplying effort, at cost ε, and facing a risk λ of being monitored, in which case the worker is fired. Both ε and λ are assumed constant over time. Firms find it profitable to pay a wage premium such that a worker is indifferent between putting in effort and shirking:

$$\varepsilon = \lambda[\Omega_p - \Omega_u] \tag{6}$$

where Ω_p denotes the expected present value of holding a primary-sector job and Ω_u denotes the expected present value of being unemployed. Workers evaluate alternatives in terms solely of the expected present value of a continuous stream of returns, discounted at a constant interest rate r over an infinite horizon. (For a fuller discussion of the contract between firm and worker, including a treatment of "good-behavior bonds," see MacLeod and Malcomson 1989.)

The present value of a primary-sector job depends on the probability of involuntary job loss. Job losses are assumed to take place at a constant rate, δ, and this is taken to be the probability faced by any individual worker in the primary sector. In a stationary state, with constant wages, the present value is stationary, and we can write

$$r\Omega_p = w_p - \varepsilon - \delta[\Omega_p - \Omega_u] = w_p - \varepsilon - \delta\varepsilon/\lambda. \tag{7}$$

Workers are recruited into the primary sector from the stock of unemployed. There is no recruitment directly from secondary-sector employment. This assumption is parallel to that made in the Harris-Todaro (1970) model of migration—see McDonald and Solow 1985. (A more realistic assumption is that there is a lower, but nonzero, probability of moving from the secondary to the primary sector.) There is assumed to be no problem of monitoring work effort in the secondary sector. (This sector may be thought of as small-scale enterprises or as home production.) This means that the present value of a secondary-sector position is, in a stationary equilibrium, simply

$$\Omega_s = (w_s - \varepsilon)/r. \tag{8}$$

There is free movement between the secondary sector and unemployment, so that

$$\Omega_s = \Omega_u. \tag{9}$$

The present value of being unemployed depends on the probability of getting a job in the primary sector. If at any time there are M matches of job vacancies with unemployed workers, and all unemployed face an equal chance of being recruited, then the probability of getting a job is M/U, and we have, in a stationary equilibrium,

$$r\Omega_u = (M/U)[\Omega_p - \Omega_u]. \tag{10}$$

From (7), (8), and (9) we can solve for

$$w_p - w_s = (r + \delta)\varepsilon/\lambda. \tag{11}$$

The wage differential between the two sectors is proportional to the cost of effort; it is not affected by changes in the levels of employment. Using (6), (8), (9), and (10), we obtain

$$w_s = \varepsilon + (M/U)\varepsilon/\lambda \tag{12}$$

and hence

$$w_p = \varepsilon + [M/U + r + \delta]\varepsilon/\lambda. \tag{13}$$

The wage paid in the secondary sector exceeds the cost of effort, since the supply price is determined by the option of being unemployed and seeking a job in the primary sector. The level of wages depends on M/U, which depends on the matching process.

In the conditions described above, a primary-sector job is always accepted by an unemployed worker; however, there is imperfect matching of unemployed workers to vacant primary-sector jobs, so that not all vacancies are filled instantaneously. I work with the special form of the matching function such that, if there are U unemployed and V vacancies, then the instantaneous rate of matching is

$$M = m\sqrt{UV}. \tag{14}$$

In that case,

$$M/U = m\sqrt{V/U} \text{ and } M/V = m\sqrt{U/V}. \tag{15}$$

The ratio V/U determines the probability of getting a primary job offer (M/U) and of a vacancy's being filled (M/V).

How is the number of vacancies in the primary sector determined? It is assumed that there is a fixed cost, c, of advertising a vacancy, which is incurred whether or not the position is filled. There is assumed to be free entry of firms, and all vacancies are equally likely to be filled. Firms maximize the expected present value of profits. We have therefore a condition equating the cost to the expected return:

$$c = (M/V)J, \tag{16}$$

where J denotes the value to a firm of a filled position. It is assumed that product prices are governed by world prices. The value of the output produced by a worker, net of monitoring costs, is y, so that in equilibrium with constant w_p and J the value of J must satisfy

$$rJ = y - w_p - \delta J. \tag{17}$$

The last term appears because each job is assumed to be subject to the same probability of involuntary termination. In equilibrium the level of employment is constant, so new matches must equal the involuntary job terminations:

$$M = \delta Lp. \tag{18}$$

Finally, in the secondary sector there is assumed to be a downward-sloping demand function for labor:

$$L_s = S\{w_s\} \text{ where } S' \leq 0, \tag{19}$$

and it is assumed that $S(\varepsilon) > N$, so that in the absence of the primary sector there would be no full-employment wage in excess of the cost of effort.

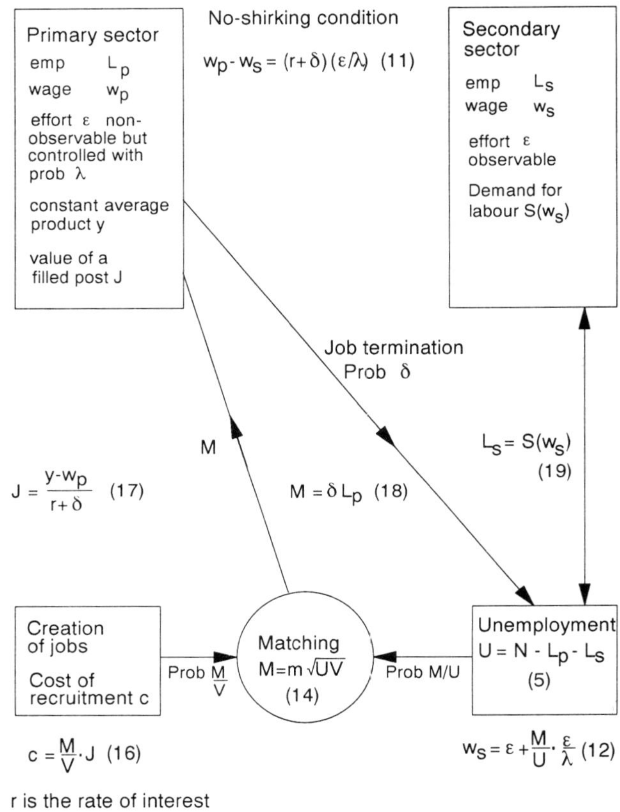

Figure 1
Structure of dual-labor-market model with efficiency wages and imperfect matching.

The elements of the model are summarized in figure 1. The stationary equilibrium is described as follows. From (15) and the free-entry condition (16),

$$M/V = m\sqrt{U/V} = c/J \tag{20}$$

and

$$M/U = m\sqrt{V/U} = m^2 J/c. \tag{21}$$

From (13) and (17),

$$(r + \delta)J = y - w_p = y - \varepsilon - [M/U + r + \delta]\varepsilon/\lambda. \quad (22)$$

Hence, from (21),

$$(r + \delta + m^2\varepsilon/c\lambda)J = y - \varepsilon - (r + \delta)\varepsilon/\lambda. \quad (23)$$

(It is assumed that y is sufficiently large that the right-hand side is strictly positive.) The equilibrium value of a job is an increasing function of c and a decreasing function of m. These are indicators of the extent to which the frictions in filling vacancies create an entry barrier protecting firms with workers in post. The equilibrium vacancy/unemployment ratio is given by

$$\sqrt{V/U} = mJ/c. \quad (24)$$

From (12) and (21),

$$w_s = \varepsilon + m^2 J\varepsilon/c\lambda \quad (25)$$

and

$$w_p = w_s + (r + \delta)\varepsilon/\lambda. \quad (26)$$

The level of employment in the primary sector is governed by the fact that in equilibrium the number of involuntary job terminations is equal to the number of matches (equation 18):

$$L_p = m^2 JU/c\delta. \quad (27)$$

Employment in the secondary sector is determined by (19) and (25). The level of unemployment follows from (5):

$$U = N - m^2 JU/c\delta - S\{w_s\}. \quad (28)$$

(A positive value follows from the assumption that $S(\varepsilon) < N$.)

In this model, unemployment arises because people "queue" for jobs in the primary sector and on account of the frictions in matching the unemployed to vacancies. These effects may be seen if we consider the impact of a rise in the productivity of a worker, y. The equilibrium value of a job, J, rises (equation 23). The equilibrium V/U ratio rises as firms create more vacancies (equation 21). Primary-sector employment rises with J, at any level of unemployment, and the ratio of primary-sector jobs to unemployment certainly rises (equation 27). This makes queuing for a primary-sector job more attractive. The equilibrium secondary-sector wage rises (equation 25), so secondary-sector employment falls (equation 19). The effect on total employment depends on whether this is outweighed by expansion of the primary sector. In what follows it is assumed that the elasticity of demand for labor in the secondary sector is sufficiently small that total employment rises if the value of J increases. Differentiating (28) and (25), we may see that this requires, after some rearrangement,

$$[-S'\{w_s\} \cdot w_s/S\{w_s\}] < [1 + \lambda/(M/U)]L_p/L_s. \tag{29}$$

If the primary sector accounts for more than half of total employment, then a sufficient condition is that the elasticity of S be less than unity.

Under the assumptions made above, unemployment is an equilibrium phenomenon. There is no demand deficiency in this economy; the output of both sectors is assumed to be sold on world markets. I do not regard the model as fully adequate to explain observed unemployment, but it provides a sufficient framework for the points I want to make about unemployment insurance.

4 The Impact of Unemployment Insurance in a Dual-Labor-Market Model

The first important feature (a*) of unemployment insurance is that benefit is paid in the case of involuntary job termination but not in the case where the worker is dismissed for industrial misconduct or quits voluntarily. I assume that in the case of dismissal for shirking there is permanent disqualification. (A more realistic treatment would allow for a probability of disqualification less than unity and for a finite period of disqualification.) This means that we have to distinguish between *insured* unemployment, in which benefit is received, and *uninsured* unemployment. It is the latter that enters the worker's calculation about shirking, since a worker who has been monitored and dismissed receives no UI. Equation 6 remains applicable, where Ω_u is the present value of being in uninsured unemployment. This is clearly different from the analysis of Stiglitz (1986) quoted in section 2, and one of the central points of the analysis is that the existence of UI does not affect the incentive to shirk in terms of the present value of a primary-sector job. At the same time, the level of wages is affected, since UI makes primary-sector employment more attractive—see below.

UI is restricted to covered employment (feature b*), and there is typically a minimum qualifying period of employment and a minimum qualifying level of earnings. I represent the effect of these restrictions by assuming that employment in the primary sector is fully covered, whereas that in the secondary sector is not covered by UI. This could be because the secondary sector is composed of home production; it could be because paid jobs in that sector do not last long enough for workers to acquire rights to UI; it could be because the secondary-sector wage is below the qualifying minimum. Therefore, a worker leaving the secondary sector enters uninsured unemployment. We have the conditions (8) and (9), as before. Those eligible for UI are workers whose primary-sector jobs are terminated. This means that

$$r\Omega_{\mathrm{p}} = w_{\mathrm{p}} - \varepsilon - \delta[\Omega_{\mathrm{p}} - \Omega_{\mathrm{i}}], \qquad (7')$$

where Ω_{i} denotes the present value of being in insured unemployment.

The level of UI payment (feature c*) is denoted by b, where this allows for both a flat-rate benefit (as in the UK) or an earnings-related benefit (in which case b is assumed to be a proportion ρ of the primary-sector wage).

Receipt of UI is conditional on making efforts to search for new employment and on accepting suitable job offers (feature d*). This is incorporated in two ways. First, the UI administration is assumed to require that a claimant put in effort in job search at cost $\eta\varepsilon$, where $0 \leq \eta < 1$. Less effort is involved than working, but nonetheless it is not pure holiday, as typically assumed. Secondly, it is assumed that refusal of a job offer in the primary sector leads to immediate termination of UI benefit (for example, because UI is administered by the state employment agency through which job matching takes place). Of course, an unemployed person could always take a job in the secondary sector. Whether this is regarded as a "suitable" job offer is a matter of interpretation. Here I assume that there is a constant probability, γ (≥ 0), that a UI recipient is monitored and his benefit terminated on the grounds that suitable employment is available in the secondary sector.

Finally, UI benefit is of limited duration (feature e*). Rather than take a fixed benefit period, for analytical convenience I assume that at any date a constant proportion, θ (> 0), of UI recipients have their benefit terminated, and that the probability of benefit termination is the same for all insured unemployed. (Treatment of a fixed benefit period would be more realistic, particularly when examining the full dynamics of the model.)

Taking these features together, the present value of insured unemployment must satisfy, in a stationary equilibrium,

$$r\Omega_i = b - \eta\varepsilon + (\gamma + \theta)[\Omega_u - \Omega_i] + M/U[\Omega_p - \Omega_i]. \tag{30}$$

There are two possible exits: to uninsured unemployment (secondary employment) and to primary-sector employment. It is assumed that the probability of receiving a job offer in the primary sector is the same for all the unemployed, regardless of their UI status. (This assumption could readily be relaxed to allow those in receipt of UI to have a higher probability of a job offer as a result of the effort devoted to job search.) For uninsured unemployment, equation 10 continues to apply. Comparing these, it is clear that the condition that the state of insured unemployment be preferred is

$$b' \equiv b - \eta\varepsilon > 0. \tag{31}$$

In other words, the net benefit allowing for the cost of the job-search requirement must be strictly positive.

The number of insured unemployed is denoted by U_i and the total number of unemployed by U. In stationary equilibrium, the inflow into insured unemployment equals the outflow to jobs in the primary sector or to uninsured unemployment:

$$\delta L_p = (M/U)U_i + (\gamma + \theta)U_i. \tag{32}$$

The level of uninsured unemployment is determined as a residual. From (18), the proportion of the total unemployed who are in receipt of UI is given by

$$\frac{U_i}{U} = \frac{M/U}{\gamma + \theta + M/U}. \tag{33}$$

The UI scheme is financed by contributions paid at the rate of τ_e by employees in the primary sector and a rate of τ_r by employers in that sector, so that

$$r\Omega_p = (1 - \tau_e)w_p - \varepsilon - \delta[\Omega_p - \Omega_i] \tag{7''}$$

and

$$rJ = y - (1 + \tau_r)w_p - \delta J. \tag{17'}$$

The budget balance for the UI fund requires that

$$bU_i = (\tau_e + \tau_r)w_p L_p = (1 - \tau_e)w_p L_p\left[\frac{1 + \tau_r}{1 - \tau_e} - 1\right]. \tag{34}$$

Defining

$$\frac{1 + \tau_r}{1 - \tau_e} - 1$$

as the total "wedge" between net wage and cost to the employer, we can see from (7″), (17′), and (34) that only the net wage and the total wedge are relevant. We may therefore set $\tau_e = 0$ without loss of generality; this is done in what follows, with τ_r capturing the wedge. The assumption that the rate of job terminations (δ) is exogenous precludes consideration of the decision to lay off workers, and the fact that δ is assumed to be the same for all jobs means that experience rating would yield the same contribution rate.

The modifications involved in introducing UI into the model are summarized in figure 2. As already noted, the introduction of UI does not affect

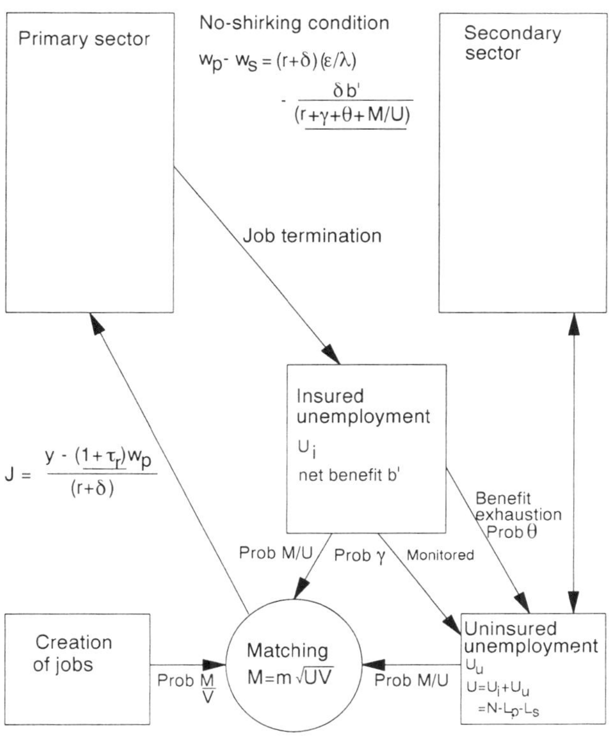

Figure 2
Effect of introducing unemployment insurance.

the relation between Ω_p and Ω_s; on the other hand, it does affect the level of wages in the primary sector. This may be seen as follows. We can use (6), (8), (9), and (10) as before to obtain

$$w_s = \varepsilon + \frac{M}{U}\frac{\varepsilon}{\lambda}.$$

In order to calculate w_p, we can solve for $(\Omega_p - \Omega_i)$ from (7″) and (30), using (6) to replace $(\Omega_p - \Omega_u)$:

$$(\Omega_p - \Omega_i)[r + \delta + \gamma + \theta + M/U] = w_p - \varepsilon - b' + (\gamma + \theta)\varepsilon/\lambda. \tag{35}$$

Even if the net benefit, b', is equal to the net wage, allowing for the cost of effort, there will still be a positive incentive to leave unemployment and accept a primary-sector job ($\Omega_p > \Omega_i$) if $(\gamma + \theta)$ is strictly positive. This brings out the importance of the conditions under which UI is administered. If there is a positive probability that benefit will be terminated, either because entitlement is exhausted or on the grounds that secondary employment is considered a "suitable" alternative, then there is no disincentive even with 100% replacement of net earnings. Substituting (35) into (7″), we can use (6), (8), (9), and (12) to obtain

$$w_p = \varepsilon + [M/U + r + \delta]\varepsilon/\lambda - \delta b'/[r + \gamma + \theta + M/U], \tag{36}$$

where b' has been left on the right-hand side, but it must be remembered that b' may depend on w_p (where the benefit is earnings-related). It is the difference between (36) and (12) that is shown in figure 2.

Comparing (36) and (13) reveals that, at any given M/U, the net wage in the primary sector is lower when the UI scheme is in effect (and this is true of both flat-rate and earnings-related schemes). (The net wage is shown on the left-hand side of (36); the first two terms on the right-hand side are the same as those on the right-hand side of (13).) UI is in this sense *complementary* to employment in the primary sector: the existence of UI makes employment in the primary sector more attractive, since it reduces the cost if the primary-sector job is terminated. In the case of a flat-rate benefit, a rise in b reduces the primary-sector wage, and with an earnings-related system a rise in the replacement rate, ρ, has the same effect (the right-hand side of (3) is a declining function of w_p). The wage also falls with an increase in the expected duration of receipt of UI (a lower value of θ) and a reduction in the risk of benefit being terminated (lower γ).

The effect of UI on the value of a filled job is

$$(r + \delta)J = y - (1 + \tau_r)w_p. \tag{37}$$

Hence, using (21) and (36), we have

$$[r + \delta + (m^2\varepsilon/c\lambda)(1 + \tau_r)]J = y - [\varepsilon + (r + \delta)\varepsilon/\lambda](1 + \tau_r) + \frac{\delta b'(1 + \tau_r)}{r + \gamma + \theta + m^2 J/c}. \tag{38}$$

(It is again assumed that the values of the parameters are such that the right-hand side is positive.) If b' were zero, the difference between (38) and the situation in the absence of UI (given by (23)) would be in the terms $(1 + \tau_r)$. These terms increase the left-hand side and reduce the right-hand side, so that, not very surprisingly, the value of a filled post is reduced by the obligation to pay UI contributions. On the other hand, if we consider the impact of the UI benefits, leaving aside the contributions ($\tau_r = 0$), we see that J rises (the right-hand side is larger for all J). The existence of UI means that primary-sector firms can offer lower wages, and this increases the value of a filled job position.

If J is reduced, then it follows that V/U falls, from equation 21, and hence M/U falls. This means that the secondary-sector wage falls (see equation 12). It follows that employment in the secondary sector rises. On the assumption (29) about the elasticity of labor demand in the secondary sector, this is not enough to outweigh the fall in primary-sector employment, and total unemployment rises. It may also be noted from equation 33 that the proportion of insured unemployment falls, irrespective of the effect on total unemployment.

From these results, we can see the effect of variation in the parameters of the UI system ignoring first of all the budget-balance requirement (assuming that the deficit on the UI fund, or the surplus, is allocated in some way that does not affect the equilibrium conditions). A rise in the rate of contribution (whether by the employee or by the employer) reduces J and has the effects just described. The same applies to a rise in the job-search requirement (η), which reduces the net value of the benefit. (Of course, the impact might be different if it raised the probability of job matching—that is, if the search was "productive.") It also applies to the rate of termination (γ). If benefits are administered more stringently, so that more people are disqualified for failing to accept secondary-sector jobs, then the value of J

falls. It may appear paradoxical that more stringent administration leads to a lower J, and hence to higher unemployment, but this greater stringency reduces the effective value of UI.

On the other hand, as we have seen, a rise in the rate of benefit, b, has the effect of raising J, and this has the reverse effects of those just described. There is a switch in employment toward the primary sector, and, on assumption 29, a rise in total employment. The same applies if benefit duration is increased (θ is smaller). UI operates, in effect, as a subsidy on the uncertain employment in the primary sector. The effect is different from that described by Shapiro and Stiglitz (1984), because those dismissed for industrial misconduct are assumed not to be eligible for UI and hence the benefit does not enter the no-shirking condition (6). Of course, if monitoring of this condition by the UI authorities is imperfect, then the results will be modified.

If we now consider a balanced-budget UI program, then—in contrast to the situation described by Shapiro and Stiglitz, where the effects of benefits and contributions reinforced one another—the effects in the model described here operate in opposite directions. As far as J is concerned, it does indeed seem possible that the gain to the employer from lower primary-sector net wages may be exactly offset by the contributions payable. Suppose that there is no job-search requirement ($\eta = 0$), so that the net benefit is b. We may write

$$w_{\mathrm{p}} = \varepsilon + [M/U + r + \delta]\varepsilon/\lambda - \delta b/[r + \gamma + \theta + M/U] \tag{39}$$

or

$$w_{\mathrm{p}} \equiv w_{\mathrm{p}}^{0} - \delta b/[r + \gamma + \theta + M/U], \tag{40}$$

where w_{p}^{0} denotes the value in the absence of UI (at any given value of M/U), and

$$(r + \delta)J = y - (1 + \tau_{\mathrm{r}})w_{\mathrm{p}} \tag{41}$$

and, from (32) and (34),

$$\tau_{\mathrm{r}} w_{\mathrm{p}}[\gamma + \theta + M/U] = \delta b. \tag{42}$$

Combining these, we can see that

$$(r + \delta)J = y - \frac{(1 + \tau_{\mathrm{r}})w_{\mathrm{p}}^{0}}{1 + \tau_{\mathrm{r}}\{[\gamma + \theta + M/U]/[r + \gamma + \theta + M/U]\}}, \tag{43}$$

from which it is clear that the value of J falls with the introduction of UI where $r > 0$. If there were no discounting, the benefit in terms of lower wage would exactly equal the contribution paid. The scheme would be purely redistributive—the wage rate in the primary sector would fall, but there would be UI benefit for those whose jobs had been terminated. It does not matter which compensation scheme (wages and UI) is adopted if they have the same actuarial value. The reason that $r > 0$ causes the UI scheme to be no longer neutral is that the scheme considered here is pay-as-you-go, so that a current job has to pay for those currently unemployed, rather than for the expected present value of future unemployment associated with that job (as is assumed by Shapiro and Stiglitz (1984, note 12). With a positive interest rate and no growth in the earnings base, this is unfavorable. (The analysis could be extended to allow for a funded UI scheme.) In this situation, the overall effect on employment may be negative (the consequences of a fall in J have been described), but it is the result of both negative and positive influences—not a purely negative effect.

Conclusions

The main purpose of this analysis has been to draw attention to the roles played by certain institutional features of unemployment insurance in countries such as the United Kingdom and the United States. Unemployment insurance is not simply a "wage when not working." There is not typically an entitlement to benefit when the person has quit employment voluntarily or has been dismissed for industrial misconduct. Entitlement depends on the past record of covered employment and on contribution conditions. The continued receipt of benefit is dependent on job search and on acceptance of suitable job offers. There is a limited duration of entitlement. As a result, a sizeable proportion of the unemployed at any one time are not in receipt of UI benefit. Others are in receipt of unemployment *assistance*, but this scheme too may disqualify those quitting voluntarily or dismissed for misconduct and may terminate payments to those refusing suitable job offers.

The aim of the simple dual-labor-market model set out here has been to provide a framework within which to examine the impact of UI, taking account of these institutional features. The UI scheme treated is necessarily stylized, but it allows for covered and uncovered employment, for the disqualification of those dismissed for "shirking" from UI benefit, for a job-search requirement, for the possibility of benefit termination for refusing employment, and for a limited duration of benefit. In the model only a proportion of the unemployed (the "insured unemployed") receive benefit; this differs from much of the theoretical literature in which it is taken for granted that all of the unemployed are in receipt of benefit.

In this model the effects of a UI program, taking both benefits and contributions together, are different from those described in many of the earlier theoretical analyses. In particular, it is necessary to take account of the benefit provided to workers by the existence of insurance against involuntary job loss, and of the way in which this reduces the equilibrium level of wages paid in the covered sector. There is a positive as well as a negative dimension to UI as far as employers, and employment, are concerned.

The total effect of a UI scheme is made up of an unfavorable effect on employment (arising from the contributions side) and a favorable effect (arising from the benefit side). This means that, if a government were to reduce benefits while leaving contributions unchanged, we would expect this to have an adverse effect on employment. Such a comparative-static analysis appears especially relevant to situations such as that in the UK in the 1980s when National Insurance unemployment benefit was cut in several different ways with no offsetting reduction in contributions. The earnings-related supplement was abolished; the contributions conditions were tightened; the period of disqualification was increased; the administration became more stringent (for details, see Atkinson and Micklewright 1989). According to the analysis presented here, such a cutback in benefits and tighter administration may have been expected to make primary-sector employment less attractive, putting upward pressure on wages in that sector. The number of vacancies in the primary sector per unemployed worker is reduced. There is a shift toward secondary-sector employment—in effect, a transfer from "good jobs" to "bad jobs." For a government seeking to encourage the development of the economy this can scarcely be seen as progress.

Acknowledgments

In writing this paper, I have drawn heavily on joint research with John Micklewright of Queen Mary College, London, and the European University Institute, Florence. He has made helpful comments on the paper but is not to be held responsible for the views expressed. I am also grateful to Nicholas Barr, Andrea Brandolini, Douglas Gale, the referee, and participants in seminars at O.F.C.E. and C.E.R.C. in Paris for their comments on the first version.

References

Atkinson, A. B. 1988. The Economics of Unemployment Insurance. Presidential address to the Econometric Society.

Atkinson, A. B., and J. Micklewright. 1989. "Turning the screw: Benefits for the unemployed 1979–88." In The Economics of Social Security, ed. A Dilnot and I. Walker. Oxford University Press.

Atkinson, A. B., and J. Micklewright. 1989a. Unemployment Compensation and Labour Market Transitions: A Critical Review. Discussion paper, London School of Economics and European University Institute.

Barr, N. A. 1988. The Mirage of Private Unemployment Insurance. Welfare State Programme discussion paper, London School of Economics.

Bowles, S. 1985. "The production process in a competitive economy: Walrasian, neo-Hobbesian and Marxian models." *American Economic Review* 75: 16–36.

Bulow, J. I., and L. H. Summers. 1986. "A theory of dual labor markets with application to industrial policy, discrimination, and Keynesian unemployment." *Journal of Labor Economics* 4: 376–414.

Burdett, K. 1979. "Unemployment payments as a search subsidy: A theoretical analysis." *Economic Inquiry* 17: 333–343.

Burdett, K., and D. T. Mortensen. 1980. "Search, layoffs, and labor market equilibrium." *Journal of Political Economy* 88: 652–672.

Calvo, G., and S. Wellisz. 1979. "Hierarchy, ability and income distribution." *Journal of Political Economy* 87: 991–1010.

Diamond, P. A. 1981. "Mobility costs, frictional unemployment, and efficiency." *Journal of Political Economy* 89: 798–812.

Diamond, P. A. 1982. "Wage determination and efficiency in search equilibrium." *Review of Economic Studies* 49: 761–782.

Doeringer, P. B., and M. J. Piore. 1971. *Internal Labor Markets and Manpower Analysis*. D. C. Heath.

Fenn, P. 1980. "Sources of disqualification for unemployment benefit, 1960–76." *British Journal of Industrial Relations* 18: 240–253.

Foster, J., and H. Wan. 1984. "Involuntary unemployment as a principal-agent equilibrium." *American Economic Review* 74: 476–484.

Hamermesh, D. S. 1979. "Entitlement effects, unemployment insurance and employment decisions." *Economic Inquiry* 17: 317–332.

Harris, J., and M. Todaro. 1970. "Migration, unemployment and development." *American Economic Review* 60: 126–142.

Hey, J. D., and K. Mavromaras. 1981. "The effect of unemployment insurance on the riskiness of occupational choice." *Journal of Public Economics* 16: 317–341.

van de Klundert, T. 1988. Wage Differentials and Employment in a Two-Sector Model with a Dual Labor Market. Unpublished.

Johnson, G., and R. Layard. 1986. "The natural rate of unemployment: Explanation and policy." In *The Handbook of Labor Economics*, volume 2, ed. O. Ashenfelter and R. Layard. North-Holland.

Lippman, S. A., and J. J. McCall. 1980. "Search unemployment." *Scandinavian Journal of Economics* 82: 253–272.

MacLeod, W. B., and J. Malcolmson. 1989. Wage Premiums and Profit Maximisation in Efficiency Wage Models. Discussion paper.

McDonald, I. M., and R. M. Solow. 1985. "Wages and employment in a segmented labor market." *Quarterly Journal of Economics* 100: 1115–1141.

Mortensen, D. T. 1977. "Unemployment insurance and job search decisions." *Industrial and Labor Relations Review* 30: 505–517.

Mortensen, D. T. 1988. The Persistence and Indeterminacy of Unemployment in Search Equilibrium. Centre for Mathematical Studies in Economics and Mangement Science Discussion Paper 810.

Oswald, A. J. 1986. "Unemployment insurance and labour contracts under asymmetric information." *American Economic Review* 76: 365–377.

Pissarides, C. 1979. "Job matchings with state employment agencies and random search." *Economic Journal* 89: 818–833.

Pissarides, C. 1984. "Search intensity, job advertising, and efficiency." *Journal of Labor Economics* 2: 128–143.

Pissarides, C. 1985. "Short-run equilibrium dynamics of unemployment, vacancies, and real wages." *American Economic Review* 75: 676–690.

Shapiro, C., and J. E. Stiglitz. 1984. "Equilibrium unemployment as a worker discipline device." *American Economic Review* 74: 433–444.

Stiglitz, J. E. 1986. "Theories of wage rigidity." In *Keynes' Economic Legacy*, ed. J. L. Butkiewicz, K. J. Koford, and J. B. Miller. Praeger.

Williams, C. A., J. G. Turnbull, and E. F. Cheit. 1982. *Economic and Social Security*, fifth edition. Wiley.

Production Fluctuations and Fiscal Policy in an Economy with Aggregate and Idiosyncratic Shocks

Oliver Hart and Eric Maskin

Ever since Lucas (1972), much of the work on the theory of business cycles has focused on asymmetric information as a culprit in aggravating fluctuations in real variables such as GNP and employment. In Lucas' own model, there are both aggregate shocks in the form of changes in the money supply and idiosyncratic shocks to individual firms' demand, but firms cannot tell these apart. When a firm observes, say, an increase in the demand for its output, it attaches positive probability to the possibility that there has been a real change in preferences. Thus, it may expand output, rather than simply raise its price as it would do if it knew for certain that the increase was due to inflation. Hence, the entangling of aggregate and idiosyncratic shocks implies that changes in the money supply have real effects: inflation induces a rise in GNP whereas deflation promotes recession.

One unattractive feature of this model is that it requires that changes in the money supply be unobservable, and such an assumption may be hard to swallow in an age where M1 through M4 are reported virtually continuously. Accordingly, various authors (e.g., Grossman and Weiss (1982)) have attempted to replace the money supply in Lucas' model with a macro variable that is more plausibly unobservable (such as the real interest rate).

Quite a different route was taken by Grossman, Hart, and Maskin (1983), who assumed that each firm knows when a macro shock occurs but not what its effect on other firms is. They showed that a shock that would have left GNP unaffected had information been symmetric will reduce GNP under such an asymmetry of information when agents are risk-averse. Risk aversion implies that firms will attempt to insure themselves against the effects of shocks. But since other agents (including insurers) cannot directly observe how a shock affects a given firm, the firm's insurance benefits must be contingent on an observable proxy, such as its level of output. Thus, a firm will have the incentive to reduce output below the first-best efficient level in order to prove that it has been adversely affected by a shock and thereby claim an insurance benefit. The overall result is a fall in GNP greater than would have occurred had information been symmetric.

In this paper we examine two models related to that of Grossman-Hart-Maskin. In the first (sections 1 and 2), we show that there is another way in which asymmetric information can aggravate fluctuations: through a mechanism resembling a Keynesian multiplier. In this model, firms have private information about their production costs, and this causes underproduction in high-cost firms. We show that an initial small aggregate endowment shock will, through its impact on production, affect income and hence aggregate demand, thereby inducing a large ultimate shift in production. This multiplier arises from the incompleteness of insurance possibilities that asymmetric information entails. Equilibrium in this model can be quite inefficient, even relative to the informational constraints we impose. Hence, we consider how welfare might be improved through taxes and subsidies. We demonstrate that, perhaps surprisingly, the optimal fiscal policy tends to drive equilibrium output further away from the first-best level. Moreover, despite the presence of a "Keynesian" multiplier, such a policy may well not consist of subsidizing demand and production but rather of taxing them.

In our second model (sections 3 and 4), the asymmetry of information concerns the demand for firms' products. The impact of aggregate demand shocks on unemployment in this case has been studied by Grossman, Hart, and Maskin (1983), and we do not consider that issue here. However, we do analyze whether there is a role for government intervention. As in the production-shock case, we find that a government, possessing the same information as the market, can improve on the market allocation. The optimal intervention in this case consists of stabilizing demand: high-final-demand products are taxed and low-final-demand products are subsidized.

1 Shocks to Production

Consider a competitive economy with two goods: one produced (soap), the other unproduced (oil). Each agent is endowed with $\tilde{K}$ units of oil, where $\tilde{K}$ is a random variable common to all agents with support $[\underline{K}, \overline{K}]$.

An agent can produce either zero or one unit of soap, and the latter requires c units of oil. For each agent, the value of c is drawn independently from a distribution that places equal probability on c_L and c_H, where $c_L < c_H < \underline{K}$.[1] We assume that there are many agents, so that, from the law of large numbers, the population divides equally between c_L and c_H. An agent's cost parameter is not known *ex ante*, but it becomes private information to the agent by the time he must decide on production. Only an agent's output (or, equivalently, sales) of soap—and not his input of oil or profit—is observable to others.

All agents have the same Cobb-Douglas preferences:

$$\alpha \ln x + (1 - \alpha) \ln y,$$

where x is consumption of soap and y that of oil. So that we can solve explicitly for equilibrium, agents are assumed to be infinitely risk-averse. That is, if consumption is represented by the random variables $\tilde{x}$ and $\tilde{y}$, an agent's von Neumann-Morgenstern utility is given by

$$\min[\alpha \ln \tilde{x} + (1 - \alpha) \ln \tilde{y}],$$

where the minimization is taken over the random variables' supports.

Because agents are risk-averse, they will wish to purchase insurance against the randomness they face. This is provided by risk-neutral, competitive insurance companies that pool risks by insuring a large number of producers (half of whom turn out to be low-cost). Since inputs are not observable, however, insurance will necessarily be incomplete. Note also that insurance companies are unable to provide insurance across aggregate states (i.e., across different values of $\tilde{K}$), because pooling is impossible in the case of aggregate uncertainty.

The timing is as follows. Before any random variable is realized, agents and insurers agree to insurance contracts. In exchange for a premium, an agent receives a benefit contingent on the realization of the "macro" variable $\tilde{K}$ and the agent's (observable) output of soap. Next, $\tilde{K}$ and agents' costs are realized, after which agents make their production decisions. Finally, agents receive their insurance benefits, and there is competitive trade in oil and soap.

Let $p(K)$ be the equilibrium price of soap in terms of oil if the realization of $\tilde{K}$ is K (oil is the numeraire throughout). Let $b_1(K)$ and $b_0(K)$ be an agent's insurance benefit (net of premium) when $\tilde{K} = K$ and he, respectively, does and does not produce soap. For each realization of $\tilde{K}$, an agent has four conceivable production plans:

(1) produce if $\tilde{c} = c_L$ and produce if $\tilde{c} = c_H$;
(2) produce if $\tilde{c} = c_L$ and not produce if $\tilde{c} = c_H$;
(3) produce if $\tilde{c} = c_H$ and not produce if $\tilde{c} = c_L$;
(4) not produce if $\tilde{c} = c_H$ and not produce if $\tilde{c} = c_L$.

We will demonstrate that for a range of parameter values there is a unique equilibrium outcome in which all the c_L agents and a fraction $\lambda(K)$ of the c_H agents produce soap. Specifically, we have the following:

PROPOSITION 1 If the realization K satisfies

$$\tfrac{1}{2}(2c_H - c_L)(1-\alpha) + \tfrac{1}{2}\alpha c_L < \alpha K < (1-\alpha)(2c_H - c_L) + \tfrac{1}{2}\alpha c_L + \tfrac{1}{2}\alpha c_H, \qquad (*)$$

then in any equilibrium $p(K) = 2c_H - c_L$ all c_L agents produce soap and so do a fraction $\lambda(K)$ of c_H agents, where

$$\lambda(K) = \frac{2K\alpha - (2c_H - c_L)(1-\alpha) - \alpha c_L}{(2c_H - c_L)(1-\alpha) + \alpha c_H}. \qquad (**)$$

To see why this proposition holds, note first that production plan 3 is impossible in equilibrium: A c_H agent produces soap in equilibrium if and only if

$$p(K) - c_H + b_1(K) \geq b_0(K). \qquad (1)$$

Inequality (1) is the c_H agent's *incentive constraint*, which arises because the value of c is private information. But (1) continues to hold when c_H is replaced by c_L—a contradiction of plan 3.

Let $b(K)$ be the *ex ante* expected net insurance benefit that a given agent receives when $\tilde{K} = K$.[2] In equilibrium, this will be allocated between $b_1(K)$ and $b_0(K)$ so as to maximize the agent's expected utility. If the agent adopts plan 2 in equilibrium, then, in view of his extreme risk aversion, his insurance contract solves

$$\max_{b_0(\cdot), b_1(\cdot)} \min\{b_0(K), p(K) - c_L + b_1(K)\} \qquad (2)$$

subject to

$$\tfrac{1}{2}b_1(K) + \tfrac{1}{2}b_0(K) = b(K), \qquad (3)$$

$$p(K) - c_L + b_1(K) \geq b_0(K), \qquad (4)$$

and

$$b_0(K) \geq p(K) - c_H + b_1(K). \qquad (5)$$

Here, (4) and (5) are the incentive constraints for c_L and c_H agents, respectively. It is readily seen that the maximized value of the agent's expected utility is

$$\tfrac{1}{2}(p(K) - c_L) + b(K). \qquad (6)$$

If instead the agent adopts plan A, his payoff is

$$b(K) \tag{7}$$

regardless of c. From (6) and (7), plan 4 can be optimal only if $p(K) \leq c_L$, which we will soon see is impossible.

Finally, if the agent adopts plan 1 his expected payoff is

$$\min\{p(K) - c_H + b(K), p(K) - c_L + b(K)\} = p(K) - c_H + b(K). \tag{8}$$

Formulas (6) and (8) imply that the agent prefers plan 1 to plan 2 if $p(K) > 2c_H - c_L$, that he prefers plan 2 to plan 1 if $p(K) < 2c_H - c_L$, and that he is indifferent between the two plans if $p(K) = 2c_H - c_L$.

Suppose, contrary to the proposition, that $p(K) > 2c_H - c_L$ in equilibrium. From the above analysis, all agents adopt plan 1. Hence, the per capita supply of soap is 1. Given the Cobb-Douglas preferences, per capita demand is

$$\frac{\alpha I}{p(K)}, \tag{9}$$

where I is per capita income. In view of the equal likelihood of c_H and c_L and our assumption that all agents adopt plan 1,

$$I = p(K) - \tfrac{1}{2}c_L - \tfrac{1}{2}c_H + K. \tag{10}$$

Now, in equilibrium, supply equals demand (i.e., (9) equals 1), and so

$$p(K) = \frac{2\alpha K - \alpha c_L - \alpha c_H}{2(1 - \alpha)},$$

which, from the right-hand inequality of (*), is less than $2c_H - c_L$. Hence, $p(K) > 2c_H - c_L$ is impossible.

Next suppose that $p(K) < 2c_H - c_L$. Let $\delta(K)$ be the fraction of agents adopting plan 2 (the rest adopt plan 4). Then per capita supply is $\frac{1}{2}\delta(K)$ and per capita demand is

$$\frac{\alpha(\frac{1}{2}p(K)\delta(K) - \frac{1}{2}\delta(K)c_L + K)}{p(K)}. \tag{11}$$

Equating per capita demand and supply, we obtain

$$p(K) = \frac{\alpha(K - \frac{1}{2}\delta(K)c_L)}{\frac{1}{2}(1 - \alpha)\delta(K)}. \tag{12}$$

The right-hand side of (12) is smallest when $\delta(K) = 1$, in which case we obtain

$$p(K) = \frac{\alpha(K - \frac{1}{2}c_L)}{\frac{1}{2}(1 - \alpha)}. \tag{13}$$

But from the left-hand inequality of (*), the right-hand side of (13) is bigger than $2c_H - c_L$, a contradiction.

We conclude that $p(K) = 2c_H - c_L$ after all. Hence, all agents adopt either plan 1 or plan 2. Let $\lambda(K)$ be the fraction adopting plan 1. Then $\lambda(K)$ adjusts to satisfy

$$\frac{\alpha((2c_H - c_L)\{[1 + \lambda(K)]/2\} - \frac{1}{2}c_L - \frac{1}{2}\lambda(K)c_H + K)}{2c_H - c_L} = \frac{1}{2} + \frac{1}{2}\lambda(K).$$

Solving for $\lambda(K)$, we obtain (**), establishing the proposition.

It is instructive to compare this equilibrium with the one that arises when there is no asymmetry of information, i.e., when insurers can observe the realizations of the agents' costs. In that case an agent can obtain perfect insurance against fluctuations in c (although not against those in K). Hence, incentive constraints such as (4) or (5) are no longer needed. We shall call equilibrium in the case of symmetric information *first-best.*

PROPOSITION 2 Given condition (*), there is a unique first-best equilibrium in which all the c_L agents produce, a fraction $\gamma(K)$ of the c_H agents produce, and the equilibrium price $p(K)$ satisfies

$$p(K) = \frac{\alpha(K - \frac{1}{2}c_L - \frac{1}{2}\gamma(K)c_H)}{[\frac{1}{2} + \frac{1}{2}\gamma(K)](1 - \alpha)}, \tag{14}$$

where, for all K,

$$\begin{aligned} &p(K) \geq c_H, \\ &\gamma(K) = 1 \text{ if } p(K) > c_H. \end{aligned} \tag{15}$$

To verify the claim, note first that, with perfect insurance, an agent's expected payoff from production plan 1 is

$$p(K) - \tfrac{1}{2}(c_H + c_L) + b(K).$$

That from plan 2 is

$\frac{1}{2}(p(K) - c_L) + b(K),$

and that from plan 4 is $b(K)$. Hence, plan 1 is optimal provided $p(K) \geq c_H$, plan 2 is optimal when $c_H \geq p(K) \geq c_L$, and plan 4 is optimal when $p(K) \leq c_L$. Now, the right-hand side of (14) takes on a maximum

$$\frac{\alpha(K - \frac{1}{2}c_L)}{\frac{1}{2}(1 - \alpha)} \tag{16}$$

when $\gamma(K) = 0$. But (16) is strictly greater than c_H, in view of the left-hand inequality in (*). Hence, there always exists a unique $\gamma(K)$ in $(0,1]$ satisfying (15). If we interpret $\gamma(K)$ as the fraction of agents adopting plan 1, it is clear from the above analysis that the behavior implicit in (14) and (15) is optimal. To see that there is no other equilibrium, suppose to the contrary that $p(K) < c_H$. Then no c_H agents will produce. Let $\delta(K)$ be the fraction of c_L agents who do. Then, from the equality between supply and demand, (12) holds, and we generate the same contradiction as that following (13).

Notice that the equilibrium price and production levels of proposition 2, which obtain when there is complete insurance, coincide with those that arise when no insurance at all is possible (i.e., when agents' production levels, as well as their input levels, are unobservable): It is easy to check that each of the production plans 1, 2, and 4 is optimal for the same range of prices in both cases.

One significant difference between the equilibria of propositions 1 and 2 is that, for the range of parameters defined by (*), the latter entails a uniformly *higher* production level. That is, for all K, $\gamma(K) > \lambda(K)$. To see this, note from (14) that

$$\gamma(K) = \frac{2\alpha K - \alpha c_L - (1 - \alpha)p(K)}{p(K)(1 - \alpha) + \alpha c_H}. \tag{17}$$

The right-hand side of (17) is decreasing in p. Moreover, when $p = 2c_H - c_L$ it coincides with (**), the expression for $\lambda(K)$. But in the range (*) the equilibrium price $p(K)$ in proposition 2 is strictly less than $2c_H - c_L$. Hence, $\gamma(K) > \lambda(K)$.

2 Multipliers and Taxes

Another notable distinction is that the proposition 1 equilibrium exhibits something resembling a Keynesian multiplier, whereas that of proposition

2—like those of all conventional competitive models—does not. Suppose that in the equilibrium of proposition 1 there is a small "oil shock"—an increase ΔK. Because ΔK increases agents' endowments, its initial effect is to induce a rise in the demand for soap of

$$\frac{\alpha \Delta K}{2c_{\mathrm{H}} - c_{\mathrm{L}}}, \tag{18}$$

given the Cobb-Douglas preferences and the equilibrium price $2c_{\mathrm{H}} - c_{\mathrm{L}}$. The equilibrium change in supply, however, is $\frac{1}{2}\lambda'(K)\Delta K$, which, from (**), equals

$$\frac{\alpha \Delta K}{(1-\alpha)(2c_{\mathrm{H}} - c_{\mathrm{L}}) + \alpha c_{\mathrm{H}}}. \tag{19}$$

Now, because $2c_{\mathrm{H}} - c_{\mathrm{L}} > c_{\mathrm{H}}$, (19) is bigger than (18). Thus, an initial shock to demand is magnified into an ultimately larger equilibrium response.

In the equilibrium of proposition 2, by contrast, an initial shock to demand $\alpha \Delta K / p$ (with the price held constant) results ultimately in the equilibrium change $\frac{1}{2}\gamma'(K)\Delta K$. Now, either $\gamma' = 0$ (when $p > c_{\mathrm{H}}$), in which case there is no change in output at all, or else (when $p = c_{\mathrm{H}}$) the change (from (17)) is

$$\frac{\alpha \Delta K}{c_{\mathrm{H}}},$$

which is exactly the same as the initial shock. Either way there is no multiplier.

Thus, because proposition 2 pertains both to symmetric information with complete insurance and asymmetric information so extreme that no insurance is possible, we conclude that the existence of a multiplier depends not only on asymmetric information but also on incomplete insurance.

Notice that in the range (*) our model exhibits constant returns to scale (CRS) at the margin (i.e., starting from less than full production. output can be expanded a bit without affecting marginal cost). The conventional argument for why there is no multiplier in a competitive CRS economy is that when there is an increase in demand, firms are willing to meet that demand at the same prices. But because these firms are earning zero marginal profit on the extra output, the higher supply generates no additional income and so the story stops there. This is precisely what occurs in the equilibrium of proposition 2. When $p(K) = c_H$, an increase in demand draws more c_H agents into production, but each of them earns $p(K) - c_H = 0$.

The situation is even worse if there are decreasing returns to scale at the margin. For an increase in demand to be met by producers, the price must rise. But if demand is downward sloping, this higher price works to dampen the initial demand increase. Thus with decreasing returns we ordinarily obtain a *divider* rather than a multiplier.

In the incomplete insurance model of proposition 1, however, marginal profit is *not* zero despite the constant returns. The equilibrium price (marginal revenue) is $2c_H - c_L$ but the marginal cost of additional output is only c_H. Hence, the marginal profit is $c_H - c_L > 0$. Thus, an increase in demand gives rise to an increase in profit, which generates more demand, and so on.

Let us compare this explanation for a multiplier with some others in the literature. First, with imperfect competition among firms it is no longer true that the marginal social surplus (the sum of consumer and producer surplus) of another unit of output is zero. Indeed, it is ordinarily positive, since firms equate marginal revenue rather than price with marginal cost. Hence, a small increase in demand will induce an increase in surplus, leading to a further rise in demand, and so on (Blanchard and Kiyotaki 1987; Hart 1982). Second, suppose that there are positive externalities in production, so that an increase in one firm's output increases the marginal profitability of other firms' production (Diamond 1982).[3] Then, an increase in demand that leads one firm to increase its production will indirectly lead others to do so as well. Finally, consider a standard competitive model but suppose that, for some reason, prices are fixed at non-Walrasian levels (Benassy 1975; Grandmont and Laroque 1976). Assume, in particular, that firms cannot sell all they would like to at these prices. Then, once again, marginal social surplus will be positive (marginal profit is positive and marginal consumer surplus is zero), and so a rise in demand will generate further rounds of increases.

Suppose that the government of our incomplete-insurance economy contemplates taxing or subsidizing the sale of soap. (For simplicity, assume that sales of oil are unmonitorable, and so a tax or subsidy on oil is impossible. This is in keeping with our assumption that inputs of oil are unobservable.) There, in fact, exists a simple policy that the government can adopt to raise equilibrium soap production to the first-best level: It can subsidize soap and finance the subsidy with a lump-sum tax. Suppose, for example, that the first-best level of soap per capita is 1 for oil level K^* and that the corresponding equilibrium price is p^* ($< 2c_H - c_L$). The government can induce this level of output in the incomplete-insurance economy by setting the consumer price of oil, q, equal to p^*, and setting the producer price, p, at a level above $2c_H - c_L$. With such a high producer price, all agents will choose to produce soap, so that the per capita output is 1. This means that per capita income is

$$K + p - \tfrac{1}{2}c_H - \tfrac{1}{2}c_L + (q - p) = K + q - \tfrac{1}{2}c_H - \tfrac{1}{2}c_L, \qquad (20)$$

where the expression in parentheses on the left-hand side corresponds to the lump-sum tax needed to finance the discrepancy between consumer and producer prices. Note that when q is set at p^* the right-hand side of (20) is just first-best per capita income.

Thus, the subsidy policy works. Moreover, by virtue of its promotion of production (and GNP), it can be thought of as a form of Keynesian "pump-priming." Indeed, analogous policies improve welfare in all the other models we mentioned that exhibit multipliers. But a subsidy is not desirable in our model. Obviously the first-best equilibrium dominates the equilibrium of proposition 1. But we saw in the preceding section that the noninsurance equilibrium (which in turn is dominated by the proposition 1 equilibrium) also has first-best-level production, suggesting that such a level is not worthwhile *per se*; the available insurance opportunities matter, too.

Indeed, we now argue that the optimal tax policy involves setting a *tax* on soap sales, leading to a *lower* production level than in proposition 1. The rationale for such a tax is that it improves insurance. A c_H agent pays less than an equal share of this tax because, with his lower income, he buys less soap than his more fortunate c_L counterparts. But he gets an equal share of the receipts from the tax. Thus, he benefits overall.

More formally, consider raising the consumer price q slightly above the producer price $p = 2c_H - c_L$. The effect on a nonproducing c_H agent's utility is

$$\frac{d}{dq}\left[\alpha \ln\left(\frac{\alpha(K + b_0 + (q - p)x)}{q}\right) + (1 - \alpha)\ln((1 - \alpha)(K + b_0 + (q - p)x))\right], \qquad (21)$$

where x is per capita demand for soap. Rewriting (21), we obtain, at $q = p$,

$$\frac{\alpha p}{K + b_0}\left[\frac{px - (K + b_0)}{p^2}\right] + \frac{1-\alpha}{K + b_0}x = \frac{1}{K + b_0}\left[x - \frac{\alpha(K + b_0)}{p}\right]. \tag{22}$$

Now, the demand for soap by the c_H agent, $\alpha(K + b_0)/p$, is less than per capita demand, x (since the agent's income is below average). Thus, the right-hand side of (22) is positive, and so a tax on soap is desirable.[4]

Why is fiscal policy necessary at all—that is, why can't the market duplicate the government's actions?

A competitive insurer—just like the government—can in principle drive a wedge between the producer and consumer prices of soap, since we assume that it can monitor sales. However, it has no incentive to do so. Suppose a large number of other insurance companies are providing such a wedge—i.e., the consumer price is $q > 2c_H - c_L$, but producers pay a tax $(q - p)$ to their insurance company and so the producer price is $p = 2c_H - c_L$ (this is as in the fiscal policy described above). Then the optimal contract for a remaining small insurance company involves *all* its producers (both high-cost and low-cost) producing soap, since the effective price of soap for this coalition is $q > 2c_H - c_L$ (see (8)). Of course, if all insurers offer such a contract, then the equilibrium price could not remain above $2c_H - c_L$. Thus, there is a pecuniary externality that the individual insurer ignores by virtue of its taking prices as given. A government internalizes this externality when it sets taxes for everyone, and therein lies its advantage. Indeed, if there were only one insurer for the whole economy, it too would internalize the externality (although then presumably we would have to worry about the exercise of monopoly power). But even in this case there would be nothing to stop a new small insurance company from setting up and eliminating the wedge.

Small insurers could nevertheless improve on the competitive outcome above if they were able to keep track of their clientele's soap *purchases* as well as sales Thanks to its ability to monitor, an insurer could (and would) offer each of its customers the following contract: pay the consumer price q rather than the producer price p, and the difference will be distributed to all the insurance company's customers as a lump-sum subsidy. In other words, each insurance company and its customers would act as a miniature government-controlled society. The customers could not avoid the tax by buying from outside soap producers, since their purchases could be monitored.

Of course, the power to monitor an agent's soap purchases considerably exceeds what we were supposing that the government could do when we considered fiscal policy. In view of the linearity of prices, that policy allowed for trade to be completely anonymous (so that the government need not keep track of any given agent's transactions at all).

Another reason why the market cannot duplicate the government's actions can also be given. Suppose insurance companies can monitor only production and not sales (the previous analysis does not depend on the possibility of sales monitoring). On the other hand, assume that consumers purchase soap in a (large) number of "established" retail stores where sales *can* be monitored. Then it is feasible for the government to drive a wedge between the producer price p and the consumer price q of soap by imposing a tax at the retail level. However, an individual insurance company cannot implement such a wedge without getting the agreement of all retail stores to buy from the producers at the price p and sell to consumers at q—something that an individual retail store has no incentive to go along with (it is better for it to let other retail stores agree to the wedge and then undercut them by selling at just below q).

3 Shocks to Demand

We next turn to a model in which aggregate shocks affect a firm's demand, along the lines of Grossman, Hart, and Maskin 1983. Specifically, we consider an economy in which each of n agents uses a single input, which we will interpret as his own labor, to produce output. There are two types of output: goods 1 and 2. Whether he produces good 1 or 2, each agent has the same production function: $f(\ell)$, where $f' > 0$, $f'' < 0$, and $f'(0) = \infty$; that is, ℓ units of labor are transformed into $f(\ell)$ units of either good 1 or good 2. Also, each agent has the same utility function: $V(U(x_1,x_2) - R\ell)$. Here U is a homogeneous-of-degree-1, twice-differentiable, concave, increasing function that transforms consumption levels of the two goods x_1 and x_2 into "utils," R represents the (real) disutility of supplying labor; and V is a strictly concave von Neumann-Morgenstern utility function representing attitudes toward risk. (In contrast to previous sections, the agent is no longer infinitely risk-averse.) For simplicity, we assume

$$U(x_1,x_2) = 0 \text{ if } x_1 \text{ or } x_2 = 0,$$

$$U_1(0,x_2) = \infty \text{ if } x_2 > 0,$$

$U_2(x_1,0) = \infty$ if $x_1 > 0$,

and

$U_{12} > 0$,

where subscripts denote partial derivatives with respect to the first or second argument. One implication of our assumption that labor disutility is constant is that there is no reason for a labor market to exist; an agent may just as well use his own labor as purchase it in the marketplace.

We suppose that the two goods are *ex ante* identical, but that, after an aggregate shock hits, one of them is in high demand. Without loss of generality, we take this to be good 2:

$$U_2(1,1)/U_1(1,1) > 1. \qquad (***)$$

We further assume that agents are affected idiosyncratically by the shock: an agent cannot predict in advance whether he will end up producing good 1 or good 2; each possibility is equally likely. This assumption is a stylized representation of a situation where the impact of an aggregate demand shock on producers is uncertain. For an alternative formulation where agents produce intermediate goods, the demands for which are stochastically related to the demand for final output, see Grossman, Hart, and Maskin 1983.

As in our model of production shocks, we suppose that an agent cannot directly insure himself against demand shocks. This assumption reflects two more basic hypotheses: that (as before) an agent's profit is unobservable, and that it may be impossible to verify *ex post* whether the agent is producing good 1 or good 2.

Hence, a contract that makes insurance contingent on an agent's output is unenforceable. For simplicity, moreover, we rule out partial insurance contingent on the employment level by supposing that it too is unverifiable. (This is in contrast to the model of sections 1 and 2, where insurance could be conditional on output.)

We evaluate agents' expected payoffs *ex ante*: formally, at date 0 (the date when insurance contracts, had they been feasible, would have been written). At date 1, each agent finds out which good he produces and, acting as a price-taker in output markets, chooses how much labor to supply accordingly. Date-1 output prices then adjust so that date-1 output markets clear. At date-1, there will be equal numbers of agents in each sector. Normalize so that $p_1 = 1$ and $p_2 = p$, where $p > 1$. Then an agent in sector 2 will solve the following problem at date 1: Choose x_1, x_2, and ℓ to maximize $U(x_1,x_2) - R\ell$ subject to $x_1 + px_2 \leq pf(\ell)$. Necessary and sufficient conditions for a solution to this (in addition to the budget constraint) are

$$U_2(x_1,x_2)f'(\ell_2) = R$$

and (23)

$$U_1(x_1,x_2)pf'(\ell_2) = R.$$

Similarly, the conditions for an agent in sector 1 are

$$U_2(x_1',x_2')\frac{f'(\ell_1)}{p} = R$$

and (24)

$$U_1(x_1',x_2')f'(\ell_1) = R.$$

Since markets clear at date 1, we must also have

$$x_1 + x_1' = f(\ell_1)$$

and (25)

$$x_2 + x_2' = f(\ell_2).$$

Together, (23)–(25) plus the two budget constraints characterize the market equilibrium.

We can simplify these conditions as follows. Since U is homogeneous of degree 1, each individual will choose to consume goods 1 and 2 in the same proportions. Hence, as long as relative prices are such that these proportions are the same as those of aggregate production $(f(\ell_1),f(\ell_2))$, budget constraints will ensure that (25) is satisfied. Therefore, using the fact that U_i is homogeneous of degree 0, we may replace (23)–(25) by the following:

$$U_2(f(\ell_1),f(\ell_2))f'(\ell_2) = R,$$

$$U_1(f(\ell_1),f(\ell_2))f'(\ell_1) = R, \qquad (26)$$

$$\frac{U_2(f(\ell_1),f(\ell_2))}{U_1(f(\ell_1),f(\ell_2))} = p.$$

It is easy to see from this that equilibrium exists and is unique. Let (ℓ_1^*,ℓ_2^*) be the unique maximizer of

$$U(f(\ell_1),f(\ell_2)) - R\ell_1 - R\ell_2,$$

and let

$$p^* = U_2((f(\ell_1^*),f(\ell_2^*))/U_1(f(\ell_1^*),f(\ell_2^*)).$$

Then (ℓ_1^*,ℓ_2^*,p^*) satisfies (26) and hence constitutes an equilibrium. On the other hand, any solution to (26) solves

$$\text{Maximize } U(f(\ell_1),f(\ell_2)) - R\ell_1 - R\ell_2$$

and hence equals (ℓ_1^*,ℓ_2^*); and so p must equal p^*.

It is useful to compare the above outcome with what a central planner could achieve under perfect information (the "first best"). *Ex post*, the planner would choose a Pareto-optimal allocation; that is, he would maximize

$$U(x_1,x_2) - R\ell_2$$

subject to

$$U(x_1',x_2') - R\ell_1 \geq \overline{U},$$

$$x_1 + x_1' = f(\ell_1),$$

$$x_2 + x_2' = f(\ell_2).$$

This also leads to the maximization of net surplus

$$U(f(\ell_1),f(\ell_2)) - R\ell_1 - R\ell_2$$

and hence to

$$(\ell_1,\ell_2) = (\ell_1^*,\ell_2^*).$$

However, the planner would engage in *ex ante* risk sharing. In particular, the planner would arrange for unlucky sector-1 producers to receive a per capita lump-sum transfer T from lucky sector-2 producers, where T maximizes the expected *ex ante* utility of a typical producer; that is, T solves

$$\text{Maximize } \tfrac{1}{2}V\left(U(f(\ell_1^*),f(\ell_2^*))\left(\frac{p\,f(\ell_2^*) - T}{p\,f(\ell_2^*) + f(\ell_1^*)}\right) - R\ell_1\right)$$

$$+ \tfrac{1}{2}V\left(U(f(\ell_1^*),f(\ell_2^*))\left(\frac{f(\ell_1^*) + T}{p\,f(\ell_2^*) + f(\ell_1^*)}\right) - R\ell_1\right).$$

The solution of this equalizes the *ex post* "utils" of sector-1 and sector-2 producers; i.e., it satisfies

$$U(f(\ell_1^*),f(\ell_2^*))\left(\frac{p\,f(\ell_2^*) - T}{p\,f(\ell_2^*) + f(\ell_1^*)}\right) - R\ell_2^*$$
$$= U(f(\ell_1^*),f(\ell_2^*))\left(\frac{f(\ell_1^*) + T}{p\,f(\ell_2^*) + f(\ell_1^*)}\right) - R\ell_1^*. \quad (27)$$

(From this it is easy to see that $T > 0$.) Of course, it is in some sense inappropriate to compare the outcome of a constrained market economy with what an omniscient planner can achieve. We now analyze the planner's problem under the assumption that he faces the same constraints as the market.

4 Optimal Fiscal Policy

Suppose that the government can subsidize or tax outputs *ex post*, and balance the budget through lump-sum transfers (as in section 2). Reasons similar to those in section 2 explain why an entrepreneur or an insurance company cannot duplicate what the government does. In particular, whereas the government can impose a tax on good 2 at the retail level, an insurance company would have to get the consent of all retailers to such an arrangement—and it would always pay an individual retailer to refuse to go along and undercut the other retailers.

As in section 2, we shall confine our attention to linear taxes and subsidies. As before, we will normalize the consumption price of good 1 to be 1 and denote the consumption price of good 2 by q. However, we now let producer prices deviate from these values to reflect taxes or subsidies—denote the producer prices of goods 1 and 2 by μ and π respectively.

A producer in sector 2 now maximizes

$$W(q)\pi f(\ell) - R\ell,$$

and a producer in sector 1 maximizes

$$W(q)\mu f(\ell) - R\ell,$$

where

$$W(q) = \max\{U(x_1,x_2)|x_1 + qx_2 \le 1\}.$$

This yields the first-order conditions

$$W(q)\pi f'(\ell) = R,$$

$$W(q)\mu f'(\ell) = R.$$

In market equilibrium,

$$\begin{aligned} &U_2(f(\ell_1),f(\ell_2))\frac{\pi}{q}f'(\ell_2) = R, \\ &U_1(f(\ell_1),f(\ell_2))\mu f'(\ell_1) = R, \\ &\frac{U_2(f(\ell_1),f(\ell_2))}{U_1(f(\ell_1),f(\ell_2))} = q. \end{aligned} \tag{28}$$

An optimal intervention policy is a choice of q, μ, π that solves

$$\text{Maximize}\ \tfrac{1}{2}V(\alpha U(f(\ell_1),f(\ell_2)) - R\ell_2) + \tfrac{1}{2}V((1-\alpha)U(f(\ell_1),f(\ell_2)) - R\ell_1)$$

subject to (28) and

$$\begin{aligned} &\alpha = \frac{\pi f(\ell_2) - T}{\pi f(\ell_2) + \mu f(\ell_1) - 2T}, \\ &T = \tfrac{1}{2}(\pi - \mathrm{q})f(\ell_2) + \tfrac{1}{2}(\mu - 1)f(\ell_1). \end{aligned} \tag{29}$$

Here T is a lump-sum tax chosen to balance the government's budget, and α is sector 2's share of net revenue (and hence of total "utils" $U(f(\ell_1), f(\ell_2))$). Solving for T and using (28) and $U_1 f(\ell_1) + U_2 f(\ell_2) = U$, we obtain as the government's objective function

$$\frac{1}{2}V\left(\frac{1}{2}\frac{Rf(\ell_2)}{f'(\ell_2)} - \frac{1}{2}\frac{Rf(\ell_1)}{f'(\ell_1)} + \tfrac{1}{2}U - R\ell_2\right)$$
$$+ \frac{1}{2}V\left(-\frac{1}{2}\frac{Rf(\ell_2)}{f'(\ell_2)} + \frac{1}{2}\frac{Rf(\ell_1)}{f'(\ell_1)} + \tfrac{1}{2}U - R\ell_1\right),$$

where the control variables are ℓ_1 and ℓ_2. The first-order conditions are

$$(V_2')\left(\tfrac{1}{2}R\left[\frac{(f'(\ell_2))^2 - f(\ell_2)f''(\ell_2)}{(f'(\ell_2))^2}\right] + \tfrac{1}{2}U_2 f'(\ell_2) - R\right)$$
$$+ (V_1')\left(-\tfrac{1}{2}R\left[\frac{(f'(\ell_2))^2 - f(\ell_2)f''(\ell_2)}{(f'(\ell_2))^2}\right] + \tfrac{1}{2}U_2 f'(\ell_2)\right) = 0 \quad (30)$$

and

$$(V_2')\left(-\tfrac{1}{2}R\left[\frac{(f'(\ell_1))^2 - f(\ell_1)f''(\ell_1)}{(f'(\ell_1))^2}\right] + \tfrac{1}{2}U_1 f'(\ell_1)\right)$$
$$+ (V_1')\left(\tfrac{1}{2}R\left[\frac{(f'(\ell_1))^2 - f(\ell_1)f''(\ell_1)}{(f'(\ell_1))^2}\right] + \tfrac{1}{2}U_1 f'(\ell_1) - R\right) = 0, \quad (31)$$

where

$$V_2' = V'\left(\frac{1}{2}\frac{Rf(\ell_2)}{f'(\ell_2)} - \frac{1}{2}\frac{Rf(\ell_1)}{f'(\ell_1)} + \tfrac{1}{2}U - R\ell_2\right)$$

and

$$V_1' = V'\left(-\frac{1}{2}\frac{Rf(\ell_2)}{f'(\ell_2)} + \frac{1}{2}\frac{Rf(\ell_1)}{f'(\ell_1)} + \tfrac{1}{2}U - R\ell_1\right).$$

It is easy to see that $\ell_2 > \ell_1$ in equilibrium (i.e., the high-demand sector produces more). Suppose not: $\ell_2 \leq \ell_1$. Then the argument of V_2' is smaller than the argument of V_1' and so $V_2' \geq V_1'$. It follows from (30) and (31) that

$$U_2 f'(\ell_2) \leq R,$$

$$U_1 f'(\ell_1) \geq R.$$

However, since good 2 is the high-demand good, $\ell_2 \leq \ell_1$ implies $U_2 > U_1$ (see (***)). Hence, $f'(\ell_2) < f'(\ell_1)$, contradicting $\ell_2 \leq \ell_1$.

Given $\ell_2 > \ell_1$, we must have $V_2' < V_1'$. It follows immediately from (30) and (31) that $U_2 f'(\ell_2) > R$ and $U_1 f'(\ell_1) < R$. Hence, by (28), $\pi < p$ and $\mu > 1$. We have established the following:

PROPOSITION 3 An optimal intervention policy involves setting

$$U_2 f'(\ell_2) > R,$$

$$U_1 f'(\ell_1) < R,$$

$$\pi < p,$$

and

$\mu > 1.$

That is, the profitable sector is taxed, and the unprofitable sector is subsidized, leading to underemployment in the former and overemployment in the latter.[5]

Note that $\ell_2 > \ell_1$, $U_2 f'(\ell_2) > R$, and $U_1 f'(\ell_1) < R$ collectively imply $U_2 > U_1$; and hence $p < 1$ from (28). That is, optimal policy stabilizes demand, but not completely. Also, if $f(\ell) = \ell^\beta$, where $0 < \beta < 1$, we can compare the equilibria with and without intervention. Under intervention

$$\frac{U_2 f'(\ell_2)}{U_1 f'(\ell_1)}$$

exceeds 1, its value under nonintervention (see (26)). Hence, ℓ_2/ℓ_1 falls as a result of intervention. It follows from (28) that p rises above p^0, the equilibrium nonintervention relative price, and also that $\pi/\mu < p^0$. That is, if $f(\ell) \equiv \ell^\beta$, we have

$$1 < \frac{\pi}{\mu} < p^0 < p \tag{32}$$

under an optimal intervention policy. In other words, the consumption relative price rises under intervention, while the production relative price falls.

Thus, as in section 2, we see that government policy can yield a Pareto improvement over the laissez-faire equilibrium even though the government has the same information that the market participants have.

Conclusions

A conclusion common to both models studied in this paper is that asymmetric-information economies exhibit externalities that cause the market outcome to be inefficient, even in a second-best sense. This conclusion has also been reached by others (see, e.g., Greenwald and Stiglitz 1984), but not in a macroeconomic setting. We have shown that in some cases the externality leads to a Keynesian-type multiplier (model 1), whereas in other cases optimal government policy bears some resemblance to a Keynesian stabilization policy (model 2).

There is an analogy between our results and those found in the literature on incomplete markets (for a recent review, see Geanakoplos 1990). Incomplete-market equilibria are also second-best suboptimal, and there is a role for government intervention. However, in most incomplete-market models the market structure is taken to be exogenous. In contrast, in the present paper we have derived the trading possibilities from primitive assumptions about which variables are observable and verifiable; in this sense, the market structure is endogenous.

Dedication

This paper is dedicated to Frank Hahn, whose insistence that every theorist has an obligation to consider a large macroeconomic issue—at least, occasionally!—has been a source of inspiration to us.

Notes

1. The second inequality ensures that high-cost producers have enough supplies of oil to produce soap even in the worst-endowment state.

2. Because all agents are *ex ante* identical and the insurers are risk-neutral and competitive, $b(K)$ will turn out to be zero for each K in equilibrium. But this fact plays no role in our analysis.

3. Actually, in Diamond's model the externality is created when an agent searches for a trading partner; this raises the marginal return to search by others. But we can interpret the effort one must exert to sell one's goods as part of the production process.

4. We are implicitly assuming here that only linear taxes are feasible.

5. We refer to "an" optimal intervention policy because there is no guarantee that it is unique. The characterization in proposition 3 applies to any optimal policy.

References

Benassy, J. P. 1975. "NeoKeynesian disequilibrium theory in a monetary economy." *Review of Economic Studies* 42: 503–523.

Blanchard, O. J., and N. Kiyotaki. 1987. "Monopolistic competition and the effects of aggregate demand." *American Economic Review* 77 (4): 647–666.

Diamond, P. 1982. "Aggregate demand management in search equilibrium." *Journal of Political Economy* 90 (5): 881–894.

Geanakoplos, J. 1990. "An introduction to general equilibrium with incomplete asset markets." *Journal of Mathematical Economics* 19: 1–38.

Grandmont, J.-M., and G. Laroque. 1976. "On Keynesian temporary equilibria." *Review of Economic Studies* 43: 53–67.

Greenwald, B., and J. Stiglitz. 1984. "Externalities and economies with imperfect information and incomplete markets." *Quarterly Journal of Economics* 101 (2): 229–264.

Grossman, S. J., O. D. Hart, and E. S. Maskin. 1983. "Unemployment with observable aggregate shocks." *Journal of Political Economy* 91: 907–928.

Grossman, S. J., and L. Weiss. 1982. "Heterogeneous information and the theory of the business cycle." *Journal of Political Economy* 90: 699–727.

Hart, O. 1982. "A model of imperfect competition with Keynesian features." *Quarterly Journal of Economics* 97 (February): 109–138.

Lucas, R. E., Jr. 1972. "Expectations and the neutrality of money." *Journal of Economic Theory* 4 (April): 103–124.

Prices and Queues as Screening Devices in Competitive Markets

Joseph E. Stiglitz

Preface

This essay owes a great deal to Frank Hahn. Frank was my supervisor at Cambridge University during 1965 and 1966. I had gone to Cambridge to write my Ph.D. dissertation, after finishing my general examinations at MIT. Although I had—and still have—unbounded admiration and respect for those who had taught me at MIT, I found something disquieting about the MIT approach to economics. The perfect-competition, perfect-information, perfect-markets models that were employed in the early 1960s (mainly to study questions of growth) seemed not up to the task of addressing many of the central questions of economics—concerns which, in part, had motivated my entering the study of economics in those idealistic days. How could one study the problems of unemployment using models that assumed market clearing, or study the problems of poverty and inequality using models in which all individuals were identical or in which differences did not seem to matter much? Even as models of growth they seemed deficient; they did not really seem to explain why some countries had been successful in their development efforts, while others had failed. To be sure, we at MIT had a much better sense of the appropriate use of models than did our colleagues at Chicago. We did not take models so seriously as to base policy prescriptions (such as the desirability of unfettered free markets) on them, as they seemed to on the shores of Lake Michigan. But I found that kind of intellectual schizophrenia hard to take.

I had left MIT to study at Cambridge hoping to find some guidance on how someone who believed that economics should address the serious problems with which I was concerned might proceed. I found more and less than I had anticipated. I was somewhat disappointed by the so-called Cambridge growth economists, whose writings had helped attract me to Cambridge. Let me pass on, however, to the brighter side—Frank Hahn.[1]

Frank believed (and still believes) that economic models ought to be relevant, that they ought to address central economic issues. When I complained about inadequacies I saw in the neoclassical models with which I had been brought up, Frank issued a challenge: Do something! Show what was wrong with the models. Construct alternative models. These were not just idle injunctions, for Frank was busily engaged with similar concerns. That work culminated in his classic 1966 paper, which, as he put it at the time, placed another golden nail in the coffin of capitalism: Without the transversality conditions provided by markets extending infinitely far into the future, the economy with its heterogeneous capital goods[2] was unstable.

I followed Frank, first in focusing on the consequences of incomplete markets (though after giving some attention to examining exactly how pervasive the "Hahn problem" was and how the market economy maintained what stability it seemed to exhibit[3] I concentrated mainly on the consequences of an incomplete set of risk markets) and later in focusing on the consequences of imperfect and costly information.

This paper is part of that aspect of my research program. Frank believed strongly that the Arrow-Debreu model provided the appropriate framework for understanding why markets did not work, as well as why they did. Keynesian models needed to be related to the A-D framework, to see precisely in what ways their assumptions differed.

One important set of assumptions concerned wage flexibility. It was during my year of studying at Cambridge with Frank that I wrote the first draft of what became my joint paper with Bob Solow, setting up a simple general-equilibrium model with fixed prices.[4] But Frank insisted on pushing back assumptions as far as possible. One needed to explain why wages and prices were rigid.

This paper was written in response. I had the opportunity to study the problem of large-scale unemployment firsthand during an extended visit to the University of Nairobi in 1969. The question was, why were wages there so much higher than market-clearing.?[5] A simple idea—a simple deviation from the standard Arrow-Debreu model—seemed to have enormous explanatory power: If wages affected productivity, they would affect profitability. It might not pay to pay low wages. Firms might maximize profits at a higher-than-market-clearing level. In a paper written at the Institute for Development Studies at Nairobi, I explored three possible explanations for why productivity might depend on wages: through an effect on labor turnover; through the quality of the individuals hired; and through the workers' incentives.[6] Developing a fully articulated, rigorous general-equilibrium model (one up to Frank's standards) exploring each of these ideas has proved difficult.[7]

This paper, originally written in 1973 and circulated ln close to this form in 1976, represents my attempt to formulate a simple model showing how wages and unemployment affect the quality of the individuals hired. The model generates a kind of wage rigidity—wages do not fall even in the presence of unemployment.

1 Introduction

This paper is concerned with the analysis of competitive equilibrium in markets where there is imperfect information. The commodities being sold on the market differ with respect to some important qualities, and these qualities cannot be directly observed. However, the mix of the qualities offered on the market is a function of the price. Thus, in such markets, prices play more than just the role of Lagrange multipliers which they play in conventional economic analysis; they provide information about what is being sold. The consequences of this for the meaning of equilibrium, for the existence of equilibrium, and for its optimality are profound, and it is the purpose of this paper to explore these implications by means of a well-developed example.

The phenomenon with which I am concerned has been noted for a long time; there is a small literature on "judging quality by price," but this literature has never been integrated with the rest of economics. Akerlof (1970) discussed the subject, with the apt title "the market for lemons." But his discussion has lead to some confusion between the phenomenon of thin markets and the non-existence of equilibrium,[8] and although he intuited correctly that these markets when they exist lacked the conventional optimality properties, he failed to demonstrate this.

The phenomenon appears, in a slightly different guise, under the rubric of adverse selection in the insurance literature; there it has been observed that the mix of policyholders with respect to their riskiness depends on the premium charged.[9]

The particular example I shall develop is that of the labor market. But before I present the model in detail, it may be useful to describe the the results of my analysis in an intuitive way. Assume that the sellers of a commodity know the quality of the commodity they are selling. The buyer knows that sellers of low-quality commodities have a greater incentive to sell their commodities than sellers of high-quality commodities; moreover, as the price is lowered, individuals with high quality commodities prefer not to trade rather than to sell. Hence, as the price is lowered, the average quality is lowered. Demanders, in equilibrium, come to know this; whether the demand for the commodity is increased or decreased as the price is lowered depends on whether, in a rough sense, quality is reduced more or less than proportionately to price. Thus, demand curves may have (depending on the distribution of sellers of different qualities) any peculiar shape, and there may be multiple equilibria, as depicted in figure 1.

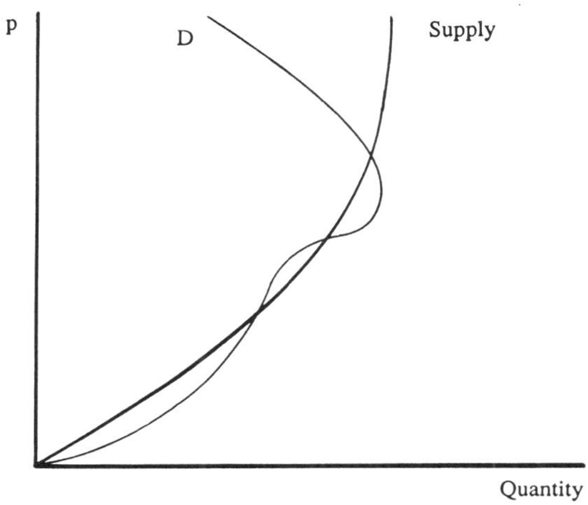

Figure 1

Indeed, among the equilibria may be a zero-price equilibrium; at that price, the quality of the goods offered is so low that there is a zero demand (only individuals with worthless commodities would offer them for sale). But note that the zero price-zero trade equilibrium is Pareto inferior to any equilibrium with a positive price. Individuals trade with one another only when they are better off, at least in an expected-utility sense; and it has been assumed that individuals do correctly foresee the composition of qualities sold on the market.

More fundamentally, the conventional notion of equilibrium as necessarily entailing supply equal to demand must be questioned. Conventional analysis argues that if supply exceeds demand, prices will fall, as suppliers attempt to underbid each other (conversely in cases of excess demand). But here, as the price changes, the mix of the qualities being offered on the market changes; in a sense, we can say that there is a different (quality) commodity offered at every price. Competitive behavior in this context entail firms (buyers) taking the wage-quality (price-quality) function as given, and on choosing the wage-quality (price-quality) function the quality (or mix of qualities) which they most prefer. Figure 2 depicts such a perceived quality-price function. Individuals choose the price that minimizes *price-per-unit quality* (e.g., with labor, the wage per *effective* laborer). But note that at p^* demand may not equal supply. If supply exceeds demand, sup-

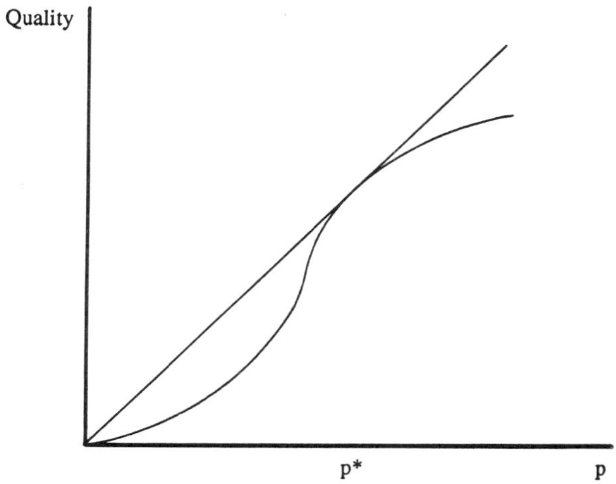

Figure 2

pliers will not "underbid," because as they lower their price they are judged to belong to a mix that has a lower average quality. It would thus appear that market equilibrium may in fact entail demand not equaling supply.

When there is an excess supply of labor, queues will form for jobs; these queues will serve as screening devices, differentiating individuals according to their characteristics. This paper develops an equilibrium theory of queues and assesses its welfare properties.

The main thrust of my analysis is to confirm the results, obtained in other contexts, showing that the analysis of markets in which there is imperfect information is qualitatively different from that of conventional economic analysis:

1. Competitive equilibrium may not entail market clearing.

2. Competitive equilibria are not Pareto optimal. (A number of different sources of inefficiency are noted below.)

3. Pareto optimality may entail some degree of unemployment, but less than in the market solution.

4. Both the market and optimal allocations may entail wage distributions (i.e., different plants paying different wages), although the observable characteristics of individuals applying at the different plants are identical. Both may also entail discrimination.

2 The Basic Model

Assume that there are two types of individuals and there are two types of jobs: each individual can be self-employed or can work in "manufacturing." The ith group has an effective productivity of A_i in manufacturing and $\gamma_i A_i$ in self-employment; i.e., those in group 1 can do in $1/A_1$ hours what those in group 2 can do in $1/A_2$ hours.

Assume that

$$A_1 > A_2;$$

i.e., in manufacturing, group 1 is more productive.[10] Group 1 has a comparative advantage in manufacturing (self-employment) if $\gamma_1 < (>) \gamma_2$.

We assume constant returns to scale in self-employment,[11] and we choose our units so that $\gamma_i A_i$ represents the wages which an individual of type i can earn in self-employment. Thus, $\gamma_i A_i$ is the reservation wage for workers of type i; i.e., below $\gamma_i A_i$ a worker of type i will not supply any labor to the market. For simplicity, we assume that each worker supplies a unit of labor, so that we can use the terms *wage rates* and *incomes* interchangeably.

Because individuals of different productivities have different reservation wages, the mix of individuals offering their services on the labor market will differ as the wage increases. Let $A(w)$ represent the mean productivity of those offering their services at wage w.[12] We call this the wage-productivity curve.

Assume that firms know that some individuals are more productive than other individuals, but there is no method by which they can ascertain which individual is the more productive. They find out, after hiring, that some workers are good and some are bad. They observe that by varying the wage they can vary the relative proportions of good and bad workers, but they still cannot predict which individual is going to be good and which is going to be bad.[13]

We can easily derive the wage-quality relationship, $A(w)$.

(i) If $\gamma_1 A_1 > A_2\gamma_2$, type 1 has absolute advantage in self-employment (see figures 3a and 3b):

$$A(w) = \begin{cases} A_2, & A_2\gamma_2 < w < A_1\gamma_1 \\ \bar{A}, & w > A_1\gamma_1. \end{cases} \tag{2.1a}$$

where

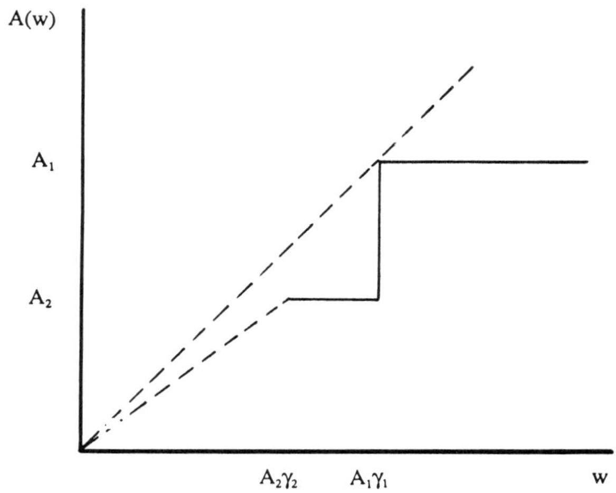

Figure 3a
$A_1\gamma_1 > A_2\gamma_2$: $A_1\gamma_1$ efficiency wage.

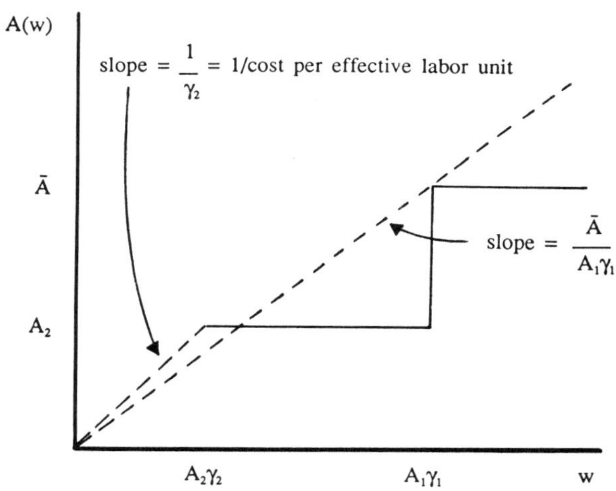

Figure 3b
$A_1\gamma_1 > A_2\gamma_2$: $A_2\gamma_2$ efficiency wage.

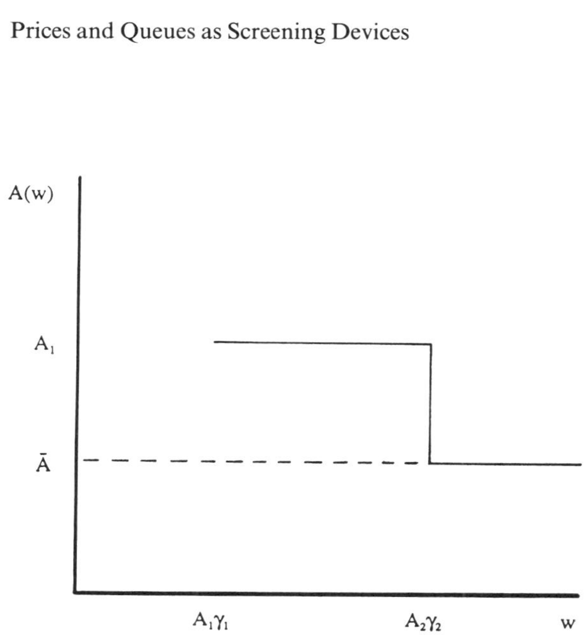

Figure 4
$A_1\gamma_1 < A_2\gamma_2$: $A_1\gamma_1$ always efficiency wage.

$$\bar{A} = \lambda A_1 + (1 - \lambda)A_2$$

represents the mean productivity of the population as a whole, where λ is the proportion of the population that is of type 1. If we let $\bar{L}$ be the total (potential) supply of labor and $\bar{L}_i$ be the total (potential) supply of laborers of type *i*, we have

$$\bar{L}_1 = \lambda \bar{L}, \quad \bar{L}_2 = (1 - \lambda)\bar{L}.$$

The wage that maximizes $A(w)/w$ is called the efficiency wage. $A(w)/w$ is given by the slope of a line from the origin to the wage productivity curve. In figure 3a $A_1\gamma_1$ is the efficiency wage; in figure 3b $A_2\gamma_2$ is.

(ii) If $\gamma_1 A_1 < A_2\gamma_2$, type 1 has absolute disadvantage in self-employment:

$$A(w) = \begin{cases} A_1, & A_1\gamma_1 < w < A_2\gamma_2 \\ \bar{A}, & w > A_2\gamma_2 \end{cases} \tag{2.1b}$$

In this case it is clear that $A_1\gamma_1$ is always the efficiency wage (see figure 4).

Two caveats concerning (2.1) should be noted: First, these quality-wage relationships obtain if there is only a single "manufacturing" firm; otherwise, the wage-quality relationship facing any single firm may depend on the wage policies of other firms. Second, the wage that is relevant is the "expected wage"[14]; as will be noted below, in equilibrium there may be excess supply of laborers, and hence the probability of not being employed may have to be taken into account. We shall return to both of these matters later.

We proceed in our analysis as follows: First, we derive, for purposes of comparison, the market equilibrium with full information. Next, we describe a rather simple case, where there is a single firm in the "employed" sector. We then compare this semi-monopsony solution (it is not complete monopsony, since individuals all have the opportunity for self-employment) with the corresponding behavior when the single firm in the employed sector is government-controlled. Finally, with these results as background, we turn to the case where there are a large number of firms in the "employed" sector.

3 The Full-Information Equilibrium

Each labor unit obtains its marginal product. Hence, if the aggregate production function in manufacturing is

$$Q = F(E), \tag{3.1}$$

where E = effective labor, we obtain a demand function for effective units of labor as depicted in figures 5 and 6.

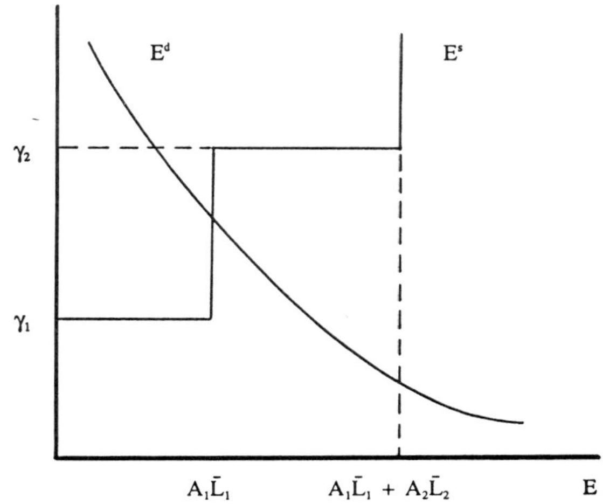

Figure 5
$(\gamma_1 < \gamma_2)$

$$E^{d} = F'^{-1}(\omega),$$

where ω is the wage *per effective labor unit*. The supply of effective labor units is as follows: If $\gamma_1 < \gamma_2$ (figure 5),

$$E^{s}(\omega) = \begin{cases} 0, & \omega < \gamma_1 \\ A_1\bar{L}_1, & \gamma_1 < \omega < \gamma_2 \\ A_1\bar{L}_1 + A_2\bar{L}_2, & \omega > \gamma_2. \end{cases} \tag{3.2a}$$

If $\gamma_1 > \gamma_2$ (figure 6),

$$E^{s}(\omega) = \begin{cases} 0, & \omega < \gamma_2 \\ A_2\bar{L}_2, & \gamma_2 < \omega < \gamma_1 \\ A_1\bar{L}_1 + A_2\bar{L}_2, & \omega > \gamma_1. \end{cases} \tag{3.2b}$$

Equilibrium is determined in the conventional way, where

$$E^{d}(\omega) = E^{s}(\omega).$$

Clearly, those workers with a comparative advantage in manufacturing work in that sector.

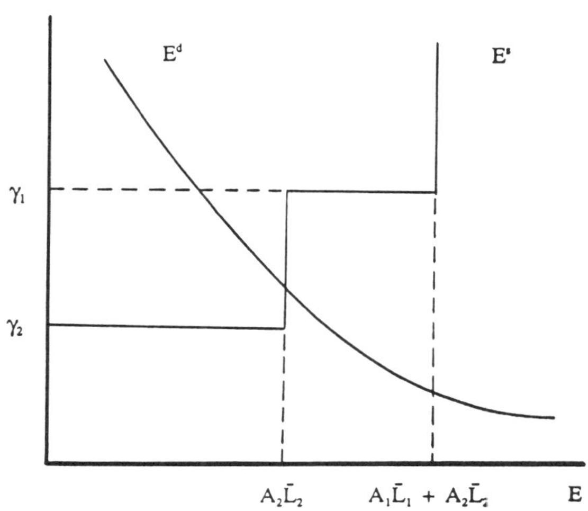

Figure 6
($\gamma_1 > \gamma_2$)

4 The Semi-Monopsony Case—Single Wage

Now assume that there is a single firm, which pays a single wage. If at the wage it offers there is excess supply, individuals who do not obtain employment may work at their self-employment occupations. We assume there is no cost of applying for a job. Thus, the quality-wage relationship is exactly as described in equation 2.1 and depicted in figures 3 and 4.

Perfect Information

The perfect-information solution to this case is simple, and is illustrated in figures 7–9. The total cost curve for efficiency units is derived from the supply curves (as depicted in figures 5 and 6). At $A_1\bar{L}_1$ there is a discontinuity (given our assumption of a single wage, here interpreted as a wage per efficiency unit in manufacturing); below this point the slope of the curve is γ_1, above it, γ_2, assuming "1" has a comparative advantage in manufacturing. (The other case is straightforward.) The total revenue curve is drawn in figures 7–9. The firm chooses the point at which profits are maximized. In figure 7 this is at the point of discontinuity, in which only those with a comparative advantage in manufacturing are hired, and at their reservation wage. In figure 8 all of the type 1 individuals are hired, and only some ($\hat{L}_2$) of the type 2's. In figure 9 only some ($\hat{L}_1$) of the type 1's are hired.

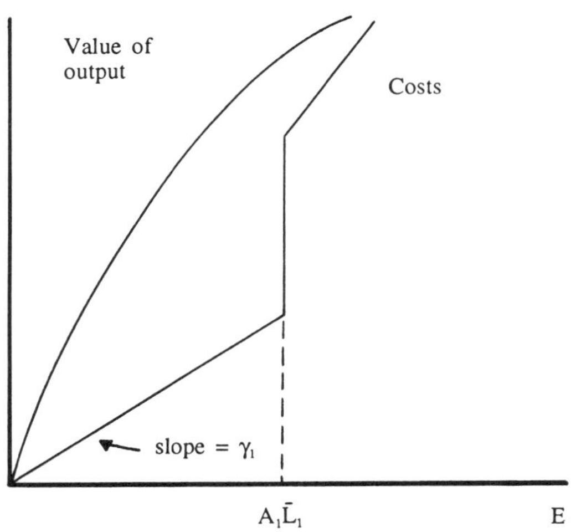

Figure 7

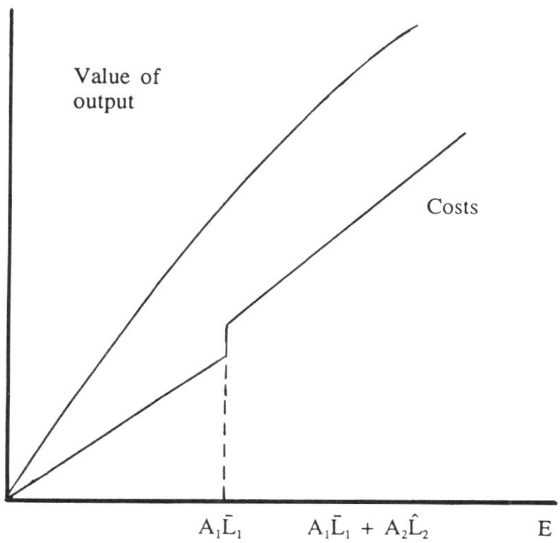

Figure 8

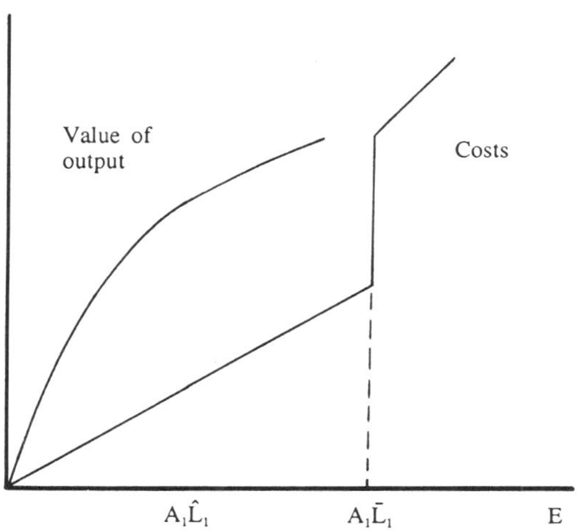

Figure 9

Imperfect Information

We now consider the behavior of the firm that knows that different individuals differ in their abilities, and knows that it cannot distinguish between the more and the less productive, but knows that the average productivity of those applying for a job will depend on the wage offered.

The firm wishes to maximize its profits, i.e.

$$\max F(A(w)L) - wL, \tag{4.1a}$$

subject to the constraint

$$L \leq L(w), \tag{4.1b}$$

where $A(w)$ denotes the dependence of the average quality of labor on the wage and where $L(w)$ is the maximum supply of labor at the given wage.

If $A_1\gamma_1 > A_2\gamma_2$,

$$L(w) = \begin{cases} 0, & w < A_2\gamma_2 \\ \bar{L}_2, & A_2\gamma_2 < w < A_1\gamma_1 \\ \bar{L}_1 + \bar{L}_2, & w > A_1\gamma_1. \end{cases} \tag{4.2a}$$

If $A_1\gamma_1 < A_2\gamma_2$,

$$L(w) = \begin{cases} 0, & w < A_1\gamma_1 \\ \bar{L}_1, & A_1\gamma_1 < w < A_2\gamma_2 \\ \bar{L}_1 + \bar{L}_2, & w > A_2\gamma_2. \end{cases} \tag{4.2b}$$

If the constraint (4.1b) is not binding, we can think of the equilibrium as a (modified) competitive one; i.e., the firm can hire all the laborers it wants at the wage it *chooses* to pay.

It is easy to show that the firm will pay either a wage of $A_2\gamma_2$ or a wage of $A_1\gamma_1$.

Its decision will depend both on the wage-quality trade-off and on the supply function. If $A(w)$ were differentiable and the supply constraint were not binding, then the firm would set

$$A(w)F' = w \tag{4.3a}$$

and

$$A'F' = 1. \tag{4.3b}$$

Dividing (4.3b) by (4.3a), we obtain

$$A' = \frac{A}{w}. \tag{4.4}$$

The solution to (4.4) is known as the *efficiency wage* (see Liebenstein 1957 and Stiglitz 1976). It is the wage that minimizes wage costs per effective laborer:

$$\min\left\{\frac{w}{A(w)}\right\}. \tag{4.5}$$

Thus, the two conditions are that the wage cost per effective unit of labor be minimized and that the marginal product equal the wage per effective labor unit.

In our example, the efficiency wage is found simply be comparing (when $A_1\gamma_1 > A_2\gamma_2$)

$$\frac{A_1\gamma_1}{\bar{A}} \quad \text{and} \quad \frac{A_2\gamma_2}{A_2},$$

which depends critically on the relative proportions of the population in the two groups. Let w^e denote the efficiency wage. Then

$$w^e = \begin{cases} A_1\gamma_1 \\ A_2\gamma_2 \end{cases} \text{as } \lambda \gtrless \lambda^* \equiv \frac{A_1\gamma_1 - A_2\gamma_2}{\gamma_2(A_1 - A_2)}. \tag{4.6}$$

Note that if $\gamma_1 > \gamma_2$, $\lambda^* > 1$, so $\lambda < \lambda^*$ and $w^e = A_2\gamma_2$. *If the type of labor that has an absolute advantage in manufacturing has a comparative advantage in self-employment, the efficiency wage is the reservation wage of the less productive group. Similarly, if the type of labor that has an absolute advantage in manufacturing has an absolute disadvantage in self-employment, then the efficiency wage is the reservation wage of the group that is more productive in manufacturing.*

The firm pays the efficiency wage if the labor constraint is not binding. Note that if the efficiency wage exceeds the minimum reservation wage, i.e.,

$$w^e > \min(A_1\gamma_1, A_2\gamma_2),$$

then, if the labor constraint is not binding, we have an equilibrium with an excess supply of laborers. There are individuals (all the individuals with a low reservation wage) who are not obtaining employment at the going wage and would be willing to work for less. In our model, the labor constraint is *not* binding if

$$F'(A(w^e)L(w^e)) < \frac{w^e}{A(w^e)}; \tag{4.7}$$

i.e., if $A_2\gamma_2 < A_1\gamma_2$ and $\lambda < \lambda^*$,

$$F'(A_2\bar{L}_2) < \gamma_2;$$

if $A_2\gamma_2 < A_1\gamma_1$ and $\lambda > \lambda^*$,

$$F'(\bar{A}\bar{L}) < \frac{A_1\gamma_1}{\bar{A}};$$

if $A_1\gamma_1 < A_2\gamma_2$,

$$F'(A_1\bar{L}_1) < \gamma_1.$$

When the labor constraint is binding, the firm sets

$$F'(A'L + AL') = L + wL'$$

or

$$AF' = \frac{w(1 + \eta^s)}{(A'w/A) + \eta^s}, \tag{4.8}$$

where η^s is the elasticity of labor supply,

$$\eta^s = \frac{L'w}{L}.$$

The marginal product exceeds the wage (that is why the labor-supply constraint is binding), and the wage exceeds the efficiency wage (i.e., $A' < A/w$). Equation 4.8 differs from the conventional formula for monopsony in that the firm takes into account the increased productivity resulting from an increase in the wage. This leads the firm to pay a higher wage than it would in the conventional monopsony case (where $\eta^s AF'/1 + \eta^s = w$).

In our particular example, the firm simply compares the profits it obtains by paying a low wage and hiring all the available labor at that wage against those it earns by paying the efficiency wage and hiring the optimal number of laborers at that wage,

$$F'(\bar{A}L) = \frac{w}{\bar{A}}.$$

In the 1976 version of the paper I provided an explicit analysis of that comparison, identifying conditions under which job rationing would occur.

5 Comparison of Semi-Monopsony Cases with Pareto Optimality

It is important in making welfare statements that we make the appropriate comparisons. That is, we should not compare a full-information equilibrium with a partial-information equilibrium. In this context, whenever $A_1\gamma_1 > A_2\gamma_2$ and $\gamma_1 < \gamma_2$ the manufacturing firm hires at least some of those with a comparative disadvantage in manufacturing employment, and this clearly is not optimal in the case of full information.

The appropriate comparison requires an analysis of the behavior of a government, faced with the same information constraints, and that of the market. Greenwald and Stiglitz (1986) provide a general result showing that when information is imperfect and markets are incomplete market equilibrium is not constrained Pareto efficient—that is, there exist government policies that respect these market imperfections and yet can make some individuals better off without making anyone else worse off. Greenwald and Stiglitz (1988) show how this argument can be extended to a version of the efficiency-wage model. Here, to develop our intuition about the nature of the market's inefficiency, we compare the behavior of the market with that of a government interested in maximizing national output. (It will be apparent that most of the differences identified below arise neither from the special notion of the social-welfare function implicit in this formulation nor from the assumption of a semi-monopsony in the market analysis.[15] These market failures arise, in perhaps modified form, in the competitive model described below.)

Formally, the problem of the government is to choose w and L so as to

$$\max F(A(w)L) - B(w)L \quad \text{s.t. } L \leq L(w), \tag{5.1}$$

where

$B \equiv A\gamma =$ productivity in self-employment

and

$B(w) \equiv$ mean opportunity cost of labor hired at wage w.

The market solution differs from the information-constrained optimal allocation because, with imperfect information, mean opportunity cost will in general differ from the wage,

$$B(w) \neq w.$$

In terms of our example, whenever

$$w = \max(\gamma_1 A_1, \gamma_2 A_2), \quad w \neq B(w)$$

i.e., if

$$w = A_1\gamma_1 \text{ and } A_1\gamma_1 > A_2\gamma_2, \tag{5.2}$$

or

$$w = A_2\gamma_2 \text{ and } A_2\gamma_2 > A_1\gamma_1,$$

then

$$\begin{aligned} B(w) &= \lambda\gamma_1 A_1 + (1-\lambda)\gamma_2 A_2 = A_1\gamma_1 - (1-\lambda)(A_1\gamma_1 - A_2\gamma_2) \\ &= A_2\gamma_2 + \lambda(A_1\gamma_1 - A_2\gamma_2) < w. \end{aligned}$$

The market may differ from the informationally constrained optimal allocation in two respects: the wage paid and the numbers of laborers hired.

If the labor constraint is not binding, the government will choose w so that

$$\frac{A'}{A} = \frac{B'}{B},$$

i.e. to maximize $\ln(A/B)$ rather than $\ln(A/w)$, and hire labor to the point where

$$AF' = B.$$

Thus, in our example, the government efficiency wage, w_g^e, is equal to the reservation wage of the group with a comparative advantage in manufacturing[16]; i.e.,

$$w_g^e = \left\{\begin{matrix} \gamma_1 A_1 \\ \gamma_2 A_2 \end{matrix} \quad \text{as } \gamma_1 \lesseqgtr \gamma_2 \right\}.$$

Thus, if $\gamma_1 > \gamma_2$ or if $\gamma_1 < \gamma_2 A_2/A_1$,

$$w_g^e = w^e,$$

but if $\gamma_2 A_2/A_1 < \gamma_1 < \gamma_2$

$$w_g^e = A_1\gamma_1 \text{ always}$$

while

$$w^e = A_1\gamma_1 \text{ if and only if } \lambda > \lambda^*.$$

The private firm pays too *low* a wage if $\lambda < \lambda^*$. Even when it pays the correct wage, when $\gamma_2 A_2/A_1 < \gamma_1 < \gamma_2$ it hires too few laborers, since $B(w) < w$ then. When $\gamma_2 A_2/A_1 < \gamma_1 < \gamma_2$ and $\lambda < \lambda^*$, output in manufacturing is greater under government control. But employment may be smaller or larger, depending on the elasticity of demand for labor in manufacturing.

Finally, the conditions under which the firm operates with a labor constraint with differ.

In the 1976 version of the paper, I provided an explicit analysis of the differing conditions under which the labor constraint will be binding, i.e., in which there will be "involuntary" unemployment.

6 Multiple-Wage Policy

There is no reason, however, that the single manufacturing firm needs to pay all individuals the same wage. It can use a multiple-wage (or, in our example, a two-wage) policy to sort individuals.

The objective in sorting out individuals is to act as a discriminating monopsonist; individuals differ in their reservation wages. The firm would like to act as a perfectly discriminating monopsonist, paying each individual only his reservation wage. It does not know which individuals have low reservation wages and which high, but by offering multiple wages it partially discriminates. Assume that an individual can apply for only one job (in the manufacturing sector); if he does not succeed in obtaining employment there, he returns to self-employment.

Assume the firm has two plants but can freely shift machines between them. At one plant it pays a wage w_H; at the other, a wage w_L, with $w_H > w_L$. At the first plant the firm hires N_H workers; at the second, N_L workers. Workers have to decide to which plant to apply. We assume that they allocate themselves to the plant with the higher expected wage; i.e., they are risk-neutral. (The analysis may be easily modified if they are risk-averse.)

We focus here on the case where type 1 has an absolute advantage in self-employment.[17] The most interesting case is that where $A_2\gamma_2$ is the efficiency wage but the firm wishes to hire more laborers than $\bar{L}_2$. We can show that the manufacturing firm maximizes its profits by paying at the high-wage plant a wage of $A_1\gamma_1$—so type 1 workers apply to the high-wage plant—and a wage in the low-wage plant which is just high enough to attract all the low-wage workers. All the type 1 workers apply to the high-wage plant, so the probability of getting a job is

$$p_{\mathrm{H}} = \frac{N_{\mathrm{H}}}{\bar{L}_1}.$$

The low-wage plant must pay a wage at least high enough to induce the low-productivity workers to apply there rather than at the high-wage plant:

$$w_{\mathrm{L}} \geq \frac{A_1\gamma_1 N_{\mathrm{H}}}{\bar{L}_1} + \left(1 - \frac{N_{\mathrm{H}}}{\bar{L}_1}\right) A_2\gamma_2.$$

The total efficiency units purchased, if the firm hires N_{H} workers at the high-wage plant, is

$$E = A_1 N_{\mathrm{H}} + A_2\bar{L}_2,$$

and the total cost is

$$C = w_{\mathrm{L}}\bar{L}_2 + N_{\mathrm{H}}A_1\gamma_1.$$

Note that the marginal cost of increasing efficiency units is greater than it would be with perfect information; in the region where the low wage has to be increased to stop type 2 individuals from applying to the high-wage plant, it is[18]

$$\bar{L}_2(A_1\gamma_1 - A_2\gamma_2)/A_1\bar{L}_1 + \gamma_1.$$

It is less expensive to increase efficiency units by using queues at the high-wage firm as a screening device, and keeping wage differentials such that they act as a perfect screening device, than in any other way.

(Though it may thus be desirable to use a wage distribution as part of a screening mechanism, it is not always desirable to do so. See the 1976 version of the paper for a fuller discussion.)

Similar arguments hold if $A_1\gamma_1 < A_2\gamma_2$; two wages are paid when the demand for labor exceeds the supply of type 1 laborers.

The results of this section could have been derived more formally from the solution to the following problem: Assume that the firm consists of a large number of identical plants, each of whose production function we denote by $F(\ )$. Let β denote the fraction paying a low wage. Then the firm maximizes

$$\max_{\{\beta, N_H, N_L, w_L\}} Y \equiv \beta F\left(\frac{N_L}{\beta} A_2\right) - N_L w_L$$

$$+ (1-\beta)F\left(\frac{N_H}{1-\beta} \frac{A_1\bar{L}_1 + A_2 L_2^A(w_H)}{\bar{L}_1 + L_2^A(w_H)}\right) - N_H A_1 \gamma_1$$

$$\text{s.t. } N_L \leq L_2^A(w_L), \quad N_H \leq \bar{L}_1 + L_2^A(w_H)$$

where $L_2^A(w_H)$ is the number of type 2 workers applying to the high-wage firm and $L_2^A(w_H)$ is the number applying to the low-wage firm.

7 Optimal Multiple-Wage Policy

A government-controlled manufacturing sector would also generally pay multiple wage rates; but the objective of the government is different. If it is indifferent as to distribution, it simply maximizes as follows:

$$\max_{\{\beta, N_H, N_L, w_H, w_L\}} Y^G \equiv \beta F\left(\frac{N_L A_2}{\beta}\right) - N_L \gamma_2 A_2 + (1-\beta)F\left(\frac{N_H}{1-\beta}\bar{A}_H\right)$$

$$- N_H\{A_1\gamma_1\rho + A_2\gamma_2(1-\rho)\}$$

(where ρ is the fraction of type 1 individuals in the high-wage manufacturing jobs, and $\bar{A}_H$ is the average ability in the high-wage firm) subject to the same constraints as before. As in section 5, the difference between the market allocation and the optimal allocation is attributed to the difference between the marginal cost of labor and the opportunity cost of labor ($A_1\gamma_1\rho + A_2\gamma_2(1-\rho)$ in the high-wage firm, $A_2\gamma_2$ in the low).

There is another important difference: While the objective of the private manufacturer in introducing differential wages is to act as a discriminating monopsonist, paying, on average, a lower wage to those with a lower reservation wage (and in this sense, the wage distribution is analogous to that discussed by Salop (1977)), from the social point of view the objective of introducing differential wages is to enable the hiring in manufacturing of a larger proportion of those who have a comparative advantage in manufacturing. That is, in the absence of wage discrimination, the manufacturing sector hires only those with an absolute disadvantage in self-employment, or it hires the two groups in the proportions in which they occur in the population.

It is thus easy to show that it is socially optimal for the firm to pay different wages in different plants if and only if the labor that has an absolute disadvantage in self-employment also has a comparative disadvantage in self-employment; by using discriminatory wage policies, the firm can increase the proportion of this group that it hires.

Thus, while both semi-monopsony and optimality may entail wage distributions, the conditions under which the wage distributions arise differ.

8 Discrimination

If there are two groups in the population, with the same ability distribution, it is immediate that the social-cost function without discrimination lies below that with discrimination; it is never optimal to have discrimination, nor will the market employ discrimination. More striking, however, is the result that if the groups differ slightly, so that the minimum cost per efficiency unit purchased at the "social efficiency wage" is less for one group than for the other, there will be both hiring and wage discrimination (i.e., members of the two groups will receive different wages; it is possible that members of only one of the two groups will be hired). Whether discrimination exists, and its nature, may differ between the market and the social optimum, however.

To see the nature of discrimination in the optimum, consider the case where it is optimal for each group to be paid the efficiency wage, $A_1^j \gamma_1^j$. The social cost of obtaining one efficiency unit from type i of group α is just γ_i^α, and from type i of group β is just γ_i^β, and of obtaining one efficiency unit at the efficiency wage is $\bar{A}^j / A_1^j \gamma_1^j \equiv e^j$. Hence, if e^β exceeds e^α, it pays to hire only group β, until all members of group β are hired, paying them a wage of $A_1^\beta \gamma_1^\beta$ (that is, the reservation wage of type 1 workers from group β). Note that this is the case even if type 1 workers from group α have a lower reservation wage, and even if type 1 workers from group α—and type

2 workers from group α, for that matter—are more productive than the corresponding workers from group β. Each of the workers of type α feels discriminated against—less productive workers of group β are being hired. The problem here is simple: firms cannot distinguish between the two types, and, given that, the opportunity cost of hiring a randomly chosen worker of group α, per expected efficiency unit within manufacturing, is higher.

9 The Competitive Solution

I have postponed the treatment of the competitive solution, because it is the most difficult; the distribution of abilities facing any single firm is a function of the actions taken by the other firms.

Earlier I stressed that the nature of the market equilibrium depends on whether firms, recognizing the dependence of quality on price (that is, productivity on wages), set their wages so as to minimize wage cost per efficiency unit. It turns out that the market equilibrium also depends critically on whether workers can apply, costlessly, to all firms simultaneously. If they cannot, then firms may be able to take actions that affect the quality of the applicant pool.

Unlimited Applications

In the case where workers can apply to all firms simultaneously, and all hiring decisions are made simultaneously, each firm will pay the efficiency wage so long as, at the efficiency wage, the total demand for labor is less than the supply; that is, if $A(w)$ is the average productivity of those applying at wage w, then w^c (the competitive wage) is the wage that minimizes $w/A(w)$, i.e.,

$$A'(w) = A(w)/w,$$

provided (in the obvious notation)

$$L^s(w^c) \geq L^d(w^c).$$

In our two-group model, with $A_2\gamma_2 < A_1\gamma_1$,

$$w^c = \begin{cases} A_2\gamma_2 & \text{if } 1/\gamma_2 > \bar{A}/A_1\gamma_1 \\ A_1\gamma_1 & \text{if } 1/\gamma_2 < \bar{A}/A_1\gamma_1. \end{cases}$$

Only One Application Allowed

To investigate the effects of costly and/or limited application, we consider here the special case where individuals can apply to only one firm, but that application is costless.[19] The results reported here are, however, general.

We first establish that there cannot exist a "pooling" equilibrium, in which all firms pay the efficiency wage. For if all firms did that, it would pay some firm to deviate by paying a slightly higher wage. If it did so, it would wind up with a longer queue. The longer queue would serve to detract all low-productivity applicants, and since the firm could thus get only high-productivity applicants its profits would be increased.

More formally, if individuals are risk-neutral, they will apply to the job that maximizes their expected income. If p^j is the probability of getting a job at firm j, and w^j is that firm's wage, then an individual of type i's expected income is[20]

$$p^j w^j + (1 - p^j) A_i \gamma_i \equiv V^i(w^j, p^j),$$

where

$$p^j = N^j / j\text{th firm applicants},$$

where N^j is the number of jobs in the jth firm. Assuming that the costs of applying to all firms are the same, individuals will, in equilibrium, sort themselves among firms so as to equate the expected incomes of all firms among which they apply (and expected income at firms at which they do not apply is lower):

$$V^i(w^j, p^j) = \overline{V}^i \text{ for all } j \text{ for which type } i\text{'s apply},$$

$$V(w^j, p^j) < \overline{V}^i \text{ for all } j \text{ for which type } i\text{'s do not apply}.$$

One small firm believes it has no effect on the level of expected income that workers of any type can obtain. It takes, in other words, $\overline{V}^i$ as given. As the firm changes its wage, queue length adjusts so as to keep the expected income of those applying the same. Figure 10 shows the indifference curves of types 1 and 2 through the putative pooling equilibrium, $\{w^*, p^*\}$. Here

$$\frac{dp}{dw} = -\frac{p^*}{w^* - A_i \gamma_i}; \tag{9.1}$$

thus, the indifference curve of the more productive workers is always

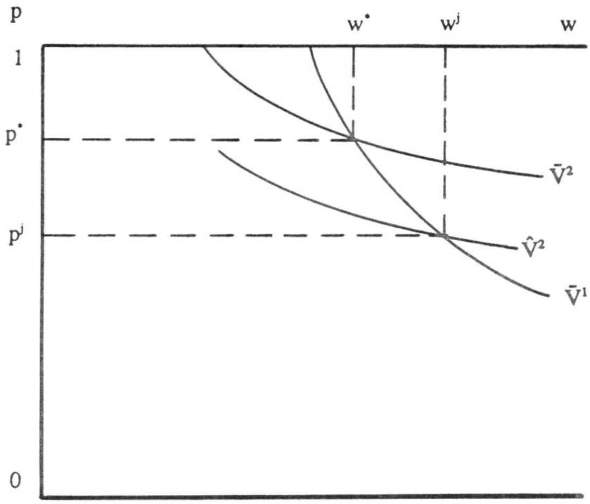

Figure 10
There cannot exist a pooling equilibrium. As a firm increases its wage, the queue increases along $\bar{V}^1$. At all points on $\bar{V}^1$, with $w > w^*$, $\hat{V}^2 < \bar{V}^2$: only type 1 applies.

steeper, as depicted in figure 10.[21] This means that any firm that raises its wage will find that as it does so, its queue length is lengthened, but as it is lengthened, eventually, all the type 2 workers stop applying, and in "equilibrium" only type 1 individuals apply. The equilibrium queue length is given by (for $w > w^*$)

$$V^1(w^*,p^*) = V^1(w^j,p^j), \tag{9.2}$$

and, since at the resulting $\{w^j,p^j\}$

$$V^2(w^*,p^*) > V^2(w^j,p^j) \equiv \hat{V}$$

(see figure 11), no individual of type 2 applies. Since there is a discrete change in the quality mix with a marginal change in the wage, any firm deviating must discretely increase its profits. Thus, there cannot exist a pooling equilibrium; there must be separation.

For future reference, note that in the special case being considered here, where individuals are risk-neutral and there are no costs of applying, the limiting "indifference curve" as V^1 approaches $A_1\gamma_1$ is a vertical straight line, as in figure 11.

We focus here on the case where type 2 has a comparative advantage in manufacturing, i.e.,[22] $1/\gamma_1 < 1/\gamma_2$.

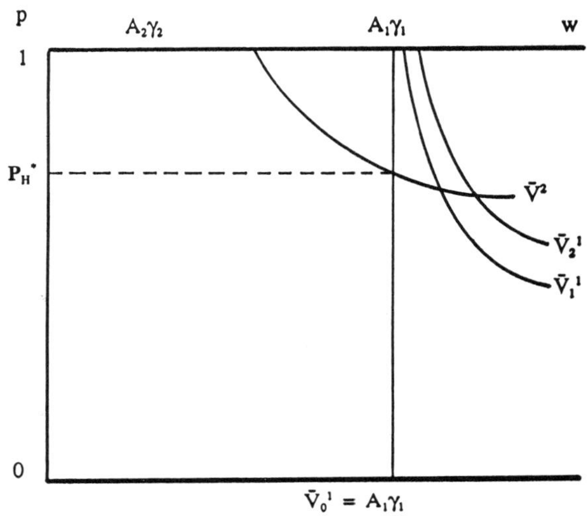

with $\bar{V}_2^1 > \bar{V}_1^1 > \bar{V}_0^1$

where subscripts of $\bar{V}^1$ denote different levels of expected utility of type 1.

Figure 11
Separating equilibrium with $w_L = \gamma_1 A_2$ and $w_H = \gamma_1 A_1$.

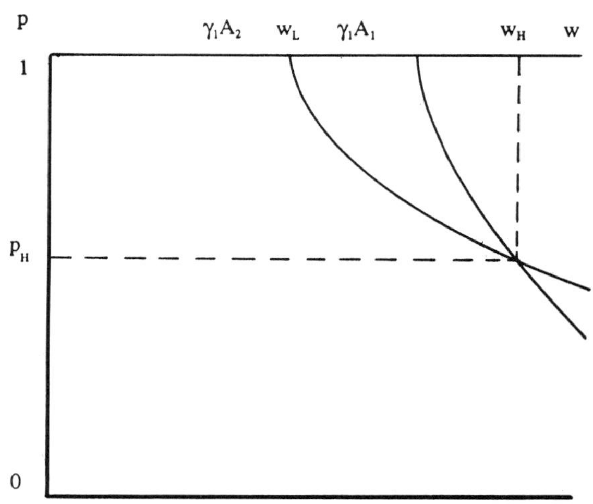

Figure 12
Separating equilibrium with $w_L > \gamma_1 A_2$ and $w_H > \gamma_1 A_1$.

The separating market equilibrium always has the following characteristics: (i) If more than one wage is paid, costs per efficiency unit are the same at both firms; if only one wage is paid, costs per efficiency unit are higher at any wage at which the other type could be obtained. (ii) There is separation; i.e., only members of one type apply to each firm. (iii) The wage equals the value of the marginal product of labor.

In the case at hand, the equilibrium is described as follows.[23] For a single wage (only type 2 hired):

(a) $w = A_2\gamma_2$ if $A_2F'(A_2\bar{L}_2) \leq A_2\gamma_2$: only some of type 2 hired;

(b) $A_2\gamma_2 \leq w \leq A_2\gamma_1$ if $A_2\gamma_1 \geq A_2F'(A_2\bar{L}_2) \geq A_2\gamma_2$: all of type 2 hired.

For a wage distribution:

(a) $w_L = A_2\gamma_1$, $w_H = A_1\gamma_1$, if $F'(A_2\bar{L}_2) > \gamma_1$ *and* $F'(A_2\bar{L}_2 + p_H * \bar{L}_1 A_1) \leq \gamma_1$, where $p_H{}^*$ is such that $V^2(w_H, p_H) = V^2(w_L, 1)$. All of type 2 hired. N_H type 1 hired, where $f'(A_2\bar{L}_2 + N_H A_1) = \gamma_1$; the size of the queue is given by $p_H = N_H/\bar{L}_1$. All type 2 hired weakly prefer to apply to the low-wage jobs. See figure 11.

(b) If $F'(A_2\bar{L}_2 + p_H * \bar{L}_1 A_1) > \gamma_1$, then the equilibrium will have $A_2\gamma_1 < w_L < w_H$; $w_H > A_1\gamma_1$; $p_H > 0$. See figure 12. More precisely, the equilibrium is described by the following three equations:

$$\frac{A_2}{w_L} = \frac{A_1}{w_H} \quad \text{(equal cost per effective laborer)},$$

$$w_L = w_H\left(\frac{N_H}{\bar{L}_1}\right) + A_2\gamma_2\left(1 - \frac{N_H}{\bar{L}_1}\right) \quad \text{(self-selection condition)},$$

$$N_H A_1 + A_2\bar{L}_2 = F'^{-1}\left(\frac{w_L}{A_2}\right) \quad \text{(demand-for-labor equation)},$$

where N_H is the number of individuals hired at the high wage.

Figure 13 provides an explicit calculation of the equilibrium (w_L^*, N_H^*) for this case.[24] w_H can be obtained from the equal cost per effective laborer condition.

The Wage-Taking Adervse Selection Model

For the sake of completeness, we mention the one final possible equilibrium configuration, where firms fail to recognize their ability to set wages. They act as wage-takers, and the equilibrium is the intersection of the demand and supply curves for labor, where firms, in determining their

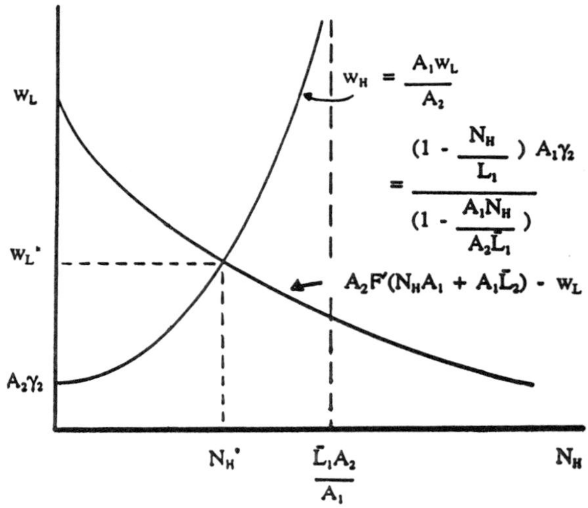

Figure 13

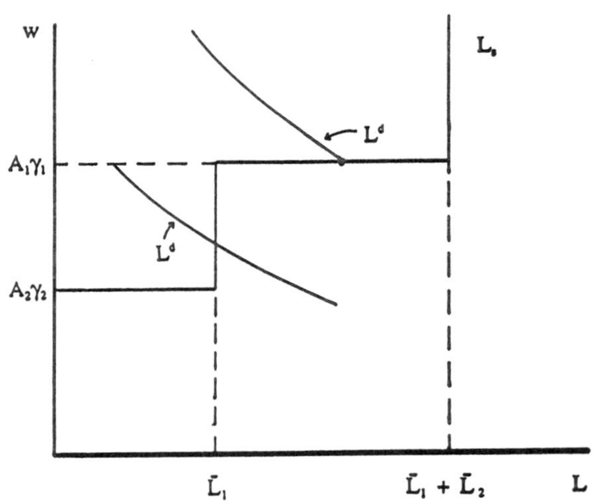

Figure 14
Wage-taking competitive equilibrium—two-group case.

demand, do recognize the dependence of productivity on wages. For the case where there are no application costs, the demand and supply for labor curves appear as in figure 14. There is a discrete increase in supply when wages rise to type 1's reservation wage; at the same point, there is a discrete *increase* in demand, since at that point there is a discrete increase in productivity. In the figure, there are multiple equilibria.

10 Constrained Pareto Efficiency of Competitive Market Equilibrium

The preceding section described a number of different competitive equilibrium configurations. Most of these are not constrained Pareto efficient; that is, the government, faced with the same information constraints, can make some individuals better off without making anyone else worse off.

The government can be thought of as facing two problems: whether to attempt to "screen" (i.e., offer a wage distribution that induces self-selection) and, if it does try to screen, what is the optimal wage-hiring policy.

No Screening Equilibria

In the above analysis, no screening equilibria arose in two cases: that where individuals could apply costlessly to as many jobs as they wished, and that where firms acted as wage takers.

In both cases, firms hire workers up to the wage that equals the (average) value of the marginal product of labor. We noticed earlier that the market solution does not maximize net national product; for it fails to recognize that the wage, on average, exceeds the opportunity cost of labor.

Unrestricted applications If the government could impose a restriction that individuals could apply to only one firm, it might be able to induce a constrained Pareto improvement. Figure 15 shows the "pooling equilibrium" and a low-productivity worker's indifference curve through the pooling equilibrium (assuming he can apply to only one job.) If the government hires a low-productivity worker at $\hat{w}_L$ (the wage that makes him just indifferent), it will improve the mix of applicants at the "pooling" equilibrium. If the government adjusts the number hired at that equilibrium, to leave p^* unchanged, all workers will be indifferent. Under certain circumstances, this perturbation will increase profits; the low-productivity worker

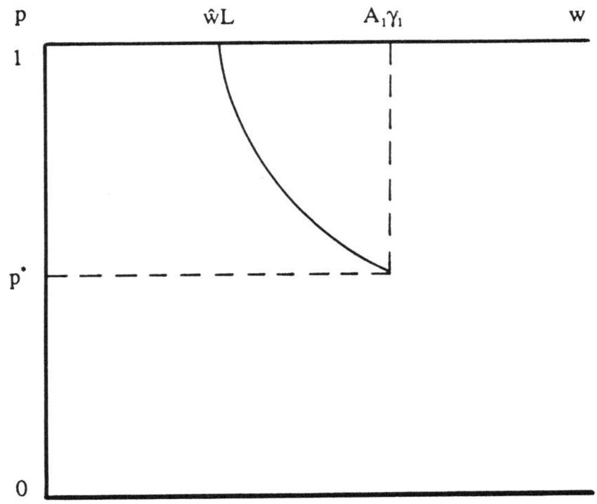

Figure 15

is willing to accept a low wage, to eliminate his risk of not getting hired, and the quality mix of the applicants at the high-wage firm is increased.

Wage-taking equilibrium The wage-taking market equilibrium may also not be constrained Pareto efficient. As was noted, there may be multiple equilibria. The low-wage equilibrium may be Pareto dominated by the high-wage equilibrium. Figure 16 illustrates such a case, where there are no application costs. In the low-wage equilibrium, the low-productivity workers are just indifferent to getting a job in manufacturing and self-employment; in the high wage equilibrium, all of the low-productivity workers who do get jobs are unambiguously better off. Moreover, if $A_1\gamma_1$ is the efficiency wage, profits are higher at the high-wage equilibrium, because costs per efficiency unit are lower.

Screening Equilibria

In the case of screening, constrained Pareto optimality entails

$$\max V^2(w_L, p_L)$$

$$\text{s.t. } V^1(w_H, p_H) \geq \bar{V}^1,$$

$$\pi \geq \bar{\pi},$$

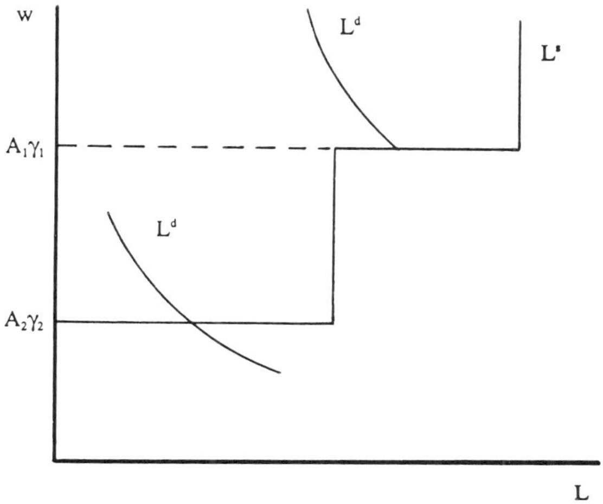

Figure 16

$$\pi + w_L p_L \bar{L}_2 + p_H \bar{L}_1 \leq \beta F\left(\frac{A_2 \bar{L}_2 p_L}{\beta}\right) + (1 - \beta) F\left(\frac{p_H \bar{L}_1}{1 - \beta}\right),$$

$$V^2(w_L, p_L) \leq V^2(w_H, p_H),$$

where π denotes total profits for firms.

Note that the problem we have formulated is the general problem of constrained Pareto optimality (Greenwald and Stiglitz 1986), which is somewhat more general than the problem of maximizing net national output analyzed earlier.

A major difference between the market solution and constrained Pareto optimality is that the former requires the cost per efficiency unit to be the same at all firms; the government can tax, say, high-wage firms to subsidize low-wage firms. Moreover, the government recognizes that policies undertaken by one (group of) firm(s) has effects on other firms: if the low-wage firms increase their wages, it lowers the wage that the high-wage firms must pay to still be able to obtain just high-productivity workers. (See figure 17.)

Thus, it is possible to show that there are conditions under which we (i) tax the high-wage firms; (ii) use the proceeds to finance a subsidy to the low-wage firms; (iii) adjust the wage and hiring policy at the high-wage firms so that there is, in equilibrium, "separation" and still leave high-

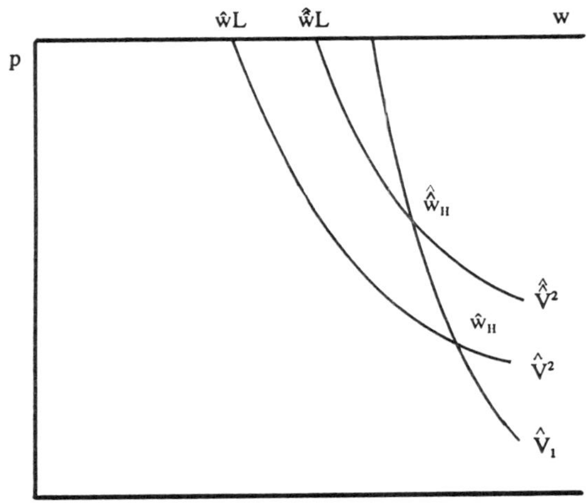

Figure 17
Raising w_L lowers the "separating" high wage.

productivity individuals on their reservation indifference curve; and (iv) still have money left over to increase profits. The low-productivity workers are better off; the high-productivity workers remain on their reservation indifference curves, and are thus unaffected; and there are profits left over, which can be used to make everyone better off.[25]

11 Concluding Remarks

The results of this paper may be looked at in two ways. As a positive theory, the interaction of wages, quality, and queues that has been explored here may provide at least part of the explanation of the high wages and unemployment in less-developed countries; it may provide part of the explanation of why laborers with seemingly similar skills are paid different wages; it may provide part of the explanation of why in parts of a recession firms do not lower wages in response to excess supply; and it may provide part of the explanation of both wage and hiring discrimination.

Alternatively, the analysis of this paper may be viewed as a criticism of the standard economic theory in which perfect information is assumed. Conventional notions of equilibrium are shown to be inappropriate, and conventional optimality results are shown not to obtain.

Postscript

I am sometimes asked why was I so tardy getting this paper published. There are two reasons. One was that I continued to look for alternative formulations, both simpler and more general; I did not succeed in doing so, at least before my attention was drawn to other problems.[26,27] The second was that I was not convinced that *this* explanation of wage rigidity and unemployment was as persuasive as the other explanations that I and others had offered in what became the fast-expanding literature on efficiency wages.[28] The model formulated in the last sections of the paper suggests that unemployment will be concentrated among the more able, as they seek to prove that they have a higher fallback wage. There may be important instances of this—Harley Street doctors and many US surgeons work short work weeks, shorter than seems plausible on the basis of standard income effects. And interpreting information-theoretic models is often tricky; the theory makes predictions about relative unemployment among groups of individuals who are otherwise observationally equivalent. It does not compare unemployment rates among doctors and blue-collar workers—these are not observationally equivalent—but rather among doctors, or among plumbers. How much of total unemployment could be attributed to this still remains problematic.

This paper represents an attempt to formulate an *equilibrium* theory of unemployment. I have increasingly come to the view that to explain cyclical unemployment one needs to focus on models of adjustment. The question is, what will happen to the quality of a firm's labor force, and therefore to its long-run profits, if, in response to some disturbance, it lowers its wages, rather than laying off a particular fraction of its workers? The kinds of "adverse selection" effects upon which I have focused here may take on first-order importance in that context.[29]

The challenges Frank Hahn posed a quarter of a century ago have given rise to a rich and fruitful literature. His influence on the profession—his insistence on intellectual rigor *and* economic relevance—has been all for the good. Capitalism is alive and well. The many golden nails that he might have thought he was putting in the coffin of capitalism have enabled us to understand better how the capitalist system really works. And out of that understanding, hopefully, will come a better-functioning economy and a better society. For this—and for his friendship over all these years—we are all grateful.

Acknowledgments

This work was supported by the National Science Foundation and the Hoover Institution. I have benefited greatly from conversations with Andy Weiss; he has dealt with some of the same issues in the context of imperfectly competitive economies (1976). His recently published book (1990) provides an excellent description of a wide range of efficiency wage models.

Notes

1. There were many other bright sides as well, both among the faculty (such as James Meade, Michael Farrell, and David Champernowne) and among the students—my long-standing collaborations and friendships with Partha Dasgupta, Tony Aktinson, Geoffrey Heal, Chris Bliss, and James Mirrlees all date back to that year.

Frank had, by then, established himself as the center of his own group at Cambridge, making the place one of the most exciting in the world. I returned in 1969–1970, and the excitement was, if anything, even greater. It was in that year that Frank decided to challenge the "secret seminar" (with its policy of excluding those who were not "right-thinking"—meaning left-thinking) that Joan Robinson had run for decades. He established his own seminar, and augmented it with visitors such as Arrow and Radner. The old secret seminar seemed simply to wither away.

2. Later literature showed that all that was required were multiple assets; models with money and a single capital good exhibited similar instabilities. See, e.g., Shell, Sidrauski, and Stiglitz 1969.

3. Shell and I studied these questions in our 1967 paper, showing, among other things, that, in the model we studied, the capital asset arbitrage equation would be violated in finite time on every path not converging to the steady state, and that with less than perfect foresight the economy was more likely to be stable. In subsequent work, I (Stiglitz 1973) and others showed that in more general models there were in fact a multiplicity of paths consistent with perfect foresight which neither converged to the steady state nor ever violated the capital asset arbitrage condition.

4. I sometimes regret that I did not pay close enough attention to Uncle Frank's injunctions to relate one's work to the standard Arrow-Debreu paradigm. In our joint work, Solow and I (1968) had simply postulated consumption functions and labor-supply equations; it seemed to us obvious that any first-year Tripos student could fill in the details of how these could be derived from utility—maximizing behavior. Yet when Barro and Grossman (1971) filled in those details, it not only was published, but launched a large subsequent literature.

5. How high wages could generate urban unemployment in LDCs had recently been modeled by Todaro (1969) and Harris and Todaro (1970). Both Todaro and Harris were visiting Nairobi at the same time that I was.

6. The idea that wages might affect productivity had earlier been introduced into the development literature, e.g. by Leibenstein (1957) (another Cambridge visitor during my sojourn there). The earlier literature had, however, focused on nutritional effects. In the case of Nairobi, this seemed inadequate to explain the level of wages then being offered.

7. The labor-turnover version of the model was explored in Stiglitz 1974 and 1985; the incentives version was explored in Shapiro and Stiglitz 1984.

8. The phenomenon of thin markets happens when, because of imperfect information, individuals are less likely to trade even though, with full information, there would be gains from exchange. Because of the uncertain quality of the commodities he purchases, the price at which the individual will become a seller of a commodity (in, say, a pure exchange economy) is considerably above the price at which the individual will become a buyer. If differences in marginal rates of substitution without trade are small, equilibrium will entail zero transactions. But this is not the same as non-existence of equilibrium!

9. Although in our discussions we assume that the seller knows what he is selling but the buyer does not know what he is buying, this is not essential for our analysis; the seller may also be uninformed, and much of what we have to say still remains valid (so long as sellers of different qualities of commodities differ in their supply responses).

10. In later analysis, it will be clear that what is of importance is whether type 1 or 2 has a comparative advantage in manufacturing, i.e. whether

$$\frac{1}{\gamma_1} = \frac{A_1}{A_1\gamma_1} > \text{ or } < \frac{1}{\gamma_2} = \frac{A_2}{A_2\gamma_2}.$$

The actual value of γ makes no difference, since production in manufacturing will be governed by a production function described below (equation 3.1), which will transform units of labor power in manufacturing into units of manufacturing goods. If we choose units so $Q = E$, where Q is output in manufacturing and E is effective labor, and so the price of manufacturing output is the same as self-employment output, then it is natural to assume that $\gamma_1 < 1$ (productivity of type 1 is greater in manufacturing than in the rural sector) but $\gamma_2 > 1$ (productivity of type 2 workers is greater in self-employment than in manufacturing).

11. And that the relative price of the output of self-employment to that of manufacturing is constant (and normalized at unity).

12. Later it will be noted that, in general, we should write $A_j(w_1, \ldots, w_n, L_1, \ldots, L_n)$. The mean ability of those offering themselves to the jth firm is a function of the wages and hiring of all firms. When we simply write $A(w)$, we are implicitly assuming that all firms in the manufacturing sector are paying the same wage, and that quality does not depend on the amount of hiring. $A(w)$ then represents the mean quality of those offering themselves for employment in the urban sector. Alternatively, we assume there is a single manufacturing firm. These matters are elaborated on below.

13. The obvious objections may be raised to these informational assumptions: First, if the firm cannot observe productivity, why do individuals work at all? The answer to this is that firms can identify abilities and productivities within a range; that is, there may be individuals who are much more productive and individuals who are much less productive, but these have been screened off. Moreover, after they have hired and trained the individual, they may be able to observe both ability and effort and thus can enforce contracts requiring a stipulated level of effort. But then, it might be asked, why do not the more able "guarantee" that they are more able? They presumably would, if they were perfectly certain of their abilities, or, if uncertain, they were risk-neutral. But if individuals are risk-averse and there is even a slight degree of uncertainty about their own abilities, individuals will be unwilling to provide complete insurance; and so long as they do not provide complete insurance, firms will be concerned with the mix of individuals they hire. The particular model developed here can be thought of as the polar case of infinitely risk-averse individuals facing infinitesimally small risks, i.e., an infinitesimally small fraction of individuals of type actually have productivity A_2; all individuals have a utility function of the form $U = \min\{w\}$, the minimum income in any state of nature. But then any payment scheme depending on the actual performance will not act as a screening device, since for both groups $\min\{w\}$ is the same.

14. Or, more generally, we need to specify both the wage and the number of individuals hired (from which we can derive the length of the queue).

15. In some instances, where there is *not* unemployment, the semi-monopsonist hires fewer workers than is efficient, with this restriction in employment arising from its noncompetitive position.

16. That is, if $A_2\gamma_2 < A_1\gamma_1$, at $w = A_2\gamma_2$,

$$\frac{B}{A} = \frac{A_2\gamma_2}{A_2}$$

while at $w = A_1\gamma_1$

$$\frac{B}{A} = \frac{\lambda A_1\gamma_1 + (1-\lambda)A_2\gamma_2}{\lambda A_1 + (1-\lambda)A_2}.$$

The latter exceeds the former if $\gamma_1 > \gamma_2$, and conversely.

17. See the 1976 version of the paper for other cases, as well as details substantiating the argument below.

18. Note that so long as

$$w_L > A_1\gamma_1\frac{N_H}{\bar{L}_1} + A_2\gamma_2\left(1 - \frac{N_H}{\bar{L}_1}\right)$$

the marginal cost of hiring additional efficiency units is just $A_1/A_1\gamma_1$.

If, instead of increasing w_L, the firm had simply allowed some of the low-productivity workers to apply to the high-wage firm, applications would have continued until

$$w_L = \frac{w_H N_H}{\bar{L}_1 + \hat{L}_2} + A_2\gamma_2\left(1 - \frac{N_H}{\bar{L}_1 + \hat{L}_2}\right),$$

where $\hat{L}_2$ is the number of type 2 individuals applying to the high-wage firm.

Now, hiring an additional worker at the high-wage firm has a deleterious effect on quality, and reduces the number of applicants at the low-wage firm.

The equations

$$E = N_H\left(\frac{A_1\bar{L}_1 + A_2\hat{L}_2}{\bar{L}_1 + \hat{L}_2}\right) + A_2(\bar{L}_2 - \hat{L}_2)$$

and

$$C = \left(\frac{\bar{L}_2 - \hat{L}_2}{\bar{L}_1 + \hat{L}_2} + 1\right)w_H N_H + A_2\gamma_2(\bar{L}_2 - \hat{L}_2)\left(1 - \frac{N_H}{\bar{L}_1 + \hat{L}_2}\right)$$

where we have made use of the expression for w_L, can be thought of as defining isocost and iso-efficiency unit curves for $N_L = \bar{L}_2 - \hat{L}_2$ and N_H:

$$\left.\frac{dN_H}{d\hat{L}_2}\right|_C = \frac{N_H}{\bar{L}_1 + \hat{L}_2} - \frac{A_2\gamma_2(N^H - (\bar{L}_1 + \hat{L}_2))}{(\bar{L}_2 - \hat{L}_2)(A_1\gamma_1 - A_2\gamma_2) + (\bar{L}_1 + \hat{L}_2)A_1\gamma_1}.$$

$$\left.\frac{dN_H}{d\hat{L}_2}\right|_E = \frac{N_H}{\bar{L}_1 + \hat{L}_2}\left(\frac{(A_1 - A_2)\bar{L}_1 + A_2(\bar{L}_1 + \hat{L}_2)^2/N_H}{A_1\bar{L}_1 + A_2\hat{L}_2}\right),$$

from which it is apparent that there will be a corner solution, with $\hat{L}_2 = 0$ under the assumed conditions.

19. In effect, the second application can be thought of as having a prohibitively high application cost.

20. More generally, if there were a cost of c_i for a type i to apply to a job, individuals of type i's expected utility from applying to firm j would be given by

$$EU^i \equiv p^j u^i(w^j) + (1 - p^j)u^i(A_i \gamma_i) - c_i \equiv V^i(w^j, p^j).$$

21. This result is true with risk-averse individuals and with application costs, so long as type 2 individuals are risk-averse than type 1 individuals.

22. More general cases, when there is risk aversion and costs to applying, may be handled similarly.

23. In the special case of risk neutrality and no costs of application, if $\gamma_1 < \gamma_2$, then there may either exist no equilibrium, or it may be characterized by a single wage, $w = A_2\gamma_2$ (e.g., if $F'(A_2\bar{L}_2) < \gamma_2$ and if $A_2\gamma_2$ is the efficiency wage) or by a two-wage distribution (w_L, w_H), with

$$V^2(w_L, 1) = V^2(w_H, p_H),$$

$$w_L/A_2 = w_H/A_1,$$

$$A_2 F'(L_2 A_2 + p_H \bar{L}_1 A_1) = w_L.$$

The conditions under which each at these may occur are spelled out in Rodriguez 1991.

24. The equilibrium just described may be given a slightly different interpretation. Assume that firms enter a market sequentially. Once workers have accepted a job, they are committed. In deciding to accept a job, they must look at the opportunities they are forgoing. The opportunity cost of accepting a job is thus *endogenous*—the inability to accept a higher-wage job, should it come along. In competitive equilibrium, (i) wages must be such that it pays workers to accept a job, rather than to turn down the job, in the hopes that a better opportunity will show up; and (ii) all firms must face the same wage costs per efficiency unit obtained.

As Guasch and Weiss (1980) note, later entrants appear to have a marked advantage over earlier entrants. Earlier entrants hire lower-productivity workers (those with "low" reservation wages); this shifts the wage-productivity curve, seeming to imply that later entrants would pay higher wages and face lower costs per efficiency unit. This is the advantage of being late. But this cannot be a competitive equilibrium; and it ignores the reaction of workers who, anticipating higher wage offers in the future, will alter their reservation wages.

Assume that there are two rounds to wage offers. In the first round, firms make an offer of w_L; in the second round they offer w_H, where w_L and w_H are as described earlier. Note that if the low-wage workers correctly anticipate the future wages and hiring probabilities, they will all apply for and accept the low-wage offers; and when they do this, the cost per efficiency unit at the low-wage–early-entrant firms is identical to that at the high-wage–later-entrant firms. There is no disadvantage to being late. Wages and probabilities of getting a job are acting as screening devices among what would otherwise appear to be observationally equivalent workers.

These results are generalized by Nalebuff and Stiglitz (1982, 1985), who also address whether job commitments will arise endogenously as part of an equilibrium.

25. This is seen most clearly in the case of constant-returns-to-scale production functions, for which $\pi = 0$, and in the separating equilibrium, for suitable choice of units, $w_L = A_2$ and $w_H = A_1$. Accordingly, under our assumptions of risk neutrality and no application costs, all the high-ability individuals apply to the high-wage firms, so $p_H = N_H/\bar{L}_1$, where N_H is the number hired at the high-wage firms and where p_H is restricted, so that the self-selection condition is satisfied. Total profits is given by

$$\pi = (A_1 - w_H)p_H\bar{L}_1 + (A_2 - w_L)\bar{L}_2.$$

If w_H is increased, then to keep type 1's on the same indifference curve

$$\frac{dp_H}{dw_H} = -\frac{p_H}{w_H - A_1\gamma_1}.$$

If w_H is lowered and p_H increased, the separating wage $\hat{w}_L$ is increased:

$$\frac{d\hat{w}_L}{dw_H} = p_H + (w_H - A_2\gamma_2)\frac{dp_H}{dw_H}$$

$$= \frac{A_1\gamma_1 - A_2\gamma_2}{w_H - A_1\gamma_1} p_H.$$

Hence, total profits are increased when w_H is reduced if

$$p_H\bar{L}_1 - p_H\bar{L}_2\frac{A_1\gamma_1 - A_2\gamma_2}{w_H - A_1\gamma_1}$$

$$= \frac{p_H\bar{L}}{w_H - A_1\gamma_1}[\lambda w_H + (1 - \lambda)(A_2\gamma_2 - A_1\gamma_1)] > 0.$$

See Rodriguez 1991 for a more general result.

26. Barry Nalebuff and I (1982, 1985) did manage to formulate some *less* simple but more general models, which were partly focused on the "advantages of being late" that Guasch and Weiss discussed (1980).

27. A few further bibliographic remarks are in order. The most widely cited paper explaining wage rigidities in terms of adverse selection is perhaps Weiss 1980, but in that paper Weiss does not formulate a competitive equilibrium market of the labor market, which I have attempted to do here. Further results are reported in Weiss 1990. A more rigorous analysis of Akerlof's model is contained in Wilson 1980.

In Stiglitz 1987, I explain in greater detail the differences between this model, the standard Arrow-Debreu model, and the Akerlof lemons model. Greenwald (1986) provides perhaps the best articulation of the Akerlof lemons model in the context of labor markets.

The use of unemployment (or more generally, the failure to engage in a transaction) as a screening device has subsequently been explored more thoroughly, e.g. in the bargaining literature. See Myerson 1985 and Farrell 1987.

28. For a survey, see Yellen 1984 or Stiglitz 1987.

29. Bruce Greenwald and I (1989) have attempted to model this adjustment process formally, showing why firms would choose not to lower wages even in the face of an excess supply of labor. See also Arnott, Hosios, and Stiglitz 1988.

References

Akerlof, G. 1970. "The market for 'lemons': Quality uncertainty and the market mechanism." *Quarterly Journal of Economics* 84 (August): 488–500.

Arnott, R., A. Hosios, and J. Stiglitz. 1988. "Implicit contracts, labor mobility and unemployment." *American Economic Review* 78 (December): 1046–1066.

Barro, R., and H. Grossman. 1971. "A general disequilibrium model of income and employment." *American Economic Review* 61: 82–93.

Farrell, J. 1987. "Information and the Coase theorem." *Journal of Economic Perspectives* 1 (2): 113–129.

Greenwald, B. 1986. "Adverse selection in the labour market." *Review of Economic Studies* 53 (3): 325–347.

Greenwald, B., and J. Stiglitz. 1986. "Externalities in economies with imperfect information and incomplete markets." *Quarterly Journal of Economics* 101 (May): 229–256.

Greenwald, B., and J. Stiglitz. 1988. "Pareto inefficiency of market economies: Search and efficiency wage models." *American Economic Review* 78 (May): 351–355.

Greenwald, B., and J. Stiglitz. 1989. "Toward a theory of rigidities." *American Economic Review* 79 (May): 364–369.

Guasch, L., and A. Weiss. 1980. "Adverse selection by markets and the advantage of being late." *Quarterly Journal of Economics* 94 (May): 453–466.

Hahn, F. 1966. "Equilibrium dynamics with heterogeneous capital goods." *Quarterly Journal of Economics* 80 (November): 633–646.

Harris, J., and M. Todaro. 1970. "Migration, unemployment and development: A Two-Sector analysis." *American Economic Review* 60 (March): 126–142.

Leibenstein, H. 1957. *Economic Backwardness and Economic Growth*. Wiley.

Myerson, R. 1985. "Analysis of two bargaining problems with incomplete information." In *Game-Theoretic Models of Bargaining*, ed. A. Roth. Cambridge University Press.

Nalebuff, B., and J. Stiglitz. 1982. Quality snd Prices. Princeton University Econometric Research Program Memorandum 297.

Nalebuff, B., and J. Stiglitz. 1985. Unemployment as a Self-Selection Mechanism. Mimeo, Princeton University.

Rodriguez, A. 1991. Non-existence and Optimality of Equilibrium in a Model with Asymmetric Information and Market Screening. Mimeo, Stanford.

Salop, S. C. 1977. "The noisy monopolist: Imperfect information, price dispersion, and price discrimination." *Review of Economic Studies* 44: 393–406.

Shapiro, C., and J. Stiglitz. 1984. "Equilibrium unemployment as a worker discipline device." *American Economic Review* 74: 433–444.

Shell, K., M. Sidrauski, and J. E. Stiglitz. 1969. "Capital gains, income and saving." *Review of Economic Studies* 36 (January): 15–26.

Shell, K., and J. Stiglitz. 1967. "The allocation of investment in a dynamic economy." *Quarterly Journal of Economics* 81: 592–609.

Solow, R., and J. Stiglitz. 1968. "Output, employment and wages in the short run." *Quarterly Journal of Economics* 82: 537–560.

Stiglitz, J. E. 1973. "The badly behaved economy with the well behaved production function." In *Models of Economic Growth*, ed. J. Mirrlees. Macmillan.

Stiglitz, J. E. 1974. "Wage determination and unemployment in LDCs: The labor turnover model." *Quarterly Journal of Economics* 88: 194–227.

Stiglitz, J. E. 1976. "The efficiency wage hypothesis, surplus labor, and the distribution of income in LDCs." *Oxford Economic Papers* 28: 185–207.

Stiglitz, J. E. 1985. "Equilibrium wage distributions." *Economic Journal* 95: 595–618.

Stiglitz, J. E. 1987. "The causes and consequences of the dependence of quality on price." *Journal of Economic Literature* 25 (March): 1–48.

Todaro, M. 1969. "A model for labor migration and urban unemployment in less developed countries." *American Economic Review* 59 (March): 138–148.

Weiss, A. 1976. "A Theory of Limited Labor Markets. Ph.D. dissertation, Stanford University.

Weiss, A. 1980. "Job queues and layoffs in labor markets with flexible wages." *Journal of Political Economy* 88 (June): 526–538.

Weiss, A. 1990. *Efficiency Wages: Models of Unemployment, Layoffs and Wage Dispersion.* Princeton University Press.

Wilson, C. 1980. "The nature of equilibrium in markets with adverse selection." *Bell Journal of Economics* 11 (spring): 108–131.

Yellen, J. 1984. "Efficiency wage models of unemployment." *American Economic Review Proceedings* 74 (March): 200–205.

II INFORMATION AND THE THEORY OF GAMES

Informational Equivalence of Signals

Kenneth J. Arrow

In decisions under uncertainty, information becomes valuable. If the consequences of an action depend on a unobserved random variable, then costless observation of another random variable not independent of the first before the choice of action may improve the expected payoff. The random variable affecting the consequences will be termed the *payoff-relevant state of nature* (usually to be abbreviated to *state of nature*). The random variable observed will be termed a *signal*, to follow the language derived from communication theory, which originated in analysis of telecommunications.

We are frequently concerned with a choice among alternative signals. That is, given a decision to be made, there are alternative signals among which to choose for observation for making the decision. Clearly, a ranking of signals in terms of their value in improving decision-making would be useful. A decision problem is defined by the space of available actions and the function relating payoff to action and state of nature. Given the decision problem, the expected payoff based on any given signal can be found. Then the optimal signal among those available can be chosen.

But it would be useful to have at least a partial ordering of signals independent of the particular decision problem. This was the aim of David Blackwell's theory of comparison of information structures (Blackwell 1951, 1953; Blackwell and Girshick 1954, chapter 12). One signal is at least as good as another in the informational sense if the expected payoff based on the one signal is at least as great at that based on the other for *every* decision problem. Blackwell gave a striking characterization of the relation "informationally at least as good as"; it was essentially that the second signal could have been a garbling of the first, in the sense that the second was a signal about the value of the first signal not affected by the state of nature.

In this language, two signals can be defined to be *informationally equivalent* if each is informationally at least as good as the other. A characterization of informational equivalence is found which is just as sharp as Blackwell's criterion. The role of garbling in Blackwell's theorem is replaced by the familiar concept of sufficiency, so important in theoretical statistics. If one signal is sufficient for another (with the state of nature as parameter), then the two are clearly equivalent. If attention is confined to signals which take on a finite number of values, then we can find, for any given signal, one which could be sufficient for it and which has a minimum number of possible values. A minimal signal in this sense defines the class of all signals for which it could be sufficient; such classes are precisely the classes of informationally equivalent signals.

In section 1, the Blackwell theory is summarized. In section 2, the notion of quasi-sufficiency and the matrix concepts used in the analysis are defined, and the basic properties of quasi-sufficiency and its characterization as multiplication by a suitable kind of matrix are proved. In section 3 the characterization of informational equivalence classes sketched above is stated precisely and derived in terms of some properties of Metzler matrices (square matrices with non-negative off-diagonal elements). In section 4, a summary of known theorems on Metzler matrices is given and a new theorem needed to prove the main result of the paper is demonstrated.

1 Decision with Information and the Comparison of Signals

A decision problem with uncertainty is defined by an action space A, a random variable, X, known as the payoff-relevant state of nature, and a function, $w(a,x)$, which is the (numerically valued) payoff if action a is chosen and X takes on the value x. In the absence of information, the decider chooses a to satisfy the imperative

$$\mathrm{Max}_a \,!\, E_x[w(a,X)]. \tag{1}$$

The possibility of information means that there is a random variable, S, known as a *signal*, which is observed before a is chosen. Once S is observed, then the decision problem is the same as before, except that the distribution of X is that conditional on the observed value of S. If S takes on the value s, then the (possibly multi-valued) *decision function*, $a(s)$, is defined for each s by,

$$\mathrm{Max}_a \,!\, E_{X|S}[w(a,X)], \tag{2}$$

which is equivalent to selecting the decision function to satisfy

$$\mathrm{Max}_{a(\cdot)} \,!\, E_{X,S}\{w[a(S),X]\}. \tag{3}$$

The expected return if signal S is used is, then,

$$V(S|A,w) = \mathrm{max}_{a(\cdot)}\, E_{X,S}\{w[a(S),X]\}, \tag{4}$$

where "max" denotes the value at the maximum.

Suppose the decision-maker (DM) has a choice of signals. Then, for the given decision problem, DM will choose S when S' is also available if and only if

$$V(S|A,w) \geq V(S'|A,w). \tag{5}$$

As is clear, what is relevant about a signal is its joint distribution with the state of nature, X. Since latter random variable is given, so is its unconditional or *prior* distribution. Hence, any one of the alternative signals can be characterized by its associated *likelihood* function, which gives the conditional probability distribution of the signal given a true value of the state of nature. For simplicity, we confine ourselves to the finite case.

ASSUMPTION 1 The state of nature X and any signal S take on only finitely many values.

Then the likelihood function can be written as a likelihood matrix,

$$L(S) = (p(s|x)), \quad s = \text{columns}, x = \text{rows}, \tag{6}$$

where $p(s|x) = \text{Prob}(S = s|X = x)$.

The likelihood matrix for any signal is clearly non-negative; further, since each row is a (conditional) probability distribution, the row sums are all equal to 1. If we let e be the column vector each component of which is 1, then the second condition can be written as $L(S)e = e$.

DEFINITION 1 A matrix M is said to be a *Markov matrix* if $M \geq 0$ and $Me = e$.

Before giving Blackwell's definition of a partial ordering of signals according to informativeness, let me discuss one case where it is clearly true that one signal is at least as good as another. Imagine a communication chain between the state of nature and the DM with one intermediate link. A signal, S, is transmitted to the intermediate link. Then, a signal S' is transmitted from the intermediate link to the DM. The signal S' is a signal about S. Implicitly, it is assumed that S' contains no information about X that is not contained in S. Formally, this is defined as follows.

DEFINITION 2 S' is a *garbling* of S if $p(s'|s) = p(s'|s,x)$ for all s, s', and x.

It would appear intuitively clear that the DM would be at least as well off observing S as observing S'. More precisely, this is true provided we assume that the DM can always randomize.

ASSUMPTION 2 The action space A always includes all randomizations over itself.

Take any decision function $a(s')$ based on S'. Suppose the DM observes S to take on the value s. The distribution $p(s'|s)$ implies a distribution of $a(S')$ given $S = s$. If the DM chooses a at random with this distribution, the expected payoff will be the same as observing S' and then using the decision function $a(s')$. Hence, the DM can always do as well by observing S as by observing S' and may of course well be able to do better by using decision functions not equivalent to those based on S'.

By the usual rules of probability theory and definition 2,

$$p(s'|x) = \sum_s p(s'|s,x)p(s|x) = \sum_s p(s'|s)p(s|x).$$

In matrix notation,

$$L(S') = L(S)G, \quad \text{with } G = (p(s'|s)),\ s = \text{row},\ s' = \text{column}. \tag{7}$$

Clearly, G is a Markov matrix.

In choosing between two signals, S and S', all that matters are their individual likelihood matrices. Their joint distribution or the conditional distribution of one given the other is irrelevant. Suppose then that the likelihood matrices are related as follows:

$$L(S') = L(S)M \quad \text{for } \textit{some} \text{ Markov matrix } M. \tag{8}$$

Then, as far as the relevant information goes, S' could be a garbling of S if in fact $M = G$. But the expected payoffs under S and S', respectively, are defined only by their likelihood functions. Since we have already argued that S must be at least good as any garbling of it, it must also be true that S is at least as useful as S' if (8) holds. This motivates the following definition.

DEFINITION 3 S' is a *quasi-garbling* of S if (8) holds.

Blackwell sought a formalization of the intuitive relation "S is at least as informative as S'," which would depend only on the intrinsic properties of the signals, that is, only on their likelihood matrices. From (4), the natural definition is the following.

DEFINITION 4 S is at least as informative as S' (to be abbreviated $S \geq_i S'$) if $V(S|A,w) \geq V(S'|A,w)$ for all decision problems (A,w), where the function V is defined by (4).

The relation $\geq_i$ is clearly a partial ordering. The previous argument shows that if S' is a quasi-garbling of S, then S is at least as informative as S'. Blackwell showed that, surprisingly, the converse is also true. The requirement that expected payoff be at least as high for *all* decision problems is so strong that only the reasonably obvious case of quasi-garbling remains. If S' is not a quasi-garbling of S, then it is always possible to exhibit some action space A and some payoff function $w(a,x)$ for which the optimal expected payoff using S' as a signal is higher than that based on S.

Blackwell's Theorem For two signals, S and S', $S \geq_i S'$ if and only if S' is a quasi-garbling of S.

2 Quasi-Sufficiency

Informational equivalence of two signals is defined in the usual way in terms of the relation "at least as informative as."

DEFINITION 5 S is informationally equivalent to S' (to be abbreviated $S =_i S'$) if S is at least as informative as S' and S' is at least as informative as S.

Informational equivalence is clearly an equivalence relation, i.e., transitive, symmetric, and reflexive. As in Blackwell's theory, I start with a case where equivalence is easily seen. The role of garbling in the ordering of signals is taken here by sufficiency. The term is given the same meaning as in statistical theory, with X playing the role of the statistical parameter, S' the sample, and S the sufficient statistic.

DEFINITION 6 S is *sufficient* for S' if S is a function of S' and S' is a garbling of S.

Since a function is a garbling with conditional probabilities equal to 1, S and S' are garblings of each other and are therefore informationally equivalent.

Notice that definition 6 implies that, as the realization of S varies, the ranges of the corresponding conditional distributions of S' must be disjoint; for if there were a value of S' with positive probabilities conditional on two different values of S, then S would not be a function of S'. The matrix $(p(s|s'))$ (with s' for rows and s for columns) must be, of course, a Markov matrix, but the positive entries in different rows must occur in disjoint sets of columns. Put another way, each column can have at most one nonzero entry. It is convenient to introduce a definition for such matrices:

DEFINITION 7 M is said to be an *s-matrix* if it is a Markov matrix with at most one positive entry in each column.

LEMMA 1 If S is sufficient for S', then $L(S)M = L(S')$, where M is an s-matrix.

Proof From definitions 2 and 6 and (7), with the remarks above.

Remark An s-matrix necessarily has at least as many columns as rows. A square s-matrix is a permutation matrix.

Parallel to the step from garbling to quasi-garbling, we define quasi-sufficiency as a relation between signals which is indistinguishable from sufficiency if only the separate likelihood matrices of the two signals are known.

DEFINITION 8 S is *quasi-sufficient* for S' (abbreviated S q.s. S') if there is a signal S'' sufficient for S' such that $L(S) = L(S'')$. Clearly,

LEMMA 2 If S q.s. S', then $S =_i S'$.

Suppose the likelihood matrices of S and S' satisfy the conclusion of lemma 1 for some s-matrix M. Then, interpreting $M = (p(s''|s))$, we can construct a joint distribution with the appropriate marginal distributions conditional on X. Conversely, of course, lemma 1 and definition 8 assure us that if S is quasi-sufficient for S', then $L(S)M = L(S')M$ for some s-matrix M.

THEOREM 1 S q.s. S' if and only if $L(S)M = L(S')$ for some s-matrix M.

NOTATION For any matrix M, let $c(M)$ be the number of columns and $r(M)$ the number of rows.

From theorem 1, $c[L(S)] = r(M)$ and $c(M) = c[L[S')]$. From the remark above, it is clear that if S q.s. S' then $r(M) \leq c(M)$. Therefore,

$$c[L(S)] \leq c[L(S')].$$

NOTATION The cardinality of a signal S (abbreviated $\# S$) is the number of distinct values it can take on, i.e., $c[L(S)]$.

LEMMA 3 If S' q.s. S, then $\# S' \leq \# S$.

Clearly the relation q.s. is reflexive and transitive; these conclusions can also be verified from the characterization of theorem 1 by noting that the identity matrix is an s-matrix and that the product of two s-matrices is an s-matrix. Consider the set of all signals S' quasi-sufficient for a given signal S. There is at least one signal, say S^*, that minimizes $\# S'$ in this set. From lemma 3, either $\# S^* < \# S$ or $\# S' = \# S$ for all signals S' quasi-sufficient for S.

DEFINITION 9 S is *s-minimal* if $\# S' = \# S$ whenever S' q.s. S.

Consider any S^* that minimizes $\# S'$ subject to S' q.s. S. Suppose it were not s-minimal. Then there would exist S'' such that S'' q.s. S^* and $\# S'' < \# S^*$. But, by transitivity, S'' q.s. S, while $\# S'' < S^*$, in contradiction to the choice of S^*.

LEMMA 4 For every signal S, there is an s-minimal signal S^* such that S^* q.s. S.

In view of lemmas 2 and 4, the characterization of informational equivalence reduces to a characterization of information equivalence among s-minimal signals. Given an equivalence class of s-minimal signals, all other equivalent signals can be found by finding those for which the s-minimal signals are quasi-sufficient.

The class of s-minimal signals can be characterized very simply. Suppose $L(S)$ has a zero column. Then clearly it can be deleted with no loss. Since each column corresponds to a possible realization value for the signal, the operation of deleting the zero column can be defined in signal terms as confounding it with another column. This defines a function; if that value is observed in the new signal, we need only choose that value with probability 1 (for any value of X) and the deleted value with probability 0. Now, suppose one nonzero column of $L(S)$ is a positive multiple of another. Let s and s' be the two signal values denoted by those columns; the assumption is that, for some $a > 0$, $L_{xs}(S) = aL_{xs'}(S)$ for all x. Form a new signal S' by letting $S' = S$ when $S \neq s,s'$, $S' = s_0$ when $S = s$ or s'. This is a function of S. Define S'' as follows: $S'' = S'$ when $S' \neq s_0$. When $S' = s_0$, let S'' take on the values s and s' with probabilities $a/(1 + a)$ and $1/(1 + a)$, respectively. Then S'' is a garbling of S', and it is easy to see that $L(S'') = L(S)$. Therefore, by definition 8, S' q.s. S. By construction $\# S' < \# S$, so S is not s-minimal.

DEFINITION 10 Two nonzero vectors are said to be *collinear* if one is a positive multiple of the other.

DEFINITION 11 A matrix is *irredundant* if no columns are zero and no two columns are collinear.

We have shown that an s-minimal signal must have an irredundant likelihood matrix. We now show the converse. Suppose $L(S)$ is irredundant. Let S' be any signal quasi-sufficient for S. By theorem 1, there exists an s-matrix M such that $L(S')M = L(S)$. But if M has any zero columns or if any two columns of M are collinear, it is easy to see that the same must be true of $L(S)$, contrary to definition 11. Hence, M is irredundant. Suppose that, for some s, $M_{ss'} > 0$ for two values of s'. Since all elements in the two columns other than element s are zero, by definition of an s-matrix, the two columns are collinear, in which case M could not be irredundant, as was just proved. Therefore, M has exactly one nonzero element in each row, which must be 1 since the row sums are 1. It has no zero columns, since it is irredundant, and therefore has exactly one nonzero element in each column. Hence M is a permutation matrix and, in particular, square. Therefore,

$$\# S = c[L(S)] = c(M) = r(M) = c[L(S')] = \# S',$$

so that every S' quasi-sufficient for S has the same cardinality as S. That is, S is s-minimal.

THEOREM 2 S is s-minimal if and only if $L(S)$ is irredundant.

We now exhibit a construction to find, for any signal S, another signal which is s-minimal and is quasi-sufficient for S. It is easy to see that the relation of collinearity is reflexive, transitive, and symmetric, that is, an equivalence relation. For any matrix L, let A_0 be the set of zero columns. Let a *collinearity set* of columns be an equivalence class of (nonzero) columns under the relation of collinearity, and let K be the class composed of the collinearity sets. We first show a representation of the structure of a collinearity set. For any given collinearity set, A, choose a fixed member, t. For any member of A (say, s), $L_{.s}$ is a positive multiple of $L_{.t}$, from definition 10; that is, there exists $a_s > 0$ so that $L_{.s} = a_s L_{.t}$, where $a_t = 1$. Let a be the row vector with components $a_s (s \in A)$. Normalize a by dividing by the sum of its elements, and multiply $L_{.t}$ by the same sum. Call the resulting row and column vectors y_A and z^A, respectively. Then $L_{\cdot s} = y_s z^A (s \in A)$, or

$$L_{\cdot A} = z^A y_A, \quad y_A e_A = 1, \quad z^A \neq 0. \tag{9}$$

Let $\# K$ be the number of members of K, i.e., the number of distinct collinearity sets. Construct a Markov matrix, N, with $r(N) = c(L)$ and $c(N) = \# K$. Let $s'(A)$ be a one-one mapping of the members of K into the columns of N. Let $A(s')$ be the (unique) A for which $s'(A) = s'$. Then require of N that

$$N_{A,s'(A)} = e_A \quad \text{for } A \in K. \tag{10}$$

Since N is a Markov matrix, the row sums are 1, and all elements are non-negative. From (10), it must be that

$$N_{A,s'} = 0 \quad \text{for } A \in K, s' \neq s'(A). \tag{11}$$

NOTATION If A is a set of rows or columns, $\sim A$ will be the complement of that set, i.e., the remaining rows or columns.

Now construct a second matrix, M, as follows: Require $r(M) = c(N)$ and $c(M) = r(N) = c(L)$. Let

$$M_{s',A(s')} = y_{A(s')}, \quad M_{s', \sim A(S')} = 0. \tag{12}$$

From (9), it is easy to see that M is a Markov matrix. Also, for any column s, $M_{s's} > 0$ only if $s \in A(s')$; since the sets $A(s')$ are mutually disjoint, this can occur for at most one value of s'. Therefore, M is an s-matrix. We will want to establish that LN is irredundant, and that $LNM = L$.

To establish the first, note that

$$(LN)_{\cdot s'} = \sum_{A \in K} L_{\cdot A} N_{A,s'} + L_{\cdot A_0} N_{\cdot A_0,s'}.$$

But $N_{A,s'} = 0$ for $s' \neq s'(A)$, $= e_{A(s')}$ for $s' = s'(A)$, by (11) and (10), while $L_{\cdot A_0} = 0$ by definition. Therefore, by (9),

$$(LN)_{\cdot s'} = L_{\cdot A(s')} e_{A(s')} = z^{A(s')} y_{A(s')} e_{A(s')} = z^{A(s')}. \tag{13}$$

Since $z^{A(s')} \neq 0$, $(LN)_{\cdot s'} \neq 0$ for all s'. If $z^{A(s')} = az^{A(t')}$ for some $s' = t'$, then for $s \in A(s')$ and $t \in A(t')$ we have

$$L_{\cdot s} = y_s z^{A(s')} = y_s a z^{A(t')} = (a y_s / y_t) L_{\cdot t},$$

which is impossible because s and t belong to different collinearity sets, $A(s')$ and $A(t')$. Therefore, from (13), no two columns of LN are collinear.

LN is irredundant.

Also,

$$(LNM)_{.A} = \sum_{s'} (LN)_{.s'} M_{s',A} = \sum_{s'} z^{A(s')} M_{s',A}.$$

If A is a collinearity set, then, by (12), $M_{s',A} = 0$ if $s' \neq s'(A)$, $= y_A$ if $s' = s'(A)$, so that

$$(LNM)_{.A} = z^A y_A = L_{.A} \quad \text{for } A \in K.$$

If $A = A_0$, then $M_{S',A_0} = 0$ for all s', so that

$$(LNM)_{.A_0} = L_{.A_0}.$$

Taken together, the last two statements show that $LNM = L$.

PROPOSITION 1 For any matrix L, we can construct a Markov matrix N and an s-matrix M such that LN is irredundant and $LNM = L$.

THEOREM 3 For any signal S, we can construct a signal S' which is s-minimal and quasi-sufficient for S by choosing $L(S') = L(S)N$, where N is constructed from $L(S)$ as in the proof of proposition 1.

Proof Since $L(S)$ and N are non-negative, so is $L(S)N$. Since both are Markov matrices,

$$L(S)Ne = L(S)e = e.$$

Therefore, $L(S)N$ is Markov, and we can choose a signal S' so that $L(S') = L(S)N$. By proposition 1, $L(S')$ is irredundant, and therefore, by theorem 2, S' is s-minimal. Now choose the s-matrix M as in proposition 1; then

$$L(S')M = L(S)NM = L(S),$$

so that S' q.s. S, by theorem 1.

3 Characterization of Informational Equivalence

Any informational equivalence class must, then, contain an s-minimal signal; for, given any signal, we find one, by theorem 2, that is s-minimal and quasi-sufficient for it, and therefore is informationally equivalent to it, by lemma 1. Consider then the entire informational equivalence class containing a given s-minimal signal.

THEOREM 4 If S is s-minimal and $S =_{\mathrm{i}} S'$, then S q.s. S'.

Proof We draw on proposition 4 (below). Since S is s-minimal, $L(S)$ is irredundant by theorem 2. By definition 5 and Blackwell's Theorem, there exist Markov matrixes M and N such that

$$L(S)M = L(S'), \quad L(S')N = L(S), \tag{14}$$

and therefore

$$L(S)MN = L(S),$$

or

$$L(S)P = 0, \quad P = MN - I.$$

Since M and N are non-negative, so is MN. Since P differs from MN only on the diagonal, P has non-negative off-diagonal elements; that is, it is a Metzler matrix. Since M and N are Markov,

$$Pe = (MN - I)e = MNe - e = Me - e = 0.$$

By proposition 4, since $L(S)$ is irredundant and P is Metzler, $Pe = 0$, it must be that $P = 0$, i.e., $MN = I$, so that

$$I_{st} = (MN)_{st} = \sum_{s'} M_{ss'} N_{s't}. \tag{15}$$

Let $A(s) = \{s' | M_{ss'} > 0\}$. Then (15) implies

$$\sum_{s' \in A(s)} M_{ss'} N_{s't} = 0 \quad \text{for } s \neq t,$$

which implies that $N_{s't} = 0$ for $s' \in A(s)$, $s \neq t$. Since this holds for all $t \neq s$, while the row sum of $N_{s'\cdot}$ is 1, it must be that $N_{s's} = 1$, or

$$N_{s'\cdot} = I_{s\cdot} \quad \text{for } s' \in A(s).$$

From this, it follows that the sets $A(s)$ must be mutually disjoint, for if $s' \in A(s)$ and $s' \in A(t)$ we would have $N_{s'\cdot} = I_{s\cdot}$ and $N_{s'} = I_{t\cdot}$, which is possible only if $s = t$. If the sets $A(s)$ are disjoint, then M must be an s-matrix, so that, from (14), S q.s. S'.

This shows that the informational equivalence classes can be generated from the s-minimal signals by attaching to each all the signals for which it is quasi-sufficient, easily found, by theorem 1, by multiplying the likelihood matrix by all possible s-matrices.

Some corollaries of theorem 4 are interesting.

COROLLARY 1 Two s-minimal signals are informationally equivalent if and only if they are the same apart from a relabeling of the signal realizations.

Proof Let S and S' be s-minimal, with $S =_{\text{i}} S'$. By theorems 4 and 1, there exist s-matrices M and N such that

$$L(S)M = L(S'), \quad L(S')N = L(S).$$

Since

$$\# S' = c(M) \geq r(M) = \# S,$$

and vice versa, it must be that M and N are square. But a square s-matrix is a permutation matrix. The converse is obvious.

Thus, if two s-minimal signals are not *permutationally equivalent*, they are not informationally equivalent.

COROLLARY 2 Two signals are informationally equivalent if and only if there is an s-minimal signal quasi-sufficient for both.

Informational equivalence can be tested with the aid of theorem 3. If S and S' are two signals, form the matrices N and N' corresponding to $L(S)$ and $L(S')$. Then $S =_{\text{i}} S'$ if and only if $L(S)N$ and $L(S')N'$ are permutationally equivalent.

4 A Proposition about Metzler Matrices

Recall that a Metzler matrix is a square (real) matrix whose off-diagonal elements are non-negative. Such matrices have many special properties. Some relevant ones are summarized here:

PROPOSITION 2 For every Metzler matrix P, there is a real characteristic root, d, with a semi-positive characteristic vector, such that the real part of any other characteristic root of P is less than d. If $Pu \leq su$ for some strictly positive u, then $d \leq s$.

The root, d, and the associated semi-positive characteristics vector, y, are referred to as the *dominant root* and the *dominant vector*, respectively.

DEFINITION 12 A square matrix P is said to be *decomposable* if there exists a proper nonempty subset of the rows (or columns), A, for which $P_{\sim A, A} = 0$. P is *indecomposable* if it is not decomposable.

PROPOSITION 3 If P is Metzler and indecomposable, then it has a strictly positive dominant vector, of which every characteristic vector associated with the dominant root is a scalar multiple.

For proofs of the statements in propositions 2 and 3, see, e.g., Debreu and Herstein 1953 and Gantmacher 1959 (vol. 1, pp. 53, 66). We now state and prove proposition 4, which was used in the proof of theorem 4 above.

PROPOSITION 4 Let P be a Metzler matrix with $Pe \leq 0$ for which there exists an irredundant matrix L for which $LP = 0$. Then $P = 0$.

Proof Index the rows of L by i. The condition $LP = 0$ can be written

$$L_{i.}P = 0 \qquad \text{for all } i. \tag{16}$$

Since all columns of L are nonzero, $L_{i.}$ must be nonzero for at least one i, so that

$$P \text{ is singular.} \tag{17}$$

Since $Pe \leq 0$, then, by proposition 2, $d \leq 0$ (d is the dominant root). But from (17), 0 is a characteristic root of P; since d is at least as large as the real part of any characteristic root, $d \geq 0$, so that

$$d = 0. \tag{18}$$

Suppose P were indecomposable. Then, by proposition 3 and (18), there is a vector y^* strictly positive such that $y^*P = 0$ and such that every characteristic vector associated with the zero root is a scalar multiple of y^*. From (16), then, for each i there is a scalar, z_i, for which

$$L_{i.} = z_i y^*.$$

Let z be the column vector with components z_i. Then $L = zy^*$. Since $L \neq 0$, $z \neq 0$. All the columns of L are proportional to z, which contradicts the assumption that L is irredundant.

$$P \text{ is decomposable.} \tag{19}$$

Let n be the number of rows or columns in P. Now proceed by induction on n. For $n = 1$, it follows from (17) that $P = 0$. Suppose the theorem is true for all matrices of order not exceeding n, and P is of order $n + 1$. From (19) and definition 12, there is a proper nonempty subset of the rows and columns of P such that

$$P_{\sim A, A} = 0. \tag{20}$$

We now show that P_{AA} satisfies all the hypotheses of proposition 4; since A is proper and nonempty, the order of P_{AA} does not exceed n, and it will follow by induction that $P_{AA} = 0$. The hypothesis $LP = 0$ implies $(LP)_{.A} = 0$, or, equivalently, $LP_{.A} = 0$, which can be written

$$L_{.A}P_{AA} + L_{., \sim A}P_{\sim A, A} = 0.$$

From (20),

$$L_{.A}P_{AA} = 0. \tag{21}$$

The hypothesis $Pe \leq 0$ implies $P_{A.}e \leq 0$, which can written

$$P_{AA}e_A + P_{A, \sim A}e_{\sim A} \leq 0. \tag{22}$$

Since P is Metzler, $P_{A, \sim A} \geq 0$, and therefore

$$P_{AA}e_A \leq 0. \tag{23}$$

Since L is irredundant, it follows by definition that $L_{.A}$ is irredundant for any nonempty A. Also, since P is Metzler, it follows by definition that P_{AA} is Metzler. From (21) and (23), all the hypotheses of proposition 4 hold for P_{AA}. Therefore,

$$P_{AA} = 0. \tag{24}$$

If (24) is substituted into (22), $P_{A, \sim A}e_{\sim A} \leq 0$. But since $P_{A, \sim A} \geq 0$, and since $e_{\sim A}$ is strictly positive, it must be that

$$P_{A, \sim A} = 0. \tag{25}$$

But (25) is the same as (20) with A and $\sim A$ interchanged, and the argument leading to (24) remains valid with the interchange, so that $P_{\sim A, \sim A} = 0$. On the basis of (20), (24), and (25) together, we can indeed conclude that $P = 0$, completing the induction.

Acknowledgments

Frank Hahn has emphasized the role of information in understanding the dynamics of economic systems. This little technical essay is offered as thanks for the many years of friendship and intellectual stimulus.

Prepared under NSF grant IRI 88-14953 at the Institute for Mathematical Studies in the Social Sciences, Stanford University.

References

Blackwell, D. 1951. "Comparison of experiments." In *Proceedings of the Second Berkeley Symposium on Mathematical Statistics and Probability*, ed. J. Neyman. University of California Press.

Blackwell, D. 1953. "Equivalent comparisons of experiments." *Annals of Mathematical Statistics* 24: 265–272.

Blackwell, D., and M. A. Girshick. 1954. *Theory of Games and Statistical Decisions*. Wiley.

Debreu, G., and I. N. Herstein. 1953. "Non-negative square matrices." *Econometrica* 21: 597–607.

Gantmacher, F. R. 1959. *The Theory of Matrices*, two volumes. Chelsea.

Informational Efficiency of Search Equilibrium

Douglas Gale

The theory of rational-expectations equilibrium, developed by Lucas, Grossman, Radner, and others, formalizes the idea that prices reveal information. Under certain circumstances, it can be shown that a rational-expectations equilibrium is informationally efficient, that is, the equilibrium prices reveal all the economically relevant information.

The definition of equilibrium used in the literature on rational expectations is essentially Walrasian. It describes a centralized auction market in which all the agents observe the same vector of equilibrium prices. In other markets, however, agents do not all have the same information about prices. For example, in labor markets, where agents search for trading opportunities, each agent will observe only a small fraction of the prices in the market. The question naturally arises whether these markets too are informationally efficient.

Wolinsky (1988) addresses this question in the framework of dynamic matching. There are two types of agents: buyers and sellers. A single, indivisible good is traded (the agents have transferable utility). Each seller wants to sell at most one unit of the good, and each buyer wants to buy at most one unit. Trade takes place at a sequence of discrete dates. Once agents have traded, they leave the market. To balance the loss of the departing agents, there are constant and equal flows of buyers and sellers into the market at every date.

Search is represented by an exogenous matching process. At each date buyers and sellers are randomly matched: every agent meets precisely one agent of the opposite type. When a buyer and a seller are matched they simultaneously call out the prices at which they are willing to trade. If the buyer's price is not less than the seller's price, they are said to agree. If the agents agree, they trade and leave the market. If they disagree, they cannot trade and must wait until the next period to be rematched.

Uncertainty is represented by a finite set of states of nature. The state of nature determines the cost to the seller of supplying the good and the value to the buyer of obtaining the good. (Note that all sellers have the same cost and all buyers have the same valuation.) The state is chosen once and for all at the beginning of the world. Some fraction of sellers and buyers are assumed to know the true state. The rest have a common prior probability distribution on the set of states.

To make the model tractable, Wolinsky imposes further simplifying assumptions on this general framework. He assumes that there are only two states of nature and that agents can choose from only two admissible prices. There are also some restrictions on payoffs.

Search is costly in the Wolinsky model because agents discount the future. Other things being equal, the longer they wait to trade the lower their respective payoffs will be. When the subjective rate of time preference is high, uninformed agents will be impatient to trade. They will gather little information, and it seems unlikely that the state will be completely revealed by prices. When the rate of time preference is low, on the other hand, the cost of search is also low and agents are able to observe a great deal at little cost. One might expect that in the limit, as the costs of search become vanishingly small, the equilibrium will be informationally efficient.

Wolinsky shows that this expectation is never realized, at least for stationary equilibria. He characterizes the stationary equilibria for positive rates of time preference and then examines the asymptotic behavior of these equilibria as the rate of time preference converges to zero. Along any convergent sequence of stationary equilibria, the true state of nature is never fully revealed. This is a surprising and somewhat worrying result. In a similar framework with complete information, it has been shown that the Walras allocations can be implemented as the outcome of a dynamic matching game when search costs are negligible (Gale 1987). By analogy, one might expect the outcome of Wolinsky's game to be a rational-expectations allocation in the limit as search costs become vanishingly small. Exactly why this result fails is not clear.

In this paper I try to shed some light on the reasons why informational efficiency may fail. In section 1 I look at a Bertrand pricing model with incomplete information. The market consists of a finite number of firms and consumers. There is one-sided uncertainty: firms have information about the state of nature; consumers do not. Firms have unconstrained capacity: they can supply any integral amount of the good at constant marginal cost. This model turns out to have nice properties. There exists an efficient and informationally efficient equilibrium under quite mild conditions. Under somewhat stronger conditions it can be shown that this is the only kind of equilibrium that satisfies a criterion of strategic stability.

In the Bertrand model, consumers observe all the prices automatically. In that case, competition among firms is sufficient to force prices to reveal all the information. In section 2, it is assumed that agents must search for prices but that the cost of search is negligible. The essential issue is whether consumers will choose to sample all prices in equilibrium. If they do, then the analysis of section 1 applies. However, even if the costs of search are zero, nonrevealing equilibria exist and are stable. The essential problem is that is that there is no *ex post* dispersion of prices in these equilibria and hence no incentive to search. Because there is no incentive to search, the model behaves like a noncompetitive model. However, these equilibria can be shown to be unstable if a small amount of heterogeneity among firms is assumed. This heterogeneity produces the price dispersion that is needed to provide the incentive to search.

This framework contains most of the elements of Wolinsky's model (search, price setting, and incomplete information), but there are significant differences. The most obvious are that my model has a finite number of agents and that it is static. However, these differences are not obviously the important ones. In section 3 I examine a dynamic-matching model that is very close to Wolinsky's. The only assumptions retained from sections 1 and 2 are one-sided uncertainty and a small amount of heterogeneity among sellers. Under certain conditions, it can be shown that this model has an approximately revealing equilibrium. This result suggests that it is the one-sided uncertainty that is crucial for Wolinsky's results. These issues are discussed further in section 4.

1 Price-Setting without Search

To fix ideas, consider a simple example of a market with incomplete information. There are M identical consumers and N identical firms. There are two states of nature, labeled "high" (H) and "low" (L). The firms produce an indivisible good subject to constant marginal cost. Marginal cost can take on two values, either high (c_{H}) or low (c_{L}), depending on the state of nature. Each consumer wants to buy at most one unit of the produced good. The utility derived from one unit of the good can also be either high (u_{H}) or low (u_{L}), depending on the state of nature. Firms are assumed to observe the state of nature directly. Consumers cannot observe the state and consequently may not know the value of the good. However, in making their purchase decisions, consumers will make use of whatever information they have in order to infer the true value of the good.

The trading process is represented by a two-stage game. First, firms observe the state of nature and simultaneously set the prices at which they are willing to trade. Second, consumers observe prices and decide how much they wish to buy from each firm.

Suppose that firms are restricted to choose one of two prices, say, a high price (p_H) or a low price (p_L). Suppose that the parameters of the model satisfy the inequality

$$c_L < p_L < u_L < c_H < p_H < u_H.$$

This means that, in each state, the value of the good to consumers is greater than the cost of production to firms. Thus, efficiency requires that each consumer buy the good in each state. The gains from trade can be shared by both parties if trade takes place at the appropriate price.

Suppose that firms charge p_H in the high state and p_L in the low state. Suppose that consumers always buy the goods at the minimum prevailing price. It is easy to see that this strategy profile constitutes a Nash equilibrium of the game. Firms cannot increase profits by unilaterally deviating from this strategy. Reducing price in the high state must lead to a loss, and any firm that increases its price in the low state will not make any sales. The equilibrium price is a sufficient statistic for the state of nature, so consumers can infer the true state by observing prices. In other words, equilibrium is informationally efficient. When they observe that all firms offer the high price, consumers know that they are in the high state and that it is optimal for them to buy. Similarly, they know that it is optimal for them to buy when they observe that all firms offer low prices.

It would be nice if all equilibria were of this kind, but there are typically many other equilibria. For example, if consumers are sufficiently optimistic, there will exist a pooling equilibrium. Let v_H and v_L denote the common prior probabilities of the high and low states, respectively. Suppose that

$$v_H u_H + v_L u_L > p_H$$

and that

$$(p_L - c_L)M < (p_H - c_L)[M/N],$$

where $[M/N]$ is the largest integer less than M/N. The first inequality says that consumers are willing to buy at the high price when they have no information (other than their prior beliefs). The second ensures that, for some distribution of demand among firms, it is not in the interest of any firm to cut price in the low state, even if by so doing it could capture the whole market. Under these assumptions, there will exist a Nash equilibrium in which all firms offer p_H, regardless of the state, and all consumers buy at the minimum price charged. This equilibrium is efficient but not informationally efficient. In more complex examples, one can find equilibria that are inefficient as well as informationally inefficient.

In the simple high-low framework, it is relatively easy to get rid of the informationally inefficient equilibrium—for example, by assuming that the incentive to cut prices is sufficiently strong. But this will not work in more complex examples. For example, suppose that there are three states, H, M, and L. In an obvious notation, suppose that

$$v_H u_H + v_M u_M + v_L u_L > p_H$$

and that

$$(p_M - c_M)M > (p_H - c_M)[M/N].$$

In this case, there is an equilibrium in which firms charge the high price in states H and M and the low price in state L, even though it appears that by cutting price in the middle state a firm could be made better off. The reason is that consumers refuse to buy if they observe a price p_M. Furthermore, this behavior is rational if they believe that the economy is in the low state, so that the value of the good is less than p_M. The problem is that the firm has to signal the state of the economy as well as the price at which he is willing to trade. The problem is more complicated than in ordinary signaling models, since the consumer's beliefs depend on information received from all the firms. The price-cutting firm may not even know what other firms are doing. In what follows, I shall attempt to show that the informationally efficient equilibria do play a distinguished role, but in order to do so it is necessary to "refine" the Nash concept of equilibrium.

The Basic Model

Uncertainty in the model is represented by a finite set Ω of states of nature. The probability of each state ω in Ω is denoted by $v(\omega) > 0$.

The set of firms is indexed by $j \in J \equiv \{1, \ldots, N\}$. Each firm has some information, not necessarily complete, about the true state of nature. The firm's information is represented by an information structure, that is, a partition of the set of states. For any cell of the partition, the firm knows whether the true state belongs to that cell or to its complement. Let $\mathcal{S}_j$ denote the information structure of firm j. For any state ω, let $S_j(\omega)$ denote the unique cell of $\mathcal{S}_j$ containing ω. $S_j(\omega)$ is called the firm's information set at ω. It represents the firm's information in that state: the firm knows precisely that the true state belongs to $S_j(\omega)$ and nothing more. Consumers have no private information.

The marginal cost of firm j in state ω is denoted by $C_j(\omega) > 0$. The cost function $C_j: \Omega \to \mathbb{R}_+$ is assumed to be measurable with respect to $\mathcal{S}_j$ for every j. A firm's utility is assumed to equal its profits. If firm j sells d units of the good at a price p in state ω, its utility is $(p - C_j(\omega))d$.

Consumers' preferences are represented by a common utility function. $U(\omega)$ is the utility derived from the consumption of one unit of the good in state ω. A consumer who purchases a unit of the good at the price p in state ω enjoys a net utility of $U(\omega) - p$.

The example discussed above can be described in this notation as follows:

$$\Omega = \{\mathrm{H},\mathrm{L}\},$$

$$C_j(\omega) = c_\omega \quad \text{for } \omega = \mathrm{H},\mathrm{L} \text{ and } j \in J,$$

$$\mathcal{S}_j = \{\{\mathrm{H}\},\{\mathrm{L}\}\} \quad \text{for } j \in J,$$

$$U(\omega) = u_\omega \quad \text{for } \omega = \mathrm{H},\mathrm{L}.$$

The Market Game

Firms and consumers are assumed to play a two-stage game. In the first stage, firms simultaneously choose prices. In the second stage, consumers observe the prices charged by all the firms and decide whether and from whom to purchase the good.

To simplify the analysis, each agent is assumed to have a finite number of strategies. For the same reason, only pure strategies are considered. Let $\mathbb{P} \subset \mathbb{R}_+$ denote a finite set of admissible prices that can be charged by firms. A pure strategy for firm j is a function $g_j: \Omega \to \mathbb{P}$, with the interpretation that $g_j(\omega)$ is the price charged by firm j in state ω. It is assumed that firm j's strategy is measurable with respect to $\mathcal{S}_j$. The measurability condition ensures that the price charged by firm j depends only on information available to the firm. Let G_j denote the strategy set of firm j, and let $G = \times G_j$ denote the set of strategy profiles for firms.

Since consumers are identical, they will be treated as a single player. The demand from consumers is represented by a vector $d = (d_1, \ldots, d_N)$, where d_j is the number of units demanded from firm j. Let D denote the set of feasible consumer demands. Since total demand cannot exceed M units,

$$D = \left\{ d \in \mathbb{Z}_+^N \mid \sum_{j \in J} d_j \leq M \right\}.$$

Consumers choose their demand from each firm as a function of the prices charged by all the firms. A pure strategy for the representative consumer is a function $f : \mathbb{P}^N \to D$. For any vector of prices $p = (p_1, \ldots, p_N)$, $f_j(p)$ denotes the number of units of the good purchased from firm $j \in J$. The consumers' strategy set is denoted by F.

If the firms choose a price vector $p = (p_1, \ldots, p_N)$ in state ω and the consumers' strategy is f, the utility of firm j is $(p_j - C_j(\omega))f_j(\omega)$. The payoff function of firm j is denoted by v_j: $F \times G \to \mathbb{R}$ and defined by putting

$$v_j(f,g) = \sum_{\omega \in \Omega} (g_j(\omega) - C_j(\omega))f_j(g(\omega))\nu(\omega), \quad \forall (f,g) \in F \times G$$

with the interpretation that $v_j(f,g)$ is the payoff to firm j when consumers and firms have chosen the strategies f and g, respectively. Similarly, if the firms have chosen a price vector $p = (p_1, \ldots, p_N)$ in state ω and the consumers' strategy is f, the expected utility of the representative consumer is

$$\sum_{j \in J} (U(\omega) - p_j)f_j(p).$$

The consumers' payoff function is denoted by u: $F \times G \to \mathbb{R}$ and defined by putting

$$u(f,g) = \sum_{\omega \in \Omega} \sum_{j \in J} (U(\omega) - g_j(\omega))f_j(g(\omega))\nu(\omega), \quad \forall (f,g) \in F \times G$$

with the interpretation that $u(f,g)$ is the payoff to the representative consumer when the consumer and firms have chosen the strategies f and g, respectively. Let Γ_0 denote the game defined by the parameters $(M, N, F \times G, u, v)$.

Equilibrium

In the usual way, we define a *Nash equilibrium* of Γ_0 to be an ordered pair $(f^*,g^*) \in F \times G$ such that

(i) $u(f^*,g^*) \geq u(f,g^*), \quad \forall f \in F$

and

(ii) $v_j(f^*,g^*) \geq v_j(f^*,g^*_{-j},g_j), \quad \forall\, g_j \in G_j, \quad \forall\, j \in J$

where

$$(g_j,g^*_{-j}) \equiv (g^*_1,\ldots,g^*_{j-1},g_j,g^*_{j+1},\ldots,g^*_N).$$

The set of Nash equilibria is denoted by $\text{NE}(\Gamma_0)$.

Nash equilibrium does not require that consumers' demands be optimal except in equilibrium. To define optimal demands for all prices, one has to specify consumers' beliefs for out-of-equilibrium situations. Let $\mathcal{M}(\Omega)$ denote the set of probability measures on Ω. A belief system is a function $\mu\colon \mathbb{P}^N \to \mathcal{M}(\Omega)$, with the interpretation that $\mu(p) \in \mathcal{M}(\Omega)$ is the consumers' posterior probability distribution on states of nature when firms choose the price vector p. A belief system μ is said to be consistent with an equilibrium (f,g) if

$$\mu(p)(S) = \text{Prob}\{g(\omega) = p \text{ and } \omega \in S\}/\text{Prob}\{g(\omega) = p\}$$

for any value of p such that $\text{Prob}\{g(\omega) = p\} > 0$. A Nash equilibrium (f^*,g^*) is said to be *sequentially rational* if there exists a belief system μ that is consistent with (f^*,g^*) and if, for any p,

$$f(p) \in \operatorname*{Arg\,Max}_{d \in D} \sum_{\omega \in \Omega} \mu(p,\omega) \sum_{j \in J} (U(\omega) - p)d_j.$$

In other words, given the posterior beliefs of the consumers, their strategy is expected-utility-maximizing for every price vector p and not just for those observed in equilibrium. Let $\text{SE}(\Gamma_0)$ denote the set of sequentially rational equilibria. Sometimes we will refer to the ordered triple (f,g,μ), where μ is the belief system that supports (f,g) as a sequentially rational equilibrium, as a *sequential equilibrium.*

Sequential rationality restricts the set of equilibria somewhat, but not very much. In fact, all that sequential rationality implies about equilibrium can be summarized by the following three properties:

(i) Consumers buy only from the firm(s) offering the lowest price.

(ii) Consumers do not buy if the lowest price is greater than $\bar{u} \equiv \sup U(\omega)$.

(iii) consumers all buy if the lowest price is less than $\underline{u} \equiv \inf U(\omega)$.

It should be clear that there is a large set of equilibria consistent with these constraints. Further refinement is required to give the theory any predictive power.

Informational Efficiency

Let $\mathbb{C}_j$ denote the range of the function C_j, and let $\mathbb{C} = \bigcup_{j \in J} \mathbb{C}_j$. Let $\mathbb{U}$ denote the range of U. The following assumption will be satisfied generically:

$$\mathbb{C} \cap \mathbb{P} = \phi = \mathbb{U} \cap \mathbb{P}. \tag{A.1}$$

Let $c(\omega)$ denote the lowest marginal cost obtained by any firm in state ω, and let $p(\omega)$ denote the smallest admissible price that is greater than $c(\omega)$. In what follows, it will be assumed that there are always positive gains from trade and that these gains can be shared between firms and consumers at some admissible price:

$$c(\omega) < p(\omega) < U(\omega), \quad \forall\, \omega \in \Omega. \tag{A.2}$$

Under this assumption, an equilibrium will be *efficient* if and only if all consumers purchase the good in every state of nature.

We may also be interested in another kind of efficiency, namely *informational efficiency*. For any random variable ξ on Ω, let $\mathscr{S}_\xi$ denote the coarsest partition $\mathscr{S}$ such that ξ is measurable with respect to $\mathscr{S}$. Each cell of $\mathscr{S}_\xi$ has the form $\xi^{-1}(x)$ for some x. A partition $\mathscr{S}$ is at least as fine as a partition $\mathscr{T}$ (denoted $\mathscr{S} \subseteq \mathscr{T}$) if each cell of $\mathscr{T}$ is the union of cells of $\mathscr{S}$. If $\mathscr{S}_U \subseteq \mathscr{S}_\xi$, then ξ is said to be a *sufficient statistic* for U. An equilibrium (f^*,g^*) is said to be *informationally efficient* if and only if the firms' joint strategy g^* is a sufficient statistic for U. In what follows it will be assumed that $p(\omega)$ is a sufficent statistic for $U(\omega)$:

$$\mathscr{S}_U \subseteq \mathscr{S}_p. \tag{A.3}$$

PROPOSITION 1 Suppose that for every $\omega \in \Omega$ there are at least two firms $j \in J$ such that $C_j(\omega) = c(\omega)$. Then there is an equilibrium that is both efficient and informationally efficient.

Proof For any $j \in J$ and $\omega \in \Omega$, put

$$g_j(\omega) = \min\{p \in \mathbb{P} \,|\, p > C_j(\omega)\}.$$

For any $p \in \mathbb{P}^N$, put $f(p) = 0$ if the lowest price is greater than $\bar{u}$. Otherwise, choose $f(p)$ so that $\Sigma_j f_j(p) = M$ and $f_j(p) = 0$ if $p_j > \min p_h$. It is straightforward to check that (f,g) so defined is an equilibrium. ■

In this equilibrium, the minimum price is always equal to $p(\omega)$. Since p is a sufficient statistic for U, consumers can infer the true value of U

in any state. Then (A.2) implies that it is optimal for them to buy at the minimum price. Since there are always at least two firms charging the minimum price, no firm can earn positive profits by unilaterally deviating. It is easy to see that this equilibrium is also sequentially rational.

As the two-state example discussed above showed, there are other equilibria that do not share the nice properties of the equilibrium in proposition 1. To eliminate these equilibria, some further refinement of equilibrium is required. One class of refinements uses the notion of a "trembling hand" to test the robustness of equilibrium. Roughly speaking, an equilibrium is strategically stable if small perturbations of the game cause only small changes in the equilibrium. In Gale 1987 I carried out a formal analysis along these lines with results similar to the ones obtained here. The basic ideas were borrowed from Kohlberg and Mertens (1986). The approach adopted here does not make use of the "trembling hand." Instead, it incorporates some of the properties of strategic stability in the sense of Kohlberg and Mertens in an "intuitive" stability criterion. Under certain conditions, all the equilibria satisfying this criterion are both efficient and informationally efficient. To fix ideas, the intuitive argument is presented first.

Let $\{\Omega_1, \Omega_2, \ldots, \Omega_n\}$ be the partition of Ω induced by U. Let $U(\omega) = u_k$ for any $\omega \in \Omega_k$ and any $k = 1, 2, \ldots, n$. Without loss of generality we can assume that $u_k < u_{k-1}$ for $k = 1, 2, \ldots, n - 1$. It is clearly a dominant strategy for all consumers to buy the good whenever a price vector p with $\min p_j < u_1$ is observed. Whatever the true state, the consumers will be better off if they buy the good than if they do not. Suppose that the true state is $\omega \in \Omega_1$. Some firms can charge a price that is less than u_1 and still make a profit. But they may choose not to do so if they can charge a higher price and still sell with positive probability. To ensure that someone charges a price lower than u_1, it is necessary to assume that the profits from price cutting are "sufficiently large." The required assumption is that, roughly speaking, if all firms were charging a price higher than u_1 in state ω, and if a firm could capture the whole market by reducing its price to slightly below u_1, then it would be profitable for the firm to do so. (This idea will be made precise below.) Since all consumers will purchase the good if the minimum price if less than u_1, it cannot be an equilibrium for all firms to charge more than u_1. This shows that, in any sequential equilibrium, if the true state is $\omega \in \Omega_1$ then the minimum price will be less than u_1 and the maximum amount of trade will take place.

This argument can be used inductively on the sets Ω_k, but it becomes more complicated when $k > 1$. If $k = 1$ then it is a dominant strategy for all consumers to purchase the good if the minimum price is less than u_k. The same is not true for $k > 1$. Consumer demand depends on beliefs. A reduction in price may have a negative effect on beliefs, so that consumers reduce their demand or even become altogether unwilling to buy. Without some restrictions on beliefs, we cannot be sure that price cutting will be profitable.

To eliminate "unreasonable" beliefs, one can argue recursively as follows. Suppose that, for some $k = 1, 2, \ldots, n$ and some sequential equilibrium (f,g,μ),

$$\min_j g_j(\omega) < u_i$$

whenever $i \leq k$ and $\omega \in \Omega_i$. Then whenever the minimum price is between u_k and u_{k+1} the consumers should infer that the true state must lie in the set $\bigcup\{\Omega_i\colon i > k\}$ and it is optimal to buy. Then, if the benefits of price cutting are sufficiently high, some firm will charge a price less than u_{k+1} whenever $\omega \in \Omega_{k+1}$. By induction it follows that in any "stable" equilibrium the minimum price charged should be below u_k if $\omega \in \Omega_k$ and all consumers should purchase the good. This is enough to ensure efficiency, and with some additional assumptions we can ensure that the equilibrium is informationally efficient as well.

These intuitive ideas can now be made precise. The essential idea behind the refinement is the following. If profile p is sometimes observed in equilibrium, but is not observed in state ω in any equilibrium, then it seems reasonable that consumers' beliefs should attach zero probability to state ω when p is observed. Accordingly, equilibria that depend on contrary beliefs are eliminated. This process of eliminating equilibria is applied recursively on the sets Ω_1, Ω_2, and so on. Let

$$S_1(p) = \{\omega \in \Omega \mid \exists (f,g) \in \mathrm{SE}(\Gamma_0),\ g(\omega) = p\}, \quad \forall\, p \in \mathbb{P}$$

denote the set of states in which the price profile p is sometimes observed in some equilibrium. Let

$$M_1 = \{\mu \in \mathcal{M}(\Omega) \mid \mu(p)(\omega) = 0,\ \forall\, p \in \mathbb{P}^N,\ \forall\, \omega \in \Omega_1 \backslash S_1(p) \text{ if } S_1(p) \neq \phi\}$$

denote the set of beliefs that put zero probability on states in Ω_1 that are inconsistent with the observed price. Then let SE_1 denote the set of sequential equilibria supported by beliefs that satisfy this condition:

$$\mathrm{SE}_1 = \{(f,g,\mu) \in \mathrm{SE}(\Gamma_0) | \mu \in M_1\}.$$

Continuing in this manner, define the sets $S_k(p)$, M_k, and SE_k recursively for $k = 2, \ldots, n$:

$$S_k(p) = \{\omega \in \Omega | g(\omega) = p, \exists (f,g) \in \mathrm{SE}_{k-1}\}, \forall\, p \in \mathbb{P}^N$$

$$M_k = \{\mu \in M_{k-1} | \forall\, p \in \mathbb{P}^N, \forall\, \omega \in \Omega_k \backslash S_k(p), \mu(p)(\omega) = 0 \text{ if } S_k(p) \neq \phi\},$$

$$\mathrm{SE}_k = \{(f,g,\mu) \in \mathrm{SE}_{k-1} | \mu \in M_k\}.$$

Then a sequential equilibrium (f,g,μ) is called *stable* if and only if it belongs to SE_n.

In order to ensure the efficiency of equilibrium, it is not enough to restrict attention to stable equilibria. There must also be a strong incentive for firms to cut prices. Because information is incomplete, it may be necessary for firms to cut prices by a non-negligible amount in order to persuade consumers to buy from them. Firms will not be willing to do this unless the profits are large. For any $\omega \in \Omega$, let $J(\omega)$ denote the set of firms whose costs are less than $U(\omega)$. Assume that every firm $j \in J(\omega)$ knows the true value of $U(\omega)$:

$$\mathscr{S}_U \subseteq \mathscr{S}_j, \quad \forall\, j \in J(\omega). \tag{A.4}$$

Suppose that by charging a price $\hat{p}(\omega) \equiv \max\{p \in \mathbb{P} | p < U(\omega)\}$ in state ω, a firm $j \in J(\omega)$ could capture the entire market. Then it would earn a profit of $(\hat{p}(\omega) - C_j(\omega))M$. Total expected profits, on the other hand, cannot exceed $(\bar{u} - \underline{c})M$, where $\underline{c} = \inf C_j(\omega')$ and the infimum is taken over all states and firms. It is assumed that

$$(\bar{u} - \underline{c}) < \sum_{j \in J} \max\{0, \hat{p}(\omega) - C_j(\omega)), \quad \forall\, \omega \in \Omega. \tag{A.5}$$

The role of (A.5) can be explained as follows. Suppose that there is an equilibrium in which all firms choose a price greater than $U(\omega)$ in some state ω. Suppose further that if one firm were to reduce its price to $\hat{p}(\omega) < U(\omega)$ it could signal that the true value of the good was at least $U(\omega)$. Then that firm would capture the whole market and its profits would be $(\hat{p}(\omega) - C_j(\omega))M$. In order for equilibrium to be maintained, then, each firm must expect its profits to be at least $(\hat{p}(\omega) - C_j(\omega))M$. Since profits must be non-negative, a lower bound for the sum of profits is given by the right-hand side of (A.5) multiplied by M. But total profits cannot be greater than $(\bar{u} - \underline{c})M$, so (A.5) yields a contradiction. This argument is not quite correct, since it does not take account of the fact that firms do not know the true state. They are maximizing *expected* profits. Nonetheless, a very similar argument is used in the proof of proposition 2 to show that when (A.5) is satisfied, if every firm $j \in J(\omega)$ thinks that by cutting its price to $\hat{p}(\omega)$ it can capture the whole market, some firm will in fact cut its price. Thus, there cannot be an inefficient equilibrium. Note that the left-hand side of (A.5) is independent of the number of elements in J, while the right-hand side is not. (A.5) can be interpreted as a requirement that the number of low-cost firms be sufficiently large.

With these assumptions it can be shown that the only equilibria satisfying the stability criterion are efficient.

PROPOSITION 2 If (f,g) is a stable equilibrium, then it is efficient.

This proposition is proved in the appendix. An immediate corollary ensures that equilibrium is informationally efficient as well if the minimum cost of production is a sufficient statistic for the utility of the good.

COROLLARY Suppose that, in addition to the maintained assumptions, $c(\omega) > u_{k-1}$ for any $\omega \in \Omega_k$ and $k = 1, \ldots, n$. Then, if (f,g,μ) is a stable equilibrium, $\min_j g_j(\omega)$ is a sufficient statistic for $U(\omega)$.

Proof In the proof of proposition 2 it is shown that, for any stable equilibrium, for each $k = 1, \ldots, n$ and $\omega \in \Omega_k$,

$$u_k > \min g_j(\omega).$$

Since the equilibrium is efficient, trade always occurs at the minimum price. Therefore,

$$\min_j g_j(\omega) > c(\omega) > u_{k-1}$$

for any $\omega \in \Omega_k$. Since $u_k > u_{k-1}$, the result is immediate. ∎

2 Price Setting with Search

This section introduces search. To keep things simple it is assumed that consumers search nonsequentially for prices. That is, consumers decide at the outset, before they have acquired any information, how many prices they will sample. They do not observe any of the prices until after the entire sample is drawn.

If search is very costly, consumers will choose small samples. As a result, the model with search will behave quite differently from the model studied in section 1. On the other hand, if the cost of search is very small, consumers may choose to sample all prices in equilibrium. In that case, the model without search will be a good approximation to the model with search and the analysis of section 1 will continue to apply. The interesting question, then, is whether consumers search exhaustively (i.e., sample all prices) when the cost of search is sufficiently small.

To show that consumers will search exhaustively when costs are sufficiently small, it is sufficient to show that consumers will search exhaustively in the limit, when the costs of search are actually zero. To see this, suppose the contrary: that even as the costs of search become vanishingly small, consumers do not sample all prices. By the usual upper-hemicontinuity argument, there must exist an equilibrium in the limit, when search costs are actually zero, in which consumers do not search exhaustively. If we could rule out this possibility, then we would have generated a contradiction that proves the desired result. The strategy of this section is to analyze the limiting case of costless search and derive conditions under which search is exhaustive. (In Gale 1987 I took a more direct approach. I examined a sequence of economies in which search costs became vanishingly small and showed that, under certain conditions, the stable equilibria corresponding to this sequence of economies became both efficient and informationally efficient in the limit.)

The trading process with nonsequential search is represented by the following four-stage game:

(1) Firms simultaneously set prices.

(2) Consumers decide how many prices to sample.

(3) Nature selects a random sample of the appropriate size, without replacement.

(4) Consumers make demand decisions based on the prices in their sample.

Call this game Γ_1. A strategy profile for firms is an element $g \in G$. A strategy for consumers consists of a number $1 \leq K \leq N$ of firms to be sampled and a demand function $f\colon \mathbb{P}^K \to \mathbb{Z}_+^K$. The definitions of payoffs and equilibrium strategies are similar to those given in section 1.

Consider the equilibrium described in proposition 1. There are always at least two firms that have the minimum cost of production, and in this equilibrium they both charge the minimum price. A consumer can therefore afford to sample only $N - 1$ firms and still observe the minimum price if the firms adopt this pricing strategy. Let $N_0 < N$ denote the minimum number of firms that can be sampled and allow the consumers to observe the minimum price with probability 1. If the cost of search is sufficiently small (or zero), it will be optimal for the consumers to search N_0 times, since otherwise they will, with positive probability, select a sample that does not contain the lowest price. Furthermore, if N_0 is sufficiently large, so that the probability that the sample contains only one minimum-cost firm is sufficiently small, then firms will still find it optimal to charge the minimum price consistent with their costs. Thus, the outcome described in proposition 2 remains an equilibrium when there is nonsequential search and the search costs are sufficiently small.

PROPOSITION 3 If N_0 is sufficiently large and the costs of search are sufficiently small, there is an efficient and informationally efficient equilibrium of Γ_0 in which $K = N_0$ firms are sampled.

Proposition 3 suggests that there is some continuity between the analysis of Γ_0 and the analysis of Γ_1. Even with zero costs, however, the behavior of the search model is quite different from that of the model without search. In section 1 it was shown that a pooling equilibrium exists if consumers are sufficiently optimistic and the incentive for firms to cut price in the high state is sufficiently low. This equilibrium of Γ_0 disappears if we assume, to the contrary, that the incentive to cut price is high:

$$M(p_L - c_L) > (p_H - c_L)[M/N].$$

Under these assumptions, however, Γ_1 still has a pooling equilibrium. Suppose that consumers decide to sample only one price and that firms always charge the high price. Consumers will be willing to buy at this price, since by assumption their beliefs are optimistic. Then charging the high price is also optimal for firms. If a firm is the only one sampled, then it makes the maximum profit. If it is not sampled, then there is no point in lowering its price. Furthermore, it can be shown that when there are small search costs this equilibrium is stable in the sense of Kohlberg and Mertens (1986). In other words, the equilibrium appears to be quite robust.

Fortunately, small changes in the model suffice to eliminate this kind of equilibrium. A crucial property of the preceding example is the absence of price dispersion in equilibrium. Without price dispersion there is no incentive to search, and without search there is no price competition. To upset the pooling equilibrium, then, we must ensure that there is some price dispersion. Suppose first of all that the consumers have insufficiently optimistic beliefs to support the completely pooling equilibrium:

$$\sum_{\omega \in \Omega} U(\omega)v(\omega) < \sup c(\omega).$$

This means that no firm can produce the good at a cost low enough to attract completely uninformed consumers. When there is a large number of states, this is a very weak condition. Second, suppose that the costs of some firms are sometimes low enough to guarantee trade:

$$\exists\ \omega \in \Omega, \quad c(\omega) < \inf U(\omega).$$

In other words, in some state some firms have sufficiently low costs that consumers will want to buy from them, regardless of their beliefs. Price dispersion is a necessary but not sufficient condition for search to have value. To ensure that search takes place, we must also ensure that the consumer has some expectation that beneficial trade will take place. The preceding assumption ensures that trade will take place. Then, if firms' strategies are admissible (i.e., not weakly dominated), there must be some price dispersion (though not necessarily dispersion conditional on ω). Finally, we assume that costs are sufficiently dispersed across firms. Then it can never be optimal for consumers to search only once, for with positive probability they will miss some price at which they would want to trade. If $K \geq 2$ and if the probability that the sample contains two firms with minimum costs is sufficiently high, then the arguments developed in the previous section can be used to show that prices low enough to guarantee trade in each state will be charged. This ensures that there is price dispersion in each state, and that in turn is sufficient to guarantee that there is a positive gain from sampling a large number of firms.

To illustrate these ideas, consider the following variant of the high-low example. As before, costs, utilities, and prices take on only two values, but now it is no longer assumed that the firms have perfectly correlated costs; nor do they have complete information. Assume that

$\mathbb{C} = \{c_{\mathrm{H}}, c_{\mathrm{L}}\}$,

$\mathcal{S}_j = \mathcal{S}_{\mathrm{C}_j}$ for $j \in J$,

$\mathbb{U} = \{u_{\mathrm{H}}, u_{\mathrm{L}}\}$,

$\mathbb{P} = \{p_{\mathrm{H}}, p_{\mathrm{L}}\}$.

The parameters are assumed to satisfy the usual condition:

$$c_{\mathrm{L}} < p_{\mathrm{L}} < u_{\mathrm{L}} < c_{\mathrm{H}} < p_{\mathrm{H}} < u_{\mathrm{H}}.$$

To rule out the pooling equilibrium, assume that

$$\sum_{\omega \in \Omega} U(\omega) v(\omega) < p_{\mathrm{H}}.$$

To ensure that some trade occurs, assume that

$$\forall\, \omega \in \Omega, \quad [U(\omega) = u_{\mathrm{L}}] \Rightarrow [\exists\, j \in J,\ C_j(\omega) = c_{\mathrm{L}}].$$

The informational assumptions imply that a firm knows only its own costs. Thus, its pricing policy can depend at most on its costs. Admissibility requires the firm to charge the high price when costs are high. The only decision it needs to make is whether to charge the high or the low price when it has low costs. It is clear that we cannot have complete pooling. In that case, the consumers would never buy, profits would be zero, and some firm would have an incentive to cut price (note that each firm is sampled with positive probability). If we do not have complete pooling, then some firm cuts price whenever its costs are low. Suppose that

$$\forall\, j \in J, \exists\, \omega \in \Omega,\ C_j(\omega) = c_{\mathrm{L}} < C_h(\omega),\ \forall\, h \in J\backslash\{j\}.$$

Then, unless consumers sample every firm, there is a positive probability that the sample will contain only high prices, even though at least one firm is charging the low price. Thus, in equilibrium all prices must be sampled. From this point on, the analysis proceeds as in section 1. Note that we have not established the existence of an informationally efficient equilibrium in pure strategies. For that we need a stronger assumption—namely that with sufficiently high probability there are two firms with low costs whenever the consumers have a low valuation for the good. What the preceding argument establishes is only that, in any pure-strategy equilibrium, all prices must be sampled.

What the analysis of this example suggests is that equilibria with incomplete search can be ruled out if sufficiently strong assumptions are imposed. (Similar arguments were developed formally in Gale 1987; they will not be pursued here.)

3 Search and Price Setting in a Dynamic Framework

In the preceding sections we saw that fully revealing equilibria exist and that under certain conditions they are the only equilibria that satisfy a criterion of strategic stability. The framework in which these results were derived was an essentially static one, quite different from the dynamic framework in which Wolinsky produced his negative result. In Wolinsky's model, agents make sequential search decisions on the basis of experience in the market. In addition, his model allows for two-sided uncertainty and restricts each agent, whether buyer or seller, to trade at most one unit of the good.

It may be doubted whether any of the results derived above are relevant to the Wolinsky analysis. In this section, we will consider a version of Wolinsky's model that suggests that the intuitions derived from the static model do have some relevance for dynamic models of markets such as Wolinsky's. The model is more special than Wolinsky's; it allows for one-sided uncertainty only. Furthermore, it differs from his model in allowing a small amount of heterogeneity among sellers. With these assumptions, it can be shown that the model possesses an approximately revealing equilibrium. From this we can draw the tentative conclusion that two-sided uncertainty is essential to explaining Wolinsky's results.

There is a continuum of buyers and sellers, each of whom wants to trade at most one unit of an indivisible good. There are two states of nature: H and L. All sellers are informed (i.e., know the true state), and all buyers are uninformed. The prior probability of state ω occurring is q_ω, where $\omega = \mathrm{H,L}$. All buyers are identical, and each gets a utility of u_ω from a unit of the good in state $\omega = \mathrm{H,L}$. There are two types of sellers. A fraction $\pi > 0$ of sellers have high costs c_H regardless of the state. The rest of the sellers have costs c_ω in state $\omega = \mathrm{H,L}$. Buyers and sellers discount their utilities using the same discount factor δ, where $0 < \delta < 1$.

Trade occurs at a sequence of dates $t = 1, 2, \ldots, \infty$. At each date, each seller is matched with exactly one buyer and each buyer is matched with exactly one seller. They play the following game: The buyer and the seller in each matched pair simultaneously call out prices. There are two admissible prices: p_H and p_L. If the buyer and the seller call out the same price, trade occurs at the agreed price. If the seller calls out a lower price than the buyer, trade occurs at the lower price. If the seller calls out a higher price than the buyer, no trade can take place and the players must wait until the next period to be rematched. Buyers and sellers search until trade takes place; then they exit from the market. Every agent who exits from the market is immediately replaced by an identical agent, so that the cross-sectional distribution of agents of each type remains constant.

We make the following assumptions:

$$c_L < p_L < u_L < c_H < p_H < u_H.$$

We can also follow Wolinsky in assuming that

$$q_L u_L + q_H u_H < p_H,$$

thus ruling out the trivial pooling equilibrium, but this is not necessary for what follows. The main differences between this setup and Wolinsky's are the informational assumptions (a special case of Wolinsky's) and the assumption of a small fraction of high-cost sellers (explicitly ruled out by Wolinsky).

The Buyers' Problem

A strategy for a buyer is a sequence of functions mapping his history at each date into a price offer. Without loss of generality, we can restrict our attention to strategies having a special form. Note that a buyer exits the market as soon as he calls out the high price or as soon as he meets a seller who calls out the low price. Thus, all buyers who are still in the market have had the same experience. In each previous period they have offered the low price and been asked for the high price in return. An optimal strategy for a buyer therefore has the form "call out a low price for n periods, then call out the high price."

High-cost sellers will always call out the high price. Suppose that the other sellers call out the high (low) price when they are in the high (low) state. Suppose that the buyer's strategy is to call out the low price for $n-1$ periods and then call out the high price in the nth period. With probability q_H, the true state is H and the buyer will never be offered a low price. In that case he must wait $n-1$ periods before he can trade. With probability q_L, the true state is L and in each of the first n periods the buyer has a probability $(1 - \pi)$ of trading at the low price. Then the buyer's payoff will be

$$U_n \equiv q_H \delta^{n-1}(u_H - p_H) + q_L \left\{ \sum_{i=1}^{n} (\pi\delta)^{i-1}(1 - \pi)(u_L - p_L) + (\pi\delta)^{n-1}\pi(u_L - p_H) \right\}$$

$$= q_H \delta^{n-1}(u_H - p_H) + q_L \left\{ \frac{1 - (\pi\delta)^n}{1 - \pi\delta}(1 - \pi)(u_L - p_L) + (\pi\delta)^{n-1}\pi(u_L - p_H) \right\}.$$

Let $\Delta_n \equiv U_{n+1} - U_n$. Then

$$\Delta_n = q_H(\delta^n - \delta^{n-1})(u_H - p_H) + q_L\{(\pi\delta)^n(1 - \pi)(u_L - p_L) + ((\pi\delta)^n - (\pi\delta)^{n-1})\pi(u_L - p_H)\}$$

$$= \delta^{n-1}\{q_H(\delta - 1)(u_H - p_H) + q_L[\pi^n\delta(1 - \pi)(u_L - p_L) + (\pi\delta - 1)\pi^n(u_L - p_H)]\}.$$

Define Δ_x in the obvious way for any real number x. Then n^* is optimal if and only if $\Delta_x = 0$ for some real number $n^* - 1 < x \leq n^*$. Solving the condition $\Delta_x = 0$ for π^x, we get

$$\pi^x = \frac{(1 - \delta)q_H(u_H - p_H)}{q_L\{\delta(1 - \pi)(u_L - p_L) + (\pi\delta - 1)(u_L - p_H)\}}.$$

The Duration of Search

So far, I have posited a particular strategy for sellers and calculated the best response of the buyers. To show that the sellers' strategy is optimal we need to know the acceptance probability for the high price, which in turn depends on the cross-sectional distribution of search times for buyers. Since the sellers' decision is trivial in the high state, we need only concern ourselves with the low state. Suppose that the low state L has occurred. At each date, the equilibrium measures of buyers and sellers are constant and equal. Let β_1 denote the measure of buyers who have just entered the market, and let β_n denote the measure of buyers who have been in the market for exactly $n - 1$ periods. Every buyer is matched every period and leaves the market as soon as he receives an offer of p_L. The probability that a buyer receives an offer of p_H and must remain until the next period is π. Hence,

$$\beta_n = \pi\beta_{n-1} = \pi^{n-1}\beta_1.$$

The total population is equal to

$$\sum_{n=1}^{n^*} \beta_n = \beta_1 \sum_{n=1}^{n^*} \pi^{n-1} = \frac{\beta_1(1-\pi^{n^*})}{(1-\pi)}.$$

The fraction of the population of buyers who accept a high offer is equal to the fraction of the population that has been searching for $n^* - 1$ periods—that is,

$$\alpha = \frac{\beta_{n^*}}{\sum_{n=1}^{n^*} \beta_n} = \frac{(1-\pi)\pi^{n^*-1}}{1-\pi^{n^*}}.$$

α is the probability that a seller charging the high price in the low state will get an acceptance at any date.

The Sellers' Problem

In the high state H all sellers must charge the high price, so we only need to consider the low state. By an earlier argument, the optimal policy for a seller is to charge the high price for n periods and then charge the low price. I claim that it is optimal for a normal seller (i.e., one with low costs) to charge the low price if and only if

$$p_L - c_L \geq \alpha(p_H - c_L) + \delta(1-\alpha)(p_L - c_L). \tag{$*$}$$

The condition can be interpreted as follows: If the seller charges the low price, his payoff is the left-hand side of $(*)$. If he charges p_H in the first period and p_L in the second, his payoff is given by the right-hand side of $(*)$. So $(*)$ says that he prefers to charge p_L right away rather than charge p_H for one period and then charge p_L. Now suppose that he prefers charging p_L right away to charging p_H for $n-1$ periods and then charging p_L. That is, suppose that

$$\begin{aligned}(p_L - c_L) &\\ \geq [\alpha + \alpha(1-\alpha)\delta + \alpha(1-\alpha)^2\delta^2 + \cdots + \alpha(1-\alpha)^{n-2}\delta^{n-2}](p_H - c_L) &\\ + (1-\alpha)^{n-1}\delta^{n-1}(p_L - c_L).&\end{aligned}$$

Substituting (∗) into this equation gives

$$(p_L - c_L)$$
$$\geq [\alpha + \alpha(1-\alpha)\delta + \alpha(1-\alpha)^2\delta^2 + \cdots + \alpha(1-\alpha)^{n-1}\delta^{n-1}](p_H - c_L)$$
$$+ (1-\alpha)^n\delta^n(p_L - c_L).$$

In other words, the seller prefers charging p_L right away to charging p_H for n periods and then charging p_L. Thus, by induction, we have shown that charging the low price this period is at least as good as any other policy, if (∗) is satisfied.

Existence

Suppose that (∗) is satisfied, so that the strategy given to firms is in fact optimal for them. Then we have demonstrated the existence of an equilibrium. Furthermore, this equilibrium is approximately revealing in the sense that, as δ gets closer to 1, the probability that a buyer will trade at the correct price, which reveals the state of nature, approaches 1.

PROPOSITION 4 Suppose that $q_H(u_H - p_H) < \pi q_L(p_L - c_L)$. Then there exists an approximately revealing equilibrium for δ sufficiently close to 1.

This proposition is proved in the appendix.

4 Discussion

The results obtained in sections 1 and 2 are consistent with the view that prices do reveal the true state of nature. This is in sharp constrast with Wolinsky's negative results. Of course, there are important differences between the Bertrand-style model studied in sections 1 and 2 and the model used by Wolinsky. However, as the example analyzed in section 3 suggests, these differences may not be crucial. The one difference that seems to be essential is the assumption that only one side of the market is informed in the Bertrand model. In Wolinsky's model, there were informed and uninformed agents on both sides of the market.

The following heuristic analysis may help to explain why two-sided uncertainty is crucial. Consider a model similar to Wolinsky's, but assume that the discount rate is zero and that there is one-sided uncertainty. For example, suppose that all sellers are informed and all buyers are uninformed. Then the following strategies should support an "equilibrium": Sellers charge p_H in the high state and p_L in the low state. Buyers play "tough" when they first enter the market; that is, they offer to pay p_L in the first period. In their second period in the market they relent and play "soft"—that is, they offer price p_H. This is equilibrium behavior for the buyers because they always get to trade at the lowest possible price. The sellers are also playing optimally. In the high state it is only optimal for the sellers to charge the high price. In the low state, however, it is never optimal for a seller to deviate from the low-price strategy: whenever he charges the high price he will be unable to trade, because with probability 1 he is matched with a new buyer who plays tough. So it looks as if full revelation is possible in this case.

Now suppose that there is two-sided uncertainty. For example, suppose that some sellers are uninformed. The "equilibrium" proposed above cannot now be implemented. The presence of the uninformed sellers introduces noise that prevents an uninformed buyer from extracting information from the price "signal." Further, the buyer cannot tell whether the sellers he meets are informed or uninformed. After any finite period of search, there is still a positive probability that he has only met uninformed sellers.

In this case, when the discount rate is zero, there may be no equilibrium. Since search is costless, an uninformed buyer will never pay the high price as long as there is a positive probability of being offered the low price. A buyer may want to search forever, which clearly is incompatible with equilibrium.

With a small but positive discount rate, further search will not be optimal when the probability of getting the low price is sufficiently small. As the rate of time preference shrinks to zero, uninformed agents are willing to search longer and longer. But since the incentive to search longer affects both sides of the market, the effectiveness of search is reduced. Uninformed agents on both sides of the market are searching longer, and so the probability of meeting an uninformed agent rises, thus adding more "noise" to the signal.

There is an obvious sense in which two-sided uncertainty is the more general case. In that sense, Wolinsky's result seems to be more robust than the results offered in this paper. Two remarks can be made in this regard. The first is that there may be good reasons for assuming asymmetry between the two sides of the market. In labor markets, for example, it may be reasonable to assume that firms have more information than workers. Moreover, asymmetric information can be taken as a proxy for different degrees of computational ability. Firms and workers may have access to the same statistics but have different abilities to process this information. Here, asymmetric information is only a crude way of representing the bounded rationality of the workers. Second, the striking effect of two-sided uncertainty depends in part on other properties of the model. The fact that agents trade at most one unit means that an informed agent can give his information away at most once. The only reward for cutting price is that it allows the seller to trade more quickly. If sellers had greater productive capacity, an informed seller might reveal his information to several buyers in an effort to capture a larger share of the market. This competitive effect is crucial in the Bertrand-type models studied in sections 1 and 2, but is missing from Wolinsky's model.

Appendix

Proof of Proposition 2

The strategy of the proof is based on an induction on the sets $\Omega_1, \Omega_2, \ldots, \Omega_n$. The first step is to show that, for any $\omega \in \Omega_1$ and any $(f,g,\mu) \in \mathrm{SE}(\Gamma_0)$,

$\min g_j(\omega) < u_1.$

STEP 1 Suppose that a price vector $p \in \mathbb{P}^N$ satisfying $\inf p_j < u_1$ is observed by consumers. Whatever the state of nature, they are better off buying. Hence, there is no sequential equilibrium (f,g,μ) such that $\Sigma_{j \in J} f_j(p) < M$ for some p containing a price less than u_1.

Suppose that for some sequential equilibrium (f,g,μ) and some $\omega_0 \in \Omega_1$ every firm charges a price greater than u_1, i.e., $g_j(\omega_0) > u_1$ for every j. Let $\Omega_1^0 = \{\omega \in \Omega_1 | g_j(\omega) > u_1, \forall j \in J\}$ and $\Omega_1^1 = \Omega_1 \backslash \Omega_1^0$. Recall that $J(\omega)$ is the set of firms that have cost less than $U(\omega)$ in state ω. Let $S(\omega)$ denote the common knowledge of the firms $j \in J(\omega)$ in state ω. That is, $S(\omega)$ is the smallest set containing ω that is the union of elements of $\mathscr{S}_j$, for all $j \in J(\omega)$. Note that from (A.4) we know that $S(\omega_0) \subseteq \Omega_1$. Let $\Pi_j(\omega)$ denote the equilibrium profits of any firm j in state ω. I claim that for any firm $j \in J(\omega_0)$

$$\mathbb{E}\{\Pi_j(\omega) | \omega \in S(\omega_0) \cap \Omega_1^0\} \geq \mathbb{E}\{(\hat{p}(\omega) - C_j(\omega))M | \omega \in S(\omega_0) \cap \Omega_1^0\}. \quad (1)$$

If not, there exists some $j \in J(\omega_0)$ and some $\omega_1 \in S(\omega_0) \cap \Omega_1^0$ such that

$$\mathbb{E}\{\Pi_j(\omega)|\omega \in S_j(\omega_1) \cap \Omega_1^0\} < \mathbb{E}\{(\hat{p}(\omega) - C_j(\omega))M|\omega \in S_j(\omega_1) \cap \Omega_1^0\}. \quad (2)$$

To obtain a contradiction, we need to show that by reducing its price to $\hat{p}(\omega_1)$ the firm could increase its expected profits. The first thing to note is that the firm is making no profits when $\omega \in S_j(\omega_1) \cap \Omega_1^1$. Since $\omega_1 \in \Omega_1^0$,

$$g_j(\omega_1) > u_1.$$

Then the measurability condition requires that $g_j(\omega) \geq u_1$ for any $\omega \in S_j(\omega_1)$. Consequently, for any $\omega \in S_j(\omega_1) \cap \Omega_1^1$, firm j is not charging the lowest price and therefore $\Pi_j(\omega) = 0$. In state ω_1, firm j may not know whether the true state belongs to Ω_1^0 or to Ω_1^1. However, since it knows that profits are zero in any case if $\omega \in S_j(\omega_1) \cap \Omega_1^1$, reducing the price to $\hat{p}(\omega_1)$ cannot hurt in that event. (Note that (2) implies that $\hat{p}(\omega) > C_j(\omega)$ for any $\omega \in S_j(\omega_1)$.) So in order to show that the firm can increase its expected profits conditional on $\omega \in S_j(\omega_1)$, it is only necessary to show that it can increase its expected profits conditional on $\omega \in S_j(\omega_1) \cap \Omega_1^0$. But the firm's expected profits, conditional on $\omega \in S_j(\omega_1) \cap \Omega_1^0$, when it charges $\hat{p}(\omega_1)$ are given by the right-hand side of (2). So (2) implies that expected profits can be increased by reducing the price to $\hat{p}(\omega_1)$. This contradicts the equilibrium conditions and proves that (1) holds.

Summing (1) over $J(\omega_0)$, we obtain

$$\sum_{j \in J(\omega_0)} \mathbb{E}\{\Pi_j(\omega)|\omega \in S(\omega_0) \cap \Omega_1^0\} \geq \sum_{j \in J(\omega_0)} \mathbb{E}\{(\hat{p}(\omega) - C_j(\omega))M|\omega \in S(\omega_0) \cap \Omega_1^0\}.$$

Then for some $\omega \in S(\omega_0) \cap \Omega_1^0$,

$$\sum_{j \in J(\omega_0)} \Pi_j(\omega) \geq \sum_{j \in J(\omega_0)} (\hat{p}(\omega) - C_j(\omega))M.$$

But this contradicts (A.5), since it is clear that

$$\sum_{j \in J(\omega_0)} \Pi_j(\omega) \leq (\bar{u} - \underline{c})M.$$

This proves that $\Omega_1^0 = \phi$. Thus, in any sequential equilibrium of Γ_0 the minimum price is less than u_1 if $\omega \in \Omega_1$.

STEP 2 The previous step showed that for any price vector p such that $\min p_j > u_1$,

$$S_1(p) \cap \Omega_1 = \phi.$$

In consequence, I would like to show that for any $\mu \in M_1$,

$$\mu(p)(\omega) = 0 \text{ if } \omega \in \Omega_1 \text{ and } \min p_j > u_1.$$

However, this conclusion will not be justified if $S_1(p) = \phi$. Therefore, the next step is to identify a set of price vectors that can occur in some equilibrium (f,g,μ).

Let $\mathscr{P}_2$ denote the set of price vectors with the property that, for some $\omega \in \Omega_2$ and precisely one firm $j \in J(\omega)$,

$$p_j = \hat{p}(\omega),$$

and for all other firms,

$$p_j > \hat{p}(\omega).$$

Then I claim that, for any $p \in \mathscr{P}_2$,

$$S_1(p) \neq \phi.$$

The proof is constructive.

Fix $\omega_0 \in \Omega_2$ and $j_0 \in J(\omega_0)$ and let $\bar{p} \in \mathscr{P}_2$ be a price vector with the property that $\bar{p}_{j_0} = \hat{p}(\omega_0)$. Define a sequential equilibrium as follows. For any $j \in J$, put

$$g_j(\omega) = \begin{cases} \min\{p' > C_j(\omega)\} & \text{if } \omega \notin S_j(\omega_0) \\ \bar{p}_j & \text{otherwise.} \end{cases}$$

Define beliefs so that

$$\mu(p)(\omega_0) = 1 \text{ if } p = \bar{p}$$

and

$$\mu(p)(\omega_1) = 1 \text{ for some } \omega_1 \in \Omega_1 \text{ if } p \notin g(\Omega).$$

Beliefs are defined along the equilibrium path by the consistency condition. Define f by putting

$$f(p) = \begin{cases} 0 & \text{if } \min p_j > \Sigma \mu(p)(\omega) U(\omega) \\ d \in D(p) & \text{otherwise,} \end{cases}$$

where $D(p) = \{d \in \mathbb{Z}^N | \Sigma d_j = M \text{ and } d_j = 0 \text{ if } p_j > \min p_j\}$. Then (f,g,μ) is a sequential equilibrium with the desired price vector on the equilibrium path. This shows that for any $p \in \mathscr{P}_2$,

$$S_1(p) \neq 0$$

and

$$S_1(p) \cap \Omega_1 = \phi.$$

Therefore, for any equilibrium $(f,g,\mu) \in \mathrm{SE}_1$,

$$\mu(p)(\omega) = 0 \text{ if } p \in \mathscr{P}_2 \text{ and } \omega \in \Omega_1.$$

STEP 3 Now suppose that similar results have been established for every $k = 1, \ldots, K$. That is, for each $k \leq K$,

$$S_k(p) \neq \phi, \quad \forall\, p \in \mathscr{P}_{k+1}$$

and

$$\forall (f, g, \mu) \in \mathrm{SE}_k, \quad \forall\, \omega \in \Omega_k, \quad \min g_j(\omega) < u_k.$$

To complete the proof by induction, it needs to be shown that the same conditions hold for $k = K + 1$. The first step is to show that, for any $(f,g,\mu) \in \mathrm{SE}_{K+1}$ and $\omega \in \Omega_{K+1}$,

$$\min g_j(\omega) < u_{K+1}.$$

To do this we use the argument of step 1.

Suppose that, contrary to what is to be proved, there is a sequential equilibrium $(f,g,\mu) \in \mathrm{SE}_{K+1}$ and a state $\omega_0 \in \Omega_{K+1}$ in which every firm charges a price greater than u_{K+1}. Let

$$\Omega_{K+1}^0 = \{\omega \in \Omega_{K+1} | g_j(\omega) > u_{K+1}, \forall\, j \in J\}$$

and

$$\Omega_{K+1}^1 = \Omega_{K+1} \backslash \Omega_{K+1}^0.$$

Let $S(\omega_0)$ denote the common knowledge of the firms $j \in J(\omega_0)$ in state ω_0. I claim that, for any firm $j \in J(\omega_0)$,

$$\mathbb{E}\{\Pi_j(\omega) | \omega \in S(\omega_0) \cap \Omega_{K+1}^0\} \geq \mathbb{E}\{(\hat{p}(\omega) - C_j(\omega))M | \omega \in S(\omega_0) \cap \Omega_{K+1}^0\}. \tag{3}$$

If not, there exists some $j \in J(\omega_0)$ and some $\omega_1 \in S(\omega_0) \cap \Omega_{K+1}^0$ such that

$$\mathbb{E}\{\Pi_j(\omega)|\omega \in S_j(\omega_1) \cap \Omega^0_{K+1}\} < \mathbb{E}\{(\hat{p}(\omega) - C_j(\omega))M|\omega \in S_j(\omega_1) \cap \Omega^0_{K+1}\}. \tag{4}$$

By the earlier argument, $g_j(\omega) \geq u_1$ for any $\omega \in S_j(\omega_1)$ so $\Pi_j(\omega) = 0$ for any $\omega \in S_j(\omega_1) \cap \Omega^1_{K+1}$. Then we can restrict attention to $S_j(\omega_1) \cap \Omega^0_{K+1}$ in what follows.

Now suppose that the firm had charged the price $\hat{p}(\omega_1) < u_{K+1}$ at the information set $S_j(\omega_1)$. In any state $\omega \in S_j(\omega_1) \cap \Omega^0_{K+1}$ the consumers would have observed a price vector $p \in \mathscr{P}_{K+1}$. By the induction hypothesis and the definition of SE_{K+1}, their beliefs are concentrated on states $\omega \notin \bigcup_{k \leq K} \Omega_k$ in that event, so they will buy the maximum amount from firm j. Then the firm's expected profits conditional on $\omega \in S_j(\omega_1) \cap \Omega^0_{K+1}$ are given by the amount on the right-hand side of (4). This contradicts the equilibrium conditions and proves that (3) holds. Summing (3) over all $j \in J(\omega_0)$, we obtain a contradiction of (A.5) in the usual way.

This proves that $\Omega^0_{K+1} = \phi$—that is, in any sequential equilibrium of SE_{K+1} the minimum price is less than u_{K+1} if $\omega \in \Omega_{K+1}$.

STEP 4 To complete the proof by induction, we need to show that for any $\bar{p} \in \mathscr{P}_{K+2}$ there exists an equilibrium $(f,g,\mu) \in \text{SE}_K$ such that $g(\omega_0) = \bar{p}$ for some $\omega_0 \in \Omega_{K+2}$. This can be done using the construction in step 2.

Let $\bar{p}$ and ω_0 be fixed as above. For any $j \in J$, put

$$g_j(\omega) = \begin{cases} \min\{p > C_j(\omega)\} & \text{if } \omega \notin S_j(\omega_0) \\ \bar{p}_j & \text{otherwise.} \end{cases}$$

Define beliefs so that

$$\mu(p)(\omega_0) = 1 \text{ if } p = \bar{p}$$

and

$$\mu(p)(\omega_1) = 1 \text{ for some } \omega_1 \in \Omega_1 \text{ if } p \notin g(\Omega).$$

Beliefs are defined along the equilibrium path by the consistency condition. Define f by putting

$$f(p) = \begin{cases} 0 & \text{if } \min p_j > \Sigma\mu(p)(\omega)U(\omega) \\ d \text{ for some } d \in D(p) & \text{otherwise,} \end{cases}$$

where $D(p) = \{d \in \mathbb{Z}^N | \Sigma d_j = M \text{ and } d_j = 0 \text{ if } p_j > \min p_j\}$. Then (f,g,μ) is a sequential equilibrium with the desired price on the equilibrium path. This shows that $S_{K+1}(\bar{p}) \neq \phi$ for any $\bar{p} \in \mathscr{P}_{K+2}$.

Thus, by induction, we have shown that, for any $(f,g,\mu) \in \mathrm{SE}_n$,

$\min g_j(\omega) < U(\omega)$ for all $\omega \in \Omega$. ■

Proof of Proposition 4

We need to show that the inequality in the proposition implies that (∗) is satisfied for δ close to 1. Rewrite (∗) as

$$\frac{\alpha}{1-\delta} \le \frac{p_L - c_L}{(p_H - c_L) - \delta(p_L - c_L)}.$$

Substitute the formula for α to get

$$\frac{\pi^{n^*-1}}{1-\delta} \le \frac{(1-\pi^{n^*})(p_L - c_L)}{(1-\pi)\{(p_H - c_L) - \delta(p_L - c_L)\}}. \tag{5}$$

Since $x \ge n^* - 1$,

$$\frac{\pi^{n^*-1}}{1-\delta} \le \frac{\pi^x}{1-\delta}. \tag{6}$$

From an earlier calculation, we know that

$$\frac{\pi^x}{1-\delta} = \frac{q_H(u_H - p_H)}{q_L\{\delta(1-\pi)(u_L - p_L) + (\pi\delta - 1)(u_L - p_H)\}}. \tag{7}$$

It is straightforward to check that as $\delta \to 1$ the right-hand side of (5) converges to

$$\frac{p_L - c_L}{(1-\pi)(p_H - p_L)}$$

and the right-hand side of (7) converges to

$$\frac{q_H(u_H - p_H)}{q_L(1-\pi)(p_H - p_L)}.$$

In view of (6), (5) must be satisfied for δ close to 1 if

$$\frac{q_H(u_H - p_H)}{q_L(1-\pi)(p_H - p_L)} < \frac{p_L - c_L}{(1-\pi)(p_H - p_L)},$$

which is equivalent to

$$q_H(u_H - p_H) < q_L(p_L - c_L),$$

the inequality in the proposition. ■

Acknowledgments

This paper is a substantial reworking of ideas from an earlier paper, "Information Revelation in Markets with Non-Sequential Search" (1987), which it now supersedes. I am grateful to seminar participants at the University of Rochester, at SUNY Buffalo, and at the CMU/Pitt Theory Workshop for their comments.

References

Burdett, Kenneth, and Kenneth Judd. 1983. "Equilibrium price dispersion." *Econometrica* 51: 955–969.

Gale, Douglas. 1987. "Limit theorems for markets with sequential bargaining." *Journal of Economic Theory* 43: 20–54.

Gale, Douglas. 1987. Information Revelation in a Market with Non-Sequential Search. University of Pittsburgh mimeo.

Kohlberg, E., and J. F. Mertens. 1986. "On the strategic stability of equilibria." *Econometrica* 54: 1003–1038.

Wolinsky, Asher. 1990. "Information revelation in a market with pairwise meetings." *Econometrica* 58: 1–24.

Irrationality in Game Theory

Robert J. Aumann

The history of game theory has been evolutionary rather than revolutionary. Over the years, the fundamental concepts of the theory have been used in an ever-increasing circle of contexts; some of the most important developments consisted of innovative ways of recasting the theory so as to apply to problems that previously appeared not to fit in. A prime example is Harsanyi's historic work (1967–68) on games of incomplete information. Before this work, it had been universally thought that for game theory to be applicable, the payoff matrix of the game must be commonly known. Harsanyi's achievement consisted of formulating games of incomplete information so that they could be seen and analyzed as games of complete information; by this achievement, he opened the door to the development of the enormous fields of informational game theory and economics as we know them today. Similarly, the theory was extended from perfect information (Zermelo) to imperfect information (Borel and von Neumann); from strategic (normal) form to extensive; from two-person to n-person; from zero-sum to non-zero-sum; and from TU (transferable utility) to NTU (non-transferable utility).

The current frontier—the one discussed here—is that of rationality. Briefly, it is suggested that game theory need not assume that the players must be rational (i.e., utility maximizers).

This may sound paradoxical to the reader. After all, rationality is what game theory is all about; game theory without rationality sounds like geology without rocks or biology without life. Yet some of the most challenging problems facing the theory concern the interface between rationality and irrationality; they are about situations that cannot be dealt with on a purely rational basis, much like geological phenomena that depend on living organisms (such as cracking of rocks by plants) or biological phenomena that are the result of the nonliving environment.

1 Approach

The underlying game model from which we take off is that presented in Aumann 1987. It starts by considering the set of all "states of the world," where the specification of a state includes all relevant factors, including the (pure) strategy that each player uses in the given game, and what he knows when he decides to do so. It then asks, *suppose* that each player is rational at each state of the world that occurs with positive probability; i.e., that the strategy that that state specifies for each player happens to be one that maximizes his utility given his information. Can we then say anything about the distribution of strategy n-tuples? Does the assumption of rationality imply any specific form for this distribution?

The point of view of this model is not normative; it is not meant to advise the players what to do. The players do whatever they do; their strategies are taken as given. Neither is it meant as a description of what human beings actually do in interactive situations. The most appropriate term is perhaps "analytic"; it asks, what are the *implications* of rationality in interactive situations? Where does it lead? This question may be as important as, or even more important than, more direct "tests" of the relevance of the rationality hypothesis.

The answer given in Aumann 1987 was that it leads to correlated equilibrium—not that the players consciously choose a correlated equilibrium according to which they play, but that, to an outside observer with no information, the distribution of action n-tuples appears as if they had.

What is proposed here is to take this framework, remove the rationality hypothesis, and see where we are led.

Needless to say, I do not simply drop the rationality hypothesis and leave it at that. Rather, I propose to use the epistemic model of Aumann 1987—whose roots extend back to Radner (1968, 1972), to Harsanyi (1967–68), to von Neumann and Morgenstern, to formal epistemologists such as Kripke and Hintikka, and to probabilists such as Kolmogorov—as a very general kind of framework for studying limited rationality; a unified framework for considering rationality in environments that may include irrationality, indeed where irrationality may be of the essence.

2 Formal Description of the Model

Formally, define an *information system* to consist of the following:

(i) a strategic (normal) form n-person game G;

(ii) for each player i, a set whose members, s_i, are called *information states* of i; and

(iii) a function that associates with each information state of each player *i*
  (a) a pure strategy of *i* in *G* and
  (b) a probability distribution on ($n - 1$)-tuples of information states of the other players.

An information system is a simultaneous representation of all the players' uncertainties. Each player makes some definite choice of a pure strategy, based on whatever he knows or believes about customs, history, personalities of the other players, and so on—in brief, based on the state of his information. He knows his own choice; that is what (iiia) says. But he does not know what the others choose, though he has some belief about this. Moreover, he does not know their information states—what information is available to them when they make their choices, what they believe about his choice, and so on.

For simplicity, we confine ourselves to information systems that are finite, i.e., in which each player has finitely many information states.

Let us use the term *surmise* for a probability distribution maintained by a player, *theory* for his surmise on the ($n - 1$)-tuple of information states of the other players, and *belief* for his surmise on the ($n - 1$)-tuple of pure strategies that the other players choose. Thus, (iiib) associates a theory with each information state of each player *i*, from which we may derive *i*'s belief. From *i*'s theory we may also derive a surmise on the theories of the others, and hence about *their* beliefs. This is called a *second-order* belief; it may be computed explicitly from the information system. Similarly, we may define and compute beliefs of any order. Note that the resulting "belief hierarchy" is derived from the information system, not given exogenously.

We call a player *rational* at a given information state if the pure strategy he chooses at that state maximizes his expected payoff when calculated according to his belief at that state. (See section 7 for a discussion of this definition.)

Let us use the term *state of the world*, or simply *world*, for an *n*-tuple of information states; it is a complete specification of all relevant parameters. A widely used regularity condition on information systems is that there exists a single probability distribution *p* on the states *w* of the world, called a "common prior," such that the theory of each player *i* at each *w* is the conditional of *p* given *i*'s information state at *w* (see Harsanyi 1967–68, p. 493ff., and Aumann 1987, section 5). Intuitively, *p* represents the surmise about the state of the world held by an outside observer with no information at all; it is assumed that if the observer had the same information as a player he would make the same surmises. When it exists, a common prior allows a particularly concise description of the information system.

For an illustration, let *G* be the game with the following matrix:

	L	**R**
T	1,1	0,0
B	0,0	2,2

(as usual, the first and second coordinates of each entry represent payoffs to the row and column players—say, Alice and Bob—respectively). Consider the information system depicted by

	L	**L**	**R**
T	1,1*	1,1*	0,0
T	1,1*	1,1	0,0*
B	0,0	0,0*	2,2*

The first two rows represent two different information states of Alice, both corresponding to her pure strategy T; the last row represents a third information state, corresponding to her pure strategy B. Similarly, the columns represent Bob's information states. There are nine states of the world. Each "star" represents a probability of 1/6; the other probabilities vanish. Alice's first information state differs from her second in her belief; in the first, she knows that Bob plays his pure strategy L, whereas in the second, she attributes half-half probabilities to Bob's two pure strategies. Similarly for Bob.

Thus, in the world *w* represented by the top left corner of the 3×3 matrix, Alice plays *T*, and Bob knows this. But she does not know that he knows it; indeed, she ascribes probability only 1/2 to this event. Similarly for Bob. Finally, each player is rational in *w*, but neither knows that the other is; indeed, each ascribes probability only 1/2 to the rationality of the other.

(Throughout this paper, the term *know* is used to mean "believe with probability 1." In the current framework one cannot even formulate the stronger meaning of *know*, which allows no exceptions at all, even with probability 0.)

The above definition of an information system is analogous to Harsanyi's (1967–68) definition of a game of incomplete information. There each player may be one of several "types," where a type determines his utility function and a distribution over $(n-1)$-tuples of types of the others. Here we replace the utility functions by actions; the information states here play the same role as the types there.

Information systems are essentially equivalent to the standard partition models of information in games (as in Aumann 1987). There the primitives are the set of worlds, and n partitions of this set, one for each player. An information state of i is then defined as an atom of i's partition. Formally, information systems are slightly more parsimonious than partition models, and are better suited to our current purposes.

The purpose of this essay is to consider information systems where some players are irrational at some states of the world, and the implications this has for behavior at other states of the world, where all players *are* rational. In particular, we will see how such considerations can resolve certain "paradoxes of rationality" arising from backward induction in "centipede games."

3 High-Order Mutual Knowledge

Recall that an event is called *common* knowledge if all players know it, all know that all know it, and so on *ad infinitum.* Call an event *mutual* knowledge if all players simply know it; *second-order* mutual knowledge if it is mutual knowledge that it is mutual knowledge; and so on for any finite order. Thus, common knowledge is the same as mutual knowledge for all finite orders simultaneously.

In a conversation at Stanford during the summer of 1987, Jay Kadane of Carnegie-Mellon University suggested that it might be worthwhile to investigate the consequences of relaxing the assumption of common knowledge of rationality that underlies Aumann 1987 (see section 1 above). At the time, the framework for carrying out such an investigation was not clear. I suggest that the framework of the previous section is appropriate for this purpose.

Indeed, in such a framework it is quite easy formally to describe a situation in which there is iterated mutual knowledge of rationality up to any given order, but not common knowledge. Thus, consider a variant of the example in the previous section, with the same game *G* as there, but with the information system

	L	L	L	L	R
T	1,1*	1,1*	1,1	1,1	0,0
T	1,1*	1,1	1,1*	1,1	0,0
T	1,1	1,1*	1,1	1,1*	0,0
T	1,1	1,1	1,1*	1,1	0,0*
B	0,0	0,0	0,0	0,0*	2,2*

where each star represents a probability of 1/10, and the other probabilities vanish. Then in the state of the world represented by the top left corner there is second-order—but not third-order—mutual knowledge of rationality.

Common knowledge of rationality seems a very strong assumption. Even mutual knowledge of rationality is quite strong. A player may be rational himself, but how can he know for sure that another person is? Even if he does, it seems highly unlikely that he will know for sure, without the slightest doubt, that the other player knows that he is rational. Yet this would only be second-order mutual knowledge of rationality; common knowledge of rationality is far stronger.

The question therefore arises as to what happens when we relax this requirement just a little, e.g. by allowing a small measure of doubt to enter at a high level of mutual knowledge. Suppose, for example, that both players are rational, both know for sure that both are rational, and both impute very high probability to this being so (i.e., to both knowing for sure that both are rational); but they do not know it for *sure*. Can this make a big difference in the outcome of a game?

We will see that it can make a very big difference indeed.

4 Paradoxes of Backward Induction

Among the most disturbing counterintuitive examples of rational interactive decision theory are the paradoxes of "backward induction." The best known example is the finitely repeated prisoner's dilemma, in which all

Nash equilibria (and also all correlated equilibria) dictate playing "greedy" ("defect") at each stage, no matter how often play is repeated. Rosenthal (1982) constructed a particularly simple class of backward-induction paradoxes—the "centipede games"—a striking instance of which, due to Megiddo (1986), is as follows: \$10.50 is lying on a table. Alice has the option of taking \$10, leaving 50 cents for Bob. If she does, the game is over. If not, the amount on the table is increased tenfold, to \$105, and it is Bob's turn to play: he can take \$10, leaving \$5 to Alice. If he does, the game is over. If not, the amount on the table is again increased tenfold. This continues for a total of at most three rounds, and then ends. If play has not terminated before, then at the last stage Bob has the opportunity of taking \$1,000,000, leaving \$50,000 for Alice; after that, play is over, whether or not Bob takes the opportunity.

At all Nash equilibria of this game, Alice "goes out" immediately —i.e., she takes the \$10 at her first move, leaving 50 cents for Bob. This is also so for all correlated equilibria.

Some readers may feel that, upon consideration, Megiddo's example is not so terribly counterintuitive; that although Alice may feel quite frustrated, a considered analysis will nevertheless lead her in the end to pick up the money at the first opportunity. After all, there is a difference between frustration and paradoxicality; the players of a one-shot prisoner's dilemma will certainly feel frustrated, but the logic of that situation *does* inexorably point to playing "greedy," and the time has long passed since this was considered paradoxical. One might even say that properly digesting Megiddo's example makes it easier to accept the equilibrium outcome of, say, the 100-times-repeated prisoner's dilemma.

But others will feel that if this is rationality they want none of it—or, more to the point, that it represents an approach that is of little practical interest, at least in this example.

5 A Resolution of the Backward-Induction Paradoxes

What is proposed here is to apply the new kind of bounded rationality suggested in section 3, in which all agents are in fact perfectly rational but there is some breakdown in the commonality of the knowledge that they are. Typically, we will be interested in situations where there is iterated knowledge ("Alice knows that Bob knows that Alice knows...") of rationality up to a specified level, but no further. We will find that an extremely small breakdown in the commonality of the knowledge of rationality is enough to justify the kind of behavior that most of us would consider intuitively "reasonable."

The Megiddo example appears in matrix form as follows:

		Bob			
		a	b	c	d
	A	10 .50	10 .50	10 .50	10 .50
	B	5 v 100	1,000 w 50	1,000 50	1,000 50
Alice					
	C	5 100	500 x 10,000	100,000 y 5,000	100,000 5,000
	D	5 100	500 10,000	50,000 z 1,000,000	0 0

The rows and columns represent pure strategies of Alice and Bob, respectively. They are arranged in the order in which they prescribe "going out;" thus, Alice's third row represents the strategy in which she takes the money—"goes out"—when (and if) it is offered to her for the third time, but not before. In each entry, the upper number represents Alice's payoff, the lower one Bob's.

Consider now the information system depicted in the above matrix. Each player has just one information state for each of his pure strategies. There is a common prior, with non-negative probabilities v, w, x, y, and z; all other probabilities vanish. Note that with probability 1 Alice "stays in" on her first move.

(When one is discussing an example, as here, common priors are a desideratum, not a restriction. In theorems one strives for generality; in examples, for "regularity," for an absence of pathology. The point is that the backward-induction paradoxes can be resolved even if we restrict ourselves to common priors; *a fortiori* if we don't.)

For simplicity, consider first the case where $x = 0.99447$, $y = 0.0055$, $z = 0.00003$, and $u = v = w = 0$. Note that Bob is rational at all three states of the world that occur with positive probability; as for Alice, she is rational at x and at y, but not at z. Thus, Bob is rational with probability 1, and Alice with a probability very close to 1; the probability that she is irrational is only 3 in 100,000.

Suppose now that the true state of the world happens to be the one that his the overwhelming probability, namely x. Then both Alice and Bob are rational; moreover, each of them knows that both are rational. Indeed, it is common knowledge that Bob is rational. And he still gets $10,000, which is surely the most he could reasonably hope for.

One can ring the changes on this in many ways. The underlying point is that for Bob to be rational everywhere, and Alice everywhere except at z, it suffices that, of the ratios v/w, w/x, x/y, and y/z that are not 0/0, none exceeds 198. The probability is then 1 that Bob is rational and gets at least $50; and at the state of the world corresponding to v, both players are rational, both know this (with certainty), both know that they know this, and both know that they know that they know this, and yet Bob collects $100. And though Alice is irrational with positive probability, that probability may be tiny: when all the above ratios are 198, the probability z that Alice is irrational (as estimated by an outside observer) is 0.000000000648—less than one in a billion. Multiplying this probability by the size of Alice's "loss" (or rather forgone profit) at z, namely $50,000, we get an "expected irrationality" of less than 1/300 of a cent, an utterly insignificant sum.

Similar considerations hold for the finitely repeated prisoner's dilemma. With extremely small—practically speaking, negligible—overall probabilities of irrationality, one can, in the 100-fold repetition, justify "cooperating" until at least the 85th or the 90th stage, and even beyond. This kind of result jibes well with observed experimental behavior, in which subjects start "defecting" more and more as the game approaches its end.

This attractive resolution for these paradoxes gives a rigorous justification to the elusive idea that, whereas one should certainly play rationally at the end, it seems somehow foolish to act from the very beginning in the most pathologically pessimistic, "play it safe" way. The above analysis shows that, contrary to what had been thought, one may act in a way that is rational—even with a high degree of mutual knowledge of rationality—and yet is quite profitable. And it reflects the fact that in real interactive situations there is a great deal of uncertainty about what others will do, to what extent they are rational, what they think about what you think and about your rationality, and so on.

6 Measuring Irrationality

In this section we confine our attention to information systems with a common prior, to which the term *probability* will refer.

The methodology of section 5 lends itself well to the task of measuring irrationality. We have already used one such measure: "expected irrationality." Formally, this is defined for each player i separately, as follows: At each of i's information states, one multiplies the probability of that state by the difference between i's expected payoff there and the maximum expected payoff that he could have gotten by changing his strategy; then one sums over all of i's information states. This measure of irrationality should be useful in comparing various approaches to approximate rationality, including the ε-rationality of Radner (1980, 1986), the "perturbations" of Kreps, Milgrom, Roberts, and Wilson (1982), and the approach of this paper. What is being suggested is that, in evaluating a specified solution in a specified context, one should take into account both the amount of irrationality (as does Radner) and its probability (as do Kreps et al.). There is an obvious tradeoff between the two that is not captured by either one separately: a player may be willing to tolerate a higher probability of an irrationality that results in the loss of $1 than one costing $1 million.

The information systems of section 5 involve "correlated" strategies: each player's choice of a pure strategy depends on his belief, with different beliefs corresponding to different choices. Effects that are similar insofar as expected irrationality is concerned can be obtained in the independent case—with "mixed" strategies, so to speak. Thus, suppose that at each of his information states Bob has the same belief about Alice's choice, represented by the probabilities $A, B, \ldots$ (see the matrix in section 5). Similarly, let $a, b, \ldots$ represent Alice's belief at each of her information states. Let $B/C = C/D = a/b = b/c = 198$, and let $A = D = 0$. Then, as in the second example in section 5, Bob's expected irrationality is 0, and Alice's is less than 1/300 of a cent. (Alice is irrational only when choosing row D.) The *probability* of irrationality is greater than in section 5; it is $D = 0.0000253$, rather than $z = 0.000000000648$. But the *size* of the irrationality (the loss in expected payoff from making that choice rather than maximizing) is smaller; not $50,000, but $\$50.000 \times c$. Hence, the expected irrationality is \$50,000 × cD. Since $c = D$, this works out to \$0.0000320, as compared with \$0.0000324 in the second example of section 5.

Thus, there is no appreciable difference in expected irrationality between the two systems; it is negligibly small in both (in fact, slightly smaller in the independent case). What makes the example of section 5 more attractive is that at v, say, it displays a much higher level of mutual knowledge of rationality. By contrast, in the independent case there is no mutual knowledge of rationality at all; at v (indeed, at all states), Bob ascribes positive probability to Alice's being irrational.

We may define the *degree* of irrationality of a player i at state w of the world as minus the maximum level of mutual knowledge of i's rationality at w. This is to be distinguished from expected irrationality as defined above, which measures the "amount" of irrationality in the system. Thus, whereas the example of section 5 has a slightly higher "amount" of irrationality than the "independent" example, it has a far lower degree.

Expected irrationality is a global measure; it applies to the information system as a whole. Degree of irrationality is a local measure; it applies to a specific state of the world. It would be desirable also to develop a local measure of expected irrationality, conditional on a specific state of the world and on the information of the players at that state. This would enable us to refer to the "amount of irrationality" that is needed in the system to justify the choice of a certain strategy pair by the players (like x in Megiddo's game), even though under the circumstances both players' choices are completely rational.

7 A Difficulty with the Definition of Irrationality

The framework of section 2 requires each player, at each state of the world, to have well-defined probabilities for the other players' information states, pure strategies, and so on. Yet it permits him sometimes to be irrational, i.e., to fail to maximize expected utility. This raises a difficulty, since personal probabilities are usually *defined* via utility maximization (Savage 1954); nonmaximizers of utility don't have probabilities.

Consider first the case when there is a common prior, as in sections 5 and 6. The underlying idea of common priors is that reasonable probability assessments are or should be based on information, so that people with exactly the same information "should" have the same probabilities. Thus, one can think of a common prior as representing the assessment of a rational outside observer who has no personal interest in the outcome of the game and no private information. If he then gets the same private information as a player who is rational, he will entertain the same probabilities as that player; and if the player is not rational, it is natural to think of the observer's probabilities as the "right" ones.

In the general case, when there need not be a common prior, the difficulty may be resolved by revising the definition of an information system (section 2). Item iiib of the definition specifies a "theory" (a complete system of probability assessments) for each player at each of his information states. The revised definition specifies whether or not that player is rational at that information state, and specifies a theory for him only when he is rational. This enables us to formulate and prove general theorems, and to define the *degree* of irrationality (see section 6); its disadvantage is that it does not enable us to measure the expected *amount* of irrationality, as in sections 5 and 6.

8 Relations with "Crazy Perturbations"

In the "crazy perturbation" literature (e.g., Kreps et al. 1982; Kreps and Wilson 1982; Milgrom and Roberts 1982; Fudenberg and Maskin 1986; Aumann and Sorin 1989; Fudenberg and Levine 1989), one looks for Nash equilibria of a repeated game in which there is a small exogenous probability that a player plays irrationally but in such a way as to motivate the other player to play in some specific way—e.g., a mutually beneficial way. Most of the results say that, in one sense or another, the rational types tend to mimic those irrational types that are in some sense "best" for the player who does the mimicking. Intuitively, one might say that the rational types "disguise" themselves as irrational; they make believe they are crazy, thus "forcing" the other player to play accordingly (i.e., to maximize against the selected irrational type).

In general, this kind of theorem gives rather sharp results; it says that *all* Nash equilibria of the perturbed game have payoffs in a sharply defined class. They thus go in the opposite direction from many of the theorems on repeated games, in which results akin to the folk theorem lead to very diffuse sets of equilibrium payoffs.

Consider now a situation in which there is mutual knowledge of some given order that all players are rational, but not common knowledge; and that if the players are not rational, then they play some specified strategy, or a strategy in some specified set (such as bounded recall strategies, as in Aumann and Sorin 1989). Can theorems of the above type still be proved in this more general context? The model outlined in section 2 provides an appropriate general framework in which to investigate this question.

For the finitely repeated prisoner's dilemma, this question was treated by Kreps et al. (1982). Suppose that it is first-order mutual knowledge that the players are rational: each player is rational and knows that the other is, but does not know that the other knows that he is. In particular, he thinks that the other may think that, with some fixed small probability, he is a tit-for-tat (TFT) automaton. In this situation, it would appear that each player will still be motivated to pretend that he is TFT, since he doesn't know that the other knows that he isn't. Once he plays TFT, the other is motivated to go along, to the mutual benefit of both.

Now what happens when mutual knowledge of rationality is taken one step further—i.e., when not only does each player know that the other is rational, but each also knows that the other knows that he is? Then the reasoning appears to break down; each player might feel that there is no sense in pretending to be crazy, since he knows that the other knows that he is rational.

But further analysis indicates that the reasoning survives this step as well. A player playing TFT indeed knows that the other knows that he is pretending; but she (the other) needn't know this. He therefore figures that she may well go along, in order to make him think that she believes that he is indeed crazy, and so encourage him to continue with the mutually beneficial TFT. So he tries, and she indeed goes along, for precisely that reason.

Indeed, it appears that one can carry mutual knowledge of rationality to any finite level short of common knowledge, and still get the same effect: that the players will be motivated to play mutually beneficial but seemingly irrational strategies.

Most of us have experienced situations where some harmful fact is perfectly well known but is studiously overlooked by everybody. In this case, the harmful fact is the players' rationality (!). More precisely, the fact itself need not be harmful, but common knowledge of it would be. The above approach enables us to understand this phenomenon within the context of the theory.

This reasoning presupposes the kind of setting where the perturbation is mutually beneficial. In other settings where the "crazy perturbation" methodology has been applied, such as the chain-store paradox, we do not know whether the results extend.

Dedication

Lovingly dedicated to Frank Hahn, who has always had a penchant for the irrational.

Acknowledgments

Research partially supported by NSF grant IRI-8814953 at the Institute for Mathematical Studies in the Social Sciences, Stanford University. I am grateful to Adam Brandenburger for some important input, and, in particular, for pointing out a serious error in a previous version.

References

Aumann, R. J. 1987, "Correlated equilibrium as an expression of Bayesian rationality." *Econometrica* 55: 1–18.

Aumann, R. J., and S. Sorin. 1989. "Cooperation and bounded rationality." *Games and Economic Behavior* 1: 5–39.

Fudenberg, D., and D. Levine. 1989. "Reputation and equilibrium selection in games with a single patient player." *Econometrica* 57: 759–778.

Fudenberg, D., and E. Maskin. 1986. "The Folk Theorem in repeated games with discounting and with incomplete information." *Econometrica* 54: 533–554.

Harsanyi, J. C. 1967–68. "Games of incomplete information played by Bayesian players" (parts I, II, III). *Management Science* 14: 159–182, 320–334, 486–502.

Kreps, D., P. Milgrom, J. Roberts, and R. Wilson 1982. "Rational cooperation in the finitely repeated prisoner's dilemma." *Journal of Economic Theory* 27: 245–252.

Kreps, D., and R. Wilson. 1982. "Reputation and imperfect information." *Journal of Economic Theory* 27: 253–279.

Megiddo, N. 1986. Remarks on Bounded Rationality. IBM Research Report RJ 54310.

Milgrom, P., and J. Roberts. 1982. "Predation, reputation and entry deterrence." *Journal of Economic Theory* 27: 280–312.

Radner, R. 1968. "Competitive equilibrium under uncertainty." *Econometrica* 36: 31–58.

Radner. R. 1972. "Existence of equilibrium plans, prices, and price expectations in a sequence of markets." *Econometrica* 40: 289–303.

Radner, R. 1980. "Collusive Behavior in Non-Cooperative Epsilon-Equilibria in Oligopolies with Long but Finite Lives." *Journal of Economic Theory* 22, 136–154.

Radner, R. 1986. "Can bounded rationality resolve the prisoners' dilemma." In *Essays in Honor of Gerard Debreu*, ed. A. Mas-Colell and W Hildenbrand. North-Holland.

Rosenthal, R. 1982. "Games of perfect information, predatory pricing, and the chain store paradox." *Journal of Economic Theory* 25: 92–100.

Savage, L. J. 1954. *The Foundations of Statistics*. Wiley.

Rational Conjectural Equilibrium and Repeated Games

Hamid Sabourian

The aim of the literature on conjectural equilibrium has been to define a set of resting positions (equilibria) such that agents do not wish to move from any of the resting positions once they get there, given their model (conjecture) of the economy. This applies as much to the works of Hahn (1977, 1978) and Negishi (1961) on conjectural equilibrium in a general-equilibrium framework as to the literature on conjectural models in partial-equilibrium oligopolistic markets since the time of Bowley. Where do these conjectures come from? One possible answer would be that the conjectures are determined "historically" by variables which are usually taken as given in abstract theoretical models, and thus one cannot deduce them solely from the behavior of the rational agents. The other possibility is to develop a dynamic learning story of how conjectures are formed (see Hahn 1989 and Fudenberg and Kreps 1988). Given the difficulties involved, one has then opted for imposing some "rationality" conditions on the conjectures. The "rationality" conditions imposed vary in the literature, but all amount to imposing some stability condition on the conjectures with respect to an equilibrium.

The aim of this paper is to give a formal interpretation of conjectural models and in particular of the notions of "rationality" common in the literature. In conjectural (and reaction-function) equilibrium models, each agent, in calculating his optimal action, takes into account how his own action will affect those of his rivals and thus has a conjecture with respect to the responses of other players to his action. In these models time is not treated explicitly; however, it is clear that a conjectural model has no meaning in a static (one-shot) game, where players are asked to choose some actions simultaneously and there is no opportunity for reactions.[1] Therefore, it seems that a conjectural model has to have some dynamics behind it; it should be regarded as a static representation (short-cut) of some dynamic story. Clearly, one could tell the conjectural story "as if" it were a static one and make no distinction between dynamics and statics and leave it at that. This is common in the literature. I believe this leads to a lot of confusion (see Makowski 1987 for some objections to this "as if" methodology). At some stage one needs to treat time explicitly. Then the conjectural models appear very similar to repeated-game (RG) models. Despite the simlarity between conjectural and RG models, the two subjects have developed independently of each other, though there are a few exceptions. To what extent can solutions to conjectural models be regarded as solutions to RG models?

In this paper I try to reformulate the "rationality" concept found in the literature in a way that allows a consistent and appealing dynamic (time-explicit) interpretation to the conjectural models.[2] In fact, I show that the conjectural model can be understood in terms of a repeated-game story with adjustment cost and/or quick response, and that the "rationality" condition on conjectures, not surprisingly, amounts to the same thing as (subgame) prefectness in the RG setting. The paper can, in fact, be regarded as an extension of the work of Marschak and Selten (1978), who also try to relate their reaction model to repeated games.

In section 1 I develop a static game-theoretic framework in order to discuss the two different "rationality" concepts in the literature. In section 2 I try to give a formal time-explicit interpretation to the conjectural models. I argue that the most common "rationality" condition used in the literature has to be understood in terms of "correctness." Moreover, in subsection 2.1 I show that this definition amounts to (almost) the same thing as sequential rationality (a kind of subgame perfection) for games having the following properties:

- They are repeated infinitely often.
- Players are "myopic"; thus, in taking an action at each stage of the game, they are concerned with payoffs in the next period after the others have responded.
- The game is sequential, and once a player changes his action he has to stick with it for more than one period.

In subsection 2.2 I extend the "rationality" condition common in the literature so that it can deal with repeated grames in which "myopic" agents choose their actions simultaneously (with some adjustment cost). This extended notion of rationality amounts to the same thing as sequential rationality (or subgame perfection) for games satisfying the first two of the above conditions and simultaneous moves with adjustment cost.

Subsection 2.3, which contains the main result of the paper, shows that a slight extension of the notion of "rational" conjectural equilibrium is consistent with subgame perfection in repeated games in which (1) the agents are not myopic and have a long (infinite or finite) time horizon and (2) the agents incur a cost in changing their actions and/or respond instantaneously to each other's actions.

I conclude the paper by making a few remarks about the usefulness of the conjectural models in the light of the results and in the light of the recent literature on "bounded" rationality.

1

Consider the game

$$G = (A_i, \pi_i)_{i=1}^n,$$

where A_i and π_i are the set of actions and the payoff function of player i, respectively. Let

$$A = \prod_{i=1}^n A_i, \quad \pi = (\pi_1, \ldots, \pi_n),$$

and let N be the set of players. (Letters with subscripts i refer to actions, payoff, etc. of player i; letters with no subscript refer to vectors of actions, payoff, etc. of all players.) Thus, π_i maps A to $\mathbb{R}$. I define x_{-i} as any vector $x = (x_1, \ldots, x_n)$ without its ith element, and (x_i', x_{-i}) as any vector $x = (x_1, \ldots, x_n)$ with its ith element replaced by x_i'.

C_{ij} is the set of functions from $A \times A_i \to A_j$, with typical element $c_{ij} \in C_{ij}$, referred to as the set of *conjectural response functions*. Here, $c_{ij}(\boldsymbol{a}; a_i') \in A_j$ is to be interpreted as what i conjectures j to do in response to a deviation by i from the status quo a (and thus the action a_i) to a_i'.[3] Moreover, I define what i conjectures all other players to do in response to a deviation by i from a_i to a_i' as

$$c_{-i}(\boldsymbol{a}; a_i') = (c_{i1}(\boldsymbol{a}; a_i'), \ldots, c_{ii-1}(\boldsymbol{a}; a_i'), c_{ii+1}(\boldsymbol{a}; a_i'), \ldots, c_{in}(\boldsymbol{a}; a_i')).$$

Since I am ultimately interested in "rational" conjectures, I will assume, for notational simplicity, that all players have the same conjectures and interpret $c_{ij}(\boldsymbol{a}; a_i')$ as what all players, other than j, conjecture j to do in response to a change of action by i from a_i to a_i'.

Next I impose a condition on the conjectural functions which is common in the literature:

$$c_{ij}(\boldsymbol{a}; a_i') = a_j \quad \text{if } a_i' = a_i \ \forall\, i \text{ and } j \in N, i \neq j. \tag{1}$$

Condition (1) says that when a "deviation" by i involves no change of action on the part of i, then the response of j is also no change of action. Finally, define the set of conjectural response functions C_{ij} and their product space, satisfying condition (1), by C^*_{ij} and C^*, respectively (thus $C^* = \prod_{i,j} C^*_{ij}$).

DEFINITION 1 Given a vector of conjectural response functions $c \in C^*$ and any status quo $a \in A$, the set of best replies of player $i \in N$ is defined as

$$B_i(a;c) = \left\{ \bar{a}_i \in A_i | \bar{a}_i \in \arg\max_{a'_i \in A_i} \pi_i(a'_i, c_{-i}(\boldsymbol{a};a'_i)) \right\}. \tag{2}$$

Thus, if a is the status quo, $B_i(a;c)$ is the set of optimal actions for i, given the vector of conjectures c. Let $B(a,c) = \{B_i(a,c)\}^n_{i=1}$.

DEFINITION 2 Given a vector of conjectural response functions $c \in C^*$, the equilibrium set for i, $E_i(c)$, is defined as

$$E_i(c) = \{a \in A | a_i \in B_i(a;c)\}. \tag{3}$$

DEFINITION 3 A n-tuple of actions a^* is a conjectural equilibrium with respect to a vector of conjectures $c \in C^*$ if

$$a^* \in \bigcap_{i=1}^{n} E_i(c), \text{ i.e., } a^* \in B(a^*,c). \tag{4}$$

In other words, a^* is a conjectural equilibrium with respect to $c \in C^*$ if all players are content (i.e., are in their equilibrium set), given that each believes others to respond according to c.

The question that arises at this stage is: how is one to interpret the conjectural models? There are several points to note. As was mentioned above, conjectural stories make sense in dynamic context where agents can respond to each other's actions. Moreover, it is clear from the definitions of conjectural equilibrium that players, in deciding on an action, are concerned with payoffs after the other players have responded. The transitory profit players can gain before others have responded is not important to them in conjectural models. One reason for players' being concerned only with payoffs after others have responded (and not caring for transitory profit) may be that the others respond instantaneously. Another reason might be the existence of some adjustment cost, which may offset any transitory gain.

Finally, note that in the conjectural models defined so far the agents are "myopic" and are concerned with payoffs one period ahead. Later on I shall consider conjectural models where agents are not "myopic" and consider sequences of deviations.

In the above definition of a conjectural equilibrium, there are no conditions on the conjectures. As a result, there will be many equilibria, each associated with one set of conjectures. To reduce the multiplicity of equilibria as well as the "subjectivity" (and thus arbitrariness) of the conjectures, one would like the conjectures to be "rational" in the sense that the response functions an agent attributes to others are in fact the ones that the others would choose. The justification for such an approach (as in the literature on rational expectations) is that if the conjectures were not "rational" then the agents would revise their conjectures (i.e., "rationality" amounts to an equilibrium condition on the conjectures). I shall discuss the justification more fully in section 2. In the remaninder of this section I shall define and compare the two types of "rationality" which have been introduced in the literature.

The first definition of "rationality" was introduced by Hahn (1978) in a general-equilibrium framework. Hart (1982) also used it in a partial-equilibrium framework. To distinguish it from the next definition, I will use Hahn's and Hart's terminology and call it *reasonable conjecture.*

DEFINITION 4 A 2-tuple of actions and conjectures $(a^*, c) \in (A \times C^*)$ is a reasonable conjectural equilibrium (ReCE) if

(i) a^* is a conjectural equilibrium with respect to c

and

$$\text{(ii) } \forall i \text{ and } \forall\, a \in \bigcap_{\substack{j=1 \\ j \neq i}}^{n} E_j(c),\ \pi_i(a^*) \geq \pi_i(a). \tag{5}$$

Condition (ii), which is the "reasonableness" condition, says that for each player i there does not exist another n-tuple of actions at which all other players (except possibly i) are in equilibrium, and at the same time, i prefers it to the equilibrium a^*. To use Hahn's terminology, it amounts to saying that for each i there does not exist an i-feasible vector of actions at which i is better off than at a^*. The i-feasible set of actions is defined as

$$\bigcap_{\substack{j=1 \\ j \neq i}}^{n} E_j(c).$$

The problem with this notion of "rationality" is that it has very little story behind it, as Hahn (1978) himself pointed out. First, it does not consider the question of attainability: there may exist an n-tuple of actions which are i-feasible and preferable to a^* for a player i, but i cannot attain such a preferable n-tuple through changes in his own action. In such a case, where i, through changes in his own action, cannot bring about a preferable i-feasible state, it may still be "rational" for i to hold onto his conjectures even though condition (5) is violated. Second, reasonableness does not imply that the conjectures are "correct"—i.e., it does not imply that the conjectures of an agent about the response of others coincide with the optimal response of the others. Before turning to the second definition of "rational" conjectures, notice that the notion of "correct" conjectures is not necessarily well defined. The conjectures of any player i are said to be "correct" if they coincide with the optimal responses of other players. But the optimal response of some other player $j \neq i$ depends on j's conjectures. Thus, there is something vague about "correctness." To avoid this and thus the problem of infinite regress, "correctness" has to have a Nash-type behavior applied to conjectures; i.e., in order to asscess the "correctness" of i's conjectures one needs to take the conjectures of every $j \neq i$ as given (in which case the optimal responses of $j \neq i$ are well defined).

The second definition of "rationality" considered in the literature does try to deal with both the questions of attainability and "correctness" (in the above sense). I shall refer to it as "rational" conjectural equilibrium I (RCEI) and define it as follows:

DEFINITION 5 $2n$-tuple $(a^*,c) \in (A \times C^*)$ is a RCEI if

(a) a^* is a conjectural equilibrium with respect to c

and

$$\text{(b) } c_{ij}(\boldsymbol{a}^*,a_i') \in B_j\{(a_i', c_{-i}(\boldsymbol{a}^*;a_i'));c\}^4, \quad \text{i.e., } (a_i',c_{-i}(\boldsymbol{a}^*,a_i')) \in E_j(c)$$

$$\forall i, \forall a_i' \text{ and } \forall\, j \neq i. \quad (6)$$

Condition (b) says that what all players expect j to do in response to a deviation by i from a_i^* to a_i',

$c_{ij}(\boldsymbol{a}^*;a_i')$,

is an optimal response for j in the following sense: if j chooses some other section, j believes that he will be worse off after the others have responded than if he had chosen $c_{ij}(\boldsymbol{a}^*;a_i')$, given j's belief that the others will respond according to $c_{-j}(\ ;\ )$ and given that $(a_i',c_{-i}(\boldsymbol{a}^*;a_i'))$, what all players are expected to do after i's deviation, is the status quo. Thus, $c_{ij}(\boldsymbol{a}^*;a_i')$ satisfying (b) is a best response for j to a deviation by i and hence satisfies "rationality" if

Table 1

Time	i's action	j's action	Status quo
t	a_i'	a_j^*	a^*
$t+1$	a_i'	?	$(a_i', c_{-i}(a^*;a_i'))$
$t+2$			

(1) player j is concerned with his payoff after the others have responded (in the case of table 1, player j in deciding on optimal action at $t+1$ is concerned with payoff at $t+2$),

(2) player j's conjecture about the response of the others to his action is $c_{-j}(\ , \ )$,

(3) player j considers $(a_i', c_{-j}(\boldsymbol{a}^*, a_i'))$, what is expected of all the players after a deviation by i, as the new status quo.

Therefore, whether (b) in definition 5 (RCEI) is an appropriate notion of "rationality" (i.e., whether $c_{ij}(\boldsymbol{a}^*;a_i')$ is a best response for j after a deviation by i) depends crucially on (i) the time story one has in mind, (ii) the appropriateness of taking the beliefs of the responder, j, as given, and (iii) what one means by the term *status quo*. I shall now deal with each of these points in turn.

(i) If after a deviation by i other players can respond once and then the game ends, then obviously $c_{ij}(\boldsymbol{a}^*;a_i')$ satisfying (b) of definition 5 is not necessarily a best response for j. An appropriate "rationality" condition in this case would be

$$\pi_j(a_i', c_{-i}(a^*, a_i')) \geq \pi_j(a_i', a_j', c_{-i,j}(\boldsymbol{a}^*;a_i'))\ ^5$$

$$\forall i, \forall a_i' \in A_i, \forall j \neq i \text{ and } \forall a_j' \in A_j. \quad (7)$$

In (7) player j is not concerned with responses to his action, since the game ends at the moment of his decision making. Therefore, $c_{ij}(\cdot, \cdot)$ satisfying (b) of RCEI is a best response only if the responder, j, is also concerned with his payoff after the others have responded to his action. Thus, an appropriate way of looking at RCEI would be to regard the conjectural story as a repeated game that goes on forever (the static one-shot game being repeated infinitely often), with each player, in choosing an action at any time (say, t) being concerned with the next-period payoff at $t+1$, after the others have responded.[6]

(ii) As was mentioned above, in order to avoid the infinite-regress problem, any definition of "rationality" has to assume a Nash-type behavior with respect to the conjectures; i.e., in assessing the "rationality" of i's conjectural function (e.g. $c_{ij}(\cdot,\cdot)$) the conjectures of other players (in the case of j, it would be $c_{-j}(\cdot;\cdot)$) has to be taken as given.[7]

(iii) $c_{ij}(\boldsymbol{a}^*;a_i')$ satisfying (b) of definition 5 (RCEI) is an optimal response for j if one interprets the model in the ways discussed in (i) and (ii) and if $(a_1',c_{-i}(\boldsymbol{a}^*;a_i'))$, which is expected at that period, is the status quo. Thus, for (b) of RCEI to imply "correctness," I also need to interpret the status quo term as what all players are expected to do at that period. If, on the other hand, the status quo term at any time referred to the set of actions in the previous period (as many papers on the subject have implicitly assumed), then $c_{ij}(\boldsymbol{a}^*,a_i')$ satisfying (b) of RCEI would not necessarily be an optimal response for j. In the case of table 1, with the latter interpretation of the status quo, the status quo term at $t+1$ would be (a^*_{-i},a_i'), the actions at t, and not $(a_i',c_{-i}(\boldsymbol{a}^*;a_i'))$, which (b) of RCEI assumes. In an earlier version of this paper, I interpreted the status quo term in this latter way and referred to conjectures satisfying (b) of RCEI as being only "ex-post rational."[8] Makowski (1987) also interprets the status quo term as what players did in the previous period, and concludes that RCEI imposes a "deus ex machina" assumption on the conjectures and thus does not satisfy "correctness." But if one interprets the status quo term in the way I mentioned first—as what players are expected to do at that period—and regards the conjectural model in terms of a repeated game discussed in (i), RCEI does seem to satisfy "rationality" in the "correctness" sense. Later on, I shall give a more formal justification for the above interpretation of the "rational" conjectural equilibrium.

In comparing RCEI with ReCE, two points should be noted. First, RCEI implies that each player, say i, is no worse off at the conjectural equilibrium a^* than at any i-feasible set of actions that are *attainable* by i. Thus, in this sense RCEI is weaker than ReCE, since the latter requires player i to be no worse off at a^* than at *any* i-feasible set of actions. Second, RCEI requires "correctness" (i.e., what players conjecture others to do is in fact the optimal response of others), whereas ReCE does not necessarily imply "correctness." In this sense, ReCE is weaker than RCEI. Therefore, in general one could not say which of the two definitions is weaker. RECI seems to be more attractive simply because it tries to consider the question of attainability (and thus has a story behind it) and that of "correctness."[9]

Hart (1982), in the context of an oligopoly example, shows that there are a large number of ReCE. Sabourian (1983) demonstrates that an abstract game has in general a large number of RCEI. The reason for the multiplicity result is very similar to that of the Folk Theorem in RG, and it hinges on constructing (rational) conjectures that punish deviations from individually rational behavior.

Hahn (1978) and Hart (1982) use ReCE; however, all other rationality" concepts in the literature are variations of RCEI. Hart (1982, 1985) defines rationality in terms of a perceived-demand curve, precisely as in the case of RCEI.[10] Ulph (1982) applies RCEI locally. Marschak and Selten's (1974, 1978) definition is the same as RCEI except that they allow "rationality" to hold with respect to deviations not only from conjectural equilibrium a^* (as in (6)) but also from any n-tuple of action at which the player who deviates is in equilibrium. Laitner (1980) and Boyer and Moreaux (1983) apply Marschak and Selten's definition locally. Other writings on the subject, such as those of Hahn (1977), Bresnahan (1981), Perry (1982), and Kamien and Schwartz (1983), define "rationality" locally. Their condition for rationality amounts to equating conjectural variation with the derivative of the response function of the other players in an oligopoly context. It can be shown that this is the same as condition (b) of RCEI (and Makowski's (1987) "only slightly more rational, rational conjecture"), if conjectural functions are smooth and only local deviations are allowed.

2

As was mentioned in section 1, conjectural models are attempts at telling a dynamic story without necessarily treating time explicitly. Thus, in a way, they are short-cuts. But such short-cuts have to be justified. Therefore, in this section I try to develop a consistent dynamic story based on our "rational" conjectural models, with time treated explicitly. I shall do this by extending the notion of "rational" conjectural equilibrium most common in the literature, RCEI, in three ways. First, I shall require "rationality" of conjectures to hold with respect to deviation from every feasible status quo, not only from a conjectural equilibrium as in RCEI. Second, I shall change RCEI so that it can deal with simultaneous moves. I shall argue in subsection 2.2 that RCEI is more consistent with sequential games than with simultaneous-move ones. Third, I shall extend RCEI so that it can deal with the case where players are not myopic and are concerned with their long-run payoff.

2.1

The rationality condition must ultimately be interpreted as an equilibrium condition on the conjectures in a learning story. Putting it differently: a vector of conjectures is "rational" if, once adopted, the agents would not revise them as time unfolds. But the agents would not revise their conjectures if one of the following holds:

(i) A conjectural equilibrium set of actions is played all the time by all the players.

(ii) Each agent has "correctly" conjectured the response of the other players and thus has nothing more to learn.

(iii) Given the costs involved, it does not pay any agent to experiment and try consciously to learn anymore concerning the response of the other players.[11]

If (i) is the case, then learning is not possible and the question of "rationality" becomes meaningless. We want to go beyond this. On the other hand, it is difficult to interpret the "rationality" conditions *in the literature* in terms of experimenting, as in condition (iii). This is because all the conjectural models, including those in section 1, are deterministic and the question of conscious learning is rarely dealt with. If the players are at an equilibrium n-tuple of actions, a^*, they are doing as well as they believe they can. Why should they consider the possibility of testing their conjectures, if they already hold those conjectures with certainty? In a deterministic conjectural model, the most obvious interpretation of "rationality" seems to me to be in terms of "correctness." "Rationality" in this context amounts to saying that the agents would not revise their conjectures even if, accidentally or otherwise, they are not at an equilibrium state (since their conjectures had "correctly" anticipated the response of the other players). However, for this to be true the conjectures must be "correct" with respect to deviations from any status quo position and not only from a conjectural equilibrium. Requiring "rationality" with respect to a deviation from a (conjectural) equilibrium may make sense only if one interprets rationality in terms of conscious testing, but, as I argued above, it is difficult to do this in a deterministic model; moreover, if one requires "rationality" in a "correctness" sense, then it must hold at any status quo which the ongoing game might get to, accidentally or otherwise. Thus, my first reformulation of RCEI is to require "correctness" with respect to deviations from any status quo position.

DEFINITION 6 A $2n$-tuple (a^*,c) is RCEII if

(a) a^* is a conjectural equilibrium with respect to c

and

$$\text{(b) } c_{ij}(\boldsymbol{a},a_i') \in B_j\{a_j',c_{-i}(\boldsymbol{a};a_i');c\} \quad \text{i.e., } (a_i',c_{-i}(\boldsymbol{a};a_i')) \in E_j(c)$$

$$\forall i \text{ and } j, i \neq j, \forall\, a_i' \in A_i \text{ and } \forall\, a \in A. \quad (8)$$

Given the multiplicty of RCEI, the above reformulation may reduce the number of equilibria as it makes the conditions stricter. Furthermore, by requiring the conjectures to be "correct" with respect to deviations from any status quo position, one can overcome some of the objections to "rational" conjectural models, such as those of Laitner (1980) and Makowski (1987). Laitner argues that although "rationality" (in the sense of RCEI) requires the conjecture of any agent i about the response of any other agent j to a deviation by i from an equilibrium position a^* to coincide with the optimal response of j, given j's conjectures, j's conjecture is not necessarily "rational" at the new status quo (after i deviates). Thus, he argues that "rational" conjectural equilibria are "rational" only at one level, and that second-order conjectures are not necessarily correct. Makowski makes a similar criticism. Clearly, the above objection is not applicable if one reformulates the definition so that conjectures are "correct" at all status quo positions. In the reformulated definition, RCEII, conjectures are "correct" at every status quo, and thus second-order conjectures are also "correct."

In addition, requiring conjectures to be "correct" with respect to deviations from any status quo position can violate condition (1), which is commonly assumed in the literature. Condition (1) says that each player conjectures that if he does not deviate from any status quo there will not be any change of actions from the status quo on the part of the other players, and the same status quo will be repeated. If one requires the conjectures to satisfy (1), then they are not "correct" (do not satisfy (8)) at any status quo that is not a conjectural equilibrium. This is because, if the status quo is not a conjectural equilibrium position, some players may want to change their actions even though no one has deviated from the status quo. Condition (1) is consistent with RCEII ("correctness" everywhere) only at status quo positions which are conjectural equilibrium. Therefore, to make the definition consistent I shall replace (1) by

$$c_j(\boldsymbol{a};a_i) = a_j \quad \text{for any } a \in \bigcap_{j=1}^{n} E_j(c). \qquad (1')$$

Condition (1′) is obviously weaker than (1) and is consistent with RCEII. Henceforth, I shall look at the space of conjectures satisfying (1′) and denote it by C.

In section 1, I discussed informally the different interpretation one could give to the conjectural models. I mentioned that an appropriate interpretation might be to regard the conjectural stories as an infinite RG in which agents are "myopic" and in which at any time when an agent makes a decision he is concerned with his payoff in the next period, after the others have responded. It is easy to show that the conjectural model satisfying RCEII can be regarded as a solution to the above game if the number of players is limited to 2 and if it is assumed that player 1 can change his action at odd periods and player 2 at even periods (i.e., the game is sequential).

Consider the game $G = (A_i,\pi_i)_{i=1,2}$ being repeated infinitely often. For each date $t = 1, 2, \ldots$, consider the set of possible histories H^t, where $H^1 = \varnothing$ (the empty set) and $H^t = A^{t-1}$, $\forall\, t \geq 2$ (A^{t-1} is the $(t-1)$-fold cartesian product of A). Each element of H^t is simply a sequence of all the actions that have been played in the stage games up to t. A strategy of a myopic player (say i) at each date t is a map s_i^t: $H^t \to A_i$. Thus, s_i^t dictates the choice of i at the tth stage of the repeated game as a function of the choices made by all the players in the preceding $t-1$ stages of the repeated game. Since the game is sequential, $(s_i^t)_{t=1}^{\infty}$ have the property that, $\forall\, t \geq 2$ and $\forall\, h^t = (a^1,\ldots,a^{t-1}) \in H^t$,

$$s_1^t(h^t) = a_1^{t-1} \quad \text{if } t \text{ is even,}$$

$$s_2^t(h^t) = a_2^{t-1} \quad \text{if } t \text{ is odd.}$$

Since I assume that agents are "myopic" and choose actions to maximize their payoffs in the next period after the others have responded, an equilibrium of such a game that satisfies sequential rationality is defined as a sequence of functions

$$(s^t(h^t))_{t=1}^{\infty} = (s_1^t(h^t), s_2(h^t))_{t=1}^{\infty}$$

such that for

$t = 1$,

$$s_1^t(\varnothing) \in \underset{a_1 \in A_1}{\arg\max}\ \pi(a_1, s_2^2(a_1)),$$

$\forall\, t \geq 2$,

and

$\forall\, h^t = (a^1, \ldots, a^{t-1})$

we have

$$s_j^t(h^t) \in \arg\max_{a_j \in A_j} \pi_j(a_j, s_i^{t+1}(h^t, a_j, s_i^t(h^t)))$$
$$= \arg\max_{a_j \in A_j} \pi_j(a_j, s_i^{t+1}(h^t, a_j, a_i^{t-1})) \tag{9}$$

if j is the player who can change his action at t. (Note that the second equality in (9) follows because at t player i canot change his action.)

One can think of the above definition as a sort of subgame-perfect equilibria (SPE). The above equilibrium concept requires the strategies of each myopic agent (agents who are concerned with the next-period payoff) to be optimal after each history, given the strategies of others. This is exactly the same as the standard definition of SPE, except that in the standard definition agents are not myopic and are fully rational. However, with some abuse of the definition I shall refer to the above equilibrium as "SPE of myopic repeated game."

PROPOSITION 1 If (a^*, c) is RCEII, then the strategy $s^t(h^t)$ defined recursively by $s_j^1(\varnothing) = a_j^*$,[12] and $\forall\, t \geq 2$ and $\forall\, h^t = \{a^1, \ldots, a^{t-1}\}$

$$s_j^t(h^t) = \begin{cases} c_{ij}(\boldsymbol{s^{t-1}(h^{t-1})}; a_i^{t-1}) & \text{if } j \text{ can change his action at } t \\ a_j^{t-1} & \text{if } j \text{ cannot change his action at } t \end{cases} \tag{10}$$

is a subgame-perfect equilibrium of the above myopic game.

Note that the above strategy, $s^t(\cdot)$, says that when a player (say j) can move, he does what $i \neq j$ expects him to do (in the conjectural model) as a funtion of what both were expected to do at the previous period (this is the status quo term) and what i actually did in the previous period.

Proof The proof follows immediately from the definitions of RCEII and $s(h^t)$. There are two cases to consider.

(i) $t = 1$ and $h^1 = \varnothing$. It follows from the definition of RCEII that

$$a_1^* \in \arg\max_{a_1 \in A_1} \pi_1(a_1, c_{12}(\boldsymbol{a^*}; a_1)).$$

Since $s^1(\varnothing) = a^*$ and $s_2^2(a_1) = c_{12}(\boldsymbol{s(\varnothing)}, a_1) = c_{12}(\boldsymbol{a^*}, a_1)$,

$$s_1^1(\varnothing) \in \arg\max_{a_1 \in A_1} \pi_1(a_1, s_2^2(a_1)).$$

(ii) $\forall\ t \geq 2$ and $\forall\ h^t = (a_1^1, \ldots, a^{t-1})$. Without any loss of generality, assume that j is the player who can change his action at t. Since (a^*,c) is RCEII (and thus satisfies (8)),

$$c_{ij}(\boldsymbol{s}^{t-1}(\boldsymbol{h}^{t-1});a_i^{t-1}) \in \arg\max_{a_j \in A_j} \pi_j(a_j, c_{ji}(\boldsymbol{c_{ij}}(\boldsymbol{s}^{t-1}(\boldsymbol{h}^{t-1}); \boldsymbol{a_i^{t-1}}), \boldsymbol{a_i^{t-1}}; a_j)). \quad (11)$$

But $a_i^{t-1} = s_i^t(h^t)$, $c_{ij}(\boldsymbol{s}^{t-1}(\boldsymbol{h}^{t-1});a_i^{t-1}) = s_j^t(h^t)$, and $c_{ji}(s^t(h^t);a_j) = s_i^{t+1}(h^t,a_j,a_i^{t-1})$. Substituting the last three equations in (11), one obtains

$$s_j^t(h^t) \in \arg\max_{a_j \in A_j} \pi_j(a_j,s_i^{t+1}(h^t,a_j,a_i^{t-1})).$$ Q.E.D.

2.2

So far I have shown that RCEII and RCEI can be consistent with a "myopic" sequential repeated game. I shall now try to argue that if players are allowed to move simultaneously, RCEII or RCEI is not necessarily an appropriate definition of "rationality" and RCEII must be extended to deal with simultaneous-move games.

For simplicity, consider a 2-player (i and j) game. The "rationality" condition in RCEII amounts to

$$(c_{ij}(\boldsymbol{a};a_i'),a_i') \in B_j\{(a_i',c_{ij}(\boldsymbol{a};a_i'));c\} \quad \forall\ a_i' \in A_i, i \neq j, \forall\ a \in A. \quad (12)$$

Condition (12) says that if j does what i conjectures him to do and i stays at a_i', and thus the new status quo becomes $(c_{ij}(\boldsymbol{a};a_i'),a_i')$, then j cannot make himself better off, given his conjecture. If the players can move simultaneously, there is something strange about the new status quo $(a_i',c_{ij}(\boldsymbol{a};a_i'))$ after i's deviation. It implies that after player i moves to a_i', player j expects i to stay put at a_i'. But why, if players can move simultaneously, should i be expected to stay put at a_i'? (Such an assumption is specially untenable if one has "correctness" interpretation of rationality.)

Table 2 illustrates the point further. At time $t = 1$, the status quo is a. At $t = 1$, player i deviates to a_i' and player j carries on with the status quo a_j. The "rationality" condition in RCEII (or RCEI) says that at $t = 2$, player j is conjectured to choose $c_{ij}(\boldsymbol{a};a_i')$ and player i is conjectured to stay at a_i', but if the game is simultaneous and at $t = 2$ both players can move, then it might be irrational (not "correct") of j to assume that i will stay at a_i'. If $c_{ii}(\boldsymbol{a};a_i')$ stands for what i is expected to do after he has just deviated from a_i to a_i' ($c_{ii}(\boldsymbol{a};a_i')$ may or may not coincide with a_i'), then, in a simultaneous game, the status quo after a deviation by i (what is expected of players after

Table 2

Time	i's move	j's move	Status quo
$t = 1$	a_i'	a_j	a
$t = 2$	a_i'	$c_{ij}(\boldsymbol{a},a_i')$	$(a_i',c_{ij}(\boldsymbol{a},a_i'))$

the deviation) should be $c(\boldsymbol{a};a_i') = \{c_{ij}(\boldsymbol{a};a_i')\}_{\forall j}$.[13] Moreover, "rationality" requires $c_{ij}(\boldsymbol{a};a_1')$ to coincide with the optimal response of j (when $c(\boldsymbol{a};a_i')$ is the status quo) for all i and j, including $j = i$. Thus, the new definition of "rational" conjectural equilibrium for a n-player simultaneous game should be as follows.

DEFINITION 7 A $2n$-tuple (a^*,c) satisfies RCEIII if
(a) a^* is a conjectural equilibrium with respect to c
and

$$\text{(b) } c_{ij}(\boldsymbol{a};a_i') \in B_j(c(\boldsymbol{a};a_i');c), \quad \text{i.e., } c(\boldsymbol{a};a_1') \in E_j(c)$$

$$\forall i \text{ and } j, \forall\ a_i' \in A_i \text{ and } \forall\ a \in A. \quad (13)$$

Note that the "rationality" condition in RCEIII implies that all players are expected to end up at a conjectural equilibrium after any deviation from any status quo.

Now consider the "myopic" repeated game described above. Assume that all players can change their actions at every period (simultaneous game) and they incur an adjustment cost every time they change their actions which offsets any transitory gain. (See condition (23) below and the discussion that follows for the precise nature of the adjustment cost.) Using similar reasoning, Sabourian (1983) shows that RCEIII can be regarded as a (subgame perfect equilibrium) solution to the above "myopic" simultaneous repeated game.

2.3

The aim of this subsection is to give a time-explicit justification for the notions of conjectural equilibrium and "rational" conjectural equilibrium in terms of a supergame model, with adjustment cost, where each player has an infinite or a finite but long time horizon. I shall first define a dynamic conjectural model where agents consider sequences of moves. I shall do this for our simultaneous conjectural model (RCEIII). The same thing could be done for the sequential conjectural model (RCEII and I). I shall show that the condition for dynamic "rational" conjectural equilibrium (dynamic RCE) is very simple (a slight extension of RCEIII). Finally, I shall show that our definition of dynamic "ratinal" conjectural equilibrium can be regarded as a (subgame perfect) solution to supergames where agents are not myopic (and have a long time horizon) and incurs some adjustment costs when they change their actions.[14]

In a dynamic conjectural model, players consider a sequence of deviations. Thus, in calculating his optimal behavior, a player takes into account the response of other players to a sequence of deviations, and his conjectured payoff depends on the final n-tuple of actions that his deviations is conjectured to bring about. More formally, for any player $i \in N$, let $\{a_i^1, \ldots, a_i^k\}$ be a sequence of k deviations by a player i from a status quo a. The process is that i announces a_i^1 and conjectures that the others respond with $c_{-i}(\boldsymbol{a};a_i^1)$. Next, i announces a_i^2 and conjectures others to respond with $c_{-i}(\boldsymbol{c}(\boldsymbol{a};\boldsymbol{a}_1^1);a_i^2)$. This continues up to the last deviation, a_i^k. The final conjectured position for others, after responding to a_i^k, would be $\hat{c}_{-i}(a,\{a_i^1, \ldots, a_i^k\})$, where $\hat{c}_{-i}$ is the extended conjectural response function defined recursively as

$$\hat{c}_{ij}(a;\{a_i^1\}) = c_{ij}(\boldsymbol{a};a_i^1), \tag{14}$$

$$\hat{c}_{ij}(a;\{a_i^1, \ldots, a_i^k\}) = c_{ij}(\hat{\boldsymbol{c}}(\boldsymbol{a},\{\boldsymbol{a}_i^1, \ldots, \boldsymbol{a}_i^{k-1}\});a_i^k) \quad \forall\, k \geq 2$$

where

$$\hat{c}(a,\{a_i^1, \ldots, a_i^{k-1}\}) = \{\hat{c}_{ij}(a,\{a_i^1, \ldots, a_i^{k-1}\})\}_{j=1}^n.$$ [15]

Now all the previous definitions of equilibrium and "rationality" can be redefined to take into account the possibility of sequences of deviations. Thus, the payoff that i perceives himself to receive after a sequence of deviations $\{a_i^1, \ldots, a_i^k\}$ depends on the final position, after others have responded to all the deviations; it is equal to

$$\pi_i(a_i^k, \hat{c}_{-i}(a,\{a_i^1, \ldots, a_i^k\})).$$

Thus, the equilibrium set for player i, when every player is concerned with payoffs after k deviations, can be defined as

$$E_i^k(c) = \{a \in A \,|\, \pi_i(a) \geq \pi_i(a_i^k, \hat{c}_{-i}(a;\{a_i^1, \ldots, a_i^k\})),$$

$$\text{for any finite sequence } \{a_i^1, \ldots, a_i^k\} \in (A_i)^k\}. \tag{15}$$

The conjectural equilibrium (definition 3) can be redefined as follows:

DEFINITION 8 An n-tuple a^* is a k-period conjectural equilibrium with respect to c if $a^* \in \bigcap_{i=1}^n E_i^k(c)$.

Thus, if a^* satisfies definition 8, no player can, through a sequence of k deviations, make himself better off, given his conjectures with respect to the response of other players.

DEFINITION 9 An n-tuple a^* is a dynamic conjectural equilibrium if a^* is a k-period conjectural equilibrium for all integers k.

"Rational" conjectural equilibria (RCEIII) can be redefined in a similar way:

DEFINITION 10 A 2-tuple (a^*,c) is a k-period RCE if

$$\text{(i)} \quad a^* \in \bigcap_{i=1}^{n} E_i^k(c) \tag{16}$$

and

$$\text{(ii)} \quad c(\boldsymbol{a};a_i') \in \bigcap_{i=1}^{n} E_i^k(c) \quad \forall i, \forall\, a_i' \in A_i \text{ and } \forall\, a \in A. \tag{17}$$

Condition (17) says that what players are expected to do after a deviation by (say) player i from any status quo coincides with their optimal responses when they are interested in payoffs after k deviations. Clearly one-period RCE is the same as RCEIII.

DEFINITION 11 A $2n$-tuple (a^*,c) is a dynamic RCE if (a^*,c) is a k-period RCE for all integers k.

Consider any one- and two-period RCE (a,c). It follows from the definition of one- and two-period RCE that

$$\pi_i(a) \geq \pi_i(a_i^2, \hat{c}_{-i}(a,\{a_i^1,a_i^2\})) \quad \text{for any } \{a_i^1,a_i^2\} \tag{18}$$

and

$$c(\boldsymbol{a},a_i^1) \in E_i^\ell(c) \quad \text{for any } a_i^1 \text{ and for any } \ell = 1,2. \tag{19}$$

In particular, (18) holds for the sequence $\{a_i^1, c_{ii}(\boldsymbol{a};a_i^1)\}$. Thus, for any two-period conjectural equilibrium (a,c)

$$\begin{aligned}\pi_i(a) &\geq \pi_i(c_{ii}(\boldsymbol{a};a_i^1), c_{-i}(\boldsymbol{c}(\boldsymbol{a};\boldsymbol{a}_i^1), c_{ii}(\boldsymbol{a};a_i^1)) \\ &= \pi_i(c(a;a_i^1)) \quad \forall\, a_i^1 \in A_i.\end{aligned} \tag{20}$$

(The last equality follows from (19) and (1′).) Thus, if agents are not "myopic" and have a time horizon beyond one period, "rationality" in conjectural models seems to imply that for any one-period conjectural equilibrium $a \in A$,

$$\pi_i(a) \geq \pi_i(c(\boldsymbol{a};a_i')), \quad \forall i, \forall a_i'. \tag{21}$$

The above condition says that no player believes he can make himself better off by deviating from a conjectural equilibrium and then choosing what everyone expects him to do. It turns out that the one-period RCE (RCEIII) plus condition (21) is equivalent to the dynamic conjectural equilibrium.

PROPOSITION 2 A $2n$-tuple (a^*,c) is a dynamic conjectural equilibrium iff (a^*,c) is a one-period RCE (RCEIII) and c satisfies (21) for any a that is a (one-period) conjectural equilibrium.

Proof *Necessity:* I have already shown that two-period RCE implies (21), and by definition 11 a dynamic RCE is always a k-period RCE, $\forall$ integers k. Therefore, a dynamic RCE is always a one-period RCE and satisfies (21) for any (one-period) conjectural equilibrium. *Sufficiency:* Suppose (a^*,c) is a one-period RCE and satisfies (21). First it must be shown that if $a \in \bigcap_{j=1}^n E_j(c)$ then $a \in \bigcap_{j=1}^n E_j^k(c)$ for any integer k. To show this, consider any $a \in \bigcap_{j=1}^n E_j(c)$ and any sequence of actions $\{a_i^1,\ldots,a_i^k\}$ by any player i. Condition (21) implies that

$$\pi_i(a) \geq \pi_i(c(\boldsymbol{a};a_i^1)). \tag{22}$$

Since c is "rational," $c(\boldsymbol{a};a_i^1) \in \bigcap_{j=1}^n E_j(c)$. It follows from (21) that

$$\pi_i(c(\boldsymbol{a};a_i^1)) \geq \pi_i(c(\boldsymbol{c(a;a_i^1)};a_i^2)). \tag{23}$$

Conditions (22) and (23) imply

$$\pi_i(a) \geq \pi_i(a_i^2,\hat{c}_{-i}(a,\{a_i^1,a_i^2\})).$$

It follows inductively that

$$\pi_i(a) \geq \pi_i(\hat{c}(a,\{a_i^1,\ldots,a_i^{k-1}\})). \tag{24}$$

Moreover,

$$\hat{c}(a,\{a_i^1,\ldots,a_i^{k-1}\}) = c(\boldsymbol{\hat{c}(a,\{a_i^1,\ldots,a_i^{k-2}\})};a_i^{k-1}).$$

Thus, it follows from "rationality" of one-period RCE, (13), that

$$\hat{c}(a,\{a_i^1,\ldots,a_i^{k-1}\}) \in \bigcap_{j=1}^{n} E_j(c).$$

Therefore,

$$\text{RHS of (24)} \geq \pi_i(a_i^k, c_{-i}(\hat{\boldsymbol{c}}(\boldsymbol{a},\{\boldsymbol{a}_i^1,\ldots,\boldsymbol{a}_i^{k-1}\}); a_i^k). \tag{25}$$

Conditions (24) and (25) imply that if $a \in \bigcap_{j=1}^{n} E_j(c)$, then

$$a \in \bigcap_{j=1}^{n} E_j^k(c) \quad \text{for all integers } k. \tag{26}$$

Since $a^* \in \bigcap_{j=1}^{n} E_j(c)$ and $c(\boldsymbol{a};c_i^1) \in \bigcap_{j=1}^{n} E_j(c)$, condition (26) implies that $a^* \in \bigcap_{j=1}^{n} E_j^k(c)$ and $c(\boldsymbol{a};a_i^1) \in \bigcap_{j=1}^{n} E_j^k(c)$ for all integers k, $\forall i$ and $\forall\ a_i \in A_i$.

Q.E.D.

The above proposition implies that I can define a dynamic RCE as a 2-tuple (a^*,c) that satisfies

$$\text{(a)} \quad a^* \in \bigcap_{j=1}^{n} E_j(c), \tag{4}$$

$$\text{(b)} \quad c(\boldsymbol{a};a_i') \in \bigcap_{j=1}^{n} E_j(c) \quad \forall i, \forall a_i' \text{ and } \forall\ a \in A, \tag{13}$$

and

$$\text{(c)} \quad \pi_i(a) \geq \pi_i(c(\boldsymbol{a};a_i')) \quad \forall i, \forall a_1' \text{ and } \forall\ a \in \bigcap_{j=1}^{n} E_j(c). \tag{21}$$

Conditions (a) and (b) are just the one-period RCE (RCEIII). Condition (c) (which is desirable for a two-or-more-priod RCE) seems a plausible equilibrium condition, since it means that no agent should be able to increase his payoff by going from one conjectural equilibrium to another attainable one. Condition (c) has a flavor similar to that of the "reasonableness" condition (8), except that the former compares the payoff between equilibria that are attainable through agents' actions whereas the "reasonableness" condition does not consider the question of attainability (see section 1).

In the definition of dynamic RCE it was argued that equations (4), (13), and (21) are simple conditions that will be satisfied if players are concerned with payoffs one or possibly two periods ahead. Now I shall show that the above three conditions are in fact sufficient to determine a solution to supergame models where each agent's time horizon is long. (I have already shown in proposition 2 that the above three equations are appropriate equilibrium and "rationality" conditions for conjectural models where agents can contemplate a sequence of deviations.) To show this, I shall now return to the repeated-game model.

Let $G = (A_i, \pi_i)_{i=1}^n$ be the stage game of the RG (supergame). Consider the case where the stage game is repeated an infinite number of times. As before, let H^t be the set of possible histories of actions up to period t. An RG (pure)[16] strategy f_i for any player $i \in N$ is a sequence of maps $f_i = \{s_i^t(\cdot)\}_{t=1}^{\infty}$, where s_i^t maps H^t to A_i. Thus, s_i^t dictates the choice of i at the tth stage of the supergame, as a function of the choices made by all the players in the preceding $(t-1)$ stage of the repeated game. The set of supergame strategies of i will be denoted by F_i. Let $F = \times_{i=1}^n F_i$.

Given $f \in F$, the outcome at t will be denoted by $\sigma^t(f)$ and is defined inductively by

$$\sigma^1(f) = (s_1^1(\varnothing), \ldots, s_n^1(\varnothing))$$

and

$$\sigma^t(f) = (s_1^t(h^t), \ldots, s_n^t(h^t)),$$

where $h^t = (\sigma^1(f), \ldots, \sigma^{t-1}(f))$. Moreover, I shall denote the sequence $\{\sigma^t(f)\}_{t=1}^{\infty}$ by $\sigma(f)$.

It remains to define the RG payoffs. I shall first consider the case where each player is interested in the long-run average payoff. Thus, the RG payoff function of player $i \in N$ if the sequence of actions $h = (a^1, a^2, \ldots)$ occurs would be

$$\pi_i^{\infty}(h) = \lim_{T \to \infty} \inf \frac{1}{T} \sum_{t=1}^{T} \pi_i(a^t).$$

I now define an inertia supergame as a repeated game in which there is some cost in changing one's action between different periods.[17] More formally, the payoff of player i in an inertia supergame, if a sequence of actions $h = (a^1, a^2, \ldots)$ occurs, is defined as

$$\pi_i^{\infty}(h) = \lim_{T \to \infty} \inf \frac{1}{T} \sum_{t=1}^{T} \{\pi_i(a^t) - M(a_i^t, a_i^{t-1})\},$$

where

$$M(a_i^t, a_i^{t-1}) = 0 \quad \text{if } a_i^t = a_i^{t-1}$$

$$M(a_i^t, a_i^{t-1}) > 0 \quad \text{if } a_i^t \neq a_i^{t-1}.$$

$M(\cdot,\cdot)$ is the cost of changing one's action. I shall assume that M is bounded and

$$\max_{a \in A} \{\pi_i(a_{-i},a_i') - \pi_i(a)\} < M(a_i',a_i) \quad \text{for any } a_i' \in A_i \text{ and } \forall\, i \in N. \tag{27}$$

Condition (23) implies that a player's net gain from changing his action can never be a transitory (one-period) gain; a change can be beneficial to him only as a result of the payoff collected, after he had maintained the new action for at least two periods.

If one is to relate conjectural models to a RG model, the usual RG model with discrete time and without inertia will not do. This is because in conjectural models it is the situation after the responses of all players have been completed that matters to a player. Any transistory profit that the player might earn before the responses are complete does not enter into a player's payoff function and thus does not influence his decision.

As was mentioned above, the neglect of transistory profit can be justified on two grounds: either that firms conjecture instantaneous responses to any change of actions, so that transistory profit cannot occur, and/or that there is a cost[18] involved in changing one's action and that the cost outweighs any transistory profit (like that in (27)). Thus, it seems that in order to put the conjectural model in a time-explicit model (a repeated game) I need either to regard time as a continuous variable or to look at a repeated game with discrete time but with adjustment cost satisfying (23). The latter is what I shall consider first. Such an adjustment cost can be justified particularly if the periods are short. In fact, a repeated game with continuous time variable can be regarded as the limit of the discrete case with adjustment cost as each period becomes smaller. (I shall come back to this.)

The first result is to put our (dynamic) conjectural equilibrium in a time-explicit framework (in an inertia supergame). More precisely, I shall show that any dynamic conjectural equilibrium can define a Nash-equilibrium strategy for the inertia supergame.

For any vector of actions and conjectures (a^*,c) define the vector of RG strategies generated by it, $f = \{s^t(\cdot)\}_{t=1}^{\infty}$, as follows: $\forall\, i \in N$ and for any history $h^t = (a^1,\ldots,a^{t-1}) \in H^t$, $s_i^t(\cdot)$ is defined recursively[19] as

$$s_i(h^t) = \begin{cases} c_{ji}(\boldsymbol{s}(\boldsymbol{h}^{t-1}),a_j^{t-1}) & \text{if } t \geq 2 \text{ and } a_{-j}^{t-1} = s_{-j}(h^{t-1}) \\ a_i^* & \text{otherwise.} \end{cases} \tag{28}$$

THEOREM 3 If a^* is a dynamic conjectural equilibrium (satisfies definition 8) with respect to a vector of conjectures c, then the RG strategy $f =$

$\{s^t(\cdot)\}$, generated by (a^*,c), defined in (28), is a Nash-equilibrium strategy in an inertia supergame.

Note that f_i is defined as choosing, at each stage $t \geq 2$, what others conjectured i to do $(c_{ji}(\cdot;\cdot))$ when every player $k \in N\backslash j$ followed f_k at the previous stage, and choosing a conjectural equilibrium action a_i^* otherwise.

Proof of Theorem 3 I need to show that for any i and $\forall \tilde{f}_i \in F_i$,

$$\pi_i^\infty(\sigma(f)) \geq \pi_i^\infty(\sigma(\tilde{f}_i, f_{-i})).$$

To show this, I denote the sequence of actions for i resulting from strategies $\tilde{f}_i$ and f_{-i} by $\{\tilde{a}_i^1, \tilde{a}_i^2, \ldots\}$. Now consider any stage $t \geq 2$. At such a stage, $\sigma^t(f) = a^*$. On the other hand, if i chooses $\tilde{f}_i$ and others choose f_{-i}, then the n-tuple of action at $t \geq 2$ will be

$$\sigma^t(\tilde{f}_i, f_{-i}) = (\tilde{a}_i^t, \hat{c}_{-i}(a^*; \{\tilde{a}_i^1, \ldots, \tilde{a}_i^{t-1}\})), \tag{29}$$

where $\hat{c}_{-i}(\cdot;\{\cdot,\ldots\})$ is the extended conjectural function defined in (14). Since a^* is a dynamic conjectural equilibrium, it follows that

$$\pi_i(a^*) \geq \pi_i(a^k, \hat{c}_{-i}(a^*; \{a^1, \ldots, a_i^k\}))$$

for any sequence of deviations $\{a_i^1, \ldots, a_i^k\} \in A_i^k$. Thus, by (25) the net payoff to i at any $t \geq 2$, if $(\tilde{f}_i, f_{-i})$ is followed, will be

$$\begin{aligned}\pi_i(\tilde{a}_i^t, \hat{c}_{-i}(a^*; \{\tilde{a}_i^1, \ldots, \tilde{a}_i^{t-1}\})) - M(\tilde{a}_i^t, \tilde{a}_i^{t-1}) &\leq \pi_i(\tilde{a}_i^{t-1}, \hat{c}_{-i}(a^*; \{\tilde{a}_i^1, \ldots, \tilde{a}_i^{t-1}\}))\\ &\leq \pi_i(a^*).\end{aligned}$$

(The first inequality here follows from (27) and the second from $a^* \in \bigcap_{j=1} E^k(c), \forall k$.) Therefore, the net payoff to i, at any stage $t \geq 2$, if the supergame strategy f_i is chosen, is greater than that of any other strategy for i, given that others chose f_{-i}. As for period $t = 1$, it is possible that player i, by choosing $\tilde{a}_i^1$, increases his payoff at $t = 1$ above what he would have obtained by following f_i and choosing a_i^*. But any one-period gain from doing so plays no role in i's long-run average payoff. Thus,

$$\forall \tilde{f}_i \in F_i, \quad \pi_i^\infty(\sigma(f)) \geq \pi_i^\infty(\sigma(\tilde{f}_i, f_{-i})).$$ Q.E.D.

One would like the supergame strategies defined in the above theorem to be in equilibrium for every subgame, for the usual reason. The dynamic RCE guarantees precisely such subgame perfectness. Before stating the subgame-perfect equilibrium (SPE) result, define the strategy induced by any $f_i = \{s_i^t(\cdot)\}_{t=1}^{\infty}$ after any history $h^t = \{a^1, a^2, \ldots, a^{t-1}\}$ as $f_i|h^t$. Thus, $f_i|h^t$ is a sequence of mapping $\{\bar{s}_i^\tau(\cdot)\}_{\tau=1}^{\infty}$ such that $\bar{s}_i^\tau(\bar{h}^\tau) = s_i^{t+\tau}(h^t,\bar{h}^\tau)$ for any history h^τ.

DEFINITION 13 An n-tuple of supergame strategies $f \in F$ is SPE if $\forall i$

$$\pi_i^\infty(\sigma(f|h^t)) \geq \pi_i^\infty(\sigma(\tilde{f}_i, f_{-i}|h^t)) \quad \forall \tilde{f}_i \in F_i, \forall\, h^t \in H^t.$$

THEOREM 4 If $(a^*,c) \in (A \times C)$ is a dynamic RCE (definition 11; i.e., (4), (13), (21)), then the RG strategy $f \in F$ generated from (a^*,c), defined recursively by (28), is an SPE, with a^* as a stationary solution.

Proof I need to show that $\forall\, i \in N$, $\forall$ integers $\tau \geq 1$, and for any history of actions $h^{\tau+1} = \{a^1, a^2, \ldots, a^\tau\}$,

$$\pi_i^\infty(\sigma(f|h^{\tau+1})) \geq \pi_i^\infty(\sigma(\tilde{f}_i, f_{-i}|h^{\tau+1})), \quad \forall f_i \in F_i.$$ [20]

To show this, let me denote the sequence of actions for i resulting from strategies $(\tilde{f}_i, f_{-i})$ after $h^{\tau+1}$ by $\{\tilde{a}_i^{\tau+1}, \tilde{a}_i^{\tau+2}, \ldots\}$. Consider any stage $t \geq \tau + 2$. There are two possibilities:

(i) $a_k^\tau = s_k(h^\tau)\ \forall\, k \in N, k \neq j$. This is the case where, at the τth stage, at most one player (say j) adopted a strategy different from that induced by $(f|h^\tau)$. If i follows f_i, then the n-tuple of actions at all $t \geq \tau + 1$, given that others follow f_{-i}, will be

$$\sigma^t(f|h^{\tau+1}) = c(\boldsymbol{s}(\boldsymbol{h}^\tau); a_j^\tau). \tag{30}$$

On the other hand, if i chooses $\tilde{f}_i$, then the n-tuple of actions at $t \geq \tau + 2$ will be

$$\sigma^t(f_{-i}, \tilde{f}_i|h^{\tau+1}) = (\hat{c}_{-i}(c(\boldsymbol{s}(\boldsymbol{h}^\tau); a_j^\tau), \{\tilde{a}_i^{\tau+1}, \ldots, \tilde{a}_i^{t-1}\}), \tilde{a}_i^t).$$

Therefore, the net payoff to i of following $\tilde{f}_i$ at $t \geq \tau + 2$, given that others follows f_{-i}, is

$$\begin{aligned} &\pi_i(\tilde{a}_i^t, \hat{c}_{-i}(\boldsymbol{c}(\boldsymbol{s}(\boldsymbol{h}^\tau); a_j^\tau), \{\tilde{a}_i^{\tau+1}, \ldots, \tilde{a}_i^{t-1}\})) - M(\tilde{a}_i^t, \tilde{a}_i^{t-1}) \\ &\quad \leq \pi_i(\tilde{a}_i^{t-1}, \hat{c}_{-i}(c(\boldsymbol{s}(\boldsymbol{h}^\tau); a_j^\tau), \{\tilde{a}_i^{\tau+1}, \ldots, \tilde{a}_i^{t-1}\})) \\ &\quad \leq \pi_i(c(\boldsymbol{s}(\boldsymbol{h}^\tau), a_j^\tau)). \end{aligned} \tag{31}$$

The first inequality follows from (27) and the second from the "rationality" condition (17). Conditions (30) and (31) imply that at any $t \geq \tau + 2$ the net stage payoff to i of following $(f_i|h^{\tau+1})$ would be no less than that of following any other RG strategy $(\tilde{f}_i|h^{\tau+1}) \in F_i$.

(ii) $a_k^\tau \neq s_k(h^\tau)$ and $a_\ell^\tau \neq s_\ell(h^\tau)$, for some k and $\ell \in N$ and $k \neq \ell$. This is the case where at the τth stage at least two players adopted strategies different from those induced by $(f|h^\tau)$. Thus,

$$\sigma^t(f|h^{\tau+1}) = a^* \quad \text{for } t \geq \tau + 1.$$

On the other hand, if i chooses $\tilde{f}_i$ and others choose f_{-i}, then

$$\sigma^t(f_{-i}, f_i|h^{\tau+1}) = (\tilde{a}_i^t, \hat{c}_{-i}(a^*, \{\tilde{a}_i^{\tau+1}, \ldots, \tilde{a}_i^{t-1}\}) \quad \text{for } t \geq \tau + 2.$$

Thus, the net payoff to i of following $\tilde{f}_i$ at $t \geq \tau + 2$ is

$$\begin{aligned} &\pi_i(\tilde{a}_i^t, \hat{c}_{-i}(a^*, \{\tilde{a}_i^{\tau+1}, \ldots, \tilde{a}_i^{t-1}\})) - M(\tilde{a}_i^t, \tilde{a}_i^{t-1}) \\ &\quad \leq \pi_i(\tilde{a}_i^{t-1}, \hat{c}_{-i}(a^*, \{a_i^{\tau+1}, \ldots, \tilde{a}_i^{t-1}\})) \\ &\quad \leq \pi_i(a^*). \end{aligned} \tag{32}$$

(The first inequality in (32) follows from (28) and the second from (16).) Thus, the net stage payoff to i at any $t \geq \tau + 2$ of following $(f_i|h^{\tau+1})$ is no less than that of following any other strategy $(\tilde{f}_i|h^{\tau+1}) \in F_i$.

Possibilities (i) and (ii) together imply that the net stage payoff of i at $t > \tau + 1$ is greatest if player i follows $(f_i|h^{\tau+1})$, given that the others use $(f_{-i}|h^{\tau+1})$. As for period $t = \tau + 1$, it is possible that i, by choosing $\tilde{a}_i^{\tau+1}$, increases his payoff above what he would have obtained by following f_i and choosing $s_i(h^{\tau+1})$ at $\tau + 1$. But any one-period gain from doing so plays no role in i's long-run average payoff. Thus,

$$\pi_i^\infty(\sigma(f|h^{\tau+1}) \geq \pi_i^\infty(\sigma(\tilde{f}_i, f_{-i}|h^{\tau+1})). \qquad \text{Q.E.D.}$$

Remark 1 The above two theorems demonstrate that conjectural models, if properly specified, can be given an explicit time story. In particular, dynamic conjectural equilibrium amounts to the same thing as Nash equilibrium in an inertia supergame, and "rationality" in dynamic conjectural models implies (not surprisingly) subgame perfectness in the context of an inertia supergame.

Remark 2 The (subgame-perfect) equilibrium strategy generated by our conjectural model, $f \in F$ satisfying (28), is quite attractive since it only requires the players to know, at each stage t, what all players had done at the previous stage of the game, at $t - 1$, and what all should have done at

$t-1$ if they had followed f at that period (i.e., $s(h^{t-1})$).[21] Since the latter ($s(h^{t-1})$) represents all a player need know at t concerning h^{t-1}, $s(h^{t-1})$ can be regarded as a state variable. Such a supergame strategy is obviously atractive, since it requires less memory than many other equilibrium RG strategies. To be more precise, f satisfying theorems 1 and 2 requires the memory to be a subset of $A \times A$. Thus, the dimension of the memory does not increase as the history unfolds.

Remark 3 Any subgame-perfect equilibrium strategy generated from a dynamic RCE, f in theorem 4, is stationary after any history; i.e., for any h^t,

$$\sigma^{t'}(f \mid h^t) = \sigma^t(f \mid h^t)$$

for any $t' \geq t$. The proof of this statement is rather trivial and can be found in Sabourian 1983.

Remark 4 One can also show a converse result to theorem 2. More precisely, one can show that any SPE of an inertia supergrame that can be supported by "low memory strategies" (see note 21 for the definition of "low memory") can generate a set of conjectures that are dynamic RCE. The result is rather trivial (Sabourian 1983), and for reasons of space the proof is omitted.

Remark 5 Theorem 2 relates dynamic RCE to the SPE of an inertia supergame whose players have an infinite time horizon. Theorem 2 also holds approximately (in the sense of Radner's (1980) ε-equilibrium) for finitely repeated games with long horizon and inertia. (See Sabourian 1983.)

It was mentioned above that another interpretation of "rational" conjectural models is in terms of repeated games in which agents respond instantaneously to each other's actions. For technical reasons, the continuous-time simultaneous repeated game is difficult to model (see Simon and Stinchcombe 1989). Anderson (1984) models the instantaneous-response game by looking at the limit of the ε-perfect equilibria of the discrete inertia supergame as the period length tends to zero.[22] In the case of no discounting the period length is unimportant, and the equilibrium solution does not depend on the period length. In the case of discounting, shortening the time that elapses before the players can change their actions could be modeled by adjusting the discount factor and the one-period payoff. More formally, Anderson considers changing the period length to an arbitrary $\tau > 0$ and calls the supergame in which players play the one-shot game G every time τ elapses G^τ (he looks at the infinite-horizon case). In this case the payoff function for player i is defined as

$$\pi_i^\tau(\sigma(f)) = \sum_{t=1}^{\infty} y_i^{(t-1)\tau}\tau\{\pi_i(\sigma^t(f)) - M(\sigma_i^t(f), \sigma_i^{t-1}(f))],$$

where y_i is player i's discount factor. Finally, Anderson defines a subgame-perfect quick-response equilibrium as follows:

DEFINITION 14 A strategy f is a subgame-perfect quick-response equilibrium if $\forall\, \varepsilon > 0$, $\exists\, \tau^0 > 0$ such that $\forall\, \tau < \tau^0$ and $\forall h^t$,[23] f is an ε-Nash equilibrium of $G^\tau | h^t$ (the subgame G^τ after the history h^t).

THEOREM 5 The strategy vector f defined in theorem 4 is a subgame-perfect quick-response equilibrium for any of discount factors $y_i > 0$.

Proof Define K as the maximum one-period gain that any player can make. Since K is finite, for any $\varepsilon > 0$, $\exists\, \tau^0$ such that $\tau^0 K < \varepsilon$. Consider any $\tau < \tau^0$. It follows from the proof of theorem 2 that if any player i chooses a strategy other than f_i after any history h^t, he can gain only at t and the gain is going to last for an interval of length τ. Thus, the maximum gain i can make after any history is $K\tau$. Since $k\tau < \varepsilon$, f is an ε-Nash equilibrium after any history h^t. Q.E.D.

Remark 6 As in the case of repeated games without adjustment cost, a result of the Folk Theorem type can also be established for inertia supergames (and thus dynamic RCE) and for quick-response equilibria (see Sabourian 1989 for a survey of repeated games and Folk Theorems). In fact, one can show that certain types of behavior, e.g. price matching, can be supoorted as subgame-perfect solutions to an inertia supergame, but not necessarily to discrete repeated games without adjustment cost (Sabourian 1983).[24]

I shall now compare the above theorems to the literature on dynamic treatment of conjectures. Friedman (1968, 1977) and Robson (1986) differ from the above in two respects: first, in Friedman's model the firm is "non-conjectural" in the sense that the conjectures do not depend on the status quo; second, Friedman deals only with Nash-equilibrium strategies. Kalai and Stanford (1981) also look at a linear conjectural model in an RG context and consider only Nash-equilibrium strategies. Laitner (1980) does consider SPE. His model has a discrete time variable, but his conjectures are instantaneous and he gives a tatonnement interpretion to them. Marschak and Selten (1978), on the other hand, relate their conjectural model to a set of strategies in an inertia supergame which they call "paraperfect." But the "paraperfect" notion does not go far beyond the usual Nash equilibrium in the supergame.[25] As was mentioned in the introduction, the present paper can be regarded as a reformulation of the works of Marschak and Selten (1974, 1978) to deal with subgame perfectness.

Concluding Remarks

In the light of the results obtained in section 2, it may be argued that RCE could at best be interpreted in terms of some equilibrium concept in a repeated-game framework. Nevertheless, the conjectural models and the notion of RCE have some attractions: they are easier to deal with than general repeated games (the optimization problems in the conjectural models are static, whereas in the repeated games one often has to deal with dynamic optimization problems), and the RG strategies they generate are very simple. In fact, one could argue that by concentrating on conjectural models, and thus on the RG strategies generated by conjectures, one is introducing some kind of "bounded rationality" into repeated games.[26] Moreover, in this paper I have dealt with rational conjectures in terms of "correctness." Rationality in terms of some learning and/or experimenting story is not dealt with in RG models. Much work needs to be done on "rational" conjecture and learning.

Acknowledgments

I would like to thank F. H. Hahn and J. Thomas for reading the earlier versions of this paper and an anonymous referee for very helpful comments.

Notes

1. In this paper, I am only referring to works on conjectural equilibrium and rational conjectural equilibrium. In some works on game theory (e.g., Bernheim 1984 and Pearce 1984), the notion of conjectures has been used in one-shot games. In these latter models, conjectures do not necessarily refer to responses.

2. This shows that Makowski's (1987) objections to conjectural models do not necessarily apply.

3. Note that each conjecture is a function of a status quo term (written in bold to avoid confusions) and a deviation term.

4. Note that $B_j\{(a_i',c_{-i}(\boldsymbol{a}^*;a_i'));c\}$ is defined as

$$\left\{a_j \in A_j | a_j \in \arg\max_{a_j' \in A_j} \pi_j(a_j',c_{-j}(\boldsymbol{a}_j',\boldsymbol{c}_{-i}(\boldsymbol{a}^*;\boldsymbol{a}_i');a_j')\right\}.$$

5. $c_{-i,j}(\boldsymbol{a}^*,a_i')$ is the vector $c_{-i}(\boldsymbol{a}^*;a_i')$ without its jth component.

6. Concern with the next-period payoff could be due to the existence of adjustment costs or instantaneous response.

7. This Nash-type assumption with respect to conjectures is common to all definitions of "rational" conjectural equilibrium, including ReCE.

8. "Ex-post" in the sense that the conjectures attributed to the others are the optimum response for the others, once they have chosen them.

9. It may be argued tht "correctness" of conjectures is not necessarily an aspect of "rational" behavior (Hart 1982). Although this may be so in general, I shall argue in section 2 that "rationality" has to imply "correctness" in our deterministic conjectural model.

10. In the literature on conjectural (perceived) demand (e.g., Hahn 1977, 1978; Hart 1982), "rationality" requires conjectures to be "correct" with respect to some signal (e.g., market price) representing aggregate action of other players. Clearly, if there is one-to-one mapping between actions of the players and the aggregate signal, "rationality" with respect to the signal is the same as that with respect to actions of all players. Sabourian (1983) discusses the case where there is no one-to-one mapping; Green (1980), Kaneko (1982), and Sabourian (1990) also discuss the same point in the context of large anonymous repeated games.

11. In a stochastic conjectural model, interpreting "rationality" in terms of experimenting is very appealing. I have been working on a stochastic conjectural model, in which conscious learning is allowed, for some time. In such a model one needs to compare the cost of experimenting with the possible gains from having more information (à la Wald).

12. Of course $s_j^1(\varnothing)$ only defines the action of $j = 1$. This is because player 2 can move at even periods. Nevertheless, to make the definition consistent I need to define $s_j^1(\varnothing)$ for $j = 2$, since $s_2^2(h^2)$ depends on $s_2^1(\varnothing)$.

13. Strictly speaking, $c(\boldsymbol{a};a_i')$ refers to what is expected of all players after a deviation by i. Therefore it has to be written as $c_i(\boldsymbol{a};a_i')$. Since the second argument of the $c_i(\boldsymbol{a};a_1')$ function refers to the deviator, for simplicity I shall drop the subscript from $c_i(\boldsymbol{a};a_1')$ and write it as $c(\boldsymbol{a};a_1')$.

14. Marschak and Selten (1978) also try to justify their notion of convolution in terms of a supergame story.

15. Notice that in these conjectural models it is conjectured that players other than i are constrained to respond only to the last deviation and status quo, not to a history of deviations and status quos. Thus, the conjectures are in a way "Markovian" and are not too complex.

16. In this paper I shall consider only pure strategies, because I am considering a deterministic conjectural model.

17. Inertia supergame was defined first by Marschak and Selten (1978).

18. Such a cost can be justified on physical, administrative, computational, and/or psychological grounds.

19. Given that $s^t(\cdot)$ does not depend on t, I shall drop the superscript on s^t and write $s^t(h^t)$ as $s(h^t)$ for convenience.

20. In the previous theorem, I have already dealt with the subgame starting at time 1.

21. Marschak and Selten (1978) call such a supergame strategy a low-memory combination. I mentioned earlier that strategies generated by conjectural models have a certain Markovian property.

22. In the supergame defined above, the period length was 1.

23. t is not an integer but a multiple of τ.

24. The reason why one can generate price matching and thus kinked demand behavior as a solution to an inertia supergame has to do with the existence of an adjustment cost which removes the possibility of transitory profit.

25. An n-tuple strategy, say f, is "paraperfect" if $\forall\ i \in N$, f_i is the best strategy for i, given that others choose f_{-i}, after any sequence of actions having the property that at most one other player had deviated from f at each previous stage of the supergame. "Paraperfectness" does not go much beyond the Nash equilibrium, because histories after which a paraperfect strategy f_i is a best reply are a very small proportion of all possible histories.

26. Given the recent popularity of "bounded rationality" in game theory, a conjectural model may become fashionable with game theorists in the near future.

References

Anderson, R. 1984. Quick Response Equilibria. Mimeo, University of California, Berkeley.

Boyer, M., and M. Moreaux. 1983. "Conjectures, rationality and duopoly theory." *International Journal of Industrial Organisation* 1: 23–41.

Bresnahan, T. F. 1981. "Duopoly models with consistent conjectures." *American Economic Review* 71: 934–945.

Friedman, J. W. 1968. "Reaction functions and the theory of duopoly." *Review of Economic Studies* 35 (3): 257–272.

Friedman, J. W. 1977. *Oligopoly and the Theory of Games.* North-Holland.

Fudenberg, D., and D. Kreps. 1988. Learning, Experimentation and Equilibrium in Games. Mimeo, Stanford University.

Green, E. J. 1980. "Non-cooperative price taking in large dynamic markets." *Journal of Economic Theory* 22: 155–182.

Hahn, F. H. 1977. "Exercises in conjectural equilibrium." *Scandinavian Journal of Economics* 79 (2): 210–226.

Hahn, F. H. 1978. "On non-Walrasian equilibrium." *Review of Economic Studies* 45 (1): 1–17.

Hahn, F. H. 1989. "Information, dynamics and equilibrium." In *The Economic Theory of Missing Markets, Information and Games*, ed. F. H. Hahn. Oxford University Press.

Hart, O. 1982. Reasonable Conjectures. Mimeo, Lonodn School of Economics.

Hart, O. 1985. "Imperfect competition in a general equilibrium: An overview of recent work." In *Frontiers of Economic Theory*, ed. K. Arrow and S. Honkapohja. Blackwell.

Kalai and Stanford. 1981. Dynamic Conjectural Equilibrium. Mimeo, Northwestern University.

Kamien and Schwartz. 1983. "Conjectural variations." *Canadian Journal of Economics* 16: 2.

Kaneko, M. 1982. "Some remarks on the Folk Theorem in game theory." *Mathematical Social Sciences.*

Laitner, J. 1980. "Rational duopoly equilibrium." *Quarterly Journal of Economics* 95 (4): 641–662.

Makowski, L. 1987. "Are 'Rational Conjectures' Rational?" *Journal of Industrial Economics* 36: 35–47.

Marschak, T., and R. Selten. 1974. *General Equilibrium with Price-Making Firms: Lecture Notes in Economic and Mathematical Systems.* Springer-Verlag.

Marschak, T., and R. Selten. 1978. "Restabilizing responses, inertia super-games and oligopolistic equilibrium." *Quarterly Journal of Economics* 92: 71–93.

Negishi. 1961. "Monopolistic competition and general equilibrium." *Review of Economic Studies* 196–201.

Perry, M. 1982. "Oligopoly and consistent conjectural variations." *Bell Journal of Economics*, spring: 197–205.

Radner, R. 1980. "Collusive behaviour in non-cooperative epsilon equilibrium with long but finite lives." *Journal of Economic Theory* 22: 136–154.

Robson, A. J. 1986. "The existence of Nash equilibria in reaction functions for dynamic models of oligopoly." *International Economic Review.*

Sabourian, H. 1983. Some Notes on Rational Conjectural Equilibrium from a Game-Theoretic Perspective, Parts I and II. Economic Theory Discussion Paper 117, Cambridge University.

Sabourian, H. 1989. "Repeated games: A survey." In *The Economic Theory of Missing Markets, Information and Games*, ed. F. H. Hahn. Oxford University Press.

Sabourian, H. 1990. "Anonymous repeated games with large number of players." *Journal of Economic Theory* 51: 92–110.

Simon, L., and M. Stinchcombe. 1989. Extensive Form Games in Continuous Time, Part I: Pure Strategies. Mimeo.

Ulph, D. 1982. "Rational conjectures in the theory of oligopoly." *International Journal of Industrial Organisation* 1 (June): 131–154.

Static Choice in the Presence of Unforeseen Contingencies

David M. Kreps

It is unremarkable to observe that contingencies sometimes arise that were not foreseen at an earlier date. It is, moreover, an article of received truth that the spectre of unforeseen contingencies plays a role in dynamic planning and in contracting. Indeed, transaction-cost economists (for example, Williamson (1985)) give a central role to adaptation to unforeseen contingencies in explaining the forms of contractual arrangements that we observe.

It seems equally apparent that choice theorists have failed to deliver the tools needed to model and study the role of unforeseen contingencies. The model of Savage (1954), which is the paradigmatic model of choice under uncertainty, seems to make no allowance for such things. Accordingly, mathematical modeling of the sorts of considerations that drive the Williamson's discussion seem be beyond our present abilities.

In this essay, I will argue that this is a something of a misreading of the situation. I will present one way to model conceptually the idea that certain contingencies may be unforeseen. The model given will imply a representation theorem that is remarkably similar to the standard Savage model. There is nothing new in the mathematics of this representation. In fact, all the (not very hard) mathematics may be found in Kreps 1979. What is novel here is an attempt to reinterpret the formalisms of that earlier paper in a way that suggests the phenomenon of unforeseen contingencies.

The attempt that is made here to model unforeseen contingencies is not completely satisfactory. For one thing, there are (at least) two aspects of unforeseen contingencies that the model presented can be said to miss. I have nothing very bright to say about these two aspects, so I will mention and then dismiss them here.

First, in the model of choice presented here, the individual is not so unsophisticated as to be taken completely by surprise when something unforeseen occurs. This individual is aware at the outset that there may arise contingencies that cannot be foreseen. The individual, aware of this, takes actions which reflect this possibility. I do not attempt to model the behavior of an individual who is truly surprised by unforeseen events, in the sense that he not only fails to anticipate what might happen but also fails to realize the possibility that he cannot anticipate all possible contingencies. The behavior of such an individual would, I imagine, look something like the behavior of agents in a temporary general equilibrium:

He thinks he knows what is going on, and so his static choice conforms to the standard models. But his static choice lacks intertemporal consistency in that his model of states of the world changes as events unfold. Such behavior may be of interest; but insofar as the motivation for this study is to provide tools for a mathematical analysis of the theories put forward by (say) Williamson, one wants to model individuals who anticipate that unforeseen contingencies will arise. If one imagines that nonclassical contractual forms—relational contracting, for example—are adopted consciously by the transacting parties because those parties wish to provide themselves with governance provisions by which the unforeseen can be met, then it seems patent that those individuals are acting in anticipation of unforeseen contingencies.

Second, I do not model behavior so far from standard that it is not representable by a preference relation on a well-defined set of objects. In particular, I do not take into account the effect that the set of objects presented to an individual may have on what contingencies the individual does foresee. I would expect that, by presenting first a smaller and then a larger menu of objects to an individual, we can influence what contingencies the individual considers salient, and we can therefore influence the rankings the individual puts on items from the smaller menu. This is an important aspect of unforeseen contingencies—and, more generally, bounded rationality—but I have nothing to say about it, and I will ignore it.

I will also ignore preferences that are incomplete. Bewley (1986, 1987) presents an analysis of "Knightian Decision Theory" which concerns both static-choice and dynamic-choice behavior for incomplete preferences. He ties this analysis to phenomena such as "surprises" that are very suggestive of the term "unforeseen contingencies." I think a comparison of the models described here with those of Bewley will be interesting, but I think such comparisons will be more fruitful once this theory is developed dynamically; for now, the reader is asked to consider models of choice that are suggestive of the presence of unforeseen contingencies and that involve, at any point in time, complete and transitive preferences over the objects among which choice is currently being made.

Two other caveats should be made at the outset. First, the very notion of a contingency suggsts some sort of temporal structure, and the static choice that we will describe is naturally embedded within a framework of dynamic choice. Notwithstanding this, in this paper only static choice/

preference will be at issue; I will be discussing only the first stage of a dynamic-choice problem. This isn't to say that dynamic aspects of choice don't play a role in the story. They do, but that role will be entirely informal. I hope someday to knit the sort of static-choice behavior considered here into a model of dynamic choice, but that awaits further development. Second, interest in the phenomenon of choice in the presence of unforeseen contingencies stems primarily from the aggregation or equilibration of individual preferences within some sort of institutional context. Put another way, the test of the choice theory described here will come when that theory is used to model economic institutions. This test can be administered only when an appropriate notion of equilibrium is advanced and when important decisions are made concerning the degree of diversity allowed in the preferences of diverse individuals. I hope someday to have something to say about multi-person decision problems, but for now only single-person decision problems will be considered.

With all these caveats in place, let me describe the development that leads to the (surprising) positive assertion that we do know how to model unforeseen contingencies.

The key to this development comes from asking and answering the following questions: What behavior at the level of individual choice do we study to discern whether the individual anticipates that unforeseen things may occur? How can we recognize behavior that reflects a self-aware inability to predict all future contingencies? To answer to these questions, I contend, we should ask the individual how much flexibility he wishes to preserve for future decisions. That is, knowing that unforeseen events may happen, the individual is unwilling today to precommit to all actions he will later wish to take, even contingent on the contingencies he can foresee. He will instead wish to preserve for himself some ability to adapt to those events as they arise. By asking questions that are pointed at getting a sense of the value this individual attaches to reserved flexibility, we get a sense of the extent to which the individual perceives himself to be at risk of things he cannot foresee. All this is discussed in the context of an example in section 1 and is formalized in section 2.

Let me be very careful here. I contend that a desire to preserve flexibility is indicative of anticipated unforeseen contingencies; but it is not necessarily logically sufficient for this phenomenon. If the individual is dealing with contingent consumption possibilities for a less than completely fine list of contingencies, then the individual may exhibit a preference for flexibility. The list of contingencies may be less than completely fine because of an inability to enforce contracts that depend on certain contingencies, even if they are foreseen, or an unwillingness, owing to the expense involved, of thinking through all foreseeable aspects. In the model presented here, the desire for retained flexibility predicated on these alternative causes is observationally equivalent to flexibility-seeking behavior that is predicated on unforeseen contingencies. Of course, this suggests the sort of representation that we will derive for unforeseen contingencies.

Once one accepts this basic modeling point, at least one sort of representation (which captures the notion that there is a desire to maintain flexibility) can be taken from the literature; i.e., the representation essentially provided in Koopmans 1964 and axiomatized in Kreps 1979. This is summarized in section 2, although the summary is quite brief and the reader may need to go back to Kreps 1979 to understand what is going on.

In section 3, I consider an aspect of unforeseen contingencies that seems to be missed by the model of sections 1 and 2, namely an inability to say just what consequences ensue in a given contingency from a given action. I will argue that this aspect is in fact part and parcel of the model of sections 1 and 2. Roughly put, one wishes to preserve flexibility because one isn't able to say just what will happen (as a function of contingencies) in the future.

Section 4 contains brief concluding remarks. In particular, I discuss lacunae remaining in the sort of theory given in sections 1 and 2 and next steps to take in the development of that theory.

1 An Example

Imagine that you are told that you will be transported to some vacation spot, somewhere in the world, in one week. You will be there for two weeks. You are given a week to pack and, if you wish, to shop. You are given a budget of $10,000, which is to be used both to shop and as spending money once you get to wherever you are going. So that you don't save all the money to spend once you get there, any cash that you don't spend before getting on the plane will be taxed at a rate of 50 percent.

It is standard to think of the problem of what to pack as a choice problem. Let C represent all the possible bundles of baggage you could take with you, where one component of $c \in C$ is the amount of money left over from your shopping expedition (after the tax). Think of C as the space of all possible bundles of baggage without regard to the budget constraint, and let B be those $c \in C$ that are budget-feasible. Then, in a standard treatment, we first get hold of your preferences over all of C and then pick out a preference-optimal bundle from the set B.

Of course, there is some uncertainty in this problem. You don't know where you will be sent, what the weather will be, and so on. So a standard treatment of the problem would run as follows: There is a state space S representing all possible resolutions of that uncertainty. And, if only as a thought experiment, we ask for your preferences not on the simple space C but on the space of "contingent-bundles"; i.e., on the space $Z = C^S$, or perhaps (following Anscombe and Aumann 1963) on the space of functions from S to probability distributions on C that have finite support. It may be that there is a contingent-baggage service out there, which will allow you (presumably at some price) to buy a contingent claim to baggage. Or it may simply be that, by thinking about your preferences on C^S, we are able to get a better handle on your preferences over C.

Being a bit more formal about this, we imagine an agent who lives and consumes at two dates, $t = 0$ and $t = 1$, and that certain events may transpire between the two dates. Consumption at date t will be denoted by c_t; think of c_t as being an element of some finite-dimensional Euclidean space. Between now ($t = 0$) and later ($t = 1$), certain events may transpire, given by the state space S: At date $t = 1$, we will be able to recognize that some s from S has in fact transpired. We therefore imagine an overall commodity space of the form $Z := C_0 \times (C_1)^S$, where C_0 is the space of all date-0 consumption bundles and C_1 is the space of all date-1 consumption bundles. For simplicity, we assume that C_1 is independent of $s \in S$. We write $z = (z_0, z_1)$ for a typical element of Z, where $z_0 \in C_0$ and $z_1 \in (C_1)^S$. There are two things worthy of note concerning this general formulation *vis à vis* the example:

• In the general formulation, we have added immediate consumption, and we do not allow immediate consumption to be contingent. Most standard treatments permit uncertain immediate consumption if they have immediate consumption at all, in order to get a more powerful theory.

• In the example, C was a space of bundles of baggage. In the general formulation, we referred to the prizes as levels of consumption. Now, in terms of the example, baggage c is not "consumption" but rather the "tools" from which consumption can (conceivably) be extracted—a component of c might be the amount of suntan oil packed away, which is useful in consuming a good tan but which isn't the same as a good tan. Put another way, one wouldn't expect that the value of a prize c in our story would be the same in all contingencies s; a lot of suntan oil is more valuable in contingencies where one's destination is Tahiti (and the sun shines) than in those contingencies that represent London in a week with intermittent rain and clouds. In this regard, the example is more indicative of our intentions for this model than is the use of the term *consumption* in the general formulation—a point that will be discussed at great length in section 3. For now, keep the example firmly in mind, and understand that we will not want to push so hard that, in the general formulation, we wind up with a classic state-independent expected utility representation.

The individual has preferences over elements of Z, given (say) by a complete and transitive binary relation $\succeq$ on Z, and in the normal run of events we would pose axioms about $\succeq$ and seek a representation theorem for those preferences. For purposes of this essay, we will make the following collection of assumptions the "standard":

ASSUMPTION 1 The set S is finite. Let n be the number of elements of S, and enumerate S as $\{s_1, \dots, s_n\}$.

ASSUMPTION 2 Both C_0 and C_1 are compact and connected subspaces of some finite-dimensional Euclidean space, and $\succeq$ is continuous on Z in the obvious product topology.

ASSUMPTION 3 The relation $\succeq$ is complete and transitive.

ASSUMPTION 4 Suppose (z_0,z_1), (z_0,z_1'), (z_0,y_1), and (z_0,y_1') (all from Z) and $T \subseteq S$ are given, such that (a) $z_1(s) = z_1'(s)$ and $y_1(s) = y_1'(s)$ for all $s \in T$ and (b) $z_1(s) = y_1(s)$ and $z_1'(s) = y_1'(s)$ for all $s \in S \backslash T$. Then $(z_0,z_1) \succeq (z_0,y_1)$ if and only if $(z_0,z_1') \succeq (z_0,y_1')$.

Assumption 4 is the natural variation on Savage's sure-thing principle in this setting. By virtue of this assumption, we can talk in the usual fashion about preference conditional on a subset of states $T \subseteq S$, given a z_0. A subset T of states is said to be *non-null* given z_0 if preference conditional on T given z_0 is not trivial; that is, some z_1 is strictly preferred to another, conditional on T and given z_0. A state $s \in S$ is non-null given z_0 if the singleton set s is non-null given z_0.

PROPOSITION 1 (Debreu 1959) Assumptions 1 through 4 imply that there exist functions $u: C_0 \times C_1 \times S \to R$ and $f: C_0 \times R^S$ such that (a) f is strictly increasing in its last S arguments, and (b) the function

$$U(z_0,z_1) := f[z_0, u(z_0,z_1(s_1),s_1), \ldots, u(z_0,z_1(s_n),s_n)]$$

is an index for $\succ$; that is, $(z_0,z_1) \succeq (z_0',z_1')$ if and only if $U(z_0,z_1) \geq U(z_0',z_1')$. Moreover, for any z_0 such that there are at least three non-null states given z_0, we can assume that f takes the form

$$g\left[z_0, \sum_s u(z_0,z_1(s),s)\right]$$

for some function g: $C_0 \times R \to R$ that is strictly increasing in its second argument.

Repeating what we said before we listed the assumptions, we do not want to push further than this; the state-utility functions $u(\cdot,\cdot,s)$ are state-dependent and do not necessarily take the form $\pi(s)u(\cdot,\cdot)$ for some set of scaling probabilities $\pi(s)$ and a state-independent utility function u. Moreover, though many parameterization of this model invoke additive separability between first-period and second-period consumption, we do not.

Returning to our example, we remark first that the assumptions listed above seem wholly appropriate to our story. One can invent reasons why they wouldn't hold—especially why the sure-thing principle is incorrect (see, for example, Loomes and Sugden (1986) on "disappointment" or Schmeidler (1989) on "co-monotonicity"). But notwithstanding the Ellsberg paradox and such attempts to provide a theoretical basis for resolving it, there is nothing particular to the story as described that would suggest that the standard treatment is any less appropriate to it than is normally the case.

We now turn to the special complication of this paper, namely unforeseen contingencies, told first in terms of our story. When told that you are to be sent on vacation, you are not told all the possible contingencies involving weather, location, etc. You are given the opportunity of listing all the contingencies you can think of, with two stipulations: (1) The contingencies must be based on objectively verifiable criteria. You may include things like "Paris in a chilly drizzle, with predictions in *Figaro* of continued rain and daily highs below 20," but you may not include things like "I would like my raincoat and several heavy sweaters." (2) All the contingencies you list must be mutually exclusive—there should no ambiguity after the fact about which one of the contingencies is valid. (We will assume that this condition can be met.) And, even if it looks like you covered all the possibilities, to be on the safe side we will always append one final state, namely "none of the above," so that, by definition, the list is exhaustive.

Of course, some of the contingencies you specify, and most particularly the last one, will be fairly coarse descriptions of what might happen. You might have some contingencies for Tahiti and some for Bora Bora, but (if your knowledge of geography is similar to my own) there might be a catch-all "some other southern Pacific island north of sixty degrees south latitude."

Finally, we allow you to consider bundles of baggage contingent on all the states that you are able to name. That is, if S is the list of states you come up with (including the "none of the above" state), we look for your preferences on C^S.

What is potentially novel here is that you may recognize that your list of contingencies may be incomplete. The "none of the above" contingency may take place, and even in those contingencies that you do describe the description may be coarser than is ideal; you may not foresee the possibility of certain climates in certain locations, or the possibility of a South Seas island where it rains perpetually. (Of course, once you have written these down, they are by definition contingencies that have been foreseen. But, one hopes, the point is taken.)

Would the recognition of this fact affect qualitative properties of your preferences over C^S? In particular, would any of the previously listed assumptions become invalid? I have little doubt that assumption 3 is more questionable now than before; the added complications might cause you to waver in your determination to rank all available alternatives, or it might make you more susceptible to violations of assumption 3 owing to framing effects, intransitivities, and the like. But, as noted in the introduction, I wish to develop a theory that maintains assumption 3. Granting you this much rationality, I ask: Are any of the other three assumptions above *less* valid because of the presence of unforeseen contingencies? Assumption 1 and the first half of assumption 2 are purely structural. Indeed, now that you are responsible for listing all the contingencies, assumption 1 is ever more reasonable. The second half of 2 is a real assumption, but continuity continues to make quite good sense. And the intuition behind the sure-thing principle seems quite as valid as before. What one receives in one event will not affect preferences over what is received in a disjoint event; what one would have received in the (now) irrelevant event is, because of that irrelevance, itself irrelevant. The Ellsberg paradox might cause us to doubt the validity of this intuition, but it seem to me that the Ellsberg paradox turns on ambiguity in the probabilities of contingencies and not on ambiguity in the list of contingencies. The latter implies the former, to some extent, but the former can be present without unforeseen contingencies (as in the classic Ellsberg paradox). So while the Ellsberg paradox may render the standard axioms invalid, they don't seem to me to be any *more* invalid in this setting.

I am claiming, in other words, that the presence of unforeseen contingencies would not affect the standard model one bit. The old conclusions and the old model are as good as before.

Where, then, can we expect to see unforeseen contingencies make a difference? How would we recognize that you may anticipate that there are contingencies that you haven't foreseen?

The answers to these questions, both in this example and in general, are to be found by modifying the set of objects over which choice is made. Assume that, in accordance with assumption 2, the set of possible bundles of baggage C is a compact, connected subset of some finite-dimensional Euclidean space. Let K be the set of all compact subsets of C, and consider $X = K^S$. The interpretation is that our contingent baggage service, which allows you to choose your baggage contingent on your destination, offers a new service: contingent baggage-opportunity sets. That is, for each contingency s that you specify, you are allowed to specify a set of possible baggage bundles $x(s) \in K$. Then, if contingency s occurs, you wire back to the company which $c \in x(s)$ you wish to have sent along. (Transmission of the message and the baggage is instantaneous.) You can choose only one $c \in x(s)$—if you think that you might want both c and c', then you have to put $c \cup c'$ in $x(s)$ to begin with. But the point of this new service is that you preserve some flexibility until you get to wherever you are going, have a look around, and (presumably) learn about all the contingencies you didn't foresee. (You may object to this, saying that all unforeseen contingencies may not resolve immediately upon arrival. That is certainly so, but it introduces to the story more than two periods—a complication I wish to leave alone for now.) We may assume that this service is not offered for free, but such considerations will enter later when we construct the budget set. For now we are trying to get straight your preferences over the entire set X. Indeed, this service may not exist at all, just as the contingent-baggage service may not exist. But, as a gedankenexperiment, we imagine this service in the hope that the structure of X and your preferences over X will help us to clarify your preferences over the things that really are on offer, even if they are nothing more complex than elements of C.

Now suppose that we were in the standard world, where S was an exhaustive list of all states of the world; all uncertainty would be resolved by $s \in S$. The standard theory would then proceed to induce preferences over X from underlying preferences on Z using dynamic programming, as follows: Assuming that preferences over Z are represented in the spirit of proposition 1 by a function

$$f[u(z(s_1), s_1), \ldots, u(z(s_n), s_n)],$$

which, for simplicity, I will rewrite as

$$f[u_1(z(s_1)), \ldots, u_n(z(s_n))],$$

the induced value of an $x \in X$ is given by

$$f\left[\max_{c \in x(s_1)} u_1(c), \ldots, \max_{c \in x(s_n)} u_n(c)\right]$$

(where, for expository convenience, I am assuming that the u_k are continuous). Consider, in this regard, two elements of X, denoted x and x', where $x(s) = x'(s)$ for all states s except for one, say s_j. And suppose that $x \succsim x'$ (which, since we can speak of conditional preference, we might write as $x(s_j) \succsim_{s_j} x'(s_j)$). Then we know that

$$\max_{c \in x(s_j)} u_j(c) \geq \max_{c \in x'(s_j)} u_j(c),$$

and so

$$\max_{c \in x(s_j) \cup x'(s_j)} u_j(c) = \max_{c \in x'(s_j)} u_j(c).$$

That is, if we form x'' by taking $x''(s) = x(s) = x'(s)$ in all contingencies except s_j, and $x''(s_j) = x(s_j) \cup x'(s_j)$, then $x'' \sim x$.

This is bad news for the new "flexibility" service offered by the contingent-baggage firm, at least insofar as it is costly to them to maintain flexibility for you. In the standard treatment, you would not pay one whit for maintained flexibility. Instead, you would figure out which bundle of baggage you want in each contingency and tell the company not to bother offering you any other options (contingent on the state).[1]

Of course, in the scenario that has been described, where you write down the list of states S, you probably would find maintained flexibility to be somewhat useful. I contend that *this* is what fruitfully distinguishes the standard situation from one in which you must list the set of contingencies S and are aware that your list of contingencies may be far from "complete." In such a case as this, it seems far from unreasonable that, for x and x' as above, you might express $x'' \succ x \succeq x'$. What does seem reasonable is that, if x and x' are such that $x'(s) \subseteq x(s)$ for all s, then $x \succeq x'$. That is, added flexibility is never a bad thing. (Someone who hates to make decisions might think otherwise. And someone who is subject to the sort of "changing tastes" analyzed by Strotz (1955–56) might think otherwise. Odysseus, for example, preferred a reduced set of options for the contingency that his vacation included a cruise past the Isle of the Sirens.)

I do not contend that you would value flexibility in the above sense only because of unforeseen contingencies. If you are asked to list all relevant contingencies, you may be able to foresee many but get writer's cramp long before all are listed. That is, you may be working with coarse list of states of nature not because you can't foresee a finer set of states but because it becomes too costly to list them all. And there may be contingencies that you would like to write down but that, by their very nature, cannot be the subjects of a contract between you and the Flexible Contingent Baggage Corporation; we see something of this in the requirement that the contingencies you list must be objectively observable. The point is that you may value flexibility in your baggage for these reasons among others. One reason why—our present focus—is that you anticipate that there are contingencies you cannot foresee. But insofar as observable behavior is meant to indicate what the individual is "thinking about," it may not be possible to separate unforeseen contingencies from other phenomena that lead to "incompletely fine" lists of contingencies. Indeed, in the formal theory being offered here this separation is impossible.

Those who have read Kreps 1979 can presumably stop here. It is clear where we are headed. Perhaps those leaders should simply skip the next section, in which I develop more formally the ideas in the discussion above, although the notation about to be developed will be needed for section 3.

2 Representation Theorems

To be formal and general about all this, let C_0 and C_1 be as in assumption 1: compact and connected subsets of finite-dimensional Euclidean space. Let K_1 be the set of all compact subsets of C_1, endowed with the Hausdorff topology (with respect to which K_1 is compact and connected). Let S be a finite list of contingencies which are mutually exclusive and exhaustive, and let

$$X = C_0 \times (K_1)^S$$

be endowed with the product topology. A typical element of X will be denoted $x = (x_0, x_1)$, where $x_0 \in C_0$ and $x_1 \in (K_1)^S$. In the usual ways, we imagine that $Z = C_0 \times (C_1)^S$ is embedded within X. We study a binary relation $\succeq$ defined on the space X.

Remarks

(1) As in the example, you are asked to think of S as a list of contingencies compiled by the individual whose preferences are represented by $\succeq$, possibly subject to some "objectively describable" constraint such as we have imposed above. One can alternatively imagine that contingencies in S are given exogenously (by some market structure). The axioms that follow apply to any list of "states" or events that satisfies our twin requirements of mutual exclusivity and exhaustiveness. However, changing the story of where S comes from changes somewhat the interpretation that we give to things.

We do require that the states listed in S be mutually exclusive and exhaustive. There must be no ambiguity concerning which state has occurred. This is not necessarily an easy condition to meet, but we assume it nonetheless. Exhaustiveness can be obtained easily (if there is no ambiguity in saying whether one of the contingencies did in fact occur) by appending to any list of contingencies the catch-all final state "none of the above." We will refer to this catch-all state repeatedly, so we give it a name: s_ω.

(2) Our use of the letter C in C_0 and C_1 suggests "consumption," and this in turn suggests that we assume the individual is choosing among state-contingent opportunity sets of consumption. One might argue that the point of unforeseen contingencies is that the consequences of a given action are not known; one doesn't know what one will be given to consume in a

given event. This is particularly true if, as suggested immediately above, one uses the s_ω contingency in order to get the list of contingencies to be exhaustive. I very emphatically do *not* mean to give to c_1 the interpretation of consumption. The set C_1 is to be thought of as something like the set of bundles of baggage in the example—something that, depending on the contingency, is quite definite. The reader may still object that there is, in many applications, *nothing* that will pass this test of contingent definiteness. For now, I want to ignore this possibility. It will be the subject of section 3.

In view of the discussion in section 1, I make without further comment the following assumptions:

ASSUMPTION 5 $\succeq$ continuous (in the obvious product topology).

ASSUMPTION 6 $\succeq$ is complete and transitive.

ASSUMPTION 7 Suppose (x_0,x_1), (x_0,x_1'), (x_0,w_1), and (x_0,w_1') (all from X) and $T \subseteq S$ are given, such that (a) $x_1(s) = x_1'(s)$ and $w_1(s) = w_1'(s)$ for all $s \in T$ and (b) $x_1(s) = w_1(s)$ and $x_1'(s) = w_1'(s)$ for all $s \in S \backslash T$. Then $(x_0,x_1) \succeq (x_0,w_1)$ if and only if $(x_0,x_1') \succeq (x_0,w_1')$.

By virtue of assumption 7, we can speak in the usual fashion about preference conditional on a subset T of S, given x_0, and about null events and null states. Debreu's theorem remains as valid as before:

PROPOSITION 2 (Debreu 1959) Assumptions 5 through 7 imply that there exist a function $u: C_0 \times K_1 \times S \to R$ and a function $f: C_0 \times R^S$ such that (a) f is strictly increasing in its last S arguments and (b) the function

$$U(x_0,x_1) := f[x_0, u(x_0, x_1(s_1), s_1), \ldots, u(x_0, x_1(s_n), s_n)]$$

is an index for $\succ$—that is, $(x_0,x_1) \succeq (x_0',x_1')$ if and only if $U(x_0,x_1) \succeq U(x_0',x_1')$. Moreover, for any x_0 such that there are at least three non-null states given x_0, we can assume that f takes the form

$$g\left[x_0, \sum_s u(x_0, x_1(s), s)\right]$$

for some function $g: C_0 \times R \to R$ that is strictly increasing in its second argument.

Using $\succsim_{s,x_0}$ to denote conditional preference, conditional on $\{s\}$, given x_0 (with $\sim_{s,x_0}$ conditional indifference and $\succ_{s,x_0}$ conditional strict preference), we consider the following three additional assumptions.

ASSUMPTION 8 For given s and x_0, if $x_1 \succsim_{s,x_0} x_1'$, then $x_1 \sim_{s,x_0} x_1 \cup x_1'$.

ASSUMPTION 9 For given s and x_0, if $x_1'(s) \subseteq x_1(s)$, then $x_1 \succsim_{s,x_0} x_1'$.

ASSUMPTION 10 For given s and x_0, if $x_1'(s) \subseteq x_1(s)$ and $x_1 \sim_{s,x_0} x_1'$, then for all x_1'',

$$x_1 \cup x_1'' \sim_{s,x_0} x_1' \cup x_1''.$$

Assumption 8 is suggested by the standard model, where all future contingencies are assumed to be foreseen and where "dynamic programming" is used to obtain the induced preferences on X from preferences on Z.

Assumption 9, formalized by Koopmans (1964), may be termed "preference for flexibility," in that it says that any opportunity set is at least as good as any of its subsets. Of course, assumption 8 implies 9.

Assumption 10 formalizes the following limitation on any strict preference for flexibility: If one is indifferent to the flexibility added by going from x_1 to x_1' (where the latter contains the former), then one doesn't strictly value the added flexibility in $x_1' \cup x_1''$ over $x_1 \cup x_1''$.

In section 1, we gave assumption 9 in uncontingent form. It may help to do so here: For given x_0, if x_1 and x_1' are such that $x_1'(s) \subseteq x_1(s)$ for all s, then $(x_0,x_1) \succsim (x_0,x_1')$. In the presence of assumptions 5, 6, and 7, this is fully equivalent to assumption 9. Also, assumption 10 can be given in equivalent uncontingent form: For x_1 and x_1' as above (i.e., $x_1'(s) \subseteq x_1(s)$ for all s), if we write $x_1 \cup x_1''$ to denote contingency-by-contingency union of the correspondences, then $(x_0,x_1) \sim (x_0,x_1')$ implies $(x_0, x_1 \cup x_1'') \sim (x_0, x_1' \cup x_1'')$. The reader may find it a useful to ponder how difficult this sort of uncontingent statement is for assumption 8.[2]

PROPOSITION 3 If, in addition to assumptions 5, 6 and 7, assumption 8 holds for a given x_0 and s, then $u(x_0, \cdot, s)$ in proposition 2 can be assumed to have the form

$$\max_{z_1 \in x_1(s)} v_{x_0,s}(z_1)$$

for some continuous function $v_{x_0,s}$ from C_1 to R.

Of course, the dynamic-programming approach that induces preferences on X from preferences on Z uses the form above as the definition of preferences on the richer domain. So we see that, in terms of $\succ$ on X, assumption 8 is equivalent to the standard model.

PROPOSITION 4 If, in addition to assumptions 5 through 7, assumptions 9 and 10 hold for given x_0 and s, then $u(x_0, \cdot, s)$ in proposition 2 can be assumed to take the following form: There is a set $\Sigma_{x_0,s}$, a function $v_{x_0,s}: C_1 \times \Sigma_{x_0,s} \to R$, and a function $V_{x_0,s}: R^{\Sigma_{x_0,s}} \to R$ such that, if $\mu_{x_0,s}: K_1 \to R^{\Sigma_{x_0,s}}$ is defined by

$$\mu_{x_0,s}(k_1)(\sigma) = \sup_{c_1 \in k_1} v_{x_0,s}(c_1,\sigma),$$

then $V_{x_0,s}$ is strictly increasing on $\mu_{x_0,s}(K_1)$, and $u(x_0,\cdot,s) = V_{x_0,s} \circ \mu_{x_0,s}$.

Proposition 4 is less gruesome than it looks. If we think of $u(x_0,k_1,s)$ as the x_0,s contingent utility of the opportunity set k_1 for the individual, then this utility is decomposable as follows: With x_0 and s fixed, there is an "auxiliary" refinement of the event s into subevents or substates. The set $\Sigma_{x_0,s}$ gives these substates. For each substate, each consumption bundle c_1 has a substate-dependent utility (which also depends on s and x_0), given by $v_{x_0,s}(c_1,\sigma)$. The x_0,s,σ contingent value of the opportunity set k_1 is just the maximum available substate-contingent utility that it can provide; this is $\mu_{x_0,s}(k_1)(\sigma)$ computed as in the display above. And then $u(x_0,k_1,s)$ is an increasing function of the vector of these maximum available substate-contingent utilities.

If this still seems gruesome, suppose that assumptions 8 and 9 hold for all x_0 and s, and imagine the following special case: (a) Suppose that C_0 is a singleton, so that we can drop all arguments of c_0. (b) Suppose that there are more than three non-null states in S, so that, by proposition 2, state-dependent utilities can be added together. (c) Suppose that the set of substates Σ_s of state s are independent of s. Write Σ for the common set of substates. (d) Suppose that Σ is finite, and V_s takes the form of componentwise addition. Then, with all these assumptions, we would have a representation for $\geq$ given by the index

$$\sum_{s \in S} \sum_{\sigma \in \Sigma} \sup_{c_1 \in k_1(s)} u(c_1,s,\sigma)$$

for some function $u: C_1 \times S \times \Sigma$. This is a form that anyone could love; the individual's preferences involve refining the foreseeable contingencies with substates and computing an additively separable index of maximal substate-state-contingent utility.

Assumption (a) will limit applications, but it wouldn't be too costly to drop it and have back C_0. Assumption (b) is absolutely standard. Assumptions (c) and (d) seem unwarranted, although one can develop natural conditions for (c). (See Kreps 1979, theorem 2.) One can also obtain (d), although the conditions needed for (d) run somewhat counter to what is needed for (c) and very much counter to what is needed for (b); (d) comes for free if C_1 is taken to be a finite set, but if C_1 is finite then obtaining additive separation across foreseeable contingencies becomes a mess. In this regard, note also that the only reason we assumed that C_1 is connected is in order to get the concluding sentence of proposition 2. If one isn't concerned about getting an additively-separable-across-S representation but is willing to settle for weak separability across S, then the assumption that C_1 is connected is completely superfluous.[3]

My point in all this (besides, perhaps, inducing the curious reader to read Kreps 1979 in order to see what the previous paragraph might possibly mean and, more generally, how all this is done) is that the "preference for flexibility" aspect of unforeseen contingencies is easy to model in a form that is quite similar to standard models and has an axiomatic footing. The basic idea is that one subdivides foreseen contingencies into substates. These substates are very much part of the subjective representation of preference, just as are the utility function and (in other sorts of choice-theoretic models) subjective probability assessments. So there is no reason to suppose that different individuals will have preferences that use the same substate structure. And, virtually by definition, we cannot imagine consumption that is contingent on the substates. But given these two complications in the standard sort of model, the standard sort of model does just fine.

3 Contingent Ambiguity of Consequences

In the formal development above, it is assumed that there is no ambiguity in a given state $s \in S$ concerning the opportunity set $x_1(s)$ from which the individual will choose. As was remarked above, we do not necessarily mean to assume that $x_1(s)$ is a set of consumption bundles. The example of section 1 shows that our intentions are more modest; we have in mind applications where $x_1(s)$ represents an opportunity set of tools or assets with which consumption will be obtained. In a sense, our representation suggests that ambiguity (or, better, uncertainty) in the consumption consequences of $x_1(s)$ is precisely what is driving matters: If one takes the utility provided by $c_1 \in x_1(s)$ as the consumption provided (and, with state-dependent utility functions, that is not unreasonable), then the representation says that, conditional on s and x_0, $v_{x_0,s}(c_1,\sigma)$ is the substate-dependent "consumption" that c_1 provides.

Consider, however, the point of view that an important aspect of unforeseen contingencies is that one doesn't even know for sure what tools one will have as a function of the contingencies one lists. If the Flexible Contingent Baggage Corporation in fact exists, shouldn't you worry about a contingency such as "the FCBC fails to deliver all the baggage requested"? And then what? How does one represent a contract with the FCBC as a contingency-determined opportunity set in this case?

The difficulty here is especially acute in precisely the sort of application that motivates this research; viz., governance of transactions. A contract, whether implicit or explicit, may be almost completely vague concerning what is entailed if none of the specified contingencies eventuate. But the form of the model that I have used requires that each party to the transaction be able to specify, even in the contingency s_ω, just what "consequences" will ensue.

At a very formal level, and at the risk of engaging in too difficult a gedankenexperiment, this sort of problem can be dealt with. We imagine an individual making a choice out of some abstract set A^*. (For now, imagine that immediate consumption is dispensed with, although it will be reintroduced momentarily.) We can imagine this individual is able to list a set of mutually exclusive and exhaustive contingencies, given by S. The problem, then, is that there may be no natural embedding of A^* within a set C^S, for any set C.

But consider taking for C precisely the set A^*. We are asking the individual to suppose that he is able to postpone his decision until the uncertainty represented by S alone resolves. The word "alone" in the previous sentence requires emphasis; the individual is to ponder the following: "You will be told precisely which $s \in S$ pertains, but no further information will be given to you. Based on this information, you select an action A^*." If the individual is able to conceive of this situation, then the standard axioms seem as reasonable as ever.

Of course, we need to go one step further. We need to have preferences not on $(A^*)^S$ but on $(K^*)^S$, where K^* is meant to be the set of (compact) subsets of A^*. Now this requires that A^* have some topological structure, but even in the most abstruse applied setting it is hard to imagine that this won't be the case. And then the appropriate *gedanken* question is this: "You will be told precisely which $s \in S$ pertains, at which point you choose a subset $k \in K^*$ of all available options. Then you are allowed to open your eyes, look around, and see which $a \in \mathrm{k}$ you prefer." If the decision maker can imagine this, then we are in business (at least, business enough that the axioms can be examined for reasonableness).

There are two remarks to make about this. First, there may be cases in which it is impossible to imagine parts of the decision being made contingent on S. There is, conceptually, no problem with this; such pieces of the decision are handled as we handled c_0 in section 2. Of course, the greater is the part of an $a \in A^*$ that is thrown into this uncontingent decision category, the less one gets from the remaining structure. Proposition 4 (and, more to the point, proposition 2) specializes to the case in which C_1 is singleton, in which case we only learn anew that a complete, transitive, and continuous binary relation admits a numerical representation. Clearly, mileage will be obtained only insofar as the special structure of contingent opportunity sets of "choices" is actually used.

Second, in a related vein, the formal identification of an abstract set of choices A^* with C_1 would seem, in applications, to be entirely useless. What more is added by all this formalism? If $>$ on A^* is complete, transitive and continuous, it admits a numerical representation. Embedding A^* into $(K^*)^S$ adds nothing to this if, in the application, all the choices are constant functions with singleton consequences. Put another way, any continuous numerical representation of $\succ$ on A^* can be extended to a representation on $(K^*)^S$ of the form in proposition 4. The extension can take many forms, the most obvious of which is this: Given $u\colon A^* \to R$, extend u by

$$u(k) = (1/n) \sum_{i=1}^{n} \max_{a \in k(s_i)} u(a).$$

The assumption that $\succ$ on A^* can be extended to a binary relation on $(K^*)^S$ that satisfies assumptions 5, 6, 7, 9, and 10 places no restrictions on $\succ$ (except for completeness, transitivity, and continuity). Put still another way, if the set of available actions A^* makes no meaningful use of the structure of "a map from contingencies to opportunity sets," and formally identifying A^* with C certainly has this feature, then representations based on that structure tell us nothing.

There are two responses that can be made. The first is that in some of the contingencies $s \in S$ it may be possible to further identify an element of A^* with particular well-defined consequences, at the level of a definite set of tools or perhaps even at the level of consumption. This is, presumably, something that can be considered fully only in a specific application, but let me suggest a plot which may in some cases prove handy: The set S is partitioned into, say, three pieces, S_1, S_2, and S_3. States in S_1 are states in which, for every available decision, there are unambiguous consumption consequences. Let C now denote consumption bundles, so for each $a \in A^*$ and $s \in S_1$ we have an associated $a(s) \in C$. For states $s \in S_2$, consumption consequences are unclear, but there are well-defined consequences at some intermediate level—say, at the level of assets or rights that the decision maker has. Letting D be the space in which such assets or rights (or suites of luggage) reside, for each $a \in A^*$ and $s \in S_2$ there is a corresponding $a(s) \in D$. And then, in states from S_3, things are very ambiguous; in such states the best we can do is to take A^* itself as the consequence space.

Now define $E = C \cup D \cup A^*$, where we imagine that things are labeled so that the three sets are disjoint. Let K be all the compact subsets of E (presuming that each of three pieces has a topological structure, and we use the union of the three topologies as a base for a topology on E), and, finally, let $X = E^S$. (For expositional simplicity, I continue to ignore immediate consumption.) We ask the decision maker for his preferences over X. Or, if we really want to dress this up, we could take Π to be the space of simple probability distributions over E, and let (in the manner of Anscombe and Aumann 1963) $X = \Pi^S$.

In looking at preferences over X we are going one level deeper into thought experiments. Now we are asking the decision maker to consider actions which lead to unambiguous opportunity sets for consumption even on states from S_3. Imagine for now that this thought experiment is feasible; we will momentarily say something about when it isn't.

Where does this take us? For one thing, it may be thought reasonable to adopt assumption 8 in two different guises. First, assumption 8 holds without qualification for those states that are in S_1, because (by assumption) there is no ambiguity about consumption in those states. Second, for $s \notin S_1$, assumption 8 holds for sets $x(s)$ and $x'(s)$ that are subsets of C.[4] That is, when we look at a made-up act x that gives unambiguous consumption in every state s, since consumption is unambiguous, flexibility is valueless.

This, of course, has substantial (and obvious) implications for the functions v_s, over the domain $C \times \Sigma_s$. And then we can use comparisons of $\succsim_s$ on sets drawn entirely from C, from C and D, and then in general, in order to define "unambiguity equivalents" for both the tools in D and (for $s \in S_3$) the general acts $a \in A^*$.[5]

Much of this would be lost if the individual couldn't conceptualize acts that led to unambiguous consumption (or tools) on states not in S_1 (or in S_3). But still, if one knows that flexibility isn't valuable in a certain sort of contingency, one gets some specificity in the representation.

This leads me to the second answer to the question of what is conceivably gained from the formal identification of C with A^*. Consider for a moment a program of embedding this sort of static choice into a dynamic context. Imagine that the decision maker faces the same decision repeatedly, with unchanging A^*. As time passes, imagine the decision maker refining his subjective picture of states of the world in three ways: He may learn just what are the consequences of a particular A^* in contingencies he is able to name, moving those contingencies from the complement of S_1 into S_1 (or, if there is some recurring noise in consumption possibilities, perhaps from S_3 to S_2); he may learn more about the possible states of nature; and he may learn something about the likelihood of surprises—just how likely is s_ω and how valuable is reserved flexibility in some of the contingencies he can name. I am using the word "learn" here in a behavioral sense; I don't imagine anything like Bayesian rational learning, but rather things such as the following: A total surprise (an occurrence of s_ω) raises the weight that is put on s_ω in future choices; the occurrence of an *a priori* unlikely subevent to a contingency s raises the value in s of tools that were valuable in the subevent, and if flexibility in the direction of those tools was not valuable *a priori* then the perceived value of general flexibility in s is enhanced. And so on. For models of this sort, even a formal identification of A^* with C will provide useful modeling structure—although any single static-choice problem may make no use of the structure, the structure provides a natural springboard for using experience to tie together static choices at different times.

4 Concluding Remarks

When the example was presented, we quietly assumed that the each member of the list S of contingencies provided by the decision maker had an objective description. That is, the individual was not allowed to have as his list of states things like "I like bundle z best." *A fortiori*, if the individual cannot map his moods into objectively describable contingencies, we are forcing the individual to live with an incomplete list of relevant contingencies. It isn't that the individual doesn't foresee the contingencies, but only that we don't allow him to have his consumption so finely conditioned as he would like. So, it can be argued, we don't have a model of unforeseen contingencies at all, but rather a standard model of incomplete contracts.

I think this comes down to a semantic argument. If an individual foresees that he might well prefer bundle z, but cannot say in what contingency this will take place (in terms that can be given described objectively), then I would say that what is unforeseen are the circumstances in which the individual's tastes are this or that. Notwithstanding this semantic dispute (about which I have argued endlessly with colleagues without achieving any consensus), the point is taken: What I am calling "unforeseen" another may well wish to call "uncontractable." Indeed, this goes directly to my main point. At the level of static choice, the two are observationally equivalent. If they cannot be separated by what we see, then whether they are two things or one is semantic. (This is not to say that we could not separate them with observed dynamic behavior. My hunch is that it will be possible to make some useful headway here. But I have nothing to say on this at the current time.)

Before the value of the constructs and notions advanced here can be evaluated, it will certainly be necessary to take (at least) another step, to develop a dynamic and retrospective choice theory. The dynamic aspect of what is needed should be clear; the term "retrospective" is meant to connote the notion that boundedly rational individuals use evidence from the past in somewhat *ad hoc* fashion to predict the future. It seems clear to me (although perhaps not to the reader) that dynamic knitting together of the sort of static-choice behavior discussed above is an ideal arena for the general notion of retrospective choice theory. For now, I conclude with the assertion with which I began: An important aspect of "unforeseen contingencies" can be modeled in a fashion that is entirely familiar.

Those of you who have read Kreps 1986 are apt to feel a bit cheated by this. In that paper, I made a big and mysterious to-do about modeling unforeseen contingencies—enough of a to-do so that you might, quite reasonably, have expected something more in the end than the resurrection of a ten-year-old paper. In my own defense, I can only state that it took me this long to get to this position. And, as I hope I made clear in the introduction and in section 3, I am not claiming that the model put forward here completely exhausts the subject. But at the same time, I believe that those aspects that it does capture are particularly important in transaction-cost economics *à la* Williamson. The proof of that pudding, though, must await its eating.

Meanwhile, before even the model of sections 1 and 2 can be brought to bear on a real problem, some serious further work remains to be done:

(1) How does all this adapt to static choice in situations with more than two time periods? Let me be clear: I mean here static-choice behavior in a world where the choices made have ramifications for more than one future period as well as the present. The way to extend the representation seems obvious: The setting is that one chooses immediate consumption and opportunity sets the elements of which are next-period consumption and further opportunity sets. And then, it would seem clear, there is a further subdivision of events at each date. But while the natural representation does seem clear, I am unable to provide any axiomatic justification for it.

(2) Given static choice as in this model, what will dynamic choice look like? This, I anticipate, will have the flavor of retrospective theory that is alluded to (but far from explained) in section 3. The sort of repeated-choice model sketched in section 3 is only one possible variation on dynamic-choice models; for example, Elchanan Ben-Porath and Paul Milgrom (among others) have independently suggested to me that an interesting and important variation would be a two-stage decision problem in which the first stage concerns how much information to gather about the set of possible contingencies.

(3) What are the consequences of this sort of representation for some recognizable multi-period, multi-person problem? I can only pose the question at this time.

Acknowledgments

I am grateful to Elchanan Ben-Porath, Eddie Dekel, Drew Fudenberg, Faruk Gul, Mark Machina, Paul Milgrom, Andy Postelwaite, and Mark Wolfson for helpful discussion. The financial support of National Science Foundation (Grants SES-8707874 and SES-8908402), the John S. Guggenheim Memorial Foundation, and the Sackler Institute for Advanced Studies at Tel Aviv University is gratefully acknowledged.

Notes

1. To be a bit more careful about this: The flexible baggage service is not useful if fully contingent baggage is allowed. If, on the other hand, the baggage company is willing, say, to offer only uncontingent contracts, but is willing to offer you flexibility in what baggage is shipped, you might well value the flexibility.

2. For further discussion of these properties of preference, and also for proofs of the propositions about to be given and for discussion of these issues generally, see Kreps 1979. That paper deals only with the case of a singleton set S, but the extension to finite S is completely straightforward.

3. The assumption that C_0 is connected has been superfluous throughout. In fact, there has never been any need to assume that C_0 is compact. As long as I am giving some technical details, it may be worth noting that the representation implies all the assumptions except for continuity, and it implies continuity if the representing functions are continuous. Continuity of the representing functions is the only lacuna in making the result necessary and sufficient. If C_1 is a finite set, then this lacuna can be removed.

4. My own opinion is that neither of these is entirely reasonable, because of the phenomenon of "uncertainty about future tastes" (which is the subject of Kreps 1979). They might be thought by others to be reasonable, and in some applications they may be good enough approximations so that they can be made with some equanimity. It is perhaps worth observing how one could "measure" the extent to which they are good approximations: In a context with initial consumption that is desirable and single-dimensional (money), fix a contingency s and, for every subset $k \in K_1$ and $c_0 \in C_0$, let

$$\mu(k) = \inf_{c_1 \in k} \{r : (r + c_0, \{c_1\}) \sim_s (c_0, k)\}.$$

Then $\mu(k)$ is a measure, in terms of immediate consumption, of the value of flexibility derived from k. One might even call $\mu(k)$ something like the "flexibility premium" of the set k. Now, for given s, if the largest $\mu(k)$ is small, then it is warranted to say that the individual, in state s, approximately satisfies assumption 8, in roughly the same sense that someone who has small risk premia on a compact domain is approximately risk neutral.

5. I think these things are difficult to evaluate outside a specific context, so I refrain from the formal development. But to get started, suppose that C is one-dimensional (money) and preferences are always strictly increasing in c. Then the "unambiguity equivalent" of a $k \subseteq A^*$ in a contingency $s \in S_3$ is that amount c such that $\{c\} \sim_s k$. Or, to take another obvious construction, we can bound the s-contingent goodness of a $k \subseteq A^*$ by the least amount c such that $\{c\} \sim_s \{c\} \cup k$ and by the greatest amount c such that $k \sim_s \{c\} \cup k$. And so on.

References

Anscombe, F. J., and R. J. Aumann. 1963. "A definition of subjective probability." *Annals of Mathematical Statistics* 34: 199–205.

Bewley, T. 1986. Knightian Decision Theory: Part I. Mimeo, Yale University.

Bewley, T. 1987. Knightian Decision Theory, Part II: Intertemporal Problems." Mimeo, Yale University.

Debreu, G. 1959. "Topological methods in cardinal utility theory." In *Mathematical Methods of the Social Sciences*, ed. K. J. Arrow, S. Karlin, and P. Suppes. Stanford University Press.

Koopmans, T. C. 1964. "On the flexibility of future preferences." In *Human Judgments and Optimality*, ed. M. W. Shelly and G. L. Bryan. Wiley.

Kreps, D. M. 1979. "A representation theorem for 'preference for flexibility.'" *Econometrica* 47: 565–577.

Kreps, D. M. 1986. "Corporate culture and economic theory." In Japanese in *Technological Innovation and Business Strategy*, ed. M. Tsuchiya. Nippon Keizai Shimbunsha Press. In English in *Rational Perspectives on Political Economy*, ed. J. Alt and L. Shepsle. Cambridge University Press, 1990.

Loomes, G., and R. Sugden. 1986. "Disappointment and dynamic consistency in choice under uncertainty." *Review of Economic Studies*, 53: 271–282.

Savage, L. J. 1954. *The Foundations of Statistics*. Wiley. Revised and enlarged edition: Dover, 1972.

Schmeidler, D. 1989. "Subjective probability and expected utility without additivity." *Econometrica* 57: 571–588.

Strotz, R. 1955–56. "Myopia and inconsistency in dynamic utility maximization." *Review of Economic Studies* 23: 165–180.

Williamson, O. 1985. *The Economic Institutions of Capitalism*. Free Press.

Lexicographic Probabilities and Iterated Admissibility

Adam Brandenburger

The implications of common knowledge of rationality in normal-form games have been explored in recent years by Aumann (1987), Bernheim (1984, 1986), Brandenburger and Dekel (1987, 1989), Pearce (1984), Tan and Werlang (1988), and others. This line of research is concerned with providing what Aumann has termed "analytic" foundations for game-theoretic solution concepts.

The most conservative approach is due to Bernheim and Pearce. Bernheim and Pearce's notion of rationalizability assumes that it is common knowledge that each player is a subjective expected utility maximizer (Savage 1954; Anscombe and Aumann 1963), but that the precise subjective probability distribution held by each player is not necessarily common knowledge. Bernheim and Pearce show that this assumption implies that players choose iteratively undominated actions.[1]

The hypothesis of subjective expected utility maximization does not preclude players from choosing actions that are weakly dominated (inadmissible). Within decision theory, admissibility has long been advanced as an important criterion for choice (see, for example, Luce and Raiffa 1957, chapter 13). On the premise that the criterion is equally reasonable in a game-theoretic context, Kohlberg and Mertens (1986, p. 1014) view "admissibility of the players' strategies as a basic requirement" of a satisfactory solution concept. Moreover, they argue in favor of an iterated admissibility requirement.[2]

This leads naturally to the following question: What are the implications of assuming, in addition to common knowledge of rationality, that it is common knowledge that players choose only admissible actions? Samuelson (1989) and Börgers (1990) have addressed this and other questions concerning the interplay between the concepts of common knowledge and admissibility. The present paper was inspired by Börgers' work in particular, and uses lexicographic probabilities to derive a result (proposition 2 below) which is analogous to a result of Börgers. Both results address the question posed at the beginning of this paragraph.

By analogy with the result linking common knowledge of subjective expected utility maximization and iterated deletion of dominated actions, one might conjecture that assuming it to be common knowledge that players choose *admissible* actions implies that they choose *iteratively admissible* actions. However, as Samuelson has demonstrated, establishing such a result seems problematic. Börgers shows that a weaker result is achievable. He shows that *approximate* common knowledge of admissibility implies that players choose actions that survive one round of deletion of weakly dominated actions followed by iterated deletion of strongly dominated actions. This latter procedure was proposed by Dekel and Fudenberg (1990), who showed it to be equivalent to iterated admissibility when players may be uncertain about other players' payoffs.

Börgers is led to assume approximate common knowledge since, in order to incorporate admissibility, he supposes that a player's subjective probability distribution assigns strictly positive weight to *all* choices of the other players. If there are any dominance relationships in the game, this condition will violate common knowledge of rationality since it requires players to place positive probability on dominated choices by other players. In order to resolve this conflict, Börgers replaces common knowledge with a notion of approximate common knowledge that builds on the definitions of Monderer and Samet (1989) and Stinchcombe (1988).

The objective of the present paper is to show how lexicographic probabilities can be used to prove a result analogous to that of Börgers.[3] Thus, instead of approximate common knowledge, I use a lexicographic analogue, which I call common first-order knowledge. To define common first-order knowledge of admissibility, I employ the non-Archimedean version of subjective expected utility theory developed by Blume, Brandenburger, and Dekel (1991a). According to this theory, a decision maker possesses, in addition to a utility function on outcomes, a *hierarchy* of probability distributions on uncertain events that is used lexicographically in ranking actions. (In conventional subjective expected utility theory, a decision maker possesses a *single* probability distribution.) Admissibility of the decision maker's choices is ensured by requiring that every event receive positive measure under some probability distribution in the hierarchy. As for common first-order knowledge, one begins by saying that the decision maker "first-order knows an event" if that event is assigned probability 1 by the first-order probability distribution in the decision maker's hierarchy. An event is then common first-order knowledge if everyone first-order knows it, everyone first-order knows that everyone first-order knows it, and so on.

1 The Result

Consider an n-person normal-form game

$$\Gamma = \langle A^1, \ldots, A^n; u^1, \ldots, u^n \rangle$$

where, for each $i = 1, \ldots, n$, A^i is player i's finite set of pure strategies (henceforth actions) and $u^i: A^1 \times \cdots \times A^n \to \mathbb{R}$ is player i's von Neumann-Morgenstern utility function. For any $i = 1, \ldots, n$, the set $A^1 \times \cdots \times A^{i-1} \times A^{i+1} \times \cdots \times A^n$ will be denoted by A^{-i}.

In developing the theory of rationalizability, Bernheim and Pearce augment the orthodox description of a normal-form game by specifying for each player not only a utility function over outcomes but also a subjective probability distribution over the uncertainty that player faces. By contrast, we are going to assume that players adhere to the non-Archimedean version of subjective expected utility theory developed by Blume, Brandenburger, and Dekel (1991a). It is therefore supposed that each player i possesses, in addition to a utility function u^i, a vector $\rho^i = (p_1^i, \ldots, p_{K^i}^i)$, for some integer K^i, of probability measures on A^{-i}, where p_1^i is player i's first-order belief about the other players' choices of action, p_2^i is player i's second-order belief, and so on. The component probability measures are used lexicographically in ranking actions. Thus, player i prefers an action $a^i \in A^i$ over another action $b^i \in A^i$ if and only if[4]

$$\left[\sum_{a^{-i} \in A^{-i}} p_k^i(a^{-i}) u^i(a^i, a^{-i})\right]_{k=1}^{K^i} \geq_L \left[\sum_{a^{-i} \in A^{-i}} p_k^i(a^{-i}) u^i(b^i, a^{-i})\right]_{k=1}^{K^i}.$$

Following the terminology of Blume, Brandenburger, and Dekel (1991a), I will refer to a vector $\rho^i = (p_1^i, \ldots, p_{K^i}^i)$ of probability measures as a *lexicographic probability system* (LPS).

An important consequence of assuming that player i adheres to the non-Archimedean version of subjective expected utility theory just described is that admissibility of i's choices can be guaranteed without at the same time ruling out the possibility that i assigns probability 0 (in a certain sense) to some of the other players' choices.

DEFINITION 1 An LPS $\rho^i = (p_1^i, \ldots, p_{K^i}^i)$ of player i has *full support* if, for each $a^{-i} \in A^{-i}$, $p_k^i(a^{-i}) > 0$ for some $k = 1, \ldots, K^i$.

PROPOSITION 1 Suppose player i's LPS $\rho^i = (p_1^i, \ldots, p_{K^i}^i)$ has full support. Then any action $a^i \in A^i$ that satisfies

$$\left[\sum_{a^{-i} \in A^{-i}} p_k^i(a^{-i})u^i(a^i,a^{-i})\right]_{k=1}^{K^i} \geq_{\mathrm{L}} \left[\sum_{a^{-i} \in A^{-i}} p_k^i(a^{-i})u^i(b^i,a^{-i})\right]_{k=1}^{K^i}$$

for all $b^i \in A^i$ is admissible.

Proposition 1 will not be proved here, since it is very closely related to theorem 4.2 in Blume, Brandenburger, and Dekel 1991a and proposition 1 in Blume, Brandenburger, and Dekel 1991b. Proposition 1 says that if player i's LPS has full support, then i's optimal choices will be admissible. Of course, the same effect could have been achieved in the case in which player i possessed a *single* probability distribution on A^{-i}, by simply requiring that distribution to have full support in the conventional sense. The advantage of the non-Archimedean formulation is that in guaranteeing admissibility of player i's choices, one does not at the same time have to forgo the possibility that certain action profiles of the other players are deemed infinitely unlikely by player i. Specifically, these are the action profiles $a^{-i} \in A^{-i}$ that are assigned first-order probability 0 by player i ($p_1^i(a^{-i}) = 0$). of course, any such action profile a^{-i} is not viewed as *completely* impossible by i, since it must be that $p_k^i(a^{-i}) > 0$ for some $k = 2, \ldots, K^i$.

For each other player j, where $j \neq i$, there is a set of j's actions that player i considers infinitely unlikely. This set consists of those actions $a^j \in A^j$ assigned probability 0 by (the marginal on A^j of) p_1^i. Similarly, there is a set of j's actions that i is almost sure contains j's choice, namely the set of actions $a^j \in A^j$ assigned positive probability by p_1^i. I will say that player i first-order knows that player j's choice lies in this latter set.

So far, no mention has been made of what player i might know about each other player j's rationality. I am going to assume that i first-order knows that j chooses an admissible action in the same manner as i does. That is, for each action $a^j \in A^j$ to which i assigns positive first-order probability, there must be an LPS $\rho^j = (p_1^j, \ldots, p_{K^j}^j)$, where each p_k^j ($k = 1, \ldots, K^j$) is a probability measure on A^{-j}, that has full support in a sense analogous to definition 1 (for each $a^{-j} \in A^{-j}$, $p_k^j(a^{-j}) > 0$ for some $k = 1, \ldots, K^j$) and is such that

$$\left[\sum_{a^{-j} \in A^{-j}} p_k^j(a^{-j})u^j(a^j,a^{-j})\right]_{k=1}^{K^j} \geq_{\mathrm{L}} \left[\sum_{a^{-j} \in A^{-j}} p_k^j(a^{-j})u^j(b^j,a^{-j})\right]_{k=1}^{K^j}$$

for all $b^j \in A^j$. But we also want to assume that player i first-order knows that player j first-order knows that each player chooses an admissible action, and so on. That is, we want it to be *common first-order knowledge* that the players choose admissible actions. In the following I say that an LPS $\rho^i = (p_1^i, \ldots, p_{K^i}^i)$ *justifies* an action a^i of player i if

$$\left[\sum_{a^{-i} \in A^{-i}} p_k^i(a^{-i})u^i(a^i,a^{-i})\right]_{k=1}^{K^i} \geq_L \left[\sum_{a^{-i} \in A^{-i}} p_k^i(a^{-i})u^i(b^i,a^{-i})\right]_{k=1}^{K^i}$$

for all $b^i \in A^i$.

DEFINITION 2 An action a^i of player i is *permissible* if there is an LPS ρ^i of player i that has full support and justifies a^i, if for each $j \neq i$ and every $a^j \in A^j$ assigned positive first-order probability by ρ^i there is an LPS ρ^j of player j that has full support and justifies a^j, and so on.

For each $i = 1, \ldots, n$, let $P^i \subset A^i$ be the set of permissible actions of player i. Then, if it is common first-order knowledge that the players choose admissible actions, each player i selects an action from P^i.

The main result of this paper relates the sets P^i to the sets of actions that survive the following elimination procedure. To define the procedure, a shorthand will be useful. Given the original game $\Gamma = \langle A^1, \ldots, A^n; u^1, \ldots, u^n \rangle$ and subsets $S^i \subset A^i$ $(i = 1, \ldots, n)$, the reduced game,

$$\langle S^1, \ldots, S^n; v^1, \ldots, v^n \rangle,$$

where, for each i, v^i is the restriction to $S^1 \times \cdots \times S^n$ of u^i, will be referred to simply as "the game $S^1 \times \cdots \times S^n$." Now, for each $i = 1, \ldots, n$, define sets

$$W^i = \{a^i \in A^i : a^i \text{ is not weakly dominated in the game } A^1 \times \cdots \times A^n\}$$

and

$$S_1^i = \{a^i \in W^i : a^i \text{ is not strongly dominated in the game } W^1 \times \cdots \times W^n\},$$

and, for $m = 2, 3, \ldots$, define inductively

$$S_m^i = \{a^i \in S_{m-1}^i : a^i \text{ is not strongly dominated in the game } S_{m-1}^1 \times \cdots \times S_{m-1}^n\}.$$

Finiteness of the original sets of actions A^i immediately implies the existence of an M such that, for all $i = 1, \ldots, n$,

$S_m^i = S_M^i \neq \varnothing$ for all $m \geq M$.

The residual sets S_M^i are the sets of actions that remain after elimination of weakly dominated actions followed by iterated elimination of strongly dominated actions. The result can now be stated.

PROPOSITION 2 For each $i = 1, \ldots, n$, the sets P^i of permissible actions is the same as the residual set S_M^i.

In light of the above argument that led to the definition of permissible actions (definition 2), proposition 2 implies that the assumption that it is common first-order knowledge that the players choose admissible actions implies that each player i selects an action from S_M^i.

Proof of proposition 2 I first show that, for any i, $S_M^i \subset P^i$. Consider an $a^i \in S_M^i$. Since a^i is not strongly dominated in the game $S_M^1 \times \cdots \times S_M^n$, the usual supporting hyperplane argument implies that there is a probability distribution p_1^i on S_M^{-i} such that

$$\sum_{a^{-i} \in S_M^{-i}} p_1^i(a^{-i})u^i(a^i,a^{-i}) \geq \sum_{a^{-i} \in S_M^{-i}} p_1^i(a^{-i})u^i(b^i,a^{-i})$$

for all $b^i \in S_M^i$. In fact, this inequality must hold for all $b^i \in A^i$. (An action b^i for which the inequality was violated could not have been eliminated.) Moreover, since $S_M^i \subset W^i$, a^i is not weakly dominated in the game $A^1 \times \cdots \times A^n$. Hence, there is a *strictly positive* probability distribution p_2^i on A^{-i} such that

$$\sum_{a^{-i} \in A^{-i}} p_2^i(a^{-i})u^i(a^i,a^{-i}) \geq \sum_{a^{-i} \in A^{-i}} p_2^i(a^{-i})u^i(b^i,a^{-i})$$

for all $b^i \in A^i$. Define an LPS ρ^i of player i by $\rho^i = (p_1^i,p_2^i)$, where p_1^i is now viewed as a distribution on the whole of A^{-i} (with support contained in S_M^{-i}). Then ρ^i has full support (since p_2^i does), and ρ^i justifies a^i.

I have argued that for each i and any $a^i \in S_M^i$ there is an LPS $\rho^i = (p_1^i,p_2^i)$ with full support that justifies a^i. Moreover, for each $j \neq i$, any action a^j assigned positive probability by p_1^i lies in S_M^j; hence, there is an LPS $\rho^j = (p_1^j,p_2^j)$ with full support that justifies a^j. And so on. This establishes that $a^i \in P^i$.

I now turn to showing that $P^i \subset S_M^i$. Consider an $a^i \in P^i$. Associated with such an a^i is a hierarchy of LPS's—the LPS ρ^i of player i that justifies a^i, for each $j \neq i$ and every $a^j \in A^j$ assigned positive first-order probability by ρ^i an LPS ρ^j of player j that justifies a^j, and so on. For each i, let $Q^i \subset A^i$ be the set of actions of i that receive positive first-order probability by some justifying LPS in the hierarchy. The proof will be completed by showing that $\{a^i\} \cup Q^i \subset S^i_M$ and, for $j \neq i$, that $Q^j \subset S^j_M$ (and hence, in particular, that $a^i \in S^i_M$, as is required).

The first step is argue that $\{a^i\} \cup Q^i \subset W^i$. To see this, note that a^i is justified by an LPS of player i with full support and hence, by proposition 1, is admissible. The same holds for any element of Q^i. An analogous argument establishes that $Q^j \subset W^j$ for $j \neq i$.

The next step is to argue that $\{a^i\} \cup Q^i \subset S^i_1$. To see this, note that if $\rho^i = (p^i_1, \ldots, p^i_{K^i})$ is the LPS that justifies a^i, then

$$\sum_{a^{-i} \in A^{-i}} p^i_1(a^{-i})u^i(a^i, a^{-i}) \geq \sum_{a^{-i} \in A^{-i}} p^i_1(a^{-i})u^i(b^i, a^{-i})$$

for all $b^i \in A^i$. In particular, this inequality holds for all $b^i \in W^i$. Moreover, by the definition of Q^{-i}, the support of p^i_1 must be contained in Q^{-i}, which is itself contained in W^{-i}. All this establishes that a^i is not strongly dominated in the (reduced) game $W^1 \times \cdots \times W^n$; that is, $a^i \in S^i_1$. The same holds for any element of Q^i. An analogous argument establishes that $Q^j \subset S^j_1$ for $j \neq i$.

Continuing in this fashion demonstrates that, for all m, $\{a^i\} \cup Q^i \subset S^i_m$ and $Q^j \subset S^j_m$ for $j \neq i$, and hence that $\{a^i\} \cup Q^i \subset S^i_M$ and $Q^j \subset S^j_M$ for $j \neq i$. ■

Dedication

Dedicated to Frank Hahn, who has always set the highest standards as a teacher and scholar.

Acknowledgments

This paper relies on earlier work with Larry Blume and Eddie Dekel on lexicographic probabilities. I am further indebted to Eddie Dekel for discussions leading to the formulation of proposition 2, and to Vijay Krishna for helpful comments. Financial support from the Harvard Business School Division of Research is gratefully acknowledged.

Notes

1. "Undominated" means "not strongly dominated." Actions that are not weakly dominated will be referred to as "admissible." This result is true when a player's beliefs about the choices of the other players are allowed to exhibit stochastic dependence (see Pearce 1984, p. 1035). Independence issues are not explored in this paper.

2. Kohlberg and Mertens (1986) observe that "one might argue that ... a strategically stable equilibrium [should] remain so when [an inadmissible] strategy is deleted (and hence, when the deletion is done iteratively)" (p. 1014) and then point out that "this requirement is incompatible with existence" (p. 1014). They therefore propose an iterated admissibility requirement that *is* compatible with existence.

3. Lexicographic probabilities have also proved useful in characterizing refinements of Nash equilibrium. See Blume, Brandenburger, and Dekel 1991b.

4. For $x, y \in \mathbb{R}^K$, $x \geq_L y$ if and only if whenever $y_k > x_k$ there exists an $\ell < k$ such that $x_\ell > y_\ell$.

References

Anscombe, F., and R. Aumann. 1963. "A definition of subjective probability." *Annals of Mathematical Statistics* 34: 199–205.

Aumann, R. 1987. "Correlated equilibrium as an expression of Bayesian rationality." *Econometrica* 55: 1–18.

Bernheim, B. D. 1984. "Rationalizable strategic behavior." *Econometrica* 52: 1007–1028.

Bernheim, B. D. 1986. "Axiomatic characterization of rational choice in strategic environments." *Scandinavian Journal of Economics* 88: 473–488.

Blume, L., A. Brandenburger, and E. Dekel. 1991a. "Lexicographic probabilities and choice under uncertainty." *Econometrica* 59: 61–79.

Blume, L., A. Brandenburger, and E. Dekel. 1991b. "Lexicographic probabilities and equilibrium refinements." *Econometrica* 59: 81–98.

Börgers, T. 1990. Weak Dominance and Approximate Common Knowledge. Working paper, Institut für Volkswirtschaft, Universität Basel.

Brandenburger, A., and E. Dekel. 1987. "Rationalizability and correlated equilibria." *Econometrica* 55: 1391–1402.

Brandenburger, A., and E. Dekel. 1989. "The role of common knowledge assumptions in game theory." In *The Economics of Missing Markets, Information, and Games*, ed. F. Hahn. Oxford University Press.

Dekel, E., and D. Fudenberg. 1990. "Rational behavior with payoff uncertainty." *Journal of Economic Theory* 52: 243–267.

Kohlberg, E., and J.-F. Mertens. 1986. "On the strategic stability of equilibria." *Econometrica* 54: 1003–1037.

Luce, R., and H. Raiffa. 1957. *Games and Decisions*. Wiley.

Monderer, D., and D. Samet. 1989. "Approximating common knowledge with common beliefs." *Games and Economic Behavior* 1: 170–190.

Pearce, D. 1984. "Rationalizable strategic behavior and the problem of perfection." *Econometrica* 52: 1029–1050.

Samuelson, L. 1989. Dominated Strategies and Common Knowledge. Working paper, Department of Economics, Pennsylvania State University.

Savage, L. 1954. *The Foundations of Statistics.* Wiley.

Stinchcombe, M. 1988. Approximate Common Knowledge. Unpublished manuscript, Department of Economics, University of California, San Diego.

Tan, T., and S. R. C. Werlang. 1988. "The Bayesian foundations of solution concepts of games." *Journal of Economic Theory* 45: 370–391.

Understanding the Past in order to Assess the Future: On Learning Equilibrium Price Processes

Mordecai Kurz

Rational-expectations equilibrium has become a standard tool employed by most researchers of markets with asymmetric information and economies with incomplete markets. The presumption is that in such equilibria prices reflect all private information and agents who do not possess this information can derive it from prices. The formulation of most models is such that once all private information is extracted and thus becomes public, the conditional forecasts of all the agents are the same and are equal to the conditional forecast of the model (for a review see Grossman 1981). It then follows that associated with every dynamic rational-expectations equilibrium is a *true* stochastic process of equilibrium prices; at any date, agents extract from prices all private information, so that the residual uncertainty in prices follows a true conditional distribution, which is known to all agents.

The concept of rational-expectations equilibrium stands in sharp contrast to the idea of "temporary equilibrium" (see, for example, Grandmont and Hildenbrand 1974), which crucially depends upon what agents think about the distribution of future prices. In a dynamic temporary equilibrium, the N agents hold probability beliefs about the sequence of all future prices. Denote those beliefs by $(G_1, \ldots, G_N)$. Current prices are then determined by the equalization of aggregate excess demand to 0 at all dates $n = 1, 2, \ldots$. This, in turn, induces an *actual* stochastic process G of prices, which may differ from all G_j. The natural criticism of the theory of temporary equilibrium is that agents do not learn from experience and do not revise their probability assessments. If they did, so goes the argument, these beliefs might converge to some G^* that was a fixed point of the implied map, and this G^* would then induce a rational-expectations equilibrium.

The positive side of the theory of temporary equilibrium is that it provides a framework for thinking about markets in which price equilibria are sensitive to and depend upon expectations. Most economists believe that such dependence is a real and perhaps important phenomenon. Yet, most economists also accept the idea that expectation should be based on the best available information, and that rational agents should therefore revise their probability beliefs when faced with new information. It is also a rather general view that extracting private information from prices is a formidable task. How could agents learn to perform such a difficult task?

A sensible way in which such learning might be accomplished is through the use of statistical methods that would be employed by an agent to discover the statistical regularity in the data. This would allow the conditional beliefs of agents to converge to the true conditional distribution of the process; hence, a rational-expectations equilibrium might be viewed as a good approximation. It is by now well known that this program faces significant difficulties. At the outset, such equilibria may not always exist (Green 1977; Kreps 1977; Radner 1979; Allen 1981; Jordan 1982a; Anderson and Sonnenschein 1982); moreover, the market implementation of such equilibria raises many difficulties (Beja 1976; Kobayashi 1977; Jordan 1982b), not the least of which is the fact that such equilibrium prices are not "incentive compatible": agents who sense that they may have an influence on market prices will distort their behavior so that prices may not reflect all their information.

The main concerns here are the process of learning and the convergence of beliefs. For a review of the literature and an in-depth evaluation of the problems encountered, see Bray and Kreps 1986. A classification proposed by Bray and Kreps suggests that the literature on learning of rational expectations equilibria has evolved with the aid of two types of models. Models of the first type (Radner 1982; Bray 1982; Blume and Easely 1982; Bray and Savin 1986) specifies an exogenous process by which the agents learn. As a result, the equilibrium is not fully compatible with the changing beliefs of the agents, and hence some of these models of behavior may be viewed as irrational. The interaction between the dynamic evolution of the economy and the learning behavior of the agents is also central to DeCanio 1979; Evans 1983, 1985, 1986; Fourgeaud, Gourieroux, and Pradel 1986; Grandmont and Laroque 1987; Marcet and Sargent 1986, 1989; and other papers. Models of the second type are identified by Bray and Kreps as involving rational learning of the unknown parameters *within* a rational-expectations equilibrium (Arrow and Green 1973; Blume and Easley 1981; Lewis 1981; Frydman 1982; Townsend 1978, 1983; Bray and Kreps 1986). Here simple examples of models with a small number of parameters are postulated. Agents know everything except these parameters, which they estimate from the data. In all simple cases, convergence to a steady state, which is a rational-expectations equilibrium, has been demonstrated. Bray and Kreps (1986) also show that Bayesian learners will have converging beliefs.

This paper goes one step beyond the concept of learning the unknown parameters within a rational expectations equilibrium. Here it is assumed that the economy is large; and with all the private signals of agents given, some intertemporal rational-expectations equilibrium is established. Thus, there is a *true* stochastic process of prices. A competitive agent who is infinitesimally small relative to the economy observes his own private information and all market prices; he makes his own intertemporal choices based on his probability beliefs at date n. With information accumulating with time, the agent attempts to learn the price process while knowing that his demand and information have no effect on the market. Assuming that the agent is rational and has unlimited computing ability, we ask whether the agent can "learn" the price process. As hinted, we shall define "learning" as the convergence of the learned conditional distribution of future prices to the *true* conditional distribution.

The view that will be adopted here ignores completely any interaction between the beliefs and actions of the agent and the market. Readers who may have been accustomed to think about this interaction as the *central* problem of learning a rational-expectations equilibrium are encouraged to think of the observing agent as a well-trained economist who is not a participant in the market at all but who uses the best available methods to learn the price process. If the concept of a rational-expectations equilibrium is to be coherent, a rational observer must be capable of learning it.

In this paper, "learning" means the discovery of the unknown conditional distribution of *future* events given the past. Although stationarity, ergodicity, or Martingale properties of the process are very useful tools which can be used to specify conditions for "learning" (or nonlearning), I shall attempt in this paper not to use them. Instead, I want to characterize the circumstances of nonlearning in terms that may correspond to the experience of an agent-econometrician working with time-series observations. To accomplish this, I make a sharp distinction between the ability of the agent to explain *past events* (in the sense of finding out their true unconditional probabilities) and his ability to predict *future events* (in the sense of discovering the true conditional probability of these events given any past events).

If $\{x_n\}_{n=1}^{\infty}$ is a stochastic process with a true probability P and if V^n is a measure (on the same measurable space) specifying the belief of an agent at stage n, then the condition of "learning" requires that the conditional probabilities $V^n(A|B)$ and $P_n(A|B)$ be close for large n. Here A is a *future* event at n and B is a *past* event at n; hence, $B \in \mathscr{F}_n$, where $\mathscr{F}_n$ is the σ-field generated by $(x_1, x_2, \ldots, x_n)$. Note that at stage n the agent assumes that past events B occurred according to the joint distribution $V_n^n(B)$, and that the error of the agent in assessing the probability of past events is measured by

$$|V_n^n(B) - P_n(B)|, \quad B \in \mathscr{F}_n.$$

The measure P_n is the restriction of P to $\mathscr{F}_n$. If $|V_n^n(B) - P_n(B)|$ does not converge to 0, then, in an intuitive sense, the learning agent was unable to "understand" or "explain" all *past* events.

The main results of the paper formulate the criteria for nonlearning of an agent in terms of *his inability to explain or understand past events.* Simply stated, the criterion proposed below says that an agent cannot learn a process (in the sense defined above) if he cannot discover precisely the unconditional probabilities of past events. This means that you cannot predict the future correctly if you do not know the past accurately! In the exact formulation of this condition, I show that nonlearning occurs if the agent continues to make a uniform error in measuring a specified class of low-P-probability past events. This brings up a subtle point.

Section 1 points out that, in order for the agent to attain learning, it is *not* necessary that the measures V^n converge to P. An example is provided according to which the marginal distribution (derived from V^n) of all future events (from n on) does not converge to the true marginal distribution but learning does take place in the sense of convergence of the conditional distributions. On the other hand, the criterion advanced by the two theorems below states that if the agent is to learn the process, then V_n^n and P_n cannot disagree too much on past events of low P-probability!

The above conclusions have interesting empirical implications. If a price process can be learned, then the probabilities of past events must be common knowledge among agents in the market; no substantial disagreements about the evaluation of the past should be encountered. I doubt very much that there are any real price processes that satisfy such a condition. Both experts and "technicians" chart past price data and seem to construct multiple theories about past behavior of prices. Moreover, there does not seem to be a market in which all the participants agree on a common explanation of past market performance. The diversity of strongly held opinions about what may explain past price movements is, perhaps, the ultimate proof that such processes cannot be learned.

1 The Conceptual Framework

We start with a complete and separable state space Ω and a measurable space $(\Omega,\mathscr{F})$ which is isomorphic to the unit interval with its Borel sets. A price process $\{x_n\}_{n=1}^{\infty}$ is defined on the probability space $(\Omega,\mathscr{F},P)$ where $x_k \in R_+^l$ and P is viewed as the true probability measure on $(\Omega,\mathscr{F})$. Since our learning agent will observe the l prices at every date, let us represent his information structure with the standard filtration $\{\mathscr{F}_n\}_{n=1}^{\infty}$, which we define as

$$\mathscr{F}_n = \sigma(x_1, x_2, x_3, \ldots, x_n), \tag{1}$$

where $\sigma(x_1, \ldots, x_n)$ is the smallest σ field generated by $(x_1, \ldots, x_n)$. Also,

$$\mathscr{F} \supseteq \mathscr{F}_\infty = \sigma\left(\bigcup_{n=1}^{\infty} \mathscr{F}_n\right). \tag{2}$$

$\mathscr{F}_n$ represents all that the agent could conceivably learn from sequences of n prices $(x_1, x_2, \ldots, x_n)$. We use the notation

$$x^n = (x_1, x_2, \ldots, x_n)$$

and

$$x = (x_1, x_2, x_3, \ldots).$$

The price process is thought of as being generated in an economy with markets for goods and assets. There is a set of N agents, each having his own resources (endowment), budget constraints, utility function, production technology, and all private information about these. Uncertainty arises from many sources. Endowments, utilities, and technology may be random; and these random outcomes may be unobservable, publicly observable, or privately observable. In addition, random and unobserved exogenous shocks may influence the performance of agents, the productivity of resources, etc. Rational agents combine all their private information with any additional information they can deduce from prices. Consequently, in a rational-expectations equilibrium all agents end up with the same information represented by the σ fields $\mathscr{F}_n$. This is precisely the information structure we are giving our learning agent. The essential difference between the active agents in the market and our learning agent is that the active agents know P and can thus deduce all the conditional distributions $P(\cdot|\mathscr{F}_n)$ for all n. Our learning agent does not know P; he observes a *single realization* $x = (x_1, x_2, x_3, \ldots)$ of the process, and as he proceeds he learns something about P. The central question of this paper is whether he asymptotically approaches the *true* conditional distribution $P(\cdot|x^n)$.

At the start of the process, our agent may already have some information about the process that could be translated into a conjecture that there exists a class $\mathscr{P}_0$ of measures on $(\Omega, \mathscr{F})$ that contains P. Moreover, if the agent were a Bayesian he would select a prior V^0. Updating V^0 given all possible information up to stage n suggests that the agent selects the conditional probability v^n:

$$v^n = V^0(\cdot|\mathscr{F}_n). \tag{3}$$

For any $A \in \mathscr{F}$, $\{V^0(A|\mathscr{F}_n), \mathscr{F}_n\}$ is a bounded martingale, and by the martingale convergence theorem it converges V^0 a.e. to the $\mathscr{F}_\infty$ measurable random variable $V^0(A|\mathscr{F}_\infty)$. Given that $\mathscr{F}_\infty$ contains all that the agent can ever learn, $V^0(A|\mathscr{F}_\infty)$ is the best posterior he can have. But, is this the correct probability? To explain this question, suppose that x is the realization of the process. Now let

$$B(x^n) = \{\omega | x_1(\omega) = x_1, \ldots, x_n(\omega) = x_n\}.$$

Since $B(x^n) \in \mathscr{F}_n$, define for $A \in \mathscr{F}$

$$v^n(A|x^n) = V^0(A|B(x^n))$$

and

$$P^n(A|x^n) = P(A|B(x^n)).$$

$v^n(A|x^n)$ is the conditional probability of A given x^n assessed by a Bayesian while $P^n(A|x^n)$ is the true distribution. It is then reasonable to say that if

$$\lim_{n\to\infty} |P^n(A|x^n) - v^n(A|x^n)| = 0 \tag{4}$$

then the Bayesian procedure was *consistent* and the agent using it learned the process.

In the formulation of our learning process we do not preclude the possibility that the agent is a Bayesian; he is allowed to be one. However, if he observes x_1 (which cannot happen under V^0) we allow him to select a new measure V^1. We thus postulate that the agent has a sequence of operators L_n such that

$$V^{n+1} = L_n(V^n, x^n). \tag{5}$$

We do not specify what L_n are. One way of thinking about the process is that at any stage the agent establishes a set $\mathscr{P}_n$ of possible measures over $(\Omega, \mathscr{F})$. Given the observations $(x_1, x_2, x_3, \ldots, x_n)$, V^{n+1} is selected so as to maximize the n-dimensional likelihood over $\mathscr{P}_n$. Such a maximum is generally not unique. Nevertheless, given the realization x, it induces a sequence $\{V^n\}_{n=1}^{\infty}$ of learned probability measures on $(\Omega, \mathscr{F})$. We postulate that the learning process converges to a measure Q:

ASSUMPTION 1 V^n converges uniformly to Q; that is,

$$\lim_{n \to \infty} \operatorname{Sup}_{A \in \mathscr{F}} |V^n(A) - Q(A)| = 0. \tag{6}$$

An immediate technical result is available:

LEMMA 1 Let $A_k \in \mathscr{F}$, where $k = 1, 2, \ldots$. Then

$$\lim_{k \to \infty} |V^k(A_k) - Q(A_k)| = 0. \tag{7}$$

Proof $|V^k(A_k) - Q(A_k)| \leqq \operatorname{Sup}_{A \in \mathscr{F}} |V^k(A) - Q(A)|$. Now take limits on both sides and use (6) to show (7). ■

As a matter of interpretation, we think of Q as the limiting probability assessment over the process x after all learning is done. We are not excluding the possibility that $Q(A|\mathscr{F}_\infty) = V^0(A|\mathscr{F}_\infty)$ for all $A \in \mathscr{F}$, and the analysis below will not depend upon this.

I will now introduce an assumption on the rationality of learning. It requires the learning agent to adopt beliefs compatible with the data he observes. To motivate first, suppose that we pick a sequence of events $H_n \in \mathscr{F}_\infty$ which are "future" events at stage n (i.e.: $H_n \in \mathscr{F}_\infty$ but $H_n \notin \mathscr{F}_n$). Suppose that, for some large n, $Q(H_n) > \varepsilon$ for some $\varepsilon > 0$. Since $V^n \to Q$ uniformly, there exists n^* such that, if $n > n^*$,

$$|V^n(H_n) - Q(H_n)| < \varepsilon/2$$

and hence

$$V^n(H_n) \geq \varepsilon/2.$$

If, however, H_n is a future set at date n, then the evaluation $V^n(H_n) \geq \varepsilon/2$ must be compatible with the observations, and we would expect that there exists $\delta > 0$ such that $V^n(H_n|x^n) \geq \delta$. This leads to the following assumption.

ASSUMPTION 2 (Rationality of Learning) For any x, there exists n^* (which may depend upon x) such that, for all $n \geq n^*$, if $H \in \mathscr{F}_\infty$ but $H \notin \mathscr{F}_n$, and if $Q(H) \geq \varepsilon$, then $V^n(H|x^n) > \varepsilon/2$.

I now introduce some notation:

$$\begin{aligned} Q^n(A|x^n) &= \text{the } Q \text{ conditional distribution of an event } A \text{ at time } n \\ &\quad\ \text{given the past } x^n, \\ Q_n(x^n) &= \text{the } Q \text{ marginal distribution of } (x_1, x_2, \ldots, x_n), \\ Q(n)(B) &= \text{the } Q \text{ marginal distribution of future events } B \text{ at time } n. \end{aligned} \tag{8}$$

Identical notation will be used for P, P^n, P_n, and $P(n)$. We need comparable concepts for V^k, but here confusion may arise when we want to take the V^n marginal distribution at time n. For this purpose we shall carry *two* superscripts; thus,

$$\begin{aligned} V^{k,n}(A|x^n) &= \text{the } V^k \text{ conditional distribution of an event } A \\ &\quad\ \text{at time } n \text{ given the past } x^n, \\ V_n^k(x^n) &= \text{the } V^k \text{ marginal distribution of } (x_1, x_2, \ldots, x_n), \\ V^k(n)(B) &= V^k \text{ marginal distribution of future event } B \text{ at time } n. \end{aligned} \tag{9}$$

$V^{n,n}(A|x^n)$, $V_n^n(x^n)$, and $V^n(n)(B)$ will have the natural meanings.

A rather technical question may arise regarding the existence of proper, regular conditional distributions $V^{k,n}(A|x^n)$, $Q^n(A|x^n)$, and $P^n(A|x^n)$. Under our assumptions about Ω and $(\Omega, \mathscr{F})$, it follows that $\mathscr{F}_n$ is countably generated. Also, from (3) the conditioning on x^n is equivalent to conditioning on $B(x^n) \in \mathscr{F}_n$. The existence of proper, regular conditional distributions $V^{k,n}(A|x^n)$, $Q^n(A|x^n)$, and $P^n(A|x^n)$ follows from theorem 4 of Blackwell and Dubins 1975. I shall also explain below that the selection of a version for any of these conditional distributions will not constitute a problem.

Returning to the question of learning, I now introduce the following:

DEFINITION 1 An agent is said to *learn the process asymptotically at x* (in short: "to learn the process") if

$$\lim_{n\to\infty} \sup_{A\in\mathscr{F}} |V^{n,n}(A|x^n) - P^n(A|x^n)| = 0. \tag{10}$$

An alternative definition would require that learning entails the requirement that, for all k,

$$\lim_{n\to\infty} \sup_{A\in\mathscr{F}} |V^{n,k}(A|x^k) - P^k(A|x^k) = 0. \tag{11}$$

A weaker version of (11) could require the weak convergence of $V^{n,k}(\cdot|x^k)$ to $P^k(\cdot|x^k)$ for all k. More precisely, for all k and all continuous bounded functions g on Ω,

$$\lim_{n\to\infty} \int g(\omega)\, dV^{n,k}(\omega|x^k) = \int g(\omega)\, dP^k(\omega|x^k). \tag{12}$$

The problem with (11) and (12) is that at time n the decision maker uses $V^{n,n}(\cdot|x^n)$ in formulating his demand. He does not use $V^{n,k}(\cdot|x^k)$, where $k \neq n$; hence, (11) and (12) require the convergence of distributions which the decision maker does not use. Moreover, the requirement that in (11) and (12) convergence is achieved at each k is a very strong condition; simple counterexamples are available when (11) and (12) are not satisfied but (10) is (Example 1 below has these properties.) To accommodate this problem, one could weaken condition (12). One simple way to do that is to require the existence of a sequence β_k declining to 0 such that

$$\left|\lim_{n\to\infty} \int g(\omega)\, dV^{n,k}(\omega|x^k) - \int g(\omega)\, dP^k(\omega|x^k)\right| \leqq \beta_k. \tag{13a}$$

On the other hand, since V^n converges uniformly to Q, one can simply require that for all bounded continuous g

$$\lim_{k\to\infty} \left|\int g(\omega)\, dQ^k(\omega|x^k) - \int g(\omega)\, dP^k(\omega|x^k)\right| = 0. \tag{13b}$$

A technical question may be raised as to when (13a) and (13b) are equivalent.

It was noted above that an intertemporal decision maker needs to use the conditional distributions in order to formulate his demand and supply correspondences for goods and assets at all dates. The requirement of weak convergence in (13a) and (13b) would have been satisfactory if all demand and supply function were continuous functions of all future prices. Since this is a bit much to ask, let us focus our attention mainly on the definition of learning as given in (10). Note also that the selection of a condition like (10) as a convergence criterion resolves the question of which versions are selected for the conditional distributions. Such differences can arise only on sets of measure 0, and condition (10) is not sensitive to them.

In adopting any of the conditions in (10), (11), (12), or (13), we are suggesting that the requirement that $Q = P$, and even the requirement that the limit marginal distributions be the same, i.e.,

$$\lim_n \sup_{A \in \mathscr{F}} |V^n(n)(A) - P(n)(A)| = 0,$$

are much too restrictive. This is an important point which needs to be explored before we turn to our concept of "complexity."

Learning a Process Does Not Require the Convergence of V^n to P

As was explained in the introduction, the central results of this paper state criteria for nonlearning by an agent in terms of the errors $V_n^n(A) - P_n(A)$ on past events ($A \in \mathscr{F}_n$). In order to understand the meaning of these criteria, it is first important to see that the convergence of V^n to P is not a necessary condition for learning. To this end, I present an example showing that the limit measure of V^n (i.e., Q) may not be equal to P. In addition, the marginal distributions of future events at n, $Q(n)$ and $P(n)$, do not get close. Nevertheless, the conditional distributions $A^n(\cdot\,|x^n)$ and $P^n(\cdot\,|x^n)$ do become uniformly close to each other as n becomes large.

EXAMPLE 1 (adapted from Blackwell and Dubins 1962) Let R be the measure on $\mathscr{F}$ determined by an experiment of independent tosses of a coin with probability $0 \leqq r \leqq 1$ of success, and let S be the corresponding measure when the coin has probability $0 \leqq s \leqq 1$ of success but $r \neq s$. Now let $0 < \mu < \lambda < 1$, and let P and Q be the mixtures[1] of R and S, where

$$P = \mu R + (1 - \mu)S$$

and

$$Q = \lambda R + (1 - \lambda)S.$$

It is clear that if we integrate Q and P over $(x_1, x_2, \ldots, x_n)$ the marginal distribution of every future event at n is the same as it was at the start. Thus, $Q(n) = Q$ and $P(n) = P$; $Q(n)$ and $P(n)$ do not get closer. Now consider the agent who observes $(x_1, x_2, \ldots, x_n)$—the results of n tosses of a coin with the true probability of heads being r if the process selected initially is R or s if the initially selected process was S. The agent who started with a prior belief that R was selected with probability λ and S with probability $(1 - \lambda)$ observes $(x_1, x_2, \ldots, x_n)$ with, say k heads and $n - k$ tails. This enables him to compute his posterior probability,

$$\lambda_n = \frac{\delta(x^n|r)\lambda}{\delta(x^n|r)\lambda + \delta(x^n|s)(1 - \lambda)},$$

where

$$\delta(x^n|r) = r^k(1 - r)^{n-k}$$

and

$$\delta(x^n|s) = s^k(1 - s)^{n-k};$$

consequently, he can compute the conditional distribution $Q^n(A|x^n)$:

$$Q^n(A|x^n) = \lambda_n R(A|x^n) + (1 - \lambda_n)S(A|x^n).$$

Similar calculations yield the conditional distribution $P^n(A|x^n)$:

$$P^n(A|x^n) = \mu_n R(A|x^n) + (1 - \mu_n)S(A|x_n).$$

However, since *either R or S* is the operating process, $\delta(x^n|r)/\delta(x^n|s)$ either converges to 0 or diverges to $+\infty$; hence, either $\lambda_n \to 0$ or $\lambda_n \to 1$. Note that this is also true for μ_n; hence, $(\lambda_n - \mu_n) \to 0$. Consequently,

$$Q^n(A|x^n) - P^n(A|x^n) = (\lambda_n - \mu_n)(R(A|x^n) - S(A|x^n)) \to 0.$$

This proves the assertion that the conditional distributions converge to each other.

Now suppose we alter the example a bit and assume that it is known that the true value of μ satisfies $\frac{1}{2} \leqq \mu \leqq \frac{3}{4}$. The observing agent who does not know μ selects candidate measures Q with parameter λ satisfying $\frac{1}{2} \leqq \lambda \leqq \frac{3}{4}$. Having observed $(x_1, \ldots, x_n)$, the agent forms the likelihood ratio for testing any $\frac{1}{2} \leqq \lambda \leqq \frac{3}{4}$ against μ. Suppose that $r > s$ and that the agent observed k heads and $n - k$ tails. The likelihood function is therefore

$$\ell_n(x_1, \ldots, x_n) = \frac{\lambda r^k(1 - r)^{n-k} + (1 - \lambda)s^k(1 - s)^{n-k}}{\mu r^k(1 - r)^{n-k} + (1 - \mu)s^k(1 - s)^{n-k}}. \tag{14}$$

It can be seen that P a.e. ℓ_n converges, and that

$$\ell_n \to \begin{cases} \dfrac{\lambda}{\mu} & \text{if } R \text{ was initially selected} \\[2ex] \dfrac{1-\lambda}{1-\mu} & \text{if } S \text{ was initially selected.} \end{cases}$$

Moreover,

$$\max_{1/2 \leq \lambda \leq 3/4} \ell_n(x_1, \ldots, x_n) \geq 1 \quad \text{for all } n,$$

and the maximized value is P a.e. $\lambda = 0.75$ if R was initially selected and is P a.e. $\lambda = 0.25$ if S was initially selected. The power of these likelihood tests is nil, but the fact is that *the agent will almost surely not discover the true process P although he will "learn the process" in the sense of our earlier definition.*

My intent is to highlight the fact that the likelihood-ratio test examines the compatibility between the data $(x_1, \ldots, x_n)$ and the alternative joint densities over x^n. However, the conclusion that is important for the understanding of this paper is that the *acceptance or rejection of the true densities of x^n is neither necessary nor sufficient for learning the process as defined above.* In the next section I shall introduce a definition of *complex processes* in terms of the behavior of the likelihood ratios. The above example should help the reader keep in mind the fact that likelihood ratios apply to the joint distribution of *past data* $(x_1, \ldots, x_n)$; their relations to the conditional distributions of future events given past observations is much more subtle.

To complete our example, suppose the agent considers any sequence of events $A_n \in \mathscr{F}_n$, such as

$$A_n = \left\{ \omega \,\middle|\, \begin{array}{l} \text{the fraction of heads observed in } n \text{ tosses} \\ \text{is strictly less than } r \end{array} \right\}.$$

By the Kolmogorov zero-one law we know that $P(A_n) \to 0$, but by (14)

$$\infty > \max_{1/2 \leq \lambda \leq 3/4} \ell_n(x_1, \ldots, x_n) > 1.$$

The sets A_n represent a sequence of rejection regions for the hypothesis that P is the true process in the sense that these observations are not likely to occur under P. Since such observations would lead to the rejection of P, the likelihood ratio exceeds 1; it is, however, bounded. Based on the fact that any interesting problem of statistical testing will have such rejection regions, our concept of a "complex process" *depends upon the behavior of the likelihood ratio in such regions.* Without defining "complexity," I point out that the process of the present example is not complex, since the likelihood ratio remains bounded on all rejection regions.

2 Complex Dynamics and Uniform Errors in Evaluating Past Events

In order to introduce the concept of complexity, which is the central concept of this paper, recall our aim of providing criteria for nonlearning in terms of the structure of errors of the agent on *past* events. This means that the criteria will specify conditions on the size of

$$|V_n^n(A) - P_n(A)|$$

over a class of sets A in $\mathscr{F}_n$. One notes immediately that it is a trivial problem to find a class of sets such that if for all n $P_n(A) = 0$ and $V_n^n(A) > 0$ on this class, learning does not occur. In this case V_n^n is not absolutely continuous with respect to P_n for all n. This creates something of a dilemma. On the one hand, the assumption $V_n^n \ll P_n$ for all n is not a natural one for a rational learning model, since it represents "extra" information about the process which the agent should be required to learn. For this reason we prefer not to make it. On the other hand, the property of absolute continuity is not needed for our development, and making it could be viewed as a technical simplification which improves the exposition and enables us to talk about complexity in terms of likelihood ratios. Keep in mind, however, that by assuming absolute continuity we are providing the agent some free information which should improve his chances of learning the process.

We have chosen a compromise of giving two definitions of complexity. First we shall make the simplifying assumption

$$V_n^n \ll P_n \quad \text{for all } n \tag{15}$$

and provide a definition of complexity (of the *first* type) using likelihood ratios. This may help some readers who may prefer a statistical formulation (see definition 2).

We next remove the assumption of absolute continuity and provide an alternate definition (see definition 3) of complexity (of the *second* type). The proof of theorem 1 is then adapted to both definitions.

To continue our development, let $x = (x_1, x_2, \ldots)$ be any realization of the process. This induces a sequence of likelihood functions denoted by $\ell_n(x^n)$, which must be defined. Under the assumption of absolute continuity in (15), we can employ the Radon Nykodym theorem to conclude that for such k there exists an $\mathscr{F}_k$ measurable random variable, denoted by dV_k^n/dP_k, such that for $k = 1, 2, \ldots$

$$V^n(A) = \int_A \left(\frac{dV_k^n}{dP_k}\right) dP \quad \text{all } A \in \mathscr{F}_k. \tag{16}$$

We shall now define ℓ_n to be the nth random variable involved in (16); that is,

$$\ell_n = \frac{dV_n^n}{dP_n}. \tag{17}$$

If P_n and V_n^n are absolutely continuous with respect to the Lebesgue measure on [0,1], then there are densities $g_n(x^n)$ of V_n^n and $f_n(x^n)$ of P_n such that $\ell_n(x^n)$ can be thought of as follows:

$$\ell_n(x^n) = \frac{g_n(x^n)}{f_n(x_n)}. \tag{18}$$

In most applications one thinks of the likelihood ratio as in (18); this intuition may be carried into the discussion below.

2.1 Complexity Expressed as Likelihood-Ratio Tests over Past Events

Returning now to the definition of "complexity," consider an agent who observes x^n and accepts V^n as his probability assessment at stage n. Since we visualize the agent as always facing a continuum of alternative hypotheses about the true P, he is not likely to select *exactly* the true P with the finite[2] data x^n. The likelihood ratio of testing V_n^n against P_n would yield $\ell_n(x^n) > 1$, where the sequence of observations x^n belongs to a sequence A_n of regions where, in accepting V^n, the agent makes type-I errors of rejecting P_n when they are true. When comparing V_n^n and P_n, it is normal in any statistical procedure to have such rejection regions. We restrict attention to a sequence of such distinct subsets that satisfy $A_n \in \mathscr{F}_n$, $A_{n+1} \notin \mathscr{F}_n$, and $P(A_n) < 1/n$. By construction, $\ell_n(y^n) > 1$ for all $y^n \in A_n$. Now, for a given realization x and the resulting sequence of V^n, we say that on A_n V_n^n *is decisive over* P_n if there exists a sequence of sets A_n as defined above and if for all $y^n \in A_n$

$$\ell_n(y^n) \geqq \varepsilon n \quad \text{for some } \varepsilon > 0. \tag{19}$$

DEFINITION 2 A process $\{x^n\}_{n=1}^{\infty}$ of prices is said to be *complex* (of the first type) if for all n

$$V_n^n \ll P$$

and for P almost every realization x there exists a sequence of distinct rejection regions

$$\{A_n\}_{n=1}^{\infty}, \quad A_n \in \mathscr{F}_n, A_{n+1} \notin \mathscr{F}_n$$

with $P(A_n) < 1/n$ and such that on A_n V_n^n is decisive over P_n.

There is a simple way of thinking about the concept of a complex price process. It deviates slightly from definition 2, but it implies the concept in the definition. It postulates that if you have studied the wheat market for many years, then the model V_n^n that you accept in 1988 to explain past price movements of wheat may be the wrong one. However, the V_n^n probability of accepting it is about the same as accepting the wrong model in 1998 and which utilized data for 10 additional years. More formally, suppose an econometrician constructs a probability model V_n^n to explain price movements from date 1 to date n. This model is not precise in the sense that the true probability is P_n, but the data x^n belonged to a region where P_n was rejected and V_n^n accepted. It is natural to expect that there will be a sequence of such rejection regions $A_k \in \mathscr{F}_n$ consisting of price sequences from date 1 to date n such that $P_n(A_k) \leqq 1/k$ but

$$V_n^n(A_k) \geqq \varepsilon_n > 0 \quad (k = 1, 2, \ldots, K, K > n).$$

At date $m > n$ the process is repeated. The econometrician obtains a model V_m^m and again has a sequence of $\mathscr{F}_m$ rejection region B_k such that $P_m(B_k) \leq 1/k$ and $V_m^m(B_k) \geqq \varepsilon_m > 0$. In the complex economy of definition 2 there exists an $\varepsilon > 0$ such that $\varepsilon_n \geqq \varepsilon$ for all n. This is the sense in which we cannot explain in 1988 past movements of wheat prices or of the Dow-Jones averages more accurately than in 1978 although ten years of additional data is available.

2.2 Complexity As Reflection of Errors in Evaluating Past Low-*P*-Probability Events

I now propose an alternative concept of complexity (not necessarily equivalent to the previous one) that utilizes neither the assumption of absolute continuity ((15)) nor the likelihood function. To motivate this second type of complexity, think of the econometrician as observing x^n and constructing a learning procedure L_{n-1} to deduce V^n. Now use the model V^n to predict the probability of "past" sets $A_n \in \mathscr{F}_n$. How accurate is the prediction $V_n^n(A_n)$ compared with the true probability $P_n(A_n)$? As with the likelihood function, we are testing *only over "past" events.* As with all statistical tests, there will exist rejection regions of P_n where $P_n(A_n) \to 0$ but $V_n^n(A_n) \geq \varepsilon$. In the case of a complex process we require a bit more.

DEFINITION 3 A process of prices $\{x_n\}_{k=1}^{\infty}$ is said to be complex (of the second type) if for P almost every realization x there exists a $\delta_x > 0$ such that, given ε, where $0 < \varepsilon < \delta_x$, there exists a sequence of "past" events A_n (i.e., $A_n \in \mathscr{F}_n$) such that $P(A_n) \leq 1/n^2$ and

$$|V_n^n(A_n) - P_n(A_n)| > \varepsilon. \tag{20}$$

One sees that in a complex environment (of the second type) there is always a sequence of past events with true P probability rapidly declining to 0 that, if evaluated with the learned models, would involve an error of at least ε. It is not easy to write down representative examples of a complex process that will capture the essential features of a market. Instead I shall swing to the other extreme and present an example of a complex process that is somewhat of an artificial curiosity since it highlights only very simple technical properties implying complexity. Although extreme, the following example helps to clarify some of the ideas involved.

EXAMPLE 2 The stochastic process $\{x_n\}_{n=1}^{\infty}$ is generated as follows. Let $\{\lambda_n\}_{n=1}^{\infty}$ be an arbitrary sequence of real numbers in $(0,1]$,

$$\lambda_k \neq \lambda_j, \quad k \neq j.$$

Let x_k be a random draw from the exponential distribution with parameter λ_k. Thus, the random variables x_k are all independent but they have different distributions. Now assume that the agent knows the structure but does not know the parameters λ_n. When he observes x_1, the best he can do is take $\mu_1 = 1/x_1$ to be the maximum-likelihood estimate of λ_1. Similarly, the maximum-likelihood estimate of λ_k is $\mu_k = 1/x_k$. Clearly it is an event of probability 0 that $\lim_{k\to\infty} |\lambda_k - \mu_k|$ exists and is equal to 0. If we associate the learned finite-dimensional distributions V_n^n with the distributions induced by the parameter estimates $(\mu_1, \mu_2, \ldots, \mu_n)$, it follows from proposition III-2-6 of Neveu 1975 that $\lim_{k\to\infty} |\lambda_k - \mu_k| = 0$ is a necessary condition to ensure that $\{x_n\}_{n=1}^{\infty}$ is not complex. With this condition violated for P almost all x, it can be shown that the conditions of definition 2 are satisfied and the process is complex. Without intricate calculations we may observe that the intuition of this example is compelling. With a new parameter arising at each stage, the econometrician has only one observation for each parameter. With the parameters arbitrary, one can hardly hope to learn all the λ_n.

The example can be modified a bit in the following way: Let $(x_1, x_2, \ldots, x_{M_1})$ be independent random variables all distributed exponentially with parameter λ_1; $(x_{M_1+1}, x_{M_1+2}, \ldots, x_{M_2})$ are independent with a common exponential distribution λ_2; and in general $(x_{M_k+1}, \ldots, x_{M_{k+1}})$ are independent with a common exponential distribution λ_{k+1}. The sequence $\{M_j\}_{j=1}^{\infty}$ is an arbitrary sequence of dates. Given the independence assumption, it is clear that the maximum-likelihood estimate of $1/\lambda_{k+1}$ is

$$\frac{1}{\mu_{k+1}} = \frac{1}{M_{k+1} - M_k - 1} \sum_{j=M_k+1}^{M_{k+1}} x_j.$$

The sequence $(\mu_1, \mu_2, \ldots, \mu_n)$ together with the fixed dates $(M_1, \ldots, M_n)$ will define V_n^n and the measure Q to which they converge. It is clear from the previous reasoning that proposition III-2-6 of Neveu 1975 still applies and the process is complex.

A further modification of the example is possible. According to this,

$$N_j = \sum_{k=1}^{j} M_k, \quad j = 1, 2, \ldots$$

may be taken as a sequence of stopping times. However, we also assume that each N_j is independent of all x_k, $k > j$. It can be shown that this is also a complex process.

The essential technical point of example 2 is that each parameter has only a finite number of independent observations which can be used to estimate it. *All future data beyond a certain point provides no information about the past.* This extreme condition is obviously sufficient for complexity.

The Impossibility of Learning a Complex Price Process

3.1 The Basic Theorem under Uniform Convergence of Learning

The objective of this subsection is to prove the central result of this paper.

THEOREM 1 Let $\{x_j\}_{j=1}^{\infty}$ be a complex price process. Then for P almost any realization x and any rational learning process, the agent cannot learn the process.

Note that the theorem does not specify which type of complexity is being assumed. The theorem is true for either type, and this point will be made in the development of the proof. As for terminology, we shall refer to "complexity of type I" as the type specified in definition 2 and "complexity of type II" as the type specified in definition 3. We shall use the notation $V^n(A|\mathscr{F}_k)$ for the conditional distribution of V^n on the sub σ-field $\mathscr{F}_k$. First, the notion of *uniform integrability* will be introduced.

DEFINITION 4 A sequence $\{y_n\}$ of random variables is said to be uniformly integrable with respect to a measure Q on $(\Omega,\mathscr{F})$ if

$$\sup_n E|x_n| < \infty$$

and

$$\lim_{a\to\infty} \sup_n \int_{|x_n|>a} |x_n|\, dQ = 0.$$

LEMMA 2 If $V_k^n \ll P_k$, then $Q_k \ll P_k$ and dQ_n/dP_n exists P a.e. for all n.

Proof Since $V^n \to Q$ uniformly, $V_k^n(A) \to Q_k(A)$ for each k and every $A \in \mathscr{F}_k$. Since $P_k(A) = 0$ implies $V_k^n(A) = 0$, it follows that $Q_k(A) = 0$ as well. Hence, $Q_k \ll P_k$ all k. By the Radon Nykodym theorem we can define the likelihood function

$$\ell_n^Q = \frac{dQ_n}{dP_n}. \tag{21}$$

■

Since under complexity of the first type we assume $V_k^n \ll P_n$, it follows from lemma 2 that ℓ_n^Q is well defined for all n.

LEMMA 3 Let x be a realization of a process $\{x_n\}_{n=1}^{\infty}$ which is complex of the first type. Then the sequence of random variables $\{\ell_n^Q\}$ is not uniformly integrable.

Proof From the definition (21) it follows that $\ell_n^Q \geq 0$ and

$$1 = \int_{\Omega} \ell_n^Q(\omega)\, dP(\omega) \quad \text{for all } n. \tag{22}$$

Hence, $E\ell_n^Q = 1$ w.r.t. P satisfying the first condition of uniform integrability. However, let $\{A_n\}$ be the sequence of sets postulated in definition 2. Let an $\varepsilon > 0$ be given as in (19). Since V^n converges uniformly to Q, there exists n^* such that for all $n \geq n^*$

$$\operatorname*{Sup}_{A \in \mathscr{F}} |V^n(A) - Q(A)| \leqq \varepsilon/2.$$

Hence,

$$Q(A_n) \geqq V^n(A_n) - \varepsilon/2. \tag{23}$$

From (19) and the condition $P(A_n) \leq 1/n$ it follows that

$$V^n(A_n) = \int_{A_n} \ell_n^Q(\omega)\, dP \geqq \varepsilon. \tag{24}$$

Combining (23) and (24), we have

$$Q(A_n) \geqq \varepsilon/2.$$

From (21) we have

$$\int_{A_n} \ell_n^Q(\omega)\, dP(\omega) = Q(A_n) \geqq \varepsilon/2 \quad \text{for all } n,$$

and this violates the second condition of uniform integrability. ■

LEMMA 4 Let x be a realization of a process $\{x^n\}_{n=1}^{\infty}$ that is complex of type I or type II. Then the limit measure Q is not absolutely continuous with respect to P.

Proof Consider first complexity of type I. Then by lemma 3 $\{\ell_n\}_{n=1}^{\infty}$ is not uniformly integrable with respect to P. To prove that $Q \not\ll P$, suppose to the contrary that $Q \ll P$. Note first that $Q \ll P$ is equivalent to the requirement that for every $\varepsilon > 0$ there exist $\delta > 0$ such that $P(A) < \delta \rightarrow$

$Q(A) < \varepsilon$ for all A. Thus, select an $\varepsilon > 0$ and a $\delta > 0$ that satisfy the above. For any real number $a > 0$ define

$$B_a^n = \{\omega: \ell_n(\omega) \geqq a\}.$$

Now select $a > 1/\delta$. Then, by $Q \ll P$,

$$P(B_a^n) < \delta$$

and

$$Q(B_a^n) < \varepsilon \quad \text{uniformly in } n.$$

However,

$$\int_{B_a^n} \ell_n \, dP = Q(B_a^n) < \varepsilon \quad \text{uniformly in } n;$$

hence, $\{\ell_n\}_{n=1}^{\infty}$ is uniformly integrable with respect to P and this is a contradiction. It follows that $Q \not\ll P$.

Next, consider complexity of type II. By definition 3, there exist a δ_x and a sequence $\{A_n\}$ in $\mathscr{F}_n$ that satisfy the definition of complexity. Let

$$\bar{A} = \lim_k \sup_{n \geq k} A_n.$$

Clearly, $\bar{A} \in \mathscr{F}_\infty$. Since $P(A_n) \leqq 1/n^2$ it follows that $\sum_{n=1}^{\infty} P(\bar{A}_n) < \infty$, and by the first Borel-Cantelli lemma it follows that $P(\bar{A}) = 0$. Now consider the claim that $Q(\bar{A}) > 0$, hence $Q \not\ll P$. To prove this assertion, note first that

$$Q(\bar{A}) \geqq Q(A_n) \quad \text{for all } n.$$

From the definition of type II complexity it follows that there exists $\varepsilon > 0$ ($\varepsilon < \delta_x$) such that

$$|V^n(A_n) - P(A_n)| > \varepsilon.$$

Since $P(A_n) < 1/n^2$, it follows that for large n

$$V^n(A_n) > P(A_n) + \varepsilon.$$

Since V^n converges uniformly to Q, there exists n^* such that for all $n > n^*$

$$|V^n(A_n) - Q(A_n)| \leqq \varepsilon/2;$$

hence,

$$Q(A_n) \geqq V^n(A_n) - \varepsilon/2$$
$$\geqq \varepsilon/2 + P(A_n) \geqq \varepsilon/2.$$

Hence,

$$Q(\bar{A}) \geqq \varepsilon/2.$$ ■

Proof of Theorem 1 All statements below are made for x a.e. P, and this will not be repeated. By lemma 4 there exists $\bar{A} \in \mathscr{F}_\infty$ such that $Q(\bar{A}) > 0$ and $P(\bar{A}) = 0$. We have $P(\bar{A}|\mathscr{F}_n) = 0$ P a.e., and hence $P(\bar{A}|x^n) = 0$. On the other hand, by the definition of $\bar{A}$ we have that $\bar{A} \in \mathscr{F}_\infty$ and $Q(\bar{A}) \geq \varepsilon/2$. Since $\bar{A} \notin \mathscr{F}_n$, assumption 2 applies. It follows that there exists n^* such that

$$V^n(\bar{A}|x^n) > \varepsilon/4 \quad \text{for all } n \geq n^*. \tag{25}$$

Since $V^n \to Q$ uniformly, it follows that

$$V^n(\bar{A}|\mathscr{F}_n) \to Q(\bar{A}|\mathscr{F}_n) \text{ a.e. } Q.$$

Hence, there exists n^{**} such that for $n > n^{**}$

$$|V^n(\bar{A}|\mathscr{F}_n) - Q(\bar{A}|\mathscr{F}_n)| \leqq \varepsilon/8 \text{ a.e. } Q, \tag{26}$$

and this implies that

$$Q(\bar{A}|\mathscr{F}_n) \geqq V^n(\bar{A}|\mathscr{F}_n) - \varepsilon/8 \text{ a.e. } Q.$$

Since $B(x^n) \in \mathscr{F}_n$, we have

$$Q(\bar{A}|x^n) \geqq V^n(\bar{A}|x^n) - \varepsilon/8, \tag{27}$$

and (25) together with (27) imply

$$Q(\bar{A}|x^n) \geqq \varepsilon/8.$$

This shows that

$$|Q(\bar{A}|x^n) - P(\bar{A}|x^n)| \geqq \varepsilon/8,$$

violating the definition of learning. ■

3.2 The Basic Theorem under Weak Convergence of Learning

If one has a preference for the weaker definition of learning (13a), one may weaken the assumptions of theorem 1. More specifically, introduce the following.

ASSUMPTION 1′ V^n converges weakly to Q. That is, for any bounded continuous function $g(\omega)$,

$$\int_\Omega g(\omega)\,dV^n(\omega) \to \int g(\omega)\,dQ(\omega).$$

Next, in the definition of complexity one may require that the sequence $\{A_n\}$ be *nested*, i.e., $A_n \supset A_{n+1}$ for all n. With this assumption and this definition, we have the following theorem.

THEOREM 2 Let $\{x_j\}_{j=1}^{\infty}$ be a complex price process with the modification that $\{A_n\}$ are nested. Then, under assumption 1′, for P almost every realization x and for any rational learning process, the agent cannot learn the process in the weak-convergence sense of (13a).

The proof of this theorem is omitted. Note, however, that the condition of $\{A_n\}$ being nested enables us to prove directly that $Q \not\ll P$ without the delicate machinery of the martingale convergence theorem or the Borel-Cantelli lemma. One may then trace each step of the proof and replace uniform convergence with weak convergence of V^n.

4 Some Final Observations

The problem addressed in this paper is similar to the statistical problem of estimating consistently the parameter of a distribution (for a recent survey, see Diaconis and Freedman 1986). Taking a Bayesian approach, Doob (1948) showed that if the parameter space is finite and the true parameter is in the support of the prior distribution, then the posterior distribution converges weakly to the mass distribution concentrating on the true parameter.

The limited applicability of this result to economic environments arises from two sources. First, economic environments may be characterized by complex, nonstationary, stochastic structures for which a finite parameter space is not sufficient. In this case the results of Freedman (1963, 1965) indicate the nature of the difficulties. Second, and more important, the statistical literature assumes that the analyst can conduct controlled experiments yielding independent observations from the given distribution. The learning economic agent does not have this option and must learn all he can from the data generated by the dynamic economy he observes. If the economy is not represented by a stochastic process that generates independent observations, the agent cannot have independent replicas of the economy.

The inability of an economist to conduct controlled experiments of the equilibrium of a single market or of the whole economy is the central reason why price processes cannot be learned in the sense defined earlier. Researchers studying price movements of commodities and assets invariably find the data from a single realization of the process to contain relatively little information, so that it is impossible to develop tests with any power at all (Summers 1986). A vast literature has developed on the analysis of time series that follow stationary second-order processes. These restrictions represent drastic stochastic limitations. However, even under these restrictions, the existence of consistent estimates normally requires that the covariance function between x_n and x_{n+k} be bounded by some rapidly declining geometric function of k. This amounts to the condition that effectively the process has only a finite number of parameters and that with growing number of observations variables that are far enough apart in time are essentially distributed i.i.d.

I do not believe that commodity-price and asset-price processes act this way. They are significantly dependent, and they often exhibit nonstationarity (which is reflected in the fact that each date brings with it new consumers, new technologies, new endowments, and new products). This complexity of price processes makes it unlikely that a rational agent can fully learn them.

Acknowledgments

Frank Hahn has had serious doubts about the usefulness of rational-expectations equilibria. Sharing his doubts, I contribute this essay in his honor. This is also to express my gratitude for many shared intellectual experiences.

This work was supported by National Science Foundation Grant IRI-8814953 at the Institute for Mathematical Studies in the Social Sciences, Stanford University.

Notes

1. Thus, there is one *initial* random selection of one of the two processes R and S.

2. This is true even in the trivial case of tossing a single coin where the probability of "heads" is not known but the prior is say, uniform on [1/4, 3/4]. Without explicitly introducing a proba-

bility on the space of all probability measures, we shall loosely think of the set of alternatives as a continuum such that an infinite sequence of observations is needed for selecting one with certainty.

References

Allen, B. 1981. "Generic existence of completely revealing equilibria for economies with uncertainty when prices convey information." *Econometrica* 49: 1173–1199.

Anderson, R. M., and H. Sonnenschein. 1982. "On the existence of rational expectations equilibrium." *Journal of Economic Theory* 26: 261–278.

Arrow, K. J., and J. R. Green. 1973. Notes on Expectations Equilibria in Bayesian Settings. Working Paper 33, IMSSS, Stanford.

Beja, A. 1976. The Limited Information Efficiency of Market Processes." Working Paper 43 Research Program in Finance, University of California, Berkeley.

Blackwell, D., and L. Dubins. 1962. "Merging of opinions with increasing information." *Annals of Mathematical Statistics* 33: 882–886.

Blackwell, D., and L. Dubins. 1975. "On existence and non-existence of proper, regular, conditional distributions." *Annals of Probability* 3: 741–752.

Blume, L. E., and D. Easley. 1981. Rational Expectations Equilibrium and the Efficient Market Hypothesis." Mimeo, Cornell University.

Blume, L. E., and D. Easley. 1982. "Learning to be rational." *Journal of Economic Theory* 26: 340–351.

Bray, M. 1982. "Learning, estimation and the stability of rational expectations equilibria." *Journal of Economic Theory* 26: 318–339.

Bray, M. 1983. "Convergence to rational expectations equilibrium." In *Individual Forecasting and Aggregate Outcomes: "Rational Expectations" Examined*, ed. R. Frydman and E. S. Phelps. Cambridge University Press.

Bray, M., and D. Kreps. 1986. "Rational learning and rational expectations." In *Arrow and the Ascent of Modern Economic Theory*, ed. G. R. Feiwel. New York University Press.

Bray, M., and N. E. Savin. 1986. "Rational expectations equilibria, learning and model specification." *Econometrica* 54: 1129–1160.

DeCanio, S. J. 1979. "Rational expectations and learning from experience." *Quarterly Journal of Economics* 93: 47–58.

Diaconis, P., and D. Freedman. 1986. "On the consistency of Bayes estimates." *Annals of Statistics* 14 (1): 1–26.

Doob, J. L. 1948. Application of the Theory of Martingales. Coll. Int. du CNRS, Paris.

Evans, G. W. 1983. "The stability of rational expectations in macro-economic models." In *Individual Forecasting and Aggregate Outcomes: "Rational Expectations" Examined*, ed. R. Frydman and E. S. Phelps. Cambridge University Press.

Evans, G. W. 1985. "Expectational stability and the multiple equilibria problem in linear rational expectations models." *Quarterly Journal of Economics* 100: 1217–1233.

Evans, G. W. 1986. "Selection criteria for models with non-uniqueness." *Journal of Monetary Economics* 18: 147–157.

Fourgeaud, C., C. Gourieroux, and J. Pradel. 1986. "Learning procedure and convergence to rationality." *Econometrica* 54: 845–868.

Freedman, D. 1963. "On the asymptotic behavior of Bayes estimates in the discrete case I." *Annals of Mathematical Statistics* 34: 1386–1403.

Freedman, D. 1965. "On the asymptotic behavior of Bayes estimates in the discrete case II." *Annals of Mathematical Statistics* 36: 454–456.

Frydman, R. 1982. "Towards an understanding of market process, individual expectations, market behavior and convergence of rational expectations equilibrium." *American Economic Review* 72: 652–658.

Grandmont, J. M., and W. Hildenbrand. 1974. "Stochastic processes of temporary equilibrium." *Journal of Mathematical Economics* 1: 247–277.

Grandmont, J. M., and G. Laroque. 1987. Stability, Expectations and Predetermined Variables. Mimeo, Paris.

Green, J. R. 1977. "The non-existence of information equilibria." *Review of Economic Studies* 44: 451–463.

Grossman, S. J. 1981. "An introduction to the theory of rational expectations under asymmetric information." *Review of Economic Studies* 48: 541–560.

Jordan, J. S. 1982a. "The generic existence of rational expectations equilibrium in the higher dimensional case." *Journal of Economic Theory* 26: 224–243.

Jordan, J. S. 1982b. "Admissible market data structures: A complete characterization." *Journal of Economic Theory* 28: 19–31.

Kobayashi, T. 1977. A Convergence Theorem on Rational Expectations Equilibrium with Price Information. Working paper 79, IMSSS, Stanford.

Kreps, D. 1977. "A note on fulfilled expectations equilibria." *Journal of Economic Theory* 14: 32–43.

Lewis, G. 1981. "The Phillips curve and Bayesian learning." *Journal of Economic Theory* 24: 240–264.

Marcet, A., and T. J. Sargent. 1986. Convergence of Least Squares Learning in Environments with Hidden State Variables and Private Information. Mimeo.

Marcet, A., and T. J. Sargent. 1989. "Convergence of least squares learning mechanisms in self referential linear stochastic models." *Journal of Economic Theory* 48: 337–368.

Neveu, J. 1975. *Discrete-Parameter Martingales.* North-Holland.

Radner, R. 1979. "Rational expectations equilibrium generic existence and the information revealed by prices." *Econometrica* 47: 655–678.

Radner, R. 1982. "Equilibrium under uncertainty." In *Handbook of Mathematical Economics* 2, ed. K. J. Arrow and M. D. Intriligator. North-Holland.

Summers, L.H. 1986. "Does the stock market rationally reflect fundamental values?" *Journal of Finance* 40: 591–601.

Townsend, R. M. 1978. "Market anticipations, rational expectations and Bayesian analysis." *International Economic Review* 19: 481–494.

Townsend, R. M. 1983. "Forecasting the forecasts of others." *Journal of Political Economy* 91: 546–588.

Transfer Payments and the Core of a Profit-Center Game

Roy Radner

If a firm is organized as a collection of profit centers, and if some profit centers use goods, services, or resources provided by other centers, then the issue arises of how the supplier centers will be compensated in accounting dollars. This is sometimes called the problem of "transfer pricing," although the term may be misleading since it suggests fixing a price per unit of the commodity that is provided.

If the profit centers—or *divisions*, as I shall call them here—are allowed to bargain freely among themselves regarding the terms of such transfers of commodities (goods, services, resources) and the corresponding transfers of accounting dollars, one might predict the outcome to be in the core of a suitably defined game, should the core be nonempty. Roughly speaking, an element of the core is a feasible production plan for the firm, together with an allocation of accounting profits among the divisions, such that no subset of divisions obtains a total profit smaller than it could get by operating "on its on." (These concepts will be defined more precisely in section 2.) Thus, an element of the core is in some sense "stable" against recontracting by groups of divisions. (See, however, the remarks at the end of this introduction.)

The nonemptiness of the core has been established for models of pure-exchange economies, and for economies with production in which every subset of consumers has available to it—in principle—the same set of production possibilities.[1] The essence of the typical firm is that different divisions have available *different* production possibilities; each division specializes in a particular set of activities (lines of business, research and development, production, marketing, etc.). On the other hand, a firm is simpler than an economy as a whole in that there are no "consumers" in the usual sense. Finally, a realistic model of the internal economics of the firm should allow for "nonconvexities," i.e., possibilities of increasing returns to scale, fixed costs, externalities, etc.

In this paper I define a "profit-center game" for a firm organized into divisions, and I make some progress toward characterizing the core for some simple models with nonconvexities. The results for these models suggest the following general conclusions:

- For the case of a single "supplier" division and several "customer" divisions, under quite general conditions, the following imputation of profit is in the core: the supplier gets all of the "surplus" that it generates within the firm. In particular, if a customer can get from the outside market inputs that are comparable to those it gets from the supplier, then the transfer price corresponding to this core imputation may be as high as the market price. In general, there will typically be other core imputations in which the customers share some of the surplus. For some special cases I examine the upper bounds on the shares of the surplus that the customers can receive, or, correspondingly, lower bounds on the transfer prices that they can pay the supplier. For example, if the supplier's cost function is linar, with a fixed cost and a constant marginal cost for each commodity, then (for an imputation in the core) the customers must pay transfer prices that are at least as large as the corresponding marginal costs, and some of them must pay strictly larger transfer prices (unless, of course, the supplier is subsidized by the headquarters, a possibility that is not envisioned in the present model).

- The core will be nonempty under a variety of non-neoclassical technological conditions that occur naturally within a firm, provided there is no competition among internal suppliers who produce close substitutes. In particular, I give some conditions under which the suppliers of strictly complementary inputs can (in the core) jointly extract all of the surplus generated by the use of those inputs by their internal "customers."
- The core may be empty if there are alternative internal suppliers of close substitutes, and their average costs are declining and then increasing in the relevant ranges of output.

This last result suggests that, in setting up profit centers, the firm will try to avoid creating "internal competition" among internal suppliers of close substitutes. However, further research is needed to determine the range of models for which these conclusions are valid.

For completeness, I also give the usual argument that establishes the nonemptiness of the core under general conditions of convexity. This argument uses the standard method of duality to impute "shadow profits" to the divisions, calculated according to the "shadow prices" corresponding to an optimal production plan.

A more fundamental extension of the model would be needed in order to study how an element of the core might be selected. Such an extension would require a more explicit consideration of the information available to the players. Although such an extension is not attempted here, a few informal remarks may help put the present paper in better perspective. At one extreme, suppose that all the data of the problem (cost and revenue functions, etc.) were known to the headquarters of the firm, and that the headquarters had the capacity to compute a profit-maximizing plan and the power to enforce its instructions to the divisions. In this case, the imputation of profits to individual divisions would be unnecessary, as would be the exercise of finding an element of the core. At the other extreme, suppose that the data about each division were initially known only to that division. If—as suggested at the beginning of this introduction—one were to rely on bargaining among the divisions (or division heads) to produce a plan and an imputation of profit, then, depending on the bargaining mechanism and the initial data, the outcome might or might not be optimal for the firm. For example, even in the case of one customer and one supplier, if the bargaining mechanism has the property that the divisions are neither "taxed" nor "subsidized" by the headquarters, then the outcome cannot be in the core for all configurations of the data.[2] On the other hand, if taxes and subsidies are allowed, then an appropriate "Groves mechanism" will produce outcomes in the core for all configurations of the data.[3]

In most firms, the typical situation will be somewhere between the two extremes sketched above. In a continuing relationship among the divisions, if a plan and a profit imputation are not in the core, this fact may be discovered by the interested parties, and they will have an incentive to change the arrangement by some means, even if this requires an evasion of bureaucratic rules. Thus, an arrangement not in the core may not be viable in the long run. On the other hand, there may be no mechanism that is guaranteed to lead to a core arrangement.

1 The Economy of the Firm

The firm is divided into *divisions*, indexed by i in I. The goods, services, and resources that are used, produced, bought, or sold by the divisions are called *commodities*. Those commodities that can be bought or sold on markets that are external to the firm are called *market commodities*; those that are owned or produced by the firm and used internally are called *nonmarket commodities*. It will be convenient to make the convention that a commodity must be either market or nonmarket, but not both. A simple device will show that this can be done without loss of generality (see below). Commodities may also be distinguished by date and location, as is normally done in the theory of production (see, for example, Debreu 1959, Chapter 2).

The *net output* of division i will be denoted by $y_i = (m_i, n_i)$, a vector with dimension equal to the total number of commodities. The subvectors m_i and n_i correspond to the market and nonmarket commodities, respectively. A coordinate of y_i is positive or negative according as the corresponding commodity is a net output or a net input of that division. The total net output of the firm is the sum of the net outputs of the individual divisions.

A division is characterized by its *production set*, Y_i, and its initial resources, r_i. The production set of the division is its set of technologically feasible net output vectors. The vector r_i of initial resources describes the quantities of nonmarket commodities that are assigned to (or owned by) division i before the process of production or before any buying or selling takes place. A *plan* for the firm is a combination of net output vectors, one for each division. A plan (y_i) is *feasible* if each division's net output vector is technologically feasible and for each nonmarket commodity the firm's total net input does not exceed its total initial resources. This can be expressed formally as follows:

$$\text{for each } i \text{ in } I,\ y_i \text{ is in } Y_i; \tag{1.1}$$

$$\sum_{i \in I} (n_i + r_i) \geq 0. \tag{1.2}$$

Suppose that the market commodities are bought and/or sold at fixed prices; denote the vector of these prices by p. (A more general treatment would allow the market prices to depend on the firm's net output vector.) The *profit* of the firm is the value of the net output of market commodities, evaluated at the market prices. Thus, the profit is the inner product pm, where m is the (vector) sum of the market-commodity net-output vectors of the divisions. Since the commodities may be dated, this formulation allows one to interpret the profit as the present discounted value of the firm's net outputs of market commodities.

If a particular good or service can serve as either a market or a nonmarket commodity, the two versions of the good or service will be distinguished formally but will be treated as perfect substitutes in production. This perfect substitutability will, of course, be expressed in the production sets of the divisions.

In modeling the initial resources of the firm, it might seem unnecessary, or even inappropriate, to assign them to the individual divisions at the beginning, before the choice of the production plan of the firm. This is, however, only a convention, and it can be interpreted in several ways. First, one of the "divisions" might be the headquarters of the firm, whose "production" consists in the assignment of centrally controlled resources to the several divisions. Second, resources that are initially assigned to one division can be reassigned to others as part of the production plan, without cost. Finally, one wants to be able to model the situation in which certain resources or "capacities" are naturally associated with certain divisions, for organizational or informational reasons that are not explicitly treated in the model in more detail.

In course of the paper, various assumptions will be made about the productions sets of the divisions. Two assumptions, however, will be maintained throughout the paper, unless otherwise noted. The first asserts that any division can do nothing, producing no outputs and using no inputs. The second asserts that commodities can be unsold or unused without using up other commodities.

A1 (inaction) For each i, Y_i contains the zero vector.

A2 ("free" disposal) For each i and each y_i in Y_i, if $y_i' \leq y_i$ then y_i' is also in Y_i.

Furthermore, it is natural to suppose that the prices of all market commodities are strictly positive. It should be pointed out, however, that in conjunction with assumption A2 this is not merely a convention. For example, if one of the "outputs" of the firm is a toxic waste, the firm may have to pay a positive price to have the waste treated and taken away. On the other hand, once one has ruled out negative prices, there is no essential further loss of generality in assuming that all prices are strictly positive.[4]

A3 The prices of all market commodities are strictly positive.

A feasible production plan for the firm is called *optimal* if it has maximum profit in the set of all feasible plans.

2 The Profit-Center Game and the Core

In order to model the organization of the firm as a collection of profit centers, I shall define a "cooperative game" whose outcome is not only a production plan but also an imputation of an "accounting profit" to each division. I shall suppose that the sum of the accounting profits of the divisions equals the profit of the firm, pm, as defined in section 1. The theory used to predict the outcome of the game is that the outcome will be in the core of the game (defined below). The basic analytical problems addressed in this paper are (1) the determination of conditions under which the core is nonempty and (2) as complete a description of the core as is possible under such conditions.

In what follows I shall consider nonempty subsets of the set of all divisions—called *coalitions*—and the maximum profit that each coalition could make if it acted as a "firm" on its own. Roughly speaking, an imputation of accounting profits to the several divisions of the firm is in the core if the total accounting profit imputed to each coalition is not less than the actual profit it could earn if it acted as a firm on its own.

Thus, for any coalition S, a nonempty subset of I, define $v(S)$ by

$$v(S) = \max p\left(\sum_{i \in S} m_i\right) \quad \text{subject to} \tag{2.1}$$

1. for each i in S, y_i is in Y_i,
2. $\sum_{i \in S} (n_i + r_i) \geq 0$.

In particular, $v(I)$ is the maximum profit of the entire firm.[5]

As a consequence of assumption A1 (inaction), the zero vector is a feasible net output for any coalition, and so the maximum in (2.1) is nonnegative. Thus,

$$v(S) \geq 0 \quad \text{for each coalition } S. \tag{2.2}$$

On the other hand, it would be quite usual for coalitions other than I (the entire firm) not to be able to make strictly positive profits on their own, so that $v(S)$ might be zero for many—or even all—coalitions other than I.

A *profit imputation* $x = (x_i)$ is a vector whose ith coordinate is to be interpreted as the accounting profit attributed to division i. A profit imputation is *feasible* if there is a feasible net output vector for the firm such that the total accounting profit of the divisions equals the total profit of the firm.

A profit imputation $x = (x_i)$ is said to be in the *core* if

$$\text{for each coalition } S, \sum_{i \in S} x_i \geq v(S) \tag{2.3}$$

and

$$\sum_{i \in I} x_i = v(I). \tag{2.4}$$

Condition (2.4) implies in particular that a profit imputation in the core is feasible. The core is thus the set of feasible profit imputations that (1) give each coalition other than I at least as much profit as it could get on its own and (2) have a total profit equal to the maximum profit of the firm as a whole.

There is nothing in the model described thus far that guarantees that the core is nonempty.

3 The Core of the Profit-Center Game is Nonempty for Convex Production

If the production set of the firm is convex, and the usual duality theory is applicable, then the core of the profit-center game is nonempty. A profit imputation in the core can be obtained as follows. Recall that a production plan for the firm is optimal if it maximizes the total value of the net output of market commodities, subject to its production and resource constraints. Corresponding to an optimal plan there will be a "shadow price" for each nonmarket commodity. Impute to each division an accounting profit equal to the sum of (1) the value of its net output of market commodities, (2) the "shadow value" of its net output of nonmarket commodities, and (3) the "shadow value" of its initial resources.

Although the above construction is well known, I shall sketch it here more formally for the sake of completeness. (The reader can skip to section 4 without loss of continuity.) I make the following assumption, in addition to A1–A3:

A4 Each production set Y_i is closed and convex.

Let $(\hat{y}_i) = ((\hat{m}_i, \hat{n}_i))$ be an optimal production plan for the firm. By standard duality theory,[6] there exists a non-negative, nonzero vector q such that

for each division i, and each (m_i, n_i) in Y_i,

$$pm_i + qn_i \leq p\hat{m}_i + q\hat{n}_i \tag{3.1}$$

and

$$q \sum_{i \in I} (\hat{n}_i + r_i) = 0. \tag{3.2}$$

An interpretation of (3.1) is that, at the optimal production plan, each division is maximizing its "shadow profit." Since q is non-negative, (3.2) implies that if the resource constraint of a nonmarket commodity is not binding, then the corresponding shadow price is zero.

Define the profit imputation $\hat{x} = (\hat{x}_i)$ as follows: For each i in I,

$$\hat{x}_i = p\hat{m}_i + q(\hat{n}_i + r_i). \tag{3.3}$$

Note that, by (3.2),

$$\begin{aligned}\sum_{i \in I} \hat{x}_i &= p \sum_{i \in I} \hat{m}_i + q \sum_{i \in I} (\hat{n}_i + r_i) \\ &= \sum_{i \in I} \hat{m}_i \\ &= v(I).\end{aligned}$$

I shall now show that $\hat{x}$ is in the core, as defined in section 2. Consider any coalition S smaller than the entire firm, and let $(y_i)_{i \in S}$ be a production plan that is feasible for S on its own, i.e., that satisfies conditions 1 and 2 of (2.1). By those conditions, together with (3.1), (3.3), and condition 2 of (2.1),

$$\begin{aligned}\sum_{i \in S} pm_i &\leq \sum_{i \in S} (p\hat{m}_i + q\hat{n}_i - qn_i) \\ &= \sum_{i \in S} (p\hat{m}_i + q\hat{n}_i + qr_i - qn_i - qr_i) \\ &= \sum_{i \in S} \hat{x}_i - q \sum_{i \in S} (n_i + r_i) \\ &\leq \sum_{i \in S} \hat{x}_i. \end{aligned} \tag{3.4}$$

Hence, $v(S)$ cannot exceed the right-hand side of (3.5).

This argument can be extended, under appropriate conditions, to cases in which the net revenue from the net output of market commodities is a concave function of the net outputs of those commodities.

4 Four Elementary Propositions about the Core

From (2.3) and (2.4) it is clear that the core is defined entirely in terms of the function v, which assigns a real number to each nonempty subset of players. The function v is usually called the characteristic function of the game. Thus, two firms that have different "economies" (as in section 1) but the same characteristic function will have the same core.

In this section I present four elementary but useful propositions about the core, which will be applied in subsequent sections. Throughout this section I make no assumption about the characteristic function, v, other than those made explicit in the statements of the propositions.

4.1 Strategically Equivalent Games

PROPOSITION 4.1 If $c = (c_i)$ is a vector with coordinates corresponding to the players i in I, and if $\tilde{v}$ and v are two characteristic functions such that, for each coalition S (a nonempty set of players),

$$\tilde{v}(S) = v(S) + \sum_{i \in S} c_i,$$

then x is in the core of v if and only if $\tilde{x} = x + c$ is in the core of $\tilde{v}$.

4.2 A Bound on Individual Imputations in the Core

PROPOSITION 4.2 If a vector x is in the core, then for each player i

$$x_i \leq v(I) - v(I \backslash \{i\}).$$

(Recall that I denotes the set of all players.)

4.3 Necessary Players

In light of proposition 4.1, there is no loss of generality in making the convention that, for each player i, $v(i) = 0$, where I use the abbreviation $v(i)$ for $v(\{i\})$. Suppose that, in addition, each set of players can get at least zero, i.e., the function v is non-negative. A player j will be called *necessary* if no set of players that does not contain j can get more than zero. The next proposition states that, under these conditions, an imputation that gives everything to a necessary player is in the core.

PROPOSITION 4.3 With the convention that, for every player i, $v(i) = 0$, suppose that, for each coalition S,

1. $0 \leq v(S) \leq v(I)$,

2. if player j is not in S, then $v(S) = 0$.

Then the core contains the vector x^* defined by

$$x_j^* = v(I),$$

$$x_i^* = 0 \quad \text{if } i \neq j.$$

Proof If j is in S, then

$$\sum_{i \in S} x_i^* = x_j^* = v(I) \geq v(S).$$

If j is not in S, then

$$\sum_{i \in S} x_i^* = 0 = v(S),$$

which completes the proof.

Note that there can be other imputations in the core, and in particular there can be more than one necessary player.

4.4 Superfluous Players

A player is called *superfluous* if deleting him from the set of all players, I, does not reduce the value of the characteristic function. Again, make the convention that $v(i) = 0$ for all i.

PROPOSITION 4.4 If $v(I) = v(I \setminus \{j\})$, then for any x in the core, $x_j = 0$.

Proof If $x_j > 0$, then

$$\sum_{i \neq j} x_i < \sum_{i \in I} x_j = v(I) = v(I \setminus \{j\}),$$

so that x cannot be in the core. On the other hand, $v(i) = 0$ implies that $x_i \geq 0$ if x is in the core.

5 One Supplier and Several Customers

In this section I consider a firm with an economy as described in section 1, but with the following special structure: one division, the "supplier," produces nonmarket commodities for the other divisions, the "customers." The customers may get inputs from the market, too, but they produce only market commodities. The supplier gets its inputs from the market, produces nonmarket commodities for customers in the firm, and may also produce market commodities. Although this structure is special, I make no special assumptions (such as convexity) about the production possibilities.

Using the elementary propositions of section 4, I show that, under very general conditions, the following imputation of profit is in the core: the supplier gets all of the "surplus" that it generates within the firm. In particular, if a customer can get from the outside market inputs that are comparable to those it gets from the supplier, then the transfer price corresponding to this core imputation may be as high as the market price.

In general, the above imputation will not be the only one in the core; there will typically be others in which the customers share some of the surplus. For some special cases I examine the upper bounds on the shares of the surplus that the customers can receive, or correspondingly, lower bounds on the transfer prices that they can pay the supplier. For example, if the supplier's cost function is linear, with a fixed cost, and a constant marginal cost for each commodity, then (for an imputation in the core) the customers must pay transfer prices that are at least as large as the corresponding marginal costs, and some of them must pay strictly larger transfer prices (unless, of course, the supplier is subsidized by the headquarters, a possibility that is not envisioned in the present model).

Let player 0 denote the supplier, and let the customers be indexed by $i \geq 1$. As before, I denotes the set of all the players. Denote by z_i the vector of nonmarket commodities supplied by 0 to i, and let z denote the vector of the total quantities of nonmarket commodities supplied by 0 to the customers, i.e.,

$$z = \sum_{i \geq 1} z_i.$$

The supply vector z is constrained to be in some set, say Z, that represents what is technically feasible for the supplier (without regard to cost). Thus far, nothing is assumed about Z except that it is some subset of the nonnegative part of the vector space whose dimension equals the number of nonmarket commodities. Let $F_0(z)$ denote the profit of the supplier (before transfers from other divisions) if it provides the vector z to the customers. The function F_0 reflects any opportunities the supplier has to produce market goods, as well as the cost of producing z. If the supplier has any capacity limitations, these will also be reflected in F_0.

For example, let $R_0(z')$ be the supplier's revenue from selling z' to the outside market, and let $C_0(z + z')$ be the supplier's cost of production.

Then

$$F_0(z) = \max_{z'} [R_0(z') - C_0(z + z')]. \quad (5.1)$$

In particular, if the supplier cannot (or may not) sell its output to the market, the $z' = 0$ and $F_0(z) = -C_0(z)$.

I now consider the customers. For $i \geq 1$, let $F_i(z_i)$ denote customer i's "gross" profit if it gets input z_i from the supplier. Here "gross" means before making any transfer payments to the supplier. F_i reflects any opportunities the customer has for buying inputs on outside markets. For example, suppose that i buys s_i on the market,[7] at cost $C_i(s_i)$, and suppose that from its total inputs $(z_i + s_i)$ it produces outputs that earn it a total revenue of $R_i(z_i + s_i)$. Then

$$F_i(z_i) = \max_{s_i} [R_i(z_i + s_i) - C_i(s_i)]. \quad (5.2)$$

Note that $F_i(0)$ is i's maximum profit if it buys all its inputs on the outside market.

Incidentally, in the notation of section 1,

$$m_0 = F_0(z),$$

$$n_0 = z,$$

$$Y_0 = \{(m_0, n_0) | m_0 = F_0(n_0), n_0 \geq 0\}.$$

For $i \geq 1$,

$$m_i = F_i(z_i),$$

$$n_i = -z_i,$$

$$Y_i = \{(m_i, n_i) | m_i = F_i(-n_i), n_i \geq 0\}.$$

A (feasible) *plan* for the firm is a specification

$$\zeta = (z_i)_{i \geq 1}$$

of the commodity z_i $(i \geq 1)$ supplied by 0 to the several customers i, such that

$$z = \sum_{i \geq 1} z_i \text{ is in } Z.$$

The profit to the firm from a plan ζ is

$$\pi(\zeta) = F_0(z) + \sum_{i \geq 1} F_i(z_i).$$

Similarly, if S is a coalition, and the supplier is in S, then a *plan*

$$\zeta_S = (z_i), \quad i \geq 1, \quad i \text{ in } S$$

is feasible for S if

$$\sum_{\substack{i \in S \\ i \geq 1}} z_i \text{ is in } Z.$$

On the other hand, if the supplier is *not* in S then all the customers in S must buy their inputs on the outside market.

I can now specify the characteristic function for this game. If the supplier is in S, then

$$v(S) = \max \left\{ F_0(z) + \sum_{\substack{i \geq 1 \\ i \in S}} F_i(z_i) | z_j = 0 \text{ for } j \notin S, z \in Z \right\}, \tag{5.3}$$

where z denotes, as above, the sum of the vectors z_i. If the supplier is not in S, then

$$v(S) = \sum_{\substack{i \geq 1 \\ i \in S}} F_i(0). \tag{5.4}$$

I assume that the maxima in (5.1) and (5.2) are attained. In particular, $v(I)$ is the maximum profit of the firm. Let $\hat{\zeta} = (\hat{z}_i)$ denote a plan that attains $v(I)$, and let $\hat{z}$ denote the corresponding vector of the total commodities supplied by 0 to the customers.

The first result of this section states that there is an imputation in the core such that the supplier gets all of the surplus due to its presence in the firm!

THEOREM 5.1 If Z contains the vector 0, then the core contains the profit imputation $x^* = (x_i^*)$ defined by

$$x_0^* = v(I) - \sum_{i \geq 1} F_i(0),$$

$$x_i^* = F_i(0), \quad i \geq 1.$$

Proof Use propositions 4.1 and 4.3.

Corresponding to the core imputation x^* in theorem 5.1 is a set of transfer payments from the customers to the supplier:

$$t_i^* = F_i(z_i) - F_i(0), \quad i \geq 1. \tag{6.5}$$

In general, there will be imputations in the core other than x^*. Bounds on what a player can obtain in a core imputation are provided by proposition 4.2.

EXAMPLE 5.1 This example,[8] although not particularly realistic, will be useful in illustrating the preceding ideas. It will also be used in section 6 to construct an example in which the core is empty.

Suppose that there are three customers and one supplier. Each customer can obtain either 1 unit or 0 units from the supplier, and nothing from the outside. The supplier's cost is c_k if it supplies a total of k units ($k = 0, 1, 2,$ or 3). Thus, in the preceding notation,

$$F_0(k) = -c_k.$$

The profit to a customer is b if he gets one unit of the input, and 0 otherwise. Thus, for $i \geq 1$,

$$F_i(1) = b > 0,$$

$$F_i(0) = 0.$$

Assume that

$$0 = c_0 < c_1 < c_2 < c_3,$$

$$c_1 > b, \quad c_2 < 2b, \quad c_3 < 3b,$$

$$c_3 - c_2 > b.$$

Then

$$v(0,i,j) = 2b - c_2, \quad \text{if } i \neq j, i \text{ and } j \geq 1,$$

$$v(0,1,2,3) = 3b - c_3,$$

$$v(S) = 0, \quad \text{otherwise.}$$

If x is in the core, then

$$\sum_0^3 x_i = 3b - c_3 = v(I),$$

so that

$$x_3 = 3b - c_3 - x_0 - x_1 - x_2$$
$$\leq 3b - c_3 - 2b + c_2$$
$$= b - (c_3 - c_2).$$

The same inequality is satisfied by x_1 and x_2, so that

$$\sum_1^3 x_i \leq 3b - 3(c_3 - c_2).$$

Also,

$$\sum_1^3 x_i = 3b - c_3 - x_0.$$

Hence, given $x_0 \geq 0$, there is an x in the core giving x_0 to 0 if and only if

$$3b - 3(c_3 - c_2) \geq 3b - c_3 - x_0,$$

or

$$\frac{c_2}{2} \geq \frac{c_3}{3} - \frac{x_0}{6}. \tag{5.6}$$

In particular, if the above inequality is satisfied, then $(x_0, b - t, b - t, b - t)$ is in the core with the transfer price t,

$$t = \frac{c_3 + x_0}{3}, \tag{5.7}$$

provided that $(b - t)$ is non-negative, i.e., that

$$x_0 \leq 3b - c_3. \tag{5.8}$$

Hence there is no x in the core with $x_0 = 0$ if

$$\frac{c_2}{2} < \frac{c_3}{3}. \tag{5.9}$$

EXAMPLE 5.2 Suppose that there is no outside market for the supplier's output, and that the supplier's cost function is linear, with a positive fixed cost, a, and a vector c of constant, positive marginal costs. In other words, in the notation of (5.1),

$$F_0(z) = -(a + cz),$$

where cz denotes the inner product ("dot product") of c and z. Suppose further that each customer can obtain corresponding inputs on the outside at constant external prices e (a vector), with each coordinate of e strictly greater than the corresponding coordinate of c, or[9] $e \gg c$. Let $\hat{z}_i$ maximize $[R(z_i) - cz_i]$, and assume that $\hat{z}_i > 0$. Also, let $\hat{z}$ (as usual) be the sum of the vectors $\hat{z}_i$, and assume that, with the plan $(\hat{z}_i)$ the firm's profit is positive, i.e.,

$$\hat{\pi} = \sum_{i \geq 1} R_i(\hat{z}_i) - a - c\hat{z} > 0. \tag{5.10}$$

It follows that (z_i) is an optimal plan for the firm, and so

$$v(I) = \hat{\pi}. \tag{5.11}$$

On the other hand, let $\tilde{s}_i$ maximize $[R_i(s_i) - es_i]$, so that in the notation of (5.2)

$$F_i(0) = R_i(\tilde{s}_i) - e\tilde{s}_i. \tag{5.12}$$

Under the firm's optimal plan, customer i's gross profit (before transfers) is

$$F_i(\hat{z}_i) = R_i(\hat{z}_i). \tag{5.13}$$

Hence, the core imputation x^* of theorem 5.1 corresponds to the following transfers from customers to the supplier:

$$t_i^* = R_i(\hat{z}_i) - R_i(\tilde{s}_i) + e\tilde{s}_i. \tag{5.14}$$

Suppose that R_i is strictly increasing, *strictly concave* (at least in the relevant region), and differentiable, and that $\tilde{s}_i$ is an interior point of the feasible set. It follows that

$$\tilde{s}_i < \hat{z}_i,$$

$$R_i(\tilde{s}_i) > R_i(\hat{z}_i),$$

$$\nabla R_i(\tilde{s}_i) = e,$$

where ∇R_i denotes the gradient of R_i. Hence,

$$\begin{aligned} R_i(\hat{z}_i) - R_i(\hat{s}_i) &< \nabla R_i(\tilde{s}_i)(\hat{z}_i - \tilde{s}_i), \\ &= e(\hat{z}_i - \tilde{s}_i), \end{aligned}$$

so that

$$t_i^* < e(\hat{z}_i - \tilde{s}_i) + e\tilde{s}_i = e\hat{z}_i. \tag{5.15}$$

In other words, the transfer price under x^* is strictly less than the external market price. (It is, of course, trivial that the transfer price corresponding to a core imputation cannot exceed the external-market price in this example.)

The transfer t_i^* is, of course, an upper bound on what a customer would pay the supplier in a core imputation. To get a lower bound, one uses proposition 4.2. I consider here only the case in which, without any one customer i, it is still profitable for the firm to supply internally all of the remaining customers' demands; i.e., for each i,

$$\sum_{j \neq i} [R_j(\hat{z}_j) - c\hat{z}_j] - a > 0. \tag{5.16}$$

In this case, proposition 4.2 implies that for an imputation in the core, for $i \geq 1$,

$$\begin{aligned} x_i &\leq v(I) - v(I \backslash \{i\}) \\ &= R_i(\hat{z}_i) - c\hat{z}_i. \end{aligned}$$

The corresponding bound on the transfer is

$$t_i \geq c\hat{z}_i. \tag{5.17}$$

This corresponds to a lower bound on the transfer price (vector) of c. Notice, however, that not every customer can pay this lower bound in a core imputation, since then the supplier would make a loss. In other words, (5.17) cannot be simultaneously binding for all customers. On the other hand, for every customer i there is a core imputation for which (5.17) is binding.

These conclusions must be modified if condition (5.16) is not satisfied. In such cases there is at least one customer j such that it is not profitable for the supplier to meet the demands of the remaining customers. Such a customer is a "necessary" player in the language of section 4, and hence there is a core imputation that gives him all of the surplus. In this case the supplier is still a necessary player, too, so it is still true that there is also a core imputation that gives the supplier all of the surplus.

6 Several Suppliers and Customers

6.1 Competition among Suppliers

An extreme case of "competition" among internal suppliers is the one in which two or more suppliers produce identical nonmarket commodities for the use of customers in the firm. If the average costs of these suppliers is declining and then increasing in the relevant range of output, but the optimal plan requires that all of the output (of this nonmarket commodity) be produced by a single supplier, then the core may be empty. The following example illustrates this phenomenon.

EXAMPLE 6.1 Consider the situation of example 5.1, but suppose that there are two suppliers instead of one, with identical cost functions. Recall that there are three potential customers, each of which can use either one unit or none. If a customer uses one unit, his benefit is $b > 0$; otherwise it is 0. The cost for a single supplier of producing k units ($k = 0, \ldots, 3$) is $C(k)$, where

$$\begin{aligned} &0 = C(0) < C(1) < C(2) < C(3), \\ &C(1) > b, \\ &C(k) < kb \text{ for } k \geq 2, \\ &kb - C(k) \text{ is increasing in } k \text{ for } 0 \leq k \leq 3. \end{aligned} \tag{6.1}$$

Note that the last line of (6.1) is equivalent to

$$C(k+1) - C(k) < b \text{ for } 0 \leq k \leq 2. \tag{6.2}$$

It follows from (6.1) that each customer should get one unit, and that one supplier should produce all three units and the other none. The characteristic function is

$$v(S) = \begin{cases} 2b - C(2) & \text{if } S \text{ has 2 customers and at least 1 supplier;} \\ 3b - C(3) & \text{if } S \text{ has 3 customers and at least 1 supplier;} \\ 0 & \text{otherwise.} \end{cases}$$

Each supplier is a "superfluous player" in the sense of subsection 4.4;

hence, for any core imputation, each supplier receives 0. Let x_k denote the imputation of profit to customer k ($k = 1, 2, 3$). For a core imputation,

$$\begin{aligned} x_1 + x_2 &\geq 2b - C(2), \\ x_1 + x_3 &\geq 2b - C(2), \\ x_2 + x_3 &\geq 2b - C(2), \\ x_1 + x_2 + x_3 &= 3b - C(3). \end{aligned} \tag{6.4}$$

Hence, for each customer k,

$$\begin{aligned} x_i &\leq [3b - C(3)] - [2b - C(2)] \\ &= b - [C(3) - C(2)]. \end{aligned}$$

Hence,

$$\sum_1^3 x_k \leq 3b - 3[C(3) - C(2)]. \tag{6.5}$$

Comparing (6.5) with the last line of (6.4), we see that the core will be empty if the right-hand side of (6.5) is strictly less than $3b - C(3)$, or if

$$\frac{C(2)}{2} < \frac{C(3)}{3}. \tag{6.6}$$

On the other hand, if the inequality in (6.6) is reversed (weakly), then the imputation

$$x_k = b - \frac{C(3)}{3}, \quad k = 1, 2, 3 \tag{6.7}$$

in which the three customers share the surplus equally, is in the core. (This is essentially the same analysis as was used in example 5.1 to determine when there was an imputation in the core that gave the single supplier 0.)

It is clear that examples of this kind can be constructed with any number of suppliers and customers, and that the commodities produced by the several suppliers need not be perfect substitutes.

On the other hand, it is well known that if average cost is declining throughout the relevant range, and other conditions are satisfied, then the core will not be empty, as the following example illustrates.

EXAMPLE 6.2 Let there again be two identical suppliers, each with cost function C. Let K denote the set of customers, and suppose that customer k has a linear profit function

$$F_k(q) = b_k q, \quad 0 \leq q \leq Q_k$$

where q is a real number and $b_k > 0$. Let $Q \equiv \sum Q_k$, and make the following assumptions:

A1 For $0 < q \leq Q$, $C(q)$ is positive, differentiable, and increasing; average cost $C(q)/q$ is minimized at $q = Q$; $C(0) = 0$.

A2 For every customer k, and for $0 < q \leq Q$, $C'(q) < b_k$.

A3 $\sum_k b_k Q_k - C(Q) > 0$.

These assumptions imply that the total profit is maximized when a single supplier produces the total input Q and each customer k gets input Q_k; the maximum profit is

$$\hat{\pi} = \sum_k b_k Q_k - C(Q).$$

Let a denote the average cost $C(Q)/Q$. It is easy to check that the following imputation is in the core: each supplier gets 0, and each customer k is charged the unit price equal to a, i.e., k receives the imputation $(b_k - a)Q_k$. In fact, we need only check that, for every subset S of customers in K,

$$\sum_S (b_k - a)Q_k \geq \left(\sum_S b_k Q_k\right) - C\left(\sum_S Q_k\right),$$

since the assumptions imply that the right-hand side is the value of the characteristic function for a set consisting of S together with one or both suppliers. But the last inequality is equivalent to

$$a = C(Q)/Q \leq C\left(\sum_S Q_k\right) \Big/ \sum_S Q_k,$$

which is true by assumption A1.

6.2 Complementary Suppliers

At the opposite pole from the case of competing suppliers is the case in which the several suppliers produce nonmarket commodities that are "strict complements." As we shall see, this case is very much like the case of a single supplier; in fact, in a very precise sense it will correspond to the case of a single supplier resulting from a "merger" of the several complementary suppliers.

I shall use a model that is close to that of section 5, but with several suppliers. Let J denote the set of suppliers and K the set of customers; J and K are disjoint, and I is the union of J and K. Let $z_{jk} \geq 0$ denote the vector of nonmarket commodities supplied by j to k, and define

$$z_{j.} \equiv \sum_k z_{jk},$$

the total supply of supplier j. The latter is constrained to be in some set Z_j; the product

$$Z \equiv \prod_j Z_j$$

corresponds to the set Z in section 5. I assume that each set Z_j contains the vector 0.

Denote by z_k the vector of nonmarket inputs that customer k receives;

$$z_k = (z_{jk})_{j \in J}.$$

We can define the profit function, F_k, for customer k, as in section 5 (e.g., as in (5.2)). We can also define the profit function, say G_j, for supplier j, in the same way that F_0 is defined in section 5 (e.g., as in (5.1)). Let ξ denote a plan, $((z_{jk}))$.

The *assumption of strict complementarity* (SC) states that, if the nonmarket input from any supplier to any customer is 0, then the maximum profit for that customer is the same as it would be if the nonmarket inputs from all the suppliers were 0. Formally,

(1) For every j in J and k in K, if $z_{jk} = 0$ then $F_k(z_k) = F_k(0)$.

I also add to SC the following conditions:

(2) For all j in J and k in K, all $z_k \geq 0$ and $z_{j.} \geq 0$ in Z_j,

$$F_k(z_k) \geq F_k(0),$$

$$G_j(z_{j.}) \leq G_j(0),$$

$$G_j(0) \geq 0.$$

For any situation defined as above, define the corresponding *one-supplier game* by replacing the set of suppliers with a single supplier whose production possibility set is Z and whose profit function is

$$F_0(z) = \sum_{j \in J} G_j(z_{j.}). \tag{6.8}$$

Thus, the corresponding one-supplier game fits the model of section 5.

The main result for complementary suppliers is as follows.

THEOREM Under the assumption of strict complementarity (SC), if $[x_0^*,(x_k^*)_{k \in K}]$ is in the core of the one-supplier game, and if

$$\sum_{j \in J} x_j^* = x_0^*,$$

where

$$x_j^* \geq G_j(0) \text{ for all } j \text{ in } J,$$

then $(x_i^*)_{i \in I}$ is in the core of the several-supplier game.

Proof First, observe that if $S \leq I$ and S does not contain every supplier, then

$$v(S) = \sum_{j \in S \cap J} G_j(0) + \sum_{k \in S \cap K} F_k(0). \tag{6.9}$$

To see this, observe that if S does not contain every supplier, then by SC the inputs of all other suppliers are worthless, so the maximum profit of customer k is $F_k(0)$. Since no customer needs any positive nonmarket inputs, the maximum profit of any supplier j in S is $G_j(0)$. These two observations imply (6.9). Second, observe that if $[x_0^*,(x_k^*)_{k \in K}]$ is in the core of the one-supplier game, then for all customers k in K

$$x_k^* \geq F_k(0) = v(\{k\}). \tag{6.10}$$

We must now consider two cases. In the first case, not every supplier is in S; then

$$v(S) = \sum_{\substack{j \in S \\ j \in J}} G_j(0) + \sum_{\substack{k \in S \\ k \in K}} F_k(0).$$

Hence,

$$\sum_{i \in S} x_i^* \geq v(S). \tag{6.11}$$

In the second case, every supplier is in S ($J \subset S$). Let $\bar{v}$ denote the characteristic function of the one-supplier game. Then

$$v(S) = \bar{v}(\{0\} \cup (K \cap S)).$$

According to section 5, $\bar{v}(T)$ is the maximum of

$$F_0(z) + \sum_{k \in T} F_k(z_k) \tag{6.12}$$

subject to the constraint that, for some feasible plan ξ with $z_k = 0$ for all k not in T,

$$\sum_k z_k = z.$$

By (6.8), the maximum of (6.12) is also $v(S)$ where $S = J \cup T$; hence (6.11) is satisfied in the second case, too, which completes the proof.

Acknowledgments

I am indebted to E. E. Zajac for having introduced me to this topic, and to P. B. Linhart, A. R. Schotter, and M. Wooders for helpful discussions. Douglas Gale provided useful comments on an earlier draft. The views expressed here are those of the author, and not necessarily those of AT&T Bell Laboratories.

Notes

1. See Scarf 1986 and Sharkey 1982. Moulin (1987) gives a very brief survey and additional references. The topic is closely related to "cost allocation." I do not here consider issues of fairness or justice; see, e.g., Zajac 1978.

2. A precise statement of this result is beyond the scope of the present paper; "outcomes" of a bargaining mechanism are assumed to be determined by Bayes-Nash equilibria of the incomplete-information game that is induced by the mechanism (see Myerson and Satterthwaite 1983).

3. See Radner 1986 for a precise statement. The Groves mechanism in question will specify a noncooperative "revelation game" in which, for each player, it is a dominant strategy to tell the truth. The corresponding outcome maximizes the firm's profit and is individually rational for both players. To achieve the latter, the headquarters may have to "subsidize" the profit centers.

4. Recall that in the model the prices of market commodities are exogenous and fixed. If the price of a market commodity were 0, then it would not enter the profit calculations, although the availability of the commodity would be reflected in the description of the production possibility sets.

5. In all the particular models investigated in this paper, the maxima in (2.1) will be attainable.

6. In fact, to obtain the desired results, some further regularity conditions must be imposed; see any standard treatment of duality theory in nonlinear programming.

7. Note that s_i and z_i are vectors in the same space. Thus, if a particular input is "computing services," part may be purchased on the market and part obtained internally.

8. This example is adapted from Zajac 1978. However, it is probably older.

9. For vectors u and w, I shall write $u \geq w$ if each coordinate of u is as large as the corresponding coordinate of w, $u > w$ if $u \geq w$ but $u \neq w$, and $u \gg w$ if each coordinate of u is strictly greater than the corresponding coordinate of w.

References

Debreu, G. 1959. *Theory of Value*. Yale University Press.

Moulin, H. 1987. "A core selection for regulating a single-output monopoly." *RAND Journal of Economics* 18: 397–407.

Myerson, R. B., and M. A. Satterthwaite. 1983. "Efficient mechanisms for bilateral trading." *Journal of Economic Theory* 28: 265–281.

Radner, R. 1986. "The internal economy of large firms." *Economic Journal* 96 (supplement): 1–22.

Scarf, H. 1986. "Notes on the core of a productive economy." In *Contributions to Mathematical Economics*, ed. W. Hildenbrand and A. Mas-Colell. North-Holland.

Sharkey, W. 1982. *The Theory of Natural Monopoly*. Cambridge University Press.

Zajac, E. E. 1978. *Fairness and Efficiency: An Introduction to Public Utility Pricing*. Ballinger.

Credible Oil Supply Contracts

David M. Newbery

The world oil market differs from the conventional textbook commodity market in three important respects. First, as oil is an exhaustible resource, current supply decisions depend on future prices, but there are no futures markets. Since future prices depend on future supplies, each producer must predict the supply plans of the other producers. Second, the market is dominated by few large suppliers who face competition from a fringe of small producers. The market structure is neither one of pure monopoly nor one of perfect competition. As an approximation it can be modeled as a dominant producer (in this case a cartel, a subset of OPEC) facing a competitive fringe. The dominant producer has the power to influence prices now and in the future by changing its supplies and planned supplies; faced with a passive price-taking fringe, it can therefore act as a Stackelberg leader (von Stackelberg 1952). If such a leader announces his intertemporal supply plan, the fringe will then respond with a supply plan, and the leader can choose his best plan given the resulting response and resulting time path for oil prices.

Third, oil is a highly politicized commodity, conferring substantial scarcity rents to those in a position to exploit them and traded between sovereign nation states. In such a situation, the only credible long-term supply contracts are those that continue to be mutually advantageous, for there is no supranational legislature to ensure that contracts are honored. Maskin and Newbery (1978, 1990) showed that this lack of internationally binding contracts had a significant adverse effect on a dominant oil importer and totally altered the nature of market equilibrium. The present paper shows that the same phenomenon can be as important and as damaging for oil exporters. The reason is simply explained, though it has been largely overlooked in earlier studies of exhaustible-resource theory. Consider the case of the large oil importer in an otherwise competitive world economy, as in Maskin and Newbery 1990. If the importer announces now that he plans to import small quantities of oil in the future, the future world demand for oil will be depressed and hence the price will be reduced. Producers will prefer to sell early, and will depress the present price to the advantage of the importer. If suppliers believed that the importer had bound itself now to carrying out this future plan, then the importer could use its future market power to benefit from cheap early oil. If the importer could later change its plan, it would choose to do so, avoiding the costs of lower-than-desired future imports. Thus, the original plan is not *dynamically consistent*; equivalently, it does not satisfy the *principal of optimality* (Bellman 1957). A plan is dynamically consistent and satisfies the principle of optimality if, when the initial stages of the plan have been implemented, the economy or system evolves to a position for which the remaining stages of the plan continue to be the best choice from the new position.

Maskin and Newbery (1978) demonstrated that for almost all model specifications, the importer's best plan drawn up on the assumption that it would be binding in the future would be dynamically inconsistent. In the absence of binding contracts, such a plan would not be credible, and producers would have to forecast the level of future imports, which would be in the importer's interest when the time comes, in order to plan their exports. What, in such a context, was a credible import plan? Fortunately, game theory provides guidance on this question. Each player chooses a strategy—in this case, a level of imports at each date—given the strategies (levels of imports) chosen by other players. This configuration of strategies is *credible* if it forms a *perfect* Nash equilibrium—that is, if it constitutes a Nash equilibrium at every node in the game tree. (This equilibrium, sometimes called *subgame perfect*, is discussed in Selten 1975.) Game theory thus draws a distinction between credibility (or perfectness) and dynamic consistency, for dynamic consistency requires only that the configuration of strategies form a Nash equilibrium at every point along the equilibrium path emanating from the starting node, but not necessarily at points off the path. This distinction will be clarified below in a discussion of alternative equilibrium concepts.

In the oil import case, Maskin and Newbery were able to solve for the credible import strategy in a simple example. The key result was that not only was such a plan less attractive to the importer than a binding contract plan, but the importer's market power might actually be disadvantageous, in that the importer could be worse off than with no market power.

In the present paper we are interested in modeling the world oil market on the assumption that a dominant producer faces a competitive fringe of other producers, and competitive importers.[1] In some ways the problem appears quite similar to the oil import problem, for in both cases a dominant agent competes with competitive agents on his side of the market and trades with competitive agents on the other side of the market. There is, however, one arguably important difference, which is best appreciated by examining the discrete-time case. The natural sequence of events for the importing case is for the dominant importer to choose a tariff at the start of the period, and for all agents, including the domestic residents in the dominant-importing country, to then choose their consumption. This sequence gives the dominant importer a first-mover advantage, and the appropriate equilibrium concept for such a game is the Stackelberg equilibrium (von Stackelberg 1952). The dominant agent chooses his actions taking into account the responses of the remaining (in this case, competitive) agents.

When the market power lies on the exporting side, however, it is less obvious that the dominant agent has a natural first-mover advantage. If production was highly decentralized, with each producer taking his own supply decisions in response to the market signals he receives, then a dominant producer would announce a production tax schedule which would internalize its market power in exactly the same way as the import tariff, and the situation would be quite symmetric. If, on the other hand, the dominant producer achieves its market power by directly controlling its supply decision, then it has a first-mover advantage only if it can announce its supply plans at the start of the period. Otherwise each producer would draw up its supply plans taking the plans of others as given, and the appropriate equilibrium concept would be Nash-Cournot.

Which, then, is the correct equilibrium concept for the case under discussion, in which there is a dominant producer? It is here that the distinction between dynamic consistency and credibility becomes important. The problem is further complicated by the fact that the agents have to choose a (finite) sequence of decisions. Moreover, each decision differs from the previous decision, as there is less oil left and hence it is available on different terms. The simplest case to solve is one in which the agents choose the whole sequence of decisions at the start of the game on the assumption that they will carry them out come what may. This gives rise to *open-loop equilibria*, in which decisions are soley a function of time and the initial state. In the open-loop Stackelberg equilibrium (OLSE) the dominant producer announces a supply plan (or, equivalently, a production tax plan) and the remaining agents then choose their best plan in response. In the open-loop Nash-Cournot equilibrium (OLNCE), each agent draws up his supply plan assuming that the supplies of other agents are given.

Now, it is one thing to argue that the Nash-Cournot equilibrium concept is the appropriate concept in a one-shot game, and quite another to argue that the OLNCE is appropriate for a multi-period game. Surely, if the dominant agent has market power, and is able to revise his plan over time, then he should be able to influence the supplies of the fringe producers, and hence choose a plan that induces a more favorable response from the fringe. This kind of reasoning suggests that the OLNCE fails to capture an important element of the market power of the dominant producer—an element present in the Stackelberg equilibrium—and is presumably the reason why some economists prefer to model dominant-agent games as Stackelberg equilibria. Unfortunately, for the class of problems under discussion here the issue is more complicated. The reason is that, although the OLSE may reflect market power better, it may also be dynamically inconsistent, whereas the OLNCE, which may fail to reflect the market power adequately, is at least dynamically consistent. For a plan to be credible, the resulting equilibrium should not only adequately reflect the market power of the dominant agent but should also be dynamically consistent. Where the OLSE is inconsistent, neither equilibrium concept is credible; that is, neither is subgame perfect.

However, it is possible to define equilibrium concepts which are subgame perfect and which satisfy the principle of optimality in the absence of binding commitments. The feedback Nash-Cournot equilibrium (FBNCE) has each producer simultaneously choosing his supply plan for the next period, taking as given the next-period supply plans of the other producers, on the assumption that all producers will choose the following periods' supplies in the same manner. In the feedback Stackelberg equilibrium (FBSE) the dominant producer announces the next period's supply at the beginning of the period (or announces the tax schedule) and then other suppliers choose their supply for that period. Again, all suppliers assume that in subsequent periods they will decide what best to do given the state in which they find themselves. These *feedback equilibria* differ from the open-loop equilibria in that decisions depend on the current state of the system and not just on the initial state and time.[2] Another way to stress the distinction is to describe feedback equilibria as *rational-expectations equilibria*, since the agents need to predict the relationship between the future state of the game and their current decisions. Depending on these current decisions, they will be placed in a more or less favorable position for the remainder of the game.

If the open-loop equilibrium is dynamically inconsistent, then it will be credible only if commitment is possible, in which case a dominant agent can use his (committed) future intentions to affect and benefit his present position. In the feedback or rational-expectations equilibrium, future actions cannot be used to influence current outcomes, and hence the dominant agents' market power is weakened (perhaps significantly).

We return then to the question of timing, and hence the correct choice of equilibrium concept. The Stackelberg equilibrium is a natural equilibrium concept for a dominant producer who can sign binding contracts, for the remaining agents, being competitive, are passive and would then be forced to react to the dominant producer. In the absence of binding contracts, the dominant producer cannot credibly announce more than his next-period supply, and there is thus much less time for the other producers to respond. If there is not time for them to respond, then the FBNCE is the appropriate concept. If there is time for them to respond, then the dominant producer must decide whether it is profitable to exploit his first-mover advantage. In part, the issue will turn on the length of a period, where the natural length of a period is dictated by the time taken to make a significant change in supply. This may well depend more on the institutional structure (whether the cartel has to meet, whether Congress has to approve a change in tax laws, etc.) than on technological factors.

The approach taken here is to concentrate on the Stackelberg equilibrium for the following reason. If the open-loop Stackelberg equilibrium is dynamically consistent, then it is a credible equilibrium, as it reflects the asymmetry in market power more convincingly than the OLNCE. If it is dynamically inconsistent, then it is interesting to compare it directly with the consistent (i.e., feedback) Stackelberg equilibrium. However, as it is difficult to decide unambiguously whether the FBSE or the FBNCE is more appropriate, the latter will also be (rather briefly) discussed.

Whereas in the dominant-oil-importer case the open-loop (or binding-contract) Stackelberg equilibrium is always inconsistent, in the case of the dominant oil exporter Ulph and Folie (1981) and Newbery (1981) have shown that (in some cases, at least) the best plan for the dominant producer is dynamically consistent, so the absence of binding contracts makes no difference to the market equilibrium. The reason is that under these plans the fringe retains sufficient oil to continue to limit the market power of the dominant producer for the entire time horizon, and hence the producer has no incentive to deviate from the plan he would have chosen were he able to precommit himself.

However, if the dominant producer wishes to continue production after the fringe has exhausted its stock of oil, then the best initial plan is likely to be dynamically inconsistent, for once the fringe has exhausted its stocks it loses its influence over the dominant producer, who is then free to deviate from his original plan and who typically would find it profitable to do so.

There are two main cases when this temptation to depart from the initial plan arises after the fringe is exhausted. The first occurs when the dominant supplier has higher extraction costs than the fringe and hence, other things being equal, has an incentive to delay extraction. Empirically this is implausible. The second case arises when the dominant supplier uses a lower discount rate in making depletion decisions, and this case is practically important. The "low absorbing" members of OPEC are forced to lend abroad at low real rates of return, since they cannot profitably absorb all their revenue domestically, and this capital-market imperfection (itself a reflection of the inability to enforce satisfactory intertemporal contracts) encourages delay. Newbery (1981) shows that this effect may more than outweigh any cost advantage for plausible estimates of rates of discount and extraction costs.[3]

Cremer and Weitzman (1976) calculate the Stackelberg equilibrium for the case in which the dominant producer uses a lower rate of discount than the fringe, and their solution will thus be dynamically inconsistent. Most economists, in calculating such a Stackelberg equilibrium, would naturally reach for the normal single-agent version of Pontryagin's Maximum Principle (or some essentially equivalent numerical optimization package). The problem is that the simple Maximum Principle tends to conceal the implicit (and unreasonable) assumption that agents must commit themselves to fulfill the plans they draw up. Without binding contracts, dynamically inconsistent plans are not equilibrium solutions, and the solutions must be found by other means.[4]

To summarize, the simple application of the (single-agent) Maximum Principle to intertemporal optimization problems gives an open-loop plan—that is, one in which actions depend only on calendar time (and the initial configuration of the system). If the agent has market power, and if choices depend on expectations of the future, the open-loop plans that reflect this market power are typically dynamically inconsistent. This has recently been noted in the context of choosing optimal macroeconomic policies in an economy in which agents make current decisions (for investment, employment, etc.) based on expectations about the future course of the economy, including expectations about future macro-policies. (The key paper here is Kydland and Prescott 1977, but see also Calvo 1978, Buiter 1980, the special issue of the *Journal of Economic Dynamics and Control* (1980) on rational expectations, and, for a recent survey, Karp and Newbery

1990.) Again, if there is no mechanism for committing the government to follow its announced plan, then plans derived from the (single-agent) Maximum Principle are not credible. Although there was initially some skepticism as to whether a dynamically consistent solution could be found in these cases, it is now accepted that such solution can be derived, though they often involve formidable computations (Chow 1980).

This first objective of this paper is to show that what appears at first sight to be the natural equilibrium concept for the oil market—that is, the open-loop Stackelberg equilibrium—is, in our model, dynamically inconsistent. As such, it would only be a credible supply plan given binding contracts, and I shall refer to it as the Binding Contract Equilibrium to stress this implicit assumption. A second objective is to show how to compute a credible supply plan in the absence of binding contracts, when all producers must forecast future actions by other suppliers. As was argued above, there are two natural candidates for the solution concept, depending on the timing of the dominant producer's supply intentions and the supply decisions of the fringe. If the fringe choose their supply in response to the dominant producer, then the correct equilibrium concept is the feedback Stackelberg equilibrium, which, to stress the importance of expectations, I shall also call the Rational Expectations Stackelberg equilibrium. If, on the other hand, all producers choose their supply before they know the plans of their competitors, then the correct equilibrium concept is the feedback Nash-Cournot equilibrium. The main contribution of this paper is to derive analytical solutions for these two equilibria in a special, simplified model, which will make it possible to examine the effect of the absence of binding contracts. Hitherto, such solutions could be derived only for the linear-quadratic case (i.e., linear dynamics, quadratic objective or loss function; see Kydland 1977; Chow 1980, p. 58), and even then it was necessary to solve for specific numerical values. In the present case, we have an alternative simple model that permits a relatively straightforward solution. The model takes a special form for two reasons: First, there appears to be no general, tractable derivation of the solution except in special cases. Second, the model was chosen to be as close as possible to that analyzed in detail in Maskin and Newbery 1978. It is an interesting question in its own right to contrast the effects of market power on the buying and selling sides.

We shall make three unrealistic assumptions to simplify the model. First, we shall consider the implausible case in which the dominant supplier has higher costs, rather than the case of differing discount rates. Together with the assumption that the fringe has zero extraction costs, this simplifies the problem while retaining the feature of dynamic inconsistency. My defense of this choice is that the only tractable model with different discount rates has zero extraction costs for all producers and gives uninteresting degenerate solutions. The second important assumption is that oil is valueless after a fixed date. The reason is that fixed-terminal-date problems are easier to solve than more complex boundary-value problems. Finally, we shall assume that all market participants have full information about supply and demand conditions and that there is no uncertainty. Specifically, they are assumed to know the demand function at every future date, and to know the extraction costs and the reserves of all suppliers. This last assumption is common to most work on exhaustible resources and can be defended by arguing that it is improbable that suppliers would be able to conceal special information about costs or reserves for very long. The assumption of no uncertainty is less realistic and is made for simplicity.

For this model the binding-contract equilibrium is easily found and shown to be dynamically inconsistent. The next section shows how to compute the dynamically consistent feedback Stackelberg equilibrium and the feedback Nash-Cournot equilibrium. These are then compared with each other, and with the benchmark of the competitive equilibrium. The main result is that both the rational-expectations Stackelberg equilibrium and the feedback Nash-Cournot equilibrium can yield lower present discounted profits to the dominant producer than the competitive equilibrium, just as Maskin and Newbery (1978) found cases in which a dominant oil *importer* could be worse off in the RESE than in the competitive equilibrium.

The other main result is that in most cases the FBNCE yields higher profits than the RESE, though there are other cases (with shorter time horizons) in which the reverse is true. Hence, the dominant producer has an incentive to avoid revealing his short-run supply plans, though, of course, he may not have this option.

The Model

Time is divided into a number of discrete periods $(0, 1, \ldots, t, \ldots, T)$. At date T oil becomes worthless because of the sudden availability of a relatively cheap and abundant substitute. There is a single dominant producer (or cohesive cartel) facing a fringe of competitive producers, each of whom acts as though it has no influence on the price at any date. In period t the key variables are

x_t sales of the dominant producer

y_t total sales of the fringe

p_t market clearing price of oil

X_t stock of oil held by the dominant producer at the start of t

Y_t total fringe stock at the start of t.

In addition, the dominant producer has a unit extraction cost of c. All producers face the same rate of interest r, or discount factor $\beta = 1/(1 + r)$. The key simplifying assumptions are that the extraction costs of the fringe producers are zero and that the demand function is unit elastic,

$$p_t = \frac{1}{x_t + y_t} \tag{1}$$

as in Maskin and Newbery 1978. The importance of the first of these assumptions is that in equilibrium the fringe will choose a pattern of supply which ensures that the price rises at the rate of interest:

$$p_t = p_0(1 + r)^t = p_0\beta^{-t}. \tag{2}$$

With these preliminaries complete, we can now define and solve for various equilibria, and test for their credibility. In the first, the dominant producer announces his supply plan for the whole period and is committed to following it. To stress this contractual feature, the equilibrium will be called the binding-contract equilibrium, or BCE.

The Binding-Contract Equilibrium (Open-Loop Stackelberg Equilibrium)

At the start of the first period ($t = 0$) the dominant producer (or leader announces his supply plan

$$\mathbf{X} = (x_0, x_1, \ldots, x_t, \ldots, x_T). \tag{3}$$

Each fringe producer chooses his supply plan to maximize the present discounted value of his profits. If follower f sells y_t^f in period t, he chooses the sequence $\{y_t^f\}$ to maximize the present value of profits:

$$\sum_{t=0}^{T} \beta^t y_t^f p_t \quad \text{subject to} \sum_{t=0}^{T} y_t^f \leq Y_0^f \tag{4}$$

(since he has zero extraction costs.) He takes the price trajectory as given, and can perfectly forecast the price. It is then readily shown (Newbery 1981; Ulph and Folie 1981) that the BCE is characterized as follows: The price rises at the rate of interest because the fringe producers have zero extraction costs and perfectly arbitrage the price. The leader increases his profits by delaying his sales as long as possible, since this lowers the present value of his costs without altering the present value of his sales. Thus, the fringe is initially the sole supplier until period τ, at which point the leader takes over as sole supplier. (In period τ both may supply in this discrete-time version.) The leader plans to sell $X \leq X_0$ in total, and the initial price, which indexes the whole price path, must be such as to equate total supply to total demand:

$$X + Y_0 = \sum_{0}^{T} \frac{1}{p_t} = \frac{1}{p_0}\left(\frac{1 - \beta^{T+1}}{1 - \beta}\right), \tag{5}$$

using (1) and (2). Given p_0, date τ is found as the time taken to exhaust Y_0:

$$\tau = \text{Max}\{t \mid \beta^t > 1 - p_0 Y_0(1 - \beta), \tau \in (0, 1, \ldots, T)\}. \tag{6}$$

The choice of X in turn maximizes the leader's initial present discounted profits.[5] Once the leader has announced plan $\mathbf{X}$ of (3), the fringe can compute the price trajectory from (3) and (5). If the leader sets $x_t < \beta^t/p_0$, $t < \tau$, the fringe will sell enough in period t to arbitrage the price to the level given by (2), whereas if $x_t > \beta^t/p_0$ the leader forgoes profits. As long as the leader is bound to follow his plan, his profit-maximizing strategy is one in which prices are perfectly arbitraged and his sales are delayed as long as possible.

The Problem of Dynamic Inconsistency

It is clear that if the leader could subsequently replan his future sales he would choose to do so, so his initial plan is dynamically inconsistent and hence is not a credible plan in the absence of binding contracts. Consider the position of the leader at date τ, when the fringe has exhausted its oil. There is nothing now to constrain the leader from raising the price above the competitively arbitraged path. Clearly, if the fringe producers anticipated this they would delay sales until after τ, and the proposed solution would not be an equilibrium. Indeed, working in continuous time, in the open-loop equilibrium the leader would choose to sell X_t^* over the period $[t, T]$ where

$$X_t^* = \sqrt{\frac{1 - e^{-r(T-t)}}{1 + e^{-r(T-t)}}\left(Y_t^2 + \frac{2Y_t}{rc}\right)} - Y_t \tag{7}$$

(Newbery 1980). Clearly, as date τ approaches, and $Y_t \to 0$, $X_t^* \to 0$; thus, the dominant supplier would like to reduce his future sales in order to drive up the price.

In short, if allowed to renegotiate his contract, the leader will wish to do so the moment $X_t^* \leq X_t$, which will certainly occur before date τ. Unless contracts are binding, therefore, the fringe will not believe the leader's announced supply strategy. In the absence of binding contracts they must predict the actual strategy that will be followed.

If the leader can announce his short-term supply plans for the next period, and hence can influence the fringe's next-period choice, the appropriate equilibrium concept is the feedback Stackelberg equilibrium, as discussed above. The alternative equilibrium, in which all producers choose the next period's supply simultaneously (the feedback Nash-Cournot equilibrium), is discussed below. For the moment, note that FBSE appears to be a better description of a cartel that periodically meets to coordinate and announce its short-run policy, and in which the fringe producers are close spectators of this process. In the absence of binding contracts, the fringe takes the next-period supply of the leader as given but has to predict future supply plans. To stress the importance of expectations, the FBSE will also be called the *rational-expectations Stackelberg equilibrium* (RESE).

The Rational-Expectations Stackelberg Equilibrium

The equilibrium must have the fringe choosing a supply plan that, together with the predicted sales of the leader, perfectly arbitrages prices, for otherwise they could profitably reallocate sales. This perfect-arbitrage condition greatly simplifies the solution, which must come from a one-dimension family of price paths, indexed by the terminal price, p_T, so that

$$p_t = \beta^{T-t} p_T, \quad t = 0, 1, \ldots, T. \tag{8}$$

Given the leader's planned cumulative future sales, X_t, and the remaining stock of the fringe at the start of period t, Y_t, the fringe can calculate the terminal price (and hence the whole price path) from the condition that total sales must equal total demand:

$$X_t + Y_t = \sum_{s=t}^{T} \frac{1}{p_s} = \frac{1}{p_T} \sum_{s=t}^{T} \beta^{s-T} \tag{9}$$

(where demand is given by (1) and (8)). With this prediction of p_T they can compute p_t. Given the announced sales, x_t, they will continue to supply in period t until the price has been driven down to p_t. The fringe producers' responses are thus completely determined by the leader's announced sales, x_t, and his predicted subsequent sales. The fringe predicts the leader's sales in period $s > t$ by assuming that the leader will maximize his profits starting from the position he finds himself in at the start of period s, given that he cannot commit himself more than one period ahead.

There are two alternative but equivalent ways of formulating the leader's maximization problem. He wishes to maximize (present-value) profits from period s to period T, subject to the responses of the fringe (or, equivalently, subject to the arbitrage condition (8)) and given that his sales from $s + 1$ to T must maximize profits from $s + 1$ on. Alternatively, since future profits depend on the future state of the game, and hence on the future stocks of the leader and the fringe, the leader must choose his current sales in period s to maximise current profits, plus discounted future profits (which depend on the future state). Stocks in period $s + 1$ are just equal to current stocks less period-s sales, and hence the leader's current sales influence both current profits and (by influencing the starting point of the game starting from $s + 1$) future profits. In both cases it is obviously necessary to work back from the future state of the system, and hence ultimately from the terminal period. It is therefore notationally convenient to subscript time periods by the number of periods yet to go before oil becomes valueless, n. Let the terminal price be p; hence, the equilibrium price in period n is, from (8),

$$p_n = \beta^n p, \quad n = T - t, \quad n = (0, 1, \ldots, T). \tag{10}$$

The leader's supply plan is found recursively as follows. In the final period the fringe producers have no alternative but to sell their remaining stocks. The leader therefore chooses x_0 to

$$\max_{x_0} W_0 = x_0(p - c) \tag{11}$$

subject to demand equals supply:

$$\frac{1}{p} = x_0 + Y_0, \quad x_0 \leq X_0. \tag{12}$$

Assuming adequate supplies, X_0, and low enough extraction costs to make supply profitable, the solution is[6]

$$x_0 = \frac{p - c}{p^2}, \quad y_0 = Y_0 = \frac{c}{p^2}. \tag{13}$$

The leader's *credible* supply makes his supply a function of the state of the system; hence, equation (13) can be written, substituting for p, as

$$x_0 = \psi_0(X_0, Y_0) \begin{cases} = \text{Max}\{\sqrt{Y_0/c} - Y_0, 0\} \text{ for } X_0 \geq X_0^c = \sqrt{Y_0/c} - Y_0 \\ = X_0 \qquad \text{for } X_0 < X_0^c. \end{cases} \tag{14}$$

The fringe supply plan also depends on the state of the system, but in the final period this necessarily has a simple form:

$$y_0 = \gamma_0(X_0, Y_0, x_0) = Y_0.$$

The price is

$$p_0 \begin{cases} = \dfrac{c}{Y_0} & \text{for } X_0 \geq X_0^c \\[2ex] = \dfrac{1}{X_0 + Y_0} & \text{for } X_0 < X_0^c \end{cases} \tag{15}$$

(except that $x_0 = 0$ if $p_0 < c$).[7] The term X_0^c is the *critical credible stock* at the start of the last period, namely, the maximum amount of oil which it would pay the leader to supply. Oil in excess of this level has zero value to the leader, and could costlessly be destroyed. If the leader has less oil, then it will pay him to sell his entire stock.

In the penultimate period the leader announces x_1; the followers must choose y_1 and hence $y_0 = Y_1 - y_1$ knowing that the leader will follow the plan of equation (14) in the last period. They thus arbitrage prices: $p_1 = \beta p$, which, from equations (1) and (15), can be written

$$\frac{1}{x_1 + y_1} = \beta\sqrt{\frac{c}{Y_1 - y_1}}. \tag{16}$$

Their supply plan can thus be written $\gamma_1(x_1, Y_1)$. The leader chooses x_1 to maximize

$$W_1 = (p_1 - c)x_1 + \beta(p_0 - c)\psi_0\{X_1 - x_1, Y_1 - \gamma_1(x_1, Y_1)\}. \tag{17}$$

Assuming adequate stocks and low enough costs, this can be written

$$\max_{x_1} W_1 = \left(\frac{1}{x_1 + \gamma_1(x_1)} - c\right)x_1 + \beta\left(\frac{1}{\beta\{x_1 + \gamma_1(x_1)\}} - c\right)\left(\sqrt{\frac{Y_1 - \gamma_1(x_1)}{c}} - \{Y_1 - \gamma_1(x_1)\}\right) \tag{18}$$

since Y_1 is given. The solution will be of the form

$$x_1 = \psi_1(Y_1) \text{ provided } X_1 \geq X_1^c(Y_1). \tag{19}$$

Again, X_1^c, the critical credible stock at the beginning of the pènultimate period, is the maximum amount that will be sold over the remaining two periods. If the leader has less oil than X_1^c, then it is readily checked that he will plan to retain $X_0^c(Y_1 - y_1)$ for the last period, and will hence set $x_1 = X_1 - X_0^c(Y_1 - y_1)$, where y_1 is set by the arbitrage condition (16). This follows because the arbitrage condition, which is imposed after the choice of x_1, makes the present-value price constant and hence makes the present value of the leader's revenue also constant. Delaying sales as long as possible (and hence delaying extraction costs) is therefore the best supply strategy.

Solving for the Rational-Expectations Stackelberg Equilibrium

Equation (18) appears intractible, but the problem can be greatly simplified by working in terms of a different state variable. As was remarked above, the perfect-arbitrage equation (10) greatly simplifies the solution, which must come from a one-dimension family of price paths, indexed by the terminal price, p. The trick is to note that, provided the leader's stock at the start of period n is at least as large as the critical credible stock level, $X_n^c(Y_n)$, the leader's sales are constrained not by his stocks but only by fringe stocks, and so his sales depend only on Y_n:

$$x_n = \psi_n(Y_n).$$

Also, prices must be such as to equate supply and demand in the remaining

$n+1$ periods, which, summing over periods and using the arbitrage condition, we can write as

$$Y_n + \sum_{s=0}^{n} \psi_s(Y_s) = \sum_{s=0}^{n} \frac{1}{p_s} = \frac{1}{p} \sum_{s=0}^{n} \beta^{-s}. \tag{20}$$

Finally, fringe sales are computed from the leader's sales and the arbitrage condition:

$$y_s = \frac{1}{\beta^s p} - \psi_s(Y_s) = Y_s - Y_{s-1}; \tag{21}$$

hence, Y_s is a function of Y_n and p, and (20) is therefore a monotonic equation relating p to Y_n. Since both the leader's sales and fringe sales are just a function of Y_n, the state of the system is completely described by Y_n, and hence can be as well described by p.

If the leader's stock is less than $X_n^c(Y_n)$, then he will sell nothing until the critical credible stock has fallen to a level equal to his stock, after which he sells at the maximum credible rate, $\psi_s(Y_s)$. Since this rate will be determined recursively, it is only necessary to solve for this rate—the number of periods for which it applies can then be determined given the available stock.

To see how this solution strategy simplifies the present problem, note that in the last period the solution from (13) can be written

$$x_0 = \frac{p-c}{p^2} = \Phi_0(p). \tag{22}$$

In the penultimate period the leader chooses his supply $x_1|_{\Phi_0(\cdot)}$, and the fringe then decides how to allocate its total stock, Y_1, to arbitrage the price, given that the index of prices, p, must be such as to equate total predicted supply to total demand:

$$Y_1 + x_1 + \Phi_0(p) = \frac{1}{p}\left(1 + \frac{1}{\beta}\right) = \frac{B_1}{p}, \tag{23}$$

where total demand from period n on is B_n/p and where

$$B_n \equiv \sum_{j=0}^{n} \beta^{-j}. \tag{24}$$

The leader thus chooses x_1 to maximize the profits:

$$\underset{x_1}{\text{Max}}\ W_1 = x_1(\beta p - c) + \beta\Phi_0(p)(p - c)$$

given that p and x_1 must satisfy (23). The Lagrangian is

$$\mathscr{L} = x_1(\beta p - c) + \beta\Phi_0(p)(p - c) - \lambda\{Y_1 + x_1 + \Phi_0(p) - B_1/p\}, \tag{25}$$

which yields, differentiating first with respect to x_1,

$$\lambda = \beta p - c,$$

and then, differentiating w.r.t. p and substituting for λ,

$$\beta\{x_1 + \Phi_0(p)\} - c(1 - \beta)\frac{d\Phi_0}{dp} - \frac{(\beta p - c)B_1}{p^2} = 0$$

or

$$X_1^c = \frac{B_1}{p} - \frac{c}{\beta}\left\{\frac{B_1}{p^2} + (1 - \beta)\frac{d\Phi_0}{dp}\right\}, \tag{26}$$

where

$$X_n^c \equiv \sum_{j=0}^{n} \Phi_j(p).$$

Thus, $X_n^c(p)$ is the total amount that the leader can credibly be expected to sell in period n and later if the terminal price is p, and is what has been termed the *critical credible stock* at n.

Equation (22) allows $d\Phi_0/dp$ to be computed and gives

$$X_1^c(p) = \frac{B_1}{p} - \frac{c}{\beta p^2}\left\{\frac{1 + \beta^2}{\beta} + 2(1 - \beta)\frac{c}{p}\right\} \tag{27}$$

and

$$x_1 = \Phi_1(p) - X_1^c(p) - \Phi_0(p) = \frac{1}{\beta p} - \frac{c}{(\beta p)^2} - \frac{2(1 - \beta)c^2}{\beta p^2}. \tag{28}$$

A recursive formula for the critical credible stock at the start of period n, X_n^c, can be derived as a function of already-computed terms $X_{n-i}^c(p)$ as follows. The leader chooses x_n to maximize

$$W_n = x_n(\beta^n p - c) + \sum_{j=n-1}^{0} \Phi_j(p)\{\beta^n p - \beta^{n-j}c\}$$

subject to

$$\frac{B_n}{p} = x_n + \sum_{n-1}^{0} \Phi_j(p) + Y_n.$$

The counterpart to (25) is

$$\mathcal{L}_n = x_n(\beta^n p - c) + \sum_{j=n-1}^{0} \Phi_j(p)\{\beta^n p - \beta^{n-j}c\} + \lambda\left\{\frac{B_n}{p} - x_n - Y_n - \sum_{n-1}^{0} \Phi_j(p)\right\}, \tag{29}$$

whence $\lambda = \beta^n p - c$, and

$$\beta^n\left\{x_n + \sum_{n-1}^{0} \Phi_j(p)\right\} - \frac{(\beta^n p - c)B_n}{p^2} + \sum_{n-1}^{0} \frac{d\Phi_j}{dp}\{c - \beta^{n-j}c\} = 0.$$

Thus,

$$\beta^n X_n = \beta^n \frac{B_n}{p} - \frac{cB_n}{p^2} - c\sum_{n-1}^{0} (1 - \beta^{n-j})\frac{d\Phi_j}{dp}. \tag{30}$$

This holds for all n, and hence for $n - 1$:

$$\beta^{n-1} X_{n-1} = \beta^{n-1} \frac{B_{n-1}}{p} - \frac{cB_{n-1}}{p^2} - c\sum_{n-2}^{0} (1 - \beta^{n-1-j})\frac{d\Phi_j}{dp}. \tag{31}$$

Multiply (31) by β and subtract from (30) to get

$$\beta^n(X_n - X_{n-1}) = \frac{1}{p} - \frac{c(B_n - \beta B_{n-1})}{p^2} - c(1-\beta)\frac{d\Phi_{n-1}}{dp} - c(1-\beta)\sum_{n-2}^{0} \frac{d\Phi_j}{dp}$$

or

$$\beta^n x_n = \beta^n \Phi_n(p) = \frac{1}{p} - c\left\{\frac{B_n - \beta B_{n-1}}{p^2}\right\} - c(1-\beta)\frac{dX_{n-1}^c}{dp}. \tag{32}$$

Equation (32) now gives x_n as a function of p, and hence determines $\Phi_n(p)$. This recursive relation involves both stock functions and flow functions, but we can write it in terms of flows by noting that

$$\frac{d\Phi_{n-1}}{dp} = \frac{dX_{n-1}^c}{dp} - \frac{dX_{n-2}^c}{dp}.$$

Rewrite equation (32) replacing n by $n-1$, and subtract from (32) to obtain

$$\beta^n \Phi_n(p) = \beta^{n-1}\Phi_{n-1}(p) - c(1-\beta)\left\{\frac{1+\beta}{\beta^n p^2} + \frac{d\Phi_{n-1}}{dp}\right\}. \tag{33}$$

Two final constraints should be noted before this is solved. The first is that sales must be non-negative. The second is that the leader will not sell if the price falls below the extraction cost, since this will not only incur immediate losses but will also, by increasing total sales, reduce price and hence profit in all subsequent periods. The general solution is then

$$\Phi_n(p) = \text{Max}\left\{0, \frac{1}{p_n} - \frac{c}{p_n^2} - \frac{1}{p_n}\sum_{j=1}^{n} A(n,j)\left(\frac{c}{p_n}\right)^{j+1}\right\}, \tag{34}$$

and, since $p_n = \beta^n p > c$,

$$n \le \text{Int}\left\{\frac{\log(c/p)}{\log \beta}\right\}, \tag{35}$$

where the coefficients $A(n,j)$ can be generated by a simple recursion relationship:

$$A(n,j) = \beta^{j+1}\{A(n-1,j) + (1+j)(1-\beta)A(n-1,j-1)\}, \qquad j = 1,\ldots,n \tag{36}$$

$$A(n,0) \equiv 1, \quad A(n-1,n) \equiv 0.$$

The sales of the fringe are now determined:

$$y_n = \gamma_n(p) = \frac{1}{p_n} - \Phi_n(p). \tag{37}$$

A simple computer-programmable solution algorithm finds the solution as follows. Given Y_0, find p on the assumption that the leader sells X_0, then with this price compute the total sales of the leader on [0,T], $X_0^c(p)$. Next, find the value of p that will generate a total demand of $Y_0 + X_0^c(p)$ on $[0, T]$, and so on to the desired degree of accuracy.[8]

The Feedback Nash-Cournot Equilibrium

In the RESE or feedback Stackelberg equilibrium, the leader announces each period's supply before the fringe producers choose their response. In the feedback Nash-Cournot equilibrium, each agent chooses his current sales before he observes the current sales of other producers. If the leader has the option of announcing his sales first, it is obviously important to ask whether he would choose to do so. Of course, he may not be able to avoid pre-announcing, since this may be the only viable way in which a cartel can coordinate its supply plans. Either way, it is interesting to compare the two feedback equilibria to see if the timing of decisions is crucial.

The Nash Equilibrium

In the present problem it is more difficult to solve for the feedback Nash-Cournot equilibrium than for the feedback Stackelberg, except for the case in which the open-loop Nash-Cournot equilibrium coincides with the feedback equilibrium. The present paper therefore confines itself to this case, for which we need to compute the open-loop solution.

The Open-Loop Nash-Cournot Equilibrium

In the open-loop Nash-Cournot equilibrium (OLNCE), each producer chooses his best supply plan as a function of time (and the initial state) before the first period, on the assumption that the supply plans of the other producers are given and will not be altered during the course of the game. It is simple to characterize and compute, and for that reason it is a popular choice of equilibrium concept for modeling the oligopolized world oil market (Salant 1976; Ulph and Folie 1980a,b; Newbery 1980, 1981; Loury 1986). It is readily computed for the present model, in which the competitive fringe again imposes a perfectly arbitraged price path in equilibrium, with the price rising at the rate of interest. In discrete time, $t \in [0, T]$ with time running forward, the dominant producer's sales are

$$x_t = \text{Max}\left\{\frac{\alpha p_t - c}{p_t^2}, 0\right\}, \quad t = 0, 1, \ldots, T \tag{38}$$

where α is a shadow price:

$$0 < \alpha \leq 1, \quad (1 - \alpha)\left(X_0 - \sum_{t=0}^{T} x_t\right) = 0 \tag{39}$$

and prices are perfectly arbitraged by the fringe as in (2) and (8). Equation (39) gives the shadow price on the dominant producer's stock of oil. If he has more oil than he plans to sell, then $\alpha = 1$; otherwise α is found from the condition that total sales are constrained by the initial stock, X_0. The price level, p_0, will be found from the condition that total sales equal total demand, as in equation (5).

The Feedback Nash-Cournot Equilibrium

The feedback equilibrium is computed recursively in the same way as the feedback Stackelberg equilibrium. There are two possibilities: either the dominant producer has a sufficiently large initial stock that the open-loop Nash-Cournot equilibrium is unconstrained by available stocks (i.e., $\alpha = 1$ in equation (39)) or he has less than this initial value. If the dominant producer has excess oil, then the open-loop Nash-Cournot equilibrium coincides with the feedback Nash-Cournot equilibrium, for the following reason. The dominant producer will sell as much as it is profitable to sell, which will depend on the sales of the fringe. As in the feedback Stackelberg solution, his sales will thus only depend on total fringe sales, and the system is completely described by one state variable, Y_t, instead of by both X_t and Y_t. Equivalently, the system can be completely described by the terminal price, p_T or p. In particular, sales in later periods will not affect the dominant producer's sales in earlier periods, since he is not constrained by the availability of oil—a situation that also occurs in the unconstrained open-loop case. Hence, the two solutions coincide. To see this in detail, consider the two-period problem with no constraint on the dominant producer's stock of oil. Once again, number periods from the date of exhaustion, as before, and observe that the last-period solution is exactly as before the feedback Stackelberg solution of equations (13) and (14). In the penultimate period the dominant producer chooses x_1 to maximize

$$W_1 = (p_1 - c)x_1 + \beta(p_0 - c)\psi_0(Y_1 - y_1^*) \tag{40}$$

subject to $y_1 = y_1^*$, given, and from (15)

$$p_0 = \sqrt{c/Y_0}, \quad p_1 = \frac{1}{x_1 + y_1^*}.$$

Clearly, since y_1^* cannot be influenced by x_1, the last period is completely independent of x_1, and hence the problem fragments into a series of one-period optimization problems. The solution is

$$x_1 = \frac{p_1 - c}{p_1^2}, \quad y_1 = \frac{c}{p_1^2}.$$

The solution for n periods, assuming excess oil is available, is

$$x_n = \text{Max}\left\{\frac{p_n - c}{p_n^2}, 0\right\}, \quad y_n = \text{Min}\left\{\frac{c}{p_n^2}, \frac{1}{p_n}\right\}. \tag{41}$$

Hence, assuming $p_n > c$,

$$Y_n = \sum_{j=0}^{n} y_j = \frac{c}{\beta^{2n} p^2}\left(\frac{1 - \beta^{2(n+1)}}{1 - \beta^2}\right). \tag{42}$$

Therefore,

$$p_n = \sqrt{\frac{c(1 - \beta^{2(n+1)})}{(1 - \beta^2) Y_n}}, \tag{43}$$

$$y_n = \left(\frac{1 - \beta^2}{1 - \beta^{2(n+1)}}\right) Y_n, \quad x_n = \frac{1}{p_n} - y_n = x_n(Y_n), \tag{44}$$

$$X_n^d = \frac{1 - \beta^{n-1}}{1 - \beta} \sqrt{\frac{(1 - \beta^2) Y_n}{c(1 - \beta^{2(n+1)})}} - Y_n. \tag{45}$$

Provided $X_n \geq X_n^d$, the amount required for this solution, the open-loop and the feedback Nash-Cournot equilibrium coincide and can be described either in terms of price, as in (41), or in terms of the fringe stock, as in (44).

When oil has a positive shadow value in the open-loop Nash-Cournot equilibrium, this argument fails, and the feedback strategy will differ from the open-loop strategy. This is best seen in the two-period case, where equation (40) can be written

$$\underset{x_1}{\text{Max}}\ x_1(p_1 - c) + \beta(X_1 - x_1)(p_0 - c)$$

$$\text{s.t. } p_1 = \frac{1}{x_1 + y_1^*}, \quad p_0 = \frac{1}{X_1 - x_1 + Y_1 - y_1^*}$$

and, in equilibrium, $p_1 = \beta p_0$. Solving:

$$p_0 \equiv p = \frac{1 + \beta}{\beta(X_1 + Y_1)},$$

$$x_1 = \frac{X_1}{1+\beta} - \frac{c(1-\beta)\beta}{(1+\beta)^3}(X_1 + Y_1)^2, \quad x_0 = X_1 - x_1. \tag{46}$$

$$y_1 = \frac{Y_1}{1+\beta} - \frac{c(1-\beta)\beta(X_1 + Y_1)^2}{(1+\beta)^3}, \quad y_0 = Y_1 - y_1. \tag{47}$$

The solution is valid for

$$X_1 < X_1^d = (1+\beta)\sqrt{\frac{Y_1}{c(1+\beta^2)}} - Y_1.$$

Unfortunately, it is no longer possible to describe the state of the system by one variable, and hence there is no obvious method for calculating a general solution.

Comparisons Between Feedback Nash-Cournot and Feedback Stackelberg Equilibria

Since at the moment it is only possible to compute the feedback Nash-Cournot equilibrium (FBNCE) for the case of excess oil, we restrict our attention to such cases. First, suppose that the terminal price p were the same in the RESE as in the FBNCE. In that case, less oil would be sold at every date but the last in the RESE than in the FBNCE, since at date t in the RESE the dominant producer's sales can be written as a shortfall, ε_t, from the FBNCE sales:

$$x_t = \operatorname{Max}\left\{\frac{p_t - c}{p_t^2} - \varepsilon_t, 0\right\}, \quad \varepsilon_t \geq 0, \quad t = \tau, \tau + 1, \ldots, T \tag{48}$$

where $t = T - n$ and where ε_t and τ are implicitly defined by (34), (35), and (41). However, the price could be the same only if the same total stock were sold in both equilibria—which is impossible if oil is in excess supply in the FBNCE, as less is sold in the RESE. Hence, the price must be higher in the RESE, tending to make for higher profits. But the dominant producer sells less in the RESE, and the time profits of sales are less favorable, being less concentrated at later dates than in the FBNCE (ε_t, the deviation, is positive). Hence, it is not obvious which equilibrium yields higher profits. In the two-period case it might be argued that the RESE should yield higher profits than the (excess-supply) FBNCE, since the dominant producer has the power to influence y_1 in the RESE but not in the FBNCE. This is indeed the case in the two-period example, but the argument fails in the many-period case for the following reason: The last period has the same algebraic form in both equilibria, and hence in the two-period case being able to influence y_1 is advantageous, since nothing untoward happens in the only other period. In the n-period case, y_n can be manipulated, but at the expense of changing the functional form of later-period strategies.

The issue was explored by numerically solving for the RESE and the FBNCE (or the open-loop NCE) in a model with 31 time periods (i.e., $n = 0, 1, \ldots, 30$). In all experiments in which oil was in excess supply, the FBNCE yielded higher profits than the RESE. One such set of examples is shown in table 1. (Note that the FBNCE is equal to the OLNCE for $c \geq 0.6$, since then total sales are less than total stocks.)

Further numerical experiments suggested that if the dominant producer sells all his stock in the RESE his profit will be higher than in the open-loop NCE. Though it is possible to unambigously rank the open-loop and feedback Stackelberg equilibria, since the latter could be chosen as an open-loop strategy, the same argument fails to hold in a comparison between open-loop and feedback Nash-Cournot equilibria.

In the Stackelberg equilibrium, the open-loop strategy dominates the feedback strategy because the latter is also a feasible (but typically unattractive) open-loop strategy yielding the same fringe response and hence the same equilibrium. In the Nash-Cournot equilibrium, since in the open-loop strategy the fringe chooses without knowing the dominant producer's strategy, it is not possible for the dominant producer to elicit the same response from the fringe as in the feedback equilibrium. Hence, it is not possible to use a revealed-preference argument to rank equilibria, and it remains an open question whether in a many-period context the RESE might yield higher profits than the FNBCE for some configurations.

Nevertheless, these numerical experiments suggest that the dominant producer may prefer not to exercise leadership in the absence of binding contracts, and raise the question as to whether he can avoid this role and hence choose between playing Stackelberg strategies and Cournot-Nash strategies.

Comparisons with the Competitive Equilibrium

It remains to compare the RESE and the FBNCE with the competitive equilibrium. Standard arbitrage arguments (first expounded in Hotelling 1931) imply that competitive rent, defined as price less marginal extraction cost, must rise at the rate of interest. In the present model the costless oil of

Table 1
The dominant producer's profits and sales in the various equilibria. $\beta = 1/1.05$, $T = 30$, $Y_0 = 30$, $X_0 = 10$, $p_T = 1.81$ ($p_0 = 0.42$) for $c \leq 0.3$.

	Presented discounted profits W in					
c^a	CE[b]		NCE[c]		RESE[d]	BCE[e]
0.1	3.654		3.471		3.711	3.719
0.2	3.271		3.010		3.363	3.401
0.3	2.890		2.648		2.973	3.082
0.4	2.510		2.317	<	2.322	2.764
0.5	2.132		1.998	>	1.691	2.404
0.6	1.762		1.571		1.250	2.126
0.7	1.465		1.215		0.931	1.801
0.8	1.118		0.939		0.696	1.485
0.9	0.759	>	0.723		0.521	1.213
1.0	0.401	<	0.555		0.389	0.990
1.1	0.046		0.422		0.289	0.803
1.2	0.00		0.317		0.213	0.647

	Total sales			
c	CE	NCE	RESE	BCE
0.1	10	10	10	10
0.2	10	10	10	10
0.3	10	10	10	10
0.4	10	10	8.29	10
0.5	10	10	5.89	10
0.6	10	7.98	4.37	10
0.7	10	6.19	3.30	10
0.8	10	4.87	2.54	8.74
0.9	10	3.86	1.98	7.38
1.0	10	3.07	1.55	6.26
1.1	10	2.45	1.21	5.32
1.2	8.97	1.95	0.96	4.51

a. Extraction cost.
b. Competitive equilibrium
c. Open loop Nash-Cournot equilibrium
d. Rational expectations Stackelberg equilibrium
e. Binding contract Stackelberg equilibrium.

Feedback NCE coincides with open-loop NCE for $c \geq 0.6$.
Underlines signal points where the graphs cross.

the fringe will be extracted first, over $[0,\tau]$, with the costly oil sold later. The price path will be kinked at τ, with the price rising less rapidly than the rate of interest thereafter. The dominant producer will clearly be worse off than in the binding-contract equilibrium, where he sells later (as in the competitive equilibrium) but at a higher price. However, in comparison with the other equilibria he has a more favorable time profile of sales (delaying extraction costs as long as possible) but a less favorable price. Again, these two factors work in different direction on his profits, and table 1 demonstrates the paradoxical result that the dominant producer may be better off in a competitive equilibrium than in either a feedback Nash-Cournot equilibrium or a rational-expectations Stackelberg equilibrium if his extraction costs are high enough. In other words, for the dominant producer to be able to unambiguously benefit from his market power, he has to be able both to precommit his strategy and to announce it. If he precommits but does not announce it, then the other players must assume that they are playing an open-loop Nash game; if he announces a strategy but is not committed to it, then the other players must assume that it may be changed, and will compute and supply the feedback equilibrium. In both cases the dominant producer can be disadvantaged by his market power, just as in Maskin and Newbery 1978 (which dealt with the dominant oil importer). The result is sufficiently striking as to be summarized in a proposition.

PROPOSITION In the absence of binding contracts, a dominant oil exporter may be disadvantaged by his market power to the extent that he earns lower profits than in the competitive equilibrium.

Needless to say, it would not be credible for the dominant producer to promise to behave competitively in the future, though it would certainly provide a disincentive for a group of currently competitive high-cost producers to form a cartel in order to exploit their market power.

What would happen if the dominant producer had zero extraction costs (i.e., were identical to the fringe producers)? Two cases must be distinguished. If in the binding-contract equilibrium the leader wishes to sell all his oil, then there is no difference between the equilibrium and the RESE, since the leader would sell first, and the fringe would retain their oil and hence retain the power to arbitrage the price paths. If, however the leader does not wish to sell all his oil in the BCE, then the two equilibria may

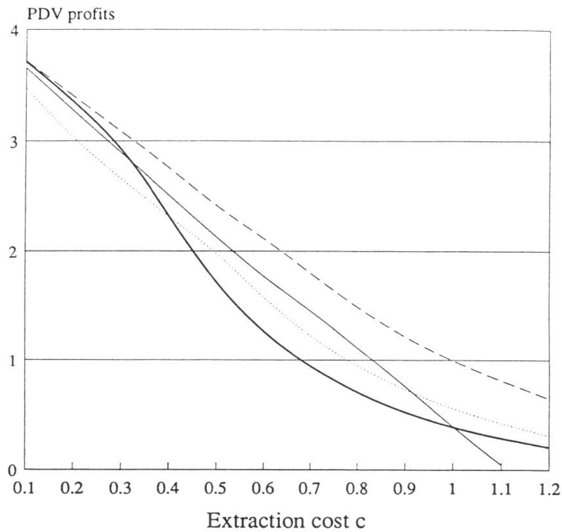

Figure 1
The dominant producer's profits. (——) competitive equilibrium; (······) open-loop Nash-Cournot equilibrium; (**——**) rational-expectations Stackelberg equilibrium; (----) binding-contract Stackelberg equilibrium.

differ, unless the leader can visibly destroy the unwanted excess in the first period; otherwise, in the RESE it would not be a credible strategy to sell the desired quantity immediately, since the fringe would expect the surplus to be sold later.

Table 1 and figure 1 demonstrate that the ordering of the various equilibria can switch and reswitch as the dominant producer's extraction costs vary (and with these costs, his total sales.) The only systematic ordering theoretically guaranteed is BCE > {CE,NCE,RESE}, though, as we observed, it seems to be true that FBNCE > RESE if $\sum x_t$(FBNCE) < X_0.

Conclusions

Where the dominant oil producer has an incentive to delay extraction, as in the model analyzed, the calculation of the market equilibrium in the absence of enforceable long-term contracts is a delicate matter. This paper provides the first explicit characterization of the dominant producer's equilibrium for a special example in which this incentive to delay takes an extreme form.

If the dominant producer can choose to announce his next-period supply before his competitors choose their supply, then the correct equilibrium concept for the resulting dynamic game is the feedback (or rational-expectations) Stackelberg equilibrium. If his supply decision is made at the same time as those of his competitors, then the correct equilibrium concept is the feedback Nash-Cournot equilibrium. Although the FBSE may yield higher profits to the dominant producer than the FBNCE in some cases, for the examples computed in the paper the reverse is true, and the dominant producer thus has an incentive to avoid announcing his intended supply. However, he may not have this option, particularly if "he" is a cartel that achieves cohesion only by publicly announcing its (short-run) supply plan.

The main result of the paper was the demonstration that the dominant oil producer might be disadvantaged by his market power and be forced to sell on less favorable terms than if he were to behave competitively. Both the feedback Nash-Cournot equilibrium and the RESE are inferior to the competitive equilibrium for high values of extraction cost. Moreover, despite the fact that the leader appears to have more power over the fringe in the RESE, where the feedback Nash-Cournot equilibrium coincides with the open-loop NCE, the FBNCE yields higher profits to the leader than the RESE.

Acknowledgments

This paper was first written in July 1980, and was revised in response to comments from Oliver Hart in March 1983. It was not published, probably because it irritated game theorists, and was not understood by economists interested in the oil market. It is very much in the spirit of the Risk project, as it addresses the question of market incompleteness arising from the inability to enforce certain kinds of contracts. It benefited from extensive collaborative work with Eric Maskin, some of which is reported in Maskin and Newbery 1990. I am also indebted to Alastair and David Ulph, Mark Machina, and Edward Prescott for helpful comments and discussions, and to Gordon Hughes for computing advice. The support of the British ESRC project Risk, Information and Quantity Signals in Economics is acknowledged with thanks.

Notes

1. There are a number of papers characterizing the intertemporal equilibrium of an exhaustible resource where there is market power on the sellers' side. See, for example, Gilbert and Goldman 1978, Gilbert 1978, Hoel 1978, Lewis et al. 1979, Loury 1986, Pindyck 1978, Salant 1976, Stiglitz 1976, and Sweeney 1977. None of these deals with the potential problem of dynamic inconsistency.

2. Definitions and discussions of the various feedback and open-loop equilibria are given in Simaan and Cruz 1973, Cruz 1975, and Kydland 1977. Since this paper was first written, it has become clear that in repeated games there typically exist a multiplicity of perfect (and therefore dynamically consistent) equilibria if agents can condition on the history of play (Fudenberg and Maskin 1986). This is known as the Folk Theorem. In the simplest example, agents agree to cooperate provided that no agent has cheated in the past; if any agent cheats, all agents expect to play noncooperatively in all future periods. This is a credible threat, since the noncooperative equilibrium is individually rational; if agents have a small enough discount rate so that their future payoffs are important to them, this threat sustains cooperation as a noncooperative strategy. Although the Folk Theorem refers to repeated games, it is widely recognized that similar results hold for dynamic games (Haurie and Pohjola 1987; Ausubel and Deneckere 1989; Gul, Sonnenschein, and Wilson 1986). (The distinction between repeated games or supergames and dynamic games is that a repeated game is an infinitely repeated one-shot game. Agents' current actions may affect future behavior, as occurs when the strategies are history-dependent, but current actions do not directly affect the structure of the game. In a dynamic game, on the other hand, current actions such as the extraction of a resource do directly affect the future game.) The equilibrium that arises depends on what agents expect would happen if some agent were to deviate from equilibrium. The requirement of perfection imposes very little restriction on these beliefs, so a great variety of equilibria can be supported. Since it is beliefs about out-of-equilibrium behavior, rather than strategic interactions, that form the basis for the multiplicity of equilibria, results similar to the Folk Theorem can be obtained even if there is a single strategic agent who confronts a continuum of nonstrategic but forward-looking agents. (See Ausubel and Deneckere 1989; Stokey 1981.)

To avoid the multiplicity of equilibria, the paper considers the refinement to Markov perfect equilibria, in which agents condition their strategies only on the current state—that is, on variables that directly affect their current and future payoffs. For further discussion, see Karp and Newbery (forthcoming).

3. There is a third case in which the problem of dynamic consistency arises. The cartel may wish to sell part of its stock at the competitive price *before* the fringe sells, in order to advance the date at which it enjoys monopoly rents. The amount the cartel plans to sell early will be an increasing function of fringe stocks. Having sold this initial amount, the cartel would typically wish to change its plan and further undercut the fringe. This case, which raises rather different problems, is discussed further in Newbery 1981 and in Groot et al. 1989.

4. There is, for example, a multi-agent version of the maximum principle that has some similarities to the method proposed below of adjoining the extra requirement that the solution be dynamically consistent.

5. There leader's profits can be written

$$W = \sum_{t=0}^{T} \beta^t x_t (p_t - c)$$

$$= \sum_{\tau+1}^{T} \beta^t \left(\frac{p_t - c}{p_t}\right) + \beta^\tau (p_\tau - c)\left(X - \sum_{\tau+1}^{T} \frac{1}{p_t}\right)$$

since the leader sells from τ on and is the sole seller from period $\tau + 1$ onward, selling $x_t = 1/p_t$

from (1). This can be written

$$W = \sum_{\tau+1}^{T} \left(\beta^t - \frac{c}{p_0} \beta^{2t} \right) + \left(1 - \frac{c}{p_0} \beta^{\tau} \right) \left(p_0 X - \sum_{\tau+1}^{T} \beta^t \right).$$

Since $p_0 = p_0(X + Y_0)$ from (5), and $\tau = \tau(Y_0)$, W is a simple function of X and Y_0.

6. Note that $Y_0 > 0$, since the fringe will always retain oil to sell in the last period (as the alternative is an unbounded terminal price).

7. The condition that $x_0 = 0$ if $p_0 < c$ is in fact implicit in the first part of equation (14).

8. This iterative process converges very quickly. The stability of the numerical calculations can be checked by halving the discount rate and doubling stocks and numbers of time periods, which provides a closer approximation to a continuous-time treatment. The results are robust.

References

Ausubel, L. M., and R. J. Deneckere. 1989. "Reputation in bargaining and durable goods monopoly." *Econometrica* 57 (3): 511–532.

Bellman, R. 1957. *Dynamic Programming.* Princeton University Press.

Buiter, W. H. 1980. "The macroeconomics of Dr. Pangloss: A critical survey of the New Classical Macroeconomics." *Economic Journal* 90 (1): 34–50.

Calvo, G. A. 1978. "On the time consistency of optimal policy in a monetary economy." *Econometrica* 46 (6): 1411–1428.

Chow, G. C. 1980. "Econometric policy evaluation and optimization under rational expectations." *Journal of Economic Dynamics and Control* 2: 47–59.

Cremer, J., and M. Weitzman. 1976. "OPEC and the monopoly price of world oil." *European Economic Review* 8: 155–164.

Cruz, F. B. 1975. "Survey of Nash and Stackelberg equilibrium strategies in dynamic games." *Annals of Economics and Social Measurement* 4 (2): 339–344.

Fudenberg, D., and E. Maskin. 1986. "The Folk Theorem in repeated games with discounting or incomplete information." *Econometrica* 54: 533–554.

Gilbert, R. J. 1978. "Dominant firm pricing policy in a market for an exhaustible resource." *Bell Journal of Economics* 9: 385–395.

Gilbert, R. J., and S. N. Goldman. 1978. "Potential competition and the monopoly price of an exhaustible resource." *Journal of Economic Theory* 17: 319–331.

Gul, F., H. Sonnenschein, and R. Wilson. 1986. "Foundations of dynamic monopoly and the Coase conjecture." *Journal of Economic Theory* 39: 155–190.

Groot, F., C. Withagen, and A. de Zeeuw. 1989. Theory of Natural Exhaustible Resources: The Cartel-versus-Fringe Model Revisited. Mimeo, Tilburg University.

Haurie, A., and M. Pohjola 1987. "Efficient equilibria in a differential game of capitalism." *Journal of Economic Dynamics and Control* 11: 65–78.

Hoel, M. 1978. "Resource extraction, substitute production, and monopoly." *Journal of Economic Theory* 19: 28–37.

Hotelling, H. 1931. "The economics of exhaustible resources." *Journal of Political Economy* (3): 137–175.

Karp, L., and D. M. Newbery. Forthcoming. "Intertemporal consistency issues in depletable resources." In *Handbook of Natural Resource and Energy Economics*, ed. J. Sweeney and A. Kneese. North-Holland.

Kydland, F. 1977. "Equilibrium solutions in dynamic dominant-player models." *Journal of Economic Theory* 15: 307–324.

Kydland, F., and E. Prescott. 1977. "Rules rather than discretion: The inconsistency of optimal plans." *Journal of Political Economy* 85: 473–491.

Lewis, T. R., S. A. Mathews, and H. S. Burness. 1979. "Monopoly and the rate of extraction of exhaustible resources: Note." *American Economic Review* 69: 227–230.

Loury, G. C. 1986. "A theory of 'oil'igopoly: Cournot equilibrium in exhaustible resource markets with fixed supplies." *International Economic Review* 27: 285–301.

Maskin, E. and D. M. Newbery. 1978. Rational Expectations with Market Power: The Paradox of the Disadvantageous Monopolist. Warwick Economic Discussion Paper and Massachusetts Institute of Economics Discussion Paper. A revised version was published as Maskin and Newbery 1990.

Maskin, E., and D. M. Newbery. 1990. "Disadvantageous oil tariffs and dynamic consistency." *American Economic Review* 80 (1): 143–156.

Newbery, D. M. 1980. Credible Oil Supply Contracts. Economic Theory Discussion Paper 34, Department of Applied Economics, Cambridge University.

Newbery, D. M. 1981. "Oil prices, cartels, and the problem of dynamic inconsistency." *Economic Journal* 91: 617–646.

Pindyck, R. S. 1978. "Gains to producers from the cartelization of exhaustible resources." *Review of Economics and Statistics* 60: 238–251.

Salant, S. W. 1976. "Exhaustible resources and industrial structure: A Nash-Cournot approach to the world oil market." *Journal of Political Economy* 84: 1079–1094.

Selten, R. 1975. "Reexamination of the perfectness concept for equilibrium points in extensive games." *International Journal of Game Theory* 4: 25–55.

Simaan, M., and J. B. Cruz. 1973. "Additional aspects of the Stackelberg strategy in non-zero-sum games." *Journal of Optimization Theory and Applications* 11: 613–626.

Stiglitz, J. E. 1976. "Monopoly and the rate of exhaustible resources." *American Economic Review* 66: 655–661.

Stokey, N. 1981. "Rational expectations and durable goods pricing." *Bell Journal of Economics* 12: 112–128.

Sweeney, J. L. 1977. "Economics of depletable resources: Market forces and intertemporal bias." *Review of Economic Studies* 44: 125–142.

Ulph, A. M., and G. M. Folie. 1980a. "Economic implications of Stackelberg and Nash-Cournot equilibria." *Zeitschrift für Nationalökonomie* 40: 343–354.

Ulph, A. M. 1982. "Modelling partially cartelized markets for exhaustible resources." In *Economic Theory of Natural Resources*, ed. W. Eichhorn et al. Physica.

Ulph, A. M., and G. M. Folie. 1980b. "Exhaustible resources and cartels: An intertemporal Nash-Cournot model." *Canadian Journal of Economics* 13: 645–658.

Ulph, A. M., and G. M. Folie. 1981. "Dominant firm models of resource depletion." In *Microeconomic Analysis*, ed. D. Curry, D. Peel, and W. Peters. Croom Helm.

von Stackelberg, H. 1952. *The Theory of the Market Economy*. Oxford University Press.

The Existence of Perfectly Competitive Equilibrium à la Wicksteed

Louis Makowski and Joseph M. Ostroy

The no-surplus approach to perfectly competitive equilibrium (Ostroy 1980; Makowski 1980) is a descendant of ideas that originated in the marginal productivity theory of distribution. In this essay, we want to emphasize a kind of "loop"—not only does our work descend from marginal productivity theory, but it also can be turned around to point to the principle of marginal productivity as the centerpiece of the theory of value. A few of the early contributors to the theory had an appreciation of its centrality, but their ideas on this score were not sufficiently developed to be understood. Reviewing the contributions of Clark and (especially) Wicksteed, we identify some of their more extraordinary assertions which have been ignored or dismissed by other commentators as the result of their reading these early marginalists without the aid of an appropriate theoretical map. This will provide the historical backdrop to the main theorem of this paper, a theorem on the existence of perfectly competitive equilibrium. Such an equilibrium will be defined as an allocation yielding each individual the marginal product of his or her contribution.

We begin by reviewing the more modest position assigned to marginal productivity theory within the traditional theory of value. In preparation for what follows, we focus on claims for marginal productivity theory by Wicksteed and Clark that go beyond its usual interpretation, and we review the critiques aimed at their extraordinary claims. After collecting the arguments on which the traditional synthesis of value theory rests, we informally outline another approach to marginal productivity. Although this alternative approach is heuristically similar to the traditional one, it is quite different in the role that it assigns to marginal productivity. Instead of regarding marginal productivity theory as one piece of the competitive theory of value, in this approach it will emerge as "the whole thing." Our aim is to show that when marginal productivity theory is viewed from this different perspective, the bolder claims of Wicksteed and Clark are not overreaching. In section 2, we put this assertion to the test by showing formally how our reformulation of the marginal productivity principle can be used to give a proof of the existence of perfectly competitive equilibrium in the spirit of Wicksteed. Our main theorem is closely related to the equivalence between the Shapley value and Walrasian equilibrium (Shapley 1953; Aumann and Shapley 1974; Aumann 1975; Champsaur 1975). In section 3 we summarize the links between our result and the value-equivalence theorem. We shall also briefly discuss the connections between the value and Clark's interpretation of marginal productivity, as well as a historical irony concerning Edgeworth's views on marginal productivity theory.

Throughout our discussion of the history and the formulation of our theorem, we shall call attention to the distinction between the view that the *commodity* is the fundamental margin and the view that the *individual* is the fundamental margin of marginal analysis. It is the change in this margin, from the commodity to the individual, that underlies the historical loop in our formulation of marginal productivity theory.

1 Some History of Marginal Productivity Theory

1.1 Marginal Productivity Theory As One Part of the Theory of Value

The marginalist revolution in the theory of value in the 1870s is mainly associated with a break with the classical theory in which utility, and in particular marginal utility,[1] was given coequal status with cost of production as a determinant of price. Wicksteed and Clark are known for their contributions to the second generation of this revolution, in the 1890s, in which marginalist principles were applied to the demand for factors of production via the marginal productivity theory of distribution.[2] Both of these contributors were criticized for overreaching in their claims for marginal-productivity theory. In comparison with Wicksteed's oblique and technical claims (see below), Clark's were regarded as something of an obvious embarrassment.

In the opening paragraph of the preface of *The Distribution of Wealth* (1899), Clark summarized his objective:

> It is the purpose of this work to show that the distribution of the income to society is controlled by a natural law, and that this law, if it worked without friction, would give to every *agent* of production the amount of wealth which that agent creates. However wages may be adjusted by bargains freely made between individual men, the results of pay that result from such transactions tend, it is here claimed to equal that part of the product of industry which is traceable to the labor itself; and however interest may be adjusted by similarly free bargaining, it naturally tends to equal the fractional product that is separately traceable to capital. At the point in the economic system where titles to property originate,—where labor and capital come into possession of the amounts that the state afterwards treats as their own, —the social procedure is true to the principle on which the right of property rests.

So far as it is not obstructed, it assigns to every one what *he* has specifically produced. [italics added]

Phrases such as "natural law" and "true to the principle on which the right of property rests" invited the charge that marginalist theory was an apology for capitalism.[3] Neoclassical economists after Clark either ignored these remarks or distanced themselves from such interpretations. Although this is not our principle focus, we shall remark (in section 3.1) that recent developments concerning perfectly competitive equilibrium and the Shapley value indicate that what has been referred to as Clark's "naive productivity ethics" may not be so naive after all.

The bold claims made by Clark for the marginal productivity principle as the unique unifying principle underlying the theory of distribution were significantly diluted in the mature neoclassical synthesis of value theory. Marginal productivity theory was, after all, merely an interpretation of the first-order conditions for profit maximization by the individual firm. As such, we might say it was a principle underlying only one fourth of the theory of value, namely (1) the demand for factors of production. The other three fourths were (2) the determinants of the supply of factors of production and (3) the determinants of the demands and (4) supplies of outputs. As a less than majority contributor to the theory of value, it was in no position to dictate what the income of society would be and how it would be distributed.[4]

Before moving on to the more interesting case of Wicksteed, we call attention to a change in the margin of analysis that occurs between the first and the last sentence in Clark's opening paragraph. In the first sentence, the "agent of production" is evidently a disembodied factor of production. However, it is clear from the last sentence that Clark intends his marginal analysis in terms of commodities as a means to an end, i.e., to extend his conclusions for the marginal productivity theory of factors of production to a marginal productivity theory for persons.

In *An Essay on the Coordination of the Laws of Distribution* (1894), Wicksteed recognized the importance of a logical consistency condition as an essential element of marginal productivity theory. What set the marginalist explanation of the pricing of inputs apart from the classical theory was that the rewards to all of the cooperating factors of production would be determined by one principle: marginal productivity. However, the validity of the principle depended upon the conclusion that when the rewards to all the factors were added up they would have to equal the total output. If they added up to more than the total, there would be a contradiction; if they added up to less than the total, it would be subject to the criticisms of the classical theory where, for example, profits were the residual. To arrive at the required consistency condition, Wicksteed appears to have rediscovered Euler's theorem on homogeneous functions, because he points out that adding up would require that the production function be linearly homogeneous.[5]

Unlike Clark, whose analysis was in the verbal tradition, Wicksteed adopted a mathematical model that is still quite familiar: it is that of a function producing one output from many inputs. The key demonstration is that if the function is homogeneous of degree 1, then payments to the factors of production according to the marginal productivity principle will just exhaust the total product.

Although the style of the *Essay* is quite distinct from that of Clark, there is one key element that the two works have in common: the production function is frequently regarded not at the level of the firm but as an aggregate function applying to the economy as a whole. From the perspective of microeconomic theory, this would seem to imply an inability to recognize or an unwillingness to face the difficult problems of aggregation. The issue of which level to use in interpreting the production function—the microeconomic level of the single firm or the macroeconomic level of the economy as a whole—is, along with the distinction between the commodity margin and the individual margin, at the heart of our "rehabilitation" of Wicksteed and of the loop we shall emphasize in turning marginal productivity theory into the centerpiece of the theory of value.

It might appear that there really is no choice in the interpretation. A single aggregate function may be posited in the manner of a representative firm, but since production does take place at the level of the individual firm this is just a convenient simplification. Just as the production function is a microeconomic concept applying to the firm, so marginal productivity theory derives from the first-order conditions for profit maximization by the firm; the two ideas fit together like hand and glove. This is certainly the standard interpretation and the one that underlies the criticisms that Wicksteed received (especially from Walras and Wicksell).

The critics pointed out that the requirement of constant returns to scale in the production functions of individual firms was an unnecessarily restrictive assumption for the validity of marginal productivity theory; i.e., adding up could be obtained under much weaker conditions. The critics argued that by emphasizing the importance of constant returns Wicksteed was ignoring the role of perfect competition. Even if firm production functions did not display constant returns but merely had U-shaped average costs, competition would drive the equilibrium allocation to the point where all producing firms would be operating at an efficient scale, at the bottoms of their average costs, and therefore the zero-profits condition of competitive equilibrium would imply that the total payments to the factors of production would add up to the total value of the output.

So, the judgment is that, though Wicksteed was an important pioneer, as pioneers often do, he did not get the story entirely right. In particular, what he failed to appreciate in his partial equilibrium analysis was the importance of the general equilibrium implications of perfect competition. That he should have fallen into such an error was to be expected, since he attempted to get at the laws determining distribution solely through the application of the marginal-productivity principle (that one-fourth of the theory of value), without (for example) invoking the importance of marginal utility. His remarkable originality with respect to the one-fourth that he helped to develop was no match for the emerging full synthesis of value theory found in Walrasian general equilibrium.

1.2 Marginal Productivity as a Complete Theory of Value

Our work on the no-surplus theory of perfect competition suggests a more sympathetic reading of Wicksteed's *Essay*. This reading puts us in a position with respect to Wicksteed's critics that is similar to how Wicksteed might have appeared to them: we would say that his critics did not have a sufficiently comprehensive command of their theory to appreciate the significance of perfect competition!

Wicksteed's claims make more sense, and the critical observations leveled against him lose their force, if the *Essay* is interpreted as making a much bolder claim than the one for which he is generally credited. What this bolder claim is, and what evidence exists that Wicksteed was attempting to make it, is the subject of this subsection.

We begin with a basic change in the interpretation of the production function from the usual concrete relation between quantities of inputs and their resulting outputs to something that is, by comparison, a "metaphorical" function. Consider a function whose output is total gains from trade, or social utility, to the economy as a whole. Thus, it is an aggregate function rather than one applying to a single microeconomic unit. More important, its output is measured in some abstract utility—or, to use Wicksteed's language, in units of "satisfaction"—rather than in units of physical output. Not only does the output of this function differ from the usual production function, but its inputs are also not the same. The inputs to this "production function for social utility" are *individuals*, the productivity of an individual being based on the tastes and endowments or production possibilities (if a firm) that characterize the individual.

To make our metaphorical function resemble the usual production function, in our formal analysis we impose two further requirements: (i) There are only a finite number of different types of individuals (similar to a finite number of different types of factors of production). (ii) Each individual is of infinitesimal scale relative to the economy as a whole (so that single individuals can be regarded as infinitesimal inputs). The quantity, or mass, of individuals of type i is denoted by r_i, and the gains from trade associated with the population $r = (r_1, \ldots, r_n)$ are denoted by $g(r)$. Although we have changed the interpretation of the function, we may still apply the concept of marginal productivity. An (infinitesimal) individual of type i is paid his or her marginal product if the quantity of "social utility" the individual receives is equal to $\partial g(r)/\partial r_i$ (assuming that this partial derivative exists). Ignoring, for the moment, what this social utility is and how the payment can be made, if this reward scheme is to be a complete and logically consistent theory of distribution, it will require that when the total output of social utility is distributed to the population according to the marginal productivity principle the total rewards must add up, i.e.,

$$\sum \frac{\partial g(r)}{\partial r_i} r_i = g(r).$$

A distribution of the total output of social utility that satisfies the marginal product reward principle and also satisfies the above adding-up requirement will be called a *marginal productivity distribution.* Evidently, therefore, to guarantee that this condition will be satisfied for every r, the gains function g will have to be homogeneous of degree 1. Fortunately, for this function such a restriction is quite reasonable. If the population were to double, then the gains from trade would also double. For example, if there were no common property resources, then all of the population would own all of the land; so doubling the population would mean that the number of acres of land would also have to double. Indeed, for the gains function to be other than homogeneous of the first degree would require certain phenomena not typically admitted into the theory of value.[6]

The first-degree homogeneity of g is perfectly consistent with the discussion of U-shaped costs cited above. Doubling the size of the economy simple doubles the number of producing firms, each operating at the bottom of its U. Indeed, one can claim even more. If the aggregate value of g were to more than double when the population doubled, this would imply that economies of scale at the level of the individual firm were so large that they would be incompatible with perfect competition. The point of this observation is that, although it is certainly true that with respect to variations in the level of *commodity* inputs there is no need to assume first-degree homogeneity of the production function for the single firm, the homogeneity of the aggregate function g, whose inputs include the firms themselves, is essential to maintain perfect competition.

Granting this change to the metaphorical aggregate gains function whose inputs are households and firms, what does this have to do with the theory of value? We know that social utility is not a measurable quantity, let alone a fungible commodity which can be transferred from one person to another. So, how do these metaphorical marginal products relate to the central issues of value theory—the pricing of inputs and outputs? A formal response to this question is the subject of section 2, but we give a brief and informal description here.

In the Walrasian (also the Marshallian) approach to value theory, there is no direct emphasis on the distribution of individual welfare. Rather, the direct focus is on the equilibrium conditions for the pricing of commodities. Once these (market-clearing) prices are known, the implications for the distribution of the gains from trade follow from, for example, the household's indirect utility function, which relates prices to the maximized value of utility. But this is not the only way to address the theory of value. It may be approached from the "opposite direction," where the direct emphasis is on the distribution of welfare. In this opposite direction, the equilibrium condition for the competitive theory of value is that each *individual* receives the marginal product he or she adds to the social gains from trade, more or less as Clark claimed. Just as the distribution of welfare follows from the commodity market equilibrium approach to the theory of value, so—when approached from the opposite direction—the theory of competitive market pricing follows from the existence of a marginal productivity distribution. In this way, the principle of marginal productivity becomes the centerpiece of the theory of value.

What does this modern revision of marginal productivity theory have to do with Wicksteed? At the beginning of his *Essay*, Wicksteed makes a distinction between two interpretations of his production function $F(A,B,C,\ldots)$:

When we have safeguarded this statement by all the explanations necessary to enable us to speak of communal desires and satisfaction, we may say that the total satisfaction (**S**) of a community is a function (F) of the commodities, services, etc. ($A,B,C,\ldots$) which it commands; or $\mathbf{S} = F(A,B,C,\ldots)$. And the exchange value of each commodity or service, if purchasable, is determined by the effect on the total satisfaction of the community which the addition or the withdrawal of a small increment would have, *all the other variables remaining constant.* [p. 8; italics in original]

A more "concrete" interpretation of the function is this:

Let the special product to be distributed (P) be regarded as a function (F) of the various factors of production ($A,B,C,\ldots$). Then the (marginal) significance of each factor is determined *by the effect upon the product of a small increment of that factor*, all the others remaining constant. [p. 8; italics in original]

The first interpretation of F as yielding the output **S** is regarded as applying to the theory of exchange,[7] the second interpretation of F as yielding the output P applies to the usual theory of distribution. Wicksteed acknowledges the measurability problems associated with satisfaction, whereas "in the case of the distribution of the product, we have something external to the claimants, *something not themselves*, which is actually sliced up and divided amongst them" [italics added]. It is Wicksteed's first interpretation of his production function F that we identify as a version of our gains function g.

Further on, the question arises as to the reasonableness of the constant returns hypothesis for F. Wicksteed makes a distinction here based on the two interpretations of the function:

The question we are examining, then, is this: If every one of the abilities, efforts, materials and advantages which contribute to production were severally increased in identical ratio, would the product also be increased in that ratio?

The crucial limitation is not simply the change in output, but what Wicksteed calls the "industrial position or vantage," by which he means revenue:

...it is still unsafe to say that if all the factors were equally multiplied the product would be increased proportionally, because we have defined the product, not as a material product but as an industrial position or vantage; and, in order that this may be doubled or trebled, it is necessary not only that all of the factors of production should be doubled or trebled, but also the *area of operations* should be capable of corresponding enlargement on the same terms that have ruled hitherto; or in other words that there should be a fresh supply of people who want, or can be made to want, the commodity or service in question, on the same terms as those who now enjoy it. And to assume this is obviously unwarrantable. [p. 34; italics in original]

The above quote refers to the P interpretation of Wicksteed's production function F. By contrast, Wicksteed observes that constant returns are built into the **S** interpretation of F:

And at this point comes dimly into view a problem of the utmost interest and importance, which will be touched upon, on one side, under section 7, paragraph (f) of this essay, and which suggests itself under another aspect here, but is far too vast to be dealt with incidentally. For the truth is that the real or "social product" is the total satisfaction accruing from the processes of industry to the whole community, including both the customer and the manufacturer; and in this sense the body of customers and their desire for the product, themselves constitute the factors of production. If *these* factors, like the others, receive a proportional increment then obviously the conditions are exactly repeated, and the product too will receive a proportional increment. [p. 34; italics in original]

As our final quotation from Wicksteed, we reproduce section 7, paragraph (f), referred to above:

Lastly, I would just touch upon the fascinating subject of the analogies between the curves of Production and the curves of Satisfaction. In the ordinary individual or person curve of consumption, the satisfaction is regarded as accruing to the individual, and the price paid is regarded as subtracted from that amount. The early amounts are regarded as yielding a surplus over their price because they yield a higher satisfaction than is represented by the marginal significance that regulates their price. Our investigations suggest another way of looking at the matter. Satisfaction may be regarded as a function of certain factors, one of them being a psyche or sensitive subject. If this be followed out it will be found that the "surplus" or "consumer's rent" is neither more nor less than the differential coefficient or marginal significance of *psyche* as a factor in the production of satisfaction! Here we once again see that when the marginal distribution has been completed there is no surplus. Our ideal is for the whole satisfaction, without deduction, to fall in distribution to psyche, so that increments of psyche would be identical with increments of a satisfaction ideally maximized in its amount per unit psyche. [pp. 48–49; italics in original]

In virtually all respects, we find this to be an accurate summary of the conditions underlying the main theorem of this paper. Translating Wicksteed's notation, we have $\partial g(r)/\partial r_i \sim \partial F/\partial K$. The function g is derived from the basic data of the economy, which include tastes and resources. With v_i the utility function of an individual of type i, there is some allocation $z = (z_i)$, where z_i is the *net trade* to individual i, that achieves the total satisfaction $g(r)$, i.e.,

$$g(r) = \sum v_i(z_i)r_i.$$

With certain qualifications, it can be shown that $\partial g(r)/\partial r_i$ exists. Therefore, since g is homogeneous,

$$g(r) = \sum \frac{\partial g(r)}{\partial r_i} r_i.$$

So,

$$\sum \left[\frac{\partial g(r)}{\partial r_i} - v_i(z_i) \right] r_i = 0. \tag{1}$$

The marginal-productivity condition for equilibrium is the existence of a z such that, for each i,

$$\frac{\partial g(r)}{\partial r_i} = v_i(z_i). \tag{2}$$

When the allocation is such that each individual is receiving his or her marginal product, then each "psyche" is extracting as a reward all the surplus contributed and we can agree with Wicksteed that "when the marginal distribution has been completed there is no surplus."

The implications for commodity pricing follow from the result that, for any z satisfying (1), there is a price vector p such that for each individual i

$$\frac{\partial g(r)}{\partial r_i} = v_i(z_i) - pz_i.$$

Therefore, the marginal productivity condition for equilibrium (2) requires that $pz_i = 0$, and this will be shown to imply that the pair $[p,z]$ is a Walrasian equilibrium.

Remark The marginal-productivity equilibrium condition is something more than a definition of Walrasian equilibrium in disguise. For example, in models with a finite number of individuals, Walrasian equilibrium rarely satisfies the marginal productivity equilibrium condition (Ostroy 1980; Makowski 1980; Anderlini 1986). Even in models with a continuum of individuals, the two can differ. The requirement that ∇g exist is a substantive restriction on the definition of equilibrium which expresses a kind of *perfect substitutability among individuals* that is part of the heuristic meaning of perfect competition. Let q be the n-tuple of individuals' net utility in a Walrasian equilibrium, i.e., $q = (q_i) = (v_i(z_i))$. When $q = \nabla g(r)$ exists, there are well-defined rates at which *individuals* can be substituted for each other while holding total satisfaction constant. These well-defined rates of person-by-person substitutability translate to well-defined rates of commodity-by-commodity substitutability in the sense that $q = \nabla g(r)$ implies that at the associated commodity prices p all others have perfect substitutes for each individual's *commodities*. Hence, each individual faces perfectly elastic demands and supplies for the goods he or she sells and buys. Under the price-taking assumption of Walrasian equilibrium, this perfect substitutability/perfect elasticity need not be a feature of Walrasian equilibrium, even in a nonatomic model. In section 3, we shall use an example due to Edgeworth to illustrate the consequences of the distinction.

The quotations and discussion above are not intended to show that Wicksteed anticipated the *proof* of the main result of section 2. What they are intended to show is that, although developments in economic theory did not prepare him to construct such a proof, the conclusion confirms his speculations on the implications of the marginal productivity theory of distribution as it applies to the theory of exchange!

Wicksteed has received considerable recognition for his part in the development of marginal productivity theory. Of necessity, this recognition has been limited by the commentators' own understanding of that theory and, as a result, some parts of his *Essay* have not been appreciated. It is easy to see that, with a conventional view of marginal productivity theory, Wicksteed's excursions into an exchange interpretation where the product is "satisfaction" and the inputs of the function are "psyche" might appear, at best, as poetic flights of fancy to be separated from his real contribution to the development of economics. As an illustration, in commenting on Wicksteed's *Essay* Stigler (1941, p. 331) writes: "As an alternative, the product may be social utility. Since marginal utility decreases, the theorem [Euler's] then holds only if consumers are included among the factors of production. This result is of no practical significance; let us pass to the third and important concept [commercial product]." What is dismissed here as having no import, we regard as pointing to an understanding of the marginal productivity principle which makes it the centerpiece of the theory of value.

2 Definitions, Theorems, and Proofs

2.1 Statement of Theorems 1 and 2

The Model Consider a nontransferable utility (NTU) model of a pure-exchange economy in net-trade form. The economy can be described by a set $\mathscr{E}_{\text{NTU}} = \{v_i: i = 1,\ldots,n\}$, where $v_i: \mathbb{R}^\ell \to \mathbb{R} \cup (-\infty)$ represents the preferences of i over trades $z_i \in \mathbb{R}^\ell$. Our convention is that positive (negative) elements of z_i represent purchases (sales), and the effective domain of v_i,

$$Z_i \equiv \{z_i \in \mathbb{R}^\ell: v_i(z_i) > -\infty\},$$

represents the set of feasible trades for i. $\mathscr{E}_{\text{NTU}}$ may be interpreted either as an economy with n individuals or as an economy with a nonatomic continuum of individuals consisting of n types, with a unit mass of each type. The second interpretation will be primary.

The following assumptions will be maintained throughout. With $\Omega = \mathbb{R}^\ell_+$, for all i:

(A.1) $Z_i = \Omega - \{\omega_i\}$ for some $\omega_i \in \Omega$.
(A.2) v_i is concave, continuous on Z_i, and for each z_i there exists z_i' s.t. $v_i(z_i') > v_i(z_i)$.
(A.3) $0 \in \text{int}(\Sigma Z_i)$ (i.e., $\omega \equiv \Sigma\omega_i \gg 0$).

With ω_i interpreted as i's resource endowment, (A.1) implies that i's consumption set is Ω.

Embedding $\mathscr{E}_{\text{NTU}}$ into a Family of Economies Preparatory to defining the central concept, it will be convenient to regard $\mathscr{E}_{\text{NTU}}$ as a particular member of a two-parameter family of economies,

$$\{\mathscr{E}_{\text{NTU}}(r,w): r = (r_1,\ldots,r_n) \in \mathbb{R}^n_+ \text{ and } w \in \mathbb{R}^\ell\}.$$

Interpret $\mathscr{E}_{\text{NTU}}(r,w)$ as an economy with a mass r_i of each type i and with w extra resources. Within this family $\mathscr{E}_{\text{NTU}}$ has a unit mass of each type i and has no extra resources; i.e., $\mathscr{E}_{\text{NTU}} = \mathscr{E}_{\text{NTU}}(e,0)$, where $e = (1,1,\ldots,1) \in \mathbb{R}^n$.

For any economy $\mathscr{E}_{\text{NTU}}(r,w)$, an allocation $z = (z_1, \ldots, z_n)$ is *attainable* if $\Sigma r_i z_i = w$, i.e., if the sum of trades equals the total extra resources in the economy. For any $r \in \mathbb{R}^n_+$ and $w \in \mathbb{R}^\ell$, let

$$A(r,w) = \{z \in \textstyle\prod_i Z_i \colon \Sigma r_i z_i = w \text{ and } z_i = 0 \text{ if } r_i = 0\},$$

$$A \equiv A(e,0).$$

$A(r,w)$ represents the set of attainable allocations in $\mathscr{E}_{\text{NTU}}(r,w)$. It is a standard exercise to verify that, under our maintained assumptions,

(1) $\forall r, \forall w$: $A(r,w)$ is compact, convex, and $A(r,w) \neq \phi$ if $w \in \Sigma r_i Z_i$.

Remark We have implicitly restricted our attention, above, to equal-treatment allocations. For our purposes this is merely a felicitous and harmless simplification. As is well known, given our assumptions that each v_i is concave and each Z_i is convex, for any attainable allocation there exists an attainable, utility-equivalent, equal-treatment allocation.

The Marginal Product of an Individual Throughout, let $\lambda = (\lambda_1, \ldots, \lambda_n) \in \mathbb{R}^n_+$, $\lambda \neq 0$. For any such λ, define the function $\psi_\lambda \colon \mathbb{R}^n_+ \times \mathbb{R}^\ell \to \mathbb{R} \cup \{-\infty\}$ by

$$\psi_\lambda(r,w) = \sup\{\Sigma r_i \lambda_i v_i(z_i) \colon \Sigma r_i z_i = w\}.$$

(Our convention is that $0 \cdot (-\infty) = -\infty$; so the above supremum equals $-\infty$ unless $z_i \in Z_i$ for all i, even i with $\lambda_i = 0$.) The number $\psi_\lambda(r,w)$ represents the maximum potential *gains from trade* in the economy $\mathscr{E}_{\text{NTU}}(r,w)$, when social utility is formed by adding the individual utilities weighted according to λ. Also define $f_\lambda \colon \mathbb{R}^\ell \to \mathbb{R} \cup \{-\infty\}$ and $g_\lambda \colon \mathbb{R}^n_+ \to \mathbb{R}$ as follows:

$$\forall w, \quad f_\lambda(w) = \psi_\lambda(e,w)$$

$$\lambda r, \quad g_\lambda(r) = \psi_\lambda(r,0).$$

So, $f_\lambda(0) = g_\lambda(e)$. The function f_λ measures the gains from trade when extra *resources* are added to $\mathscr{E}_{\text{NTU}}$, while g_λ measures the gains from trade when $r - e$ extra *individuals* are added to $\mathscr{E}_{\text{NTU}}$. It is a standard exercise to verify that f_λ and g_λ are well defined (e.g., the sup in the definition of f_λ never equals $+\infty$) concave functions. More specifically, for future reference:

(2) $\forall \lambda$, f_λ is concave and satisfies, for any w,

- $f_\lambda(w) = -\infty$ if $A(e,w) = \phi$,

• $f_\lambda(w) = \max\{\Sigma\lambda_i v_i(z_i): z \in A(e,w)\}$ if $A(e,w) \neq 0$ (and this maximum exists).

(3) $\forall\lambda$, g_λ is concave, positively homogeneous (of degree 1), and satisfies, for any r,

$g_\lambda(r) = \max\{\Sigma\lambda_i v_i(z_i)r_i: z \in A(r,0)\}$ (which exists).

Further, letting

$\zeta(\lambda) = \arg\max\{\Sigma\lambda_i v_i(z_i): z \in A \equiv A(e,0)\}$,

then ζ is a u.h.c, convex-valued correspondence on

$\Lambda \equiv \{\lambda \in \mathbb{R}^n_+ : \Sigma\lambda_i = 1\}$.

Now we are prepared for the key definitions. The main idea of our approach to perfectly competitive equilibrium is that, under perfectly competitive conditions, the rewards that individuals receive are equated to their marginal social contributions. When there is a continuum of agents, the latter can be computed using the calculus, just like ordinary marginal products. More specifically, for any given λ, the "marginal product of individual i" is the marginal social contribution of an infinitesimal additional mass of type i to the economy $\mathscr{E}_{\text{NTU}}$, when social utility is computed according to the weights λ. Formally, the idea is expressed in terms of the directional derivative of the gains function g_λ.

DEFINITION The *marginal product* of an infinitesimal individual of type i under λ is given by $g'_\lambda(e;e_i)$, where

$$g'_\lambda(e;e_i) = \lim_{t\to 0_+} \frac{g_\lambda(e + te_i) - g(e)}{t}$$

and e_i is the ith unit vector in $\mathbb{R}^n$.

Our main result is an existence theorem specifying conditions under which each individual receives his or her marginal product.

DEFINITION The pair (z^0,λ^0) is a *marginal productivity (MP) equilibrium* for $\mathscr{E}_{\text{NTU}}$ if $z^0 \in A$, $\lambda^0 \gg 0$, and for each i

$\lambda_i^0 v_i(z_i^0) = g'_{\lambda^0}(e;e_i)$.

It will also be convenient to have the following terms based on an MP equilibrium. Say that z^0 is an MP *allocation* for $\mathscr{E}_{\text{NTU}}$ if $\exists\ \lambda^0 \gg 0$ such that

(z^0, λ^0) is an MP equilibrium. Also, say that $q = (q_i)$ is an MP *distribution* for $\mathscr{E}_{\text{NTU}}$ under λ^0 if $q = \nabla g_{\lambda^0}(e)$, where $\nabla g_{\lambda^0}(e)$ is the gradient of g_{λ^0} at e.

Two Additional Assumptions A key step in proving the existence of an MP equilibrium will involve showing that, $\forall \lambda$, g_λ is differentiable at e. For this part of the proof, an additional assumption is crucial: we will require preferences to be smooth. For each $z_i \in Z_i$, define the cone generated by Z_i from z_i as

$$C_i(z_i) = \{d \in \mathbb{R}^\ell : \exists\, t > 0 \text{ s.t. } (z_i + td) \in Z_i).$$

$C_i(z_i)$ represents the set of feasible directions in which it is possible to go from z_i while staying in Z_i. It is well known that C_i inherits the closure and convexity properties of Z_i. Let $v_i'(z_i;d)$ represent the directional derivative of v_i at z_i in the direction d.

DEFINITION v_i is *smooth* if $\forall\, z_i \in Z_i\ \exists\ \nabla v_i(z_i) \in \mathbb{R}^\ell$ s.t.

$$v_i'(z_i;d) = \nabla v_i(z_i) d \text{ for all } d \in C_i(z_i),$$

and $\nabla v_i(\cdot)$ is continuous on Z_i.

It should be obvious that v_i is smooth if there exists a continuously differentiable function $\bar{v}_i$ defined on an open set containing Z_i, with the property that $\bar{v}_i(z_i) = v_i(z_i)$ for all $z_i \in Z_i$.

To prove the main result, we will assume

(A.4) $\forall i$, v_i is smooth.

At almost the final step in proving the existence result, we will need a resource-relatedness assumption (in the sense of Arrow and Hahn 1971).

DEFINITION Individual j is *resource related* to individual k if, $\forall\, z \in A$, $\exists\, w \in \Omega$ and $\exists\, z' \in A(e,w)$ s.t.

(a) $\forall i\ v_i(z_i') \geq v_i(z_i)$, with $v_k(z_k') > v_k(z_k)$

(b) for all commodities h $(h = 1, \ldots, \ell)$, $w^h > 0$ only if $\omega_j^h > 0$.

The idea is that the economy would be no worse off, and k could be made better off, with w extra resources, where only resources h are added that j could supply.

DEFINITION Individual j is *indirectly resource related* to individual k if there is a sequence $i_1, \ldots, i_{m'}, \ldots, i_m$ where $i_1 = j$, $i_m = k$, and $i_{m'}$ is resource related to $i_{m'+1}$ for $m' = 1, \ldots, m - 1$.

Our last assumption will be the following:

(A.5) Every individual is indirectly resource related to every other individual.

The maintained assumptions, (A.1)–(A.3), along with the assumption to guarantee the differentiability of g_λ at e, (A.4), and the indirect-resource-relatedness assumption, (A.5), will suffice to prove that an MP equilibrium exists for $\mathscr{E}_{\mathrm{NTU}}$. As will be seen, there is an intimate connection between an allocation satisfying the MP definition of equilibrium and a Walrasian allocation for $\mathscr{E}_{\mathrm{NTU}}$.

DEFINITION $[p,z]$ is a *Walrasian equilibrium* for $\mathscr{E}_{\mathrm{NTU}}$, denoted by $[p,z] \in \mathrm{WE}(\mathscr{E}_{\mathrm{NTU}})$, if $p \in \mathbb{R}^\ell$, $z \in A$, and for each i

$$pz_i = 0$$

and

$$v_i(z_i) = \sup\{v_i(z_i'): pz_i' = pz_i\}.$$

MAIN RESULT (THEOREM 1) In addition to the maintained assumptions, assume (A.4) and (A.5). Then there exists an MP equilibrium, i.e., a $\lambda^0 \gg 0$ and a $z^0 \in \zeta(\lambda^0)$ s.t. $\forall i$

$$g'_{\lambda^0}(e;e_i) = \lambda_i^0 v_i(z_i^0).$$

Moreover, for any such z^0 and λ^0 there exists $p(\lambda^0) = \nabla f_{\lambda^0}(0)$ such that

$$[p(\lambda^0), z^0] \in \mathrm{WE}(\mathscr{E}_{\mathrm{NTU}}),$$

where $p(\lambda^0)$ is the gradient of f_{λ^0} at 0 (which exists).

We know from theorem 1 that marginal product allocations are Walrasian. But if preferences are not smooth, the converse may not hold. (A classical example is Edgeworth's master-servant example; see section 3.2.) As our other result, we show that, assuming smoothness, the converse does hold. The result is implied by Aumann's proof of the equivalence between value allocations and Walrasian allocations in continuum NTU economies (see, in particular, Aumann 1975, lemma 14.1). However, we prefer to give an alternative proof that is more in the spirit of this paper, with its emphasis on the geometric properties of concave functions.

THEOREM 2 In addition to the maintained assumptions, assume (A.4) and (A.5) and that preferences are weakly monotonic (i.e., $\forall i \; \forall \, z_i \in Z_i$: $z_i' \geqq z_i$

implies $v_i(z_i') \geqq v_i(z_i)$). Then, for any $[p,z] \in \mathrm{WE}(\mathscr{E}_{\mathrm{NTU}})$, $\exists\, \lambda \gg 0$ s.t. $\forall i$

$$g_\lambda'(e;e_i) = \lambda_i v_i(z_i).$$

2.2 Proof of Theorem 1

The proof involves two steps. First, an analog of theorem 1 is displayed for a family of transferable utility (TU) economies. Second, a fixed-point argument is used that builds on the TU analog.

A Supplementary Construction For any given λ, it is convenient to associate $\mathscr{E}_{\mathrm{NTU}}$ with a transferable utility economy with $\ell + 1$ commodities, in which each i evaluates any trade $(z_i,m_i) \in \mathbb{R}^\ell \times \mathbb{R}$ according to the quasi-linear utility function $u_i^\lambda(z_i,m_i) = \lambda_i v_i(z_i) + m_i$. The associated economy can thus be described by the set $\mathscr{E}_{\mathrm{TU}}^\lambda = \{u_i^\lambda\colon i = 1,\ldots,n\}$.

The proof of theorem 1 builds on the interesting fact that for any given λ there is a one-to-one correspondence between the subgradients of f_λ at 0 and the Walrasian prices for $\mathscr{E}_{\mathrm{TU}}^\lambda$. Formally expressed, for any λ, let $\partial f_\lambda(0)$ represent the set of subgradients of f_λ at 0. Note that this set is nonempty, since, by (2), f_λ is concave and, by (A.3), 0 is in the interior of f_λ's effective domain.

DEFINITION $[p,z]$ is a *Walrasian equilibrium* for $\mathscr{E}_{\mathrm{TU}}^\lambda$, denoted by $[p,z] \in \mathrm{WE}(\mathscr{E}_{\mathrm{TU}}^\lambda)$, if $p \in \mathbb{R}^\ell$, $z \in A$, and for each i

$$\lambda_i v_i(z_i) - pz_i = \sup\{\lambda_i v_i(z_i') - pz_i'\colon z_i' \in \mathbb{R}^\ell\}.$$

Note that the last condition in the definition just says that, $\forall i$, p is a subgradient of $\lambda_i v_i$ at z_i, i.e.,

$$p \in \partial \lambda_i v_i(z_i).$$

More conventionally expressed, it says that, $\forall i$, $(z_i, -pz_i)$ maximizes u_i^λ over all (z_i',m_i') s.t. $pz_i' + m_i' = 0$. But the former viewpoint is more useful here, because it is a well-known fact (e.g., see Mas-Colell 1985, chapter 4) that

$$\text{(4)}\quad \forall \lambda\, \forall z \in \zeta(\lambda)\colon p \in \partial f_\lambda(0) \quad \text{iff } p \in \partial \lambda_i v_i(z_i)\ \forall i.$$

Recall from result (3) that $\zeta(\lambda)$ is the set of all attainable allocations that maximize the gains from trade under λ. The characterization (4) implies that any $p \in \partial f_\lambda(0)$, when combined with any $z \in \zeta(\lambda)$, forms a $\mathrm{WE}(\mathscr{E}_{\mathrm{TU}}^\lambda)$.

The proof of theorem 1 for $\mathscr{E}_{\mathrm{NTU}}$ is based on the following analogous result for any economy $\mathscr{E}_{\mathrm{TU}}^\lambda$.

THEOREM 3 In addition to the maintained assumptions, assume preferences are smooth, (A.4). Then, for any λ, f_λ is differentiable at 0 with gradient denoted by $p(\lambda)$. Further, for any λ, any $z \in \zeta(\lambda)$, and all i,

$$g'_\lambda(e;e_i) = \lambda_i v_i(z_i) - p(\lambda)z_i,$$

where $p(\cdot)$ is continuous on Λ.

The proof of theorem 3 appears in the next section. First we show that, with the aid of a standard fixed-point argument, theorem 3 implies our main result.

A Fixed-Point Argument For any $\lambda \in \Lambda$, let

$$\eta(\lambda) = \{\xi = (\xi_i) \in \mathbb{R}^n: \quad \xi = (-p(\lambda)z_1, \ldots, -p(\lambda)z_n) \quad \text{for some } z \in \zeta(\lambda)\}.$$

Note that $\{\eta(\lambda): \lambda \in \Lambda\}$ is a bounded subset of $\mathbb{R}^n$. Indeed, $\{p(\lambda): \lambda \in \Lambda\}$ is bounded, since, by theorem 3, $p(\cdot)$ is a continuous function on a bounded set; while $\{\zeta(\lambda): \lambda \in \Lambda\}$ is contained in $A \equiv A(e,0)$, which is a compact set by (1). Let B be any compact, convex subset of $\mathbb{R}^n$ containing $\{\eta(\lambda): \lambda \in \Lambda\}$. We can then regard η as a correspondence from Λ to B. Further, it is a u.h.c., convex-valued correspondence, since, by (3), ζ is u.h.c. and convex-valued on Λ and, by theorem 2, $p(\cdot)$ is continuous on Λ.

Given any $\xi \in B$, let $\mu(\xi) = \{\lambda \in \Lambda: \lambda\xi \geqq \lambda'\xi \text{ for all } \lambda' \in \Lambda\}$. It is well known that μ is a u.h.c., convex-valued correspondence on B (e.g., see Debreu 1959, 5.6(1)).

Now consider the correspondence ϕ from $\Lambda \times B$ to itself defined by

$$\phi(\lambda,e) = \mu(\xi) \times \eta(\lambda).$$

Since it is u.h.c. and convex-valued, it has a fixed point (λ^0,ξ^0). Thus,

(i) $\lambda\xi^0 \leqq \lambda^0\xi^0 \; \forall \; \lambda \in \Lambda$, where
(ii) $\xi^0 = (-p(\lambda)z_1^0, \ldots, -p(\lambda)z_n^0)$ for some $z^0 \in \zeta(\lambda^0)$.

Note that $z^0 \in \zeta(\lambda^0)$ implies $z^0 \in A$; consequently, $\Sigma\xi_i^0 = 0$. So, $\lambda^0 \in \mu(\xi^0)$ implies $\lambda_i^0 = 0$ whenever $\xi_i^0 < 0$. But if $\lambda_i^0 = 0$, then, since $p(\lambda^0) \in \partial\lambda_i^0 v_i(z_i^0)$ by (4),

$$\xi_i^0 \equiv -p(\lambda^0)z_i^0 \geqq -p(\lambda^0)Z_i \geqq 0,$$

where the last inequality follows from (A.1), specifically from the fact that $0 \in Z_i$. We conclude that

(iii) $\xi_i^0 = 0, \quad \forall i.$

It now follows from theorem 3 that $\forall i$

(iv) $g'_{\lambda^0}(e;e_i) = \lambda_i^0 v_i(z_i^0).$

There only remains to be shown that

(v) $\lambda_i^0 > 0 \quad \forall i,$

and that $[p(\lambda^0), z^0] \in \mathrm{WE}(\mathscr{E}_{\mathrm{NTU}})$. The former will readily imply the latter.

It is a straightforward, although slightly involved, exercise to verify that

(5) $\forall \lambda$, and all individuals j and k: if j is resource related to k and if $\lambda_j = 0$ while $\lambda_k > 0$, then $g'_\lambda(e;e_j) > 0$.

(See the appendix for a proof.) Now observe that since $\lambda^0 \in \Lambda$, $\exists$ a type k s.t. $\lambda_k^0 > 0$. Further, by (A.5), any type j is indirectly resource related to k. So, $\exists$ a sequence $i_1, \ldots, i_{m'}, \ldots, i_m$ with $i_1 = j$, $i_m = k$, and $i_{m'}$ resource related to $i_{m'+1}$ for $m' = 1, \ldots, m-1$. Since i_{m-1} is resource related to k and $\lambda_k^0 > 0$, if $\lambda_{i_{m-1}}^0 = 0$ then (5) would imply that $g'_{\lambda^0}(e;e_{i_{m-1}}) > 0$, which would contradict (iv) for $i = i_{m-1}$. So, $\lambda_{i_{m-1}}^0 > 0$. Repeating the above argument, since i_{m-2} is resource related to i_{m-1} and $\lambda_{i_{m-1}}^0 > 0$, $\lambda_{i_{m-2}}^0 = 0$ would again lead to a contradiction. So, $\lambda_{i_{m-2}}^0 > 0$. Continuing to repeat the argument, we finally come to the conclusion that $\lambda_{i_1}^0 \equiv \lambda_j^0 > 0$. So, for any individual j, $\lambda_j^0 > 0$, as was to be shown.

There only remains to be shown that $[p(\lambda^0), z^0] \in \mathrm{WE}(\mathscr{E}_{\mathrm{NTU}})$, in particular, that, $\forall i$,

$$v_i(z_i^0) = \sup\{v_i(z_i)\colon p(\lambda^0)z_i = 0\}.$$

But since by (4) $p(\lambda^0) \in \partial \lambda_i^0 v_i(z_i^0)$ $\forall i$, $\forall i \forall z_i$

$$\lambda_i^0 v_i(z_i) - \lambda_i^0 v_i(z_i^0) \leqq p(\lambda^0)z_i - p(\lambda^0)z_i^0.$$

Or, since $\lambda_i^0 > 0$ and $p(\lambda^0)z_i^0 = 0$, $v_i(z_i) \leqq c_i(z_i^0)$ whenever $p(\lambda^0)z_i = 0$. So, theorem 1 is proved.

Remark The mapping ϕ is an adaptation of the mapping used by Debreu (1959, 5.6(1)) to prove the existence of a WE. There is also some relation to the mapping by Arrow and Hahn (1971, chapter 5).

2.3 Proof of Theorem 3

The proof involves three steps. First, a simple relation between the subdifferentials of f_λ and g_λ is demonstrated. Second, under smoothness of preferences, it is shown that both subdifferentials are unique. The proof of theorem 3 then follows readily.

The Relation Between the Marginal Product of Individuals and the Marginal Product of Commodities For any given λ, let $\partial g_\lambda(e)$ represent the set of subgradients of g_λ at e. This set is nonempty since, by (3), g_λ is concave, and e is in the interior of g_λ's domain, $\mathbb{R}^n_+$.

The proof of theorem 3 is based on a simple relation between the prices of commodities, $p \in \partial f_\lambda(0)$—reflecting the marginal social valuations of resources when social utility is formed by adding the individual utilities weighted according to λ—and the prices of people, $q \in \partial g_\lambda(0)$—reflecting the marginal social valuations of individuals under the weights λ. As we shall see, the relation between the two (theorem 4 below) can be interpreted as a Core Equivalence Theorem.

In the terminology of Rockafellar (1970), for any given λ, let $v^*_{\lambda_i}: \mathbb{R}^\ell \to \mathbb{R} \cup \{+\infty\}$ represent the *conjugate* of $\lambda_i v_i$, defined by

$$v^*_{\lambda_i}(p) = \sup\{\lambda_i v_i(z_i') - pz_i' : z_i' \in \mathbb{R}^\ell\}.$$

Note that $v^*_{\lambda_i}$ has a nonempty effective domain (i.e., for some p, $v^*_{\lambda_i}(p) < \infty$) since, by (4), $\forall p \in \partial f_\lambda(0)$, $\forall z \in \zeta(\lambda)$, $\forall i$,

$$v^*_{\lambda_i}(p) = \lambda_i v_i(z_i) - pz_i.$$

Let $v^*_\lambda(p) = (v^*_{\lambda_1}(p), \ldots, v^*_{\lambda_n}(p))$. The relation between $\partial g_\lambda(e)$ and $\partial f_\lambda(0)$ is given by the following theorem:

THEOREM 4 $\forall \lambda, \partial g_\lambda(e) = v^*_\lambda[\partial f_\lambda(0)]$.

Once these terms are suitably interpreted, theorem 4 is an instance of the well-known Core Equivalence Theorem for the nonatomic TU economy consisting of n types of individuals, where type i has the utility function $\lambda_i v_i$ and there is unit mass of each type. The set $\partial g_\lambda(e)$ represents the elements of the core of this economy, i.e., the set of $q = (q_1, \ldots, q_n)$ such that

$$qe = g_\lambda(e)$$

and

$$0 \leq r \leq e \text{ implies } qr \geq g_\lambda(r).$$

This description takes advantage of the fact that in a type economy members of the same type are always equally treated in the core in terms of utility.

Since g_λ is positively homogeneous, it is well known that $q \in \partial g_\lambda(e)$ if and only if

$$qe = g_\lambda(e)$$

and

$$\forall r \geq 0, \quad qr \geq g_\lambda(r).$$

The positive homogeneity of g_λ implies that the second condition in the above description of the core implies the second condition in the characterization of the subdifferential.

To prove theorem 4 in one direction, suppose $p \in \partial f_\lambda(0)$. We will show that $q \equiv v_\lambda^*(p) \in \partial g_\lambda(e)$. Let $z \in \zeta(\lambda)$. Then, by (4), $[p,z] \in \mathrm{WE}(\mathscr{E}_{\mathrm{TU}}^\lambda)$. So q is in the core of $\mathscr{E}_{\mathrm{TU}}^\lambda$, which implies, as argued above, that $q \in \partial g_\lambda(e)$.

To prove the converse, suppose $q \in \partial g_\lambda(e)$ or, equivalently, suppose q is in the core of $\mathscr{E}_{\mathrm{TU}}^\lambda$. We need to show that $q = v_\lambda^*(p)$ for some $p \in \partial f_\lambda(0)$. Let

$$\Gamma_i = \{(z_i, m_i) \colon \lambda_i v_i(z_i) + m_i > q_i\}, \quad \Gamma = \mathrm{co}(\bigcup \Gamma_i).$$

From this point onward, the proof follows the classic proof of core equivalence by Debreu and Scarf (1963). One shows that there exist prices $(p, 1) \in \mathbb{R}^\ell \times \mathbb{R}$ that separate Γ from 0; then, using (4), one shows $p \in \partial f_\lambda(0)$. The details are left to the interested reader to fill in.

The Differentiability of f_λ at 0 and of g_λ at e Although g_λ is not necessarily differentiable at e (i.e., $\partial g_\lambda(e)$ is not necessarily single-valued), it will be under the additional assumption that preferences are smooth, (A.4). Indeed, given (A.4), f_λ will be differentiable at 0, which immediately implies, by theorem 4, that g_λ will be differentiable at e.

LEMMA In addition to the maintained assumptions, assume (A.4). Then, for any λ, f_λ is differentiable at 0.

To prove the lemma, we must show that $\partial f_\lambda(0)$ is single-valued. Suppose $p \in \partial f_\lambda(0)$ (recall $\partial f_\lambda(0) \neq \phi$). Then, by (4), $\forall z \in \zeta(\lambda)\ \forall i$,

$$p \in \partial \lambda_i v_i(z_i),$$

i.e.,

$$p(z_1' - z_i) \geqq \lambda_i(v_i(z_i') - v_i(z_i)) \quad \forall z_i'.$$

Let $z_i' = z_i + t\tilde{e}_h$, where $\tilde{e}_h$ is the hth unit vector in $\mathbb{R}^\ell$. Then $\forall i, \forall t > 0$,

$$tp^h \geqq \lambda_i(v_i(z_i + t\tilde{e}_h) - v_i(z_i)).$$

Dividing by t and letting $t \to 0_+$ shows that

(i) $\forall i,\ p^h \geqq \lambda_i v_i'(z_i;\tilde{e}_h)$.

Similarly, it is shown that

(ii) $\forall i,\ -p^h \geqq \lambda_i v_i'(z;-\tilde{e}_h)$.

Now, by (A.3), $\omega \gg 0$. Hence, since $z \in A$,

$$\Sigma z_i^h = 0 > \Sigma(-\omega_i^h)$$

for each commodity h. That is, $\forall h\ \exists i$ s.t. $z_i^h > -\omega_i^h$; alternatively expressed, $\forall h\ \exists i$ s.t. $\tilde{e}_h$ and $-\tilde{e}_h$ are both in $C_i(z_i)$. So, $\forall h\ \exists i$ s.t.

$$v_i'(z_i;\tilde{e}_h) = -v_i'(z_i;-\tilde{e}_h) = \nabla v_i(z_i)\cdot\tilde{e}_h.$$

Or, using (i)–(ii),

(iii) $\forall p \in \partial f_\lambda(0)\ \forall h$: $p^h = \lambda_i \nabla v_i(z_i)\tilde{e}_h$ for some i.

Thus, $\partial f_\lambda(0)$ is single-valued, so the lemma is proved.

Completing the Proof of Theorem 3 The lemma, when combined with theorem 4, implies that, for any λ, g_λ is differentiable at e. In particular, letting $q(\lambda) = (q_1(\lambda), \ldots, q_n(\lambda))$ represent the gradient of g_λ at e, we have, $\forall i$,

$$q_i(\lambda) = v_{\lambda_i}^*(p(\lambda)),$$

where $p(\lambda)$ is the gradient of f_λ at 0. More specifically, recall from (4) that if $p \in \partial f_\lambda(0)$ then $\forall z \in \zeta(\lambda), \forall i$:

$$v_{\lambda_i}^*(p) = \lambda_i v_i(z_i) - pz_i.$$

Since $g_\lambda'(e;e_i) = q_i(\lambda)$, we conclude that for any λ, any $z \in \zeta(\lambda)$, and all i

$$g_\lambda'(e;e_i) = \lambda_i v_i(z_i) - p(\lambda)z_i.$$

At this point the proof of theorem 3 is essentially complete. It remains only to be shown that

(6) Under the assumption of theorem 2, $p(\cdot)$ is continuous on Δ.

Since this is entirely routine, the proof of (6) is relegated to an appendix.

2.4 Proof of Theorem 2

As a preliminary to proving theorem 2 we will show that, for every individual j, $p\omega_j > 0$. Since, by (A.5), j is resource related to some individual $k \neq j$, there exist a w and a $z' \in A(e,w)$ satisfying conditions (a) and (b) in the definition of resource relatedness. Thus, $pz'_i \geqq pz_i$ for all i, with $>$ for $i = k$. Summing shows $\Sigma pz'_i > \Sigma pz_i = 0$; that is, $pw = p\Sigma z'_i > 0$. But $w^h > 0$ only if $\omega_j^h > 0$, and $p \geqq 0$ since preferences are monotonic. Thus, $p\omega_j > 0$.

For every individual i, define the function $V_i^*: \mathbb{R} \to \mathbb{R} \cup \{-\infty\}$ by

$$V_i(m) = \sup\{v_i(z'_i): pz'_i \leqq m\}.$$

It is well known (e.g., see Mas-Colell 1985, proposition 4.2.22) that, since $p\omega_i > 0$, V_i^* is a well-defined (i.e., $V_i^*(m) < \infty$ for all m), increasing, concave function. Further, pz_i is in the interior of V_i^*'s effective domain, since $pz_i = 0 > \min pZ_i = p(-\omega_i)$. Thus, letting $\partial V_i^*(pz_i)$ represent the set of subgradients of V_i^* at pz_i, $\partial V_i^*(pz_i) \neq \phi$.

For each i, let $\mu_i \in \partial V_i^*(pz_i)$. Then $\mu_i > 0$, since, by definition of a subgradient,

$$V_i^*(m) - V_i^*(pz_i) \leqq \mu_i m - \mu_i pz_i, \quad \forall m.$$

If $\mu_i \leqq 0$, then the nonsatiation assumption in (A.2) would be violated.

For each i, let $\lambda_i = 1/\mu_i$ (i.e., the inverse of the marginal utility of income). Then

$$\lambda_i V_i^*(m) - m \leqq \lambda_i v_i(z_i) - pz_i, \quad \forall m.$$

But, by definition of V_i^*,

$$\lambda_i v_i(z'_i) - pz'_i \leqq \lambda_i V_i^*(pz_i), \quad \forall z'_i.$$

Hence,

$$\lambda_i v_i(z'_i) - pz'_i \leqq \lambda_i v_i(z_i) - pz_i, \quad \forall z'_i,$$

i.e., $p \in \partial \lambda_i v_i(z_i)$ for each i. Thus, $[p,z] \in \mathrm{WE}(\mathscr{E}_{\mathrm{TU}}^{\lambda})$. Now, since $pz_i = 0$ for each i, theorem 2 implies

$\forall i\colon g'_\lambda(e;e_i) = \lambda_i v_i(z_i)$,

as was to be proved.

3 Concluding Remarks

The results of section 2 concern the existence and characterization of an MP equilibrium, i.e., an allocation $z^0 = (z_i^0)$ and weights $\lambda^0 = (\lambda_i^0)$ such that, for each infinitesimal individual of type i,

$\lambda_i^0 v_i(z_i^0) = g'_{\lambda^0}(e;e_i)$.

Besides our maintained hypotheses, (A.1)–(A.3), sufficient conditions for the existence of such an equilibrium are the smoothness condition (A.4) and the resource-relatedness condition (A.5). Although an MP equilibrium does not say anything directly about commodity pricing, associated with any MP allocation are prices that clear all commodity markets and realize the allocation as a Walrasian equilibrium. Conversely, any Walrasian equilibrium satisfying all of the above assumptions and a weak monotonicity condition will be a marginal productivity equilibrium.

Proofs of theorems 1 and 2 could have been obtained by other means. They could have been demonstrated as corollaries of other results involving the characterization of the value and its connection to Walrasian equilibria. The first step would be to cite the Value Equivalence Theorem of Aumann (1975), which is based on the work of Aumann and Shapley (1974). In what has become an acceptably loose way of describing it, the formula for the value yields for each individual the "average marginal product," where the average is taken over all the groups in the economy which the individual might join. In the context of a nonatomic model of an exchange economy, the average group can be shown to be almost surely close to a representative sample of the entire population; e.g., in the type economy with population $r = (r_i)$, a representative sample will consist of $\hat{r} = (\hat{r}_i)$, where $\hat{r}_1/\hat{r}_2/\cdots/\hat{r}_n \sim r_1/r_2/\cdots/r_n$. Since the g function is postively homogeneous, there will be effectively no difference between the value computed as the average marginal product to a representative sample sub-economy and what we have called an MP distribution, where the individual's marginal product is defined with respect to that group consisting of the economy as a whole. Thus, in the context of nonatomic exchange economies, the value coincides with an MP distribution. Aumann showed that it is precisely under these conditions, in which there is no difference between the *average* marginal product and what we have called *the* marginal product of an individual, that the value coincides with Walrasian equilibria. (Aumann did not confine himself to the assumption of a finite number of types.)

The remaining step leading to the results in theorems 1 and 2 would be to cite an existence theorem for Walrasian equilibria. In the finite type context, appeal could have been made to Debreu 1959 or to Arrow and Hahn 1971.

However, such a method of proof would have been contrary to our goal of putting the marginal productivity equilibrium condition on a footing independent of the value and of Walrasian equilibrium. Thus, instead of relying on the existence of Walrasian equilibrium plus some additional smoothness qualifications to demonstrate the existence of an MP allocation, we reversed the line of causation to show how the existence of an allocation satisfying the marginal productivity equilibrium condition implies Walrasian equilibrium. Similarly, we wanted to clearly demonstrate the stand-alone properties of an MP distribution apart from the value.

Having shown that conditions for its existence can be independently obtained, we now want to comment on the relation between an MP equilibrium on the one hand and the value and Walrasian equilibrium on the other.

3.1 The Shapley-Clark Connection

We interpret theorem 1 as giving a certain logical respectability to Clark's zealous interpretation of marginal productivity theory. There are two interrelated parts to his zeal. The first is that marginal productivity is the central feature of the perfectly competitive theory of value. Although marginal utility is certainly acknowledged, in Clark's hands marginal productivity stands out as the most important implication of the marginal revolution. Contrast this with the more conventional view that the two conceptual margins are of equal importance, or that if one is more important it is marginal utility. After all, marginal utility alone suffices to provide a theory of value in exchange economies, whereas marginal productivity alone provides only a theory of the demand for factors of production. Comparing Clark and Wicksteed, however, we do not see any evidence that Clark thought of applying the concept of marginal productivity to exchange, and we do not credit him with this position.

The second and better-known component of Clark's zeal has to do with the "ethics" of marginal productivity, and here we think that the concept of the value lends some support to his claims. Consider Clark's position that giving each individual his or her marginal product is "the social procedure [that] is true to the principle on which the right of property rests." As it stands, this can only be true by definition, because Clark did not say what the general principles are that would make it true. This is where the value enters.

The value is an attempt to define axiomatically how to share the surplus, or gains from trade. It can be interpreted as an "arbitration scheme"[8] that makes each player's share depend in a kind of unbiased way on the contribution the player can make to others. The scheme is, however, conditioned on the rules of the game, so it might be described as a "conditionally neutral arbitration scheme." Taking the counterpart of the rules of the game as the initial assignment of property, Clark recognizes the conditional nature of the marginal productivity reward principle.[9]

Not only did Clark not say what the general principles were that define a social procedure true to the principles of private property, but he also did not say what those principles or their consequences could possibly be in the absence of perfect competition, i.e., in environments that failed to exhibit adding-up (in terms of individuals). Shapley did both—he provided axioms that applied to conditions that were not necessarily, indeed not typically, perfectly competitive. Thus, the value is an axiomatic characterization of an arbitration scheme applicable to all environments, not only perfectly competitive ones.

The remarkable result, the Value Equivalence Theorem, is that in perfectly competitive environments the social arbitration procedure defined by the value coincides with an MP distribution. Thus, Clark's assertions that the division of the surplus under conditions of perfect competition exhibits a kind of "conditionally rational" division of the gains from trade is supported by its coincidence with the value.

Remark The existence of an MP equilibrium implies that each individual is fully appropriating the gains he or she contributes. Thus, when a value allocation coincides with an MP allocation, the two principles of distribution evidently coincide. Is the value, therefore, an extension of perfectly competitive theory to noncompetitive environments? In our view, the answer is No. Elsewhere (Makowski and Ostroy 1987, 1988) we have emphasized the remarkable incentive properties of full appropriation for achieving efficiency, properties that would not be shared by the value allocation—or any feasible allocation—in noncompetitive environments. Without full appropriation, the first-best efficiency, which is a part of the value, is not implementable.

3.2 The Edgeworth-Wicksteed Connection

Theorems 1 and 2 describe conditions under which an MP equilibrium coincides with a Walrasian equilibrium. In this subsection we focus on reasons why the two equilibrium conditions differ, and, more specifically, why a Walrasian equilibrium might not satisfy—even in a nonatomic model—the marginal productivity conditions for equilibrium. We shall point out these differences using an example due to Edgeworth.

Besides homogeneity of the first degree, which is a built-in feature of g, the existence of an MP equilibrium requires that the gradient of g exist at e, i.e., that $\partial g(e)/\partial e_i$ exist for each i. Because g is an aggregate function constructed from the characteristics of the individuals in the population, there is no need to require that differentiability hold at the level of the individual since smoothing can occur through aggregation. However, if we did not impose smoothness on the characteristics of all the individuals, we could obtain only a generic existence theorem on MP equilibria.

Existence problems for ∇g are related to traditional concerns about the legitimacy of marginal analysis. One of the criticisms of marginal productivity was that the marginal product need not exist. The two recognized sources of nonexistence were (1) that resources may be indivisible, so that infinitesimal margins were irrelevant to the firm's calculations, and (2) that, even if resources were divisible, production functions need not be differentiable. The skepticism that greeted efforts to apply marginal productivity to the entrepreneur's return was a favorite instance of the first problem; fixed-coefficient production functions were pointed out as an instance of the second.[10]

The above two issues are of unequal importance when one is dealing with the differentiability of g. The problems posed by resource indivisibility effectively vanish in an economy with a large number of participants because the individual, who is an indivisible unit, is an infinitesimal unit at the level of the economy as a whole. When evaluating the marginal product of an individual, we are considering the (infinitesimal) difference between having and not having that individual with his *entire package* of resources whether or not those resources are divisible. Thus, the marginal product of an individual supplying entrepreneurial services is not any more problematic than the marginal product of an individual supplying other kinds of labor services.[11] The second difficulty does not disappear. In those cases where smoothing is not achieved by aggregation, the failure of differentiability at the micro level can have macro consequences for the existence of an MP equilibrium.

To illustrate this point we shall consider Edgeworth's master-servant example. In his *Mathematical Psychics* (1881), Edgeworth was concerned to show how a more fundamental approach involving bargaining could be used to demonstrate perfectly competitive equilibrium. For Edgeworth, the crux of the matter was to show that the outcome of bargaining would be *determinate*. To the extent that the outcome of bargaining was indeterminate, the market was subject to imperfections. For example, "... *contract is more or less indeterminate according as the field is less or more affected with the first imperfection*, limitation of numbers" [p. 42; italics in original]. Edgeworth noted, however, that large numbers did not necessarily guarantee determinacy:

> The *second* indeterminacy may be operative in many cases of contract for personal service. Suppose a market, consisting of an equal number of masters and servants, offering respectively wages and service; subject to the condition that no man can serve two masters, no master can employ more than one man; or suppose equilibrium already established between such parties to be disturbed by a sudden influx of wealth into the hands of the masters. Then there is no *determinate*, and very generally *unique*, arrangement towards which the system tends under the operation of, may we say, a law of Nature, and which would be predictable if we knew beforehand the real requirements of each, or of the average, dealer; but there are an indefinite number of arrangements *à priori* possible, towards one of which the system is urged *not* by the concurrence of innumerable (as it were) neuter atoms eliminating chance, but (abstraction being made of custom) by what has been called the Art of Bargaining—higgling dodges and designing obstinacy, and other incalculable and often disreputable accidents. [p. 46, italics in original]

The phenomenon that Edgeworth attributes to indivisibility can be reproduced under the assumption of divisible resources but nondifferentiable utility functions. Let the masters have two units of the first commodity and the servants have two units of the second commodity. A master's utility function for net trades is $v_1(z_1) = \min(2 + z_{11}, z_{12})$, and a servant's is $v_2(z_2) = \min(z_{21}, 2 + z_{22})$. Whatever the number of masters and servants, an optimal $z = (z_1, z_2)$ will be such that $z_1 = (-1, 1) = -z_2$ whenever $z_i \neq 0$; i.e., each (employed) servant will serve only one master, and each (employing) master will hire only one servant. It is readily verified that for this example $g(r) = \min(r_1, r_2)$.[12] Therefore, with unit mass of both masters and servants, $\partial g(e) = \{(\alpha, 1 - \alpha): \alpha \in [0,1]\}$. As Edgeworth noted but did not emphasize, the difficulty occurs only when the numbers on each side of the market are the same ($r_1 = r_2$). In more contemporary language, it can be shown that when $r_1 = r_2$ the "higgling dodges and designing obstinacy" present opportunities for *manipulation* of a Walrasian equilibrium by groups of individuals of arbitrarily small size. However, when $r_1 \neq r_2$, then, even though the market continues to exhibit features of indivisibility, the outcome of bargaining is perfectly determinate in the sense that $\nabla g(r) = (1,0)$ or $(0,1)$ whenever $r_1 < r_2$ or $r_2 < r_1$, respectively, and the outcome is *not manipulable*.

There is a historical irony in this analysis of Edgeworth's example. Determinacy holds (fails) precisely when the formula

$$\nabla g(r) \cdot r = g(r)$$

can (cannot) be applied. One might therefore imagine that Edgeworth would have been sympathetic to marginal productivity theory in general and to Wicksteed's *Essay* in particular. In fact, he was critical of both. It is interesting to speculate why.

Wicksteed was able to make the bridge between the marginal productivity theory of distribution and the theory of exchange. Before introducing his metaphorical function, the output of which was satisfaction **S**, he says: "The modern investigations into the theory of value have already given us the lead we require. Indeed the law of exchange value itself is the law of distribution of the general resources of society." (pp. 7–8) Edgeworth, however, was not convinced that such a bridge could be made; if there were a bridge, he seems to believe, it would carry traffic in only one direction. He was quite willing to say that "distribution is a species of exchange,"[13] but he was reluctant to accept Wicksteed's position that, in effect, exchange could be regarded as a species of distribution. Indeed, he refers disapprovingly to the sentence of Wicksteed quoted in this paragraph.

Edgeworth, whose remarkable treatment of competitive equilibrium lay in his ability to go beyond price-taking in terms of *commodities* to its bargaining foundations in terms of *individuals*,[14] would seem to be the nineteenth-century economist most capable of appreciating and reorienting marginal analysis away from commodities and toward individuals. But his comments on marginal productivity were surprisingly conventional. He insisted on treating marginal productivity theory on a par with marginal utility theory, which meant that increments from "last doses" of commodities were literally applied.[15]

In this paper the historical emphasis has been on some of the bolder claims of Clark and Wicksteed, specifically on ones which we have found to be logically justifiable. The key to this justification is a reorientation of marginal analysis away from the commodity and toward the individual as the fundamental margin of analysis. Considering developments in mathematics and game theory since the marginalist revolution, it is easy to see why such a reorientation would have been beyond the technical capabilities of its founders. One can only guess how they would have responded to the claim that their revolution could have been stated, and also given more unity, by revising the margin.

Appendix A: Proof of (5)

We must show that $g'_\lambda(e;e_j) > 0$. Let $z \in \zeta(\lambda)$, and let w and z' satisfy the conditions in the definition of j being resource related to k.

As a preliminary step, we show $\exists w''$ and $\exists z'' \in A(e,w'')$ s.t.

(i) $\forall i$, $v_i(z_i'') \geqq v_i(z_i)$, with $v_k(z_k'') > v_k(z_k)$,

where $0 \leqq w'' \leqq \omega_j$. Indeed, pick $\bar{t} \in (0,1)$ s.t. $w'' \equiv \bar{t}w \leqq \omega_j$. (Such a $\bar{t}$ exists, since $w^h > 0$ only if $\omega_j^h > 0$.) Let $z_i'' = (1-\bar{t})z_i + \bar{t}z_i'$. The convexity of Z_i implies each $z_i'' \in Z_i$. Further, $z'' \in A(e,\bar{t}w)$, since

$$\Sigma z_i'' = (1-\bar{t})\Sigma z_i + \bar{t}\Sigma z_i = \bar{t}w.$$

That z'' satisfies (i) follows from the concavity of preferences and the fact that z' satisfies condition (a) of the definition of resource relatedness.

We next show that for any $t \in (0,1)\ \exists\ z(t) \in A(e + te_j, 0)$ s.t.

(ii) $\forall i \neq j$, $v_i(z_i(t)) \geqq v_i(z_i)$, with $v_k(z_k(t)) > v_k(z_k)$.

Indeed, let

$$z_j(t) = \frac{[(1-t)z_j + tz_j''] + t[-w'']}{1+t}$$

and, $\forall i \neq j$, let

$$z_i(t) = (1 - t)z_i + tz_i''.$$

Obviously, $\forall i \neq j$, $z_i(t) \in Z_i$. To see that $z_j(t) \in Z_j$, observe that $(1 - t)z_j + tz_j'' \in Z_j$ since Z_j is convex; and $-w'' \in Z_j$ since, by construction, $-w'' = -\bar{t}w \geqq -\omega_j$. Thus, $z_j(t) \in Z_j$, since it is just a convex combination of two points in Z_j. Further, $z(t) \in A(e + te_j, 0)$, since

$$\sum_{i \neq j} z_i(t) + (1 + t)z_j(t) = (1 - t)\Sigma z_i + t\Sigma z_i'' + t(-w'')$$

$$= tw'' - tw'' = 0.$$

That $z(t)$ satisfies (ii) follows from the concaving of preferences and the fact that z'' satisfies (i). Indeed, by concavity, $\forall t \in (0,1)$, $\forall i \neq j$:

$$v_i(z_i(t)) \geqq (1 - t)v_i(z_i) + tv_i(z_i'')$$

or

$$\frac{v_i(z_i(t)) - v_i(z_i)}{t} \geqq v_i(z_i'') - v_i(z_i).$$

Since $z(t) \in A(e + te_j, 0)$, we have, $\forall t \in (0,1)$,

$$\frac{g_\lambda(e + te_j) - g_\lambda(e)}{t} \geqq \frac{\Sigma\lambda_i v_i(z_i(t)) - \Sigma\lambda_i v_i(z_i)}{t}$$

$$\geqq \Sigma\lambda_i(v_i(z_i'') - v_i(z_i)) > 0.$$

Letting $t \to 0^+$ shows $g_\lambda'(e;e_j) > 0$, which was to be proved. ∎

Appendix B: Proof of (6)

Preliminary to showing that $p(\cdot)$ is continuous on Λ, we verify that $\{p(\lambda): \lambda \in \Lambda\}$ is bounded. Observe that, since by assumption $\nabla v_i(\cdot)$ is continuous on Z_i and since by (1) A is compact, $\forall i$

$$\{\lambda_i \nabla v_i(z_i): \lambda_i \in [0,1], z_i \in Z_i, \text{and } z_i \text{ is a part of some } z \in A\}$$

is bounded. Thus, since by (iii) of subsection 3.2, $\forall \lambda \in \Lambda$ and $\forall h$, $p^h(\lambda)$ is in one such set, $\{p(\lambda): \lambda \in \Lambda\}$ is bounded.

Given the boundedness of $\{p(\lambda): \lambda \in \Lambda\}$, to verify that $p(\cdot)$ is continuous on Λ it suffices to show that "$\lambda_m \in \Lambda$, $\lambda_m \to \lambda$, $p_m \equiv p(\lambda_m) \to p$" implies "$p = p(\lambda)$." Since $p_m \in \partial f_{\lambda_m}(0)$,

$$f_{\lambda_m}(w) - f_{\lambda_m}(0) \leqq p_m w \quad \forall w \in \mathbb{R}^{\ell}.$$

We want to show that

$$f_{\lambda}(w) - f_{\lambda}(0) \leqq pw \quad \forall w \in \mathbb{R}^{\ell}.$$

If $w \notin \Sigma Z_i$, then $f_{\lambda}(w) = -\infty$ while $f_{\lambda}(0) > -\infty$; therefore the conclusion holds. If $w \in \Sigma Z_i$ then, by (2),

$$f_{\lambda_m}(w) = \max\{\Sigma\lambda_{m,i}v_i(z_i)\colon z \in A(e,w)\}$$

and

$$f_{\lambda}(w) = \max\{\Sigma\lambda_i v_i(z_i)\colon z \in A(e,w)\}.$$

Thus, since $\lambda_m \to \lambda$,

$$f_{\lambda_m}(w) \to f_{\lambda}(w)$$

and

$$f_{\lambda_m}(0) \to f_{\lambda}(0).$$

(Formally, this follows from Debreu 1959, 2.8(4).) So, the conclusion again hold. This completes the proof of (6). ■

Acknowledgment

Research supported by National Science Foundation.

Notes

1. It was Wicksteed who introduced the term "marginal" utility to replace Jevons' "final degree of" utility.

2. Stigler's *Production and Distribution Theories* (1941) is a masterful survey of the development of marginal productivity theory.

3. Stigler (1941), p. 297.

4. Blaug (1985, p. 425) is particularly emphatic in wanting to limit the claims of the theory to nothing more than the underpinnings for the theory of factor demand. In contrast, Schumpeter (1954, pp. 912–913)—coming from the Mengerian tradition, where marginal productivity is more seamlessly incorporated into value theory—gives it a more generous interpretation.

5. Flux (1894) is credited with placing Wicksteed's contribution as an application of Euler's Theorem.

6. For example, common property resources are not typically admitted into the standard presentation of the theory of value. Their presence would, however, imply that a doubling of the population would not double all the relevant resources and thus may lead to decreasing returns.

7. "Indeed the law of exchange value is itself the law of distribution of the general resources of society." (pp. 7–8)

8. See Luce and Raiffa 1957, pp. 250–252.

9. See the next-to-last sentence of the opening paragraph of the preface of *The Distribution of Wealth* (quoted above).

10. For example, Pareto commented: "Thus, in a chocolate factory, you may increase as much as you wish the labor, the area occupied by the factory, the machines and yet if you do not increase the quantity of cacao, you will not appreciably increase the chocolate." (Quoted in Stigler 1941, p. 365.)

11. Several years ago, Frank Hahn brought to our attention Chapman's "Remuneration of Employers" (1906). It is remarkable for its analysis of a model with a continuum of workers and employers in which marginal product of an employer is obtained as the derivative of an aggregate production function.

12. Among game theorists, a model such as this would be called a "glove market." See Aumann and Shapley 1974, pp. 201–204.

13. Edgeworth 1925, vol. I, p. 13.

14. "Here it is attempted to proceed without postulating the phenomenon of uniformity of price [he references Walras] by the longer route of *contract-curve*." (Edgeworth 1881, p. 40; italics in original)

15. Edgeworth 1925, vol. I, pp. 28 and 52.

References

Anderlini, L. 1986. On Autarkic Communities and Finite No Surplus Economies. Economic Theory Discussion Paper 96, Department of Applied Economics, Cambridge University.

Arrow, K. J., and F. Hahn. 1971. *General Competitive Analysis.* Holden-Day.

Aumann, R. J. 1975. "Values of markets with a continuum of traders." *Econometrica* 43 (4): 611–646.

Aumann, R. J., and L. S. Shapley. 1974. *Values of Non-Atomic Games.* Princeton University Press.

Blaug, M. 1985. *Economic Theory in Retrospect*, fourth edition. Cambridge University Press.

Champsaur, P. 1975. "Cooperation versus competition." *Journal of Economic Theory* 11(3): 394–417.

Chapman, S. J. 1906. "The remuneration of employers." *Economic Journal* 16: 523–528.

Clark, J. B. 1899. *The Distribution of Wealth: A Theory of Wages, Interest and Profits.* Macmillan.

Debreu, G. 1959. *Theory of Value.* Wiley.

Debreu, G., and H. Scarf. 1963. "A limit theorem on the core of an economy." *International Economic Review* 4: 236–246.

Edgeworth, F. Y. 1881. *Mathematical Psychics.* Kegan Paul.

Edgeworth, F. Y. 1925. *Papers Relating to Political Economy*, volumes 1–3. Royal Economic Society, London.

Flux, A. W. 1894. "Review of Wicksteed's Essay on the Laws of the Coordination of Distribution." *Economic Journal* 4: 311.

Luce, R. D., and H. Raiffa. 1957. *Games and Decisions*. Wiley.

Makowski, L. 1980. "A characterization of perfectly competitive economies with production." *Journal of Economic Theory* 22 (2): 208–221.

Makowski, L., and J. M. Ostroy. 1987. "Vickrey-Clark-Groves mechanisms and perfect competition." *Journal of Economic Theory* 42 (2): 244–261.

Makowski, L., and J. M. Ostroy. 1988. "Groves mechanisms in continuum economies: Characterization and existence." *Journal of Mathematical Economics.*

Mas-Colell, A. 1985. *The Theory of General Economic Equilibrium: A Differentiable Approach.* Cambridge University Press.

Ostroy, J. M. 1980. "The no-surplus condition as a characterization of perfectly competitive equilibrium." *Journal of Economic Theory* 22 (2): 183–207.

Rockafellar, R. T. 1970. *Convex Analysis*. Princeton University Press.

Schumpeter, J. A. 1954. *History of Economic Analysis*. Oxford University Press.

Shapley, L. 1953. "A value for *n*-person games." In *Contribution to the Theory of Games*, volume II, ed. H. W. Kuhn and A. W. Tucker. Princeton University Press.

Stigler, G. 1941. *Production and Distribution Theories*. Macmillan.

Wicksteed, P. H. 1894. *An Essay on the Co-ordination of the Laws of Distribution*. Macmillan. Reprinted as no. 12 in LSE Series of Reprints of Scarce Tracts in Economics and Political Science, 1932.

III OPTIMALITY AND EQUILIBRIUM WITH MISSING MARKETS

The Value of Money in a Finite-Horizon Economy: A Role for Banks

Pradeep Dubey and John Geanakoplos

Frank Hahn (1965), among others, has argued that it is difficult to prove, or even to justify, a positive price for fiat (i.e., paper) money in economic equilibrium. The problem is particularly serious when there are only a finite number of time periods. In the last period nobody will want to hold a positive amount of it, if its price is positive. Hence, if there is a positive supply of money, equilibrium requires its price to be zero in the last period. But then in the second-to-last period nobody will want to consume it, or hold it, since it brings no reward in the last period. Again its price must be zero if its supply is positive. Working backward to the beginning, it follows that the value of money is always zero if it is in positive supply, in a finite-horizon economy.

This argument is not affected by the stipulation that all trade must be conducted between goods and money, provided that preferences for commodities are strictly monotonic. If the world is expected to come to an end in exactly 1 billion years, then no trade can take place through money in all the intervening years, no matter how horrible the initial distribution of commodities.

There are at least four ways around these problems. One could postulate an infinite-horizon model, so that there is no last period. This was done by Samuelson (1958), who made the agents finitely-lived, and also by Grandmont and Younes (1973), who had infinitely-lived agents that faced a transactions constraint. Alternatively, one could model the present, leaving the future as part of exogenous expectations. As long as these expectations suppose positive prices of money (Grandmont and Younes 1972) in the future, no matter what the conditions today, or at least levels of prices that are not too much higher than those today (Hool 1976), money will have positive price in today's temporary equilibrium. Third, one could postulate the existence of an external agent who stands ready to trade commodities for money at prearranged prices. Finally, following Lerner (1947), one could postulate the existence of a government that is owed in taxes (payable only in money) an amount precisely equal to the cash balances of all the individuals. In the first two approaches, money has value in any period because it is a store of value, and will by hypothesis have value in the next period; in the last two approaches, money has value because an external agent gives something (either commodities or relief from taxes) in exchange for it. In the Lerner model the delicate balance of money and debt implies that the net supply of outside money is zero.

We propose to add another explanation for the value of money by introducing a competitive banking sector. The "banking sector" is endowed with fiat money and wishes only to get more money. Agents also have endowments of money that they own free and clear, with no offsetting debts to an outside government or bank. In contrast to the first two approaches to money, its value to the agents can be derived from its transaction role alone, quite apart from any store-of-value role it might also have. Moreover, unlike the external agent mentioned in the last two approaches above, the banking sector does not have anything to offer in exchange for money. It does, however, have the power to lend money to voluntary borrowers, and to enforce the collection of the ensuing debts.

Consider an Arrow-Debreu economy in which there is some commodity that every agent has in positive supply. Suppose that one of the agents is endowed only in this good and cares only about consumption of this one good (in which he is never satiated), and that the rest have no utility for the good. Curiously, there can be no Arrow-Debreu equilibrium. If the good has positive price, then the first agent will demand exactly his endowment and the others nothing, so supply will exceed demand. If the price is zero, the first agent will demand an infinite amount of it, and so demand will exceed supply. If we think of the first agent as the banking sector, and the privileged commodity as fiat money, then we see that adding the banking sector to the standard general-equilibrium model can create still more problems: instead of getting an equilibrium in which money has a price of zero, we get an economy with no equilibrium at all!

Our model is therefore further enriched by postulating a cash-in-advance constraint along the lines of Clower 1965. All trades of commodities must be in exchange for money. Agents who wish to spend more than their endowments of cash can borrow money from the banking sector, at some endogenously determined interest rate. They repay the bank out of the cash receipts from the sale of goods. The banking sector is endowed with an exogenously fixed stock of money, M. In equilibrium, which exists under quite general conditions, the demand for money is equal to M, and the value of money is positive. By adding a banking sector and a cash-in-advance constraint to the traditional general-equilibrium model, we are able to show what neither modification alone can generate: that money has value because of its transactions role.

The crucial idea behind our analysis is that agents, who do not initially owe the bank anything, are driven by their own optimizing behavior to borrow and incur debts until their endowments are owed to the bank. More precisely, the money market for cash borrowing will clear only when the interest rate reaches at least a level θ so high that the money owed back to the bank, $(1 + \theta)M$, is at least equal to the sum $M + \sum_{\alpha \in H} m^{\alpha}$ of bank money and the private endowments $\{m^{\alpha}\}_{\alpha \in H}$ of fiat money owned by the agents. Although the result is superficially similar to the Lerner model, in that all outside money is finally owed to an external agency, each agent in our model begins with outside money, which he considers real wealth. There is no artificial requirement that the stock of money precisely balance government taxes.

When $\sum_{\alpha \in H} m^{\alpha} > 0$, the set of monetary equilibria is determinate; i.e., there are (generically) only a finite number of equilibria. Supply and demand determine not only the relative prices but also the level of prices and the interest rate. As $M/\sum_{\alpha \in H} m^{\alpha} \to \infty$, the interest rate goes to 0, and the monetary equilibrium commodity allocations converge to the Arrow-Debreu equilibrium allocations of the underlying nonmonetary economy.

Our existence theorem for monetary equilibrium provides a completely new proof of the existence of Arrow-Debreu equilibrium, by taking the limit as $M \to \infty$ (see Dubey and Geanakoplos 1989b). When $\sum_{\alpha \in H} m^{\alpha} = 0$, and agents honor all their debts, the price level is indeterminate, but all monetary equilibrium allocations are Arrow-Debreu allocations.

By contrast, in the Lerner model, the monetary equilibrium commodity allocations are always indeterminate. (See Balasko and Shell 1983.) Adding a cash-in-advance constraint implies that are also disjoint from the Arrow-Debreu commodity allocations.

In our model the banking sector "earns" a positive rate of interest on worthless paper by exploiting the agents' need to transact through money. If one thinks of the banking sector as a central bank, then it is easy to see that the bank could acquire real commodities in exchange for printed paper (exactly the opposite flow envisaged in the third approach to monetary equilibrium mentioned above, in which the government gives goods for money). Even when the banking sector is content to acquire only paper, its gains still cause a deadweight loss for the agents on account of the interest rate. Since a positive interest rate puts a wedge between buying and selling prices, it inhibits trade unless the gains to be made are sufficiently large. We are thus led to introduce a measure $\gamma^*(x)$ for the available gains to trade at any allocation x, which may be of some value in its own right. Our existence theorem for monetary equilibrium (which implies a positive price for money) depends on the hypothesis that the gains to trade $\gamma^*(e)$ at the initial endowment e exceed $\sum_{\alpha \in H} m^\alpha / M$.

Our model displays some of the rudimentary properties of a full-fledged monetary economy when the private stocks of money are positive. Injections of bank money are not neutral. They tend to cause inflation, but to lower the interest rate. On the other hand, gifts of fiat money to agents also cause inflation, but raise the interest rate. The former injections are analogous to open-market operations and the latter to fiscal policy. In this simple model, injections of bank money tend to push the economy toward the Pareto frontier, but the resulting inflation may make agents with large endowments of fiat money worse off. As Friedman (1969) and Bewley (1980) suggested, albeit in different contexts, monetary equilibria for economies with $\sum_{\alpha \in H} m^\alpha > 0$ become efficient only when $M \to \infty$ and $\theta \to 0$. When $\sum_{\alpha \in H} m^\alpha = 0$, changes in the stock of bank money M are neutral. But the moment $\sum m^\alpha$ exceeds zero, equilibrium price levels become determinate, and money is no longer neutral, as explained above (except, of course, with respect to the joint scaling up of bank money and private endowments, which is tantamount to changing dollars into cents).

A more realistic model of a monetary economy would involve many possible periods of trade, and uncertainty. Money as a durable good would then have a store-of-value role as well as a transactions role to play. If there were other assets in the economy, money would have to compete with them in each agent's portfolio, and we could speak of the speculative demand for money. If we added production to the model, we could examine the effects of increasing the stock of money on firms' output. And if we further allowed for durable goods other than money, we could discuss the velocity of money as well. (None of these features is present in the current work; the interested reader is referred to Dubey and Geanakoplos 1989a and 1989c.)

Shubik and Wilson (1977) first introduced a banking sector into a general-equilibrium model. They computed the equilibrium in an example, but did not give a general statement or proof of the existence of equilibrium. Nor did they note the possibility that money would have positive value even if the stock of privately held money was positive. They did, however, introduce bankruptcy penalties to represent the idea that the banking sector might only imperfectly be able to enforce the repayment of its loans. In their formulation, an agent suffered a loss of utility proportional to the number of dollars of his unpaid bank loan.

We investigate the existence of equilibrium when there are finite bankruptcy penalties. If the penalties are sufficiently high, then bankruptcy will not occur, and we are back in the situation described above. For lower penalty rates, bankruptcy must occur in equilibrium. Yet we are able to show that, no matter what level of penalty rates, so long as the rate is multiplied by the number of dollars owed, a monetary equilibrium will exist, given the above condition on gains to trade. Some agents will fail to repay the banks, but the equilibrium interest rate will be so high that the banking sector will recover the same amount of money in the aggregate as it did when there was no chance of default. The interpretation we make of the banking sector is that banks have no information about the reliability of particular customers and so stand ready to lend as much as is desired (up to their total holdings) to any customer at the going rate of interest. In the regime of low penalties, with bankruptcies occurring in equilibrium, scaling both the stock of bank money and the private endowments of money will have non-neutral effects (as has been noted by Shubik and Wilson) when the penalty rates are multiplied by the nominal debts.

We also consider real penalties, where the punishment depends on the size of the unpaid debt deflated by some price index. Here we find that there is a minimum threshold to the harshness of the penalty that is necessary to maintain the integrity of the banking system and the value of money. This threshold level is, however, low enough so that there can be considerable bankruptcy in equilibrium. Once we permit the harshness of the penalties to depend on the level of prices, it is only natural to extend the analysis to allow for them to depend on other macro variables, such as the volume of trade. We conclude by developing a much more general scheme for penalizing the nonpayment of debts and showing that the crucial property that must hold to guarantee the existence of monetary equilibrium, when there are sufficient gains to trade, is that the penalty becomes harsh as the volume of trade goes to zero.

1 The Economy with Fiat Money

Let $H = \{1, \ldots, h\}$ and $L = \{1, \ldots, \ell\}$ be the sets of agents and commodities, respectively. Thus, the commodity space may be viewed as $\mathbb{R}^L_+$, whose axes are indexed by the elements of L. Agent $\alpha \in H$ has initial endowment

$e^\alpha \in \mathbb{R}^L_+$ and utility function $u^\alpha: \mathbb{R}^L_+ \to \mathbb{R}$. We assume that

$$e^\alpha = (e^\alpha_1, \ldots, e^\alpha_\ell) \neq 0,$$

$$\sum_{\alpha \in H} e^\alpha \gg 0,$$

and, further, each u^α is concave and continuously differentiable (we assume smoothness throughout only for ease of exposition), and

$$D_j u^\alpha \equiv \frac{\partial u^\alpha}{\partial x_j} > 0 \quad \text{for } j \in L, \alpha \in H, x \in \mathbb{R}^L_+.$$

There is fiat money in the economy, and it is the stipulated medium of exchange. Let $M > 0$ be the supply of money at the bank, and let $m^\alpha \geq 0$ be the private endowment of money for $\alpha \in H$.

To describe the budget set and the optimization problem faced by an agent α, it will be handy to represent the sequence of events as a tree (see figure 1). Let $\theta \in (-1, \infty)$ and $p \in \mathbb{R}^L_{++}$, where θ is the money rate of interest and p_j is the price of $j \in L$ (quoted in terms of money). Both θ and p are taken by α as exogenously fixed.

At the start, α borrows $c^\alpha \in \mathbb{R}_+$ units of money from the bank. Thus, α owes $\mu^\alpha = (1 + \theta)c^\alpha$ to the bank. Next α trades in the L commodities, using money for purchases. The choices available to him at this point are then given by

$$\left\{(b^\alpha, q^\alpha) \in \mathbb{R}^L_+ \times \mathbb{R}^L_+ : q^\alpha_j \leq e^\alpha_j \text{ for } j \in L; \text{ and } \sum_{j \in L} b^\alpha_j \leq c^\alpha + m^\alpha \equiv \frac{\mu^\alpha}{1+\theta} + m^\alpha \right\}.$$

Here b^α_j is the money spent by α for purchase of commodity j, and q^α_j is the

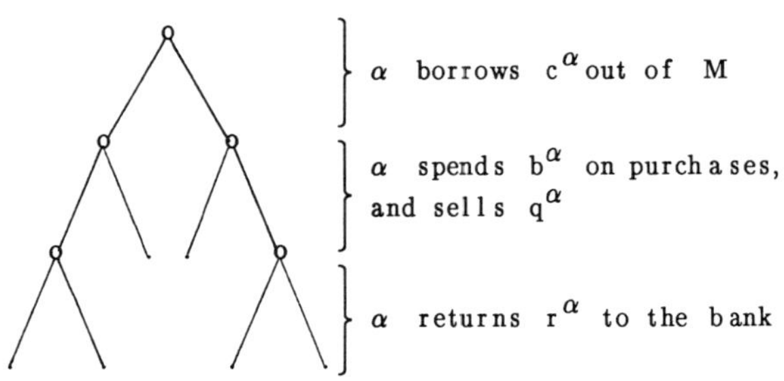

Figure 1

quantity of j that he puts up for sale. Thus, α winds up with the commodity bundle $x^\alpha \in \mathbb{R}^L_+$, where

$$x^\alpha_j = x^\alpha_j(b^\alpha,q^\alpha,p) = e^\alpha_j - q^\alpha_j + \frac{b^\alpha_j}{p_j} \tag{I}$$

for $j \in L$, and the amount of money

$$\bar{c}^\alpha = c^\alpha + m^\alpha - \sum_{j\in L} b^\alpha_j + \sum_{j\in L} p_j q^\alpha_j.$$

Finally α chooses to repay $r^\alpha \leq \bar{c}^\alpha$ on his loan. Consequently, his debt outstanding at the bank is

$$d^\alpha = d^\alpha(\mu^\alpha,r^\alpha) = \mu^\alpha - r^\alpha. \tag{II}$$

In summary, the *choice set* of agent α is

$$\Sigma^\alpha(\theta,p) = \Bigg\{(\mu^\alpha,b^\alpha,q^\alpha,r^\alpha) \in \mathbb{R}_+ \times \mathbb{R}^L_+ \times \mathbb{R}^L_+ \times \mathbb{R}_+ : q^\alpha_j \leq e^\alpha_j \text{ for } j \in L;$$

$$\sum_{j\in L} b^\alpha_j \leq \frac{\mu^\alpha}{1+\theta} + m^\alpha; r^\alpha \leq \frac{\mu^\alpha}{1+\theta} + m^\alpha - \sum_{j\in L} b^\alpha_j + \sum_{j\in L} p_j q^\alpha_j \Bigg\}.$$

The outcome functions x^α_j and d^α are continuous functions from

$$\Sigma^\alpha(\theta,p) \times \mathbb{R}^L_{++}$$

into $\mathbb{R}_+$, and for any fixed $(\theta,p) \in (-1,\infty) \times \mathbb{R}^L_{++}$ they are linear on $\Sigma^\alpha(\theta,p)$.

It may help to illustrate the attainable consumption bundles of α when $h = 2$ and $\ell = 2$ for fixed p and $\theta > 0$. (See dark lines in figure 2 and 3.)

Note that when $\theta = 0$, $m^\alpha = 0$, and α chooses to have $d^\alpha = 0$, figures 2 and 3 reduce to the classical Walrasian budget set.

Note also that, for any fixed (p,θ,d^α), the consumption set is convex if we allow free disposal.

We must now specify the utility U^α, to α, of the outcome (x^α,d^α). Were there no incentive to return money to the bank, the agent would always choose $r^\alpha = 0$ and b^α and d^α very large. Prices would be driven to infinity, and the value of money to zero. It almost goes without saying that, since agents are not rationed in borrowing from the bank, there must be some compulsion to return their loans if money is to have value. We model this

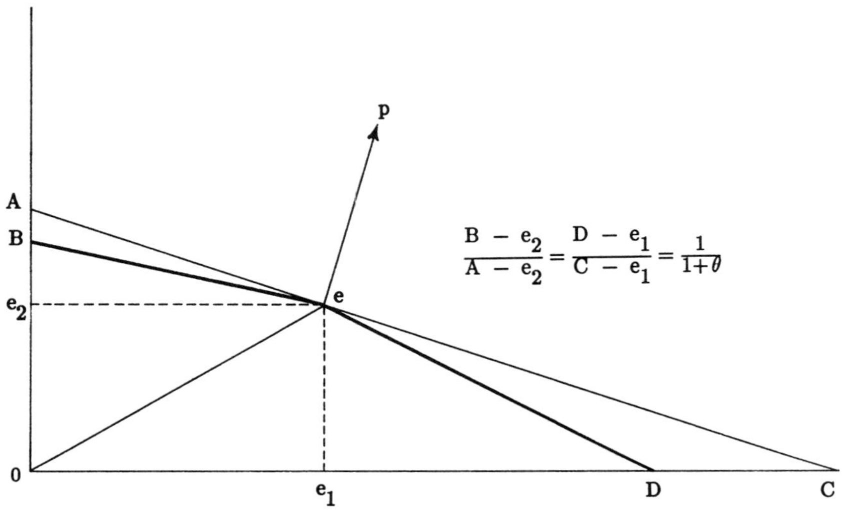

Figure 2
$(m^\alpha = 0, d^\alpha = 0.)$

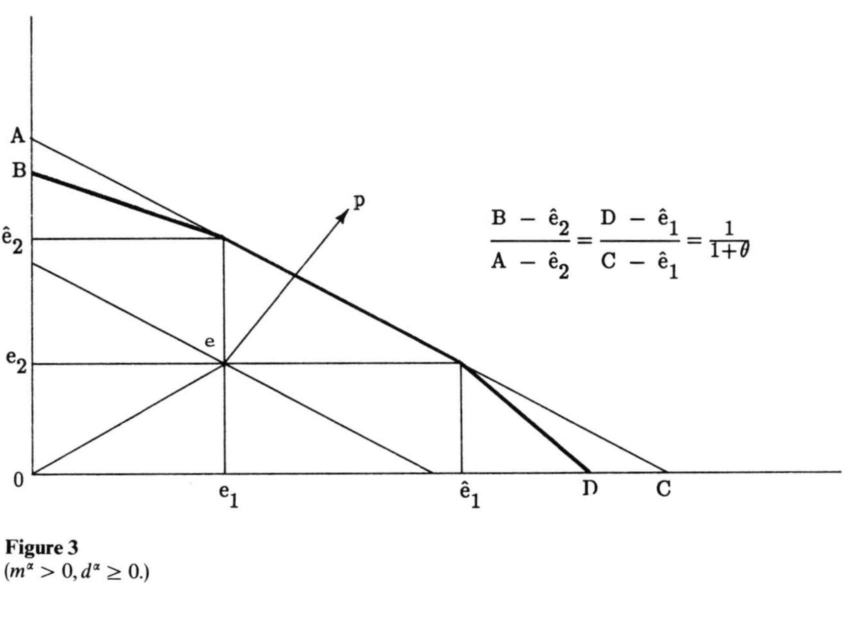

Figure 3
$(m^\alpha > 0, d^\alpha \geq 0.)$

through U^α, in terms of an "extra-economic penalty" that is levied on α when $d^\alpha > 0$, and that has the effect of reducing α's utility. The simplest form for U^α is

$$U^\alpha(x^\alpha,d^\alpha) = u^\alpha(x^\alpha) - \lambda^\alpha d^\alpha_+,$$

where $c_+ \equiv \max\{c,0\}$ for any real number c. (Note that, for fixed θ and p, U^α is a concave function of the outcome variables (x^α,d^α), which in turn are linear in the choice variables $(\mu^\alpha,b^\alpha,q^\alpha,r^\alpha)$.)

The function U^α incorporates a bankruptcy penalty via a flat rate λ^α. The penalty increases in harshness directly with the size of the debt. By thinking of λ^α as infinity, or a fixed constant, or a function of prices, we can describe many different kinds of bankruptcy laws.

Case 0: Infinite Penalties

If we imagine $\lambda^\alpha = \infty$, or indeed sufficiently large λ^α, agent α will never choose to go bankrupt, and his budget set Σ^α is effectively modified by the requirement that $d^\alpha = 0$, i.e., $r^\alpha = \mu^\alpha$. This may be reformulated as follows. Let

$$z = x^\alpha - e^\alpha \in \mathbb{R}^L$$

denote the net trade. Then the net trades available to α are

$$\left\{z \in \mathbb{R}^L\colon e^\alpha + z \geq 0,\ p\cdot z^+ + \frac{1}{1+\theta}p\cdot z^- \leq m^\alpha\right\},$$

where $z_j^+ \equiv \max\{0,z_j\}$ and $z_j^- \equiv \min\{0,z_j\}$.

When $\theta = 0$, this is the conventional Walrasian budget set. For $\theta > 0$, the available net trades are reduced. There is a "float loss" caused by the fact that purchases require the use of money. Since purchases and sales occur simultaneously, in markets where goods trade for money and not directly for each other, the money receipts from sales are obtained too late to be used directly for the purchases. This makes it necessary for α to borrow $(p\cdot z^+ - m^\alpha)_+$ from the bank. To avoid bankruptcy (i.e., to ensure $d^\alpha = 0$), α must choose

$$(1+\theta)(p\cdot z^+ - m^\alpha)_+ \leq -p\cdot z^-.$$

(See figures 2 and 3.)

Case I: Nominal Penalties

Let $\lambda^\alpha > 0$ be a fixed scalar. In this case agents may choose to go bankrupt (i.e., choose $d^\alpha > 0$), and they are punished by a utility loss proportional to the number of dollars they fail to return, regardless of the prevailing price levels. This is not fanciful. Historically, bankruptcy laws and penalties (such as the threshold above which a misdemeanor becomes a felony) have not quickly adjusted to inflation. Such nominal penalties were, as we said, first introduced by Shubik and Wilson (1977).

Case II: Real Penalties

Let $a \in \mathbb{R}^L_+$, $a \neq 0$, and

$$U^\alpha(x^\alpha, d^\alpha, p) \equiv u^\alpha(x^\alpha) - \frac{\lambda^\alpha}{p \cdot a} d^\alpha_+ .$$

Here we allow for bankruptcy penalties to adjust instantaneously to the price level. The vector $a \in \mathbb{R}^L_+ \setminus \{0\}$ serves as a "price deflator" with respect to which penalties are measured.

Case III: Endogenous Penalties

Once we have admitted the possibility that the penalty rates can depend on price levels, as in case II, it is only natural to consider penalties that depend on other macro-variables of the economy, such as interest rates, the total volume of trade, or the total volume of debt. To describe such penalties, let $A = \{(\theta, p, x) \in (-1, \infty) \times \mathbb{R}^L_+ \times (\mathbb{R}^L_+)^H\}$ denote the set of all interest rates, prices, and allocations, and let

$$\eta \colon A \to \Omega$$

be a map from A into a (Euclidean) signal space Ω. For each $\alpha \in H$, consider

$$\lambda^\alpha \colon (-1, \infty) \times \mathbb{R}^L_+ \times \Omega \to \mathbb{R}_{++}.$$

Both η and λ^α are assumed continuous. The term $\lambda^\alpha(\theta, p, \omega)$ is interpreted to be the penalty rate for α when interest rates θ and prices p prevail, and when other relevant macrovariables in the economy are according to ω. Thus, the utility to α is

$$U^\alpha(x^\alpha, d^\alpha, \theta, p, \omega) = u^\alpha(x^\alpha) - \lambda^\alpha(\theta, p, \omega) d^\alpha_+ .$$

One scenario that is of central importance in the current case occurs if penalty rates are harsh when the total volume of trade in the economy is close to zero, and progressively more lenient as the volume expands.

2 Monetary Equilibrium

We say that $\{\theta,p,y\}$, where $y = (y^1,\ldots,y^h)$ and $y^\alpha \in \mathbb{R}^L_+$ for $\alpha \in H$, is a *monetary equilibrium* (M.E.) if there exist $(\mu^\alpha,b^\alpha,q^\alpha,r^\alpha)_{\alpha \in H}$ such that

(i) for $\alpha \in H$,

(a) $(\mu^\alpha,b^\alpha,q^\alpha,r^\alpha) \in \underset{(\mu,b,q,r)\in\sum^\alpha(\theta,p)}{\text{Arg max}} \quad U^\alpha(x^\alpha(b,q,p), d^\alpha(\mu,r),\theta,p,\omega)$

(b) $y^\alpha = x^\alpha(b^\alpha,q^\alpha,p)$,

(ii) $\omega = \eta(\theta,p,y)$,

(iii) $\sum_{\alpha \in H} y^\alpha = \sum_{\alpha \in H} e^\alpha$,

(iv) $\sum_{\alpha \in H} \dfrac{\mu^\alpha}{1+\theta} = M.$

In other words, each agent optimizes (i), correctly anticipating the macro-variables ω (ii); commodity markets clear (iii); and the money market clears (iv).

By the very definition of an M.E. we guarantee that, if it exists, money will have positive value. (Commodity prices are not allowed to be infinite at an M.E.)

But the only role for fiat money in our model is to facilitate trade. When the endowments are Pareto optimal there are no gains to trade. In such a situation, money cannot be expected to have positive value, and M.E. will not exist.

Furthermore, the presence of money does not of itself make for frictionless trade. For instance, suppose the interest rate is positive. Then, as already discussed (see figures 2 and 3), a float loss is imposed which inhibits trade unless the gains to be made are sufficiently large.

It turns out that if the initial endowment of fiat money is positive, a positive interest rate is inevitable in any M.E. No agent will want to hold money at the end, since it is fiat and has no direct utility of consumption for him. Thus, all of M + $\sum_{\alpha \in H} m^\alpha$ will be returned to the bank at the end of trade. On the other hand, no agent will return more than he owes (otherwise he could spend further on purchases without going bankrupt, and improve his utility), so that at least $M + \sum_{\alpha \in H} m^\alpha$ is owed to the bank.

The upshot is that $\sum_{\alpha \in H} m^\alpha/M$ represents a "floor" on the money rate of interest, which is achieved precisely when all debts d^α are 0 for $\alpha \in H$.

3 A Measure of Gains from Trade

Positive endowments of money imply a positive money interest rate, and a positive money rate of interest inhibits trade. It follows that the question of sufficient gains to trade must arise in the analysis of existence of M.E. We now give a measure of the gains to trade available at any allocation $y \equiv (y^1, \ldots, y^h)$.

DEFINITION Given utilities $(u^\alpha)_{\alpha \in H}$ and $\gamma \in \mathbb{R}_+$, define the allocation $(y^1, \ldots, y^h)$ to be *γ-Pareto optimal* iff there do not exist feasible net trades $z^1, \ldots, z^h$ (i.e., $z^\alpha \in \mathbb{R}^L$, $y^\alpha + z^\alpha \in \mathbb{R}^L_+$ for all $\alpha \in H$; and $\sum_{\alpha \in H} z^\alpha = 0$) such that

$$u_j^\alpha(z) \equiv u^\alpha(y^\alpha + z^\alpha(\gamma)) \geq u^\alpha(y^\alpha)$$

for all $\alpha \in H$, with strict inequality for at least one α; where $z_j^\alpha(\gamma) = \min\{z_j^\alpha, z_j^\alpha/(1+\gamma)\}$ for $\alpha \in H, j \in L$. If $z_j^\alpha > 0$, then $z_j^\alpha(\gamma) < z_j^\alpha$, while $z_j^\alpha(\gamma) = z_j^\alpha$ for $z_j^\alpha < 0$. (Recall that positive (negative) components of z^α denote purchases (sales) by α.)

Figure 4 illustrates an allocation that is γ-Pareto optimal but not Pareto optimal.

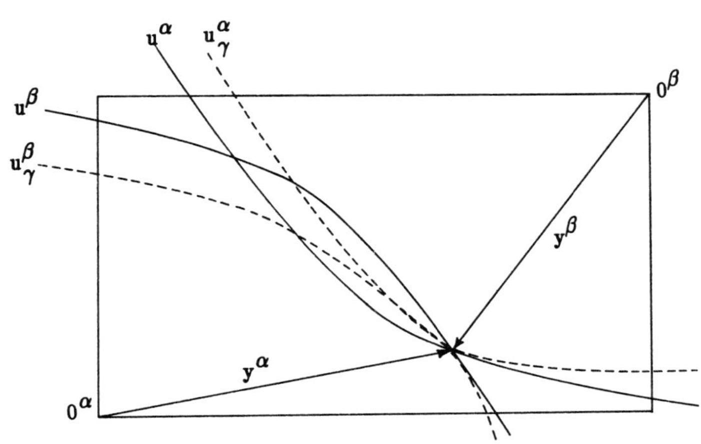

Figure 4

The indifference curve for u_j^α through y^α lies strictly inside the preferred set for u^α through y^α. Moreover, it has a kink at y^α.

Remark 1 If $(y^1,\dots,y^h)$ is not Pareto optimal, then for small enough $\gamma > 0$, $(y^1,\dots,y^h)$ is still not γ-Pareto optimal. On the other hand, for large enough γ, $(y^1,\dots,y^h)$ is γ-Pareto optimal. Note that for any allocation $y = (y^1,\dots,y^h)$ there is a minimum $\gamma^* \geq 0$ for which y is γ-Pareto optimal. *This $\gamma^* \equiv \gamma^*(y)$ can be thought of as a measure of how far y is from Pareto optimality.*

Remark 2 We could also define γ-Pareto optimality of $(y^1,\dots,y^h)$ by requiring that there are no feasible trades $(z^1,\dots,z^h)$ such that $u^\alpha(y^\alpha + z^\alpha(\gamma)) > u^\alpha(y^\alpha)$ for all $\alpha \in H$. By the usual arguments, this coincides with the other definition, since utilities are strictly monotonic.

Remark 3 The initial endowment allocation $e = (e^1,\dots,e^h)$ is γ-Pareto optimal if and only if there exists $p \gg 0$ such that for all $\alpha \in H$

$$0 \in \operatorname*{Arg\,max}_{z \in R^L} \{u^\alpha(e^\alpha + z(\gamma)) \colon e^\alpha + z \geq 0, p \cdot z \leq 0\}.$$

Equivalently,

$$0 \in \operatorname*{Arg\,max}_{z \in R^L} \{u^\alpha(e^\alpha + z)) \colon e^\alpha + z \geq 0, (1 + \theta) p \cdot z^+ + p \cdot z^- \leq 0\}.$$

To see why this is so, let

$$u_\gamma^\alpha(z) \equiv u^\alpha(e^\alpha + z(\gamma)) \text{ for } z \geq -e^\alpha.$$

Since the map from $z_j \to z_j(\gamma)$ is coordinate-wise concave, and u^α is strictly monotonic and concave, it follows that u_γ^α is concave. Moreover, it is trivial to check that u_γ^α is strictly monotonic. Remark 3 therefore follows from the standard first and second welfare theorems applied to the utilities u_γ^α.

4 The Existence of Monetary Equilibrium with Nominal or Real Penalties

The crucial condition we place on the economy is the following:

(CI) The initial endowment is not $\sum_{\alpha \in H} m^\alpha / M$-Pareto optimal; i.e., $\gamma^*(e) > \sum_{\alpha \in H} m^\alpha / M$.

Remark 4 If $\gamma = 0$, the notion of γ-Pareto optimality reduces to standard Pareto optimality. Thus, if the initial endowment of fiat money is zero (i.e., $m^\alpha = 0$ for $\alpha \in H$), then CI is tantamount to requiring that the initial endowment is not Pareto optimal.

Remark 5 It is evident that CI rules out the case where $\# L = 1$.

Our first result is now easily stated.

THEOREM 1 Consider case I with nominal penalties. Suppose condition CI holds. Then so long as $(\lambda^\alpha)_{\alpha \in H} \gg 0$, an M.E. exists.

To guarantee the existence of M.E. when the debts are measured in real terms, penalty rates cannot be allowed to be arbitrarily low. Let $Du^\alpha = (D_1 u^\alpha, \ldots, D_\ell u^\alpha)$ denote the gradient of u^α, and let $\cdot$ stand for dot product.

(CII) For $\alpha \in H$: $a_j > 0 \Rightarrow e_j^\alpha > 0$ for $j \in L$, and $(Du^\alpha(e^\alpha)) \cdot a < \lambda^\alpha$.

THEOREM 2 Consider case II with real penalties. Suppose conditions CI and CII hold. Then an M.E. exists.

THEOREM 3 Consider the case of either real or nominal penalties (case I, II). For all sufficiently large λ^α, no agent goes bankrupt at any M.E. In particular, equilibrium exists in case 0 of infinite λ^α under condition CI.

COROLLARY Let $m^\alpha = 0$ for $\alpha \in H$. For all sufficiently large λ^α, every M.E. yields Walrasian prices and allocations (in cases I and II, and obviously also in case 0).

Remark 6 An M.E. with nominal penalties can always be interpreted as an M.E. with real penalties suitably adjusted to reflect the price levels, and vice versa. However theorems 1 and 2 are not equivalent, since one must know the price levels to effect the transformation between nominal and real penalties, and the price levels are endogenous to the M.E.

5 General Bankruptcy Penalties

We could now turn to case III, which includes cases 0, I, and II, and develop the analogue of CII to ensure the existence of M.E. But in fact we have a still more general setup, of which the existence theorems 1 and 2 are corollaries. In addition to allowing for bankruptcy penalties that depend upon macrovariables, we no longer require that the penalty is linear or even separable from consumption.

Consider

$$U^\alpha: \mathbb{R}^L_+ \times \mathbb{R} \times (-1,\infty) \times \mathbb{R}^L_{++} \times \Omega \to R$$

and assume the following:

(i) U^α is continuous.

(ii) $U^\alpha(x^\alpha,d^\alpha,\theta,p,\omega)$ is concave in (x^α,d^α) for any fixed choice of θ, p, ω.

(iii) $U^\alpha(x^\alpha,d^\alpha,\theta,p,\omega) = u^\alpha(x^\alpha)$ if $d^\alpha \leq 0$.

(iv) (a) $\partial U^\alpha/\partial d^\alpha$ exists, is continuous, and is negative if $d^\alpha > 0$.

(b) $\dfrac{\partial U^\alpha}{\partial x_j}(x^\alpha,d^\alpha,\theta,p,\omega)$ exists, is continuous and positive; and

$$\sup\left\{\frac{\partial U^\alpha}{\partial x_j}(x^\alpha,d^\alpha,\theta,p,\omega)\text{: } j \in L,\ x^\alpha \text{ lies in a compact set, } d^\alpha \in \mathbb{R},\ \theta \in (-1,\infty),\ \omega \in \Omega\right\} < \infty,$$

and

$$\inf\left\{\frac{\partial U^\alpha}{\partial x_j}(x^\alpha,d^\alpha,\theta,p,\omega)\text{: } j \in L,\ x^\alpha \text{ lies in a compact set, } d^\alpha \in \mathbb{R},\ \theta \in (-1,\infty),\ \omega \in \Omega\right\} > 0.$$

(v) For any trader $\alpha \in H$, and any sequence $(x^\alpha(n), p(n))$ that is uniformly bounded, suppose that $(d^\alpha(n), \theta(n)) \to \infty$. Then

$$\liminf_n U^\alpha((x^\alpha(n), d^\alpha(n), \theta(n), p(n), \eta(\theta(n), p(n), x(n))) < u^\alpha(e^\alpha).$$

Conditions (i) and (ii) are technical. The remaining three conditions incorporate the essential properties of fiat money and bankruptcy penalties: fiat money has no direct utility of consumption (iii); unpaid bank debts are penalized and cause disutility (iv); if prices and consumptions stay bounded, then for sufficiently large debts and interest rates the bankruptcy penalties are harsh enough that an agent would prefer not to have traded at all (v).

This generalized setup clearly includes all the previous cases, without relying on the artificial separability between consumption and bankruptcy penalties. It might well be, for example, that the penalty represents a term in jail, and that could in turn affect the relative marginal utilities of consumption goods.

The analogue of condition CII in the general setting is as follows. Let

$$\lambda^{\alpha}(p) = \inf\left\{\left|\frac{\partial U^{\alpha}}{\partial d^{\alpha}}(e^{\alpha}, d^{\alpha}, \theta, p, \eta(\theta,p,e))\right| : d^{\alpha} > 0, \theta \geq 0\right\}$$

and

$$\nu^{\alpha}(p) = \sup_{d^{\alpha},\theta} \inf_{a} \left\{ \frac{\left(\frac{\partial U^{\alpha}}{\partial x}(e^{\alpha}, d^{\alpha}, \theta, p, \eta(\theta,p,e))\right)\cdot a}{p\cdot a} : a \in \mathbb{R}^{L}_{+}\setminus\{0\}, \; a \leq e^{\alpha}, d^{\alpha} > 0 \text{ and } \theta \geq 0 \right\}.$$

Then require, for every sequence $p \to \infty$,

$$\text{(CIII)} \quad \limsup_{p\to\infty} \frac{\lambda^{\alpha}(p)}{\nu^{\alpha}(p)} > 1.$$

Note that $\lambda^{\alpha}(p)$ is the minimum utility loss to α if he owes a dollar to the bank and goes bankrupt (when no trade is taking place in the economy). On the other hand, $\nu^{\alpha}(p)$ is the utility loss to α if he raises a dollar by forgoing consumption (and making sales) at his initial endowment. Thus, condition (CIII) states that if

$p_j \to \infty$ for all $j \in L$

and

$x^{\alpha} \to e^{\alpha}$ for all $\alpha \in H$,

then the marginal disutility of a dollar's unpaid debt > the marginal disutility of a dollar's credit (taken out of consumption) for each $\alpha \in H$.

THEOREM 4 Consider the case of general penalties. Suppose conditions CI and CIII hold. Then an M.E. exists.

Remark 7 (Neutrality of Money) If we double M and each m^{α}, then clearly the M.E. remain unaffected in the case of real penalties, except that all prices are also doubled. This happens in the nominal case as well, except that it is now also necessary to halve the penalty rates λ^{α} (unless the λ^{α} were sufficiently high to have ruled out bankruptcy in the first place). These changes are analogous to a change in units, and it would be surprising indeed if a switch from dollars to cents caused rational agents to behave differently. But it is worth reiterating that even such a change in units will be non-neutral if the "courts" are not directed (in the nominal case) to suitably adjust the bankruptcy laws (i.e., the λ^α).

Remark 8 (Non-Neutrality of Money) Suppose the penalities are harsh enough to rule out bankruptcy (in accordance with theorem 3)—indeed, take $\lambda^\alpha = \infty$ for all α—and that $\sum_{\alpha \in H} m^\alpha > 0$. Then the interest rate is $\sum_{\alpha \in H} m^\alpha / M$ at any M.E. Thus, an injection of bank money (with endowments of money held fixed) will lower the interest rate, while gifts of fiat money to agents (hold the supply of bank money fixed) will raise it. In either case there will be inflation and the M.E. allocation of commodities will be affected.

When there is bankruptcy, the effect of injections of bank money or private endowments will be non-neutral, and the effects on the interest rates and inflation will tend to be in the direction specified above, but not necessarily always.

Remark 9 (Dropping the Gains-from-Trade Hypothesis) Consider an economy for which the initial endowment is not Pareto optimal. As $M \to \infty$,

$$\sum_{\alpha \in H} m^\alpha / M \to 0$$

and we reach a level M^* such that condition CI holds automatically for all $M \geq M^*$, ensuring (by theorems 1, 2, and 4) the existence of an M.E. (given, of course, condition CII or CIII for real or general penalties).

More generally, let us fix utilities and the m^α and suppose that endowments vary in some hypercube in $(\mathbb{R}_+^L)^H$. Then the "volume" of economies for which condition CI fails (and hence, possibly, M.E. also fail to exist) will go to 0 as $M \to \infty$.

Remark 10 (M.E. vs. Walrasian Equilibria) Suppose throughout there is no bankruptcy (e.g., $\lambda^\alpha = \infty$). If $\sum_{\alpha \in H} m^\alpha = 0$, then the interest rate $\theta = 0$, and it is immediate that the M.E. prices and allocations are Walrasian. If $\sum_{\alpha \in H} m^\alpha > 0$, then $\theta = \sum m^\alpha / M \to 0$ as $M \to \infty$. It follows that the wedge between buying and selling prices approaches zero, and the M.E. outcomes converge to Walrasian. (Indeed, if we specialize to the nominal case, then, as $M \to \infty$, bankruptcies will disappear even if the penalties were not harsh enough to begin with, and Walrasian outcomes will occur in the limit.) Thus, our existence theorem for M.E. provides an alternative proof of the existence of Walras equilibrium (see Dubey and Geanakoplos 1989b).

Remark 11 (Distinction of M.E. from Walras Equilibria) We have already seen that when $\sum_{\alpha \in H} m^\alpha > 0$, the interest rate $\theta > 0$ and then the M.E. outcomes are not Walrasian.

Let $\sum_{\alpha \in H} m^\alpha = 0$. At any Walras equilibrium there is an implicit penalty rate for each agent, given by his "marginal utility of income" (with $p \cdot a \equiv$ one unit of income). Thus, if we choose $\eta(\theta,p,x) \equiv \eta(x)$ and each $\lambda^\alpha(d^\alpha, p, \eta(x))$ strictly smaller than these implicit rates, as (p,x) ranges over all Walras equilibria, no M.E. (in the case of real penalties) will be Walrasian. Thus, our model provides a new type of equilibrium, distinct from the Walrasian, in which liquidity constraints come to the fore. (Of course, under the conditions given in remark 10, we get Walras equilibrium as a special case of M.E.)

6 Determinacy of M.E. and the Value of Money

Let $\lambda^\alpha = \infty$ for $\alpha \in H$, and $\sum_{\alpha \in H} m^\alpha = 0$. As we saw, the M.E. are Walrasian; but it is equally clear that there is great indeterminacy of the commodity price levels: they can be scaled down arbitrarily (with agents hoarding increasing amounts of bank money M) without disturbing the M.E.

But the moment $\sum_{\alpha \in H} m^\alpha > 0$ we must have $\theta = \sum_{\alpha \in H} m^\alpha / M > 0$. Consequently there is no hoarding and the above indeterminacy abruptly disappears. In particular, the value of money (given by the price levels) is determinate.

We can state this intuition formally as follows. Let $\mathscr{U}$ be a finite-dimensional vector space of infinitely differentiable utilities which satisfies the property that if $c \in \mathbb{R}^L$ is small enough, and $u \in \mathscr{U}$, then $v \in \mathscr{U}$, where v is defined by $v(x) \equiv u(x) + c \cdot x$.

THEOREM 5 For an open, dense, and full measure set $\mathscr{E}$ of vectors

$$E = (M, (\lambda^\alpha, e^\alpha, m^\alpha, u^\alpha)_{\alpha \in H}) \in \mathbb{R}_{++} \times (\mathbb{R}_{++} \times \mathbb{R}^L_{++} \times \mathbb{R}_{++} \times \mathscr{U})^H,$$

the set of M.E. for the economy defined by E is finite in number, where λ^α refers to either real or nominal bankruptcy penalties.

Remark 12 This theorem applies whether or not there is bankruptcy.

7 Exogenous Debts

We can extend our model to allow for the possibility that agents have exogenous debts to the bank, on account of unpaid loans from the past (which have been rolled over into the current period). Let Δ^α denote such a debt of $\alpha \in H$. If Δ^α is positive, then this means that α owes Δ^α to the bank; if it is negative, the bank owes $-\Delta^\alpha$ to α. (In the interpretation, agents may owe each other money, with the banking sector acting like a "clearing house" through which all debts are channeled.)

Define M.E. exactly as before, with one amendment: d^α is replaced by $d^\alpha + \Delta^\alpha$ throughout, in the argument of U^α, for all $\alpha \in H$. Thus, the payment of Δ^α is called for at the end of trade, and the current debt d^α (incurred in trade) is adjusted by the exogenous debt Δ^α, to arrive at the net final debt $(d^\alpha + \Delta^\alpha)_+$ of α to the bank.

We extend the gains-from-trade hypothesis (CI) to allow for debts:

(CI*) The initial endowment is not

$$\left(\frac{\sum_{\alpha \in H} m^\alpha - \sum_{\alpha \in H} \Delta^\alpha}{M}\right)_+ \text{-Pareto optimal,}$$

i.e.,

$$\gamma^*(e) > \left(\frac{\sum_{\alpha \in H} m^\alpha - \sum_{\alpha \in H} \Delta^\alpha}{M}\right)_+ .$$

THEOREM 6 Consider the case of general penalties. Suppose conditions CI* and CIII hold, and furthermore

$$\sum_{\alpha \in H} m^\alpha - \sum_{\alpha \in H} \Delta^\alpha \geq 0.$$

Then an M.E. exists. Moreover, if penalties are nominal or real (cases II and III), then for large enough $(\lambda^\alpha)_{\alpha \in H}$ there is no bankruptcy at any M.E.

With nominal penalties, existence is guaranteed no matter how large, or what the sign, of the Δ^α.

THEOREM 7 If penalties are nominal and CI* holds, then for any $\{\Delta^\alpha\}_{\alpha \in H}$ an M.E. exists.

Theorem 7 holds without the artificial assumption of separability between consumption and penalties. We now define general nominal penalties, and then restate the theorem.

DEFINITION $U^\alpha(x^\alpha, d^\alpha, \theta, p, \omega)$ corresponds to *general nominal penalties* if, in place of conditions iva and v of general penalties, we assume that for $x^\alpha \leq \sum_{\beta \in H} e^\beta$ and any θ, p, ω,

(i)** there exists $\bar{c} > 0$ such that, for $d^\alpha + \Delta^\alpha > 0$,

$$\text{(a)} \quad -\frac{\partial U^\alpha}{\partial d^\alpha}(x^\alpha, d^\alpha + \Delta^\alpha, \theta, p, \omega) < \bar{c}$$

$$\text{(b)} \quad -\frac{\partial U^\alpha}{\partial d^\alpha}(e^\alpha, d^\alpha + \Delta^\alpha, \theta, p, \eta(\theta, p, e)) > 1/\bar{c}.$$

(ii)** there exists $\bar{D} > 0$ such that, for $d^\alpha > \bar{D}$,

$$U^\alpha(x^\alpha, d^\alpha + \Delta^\alpha, \theta, p, \omega) < U^\alpha(e^\alpha, \Delta^\alpha, \theta, p, \omega).$$

THEOREM 8 Consider the case of general *nominal* penalties. Suppose condition CI* holds. Then, for any $\{\Delta^\alpha\}_{\alpha \in H}$ an M.E. exists.

8 Proofs

Proof of Theorem 4 For any $\varepsilon > 0$, we construct an extensive game Γ^ε, with a continuum of players, that is partitioned into h types. An M.E. is then obtained as a limit of plays of type-symmetric strategic equilibria of Γ^ε, $\varepsilon \to 0$.

The set of players is the interval $[0, h)$ equipped with the Lebesgue measure, and for $t \in [\alpha - 1, \alpha)$ we have

$$e^t = e^\alpha, \quad m^t = m^\alpha, \quad U^t = U^\alpha,$$

where $1 \leq \alpha \leq h$. At the start, all $t \in [0, h)$ simultaneously send an "I.O.U. note" $\mu^t \in [\varepsilon, 1/\varepsilon]$ to the bank. The interest rate θ forms according to the rule

$$1 + \theta = \frac{\int_0^h \mu^t \, dt}{M}, \tag{1}$$

and t obtains

$$c^t = \frac{\mu^t}{1 + \theta} \tag{2}$$

units of bank money. In the second stage of the game, all $t \in [0,h)$ simultaneously choose $(b^t,q^t) \in \mathbb{R}_+^L \times \mathbb{R}_+^L$ subject to the constraints

$$\sum_{j \in L} b_j^t \leq \varepsilon + m^t + c^t \tag{3}$$

and

$$q_j^t \leq e_j^t. \tag{4}$$

Here b_j^t is the money sent by t for purchase of commodity j, and q_j^t is the quantity of j put up by him for sale. In the final stage of the game, each $t \in [0,h)$ returns all the money he has to the bank, which is optimal for him since money yields no utility. For each $j \in L$, the price p_j is formed by

$$p_j = \frac{\varepsilon + \int_0^h b_j^t \, dt}{\varepsilon + \int_0^h q_j^t \, dt} \tag{5}$$

and t obtains the final bundle $x^t \in \mathbb{R}_+^L$, and the debt d^t, as given by the right-hand sides of equations (I) and (II) in section 1 (after substituting t for α, and $\varepsilon + m^t$ for m^α, and the money t has on hand after trade for r^α); i.e.,

$$x_j^t = e_j^t - q_j^t + \frac{b_j^t}{p_j} \text{ for } j \in L, \tag{6}$$

$$d^t = \mu^t - \left(c^t + m^t + \varepsilon - \sum_{j \in L} b_j^t + \sum_{j \in L} p_j q_j^t\right). \tag{7}$$

The payoff to t is then

$$U^t(x^t,d^t,\theta,p,\omega),$$

where

$$\omega = \eta\left(\theta, p, \int_0^1 x^t \, dt, \ldots, \int_{h-1}^h x^t \, dt\right).$$

Finally, assume that at the end of stage 1 each t observes the interest rate θ. This completes the description of the extensive game Γ^ε.

A strategic equilibrium (S.E.) is a choice of strategies by all the players in $[0,h)$ such that no player can improve his payoff by a unilateral change of strategy. It is called type-symmetric (and denoted T.S.S.E.) if, for each $\alpha \in H$, all $t \in [\alpha - 1, \alpha)$ choose the same strategy.

Note that in the game Γ^ε the effect of the "ε-perturbation" is threefold:

(a) Each player has an extra endowment ε of fiat money.

(b) Each player is constrained to keep his I.O.U. note within the range $[\varepsilon, 1/\varepsilon]$.

(c) In each commodity market, an "external agency" supplies ε units of money and ε units of the commodity.

CLAIM 1 A T.S.S.E. exists in Γ^ε for any $\varepsilon > 0$.

Proof Each $t \in [0,h)$ chooses $\mu^t \leq 1/\varepsilon$, and θ forms as in (1), so we must have

$$\frac{h\varepsilon}{M} \leq 1 + \theta \leq \frac{h/\varepsilon}{M}.$$

So consider a "generalized game" in which each $t \in [\alpha - 1, \alpha)$ has the *ambient* strategy set

$$\sum\nolimits^\alpha = \left\{ (\mu^\alpha, b^\alpha, q^\alpha) \in \mathbb{R}_+ \times \mathbb{R}_+^L \times \mathbb{R}_+^L : \varepsilon \leq \mu^\alpha \leq \frac{1}{\varepsilon}, q^\alpha \leq e^\alpha, \right.$$
$$\left. \sum_{j \in L} b_j^\alpha \leq \varepsilon + m^\alpha + \frac{\mu^\alpha}{h\varepsilon/M} \right\},$$

which is compact and convex. For a *type-symmetric* choice

$$\sigma = (\sigma^1, \ldots, \sigma^h) \in \Sigma^1 \times \cdots \times \Sigma^h$$

by the players in $[0,h]$, where $\sigma^\alpha = (\mu^\alpha, b^\alpha, q^\alpha)$, the formulas for θ, p, etc. simplify to the following:

$$1 + \theta(\sigma) = \frac{\sum_{\alpha \in H} \mu^\alpha}{M},$$

$$p_j(\sigma) = \frac{\varepsilon + \sum_{\alpha \in H} b_j^\alpha}{\varepsilon + \sum_{\alpha \in H} q_j^\alpha}, \quad j \in L$$

$$x_j^\alpha(\sigma) = e_j^\alpha - q_j^\alpha + \frac{b_j^\alpha}{p_j(\sigma)}, \quad j \in L \text{ and } \alpha \in H$$

$$\eta(\sigma) = \eta(\theta(\sigma), p(\sigma), x^1(\sigma), \ldots, x^h(\sigma)).$$

Note that θ, p, and η are continuous functions of σ. Also, for $\sigma \in \Sigma^1 \times \cdots \times \Sigma^h$ and $\alpha \in H$, define

$$\Sigma^\alpha(\sigma) = \left\{(\mu^\alpha, b^\alpha, q^\alpha) \in \Sigma^\alpha \colon \sum_{j \in L} b_j^\alpha \leq \varepsilon + m^\alpha + \frac{\mu^\alpha}{1 + \theta(\sigma)}\right\}$$

to be the *feasible* strategy set of $t \in [\alpha - 1, \alpha)$ when all others choose strategies according to σ. Since, as already remarked,

$$1 + \theta(\sigma) \geq h\varepsilon/M \text{ for } \sigma \in \Sigma^1 \times \cdots \times \Sigma^h,$$

we have

$$\Sigma^\alpha(\sigma) \subset \Sigma^\alpha$$

for all such σ. It is also clear that $\Sigma^\alpha(\sigma)$ is compact and convex, and continuous in σ. Now define

$$\tilde{\Sigma}^\alpha(\sigma) = \operatorname*{Arg\,max}_{\tau \in \Sigma^\alpha(\sigma)} U^\alpha(x(\tau,\sigma), d(\tau,\sigma), \theta(\sigma), p(\sigma), \eta(\sigma)),$$

where, with $\tau \equiv (\mu, b, q)$, we mean

$$x_j(\tau,\sigma) = e_j^\alpha - q_j + \frac{b_j}{p_j(\sigma)} \quad \text{for } j \in L,$$

$$d(\tau,\sigma) = \mu - \left(\varepsilon + m^\alpha + \frac{\mu}{1 + \theta(\sigma)} - \sum_{j \in L} b_j + \sum_{j \in L} p_j(\sigma) q_j\right).$$

In other words, $\tilde{\Sigma}^\alpha(\sigma)$ is the best-response set of $t \in [\alpha - 1, \alpha)$, when others make the (type-symmetric) choice of σ, so that t now faces *fixed* $\theta(\sigma)$, $p(\sigma)$, and $\eta(\sigma)$. The map

$$\tau \mapsto U^\alpha(x(\tau,\sigma), d(\tau,\sigma), \theta(\sigma), p(\sigma), \eta(\sigma))$$

is continuous and concave by assumptions (i) and (ii) on U^α and the fact that $\tau \mapsto (x(\tau,\sigma), d(\tau,\sigma))$ is linear. We conclude that $\tilde{\Sigma}^\alpha(\sigma)$ is nonempty, compact and convex, and upper semi-continuous in σ.

Then the correspondence

$$\sigma \mapsto \tilde{\Sigma}^1(\sigma) \times \cdots \times \tilde{\Sigma}^h(\sigma),$$

satisfies all the conditions of Kakutani's fixed-point theorem. Any fixed point is easily seen to be a T.S.S.E. of our generalized game. Using these moves on the tree, and defining arbitrary but type-symmetric moves at other positions on the tree, we then obtain a T.S.S.E. of Γ^ε. This proves claim 1. ■

Let

$$\theta(\varepsilon), p(\varepsilon), x^1(\varepsilon), \ldots, x^h(\varepsilon), d^1(\varepsilon), \ldots, d^h(\varepsilon)$$

denote the outcome at a T.S.S.E. of Γ^ε in all steps below, and let $\mu^\alpha(\varepsilon)$, $b^\alpha(\varepsilon)$, and $q^\alpha(\varepsilon)$ denote the moves by players of type α along the T.S.S.E. play of the game.

CLAIM 2 $\theta(\varepsilon) \geq (h\varepsilon + \sum_{\alpha \in H} m^\alpha)/M > 0$ for sufficiently small ε.

Proof Choose ε small enough to ensure

$$\frac{1/\varepsilon}{M} > \frac{h\varepsilon + \sum_{\alpha \in H} m^\alpha + M}{M}.$$

If $\mu^\alpha(\varepsilon) = 1/\varepsilon$, for any α, then clearly the claim is true. So assume $\mu^\alpha(\varepsilon) < 1/\varepsilon$ for $\alpha \in H$ from now on.

Clearly at a T.S.S.E. no agent will end up with a negative debt; for if $-d^\alpha(\varepsilon) = K > 0$ then he could borrow an additional

$$0 < \frac{\Delta}{1 + \theta(\varepsilon)} < \frac{K}{1 + \theta(\varepsilon)}$$

from the bank (by raising $\mu^\alpha(\varepsilon)$ by Δ), use this money to buy any commodity he liked, and defray the loan by increasing $d^\alpha(\varepsilon)$ by Δ without incurring any default penalty. This improves his utility, a contradiction.

Since all the money in the system is returned to the bank, the total I.O.U. notes sent to the bank are at least

$$h\varepsilon + M + \sum_{\alpha \in H} m^\alpha,$$

proving Claim 2. ■

CLAIM 3 There is an $R > 0$ such that

$$\frac{p_i(\varepsilon)}{p_j(\varepsilon)} < R$$

for any $i \in L, j \in L$, and all sufficiently small ε.

Proof By claim 2, $\theta(\varepsilon) > 0$, and at least one agent type chooses $\mu^\alpha(\varepsilon) > \varepsilon$. We claim that no agent whose I.O.U. note exceeds ε will hoard the bank money that he borrowed (i.e., not spend it on purchases). Otherwise, let him reduce his I.O.U. note by δ and spend an extra $\delta\theta/(1 + \theta)$ on any good. His debt remains unchanged, but his consumption increases, so his utility goes up, a contradiction.

Clearly such agents (whose I.O.U. notes exceed ε) acquire at least $M - (h - 1)\varepsilon$ units of bank money (since $\theta(\varepsilon) > 0$). Choose ε small to ensure $M - (h - 1)\varepsilon > M/2$. Since they do not hoard, there is at least one commodity j^* with

$$p_{j^*}(\varepsilon) \geq \frac{M}{2\ell Q} \equiv \bar{Q} \text{ (say)},$$

where

$$Q = 1 + \max_{j \in L} \left\{ \sum_{\alpha \in H} e_j^\alpha \right\},$$

and we take $\varepsilon \leq 1$. (Q is the maximum offering of commodities, including the external agent's ε.) Let $I \subset L$ be the set of commodities that are being purchased by some agent in H, and let $J = L \backslash I$. Note that $j^* \in I$.

If $i \in I$, let α be a player-type that is purchasing i. Then we must have

$$\frac{D_i U(x^\alpha(\varepsilon), \ldots)}{D_k U(x^\alpha(\varepsilon), \ldots)} \geq \frac{p_i(\varepsilon)}{p_k(\varepsilon)}$$

for any $k \in L$. Otherwise, let $t \in [\alpha - 1, \alpha)$ spend Δ less on i and use Δ to purchase k; his gain in utility will be

$$D_k U^\alpha(x^\alpha(\varepsilon), \ldots)\frac{\Delta}{p_k} - D_i U^\alpha(x^\alpha(\varepsilon), \ldots)\frac{\Delta}{p_i} > 0,$$

a contradiction. Put

$$\tilde{Q} = \sup\left\{\frac{D_i U^\alpha(x, \ldots)}{D_k u^\alpha(x, \ldots)} : \alpha \in H, i \in L, k \in L, x_j \leq Q \text{ for } j \in L\right\}.$$

(Note that $\tilde{Q}$ is finite on account of condition (iv) (b) on the U^α.) We conclude that if $i \in I$ and $k \in L$,

$$\frac{p_i(\varepsilon)}{p_k(\varepsilon)} \leq \tilde{Q}.$$

Now take $i \in J$. Then

$$p_i(\varepsilon) = \frac{\varepsilon}{\varepsilon + \sum_{\alpha \in H} q_i^\alpha(\varepsilon)} \leq 1.$$

So for any $k \in L$,

$$\frac{p_i(\varepsilon)}{p_k(\varepsilon)} = \frac{p_i(\varepsilon)}{p_{j^*}(\varepsilon)} \cdot \frac{p_{j^*}(\varepsilon)}{p_k(\varepsilon)} \leq \frac{1}{\overline{\overline{Q}}} \cdot \tilde{Q}.$$

Take $R = \max\{\tilde{Q}, \tilde{Q}/\overline{\overline{Q}}\}$. ■

CLAIM 4 There is a $\underline{B} > 0$ such that $p_j(\varepsilon) > \underline{B}$ for $j \in L$ and sufficiently small ε.

Proof This follows from claim 3 and the fact (proved inside claim 3) that there is a $j^* \in L$ with

$$p_{j^*}(\varepsilon) \geq \frac{M}{2\ell\left(1 + \max_{j \in L}\left\{\sum_{\alpha \in H} e_j^\alpha\right\}\right)}.$$ ■

Consier a sequence of T.S.S.E. of Γ^ε as $\varepsilon \to 0$.

CASE A There exists a subsequence and a $\overline{B} > 0$ such that

$$p_j(\varepsilon) < \overline{B}$$

for all $j \in L$ and all ε.

CLAIM 5 In case A, there is a $\tilde{B}$ such that $\theta(\varepsilon) < \tilde{B}$ and $\mu^\alpha(\varepsilon) < \tilde{B}$ for $\alpha \in H$ and sufficiently small ε.

Proof Note that $\theta(\varepsilon) \to \infty$ if and only if there exists an $\alpha \in H$ such that $\mu^\alpha(\varepsilon) \to \infty$ on a further subsequence. If $\mu^\alpha(\varepsilon) \to \infty$, then

$$d^\alpha(\varepsilon) \geq \mu^\alpha(\varepsilon) - \left(M + \sum_{\alpha \in H} m^\alpha + h\varepsilon\right) \to \infty.$$

Then, by condition (v) on the U^α, $t \in [\alpha - 1, \alpha)$ would do better by not trading at all sufficiently far down in the sequence, a contradiction. ■

Thus, in case A we can select a subsequence so that

$$\mu^\alpha(\varepsilon), b^\alpha(\varepsilon), q^\alpha(\varepsilon) \to \mu^\alpha, b^\alpha, q^\alpha$$

for all $\alpha \in H$; moreover,

$p_j(\varepsilon) \to p_j$ for $j \in L$,

$\theta(\varepsilon) \to \theta$,

and

$x^\alpha(\varepsilon), d^\alpha(\varepsilon) \to x^\alpha, d^\alpha$ for $\alpha \in H$.

It is readily verified that the limit points yield an M.E. (Note that the constraint of $1/\varepsilon$ on μ^t is not binding since $\mu^\alpha < \tilde{B} < 1/\varepsilon$ for small enough ε. Then since $U^t \equiv U^\alpha$ is concave in μ^t, b^t, q^t for any *fixed* p, θ, ω, it follows that we could have dropped the $1/\varepsilon$ constraint altogether.)

CASE B Case A does not occur. Then, using claim 3, there is a subsequence such that $p_j(\varepsilon) \to \infty$ for all $j \in L$. But

$$p_j(\varepsilon) \le \frac{\varepsilon + \sum_{\alpha \in H} b_j^\alpha(\varepsilon)}{\varepsilon + \sum_{\alpha \in H} q_j^\alpha(\varepsilon)} \le \frac{\varepsilon + h\varepsilon + M + \sum_{\alpha \in H} m^\alpha}{\varepsilon + \sum_{\alpha \in H} q_j^\alpha(\varepsilon)}.$$

Hence, $\sum_{\alpha \in H} q_j^\alpha(\varepsilon) \to 0$ for $j \in L$, i.e., $q^\alpha(\varepsilon) \to 0$ for $\alpha \in H$. Then

$$x_j^\alpha(\varepsilon) = e_j^\alpha - q_j^\alpha(\varepsilon) + \frac{b_j^\alpha(\varepsilon)}{p_j(\varepsilon)} \to e_j^\alpha$$

for $\alpha \in H, j \in L$; i.e., $x^\alpha(\varepsilon) \to e^\alpha$ for $\alpha \in H$.

We break the analysis of case B into two subcases.

SUBCASE BI $\exists$ a type α and a subsequence of T.S.S.E. such that α goes bankrupt throughout the subsequence.

Then it must be that, for small enough ε,

$$\inf \left\{ \frac{\dfrac{\partial U}{\partial x}(x^\alpha(\varepsilon), d^\alpha(\varepsilon), \theta(\varepsilon), p(\varepsilon), \eta(\theta(\varepsilon), p(\varepsilon), x(\varepsilon))) \cdot a}{p(\varepsilon) \cdot a} : a \in \mathbb{R}_+^L \setminus \{0\}, a \le e^\alpha \right\}$$
$$\ge \left| \frac{\partial U^\alpha}{\partial d^\alpha}(x^\alpha(\varepsilon), d^\alpha(\varepsilon), \theta(\varepsilon), p(\varepsilon), \eta(\theta(\varepsilon), p(\varepsilon), x(\varepsilon))) \right|.$$

Otherwise (recalling that $x^\alpha(\varepsilon) \to e^\alpha$) any $t \equiv [\alpha - 1, \alpha)$ could choose $\tilde{a}(\varepsilon) \in \mathbb{R}_+^L \setminus \{0\}$, such that (i) $\tilde{a}(\varepsilon) < e^\alpha$ and (ii) for all $\Delta > 0$,

$$\Delta \frac{\dfrac{\partial U}{\partial x}(x^\alpha(\varepsilon), d^\alpha(\varepsilon), \theta(\varepsilon), p(\varepsilon), \eta(\theta(\varepsilon), p(\varepsilon), x(\varepsilon))) \cdot \tilde{a}(\varepsilon)}{p(\varepsilon) \cdot \tilde{a}(\varepsilon)}$$

$$< \Delta \left| \frac{\partial U^\alpha}{\partial d^\alpha}(x^\alpha(\varepsilon), \ldots, \eta(\theta(\varepsilon), p(\varepsilon), x(\varepsilon)) \right|.$$

But then t would sell the vector $\Delta \tilde{a}(\varepsilon)/p \cdot \tilde{a}(\varepsilon)$ of commodities and raise Δ units of money for defraying his unpaid bank loan. The loss in his payoff (for small Δ) is given by the LHS and the gain by the RHS, so that he can improve his payoff, a contradiction.

Let $\varepsilon \to 0$, and recall that $x^\alpha(\varepsilon) \to e^\alpha$ for all $\alpha \in H$. Taking limits on the inequality, we contradict condition CIII. So subcase BI cannot occur. This leaves us with subcase BII:

SUBCASE BII Subcase BI does not occur.

Then no one goes bankrupt throughout the sequence. This implies that

$$1 + \theta(\varepsilon) = \frac{h\varepsilon + M + \sum_{\alpha \in H} m^\alpha}{M}$$

for all ε, and hence

$$\theta(\varepsilon) \to \frac{\sum_{\alpha \in H} m^\alpha}{M} \equiv \tilde{\gamma}.$$

Now it is easy to check that $e = (e^1, \ldots, e^h)$ is $\tilde{\gamma}$-Pareto optimal, contradicting condition CI.

Indeed, note that by claim 3 relative prices are uniformly bounded; hence, there is some $p \gg 0$ such that on a subsequence

$p_i(\varepsilon)/p_j(\varepsilon) \to p_i/p_j$ for all $i, j \in L$.

But then, if $p(\varepsilon) \cdot z \leq 0$ and $z \geq -\frac{1}{2}e^\alpha$, we must have

$u^\alpha(x^\alpha(\varepsilon) + z(\theta(\varepsilon)) \leq u^\alpha(x^\alpha(\varepsilon))$

for small ε. Passing to the limit, we see that if $p \cdot z \leq 0$ then

$u^\alpha(e^\alpha + z(\tilde{\gamma})) \leq u^\alpha(e^\alpha)$,

recalling the notation

$$z_j(\gamma) = \min\left\{z_j, \frac{z_j}{1+\gamma}\right\}.$$

By remark 3, $(e^1,\ldots,e^h)$ is $\tilde{\gamma}$-Pareto optimal.

This eliminates case B altogether, leaving us with case A as the only viable one and concluding the proof of theorem 4. ■

Proof of Theorem 1 It is easily checked that if

$$U^\alpha(x^\alpha,d^\alpha,\theta,p,\omega) = u^\alpha(x^\alpha) - \lambda^\alpha d_+^\alpha$$

then assumptions (i), (ii), (iii), (iv), and (v) on U^α hold. Further,

$$\lambda^\alpha(p) = \lambda^\alpha.$$

Let $E = \max D_j u^\alpha(e^\alpha)$. Then, if $\sum_{j\in L} a_j = 1$,

$$\frac{Du^\alpha(e^\alpha)\cdot a}{p\cdot a} \leq \frac{E}{\min\limits_{j\in L} p_j}.$$

This implies that

$$v^\alpha(p) \leq \frac{E}{\min\limits_{j\in L} p_j}.$$

We conclude that

$$\frac{\lambda^\alpha(p)}{v^\alpha(p)} \geq \frac{\lambda^\alpha \min\limits_{j\in L} p_j}{E} \to \infty \quad \text{as } p \to \infty,$$

and so condition CIII holds. Then, by theorem 4, an M.E. exists in case II of nominal penalties. ■

Proof of Theorem 2 Here

$$U^\alpha(x^\alpha,d^\alpha,\theta,p,\omega) = u^\alpha(x^\alpha) - \frac{\lambda^\alpha}{p\cdot a} d_+^\alpha$$

and, once again, assumptions (i)–(v) of U^α are easily seen to hold. Here

$$\lambda^\alpha(p) = \frac{\lambda^\alpha}{p\cdot a}$$

and

$$v^\alpha(p) \leq \frac{(Du^\alpha(e^\alpha))\cdot a}{p\cdot a},$$

so

$$\frac{\lambda^\alpha(p)}{v^\alpha(p)} \geq \frac{\lambda^\alpha}{(Du^\alpha(e^\alpha))\cdot a} > 1$$

by condition CII. So condition CIII holds, and by theorem 4 an M.E. exists. ■

Proof of Theorem 3 First consider the case of real penalties, i.e.,

$$U^\alpha(x^\alpha,d^\alpha,p) \equiv u^\alpha(x^\alpha) - \frac{\lambda^\alpha d_+^\alpha}{p\cdot a}.$$

Let

$$Q^* = 1 + \max\left\{\frac{D_i u^\alpha(x)}{D_k u^\alpha(x)}: \alpha \in H, i \in L, k \in L, x \in \square\right\},$$

where

$$\square = \left\{x \in \mathbb{R}_+^L: x_j \leq 1 + \max_{j\in L} \sum_{\alpha\in H} e_j^\alpha\right\}.$$

Put

$$\hat{\lambda}^\alpha = \ell^2 Q^* \bar{a} \max\{D_j u^\alpha(x): j \in L, x \in \square\},$$

where

$$\bar{a} = \max_{i\in L} a_i.$$

It will be shown that if $\lambda^\alpha > \hat{\lambda}^\alpha$ for all $\alpha \in H$, there can be no bankruptcy at any M.E.

Suppose, to the contrary, that β is going bankrupt in such a situation. Let

$$L^* = \{j \in L: a_j > 0\},$$

$$J^* = \{j \in L: q_j^\beta < e_j^\beta\} \cap L^*,$$

$$K^* = L^* \backslash J^*.$$

Since, by assumption CII, $e_j^{\beta} > 0$ for $j \in L^*$, we see that there is positive trade in commodities in K^* (indeed, β has sold them); hence, there are buyers of K^*, and then (as was shown in the proof of claim 3)

(i)* $p_k \leq Q^* p_i$ for all $i \in L$, $k \in K^*$.

If $K^* = \phi$, let β sell εa (which is certainly feasible for him) and use the money to repay the bank. His loss in utility is

$$\varepsilon[Du^{\beta}(x^{\beta}) \cdot a] \leq \varepsilon\hat{\lambda}^{\beta}$$

and gain is

$$\frac{\varepsilon\lambda^{\beta} p \cdot a}{p \cdot a} = \varepsilon\lambda^{\beta}.$$

Since $\lambda^{\beta} > \hat{\lambda}^{\beta}$, α improves his payoff, a contradiction.

If $K^* \neq \phi$, then β has sold goods in K^* so he must have bought some good j. Let β buy $\varepsilon\ell Q^*\bar{a}$ less of good j, and sell εa_i of each good $i \in J^*$. Then the money available to β to repay the bank is

$$\text{(ii)*} \quad \varepsilon \sum_{i \in J^*} p_i a_i + \varepsilon p_j \ell Q^* \bar{a} \geq \varepsilon \sum_{i \in J^*} p_i a_i + \varepsilon \sum_{k \in K^*} p_k a_k$$
$$= \varepsilon p \cdot a.$$

(The inequality follows from (i)*.) His loss in utility is at most

$$\varepsilon\left[\sum_{i \in J^*} D_i u^{\beta}(x^{\beta}) a_i + D_j u^{\beta}(x^{\beta}) \ell Q^* \bar{a}\right] < \varepsilon\hat{\lambda}^{\beta},$$

and gain is at least (using (ii)*)

$$\frac{\varepsilon \cdot \lambda^{\beta} p \cdot a}{p \cdot a} = \varepsilon\lambda^{\beta},$$

again a contradiction, since $\lambda^{\beta} > \hat{\lambda}^{\beta}$.

This proves theorem 3 for real penalties. The proof for nominal penalties is even simpler. Note that there is bankruptcy $\Rightarrow \theta > 0 \Rightarrow$ there is no hoarding $\Rightarrow$ all of M is spent $\Rightarrow$

$$p_{j^*} \geq \frac{M}{\max_{j \in L} \sum_{\alpha \in H} e_j^{\alpha}} \equiv C \text{ (say)}$$

for some $j^* \in L \Rightarrow C \leq p_{j^*} \leq Q^* p_j$ for all $j \in L$. (The last implication follows, as in (i)*, from the proof of claim 3.) Thus, $p_j \leq C/Q^*$ for all $j \in L$.

Suppose β is going bankrupt. Then he must be purchasing some good j. Let him reduce his purchase by ε and return ε to the bank. His loss in utility is at most

$$\frac{\varepsilon D_j u^\beta(x^\beta)}{p_j} \leq \frac{\varepsilon D_j u^\beta(x^\beta) Q^*}{C}$$

and gain is at least $\varepsilon\lambda^\beta$. So if we take each

$$\lambda^\alpha > \frac{Q^*}{C} \max\{D_j u^\alpha(x^\alpha) \colon \alpha \in H,\, j \in L,\, x^\alpha \in \square\}$$

it is clear that no agent will go bankrupt. ∎

Proof of Theorem 5 (Sketch) At any M.E. $(\theta, p, (x^\alpha)_{\alpha \in H}) \gg 0$, the following conditions must hold. (We write out the conditions for nominal penalties.)

$$\sum_{\alpha \in H} (x^\alpha - e^\alpha) = 0; \tag{1}$$

$$\left.\begin{aligned} &\frac{\partial U^\alpha}{\partial x_j} - t_\alpha p_j (1 + \theta) = 0 \text{ if } \alpha \text{ buys } x_j \\ &\frac{\partial U}{\partial x_j} - t_\alpha p_j = 0 \text{ if } \alpha \text{ sells } x_j \end{aligned}\right\} \text{ if } \alpha \text{ borrows money,} \tag{2}$$

$x_j^\alpha - e_j = 0$ if α neither borrows nor sells j;

$$p \cdot (x^\alpha - e^\alpha)_+ (1 + \theta) + p \cdot (x^\alpha - e^\alpha)_- - (1 + \theta) m^\alpha - d^\alpha = 0 \text{ for all } \alpha \in H; \tag{3}$$

$d^\alpha = 0$ for all α that do not go bankrupt,

$$\frac{dU^\alpha}{\partial x_j} \frac{1}{p_j} - (1 + \theta)\lambda^\alpha = 0 \text{ for all } \alpha \text{ that do go bankrupt, if } \alpha \text{ is buying } j; \tag{4}$$

$$\sum_{\alpha \in H} p \cdot (x^\alpha - e^\alpha)_+ - \left(M + \sum_{\alpha \in H} m^\alpha\right) = 0. \tag{5}$$

Equation (1) simply says that all commodity markets clear; (2) and (4) reflect the fact that α has maximized U^α, where $t_\alpha \equiv$ marginal utility of money for α; (3) may be viewed as a definition of the debt d^α. If α does not borrow, then with $\theta > 0$, α spends exactly m^α, sells nothing, and

$$\frac{\partial U^\alpha}{\partial x_j} = t_\alpha p_j k$$

for goods j that α buys, where $1 \leq k \leq (1 + \theta)$. The variable k is new, but we also add a new equation $m^\alpha = p \cdot (x - e^\alpha)_+$.

The crucial equation is (5), which asserts that total expenditures are equal to the total stock of money. Note that this equality must hold when $\theta > 0$, since (as we have seen before) when $\theta > 0$ there can be no hoarding. An agent who has a dollar will always spend it, even if he has borrowed it. (Equation (1) implies that

$$\sum_{\alpha \in H} p \cdot (x^\alpha - e^\alpha)_+ = \sum_{\alpha \in H} p \cdot (x^\alpha - e^\alpha)_-,$$

that is, money spent on purchases equals money obtained from sales. Also, (3) and (5) together yield $\theta = (\sum_{\alpha \in H} m^\alpha + \sum_{\alpha \in H} d^\alpha)/M$.)

Note that in (4), if α is going bankrupt, he must be borrowing, and purchasing some good j; hence, he could contemplate a dollar less or more of borrowing, spending a dollar less or more on good j. If neither direction is to increase his utility, then the second statement in (4) must hold.

So let the map

$$f: \mathscr{E} \times \mathbb{R}^L_{++} \times \mathbb{R}_{++} \times (\mathbb{R}^L_{++})^H \times \mathbb{R}^H \times \mathbb{R}^H \to \mathbb{R}^L \times \mathbb{R}^{LH} \times \mathbb{R}^H \times \mathbb{R}^H \times \mathbb{R}$$

be given by

$$f((M, (\lambda^\alpha, e^\alpha, m^\alpha, u^\alpha)_{\alpha \in H}, (p, \theta, (x^\alpha)_{\alpha \in H}, (d^\alpha)_{\alpha \in H}, (t^\alpha)_{\alpha \in H})$$
$$\equiv \text{the LHSs of the above equalities.}$$

We can check immediately that $f \pitchfork 0$, as follows: By varying M, we perturb (5) however we like, without disturbing any other equation. By varying m^α, we can perturb (3) without changing anything except (5), which is already "controllable" (i.e., it can be compensated for by a change in M). By varying d^α or λ^α, we can perturb (4) however we like, disturbing only (3) and (5), which are controllable. By perturbing U^α, we perturb (2) however we like (presuming there is trade by every individual in every good), affecting only (4), which is under control. Finally, we can perturb x^α to control (1), and that may affect all of (2)–(5), but that is no matter, since they are all under control.

It remains only to check that if some α does not trade j, then the same argument goes through. If j is being purchased by some other agent β, then (1) can be perturbed by varying x_j^β, and (2) can be controlled by varying $\partial U^\beta/\partial x_j$, as we have seen. To perturb $x_j^\alpha - e_j$ for α (not trading j), vary x_j^α; this can be compensated by varying x_j^β, and (2) β can be compensated by varying $\partial U^\beta/\partial x_j$.

For now, let us restrict attention to the open set of endogenous variables $\hat{V}$ at which for every j there is some β with $x_j^\beta - e_j^\beta \neq 0$. We have just proved that $f\colon \mathscr{E} \times \hat{V} \to \mathbb{R}^{L+LH+2H+1}$ is transverse to 0. Since the dimension of $\hat{V}$ is also $L + LH + 2H + 1$, we deduce from the transversality theorem that for almost all parameters $(M,(\lambda^\alpha,e^\alpha,m^\alpha,u^\alpha)_{\alpha\in H})$ the resulting economy has a finite number of equilibria with endogenous variables in $\hat{V}$.

To finish the proof, let $\hat{L} \subset L$ be any nonempty subset of L. For all $j \notin \hat{L}$, fix $x_j^\alpha = e_j^\alpha$ for all $\alpha \in H$, defining the subeconomy on $\hat{L}$. For this subeconomy the above argument shows that, for a generic set of parameters, there are only a finite number of equilibria with endogenous variables in $V_{\hat{L}}$ (where for each $j \in \hat{L}$, $x_j^\alpha - e_j^\alpha \neq 0$ for some α).

Since $m^\alpha > 0$, each agent is buying some good at equilibrium. Hence, any equilibrium of the original economy will be an equilibrium of the subeconomy $\hat{L}$ with endogenous variables in $V_{\hat{L}}$, for some nonempty set $\hat{L} \subset L$ of traded goods. Since there are only a finite number of subsets $\phi \neq \hat{L} \subset L$, the result follows for nominal penalties.

The proof of real penalties is exactly the same, except that in (4) we substitute $\lambda^\alpha/p\cdot a$ for λ^α. ■

Proof of Theorem 6 Define Γ_ε as before, with the following substitution:

$d^t \to d^t + \Delta^t$ (where $\Delta^t \equiv \Delta^\alpha$ for $t \in [\alpha - 1, \alpha)$)

in the argument of U^t, for $t \in [0,h)$. Then a T.S.S.E. exists exactly as in claim 1. (We have not altered the strategy sets of the agents, or their payoff functions. Only the outcome has got adjusted as indicated above.)

Now reread the proof of claim 2 as follows. As before, no agent will hold positive amounts of fiat money at the end of trade, so all the money in the system,

$$h\varepsilon + \sum_{\alpha\in H} m^\alpha + M,$$

is returned to the bank. Now, however, agents may well repay more than their I.O.U. notes to the bank (in an effort to clear their exogenous debts), but clearly (by the same argument as in the proof of claim 2) no agent t of type α will repay more than his total debt,

$$\mu^t(\varepsilon) + \Delta^t \equiv \mu^\alpha(\varepsilon) + \Delta^\alpha,$$

at a T.S.S.E. Hence,

$$\sum_{\alpha \in H} \mu^\alpha(\varepsilon) + \sum_{\alpha \in H} \Delta^\alpha \geq h\varepsilon + \sum_{\alpha \in H} m^\alpha + M,$$

which implies that

$$\sum_{\alpha \in H} \mu^\alpha(\varepsilon) \geq h\varepsilon + \sum_{\alpha \in H} m^\alpha - \sum_{\alpha \in H} \Delta^\alpha + M.$$

Since

$$\sum_{\alpha \in H} m^\alpha - \sum_{\alpha \in H} \Delta^\alpha \geq 0$$

by assumption, we have

$$\sum_{\alpha \in H} \mu^\alpha(\varepsilon) \geq h\varepsilon + M > M,$$

and hence

$$\theta(\varepsilon) = \frac{\sum_{\alpha \in H} \mu^\alpha(\varepsilon)}{M} - 1 > 0.$$

The rest of the proof of theorem 6 goes through like the proof of theorem 4, replacing d^α by $d^\alpha + \Delta^\alpha$ throughout (in the argument of U^α). Similarly, the proof of theorem 3 goes through as well. ■

Proof of Theorem 8 (and thus also theorem 7) Define Γ_ε as in the proof of theorem 6, and note that a T.S.S.E. exists.

CLAIM 6 $\exists\, \underline{B}^*$ such that, for sufficiently small ε,

$$p_j(\varepsilon) > \underline{B}^*$$

for $1 \leq j \leq l$.

Proof Suppose $\theta(\varepsilon) \to \infty$. Then the total debt of all agents is at least

$$\theta(\varepsilon)M + \sum_{\alpha \in H} \Delta^\alpha,$$

and so agents of some type β have debt at least

$$\frac{\theta(\varepsilon)M + \sum_{\alpha \in H} \Delta^\alpha}{h} \to \infty$$

and hence, by (ii)**,

$$U^\beta(x^\beta(\varepsilon), d^\beta + \Delta^\beta, p(\varepsilon), \theta(\varepsilon), \eta((\theta(\varepsilon), p(\varepsilon), x(\varepsilon)))$$

$$< U^\beta(e^\beta, \Delta^\beta, p(\varepsilon), \theta(\varepsilon), \eta(\theta(\varepsilon), p(\varepsilon), x(\varepsilon)))$$

for small enough ε. Then any agent of type β would do better not trading at all, a contradiction.

We conclude that $\theta(\varepsilon)$ is bounded from above, hence so is each $\mu^\alpha(\varepsilon)$, and therefore the bound of $1/\varepsilon$ on the I.O.U. notes is not binding for small enough ε.

Suppose $p_j(\varepsilon) \to 0$ for some $j \in L$. Let any agent of type α increase his I.O.U. note by δ, obtain

$$\frac{\delta}{1 + \theta(\varepsilon)}$$

units of bank money, and purchase

$$\frac{\delta}{(1 + \theta(\varepsilon))p_j(\varepsilon)}$$

of j. His gain in utility (for small ε) is at least

$$\frac{\partial U^\alpha}{\partial x_j}(x^\alpha(\varepsilon), d^\alpha(\varepsilon), p(\varepsilon), \theta(\varepsilon), \eta(\theta(\varepsilon), p(\varepsilon), x(\varepsilon)))\frac{\delta}{(1 + \theta(\varepsilon))p_j(\varepsilon)}$$

and loss is at most (using (i)**)

$$\bar{c}\delta.$$

Since $\theta(\varepsilon)$ is bounded from above, and $\partial U^\alpha/\partial x_j$ is bounded away from zero, we see that he can improve his payoff, a contradiction. This establishes claim 6.

Since condition CIII is obviously implied by hypothesis (b), the rest of the proof of theorem 7 proceeds exactly as the proof of theorem 4 (after claim 4). ∎

Remark 13 (on a variation of condition CII) We can drop the requirement that $a_j > 0$ only if $e_j^\alpha > 0$ for all $\alpha \in H$ by making the λ^α harsher. More precisely, let

$$\bar{Q} = \frac{M}{2\ell \max_{j \in L} \sum_{\alpha \in H} e^{\alpha}},$$

$$\hat{Q}^* = 1 + \max \left\{ \frac{D_i u^{\alpha}(e^{\alpha})}{D_k u^{\alpha}(e^{\alpha})} : \alpha \in H, i \in L, k \in L \right\},$$

$$R^* = \max \left\{ \hat{Q}^*, \frac{\hat{Q}^*}{\bar{Q}} \right\}.$$

Assume

(CII)* $\lambda^{\alpha} > \ell^2 R^* \bar{a} \max\{D_j u^{\alpha}(e^{\alpha}) : j \in L\}$ for $\alpha \in H$,

where (recall)

$$\bar{a} = \max_{j \in L} a_j.$$

Then our results hold with (CII)* in place of (CII). To see this, reread the proof of theorem 3, remembering that as $p(\varepsilon) \to \infty$

$$x^{\alpha}(\varepsilon) \to e^{\alpha},$$

and obtain the same contradiction. (Note that, as in claim 3, $p_i(\varepsilon)/p_k(\varepsilon) < R^*$, so we can substitute R^* for Q^* in rereading the proof of theorem 3.)

References

Balasko, Y., and K. Shell. 1983. Lump-Sum Taxation: The Static Case. CARESS discussion paper.

Bewley, T. 1980. "The optimum quantity of money." In *Models of Monetary Economies*, ed. J. H. Kareken and N. Wallace. Federal Reserve Bank of Minneapolis.

Clower, R. W. 1965. "The Keynesian counterrevolution: A theoretical appraisal." In *The Theory of Interest Rates*, ed. F. H. Hahn and F. P. R. Brechling. Macmillan.

Dubey, P., and J. Geanakoplos. 1989a. Liquidity and Bankruptcy with Incomplete Markets: Pure Exchange. CFDP 900.

Dubey, P., and J. Geanakoplos. 1989b. Existence of Walrasian Equilibrium without a Price Player or a Generalized Game. CFDP 912.

Dubey, P., and J. Geanakoplos. 1989c. Liquidity and Bankruptcy with Incomplete Markets: Production. Mimeo.

Friedman, M. 1969. *The Optimum Quantity of Money and Other Essays*. Aldine.

Grandmont, J.-M., and Y. Younes. 1972. "On the role of money and the existence of a monetary equilibrium." *Review of Economic Studies* 39: 355–372.

Grandmont, J.-M., and Y. Younes. 1973. "On the efficiency of a monetary equilibrium." *Review of Economic Studies* 40: 149–165.

Hahn, F. H. 1965. "On some problems of proving the existence of an equilibrium in a monetary economy." In *The Theory of Interest Rates*, ed. F. H. Hahn and F. P. R. Brechling. Macmillan.

Hool, R. B. 1976. "Money, expectations and the existence of a temporary equilibrium." *Review of Economic Studies* 43: 439–445.

Lerner, A. 1947. "Money as a creature of the state." *American Economic Review Special Proceedings*, May: 312–317.

Samuelson, P. 1958. "An exact consumption loans model of interest with or without the social contrivance of money." *Journal of Political Economy*.

Shubik, M., and C. Wilson. 1977. "The optimal bankruptcy rule in a trading economy using fiat money." *Zeitschrift für Nationalökonomie* 37: 3–4.

The Lucas Equation, Indeterminacy, and Non-Neutrality: An Example

Pierre-André Chiappori and Roger Guesnerie

Lucas' model (1972) has received widespread and deserved attention from the economic profession. His influential message rests upon the analysis of a stylized model. Stationary equilibria of this model ("rational expectations equilibria," in Lucas' terminology) are identified with functions which are solutions of a functional equation. The study of this functional equation, which is at the heart of Lucas' analysis, is the subject of the present article.

Our study has three main purposes:

First, we consider the only model (to the best of our knowledge) in which an explicit analytical solution of the Lucas model has been exhibited, namely the model used in the pedagogical presentation of Azariadis (1981). In this simplified framework, as well as in a more general setting, the basic functional equation has a unique solution within the class of functions which are linear in one of the observable variables, the past-period money supply. Removing the restriction to this class of linear (in money) solutions, we exhibit other solutions, still under analytical form. The first objective of this study is thus to attempt a more comprehensive study of the Lucas equation in a specific case accessible to computation.

A second objective, of independent interest, is to propose a method for the resolution of functional equations arising from the theory of rational expectations, which is (again to the best of our knowledge) original in the economic literature. This method is conceptually natural—the solution is expressed under the form of a power series—but analytically difficult.

Third, our example provides another illustration of the possible indeterminacy of rational-expectations equilibria—an illustration which has, as we shall argue, original features. To this point let us mention that we exhibit a one-dimensional family of solutions in which the Lucas solution is a limit case of a zero value for the indexing parameter. We can also already note that all solutions but the Lucas solution are nonlinear in past money and invalidate the special version of money neutrality imbedded in the Lucas solution.

Naturally, we hope that the text reflects the influence of Frank Hahn's demanding requirements and intellectual flair on our own production. At least, the content of the text is not, we believe, foreign to Hahn's preoccupations. He repeatedly insisted on the need for a better assessment of the theoretical foundations of the thought of the new neoclassical school, and he contributed substantially (Hahn 1980, 1988a, 1988b) to the clarification of this field. The present text attempts to provide some additional thoughts on this issue.

1 The Lucas-Azariadis Model

Lucas considers a Samuelsonian overlapping-generations economy, in which the "old" generation only consumes. Total labor supply from the young is θy, where y is the labor supply of a representative young producer and θ is a random coefficient associated with a real shock in the economy. Demand from the old generation, which only holds money, equals mx/p, where mx is the money stock (the product of m—previous money stock—and x—a monetary shock). Moreover, θ and x satisfy $\mathbb{E}(x) = \mathbb{E}(\theta) = 1$.

Azariadis' simplifying assumption is that the utility function of the representative consumer is

$$U = c' - \tfrac{1}{2}y^2, \tag{1}$$

where c' is future consumption. (Note that "young" people do not consume.) When young agents choose their labor supply, future consumption may be random; then they maximize

$$E(U/I) = E(c'/I) - \tfrac{1}{2}y^2,$$

where I denotes the information available at that date.

Since future consumption is simply $c' = ypx'/p'$, every interior solution to the maximization problem of the typical goods supplier satisfies

$$y = E\left[\frac{px'}{p'} \bigg/ I\right],$$

the expectation being taken conditionally on present information I.

Lucas and Azariadis assume that I is the current equilibrium price p, so the market-equilibrium condition is

$$E\left[\frac{px'}{p'} \bigg/ p\right] = \frac{mx}{\theta p}. \tag{3}$$

At this point, the basic idea in Lucas' paper is to define an equilibrium price to be a *function* $p(m,x,\theta)$. The agent's expectations will be said to be rational if (3) is satisfied—that is, if

$$E\left[\frac{p(m,x,\theta)\cdot x'}{p(mx,x',\theta')}\Big/ p(m,x,\theta)\right] = \frac{mx}{\theta p(m,x,\theta)}. \tag{4}$$

An important property of (4) is the following:

LEMMA 1 (Lucas 1972) For any solution of (4),

$$\frac{x_1}{\theta_1} \neq \frac{x_2}{\theta_2}$$

implies

$$p(m,x_1,\theta_1) \neq p(m,x_2,\theta_2).$$

Proof Suppose $p(m,x_1,\theta_1) = p(m,x_2,\theta_2)$. Then (4) immediately implies

$$\frac{x_1}{\theta_1} = \frac{x_2}{\theta_2}.$$

Note, however, that the reciprocal of lemma 1 does *not* hold in general. For any solution of (4), the equilibrium price reveals the shock ratio $z = x/\theta$ (lemma 1), but it might well reveal "more" than z. In other words, there might exist solutions of (4) in which different values of x and θ are associated to the *same* ratio $z = x/\theta$, but to *different* equilibrium prices $p(m,x,\theta)$. (See Lucas 1983.)

An immediate consequence of this point is that equation (4) cannot be solved under this most general form. Following Lucas' erratum (1983), we shall restrict our attention to a special subclass of solutions—namely, to the function p, which can be written in the form

$$p(m,x,\theta) = \psi(m,z) \text{ with } z = x/\theta. \tag{5}$$

In this case, (4) becomes

$$E\left[\frac{\psi(m,z)x'}{\psi(mx,z')}\Big/ \psi(m,z)\right] = \frac{mx}{\theta\psi(m,z)}. \tag{6}$$

Under this restriction, a consequence of lemma 1 is that each solution of ψ of (6) defines a one-to-one correspondence between prices and shock ratios. This, in turn, shows that the expectation in (6) can equivalently be taken conditionally on z, i.e., that solutions of (6) are solutions to

$$E\left[\frac{\psi(m,z)x'}{\psi(mx,z')}\bigg/ z\right] = \frac{mx}{\theta\psi(m,z)}. \tag{7}$$

However, a solution of (7) is a solution of (6) if and only if it meets the condition stated in lemma 1—i.e., if $z_1 \neq z_2$ implies $\psi(m,z_1) \neq \psi(m,z_2)$.

Defining

$$\varphi(m,z) = \frac{mz}{\psi(m,z)} \text{ (=per capita labor supply)}$$

leads to the *Lucas-Azariadis equation*:

$$E\left[\frac{\theta'}{\theta}\varphi(mx,z')/z\right] = [\varphi(m,z)]^2. \tag{8}$$

The above discussion shows that any solution of (8) that satisfies lemma 1 will be a solution of (6), and hence of (4). It is then a rational expectation, or a self-fulfilling theory. The remaining of the paper is devoted to the study of a family of solutions to the basic functional equation (8).[1]

2 Solutions to the Lucas-Azariadis Equation

The Lucas-Azariadis Solution

Lucas and Azariadis solve (8) under the following additional hypothesis:

(H) $\varphi(m,z)$ does not depend on m.

Note that (H) implies that the price $p = \psi(m,z)$ is proportional to m. That is, (H) can be understood as a neutrality-like assumption: the component m of the money stock, which is common knowledge when the agents make their decision, has no real effect.

PROPOSITION 1 (Lucas, Azariadis) Under hypothesis (H), the *unique* solution of equation (8) is

$$\varphi(m,z) = u_0\sqrt{\chi_0(z)},$$

where

$$\chi_0(z) = E\left[\frac{1}{\theta}\bigg/ z\right]$$

and

$$u_0 = E[\theta' \sqrt{\chi_0}(z')].$$

Proof Under (H), equation (8) becomes

$$E[\theta'\varphi(z')] \cdot E\left[\frac{1}{\theta}\bigg/ z\right] = \varphi(z)^2.$$

Since $E[\theta'\varphi(z')]$ is a constant, $\varphi(z)$ must be of the form $u_0 \cdot \chi_0^{1/2}(z)$; then the computation of u_0 is straightforward.

The Existence of a Non-Lucas Solution

Lucas' uniqueness result of proposition 1 relies on the neutrality hypothesis (H). Note, however, that (H) does *not* stem from Lucas' definition of rational expectations; rather, it appears as a totally independent assumption. A natural question is whether equation (8) admits solutions that do not satisfy (H).

We now show, from an example, that the answer is positive. Assume that the distributions of x and θ are log normal, with respective densities

$$f_x(t) = \frac{1}{t\sigma\sqrt{2\pi}} \exp\left[-\frac{1}{2\sigma^2}\left(\operatorname{Log} t + \frac{\sigma^2}{2}\right)^2\right]$$

and

$$f_\theta(t) = \frac{1}{t\mu\sqrt{2\pi}} \exp\left[-\frac{1}{2\mu^2}\left(\operatorname{Log} t + \frac{\mu^2}{2}\right)^2\right],$$

where σ and μ are positive parameters.[2] Note that these densities satisfy Lucas' requirement that $E(x) = E(\theta) = 1$.

The basic idea, at that point, is to look for a solution of (8) that can be written in the form[3]

$$\varphi(m,z) = \sum_{k=0}^{\infty} a_k(z) m^{-\lambda k}, \tag{9}$$

where λ is a real positive number to be determined. The complete construction requires four steps.

Step 1: Necessary Condition For a function (5) to be a solution of (4), we must have

$$\sum_{k=0}^{\infty} E\left\{\frac{\theta'}{\theta} a_k(z')m^{-\lambda k}x^{-\lambda k}\middle| z\right\} = \sum_{k=0}^{\infty}\sum_{i=0}^{k} [a_i(z)a_{k-i}(z)]m^{-\lambda k}. \tag{10}$$

With the factors of $m^{-\lambda k}$ identified on both sides, the (infinite) following set of conditions obtains:

$$E\left(\frac{\theta'}{\theta} a_0(z')|z\right) = a_0^2(z), \tag{11}$$

$$E\left(\theta' a_1(z')\frac{x^{-\lambda}}{\theta}|z\right) = 2a_0(z)a_1(z), \tag{12}$$

$$E\left(\theta' a_k(z')\frac{x^{-\lambda k}}{\theta}|z\right) = \sum_{i=0}^{k} a_i(z)a_{k-i}(z), \quad k \geq 2. \tag{13}$$

Step 2: A Solution of (11) and (12) We already know the solution of (11), since it is nothing else than the Lucas-Azariadis solution. Equation (12) can be written

$$E\{\theta' a_1(z')\} \cdot E\left\{\frac{x^{-\lambda}}{\theta}|z\right\} = 2a_0(z)a_1(z).$$

Conforming with previous notation, we write

$$E\left\{\frac{x^{-\lambda}}{\theta}|z\right\} = \chi_\lambda(z).$$

Then $a_1(z)$ must be of the form

$$\frac{K_1\chi_\lambda(z)}{a_0(z)}.$$

From equation (12), we have

$$K_1 = \tfrac{1}{2}E\{\theta' a_1(z')\} = \frac{K_1}{2}E\left\{\frac{\theta'\chi_\lambda(z')}{a_0(z')}\right\}.$$

K_1 can be any arbitrary real number (in the following, we shall take it positive), provided that

$$E\left\{\frac{\theta'\chi_\lambda(z')}{a_0(z')}\right\} = 2.$$

Using (11), this is equivalent to

$$E\left\{\frac{\theta'\chi_\lambda(z')}{\sqrt{\chi_0}(z')}\right\} = 2E(\theta'\sqrt{\chi_0}(z')). \tag{14}$$

For $\lambda = 0$, the left-hand side of (14) equals $E\{\theta'\sqrt{\chi_0}(z')\}$, which is smaller than the right-hand side. We show now that for λ large enough, the left-hand side becomes bigger than the right-hand side. For the sake of simplicity, we use the lognormal assumption to prove this property (but it holds under more general assumptions on the distribution).

With the lognormal distribution, it can be shown that

$$E\left(\frac{x^s}{\theta}\middle| z\right) = A^{s^2-4s+3}z^{\alpha s+\beta}, \tag{15}$$

with

$$A = \exp\left\{\frac{\mu^2\sigma^2}{2(\mu^2+\sigma^2)}\right\},$$

$$\alpha = \frac{\sigma^2}{\mu^2+\sigma^2},$$

and

$$\beta = \frac{\mu^2}{\mu^2+\sigma^2} = 1-\alpha,$$

and that

$$E\{z'^{\alpha s+\beta/2}\theta'\} = BC^{s^2-s},$$

with

$$B = \exp\left\{-\frac{\mu^2}{8}\frac{\mu^2+2\sigma^2}{\mu^2+\sigma^2}\right\}$$

and

$$C = \exp\left\{\frac{\sigma^4}{2(\mu^2+\sigma^2)}\right\}.$$

It follows that

$$E\left\{\frac{\theta'\chi_\lambda(z')}{\sqrt{\chi_0(z')}}\right\} = \frac{A^{\lambda^2}+4\lambda+3}{A^{3/2}} E\left\{\frac{\theta' z'^{-\alpha\lambda+\beta}}{(z')^{\beta/2}}\right\}$$

$$= A^{\lambda 2+4\lambda+3/2} E\{\theta' z'^{-\alpha\lambda+\beta/2}\}$$

$$= A^{\lambda 2+4\lambda+3/2} BC^{\lambda 2+\lambda}$$

and

$$E\{\theta'\sqrt{\chi_0}(z')\} = A^{3/2}E\{\theta' z'^{\beta/2}\} = A^{3/2}B.$$

For λ large enough, obviously

$$A^{\lambda 2}\cdots BC^{\lambda 2}\cdots > A^{3/2}B.$$

Furthermore, here, there is a unique $\lambda_0 > 0$ for which equation (14) holds. It is defined by

$$A^{\lambda_0^2+4\lambda_0}C^{\lambda_0^2+\lambda_0} = 2.$$

So the log-normality assumption leads to

$$a_0(z) = A^3 B z^{\beta/2} \stackrel{\text{def}}{=} u_0 z^{\beta/2} \tag{17}$$

and

$$a_1(z) = u_1 z^{-\alpha\lambda_0+\beta/2}, \tag{18}$$

where u_1 is an arbitrary (non-negative) real number.

Step 3: A Solution of (13) Now we come back to the general term. Equation (13) can be written as

$$2a(z)a_k(z) = K_k \chi_{\lambda_0 k}(z) - \sum_{1}^{n-1} a_i(z)a_{k-i}(z), \tag{19}$$

where

$$K_k = E(\theta' a_k(z')). \tag{20}$$

We first show, by induction, the following:

LEMMA 1 Take $a_0(z)$ as defined in (17), choose an arbitrary u_1, and compute $a_1(z)$ as in (18). Then, any solution to equations (19) and (20) for $k \geq 1$ is of the form

$$a_k(z) = u_k z^{-\alpha\lambda_0 k + \beta/2},$$

where u_k is positive. Furthermore, u_k is of the form $\zeta_k u_1^k$.

Proof Note first that $a_0(z)$ and $a_1(z)$ actually have the form assumed here. Now assume that the property is true for $2, \ldots, k-1$; we show that it is true for k. Note first that (19) writes down

$$2a_0(z)a_k(z) = K_k A^{\lambda_0^2 k^2 + 4\lambda_0 k + 3} z^{-\alpha\lambda_0 k + \beta} - \left(\sum_{i=1}^{k-1} u_i u_{k-i}\right) z^{-\alpha\lambda_0 k + \beta},$$

or

$$a_k(z) = \frac{1}{2A^3 B}\left[K_k A^{\lambda_0^2 k + 4\lambda_0 k + 3} - \left(\sum_{i=1}^{k-1} u_i u_{k-i}\right)\right] z^{-\alpha\lambda_0 k + \beta/2}.$$

This shows that $a_k(z) = u_k z^{-\alpha\lambda_0 k + \beta/2}$. It remains to show that $u_k > 0$. From (20), K_k is determined by

$$K_k = \left(\sum_{1}^{k-1} u_i u_{k-i}\right) \frac{C^{\lambda_0^2 k^2 + \lambda_0 k}}{-2A^3 + A^{\lambda_0^2 k^2 + 4\lambda_0 k + 3} C^{\lambda_0^2 k^2 + \lambda_0 k}}.$$

Hence,

$$u_k = \frac{1}{u_0}\left[\frac{\sum_1^{k-1} u_i u_{k-i}}{A^{\lambda_0^2 k^2 + 4\lambda_0 k} C^{\lambda_0^2 k^2 + \lambda_0 k} - 2}\right], \quad k > 1. \tag{21}$$

As announced, u_k is positive since the denominator is strictly positive for $k > 1$. Also, if u_i and u_{k-i} are proportional to $(u_1)^i$ and $(u_1)^{k-i}$, u_k is proportional to $(u_1)^k$. This terminates the induction proof.

Note that (21) uniquely defines the sequence u_k for any given u_1 (and, by the way, that the positivity of u_1 is crucial for the argument).

Step 4 It remains only to show that the series

$$\sum_{0}^{\infty} u_k (z^{-\alpha\lambda_0 k + \beta/2}) m^{\lambda_0 k}$$

converges for any couple $(z,m) \in \mathbb{R}_+^2$. For the sake of notational simplicity, let

$$D(k) = u_0[A^{\lambda_0^2 k^2 + 4\lambda_0 k} C^{\lambda_0^2 k^2 + \lambda_0 k} - 2].$$

Note that for any $\gamma > 1$, $D(k)$ becomes greater at infinity than $k\gamma^{k^{3/2}}$. More precisely, choose some $\gamma > 1$; then

$$\exists\, K \mid \forall k \geq K,\ D(k) > k\gamma^{k^{3/2}}. \tag{22}$$

Let us then define

$$M = \operatorname{Min}\left(1, \min_{2 \leq k \leq K-1} \frac{D(k)}{k\gamma^{k^{3/2}}}\right). \tag{23}$$

Note that M is strictly greater than zero and that for any $k \leq K$

$$\frac{kM}{D(k)} \leq \gamma^{-k^{3/2}}. \tag{24}$$

Then the following can be shown:

LEMMA 2 If $u_1 < \bar{u}_1 = M/\gamma$, then $u_k < M\gamma^{-k^{3/2}}$, $k \geq 1$.

Proof We proceed by induction, and assume that the property holds true for any u_i, $1 \leq i < k$. Then, in particular, $u_i < M$, $i < k$, and

$$u_k = \frac{\sum_{i=1}^{k-1} u_i u_{k-i}}{D(k)} < \frac{kM^2}{D(k)} \left(= M \frac{kM}{D(k)}\right). \tag{25}$$

If $k > K$, then by (16)

$$\frac{k}{D(k)} < \gamma^{-k^{3/2}}$$

and by (23) $M \leq 1$; hence, $u_k < M\gamma^{-k^{3/2}}$. And if $k \leq K$, the same conclusion follows from (24) and (25). This terminates the proof of the lemma.

Note that the power series we are considering is absolutely dominated by

$$M \sum_{0}^{\infty} \gamma^{-k^{3/2}} (z^{-\alpha\lambda_0 k + \beta/2}) m^{\lambda_0 k},$$

which converges for any z and m. Hence, for some values of u_1, the power series we are considering converges for any z and m. However, this is sufficient for the convergence of the series of *any* u_1, z, and m:

LEMMA 3 If there exists a $u_1^* > 0$ such that the series converges for any z and m, then the series converges for any u_1, m, and z.

Proof Suppose that the power series

$$\varphi^*(z,m) = \sum_0^\infty u_k^* m^{-\lambda_0 k} z^{-\alpha\lambda_0 k+\beta/2},$$

where the u_k^* are deduced from u_1^* by (23), converges for any m and z. Consider the series

$$\overline{\varphi}(z,m) = \sum_0^\infty u_k m^{-\lambda_0 k} z^{-\alpha\lambda_0 k+\beta/2},$$

where the u_k are obtained according to (21), from some $u_1 \neq u_1^*$. Pose $w = u_k^*/u_1$; then, from lemma 1,

$$\forall k,\ u_k = \frac{u_k^*}{w^k}.$$

Thus,

$$\overline{\varphi}(z,m) = \sum_0^\infty u_k^* \frac{m^{-\lambda_0 k}}{w^k} z^{-\alpha\lambda_0 k+\beta/2}$$

$$= \varphi^*\left(\frac{m}{w^{-1/\lambda_0}}, z\right), \text{ which converges.}$$

We can now recapitulate the conclusion:

Take $u_0 = A^3 B$. Take λ_0 such that

$$A^{\lambda_0^2+4\lambda_0} C^{\lambda_0^2+\lambda_0} = 2.$$

After fixing u_1, compute recursively

$$u_k = \frac{\sum_1^{k-1} u_i u_{k-i}}{u_0[A^{\lambda_0^2 k^2+4\lambda_0 k} C^{\lambda_0^2 k^2+\lambda_0 k} - 2]}, \quad k > 1.$$

For any $u_1 > 0$, the power series

$$\sum_0^\infty u_k z^{-\alpha\lambda_0 k+\beta/2} m^{-\lambda_0 k}$$

converges toward a positive function $\varphi(m,z)$ which is a solution to the functional equation (8). The limit solution corresponding to $u_1 = 0$ is nothing else than the Lucas solution. We can thus state the following result:

PROPOSITION 2 There exists a continuum S of solutions to equation (8), indexed by a non-negative parameter u_1. All of them are also solutions to equation (6), hence to equation (4). The limit solution corresponding to $u_1 = 0$ is the Lucas-Azariadis solution. For all strictly positive values of u_1, the corresponding solutions do not satisfy (H).

It may be interesting to consider the (limit) case in which there is no real shock. Technically, the random variable θ becomes certain, which corresponds to the condition $\mu = 0$. Then the observation of z fully reveals x; the basic equation (8) becomes

$$\underset{x'}{\mathrm{E}}\,[\varphi(mx,x')] = [\varphi(m,x)]^2. \tag{8'}$$

The results of proposition 2 immediately apply to this particular case:

COROLLARY 1 Equation (8′) has a continuum of solutions, indexed by a non-negative parameter u_1. The (limit) solution corresponding to $u_1 = 0$ (i.e., Lucas' solution) is constant. For all other values of u_1, the labor supply strictly decreases with both m and x.

Proof For $\mu = 0$, we get $A = B = 1$ and $C = e^{\sigma^2/2}$. Lucas' solution, $\overline{\varphi}$, then degenerates to $\overline{\varphi} \equiv 1$. Other solutions are defined, for any given $u_1 > 0$, by

$$\varphi_{u1}(m,z) = \sum u_k(mz)^{-\lambda k},$$

where λ is the positive root of $\lambda^2 + \lambda = (2 \ln 2)/\sigma^2$ and where the u_k are sequentially defined by

$$u_k = \frac{\sum_1^{k-1} u_i u_{k-i}}{C^{\lambda^2 k^2 + \lambda k} - 2}, \quad k > 1.$$

The remainder of the proof is straightforward.

A conclusion is that the real shock—hence, the presence of imperfect transmission of information—is *not* necessary for non-Lucas solutions to exist. (We shall come back, in the conclusion, to the interpretation of this case.) To the contrary, non-Lucas solutions disappear if we assume away the *money* shock ($\sigma = 0$), as the reader may easily check.

3 Lucas versus Non-Lucas Solutions

We shall now compare the "non-Lucas" solutions described in proposition 2 with the (traditional) Lucas-Azariadis one. In what follows, the former (corresponding to $u_1 > 0$) will be referred to as *non-strongly-neutral* solutions. That is, they do not satisfy the (strong) neutrality requirement (H): once a specific solution φ (i.e., a specific self-fulfilling theory) has been chosen, real output along the corresponding trajectory does depend on the first-period quantity of money m, as well as on the shock ratio z. Note, however, that the solutions we derive still satisfy a (weak) form of neutrality: the *set* of solutions is not affected (in real terms when the initial quantity of money is modified).[4]

Qualitative Properties

Let us first consider the qualitative properties of the solutions (figures 1, 2).[5]

For "high" values of z and/or m, non-neutral solutions behave as the Lucas one; in particular, both price and labor supply tend to infinity with z. For "low" values of m and z, however, labor supply tends to infinity in the non-neutral solutions, whereas it tends to zero in the Lucas one.

Also, note that for any non-neutral solution, the corresponding price function,

$$\psi(m,z) = mz/\varphi(m,z),$$

is strictly monotonic in z. That is, lemma 1 is satisfied; hence, ψ is a solution of (6).

In particular, it must be stressed that, for *all* solutions (including the Lucas-Azariadis one), labor supply is unbounded; moreover, in non-strongly-neutral solutions, labor supply is bounded away from zero, whereas it is not in the strongly neutral one. From a stochastic viewpoint, since the support of z is $]0, +\infty[$, this means that, in *all* solutions, labor supply may take arbitrarily large values with positive probability. This fact—which, in a sense, contradicts Lucas' (1972) original result—is closely linked to the particular utility function chosen, for convenience, by Azariadis. Again, it must be reminded that Azariadis' paper is (to our knowledge) the only example of analytic resolution of Lucas' equation; in fact, analytical resolution requires a very simplified framework. The fact that labor supply may become arbitrarily large, unrealistic as it seems, must hence be considered as a "red herring," due to particular functional forms. In Chiappori and Guesnerie 1989, we claim that the present set of solutions only illustrates a more general class, which can be associated to heteroclinic orbits[6] of a dynamical system (which, in turn, is associated to

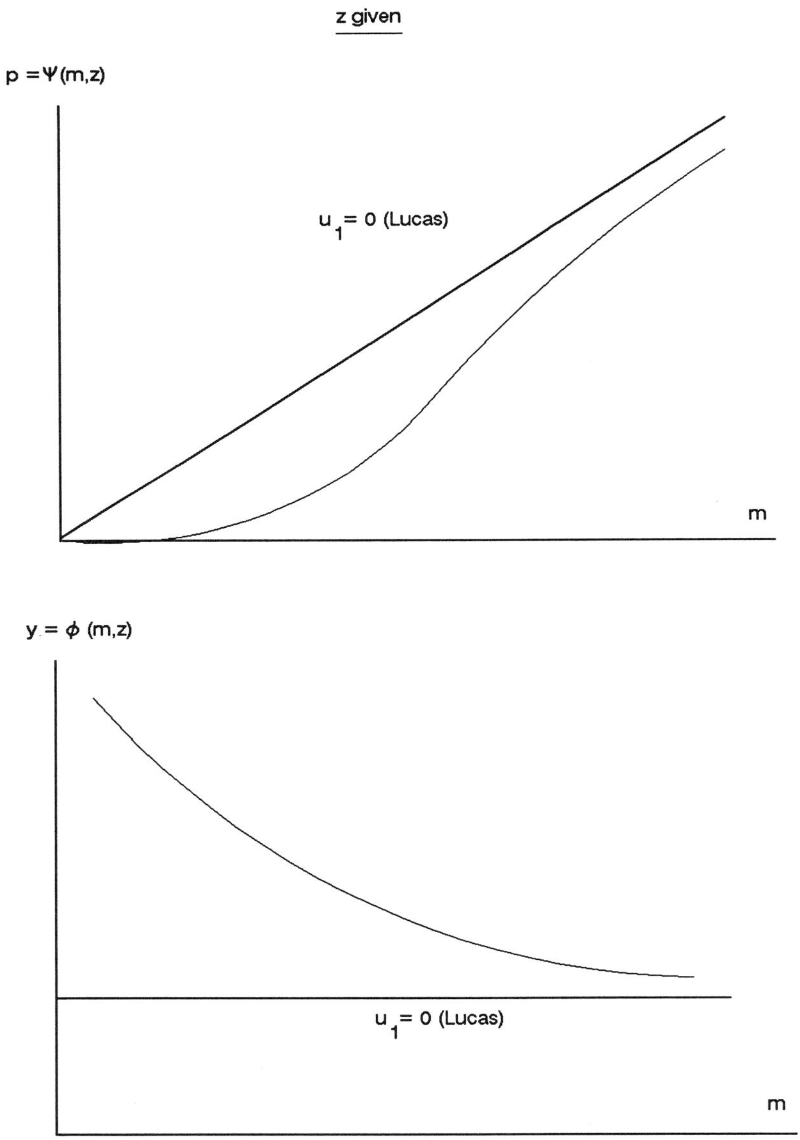

Figure 1

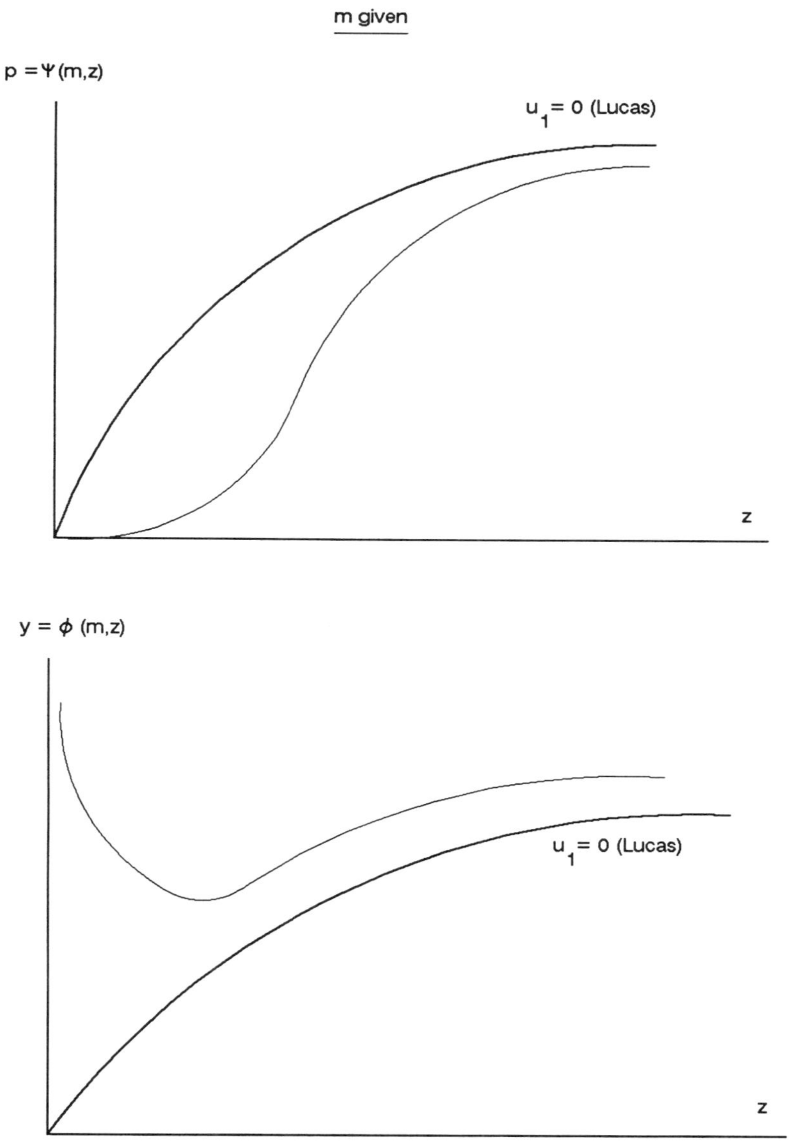

Figure 2

the existence problem). From this point of view, infinite labor supply simply corresponds to a particular stationary point of the system. In particular, in a slightly different context, the existence of *bounded* solutions of this kind can be demonstrated; but an analytical expression, in those cases, seems technically out of reach.

Stochastic Properties

On the other hand, the stochastic behaviors of Lucas and non-Lucas solutions are not identical. Specifically, in Lucas solution, the stochastic process followed by labor supply is uncorrelated through time; i.e., labor supply at date t is totally independent of labor supply at date $t' < t$. In particular, it is (trivially) stationary, in the probabilistic sense. To the contrary, in the non-Lucas solutions described in proposition 2, labor supply at date t depends on money supply at that date; since the money process is autocorrelated, autonomous, and nonstationary in the probabilistic sense,[7] the labor-supply process inherits the same properties. In other words: nonstationarity of labor supply, in our solution, can be seen as an immediate consequence of both Lucas' money process *and* the "strong non-neutrality" hypothesis that labor supply may depend on money stock

Welfare Comparison

It is possible to rank the solutions obtained above from a welfare viewpoint. To be more precise:

PROPOSITION 3 The *ex ante* welfare of each generation is an increasing function of u_1. In particular, any non-neutral solution Pareto dominates the Lucas solution.

Proof Per capita labor supply during the generation's first period of life is $y = \psi(m,z)$, m being the currently available quantity of money. Total production during the second period is $\theta'\psi(mx,z')$, to be divided among θ agents. Hence, each agent's expected utility is

$$E(U) = E\left[\frac{\theta'}{\theta}\varphi(mx,z')\right] - \tfrac{1}{2}E[\varphi(m,z)^2].$$

But the basic functional equation, (8), becomes

$$\underset{\theta',z'}{\mathrm{E}}\left[\frac{\theta'}{\theta}\varphi(mx,z')\right] = \varphi(m,z)^2.$$

Taking both sides' expectations with respect to z and θ gives, from a classical property of conditional expectations,

$$\underset{\theta,z,\theta',z'}{\mathrm{E}}\left[\frac{\theta'}{\theta}\varphi(mx,z')\right] = \underset{z}{\mathrm{E}}\,[\varphi(m,z)^2].$$

Hence,

$$\mathrm{E}(U) = \tfrac{1}{2}\mathrm{E}[\varphi(m,z)^2].$$

Since, for any m and z, φ is increasing with respect to u_1 (see the figures), a higher u_1 generates a higher expected utility.

Conclusion

We should briefly compare the achievements of the paper with the objectives stated in the introduction.

Concerning the first objectives, although we have not exhausted the study of the set of solutions of equation (8) in the model under consideration we have indeed exhibited a new class of solutions to the Lucas equation in the specific model under consideration. Naturally these new solutions may be challenged for economic reasons (see the previous section). But as far as existence is concerned, they are relevant and cannot be dismissed *a priori.*

Second, the paper demonstrates that the method of resolution we propose is indeed feasible. It is, however, incomparably more difficult to implement than standard methods of unknown coefficients used in previous studies of linear rational-expectations equations. (See, for example, Broze, Gourieroux, and Szafarz 1985.) Here, an infinity of unknown coefficients must be identified, and it must be shown that the corresponding power series has an adequate radius of convergence[8]; moreover, the difference-of-martingales technique does not apply here, because of the imperfect information component.

Third, and finally, the contribution of the paper to the understanding of the general indeterminacy issue is the subject of further studies. The main question concerns the theoretical status of our "new" solutions. Part of their originality relies upon the analysis they provide of the specific relative influence of real and monetary shocks in heterodox solutions.

Forgetting about real shocks and concentrating on solutions of the form given by corollary 1, one can argue that those are now *sunspot* solutions.

The reason is that money, intrinsic in the general model, is now *extrinsic*: it is not a fundamental of the economy, i.e., one of the factors that influence its *real* behavior. Hence, the real effect of money, as described by corollary 1, can be viewed as an example where an extrinsic signal "matters." This is exactly the definition of a sunspot equilibrium. (See Chiappori and Guesnerie 1991 for a presentation.) This interpretation, and specifically the exact status of the particular solutions we find, are examined in Chiappori and Guesnerie 1989.

Some points can, however, be made here.

Our solutions—in the limit case of the absence of real shocks —have features which make them qualitatively different (for example, in view of the stochastic properties of economic variables) from classical sunspot solutions. They differ from the Azariadis (1981) and the Azariadis-Guesnerie (1986) solutions (which require backwards-bending labor supply), and from the Farmer-Woodford (1984) solutions (which do not exist in the present model). The findings of Peck (1988), who constructs time-dependent sunspot equilibria converging to autarky with probability 1, have no direct implications for our study.

In Chiappori and Guesnerie 1989 we attempt a partial although reasonably general classification of sunspot solution in one-dimensional, one-step-forward-looking dynamical systems. We identify sunspot solutions with the trajectories—possibly degenerated—of some associated dynamical system. Some of the solutions are indeed associated with a heteroclinic orbit of the system; they are called heteroclinic solutions. It turns out that the solutions computed in the present paper are "sunspot connected" with such solutions; i.e., they coincide with these heteroclinic solutions when the intrinsic noise disappears. In view of that, the controversial issue of a possibly infinite labor supply is a somewhat red herring: heteroclinic trajectories going to plus infinity are nothing more than particular heteroclinic trajectories.

Acknowledgment

We are indebted to J.-M. Grandmont for helpful comments.

Notes

1. J.-M. Grandmont has pointed out to us that the set of *all* solutions to this equation could be characterized using the following trick, directly borrowed from the study of linear systems

(Broze, Gouriéroux, and Szafarz 1987). Equation (8) can be written as

$$(\theta/\theta')\cdot\varphi(mx,z') = [\varphi(m,z)]^2 + \varepsilon',$$

where ε' satisfies $\mathbb{E}(\varepsilon'/z) = 0$. Then solving this new functional equation in φ, for an arbitrary ε, provides us with a general solution of (8). Of course, the power-series method described in the paper can clearly help solving the equation. However, this approach is not helpful here, since our aim is to *characterize the behavior* of the solutions we find.

2. Since both real and monetary shocks are multiplicative in the model, the lognormality assumption is very natural; it will hold, for instance, if θ and x can be considered as products of "numerous" independent, identically distributed "small" random shocks.

3. In Chiappori and Guesnerie 1990 we instead consider solutions of the form $\sum_{k=0}^{\infty} a_k(z)m^{\lambda k}$. These solutions have different boundary properties (especially when m tends to zero or infinity); moreover, they raise some difficulties linked with the revelation of information through prices.

4. More precisely, consider any solution φ belonging to S; let m_0 be the intial quantity of money. Suppose, now, that m_0 is changed into some $m_0' > 0$. It is easy to show that there exists a function φ' in S, such that

$$\varphi(m_0',z) = \varphi'(m_0,z)$$

for all z. That is to say, changing m_0 into m_0', and keeping φ constant, is always equivalent to changing φ into some (conveniently chosen) φ' in S, m_0 remaining unchanged.

5. The diagrams were obtained by numerical computation of the power series. However, their qualitative properties can be derived formally.

6. A heteroclinic orbit is a stable orbit linking two stationary points.

7. To see this, note that $\text{Log}m_{t+1} = \text{Log}m_t + \text{Log}x_t$. Taking the stationary distribution for m_t and m_{t+1} gives

$$\text{E}[\text{Log}m_{t+1}] = \text{E}(\text{Log}m_t) + \text{E}[\text{Log}x_t],$$

hence $\text{E}(\text{Log}x_t) = 0$—a contradiction with $\text{E}(x_t) = 1$ unless x_t is not random.

8. The mere fact that the power series actually converge was not totally expected a priori. It must be remembered that in numerous cases—particularly in the physical sciences (including the well-known "three-body" problem)—*all* power series derived from the resolution of a functional equation diverge, though it is clear that the equation does admit solutions (see Poincaré 1890). In this sense, the functional equations derived from the rational-expectations framework—at least for the Lucas-Azariadis model—are "well behaved"!

References

Azariadis, C. 1981. "A reexamination of natural rate theory." *American Economic Review* 71 (5): 944–960.

Azariadis, C., and R. Guesnerie. 1986. "Sunspots and cycles." *Review of Economic Studies* 111: 725–737.

Broze, L., C. Gourieroux, and A. Szafarz. 1985. "Solutions of linear rational expectations models." *Econometric Theory* 1: 341–368.

Chiappori, P.-A., and R. Guesnerie. 1989. Self-Fulfilling Theories: The Sunspot Connection. Working paper 8919, DELTA, Paris.

Chiappori, P.-A., and R. Guesnerie. 1990. "Anticipations, indetermination et non-neutralite de la monnaie." *Annales d'Economie et de Statistiques* 19: 1–25.

Chiappori, P.-A., and R. Guesnerie. 1991. "Sunspot equilibria in sequential markets model." In *Handbook of Mathematical Economics*, volume 4, ed. Hildenbrand and Sonnenschein. Forthcoming.

Farmer, R., and M. Woodford. 1984. Self-Fulfilling Prophecies and the Business Cycle. Working paper 84-12, University of Pennsylvania.

Lucas, R. E. 1972. "Expectations and the neutrality of money." *Journal of Economic Theory* 4: 103–124.

Lucas, R. E. 1983. "Expectations and the neutrality of money: A corrigendum." *Journal of Economic Theory* 31: 197–199.

Peck, J. 1988. "On the existence of sunspot equilibria in an overlapping generation model." *Journal of Economic Theory* 44 (1).

Poincaré H. 1890. "Sur les équations de la dynamique et le problème des trois corps." *Acta Mathematica* 13: 1–270.

Three Observations on Sunspots and Asset Redundancy

Andreu Mas-Colell

In this paper I make the following three observations (of which the second is perhaps the most significant):

- Suppose we have a sequential, finite-horizon, *complete* market economy. Let some uninsurable publicly observed sunspot signals occur after trade takes place in period 1 but before it takes place in period 2. Nontrivial sunspot equilibria are then possible. (*Nontrivial* means that the realizations of the equilibria are not equilibria of the model without sunspots.) This will come as no surprise, but no example making precisely this point seems to be available. The seminal reference on sunspot equilibria is Cass and Shell 1983 (see also Shell 1987). Various examples can be found in Cass and Shell 1983 and also in Aumann, Peck, and Shell 1988, Balasko 1987, Balasko, Cass, and Shell 1988, Guesnerie and Laffont 1988, Maskin and Tirole 1987, and Peck and Shell 1988.
- The presence of redundant assets may help to immunize an otherwise complete economy against sunspot contamination.
- Redundant assets may actually influence the disequilibrium properties of spot equilibria; for example, the presence of a redundant asset may help to guarantee the tâtonnement stability of a spot equilibrium. This last observation is not related to sunspot issues.

The power and the failures of the Invisible Hand have been at the center of Frank Hahn's research. In a modest way these three observations deal also with this grand topic. The presentation lacks, I am afraid, the flair that Frank would undoubtedly have given to it. But the thought of what he could do with them persuades me to dedicate these three observations to him.

1 Nontrivial Sunspot Equilibria

Our initial datum is a conventional Walrasian exchange economy at date $t = 1$. There are ℓ commodities and two (types of) consumers, $i = 1, 2$, with endowments $\omega_i \in R^\ell_+$ and utility functions u_i: $R^\ell_+ \to R$ satisfying the usual conditions (including strict concavity and differentiability). Price vectors are denoted by p. A Walrasian price vector p and allocation $\bar{x} = (\bar{x}_1, \bar{x}_2)$ are defined, in the familiar way, by the following conditions:

$$\bar{x}_1 + \bar{x}_2 \leq \omega_1 + \omega_2,$$

$$x_i \text{ maximizes } u_i(x_i) \text{ subject to } p \cdot x_i \leq p \cdot \omega_i.$$

Note that nothing prevents us, either here or in later developments, from interpreting some of the ℓ commodities as state-contingent Arrow-Debreu commodities. There is no need, however, to keep track of this separately. The key fact is that *our basic economy is a complete one.*

Suppose now that at the beginning of period 1 an extrinsic, payoff-irrelevant, publicly observable state $s \in S$, for short a sunspot, occurs with probability $\pi(s)$ (see Aumann et al. 1988, Maskin and Tirole 1987, and Peck and Shell 1991 for models without public observability). We take $\# S < \infty$. Under the hypothesis of rational expectations the equilibrium is then an assignment $p(s),x(s)$ such that for every s, $p(s),x(s)$ is Walrasian for the original economy. If the latter has several equilibria, then the *ex post* equilibrium realization may depend on the sunspot. This is an obvious and, for current purposes, not terribly interesting fact. After all, *ex post* the presence of sunspots is undetectable. In this paper we concern ourselves with nontrivial sunspot equilibria, defined as those where with positive probability the *ex post* realization of the equilibrium is not an equilibrium of the original economy.

For the sunspot equilibrium function to be something other than a selection of the equilibria of the original economy, we need to extend our primitive model to include some decision variables at $t = 0$ that are payoff-relevant and therefore capable of being influenced by price expectations. Perhaps the simplest way to proceed is to assume that there is a given list of assets tradable at $t = 0$ and having returns at $t = 1$.

Suppose first that the assets available at $t = 0$ can have payoffs contingent on the sunspot signal. Assume in fact that there is an Arrow security for every s (that is, security s pays \$1 if and only if s occurs). Then, if every trader has free access to the securities markets, complete insurance is possible and risk aversion rules out the possibility of (even trivial) sunspot equilibria (Cass and Shell 1983). Cass and Shell (1983), Balasko (1987), and Balasko et al. (1988) have shown that if access to the asset markets is asymmetric (i.e., if only some consumers can use them) then nontrivial sunspot equilibria are possible. Guesnerie and Laffont (1988) arrive at the same conclusion under the hypothesis that access is symmetric but the original economy is not itself complete. The case where sunspot-contingent contracts are possible is therefore well understood (but see the remark at the end of this section).

In this paper we consider the situation where assets cannot be sunspot-contingent but otherwise the original economy is complete (thus, this case is complementary to that of Guesnerie and Laffont 1988). Informally, the interest of this case can be argued as follows. Suppose that we live in a fairly perfect world (i.e., one where complete markets emerge) but suppose also that the world is exposed to a multitude of sunspot signals—so many, in fact, that they cannot even be listed *a priori* and, as a consequence, the task of developing insurance institutions that will automatically guarantee sunspot-freeness is unfeasible. This "perfect" world will have to be more reactive. Insurance institutions (perhaps contingent markets, but see the next section for another suggestion) will develop as particular sunspot variables find their way into the equilibrium, and with the targeted intention of counteracting and nullifying them. Obviously, it would be neater if the system did not have to worry about all this because the underlying completeness made it immune to (nontrivial) sunspots. It will, probably, come as no surprise that this is not so. Nonetheless, it will be useful to have a class of examples, and this section is devoted to providing it.

We proceed to extend the original model by including asset trade at $t = 0$. The assets are sunspot-independent and pay in goods at $t = 1$. To be specific, we assume there are two assets with return vectors $r_1, r_2 \in R^{\ell}_{+}$. (Because of the budget constraint, a single asset would not allow any trade.) A sunspot equilibrium is now a four-tuple $(\bar{q}, \bar{y}, \bar{p}, \bar{x})$ composed of an asset price vector $\bar{q} \in R^2$, asset trade vectors $\bar{y}_i \in R^2$ $(i = 1,2)$, a spot equilibrium price function $\bar{p}(s) \in R^{\ell}$ $(s \in S)$, and consumption allocations $\bar{x}_i(s) \in R^{\ell}_{+}$ $(s \in S, i = 1,2)$ satisfying the following:

(a) $\sum_i \bar{x}_i(s) \leq \sum_i \omega_i, s \in S, \sum_i \bar{y}_i \leq 0$.

(b) For every $i = 1,2$, $\bar{y}_i, \bar{x}_i$ solve

$$\text{Max} \sum_s \pi(s) u_i(x_i(s))$$

$$\text{s.t. } \bar{p}(s) \cdot x_i(s) \leq \bar{p}(s) \cdot (\omega_i + r_1 \bar{y}_{i1} + r_2 \bar{y}_{i2}), s \in S, \text{ and } q \cdot y_i \leq 0.$$

The sunspot equilibrium is nontrivial if, for some $s \in S$, $\bar{x}(s)$ is not an equilibrium allocation of the original economy.

Without the sunspots, the asset structure is redundant (the original economy is complete). The assets are not needed at equilibria, although there may be asset trades. More precisely, there may be a continuum of consumption equivalent asset trades and every equilibrium consumption can be reached with zero asset trades (see the next section for more on redundancy). This is not an essential feature of our analysis, the important point is that the economy, extended with the asset trades, is complete. This may happen because (as in our case) the original economy is complete, or as a consequence of the asset trading possibilities.

In the presence of sunspots the option to trade in assets becomes very relevant, so much so that nontrivial sunspot equilibria are now a possibility. In particular, we have the following proposition:

PROPOSITION 1 Suppose that the basic economy (u_i,ω_i), where $\omega_i \gg 0$ and $i = 1,2$, admits three linearly independent equilibrium price vectors p_1, p_2, p_3 (this implies $\ell > 2$). Suppose also that $\# S > 2$. Then we can find endowments ω_i' $(i = 1,2)$ and asset-return vectors r_1, r_2 such that the economy (u_i,ω_i'), $i = 1, 2$, admits nontrivial sunspot equilibria.

Proof The idea is to construct the ω_i' and the vectors of asset returns in such a way that after equilibrium asset trade we get the original economy ω_i and, depending on the sunspot signal, some of the equilibrium prices p_1, p_2, p_3.

Without loss of generality we let $S = \{s_1,s_2,s_3\}$ and the three states be equiprobable. Let λ_j^i $(i = 1,2,\ j = 1,2,3)$ be the marginal utility of income of consumer i at the equilibrium corresponding to p_j. Choose a vector $a = (a_1,a_2,a_3) \neq 0$ such that $\sum_j \lambda_j^i a_j = 0$ for $i = 1,2$. Because the price vectors p_j are linearly independent, we can find $r \in R^\ell$ such that $p_j \cdot r = a_j$ for every j. Of course, $r \neq 0$. We can express $r = r_1 - r_2$ with $r_1 \geq 0$ and $r_2 \geq 0$. These are going to be the two assets. Note that because we can choose a to be arbitrarily small the returns r are also small—sufficiently small, in fact, for

$$\omega_1' = \omega_1 + r \geq 0, \omega_2' = \omega_2 - r \geq 0.$$

We claim that the following describes a nontrivial sunspot equilibrium for the economy (u_i,ω_i'), where $i = 1, 2$: Take $q = (1,1)$, $y_1 = (1,-1)$, $y_2 = (-1,1)$, $p(s_1) = p_1$, $p(s_2) = p_2$, and $p(s_3) = p_3$. Indeed, $\sum_j \lambda_j^i p_j(r_1 - r_2) = 0$ for $i = 1, 2$ guarantees that we have an equilibrium. For the nontriviality, note that, for some j,

$$p_j \cdot \omega_j' = p_j \cdot \omega_j + p_j \cdot r = p_j \cdot \omega_j + a_j \neq p_j \cdot \omega_j. \qquad \blacksquare$$

We end this section with a few remarks on the hypothesis of proposition 1.

The proof makes clear that we need to randomize at least three price vectors, and therefore we need at least three states. The next section will further clarify this.

We do not know if there is an example with $\ell = 2$.

The need of multiple equilibria from some endowment is clear. Sunspots can matter only if they induce randomness. However, the *ex post* economy is nonrandom, and therefore randomness can only come from a nonuniform equilibrium selection for the *ex post* economy.

The need of multiple equilibria is not so obvious if sunspot-contingent assets are possible. The following statement may be true, but, so far as we know, it is unproven, and a proof does not seem easy: "Suppose that the utility functions of the N consumers at $t = 1$ are such that the equilibrium is unique for any distribution of endowments. Then for any asset structure at $t = 0$ (sunspot-contingent assets allowed) every equilibrium is sunspot-free." Note that the statement is true in the two extreme cases (where there are no sunspot-contingent assets and where there are enough of them to allow complete insurance). The problem is in the intermediate cases. [Note added in May 1990: The above question has been settled by Hens (1990). Alas, for the more natural interpretations of the expression "the equilibrium is unique for any distribution of endowments" the statement is false. See Hens 1990 for a thorough analysis.]

2 Redundant Assets and Sunspots

In this section I shall argue, by means of a trivial example, that the existence of redundant assets may help to immunize an economy against the presence of sunspots. The reason is that with more assets there are more possibilities that the economy finds a way to coordinate itself so that trade takes place before the sunspot signal occurs—which is like saying that the agents of the economy agree not to look at the sunspot.

As in the previous section, at $t = 1$ there are spot markets for ℓ goods. We do not, however, require now that the market structure be complete at $t = 1$. It is possible that, for example, one of the characteristics defining a commodity be a set of (payoff-relevant, non-sunspot) states of the world, and that each of these leads to a separate budget constraint. We need not be explicit about the particular spot market structure.

At time $t = 0$, there is trade in J assets. We assume that the family of payoff vectors $\{r_1, \ldots, r_J\} \subset R^\ell$ has maximal possible rank, i.e., the rank equals the minimum of J and ℓ.

Depending on the spot market structure, the assets may or may not be redundant. In section 1 all the assets were redundant because the system of spot markets was complete to begin with. More generally, suppose that we had G physical goods and M payoff-relevant states. Then $\ell = GM$, and if there is a budget constraint per state we have redundancy only if $J > M$.

The number of traders is N.

As in section 1, at the beginning of period 1 the publicly observable sunspot state $s \in S$ occurs. The cardinality of the set S is not restricted in any way (except that for simplicity we take it to be finite). A sunspot equilibrium $(\bar{q}, \bar{y}, \bar{p}, \bar{x})$ is defined as in section 1. (Note that if the spot market structure requires several budget constraints, even after the occurrence of s, then the budget restriction in part (b) of the definition in section 1 must be modified accordingly.)

The example in section 1, or for that matter any trivial (but nonconstant across sunspots) sunspot equilibrium, shows that sunspot equilibria may not be Pareto-optimal. If we could create a complete set of sunspot-contingent assets, then the Pareto-optimality of equilibria would be restored. Proposition 2, which is a version of the First Fundamental Theorem, shows that there is another possibility: if $J = \ell$, then any sunspot equilibrium is optimal (that is, it is sunspot-free). Note that ℓ *may be quite smaller than* S, which means that even if $J = \ell$ and, from the standpoint of the original economy, there is much redundancy, we may still be quite far from completeness inclusive of sunspots (that is, insurance contracts against sunspots may remain unavailable).

There is no mystery in this result. Think of the J assets as future contracts. Then the hypothesis $J = \ell$ says that any trade can be guaranteed by future contracts. Hence, even if there are no exogenously given insurance contracts on sunspot signals, there is nonetheless an endogenous insurance mechanism: future contracting before the signal occurs. In a related guise all this is very familiar. The traditional interpretation of the Arrow-Debreu equilibrium is in terms of contracting at time 0 for any future delivery of goods (which could be contingent on the occurrence of some payoff-relevant state). Clearly, any subsequently occurring sunspot signal will not affect anything. All trade has taken place at time 0. As Arrow (1953) observed, if the equilibrium is recast as taking place sequentially then there is much asset redundancy in the traditional interpretation (only one contingent commodity for every payoff-relevant state is needed). In turn, my point is simply that this redundancy is not entirely useless: it makes sunspot infection more difficult.

Formally,

PROPOSITION 2 If $J \geq \ell$ then every sunspot equilibrium is Pareto-optimal.

Proof As indicated, no more is involved than the usual proof of the First Fundamental Theorem. Suppose that $(\bar{q},\bar{y},\bar{p},\bar{x})$ is a sunspot equilibrium and that the allocation x Pareto-dominates $\bar{x}$. Because the rank of $\{r_1,\ldots,r_J\}$ is ℓ, we can find $y = (y_1,\ldots,y_N)$ such that $\sum_i y_i = 0$ and $x_i = \sum_j r_j y_{ij}$. If $\bar{q}\cdot y_i \leq 0$ then agent i could attain the consumption x_i at prices $(\bar{q},\bar{p})$. Hence $\bar{q}\cdot y_i \geq 0$ for all i and $\bar{q}\cdot y_i > 0$ for at least one i. But this contradicts $\sum_i y_i = 0$. ■

3 More on Redundancy

In the previous section we saw by means of an example how the presence of redundant assets may prevent the occurrence of some unsuitable phenomena. This point can be deepened and made much more general. Even in a context of complete markets (where the set of equilibrium allocations is invariant to the addition or deletion of redundant assets) the properties of particular equilibria may depend on the precise set of available assets. As an illustration, it is shown in this section that an Arrow-Debreu equilibrium that with probability 1 is *ex post* tâtonnement stable and unique can become *ex post* unstable and nonunique with positive probability if a redundant asset is dropped.

Suppose that at $t = 1$ one of two states $s = 1, 2$ can occur. In state 2 there is a single physical commodity; in state 1 there are two. We have two traders with utility functions of the form

$$u_i(x_i,y_i) = v_i(x_i) + y_i,$$

where $x_i \in R^2_+$ and $y_i \in R_+$ are, respectively, the consumptions in states 1 and 2 (obviously, these functions can be viewed as von Neumann-Morgenstern utility indicators). We assume that $v_i(\cdot)$ is strictly concave, increasing, and continuously differentiable in R^2_+. The endowment vectors are denoted $(\omega_i, z_i) \in R^2_+ \times R_+$. The following fact is well known:

LEMMA 3 Given $v_i(\cdot)$, ω_i, $i = 1, 2$, there is a $k > 0$ large enough that if $z_i > k$, $i = 1, 2$, then

$$\{(u_i(x_i) + y_i, \omega_i, z_i)\}_{i=1}^2$$

has a single Arrow-Debreu equilibrium.

Proof Let $\omega_i < re$, $e = (1,1)$, for $i = 1, 2$ and $t > \partial_j v_i(x_i)$ for $i = 1, 2, j = 1, 2$, and $x_i \leq re$. Take then $k > 4rt$. There can be only an equilibrium allocation with $y_i > 0$ for $i = 1, 2$. This is simply due to the quasi-linearity of the utility functions. Suppose there was an equilibrium allocation $(\bar{x}_i, \bar{y}_i)$ with $\bar{y}_1 = 0$. Normalizing to $p_3 = 1$, the corresponding equilibrium price vector is denoted $p = (p_1, p_2)$. We must have

$$k \leq p \cdot \omega_1 + z_1 \leq p \cdot \bar{x}_1 \leq p \cdot (\omega_1 + \omega_2) \leq 2rp \cdot e.$$

Hence, $p \cdot e \geq k/2r > 2t$. On the other hand, for each $j = 1, 2$ there should be an i with $\bar{x}_{ij} > 0$. From the first-order conditions, $\lambda_i p_j = \partial_j v_i(x_i)$ and $\lambda_i \geq 1$. Therefore, $p_j \leq \partial_j v_i(x_i) < t$, and so $p \cdot e < 2t$. This contradiction shows that there cannot be more than one equilibrium. ■

Denote by $f_i(p)$, $p \in R^2_{++}$, the excess demand of consumer i in the spot economy of state 1 determined by the utility functions $v_i(\cdot)$ and the endowments ω_i. Letting $e = (1,1)$, suppose that $f_1(e) + f_2(e) = 0$ and $\partial v_i(\omega_i + f_i(e)) = e$. What restrictions does all this impose on $f(p) = f_1(p) + f_2(p)$? As it is well known (see Shafer and Sonnenschein 1982 or section 5.5 of Mas-Colell 1985), the answer is "almost none." In particular, we may choose $f(\cdot)$ to have as many zeroes as we wish, and we can also predetermine the matrix $\partial f(e)$. Thus, for example, the equilibrium price vector e could be unstable.

On the other hand, if the z_i $(i = 1, 2)$ are large enough, lemma 3 ensures that the overall Arrow-Debreu economy has a single equilibrium, which, normalizing to $p_3 = 1$, cannot be any other than $(p_1, p_2) = e$.

We have the following situation. Consider three assets with returns $r_1 = (1,0,0)$, $r_2 = (0,1,0)$, and $r_3 = (0,0,1)$. Thus, r_1 and r_2 are contingent assets on state 1 but with returns in different commodities. If the asset structure is $\{r_1, r_2, r_3\}$ one of the two first assets is redundant but we can sustain the Arrow-Debreu equilibrium very nicely. In fact, we can even guarantee that in the *ex post* spot economy of state 1 the equilibrium price vector e is a no-trade equilibrium, hence unique and stable. However, if we drop one redundant asset the Arrow-Debreu equilibrium can be reached only with zero trade in assets, which means that in the *ex post* spot economy of state 1 the equilibrium price vector e may not be particularly nice (it could be nonunique, unstable, etc.). There is, therefore, a definitive loss in deleting the redundant asset.

A similar point has been made by Samuelson (1974) in the context of lump-sum taxation. There the redundancy issue is that the same wealth transfer can be accomplished by in-kind transfers denominated in any commodity.

Acknowledgments

I am thankful to O. Hart, T. Hens, and an anonymous referee for comments.

References

Arrow, K. 1953. Le rôle des valeurs boursières pour la repartition la meuillere des risques. Cahiers du Séminaire d'Econometrie, CNRS, Paris.

Aumann, R., J. Peck, and K. Shell, 1988. Asymmetric Information and Sunspot Equilibria: A Family of Simple Examples. CAE WP 88-34, Cornell University.

Balasko, Y. 1987. Equivariant General Equilibrium Theory. Mimeo, Université de Geneve.

Balasko, Y., D. Cass, and K. Shell. 1988. Market Participation and Sunspot Equilibria. CAE WP 88-11, Cornell University.

Cass, D., and K. Shell. 1983. "Do sunspots matter?" *Journal of Political Economy* 91: 193–227.

Guesnerie, R., and J. J. Laffont. 1988. Notes on Sunspot Equilibria in Finite Horizon Models. Mimeo, Paris.

Hens, T. 1990. Which is the appropriate uniqueness concept? Private communication.

Mas-Colell, A. 1985. *The Theory of General Economic Equilibrium: A Differentiable Approach.* Cambridge University Press.

Maskin, E., and J. Tirole. 1987. "Correlated equilibria and sunspots." *Journal of Economic Theory* 43 (2): 364–373.

Peck, J., and K. Shell. 1991. "Correlated and sunspot equilibria in imperfectly competitive economies." *Review of Economic Studies* 58 (in press).

Samuelson, P. 1974. "A curious case where reallocation cannot achieve optimum welfare." In *Public Finance and Stabilization Policy*, ed. W. Smith and J. Culbertson. North-Holland. Also in volume 4 of Samuelson's *Collected Papers*, ed. H. Nagatani and K. Crowley. MIT Press, 1977.

Shafer, W., and H. Sonnenschein. 1982. "Market demand and excess demand functions." In *Handbook of Mathematical Economics*, Volume 2, ed. K. Arrow and M. Intriligator. North-Holland.

Shell, K. 1987. "Sunspot equilibrium." In *The New Palgrave: A Dictionary of Economics*, ed. J. Eatwell, M. Milgate, and P. Newman. Macmillan.

On the Aggregate Effects of Individual Risks

Jayasri Dutta and Heraklis Polemarchakis

Where does aggregate risk come from?

Models of aggregate activity with risk typically start from the premise that aggregate production is subject to stochastic influences or productivity shocks. Firms and individuals optimize relative to this uncertainty, markets clear, and the resulting equilibrium paths usually display cyclical properties (Kydland and Prescott 1982).

These models are able to produce equilibrium paths that mimic the qualitative properties of observed aggregates with varying degrees of success. Nevertheless, they have been criticized, often vociferously. Methodologically, they appear to be assuming the results: the exogenous aggregate shocks are usually endowed with rather elaborate process properties; allocations and prices, at equilibrium, inherit these properties and, not surprisingly, display the path properties of the shocks themselves. More important, these models rely on aggregate or at least heavily correlated individual risks: it is hard to point to examples of any empirical relevance that describe persistent stochastic influences on the aggregate economy, much less to justify their sophisticated path properties.

This criticism can be understood, more generally, as posing the following question: Is it compatible with competitive equilibrium that endogenously determined aggregates (prices and allocations) display more risk than the primitive structure of the economy (the endowments and preferences of individuals and the technologies of firms)? For example, suppose that individual endowments vary stochastically; and that this variation is appropriately small and independent across individuals in the sense that per capita endowments are essentially constant according to a law of large numbers. Then an optimal competitive allocation obeys a law of large numbers as well, so that endogenous aggregates do not display more risk than the primitives (Malinvaud 1972, 1973).

In economies that extend over infinite time, this is no longer true: at a competitive equilibrium, endogenous aggregates can vary more than the primitive structure. The most striking examples are periodic cycles, even chaos (Benhabib and Day 1982, Grandmont 1985) and sunspot equilibria (Azariades 1981, Azariades and Guesnerie 1987), which show that even a nonrandom economy can possess equilibrium paths that display apparently random properties. Nevertheless, such an economy possesses time-invariant equilibrium paths or steady states, so the question is answered only in part.

An alternative approach focuses on the role of the asset structure in achieving the relative constancy of equilibrium aggregates. When the asset structure is incomplete (possibly because of the demographic structure), sunspot equilibria may exist. This is the case even in an economy with a finite time horizon (Cass and Shell 1983). Possibly more in tune with macroeconomic models, consider an economy in which an optimal allocation is time-invariant or independently and identically distributed in time; this allocation is achieved at a competitive equilibrium if individuals have access to a perfect capital market. Nevertheless, a competitive equilibrium displays risk and cyclical persistence if individuals face borrowing constraints (Scheinkman and Weiss 1986) or, more generally, if the asset market is incomplete (Dutta and Polemarchakis 1990). Furthermore, all equilibrium paths display more risk than the primitives. The weakness of this argument is that it does not stand up in an economy of large numbers. Suppose that individual risks are small enough for a law of large numbers to operate; as the size of the economy increases, the equilibrium with an incomplete asset market converges to a time-invariant or an identically and independently distributed inefficient allocation.

Here, we provide an alternative argument for the aggregation of small risks that is immune to a law of large numbers. The risk of endogenous aggregates increases with the size of the economy.

Consider an economy in which production is carried out in many small firms. Productivity in each firm is random; suppose, even, that this randomness is independently and identically distributed. Obviously, this could be an ideal situation for a law of large numbers to operate, which would ensure that, as the number of firms increased, prices and allocations would converge to those achievable by a nonstochastic limit economy. This is indeed true, provided that enough decisions are taken *ex ante*, before the realization of uncertainty. On the contrary, if investment can be reallocated across firms *ex post*, after the realization of the productivity shocks, or if firms can anticipate their productivities, in a large economy, a competitive equilibrium preserves and even magnifies risk in the aggregate.

Technically, our argument relies on a very simple observation. A law of large numbers holds with respect to averages; in particular, for a sequence of independent realizations of a random variable, a weighted average converges to a constant, the expectation, with probability 1, whenever the maximal weight converges to 0. If investment is allocated before the realization of uncertainty, aggregate output depends on a weighted average of productivity shocks which obeys a law of large numbers. If investment can be reallocated *ex post*, aggregate production depends asymmetrically on individual shocks, assigning much greater weight on their maximal value. The preservation of risks in the aggregate results from the fact that the extremal values of an identically and independently distributed sequence do not converge with probability 1.

The critical factor in our analysis is the timing of investment decisions relative to the realization of the productivity shocks. When is it likely that the allocation of investment is contingent on the realization of productivities? We may think of this in two ways: either that capital is shiftable and some part of it is retraded once productivity is observed; or that firms receive information and act as if their investment decisions are made *ex post*. Suppose, first, that capital is shiftable. At any point in time, firms hold capital that includes investment made in the preceding period. The state of nature realizes; at each such state, firms differ in their productivities. Some amount of capital, for example the most recent investment, can be retraded upon the observation of productivities. Unlucky firms prefer to sell their machinery to lucky ones, since this is more profitable than producing. As a result, the firm with the maximal realization produces a large proportion of aggregate output; at the limit, if all capital is shiftable, only the luckiest firms produces at all, up to diminishing returns to scale. Aggregate production reflects this asymmetry, and preserves risk precisely because of it. The equilibrium that realizes is exactly as if investment were fully contingent on foreknowledge of the state of nature. A more direct argument that yields the same equilibrium paths is based on information. Suppose that each firm can anticipate its own productivity. This is a first approximation to a world in which management receives enough information about the production possibilities of the firm to affect investment decisions. Of course, anticipation need not be perfect; the qualitative results survive in a world of imperfect anticipation as well (Donaldson and Dutta 1989).

This argument is not specific to a particular model. We illustrate the properties of equilibrium paths in an overlapping-generations economy with production and a sequentially complete asset market, which allows for explicit characterizations. We begin by showing that a large-numbers property holds as long as investment decisions by individual firms are made *ex ante*. Next, that the argument fails when investment decisions are made *ex post*. An explicit example demonstrates that aggregate variability increases as the size of the economy (the number of firms) increases; output is serially correlated, and the real rate of interest varies countercyclically.

1 The Economy

Time,

$$t = \dots, -1, 0, 1, \dots,$$

extends from the indefinite past to the indefinite future.

Each period, an individual is born and lives for two periods. Individuals are identical aside from for the calendar time of their birth. An individual is endowed with one unit of labor when young, and none when old. There is one consumption-investment good each period. The cardinal utility function of the individual born at t,

$$U(C_t^t, C_{t+1}^t) = U(C_t^t) + \rho\, U(C_{t+1}^t), \quad \rho > 0$$

is smooth, strictly monotonically increasing and strictly concave. Obviously, the one unit of labor is supplied inelastically each period.

The single good is produced each period by a large number of firms,
$n = 1, \dots, N,$
which have the same technology to use capital, k, and labor, l, to produce output, x, Firms are subject to similar, but not identical, stochastic variations of productivity each period. The production technology of a typical firm, invariant over time, is

$$x_{n,t} = \theta_{n,t} k_{n,t}^{(1-\alpha)} l_{n,t}^{\alpha}, \quad 0 < \alpha < 1.$$

Productivity, θ, varies stochastically across firms and over time. At each time period, the realization of uncertainty is described by the vector

$$\theta_{t,N} = (\dots, \theta_{n,t}, \dots).$$

The good can be either consumed or invested. Investment, x, by a firm transforms costlessly into capital the next period. Capital depreciates by a factor δ each period. The accumulation of capital in each firm is described by

$$k_{n,t} = (1 - \delta) k_{n,t-1} + z_{n,t}, \quad 0 < \delta < 1.$$

ASSUMPTION 1 The vectors of productivities $\theta_{t,N}$ are strictly positive, and they are independently, identically distributed according to a nondegenerate probability distribution.

This is an assumption about the variation of the entire vector of productivities across time, which specifies that the economy has a stationary and memoryless structure. Differences in information structure lead to the preservation of randomness, and induce persistence, even in an economy that allows for a law of large numbers and a limiting steady state. Obviously, persistence would be more easily derived in an economy in which the exogenous characteristics were assumed to possess it.

The nondegeneracy of the distribution limits the cross-sectional correlation structure; there cannot be exact linear relations between the productivities of different firms at each point in time. Of course, this is trivially satisfied if productivities are independent across firms as well as across time.

ASSUMPTION 2 At each t, the productivities $\theta_{n,t}$ are positive, and they are identically distributed according to the probability distribution P.

This ensures that the firms in this economy have access to identical technologies, identical up to the realization of the productivity shocks. With constant returns to scale. renaming "firms" appropriately always achieves this. That the marginal distributions be the same imposes no restrictions on their dependence; productivity may be correlated across firms.

Spot markets for labor open after the realization of productivites each period; and also, after the determination of the capital employed by each firm. The output is numeraire. Firms, which maximize profits, buy labor at wage w, which clears the labor market.

A firm employs labor

$$l_{n,t} = \alpha^{1/(1-\alpha)}\theta_{n,t}^{1/(1-\alpha)}w_t^{-1/(1-\alpha)}k_{n,t}.$$

The output of the firm is

$$x_{n,t} = \alpha^{\alpha/(1-\alpha)}\theta_{n,t}^{1/(1-\alpha)}w_t^{-\alpha/(1-\alpha)}k_{n,t},$$

and its profit is

$$\pi(k_{n,t},w_t,\theta_{n,t}) = (1-\alpha)x_{n,t} = (1-\alpha)\alpha^{\alpha/(1-\alpha)}\theta_{n,t}^{1/(1-\alpha)}w_t^{-\alpha/(1-\alpha)}k_{n,t}.$$

This is the objective function for the investment decisions of the firm. Note that it is linear in the capital employed by the firm.

Labor-market clearing requires that

$$L_{t,N} = \sum_{n=1}^{N} l_{n,t} = 1,$$

so that

$$w_{t,N} = \alpha\left(\sum_{n=1}^{N} \theta_{n,t}^{1/(1-\alpha)} k_{n,t}\right)^{1-\alpha}.$$

The aggregate capital stock is

$$K_{t,N} = \sum_{n=1}^{N} k_{n,t}.$$

Aggregate output is

$$X_{t,N} = \sum_{n=1}^{N} x_{n,t} = \left(\sum_{n=1}^{N} \theta_{n,t}^{1/(1-\alpha)} k_{n,t}\right)^{1-\alpha}.$$

This is a function of the realizations of the productivity shocks and of the capital holdings by firms,

$$k_t = (\ldots, k_{n,t}, \ldots).$$

Individuals work when they are young, and consume in both periods. Their lifetime income is realized in the first period of their lives, and is split between consumption and savings. The asset structure determines the form in which income may be carried across time and states of nature. Given a menu of assets, savings is carried as a portfolio of claims on output, which is fully redeemed in old age. The firm borrows in the asset market and uses its profits to pay off claims. Aggregate investment is

$$Z_{t,N} = \sum_{n=1}^{N} z_{n,t}.$$

The structure of the asset market determines the distribution of consumption between individuals in the first and second periods of their lives and, more important, between aggregate savings and investment at equilibrium; it also determines the allocation of investment to individual firms, the vector

$$z_{t,N} = (\ldots, z_{n,t}, \ldots).$$

We consider first the allocation of investment across firms, abstracting from the aggregate savings decision; this is possible because in this economy firms are identical *ex ante*, even though they differ *ex post*. We do this to focus attention on the role of investment allocations in smoothing or magnifying the aggregate effects of individual risks; we consider separately and then contrast the case of irreversible investment and no anticipation and the case of anticipation or shiftable investment.

Finally, we examine the role of the asset structure in determining aggregate investment, and we characterize competitive equilibrium paths when the asset market is sequentially complete. To illustrate the characteristics of equilibrium paths, we use the example of the log-linear economy,

$$U(C) = \ln C,$$

which allows for explicit solutions.

2 Small Risks

Suppose, first, that when its investment decision is made, at $t - 1$, a firm can forecast its future productivity, $\theta_{n,t}$, only in stochastic terms; since productivities are independent over time, this is independent of history. Furthermore, capital is firm-specific and, once in place, can be used only by the firm that invested it. Investment is thus irreversible. The resulting path of capital accumulation has the property that aggregate randomness obeys a law of large numbers; hence, as the number of firms increases, the stationary competitive equilibrium converges to a time-invariant steady state.

Since their productivities are identically distributed, and since they are price takers in the labor market, all firms face exactly the same decision problem. A symmetric path preserves the symmetric nature of the optimization problem, so the aggregate capital stock is

$$K_{t,N} = Nk_{n,t}.$$

Aggregate output is

$$X_{t,N} = v_{t,N} K_t^{(1-\alpha)},$$

where

$$v_{t,N} = \left(\frac{1}{N}\sum_{n=1}^{N} \theta_t^{1/(1-\alpha)}\right)^{(1-\alpha)}$$

is a functional average of the individual shocks, which is bounded below by the arithmetic average and above by the maximal element. Evidently, this acts as an aggregator of randomness in production. Since the level of aggregate production suffices to describe randomness in this economy, the state of nature is fully described by the realization or the aggregate productivity shock.

The aggregate shock is distributed independently in time. Furthermore, being a functional average, it obeys a law of large numbers. As the size of the economy (the number of firms) grows without bound, the aggregate shock converges to a positive constant with probability 1; this is a straightforward application of the strong law of large numbers. Hence, the aggregate production function is constant in the limit. The limit economy is defined by this technology, preserving preferences and endowments as before. This limit economy is time-invariant and admits time-invariant paths of capital accumulation (steady states); two such steady-state paths are usually referred to as the *golden rule or the efficient steady state* and the *autarkic or inefficient steady state*, respectively. Properties of the aggregate savings function allow these steady states to be achieved as limits of competitive-equilibrium paths in economies with finitely many firms.

ASSUMPTION 3 There exists $k < \infty$ such that, at each t, $\theta_{n,t}$ is stochastically independent of $\theta_{m,t}$ whenever $|m - n| > k$. Also,

$$\mathrm{E}\theta_{n,t}^{1/(1-\alpha)} < \infty \quad \text{for } l \leq 4.$$

This strengthens assumption 2. That the dependence of stochastic shocks be limited to k neighborhoods is not implausible as a model of cross sectional dependence; Malinvaud (1973) assumes a slightly different dependence structure, with the stochastic dependence of $\theta_{m,t}$ and $\theta_{n,t}$ decaying smoothly with $|m - n|$. It is slightly stronger than necessary in order to derive a law of large numbers, as is the moment condition.

LEMMA 1 At each t,

$$\mathrm{Prob}\left(\lim_{N\to\infty} v_{t,N} = \mu^{1-\alpha}\right) = 1.$$

Proof The proof is standard. Define

$$y_{n,t} = \theta_{n,t}^{1/(1-\alpha)} - \mu$$

and

$$y_{t,N} = \frac{1}{N}\sum_{n=1}^{N} y_{n,t}.$$

By construction,

$$\mathrm{E}y_{t,N} = 0.$$

The result holds whenever

$$\sum_{N=1}^{\infty} \mathrm{Prob}(|y_{t,N}| > \varepsilon) < \infty,$$

by the Borel-Cantelli lemma. From Chebyshev's inequality,

$$\mathrm{Prob}(|y_{t,N}| > \varepsilon) < \int \left(\frac{y_{t,N}}{\varepsilon}\right)^4 P(dy_{t,N}) \leq \frac{\mathrm{E}y_{t,N}^4}{\varepsilon^4} = \frac{\mathrm{E}(\sum_{n=1}^{N} y_{n,t})^4}{N^4\varepsilon^4}.$$

Since each $y_{n,t}$ has zero expectation and is correlated with at most $2k$ of its neighbors, and since all moments up to $4/(1-\alpha)$ exist,

$$\mathrm{E}\left(\sum_{n=1}^{N} y_n\right)^4 < b_k N^2$$

for an appropriately defined constant $b_k < \infty$. The fourth moment of $y_{t,N}$ is of $O(1/N^2)$, and hence

$$\lim_{N\to\infty} \sum_{N=k}^{\infty} \mathrm{Prob}(|y_{t,N}| > \varepsilon)$$

is bounded. Since almost sure convergence is preserved by continuous transformations, the result follows. ■

Thus, with irreversible investment, in a large economy, aggregate productivity is essentially riskless.

The Limit Economy

The limit economy preserves the demographic structure and the individual preferences and endowments.

The aggregate technology is

$$X_t = \nu K_t^{1-\alpha} L_t^{\alpha},$$

where

$$\mu = \mathrm{E}\theta^{1/(1-\alpha)},$$

which exists, and

$$\nu = \mu^{1-\alpha};$$

thus, the limit economy has no risk.

Capital accumulation writes as

$$K_{t+1} = (1 - \delta)K_t + Z_t.$$

The properties of steady state equilibria in this model are well known. This, of course, is the economy of Diamond 1967.

The economy possesses two steady states, both of which can be supported as competitive equilibria. The fact that these can actually be obtained by solutions to alternative optimization exercises displays the autarkic nature of the inefficient solution.

At a steady state, employment, capital, output, and consumption are constant over time. Evidently,

$$L = 1.$$

The capital stock is

$$K_t = K,$$

and consumption is

$$C_t^t = C \quad \text{and} \quad C_t^{t-1} = C'.$$

Output is

$$X_t = X = \nu K^{1-\alpha},$$

and investment just replaces depreciation with

$$Z_t = Z = \delta K.$$

The aggregate feasibility constraint is

$$C + C' + Z \leq X.$$

The golden rule or efficient steady state maximizes the representative utility

$$U(C) + \rho\, U(C')$$

subject to the feasibility constraints. It follows that, irrespective of preferences, the golden rule is characterized by

$$K_g = \left(\frac{1-\alpha}{\delta} v\right)^{1/\alpha}$$

or

$$K_g = \sigma_g X_g,$$

where

$$\sigma_g = \frac{1-\alpha}{\delta}.$$

The autarkic path is obtained by performing the same optimization subject to the additional constraint

$$C + K \leq \alpha X,$$

which essentially imposes a borrowing constraint on the young: the consumption and savings of the young cannot exceed their wage income. Since this is in addition to the feasibility constraint, it is typically inefficient. Nevertheless, both can be decentralized as competitive equilibria. The autarkic path has the property that, irrespective of preferences,

$$C' = (1-\alpha)X + (1-\delta)K,$$

so that capital income equals the consumption of the old. In the log-linear economy, the level of capital stock at autarky is

$$K_{\mathrm{a}} = \left(\frac{\rho\alpha}{1+\rho} v\right)^{1/\alpha}$$

or

$$K_{\mathrm{a}} = \sigma_{\mathrm{a}} X_{\mathrm{a}},$$

where

$$\sigma_{\mathrm{a}} = \frac{\rho\alpha}{1+\rho}.$$

The Structural Stability of a Steady State

For every finite economy, aggregate productivity varies stochastically over time, even though its variability may be very small, and, as a result, an exact-steady state solution cannot be sustained.

The transition equation is the accumulation rule

$$K_{t,N} = (1 - \delta)K_{t-1,N} + Z_{t,N}.$$

This suffices to describe aggregate dynamics, since individual firms behave symmetrically. In principle, the level of aggregate investment can depend on all variables observable at each point in time, the full history of the realizations of uncertainty, possibly in a nonstationary way.

As an expositional device, we will start by assuming that investment is a function of current and past outputs and capital stocks; this allows us to examine the properties of the investment function which ensure that the resulting path is well behaved—in particular, that the path of capital stocks converges to a steady state as the size of the economy increases. Obviously, investment is a result of optimization by agents, so the function cannot be arbitrary. This will depend on what assets are available to transfer value across time and across states of nature. In a later section, we derive the aggregate investment function in an economy where asset markets are sequentially complete.

A continuous, stationary investment function is

$$Z_{t,N} = F_N(K_{t,N}, \ldots, K_{t-\tau,N}, v_{t,N}, \ldots, v_{t-\tau,}N);$$

obviously, this can be written equivalently as a function of a finite history of outputs, $X_{t-j,N}$, and capital stocks. The associated accumulation rule is of the form

$$K_{t+1,N} = Q_{F_N}(K_{t,N}, \ldots, K_{t-\tau,N}, v_{t,N}, \ldots, v_{t-\tau,}N).$$

We will consider only stationary rules, which involve time-invariant functions F and Q_F. Nonstationary investment functions would generate solution paths which converge to nonconstant paths in the limit.

Without loss of generality, we will assume that $\tau = 0$ so that the investment and accumulation functions involve only one lag. The results carry over, with very little modification, to situations where τ is finite, and the accumulation rule involves finite histories.

At each t, the aggregate shock converges to a constant as $N \to \infty$. Investment, $Z_{t,N}$ depends on $K_{t,N}$ and the aggregate shock $v_{t,N}$. Define the continuous nonstochastic function

$$Z_t = F(K_t, v)$$

and the corresponding transition equation

$$K_{t+1} = Q_F(K_t, v).$$

This is the transition equation for the limit economy. At each t and K_t, investment $Z_{t,N}$ converges to the value of $F(K_t, v)$ as $N \to \infty$.

A steady state of the limit economy is a positive fixed point of Q_F; this is a constant level of capital stock, K_F, which can be maintained for all time in the economy without risk. Clearly, the existence and possible uniqueness of this solution is a property of the investment function F. Since we take this function as a primitive for the moment, we will assume that a solution exists and is locally unique. Obviously, this must be verified for the investment rule that results from the particular asset structure. By definition, K_F is a solution to

$$\delta K - F(K, v) = 0.$$

The convergence of the stochastic paths $K_{t,N}$ $(t = \ldots, 0, 1, \ldots)$ requires an additional property of Q_F. We will say that k_F is locally structurally stable whenever there exists $c \in (0,1)$ such that $k \in [cK_F, (1/c)K_F]$ implies

$$\lim_{i \to \infty} Q_F^i(k) = K_F.$$

Clearly, there may be functions Q_F that have no structurally stable fixed points and others that have several. A sufficient condition for K_F to be structurally stable is that

$$\left.\frac{\partial Q_F}{\partial K}\right|_{K_F} < 1.$$

PROPOSITION 1 Consider sequences

$$t = 0, 1, \ldots, T_N, \quad N = 1, \ldots,$$

such that

$$\lim_{N \to \infty} \frac{T_N}{N} = r > 0.$$

Whenever $K_0 \in [cK_F, (1/c)K_F]$,

$$\text{prob}\left(\lim_{N\to\infty} K_{T_N} = K_F\right) = 1.$$

Proof Define

$$Q_{t,N} = (1-\delta)K + \sigma v_{t,N} K^{1-\alpha}.$$

This is a continuous function of $v_{t,N}$, and hence uniformly continuous. For each t, it must converge uniformly, almost surely, to the limit Q. Further, the composition of uniformly continuous functions is also uniformly continuous. It follows that, for each $r > 0$, Q^{rN} converges uniformly almost surely to the constant function. ■

This is useful because it distinguishes between alternative steady states of the limit economy: not all steady states are achievable as limits of stationary paths. To take a concrete example, suppose that K_1 and K_2 are such that $K_i = \delta F(K_i)$ for $i = 1, 2$; and only K_1 is structurally stable. Clearly, the associated steady state can be achieved as the limit of stationary equilibria in economies with risk. The unstable steady state cannot be achieved with probability 1, since any perturbation $v_{t,N}$ will take $K_{t,N+1}$ further away from K_2; K_1 is an attractor for stochastic equilibria, while K_2 is not.

The additional property of local structural stability determines whether, as the distribution of aggregate risk collapses, the stationary equilibrium paths collapse to the particular steady state . The fact that $v_{t,N}$ continues to be stochastic for each finite N builds in a tremble which rules out unstable steady states as limit equilibria. Evidently, the structural stability of a steady state does not imply that it is the limit of equilibrium paths in an economy with risk; this requires that the initial capital stock be in the invariant set.

3 Aggregate Risk

Suppose, alternatively, that investment can be reallocated across firms after the realization of the productivity shocks. Equivalently, when its investment decision is made, at $t-1$, a firm can forecast its productivity exactly.

The spot market for labor clears after the reallocation of capital across firms. Since profit is linear in the capital employed by the firm, capital-market clearing requires that the capital stock employed by a firm be

$$k_{n,t} = (1 - \delta)k_{n,t-1} + \Delta_{n,t}Z_{t-1,N},$$

where

$$\Delta_{n,t} = \begin{cases} 1 & \text{if } \theta_{n,t} > \theta_{m,t}, \quad m = 1, \ldots, N \\ 0 & \text{otherwise.} \end{cases}$$

The production functions of firms display constant returns to scale and are otherwise identical, and it makes no difference to assume that only one firm has productivity equal to the maximum.

Define

$$\hat{\theta}_{t,N} = \sum_{n=1}^{N} \Delta_{n,t}\theta_{n,t} = \max_{n=1,\ldots,N} (\theta_{n,t}).$$

This extremal value is a random variable which is independently and identically distributed through time. The preservation of randomness in the aggregate comes precisely from the fact the extremal value of an expanding sequence does not obey a law of large numbers, and, as a result, the aggregate production function does not converge to a nonstochastic limit as the size of the economy increases.

The aggregate capital stock is

$$K_{t,N} = (1 - \delta)K_{t-1,N} + Z_{t-1,N}.$$

Aggregate output is

$$X_t = \left[(1 - \delta) \sum_{n=1}^{N} \theta_{n,t}^{1/(1-\alpha)} k_{n,t-1} + \hat{\theta}_{t,N}^{1/(1-\alpha)} Z_{t-1,Z} \right]^{1-\alpha}$$

or

$$X_t = v_{t,N} K_t^{1-\alpha},$$

where

$$v_{t,N} = \left(\frac{(1 - \delta)\mu_{t,N} + \dfrac{Z_{t-1,N}}{K_{t-1,N}} \hat{\theta}_{t,N}^{1/(1-\alpha)}}{(1 - \delta) + \dfrac{K_{t-1,N}}{Z_{t-1,N}}} \right)^{1/\alpha}$$

is the aggregate productivity shock. The quantity

$$\mu_{t,N} = \sum_{n=1}^{N} \frac{\theta_{n,t}^{1/(1-\alpha)} k_{n,t-1}}{K_{t-1,N}}$$

is a weighted average of productivities, weighted by individual firms' shares in the aggregate capital stock.

The aggregate productivity shock $v_{t,N}$ has two components. Sunk capital earns the average return, $\mu_{t,N}$, while new capital, or investment, earns the maximal return $\hat{\theta}_{t,N}$. This is precisely what results in the preservation and magnification of randomness in the aggregate. If $\delta = 1$, so that capital depreciates fully,

$$v_{t,N} = \hat{\theta}_{t,N};$$

aggregate productivity is independently and identically distributed over time. In addition, for every finite N, the variability of $\theta_{t,N}$ is greater than that of $\mu_{t,N}$, the average productivity shock.

Extremal Values

If investment can be reallocated *ex post*, aggregate productivity depends on the extremal value of a sequence of identically distributed random variables. Clearly, this is stochastically increasing in the size of the economy. Here, we examine the limiting behavior of aggregate quantities as the economy grows without bound.

Typically, the extremal value does not converge to a constant even for bounded random variables. However, the limiting behavior of the maximal value is not invariant to the shape of the finite sample distribution. We explore the implications of a specific distribution, with bounded, positive support, which is attracted to an extremal distribution.

ASSUMPTION 4 At each t, the productivities $\theta_{n,t}$ are identically and independently distributed according to the probability distribution

$$\text{Prob}(\theta_{n,t} < \Theta) = 1 - (1 - \Theta)^r, \quad 0 < \Theta \leq 1, \quad r > 0.$$

This strengthens and specializes assumption 2. An explicit functional form is required for the limit distribution of the extremal value to be characterized.

PROPOSITION 2 At each t,

$$1 + \left(\frac{Z_{t-1}}{K_t}\right)^{-(1-\alpha)} \frac{v_{t,N}}{N^{1/r}} \Rightarrow_N y,$$

where $\Rightarrow_N$ refers to weak convergence as $N \to \infty$; and y is a positive random variable with probability distribution

$$\text{Prob}(y \leq Y) = \exp(-|Y|^r) = H_r(Y).$$

Proof The probability distribution of the individual shocks is such that

$$\lim_{\varepsilon \to 0} \frac{1 - \text{Prob}(1 - g\varepsilon)}{1 - \text{Prob}(\varepsilon)} = g^r$$

for each $g > 0$. This suffices for $\hat{\theta}_{t,N}$ to be attracted to an extremal distribution as $N \to \infty$. In particular, at each t,

$$1 + \frac{\hat{\theta}_{t,N}}{N^{1/r}} \Rightarrow_N y.$$

Now,

$$v_{t,N} = \left[(1 - \delta)\mu_{t,N} + \frac{Z_{t-1,N}}{K_{t-1,N}} \hat{\theta}_{t,N}^{1/(1-\alpha)} \right]^{1-\alpha} \frac{K_t^{1-\alpha}}{K_{t-1}}.$$

Note that $\mu_{t,N}$ is a weighted average, at each t, so that it converges to μ in probability as $N \to \infty$ for each t. Hence,

$$\operatorname*{plim}_{N \to \infty} \frac{\mu_{t,N}}{N^k} = 0$$

for all $k > 0$ and each t. Choose $k = 1/r(1 - \alpha)$; it follows that, at each t,

$$\frac{v_{t,N}}{N^{1/r}} \frac{Z_{t-1}^{-(1-\alpha)}}{K_t} \Rightarrow_N \frac{\hat{\theta}_{t,N}}{N^{1/r}}.$$ ■

This proposition demonstrates that the limit economy is not riskless; and derives the limiting distribution for the aggregate productivity shock $v_{t,N}$ as the size of the economy, indexed by the number of firms, increases. In the limit, the productivity shock is serially correlated if and only if $\delta < 1$. Obviously, if $\delta = 1$, $Z_{t-1} = K_t$ at each t, and the limiting distribution of $v_{t,N}/N^{1/r}$ does not depend on t. Otherwise, the quantity Z_{t-1}/K_t depends on lagged output, through the investment decision, as a result, $v_{t,N}$ is autocorrelated.

The nature of serial dependence in aggregate productivity depends on the investment function. To illustrate, consider linear capital-accumulation rules of the form

$$K_{t+1} = \sigma X_t, \quad 0 \le \sigma \le 1.$$

In this case,

$$\frac{Z_t}{K_{t+1}} = 1 - \frac{1-\delta}{v_{t,N}} \prod_{j=0}^{\infty} (v_{t-j-1,N})^{\alpha(1-\alpha)^j}.$$

The distribution of $v_{t,N}$, conditional on its own history, carries infinite memory.

The transition equation for aggregate output has a simpler representation for large N.

LEMMA 2 At each t,

$$X_t^* = \sigma^{1-\alpha}(X_{t-1}^* - (1-\delta)X_{t-2}^*)^{1-\alpha}(y_t - 1) + O(N^{-(1-\alpha)/r\alpha}),$$

where

$$X_t^* = \frac{X_t}{N^{1/r\alpha}},$$

and y_t is a sequence of independent random variables with probability distribution H_r.

Proof Write

$$X_t = v_{t,N}(\sigma X_{t-1})^{1-\alpha},$$

and define

$$y_t = 1 + \left(\frac{Z_{t-1}}{K_t}\right)^{-(1-\alpha)} \frac{v_{t,N}}{N^{1/r}}.$$

The result follows from the facts that

$$\frac{Z_{t-1}}{K_t} = 1 - (1-\delta)\frac{X_{t-2}}{X_{t-1}} = 1 - (1-\delta)\frac{X_{t-2}^*}{X_{t-1}^*},$$

and

$$\frac{X_t}{X_{t-1}^{1-\alpha}} = N^{1/r}\frac{X_t^*}{(X_{t-1}^*)^{1-\alpha}}. \qquad ■$$

This defines the limiting transition equation for X_t^*. To specialize further, suppose that $\delta = 1$; in this case, the quantity $x_t^* = \ln X_t^*$ is a linear autoregressive process, with correlation less than unity; it must possess an invariant distribution; similarly, X_t^*. Since $X_t = N^{1/r\alpha}X_t^*$, and X_t^* is stationary, it follows that X_t is stochastically increasing in N. Thus, for example, the mean and the standard deviation of X_t must be of order $N^{1/r\alpha}$. Further, X_t has finite memory and displays positive first-order autocorrelation.

4 Assets and the Investment Function

So far, we have specified that investment depend on output and capital stock, and derived the implications for the path of capital stocks. Clearly, investment is the outcome of individual portfolio decisions at equilibrium; thus, the equilibrium investment function depends on the structure of assets which allow transfers across time and across states of nature. Here, we derive the investment function, and the output process at competitive equilibrium, when the asset market is sequentially complete. We restrict attention to the log-linear economy, which allows for explicit solutions for equilibrium aggregates.

When the probability distribution of the aggregate productivity shock collapses, as is the case if investment is decided *ex ante*, equilibrium paths converge to a steady state of the limit economy. When the aggregate shock does not degenerate, as is the case if investment can be reallocated *ex post*, the aggregate investment function at equilibrium determines the path properties of aggregate variability for sequences of economies with increasing size.

We consider an asset market that is sequentially complete, so that elementary securities are traded every period, which pay off on different realizations of aggregate productivity. Here, in the absence of heterogeneity among investors, "fiat money" would implement the same allocations at equilibrium.

Aggregate productivity is the source of risk in this economy. The aggregate production function is

$$X_t = v_t K_t^{1-\alpha} L_t^{\alpha},$$

where v_t, the aggregate productivity shock, is a random variable. Clearly, the properties of this random variable are derived from the primitive assumptions on the firm-specific shocks and the information structure. The probability distribution of the shock at $t + 1$ conditional on all information available at time t is described by the density function

$$\pi_t(v_{t+1}).$$

In each period, individuals can trade in elementary securities that pay off in the following period contingent on the realization of aggregate productivity. The prices of the elementary securities traded at t are

$$q_t(v_{t+1}).$$

The individuals born at t maximize expected utility

$$\ln C_t^t + \rho \int \ln C_{t+1}^t(v_{t+1})\pi_t(v_{t+1})dv_{t+1}$$

subject to the budget constraint

$$C_t^t + \int C_{t+1}^t(v_{t+1})q_t(v_{t+1})dv_{t+1} \leq \alpha X_t.$$

The demand for consumption by the individuals in the first and second periods of their lives are

$$C_t^t = \frac{1}{1+\rho}\alpha X_t$$

and

$$C^{t-1}(v_t) = \frac{\rho}{1+\rho}\frac{\pi_{t-1}(v_t)}{q_{t-1}(v_t)}\alpha X_{t-1},$$

respectively.

Since the objective function of firms in the capital market is linear, competitive equilibrium requires that firms make zero profits, which reduces to

$$\int [(1-\alpha)v_{t+1}K_{t+1}^{-\alpha} + (1-\delta)K_{t+1}]q_t(v_{t+1})dv_{t+1} = 1.$$

The market for the good clears whenever

$$C_t^t + C_t^{t-1} + Z_t = X_t;$$

the wage is set so as to clear the labor market, while the asset market clears as a residual.

Prices for elementary securities

$$\hat{q}_t(v_{t+1}) = \frac{\pi_t(v_{t+1})\hat{K}_{t+1}}{(1-\alpha)\hat{X}_{t+1} + (1-\delta)\hat{K}_{t+1}},$$

by construction, yield a competitive equilibrium.

Evidently, there is no presumption that this is the unique competitive equilibrium. In particular, note that prices

$$\tilde{q}_{ht}(v_{t+1}) = \hat{q}_t(v_{t+1})h(v_{t+1})$$

clear spot markets whenever h is a strictly positive function with expectation 1.

In each period, the real risk-free rate of interest is

$$R_t = \frac{1}{\int q_t(v_{t+1})dv_{t+1}} - 1.$$

At equilibrium, investment is

$$Z_t = X_t - \frac{1}{1+\rho}\alpha X_t - \frac{\rho}{1+\rho}\frac{\pi_{t-1}(v_t)}{q_{t-1}(v_t)}\alpha X_{t-1}.$$

Substituting, we obtain the stochastic transition equation for the capital stock, at a competitive equilibrium with a sequentially complete market:

$$\begin{aligned} K_{t+1} &= Q(K_t, K_{t-1}, v_t, v_{t-1}) \\ &= (1-\delta)K_t + \frac{1}{1+\rho}[(1+\rho-\alpha)v_t K_t^{1-\alpha} - \alpha\rho(1-\alpha)v_t v_{t-1} K_t^{-\alpha} K_{t-1}^{1-\alpha} \\ &\qquad - \rho\alpha(1-\delta)v_{t-1}K_{t-1}^{1-\alpha}]. \end{aligned}$$

The solutions to this transition equation are the equilibrium paths of capital; output paths result from this and the aggregate production function. We are now in a position to examine the path properties of equilibrium, with or without aggregate risk. We will restrict the discussion to stationary equilibria.

First, note that the transition equation admits of an exact stationary solution, where the capital : output ratio is time invariant. Write the capital : output ratio as

$$\sigma_t = \frac{K_{t+1}}{X_t}.$$

The transition equation is

$$\sigma_t = \sigma_{t-1}(1-\delta)\frac{X_{t-1}}{X_t} + \left(1 - \frac{\alpha}{1+\rho}\right) - \frac{\alpha\rho}{1+\rho}\left[\frac{1-\alpha}{\sigma_{t-1}} + (1+\delta)\frac{X_{t-1}}{X_t}\right];$$

this can be written as

$$\sigma_t = Q_*\left(\sigma_{t-1}, \frac{X_t}{X_{t-1}}\right).$$

This equation has exactly one stationary solution, where $\sigma_t = \sigma$ for each t, and all X_t. This is the autarkic solution,

$$\sigma_{\mathrm{a}} = \frac{\rho\alpha}{1+\rho}.$$

Thus, the autarkic accumulation rule

$$K_{t+1} = \sigma_{\mathrm{a}} X_t$$

is a stationary equilibrium irrespective of the nature of aggregate risk.

We will examine the properties of equilibrium paths evaluated at this stationary autarkic solution. Other stationary equilibria exist: these must have σ_t varying over time or over states of nature. Since we want to examine the qualitative properties of stationary equilibria, the particular solution chosen does not matter very much.

First, suppose that investment cannot be reallocated after productivity is observed. As we showed, this implies that the aggregate productivity shock converges almost surely to constant as the size of the economy increases. Evaluated at this limit, the transition equation is nonstochastic. Note that

$$K - Q(K,K,v,v) = \delta K^{1-2\alpha}\left(\frac{K}{X} - \sigma_g\right)\left(\frac{K}{X} - \sigma_{\mathrm{a}}\right),$$

and thus the two positive solutions of the equation are the capital stock at the golden rule, $K = K_g$, and that at autarky, $K = K_{\mathrm{a}}$. This confirms that these are the two steady states of the limit economy.

Of course, we know more than this. The autarkic equilibrium is a stationary solution for each N, and not just in the limit; the golden rule is not. It is then trivial to show that the stationary solution is dynamically stable, and, as time and the size of the economy grow simultaneously without bound, the capital stock converges to the autarkic level, K_a, with probability 1: in the limit economy, the stationary solution implies that

$$K_t = v(\sigma_a K_{t-1})^{1-\alpha},$$

which is a contraction. Thus, the autarkic equilibrium is achievable as the limit of stationary competitive equilibria.

If it is possible to reallocate investment after productivity is observed, the aggregate productivity shock does not degenerate. At each t, and for all N, the aggregate production function is stochastic; as a result, capital stock and output at equilibrium are stochastic processes described by the stochastic transition rule. We can characterize their path properties for large economies; we will evaluate these properties at the stationary solution $\sigma_t = \sigma_a$.

From lemma 2, we can write the leading term of the equation for aggregate output as

$$X_t^* = (\sigma_a)^{1-\alpha}[X_{t-1}^* - (1-\delta)X_{t-2}^*]^{1-\alpha}(y_t - 1),$$

where

$$\hat{X}_t^* = \frac{\hat{X}_t}{N^{1/r\alpha}}$$

and where y_t is a random variable carrying the extremal distribution H_r.

Both output and capital are serially correlated, with autocorrelation positive in the first order and negative in the second order.

Consider the solutions in the special case where $\delta = 1$, for convenience. In this case, the transition relations are all log- linear. For $x_t = \ln X_t$, the last expression can be written as

$$x_t = c_N + (1-\alpha)x_{t-1} + e_t,$$

where e_t is a random variable with zero mean, independent over time, and where

$$c_N = (1/r)\ln N + \mathrm{E}\ln(y_t - 1) + (1-\alpha)\ln\sigma_a.$$

Similarly, $k_t = \ln K_t$ yields

$$k_t = c_N + \alpha\ln\sigma + (1-\alpha)k_{t-1} + e_{t-1}.$$

Writing $r_t = \ln(1 + R_t)$ for the interest rate and substituting, we can write the leading term of the equation for the interest rate as

$$r_t = d_N - \alpha x_t,$$

where

$$d_N = (1/r)\ln N - \ln \mathrm{E}\frac{1}{y_t - 1} - \ln(1 - \alpha) - \alpha \ln \sigma;$$

equivalently,

$$r_t = r_{t-1} - \alpha(x_t - x_{t-1}).$$

Clearly, the interest rate is countercyclical. This can be understood as follows. When productivity is high, there is an increase in the savings of the young. As a consequence, asset prices must move procyclically, thus decreasing the interest rate. For each fixed N, x_t and k_t are stationary stochastic processes, with

$$\mathrm{E}x_t = \frac{c_N}{\alpha} \quad \text{and} \quad \mathrm{E}\hat{k}_k = \ln \sigma + \mathrm{E}x_t.$$

Obviously, the average levels of output and capital stock increase as the size of the economy increases: the larger the number of firms, the larger the expected value of the maximum productivity, and as a result, increasing the sources of randomness increases aggregate productivity and hence output. The expected value of the interest rate is $\mathrm{E}\hat{r}_t = d_N - c_N$, which does not depend on N. Asset prices, and the interest rate, are stationary over time and invariant to the size of the economy.

Conclusion

It is often claimed that competitive markets smooth the effects of individual risks and hence that one should expect to observe far less variation in aggregates—whether prices or quantities—than in the individual components. A heuristic argument invoking the law of large numbers is rather common. The formal argument, which recognizes that the law of large numbers applies to averages and not to aggregates, was made by Malinvaud (1972, 1973). Optimal allocations must be state-independent if the aggregate endowment is. Since in a finite economy competitive equilibria are optimal it follows that variations in individual endowments cannot affect prices and allocations in such a world. This is, of course, the no-sunspot result of Cass and Shell (1983). The argument is completed by noting that normalized or per capita endowments are virtually state-independent in a large exchange economy whenever individual variations are independent and identically distributed.

Averaging is indeed desirable when all uncertainty is in endowment variations; it is not when productivities vary. A planner would prefer to shift resources to more productive firms, or technologies, to the extent possible. Indeed, with constant returns to scale it is best to shift all possible resources to more productive firms. But this is precisely what destroys the validity of the law-of-large numbers argument in this world. Certainly the optimal level of output will not involve averaging, and hence will not be state-independent.

This is an argument about the optimum; the competitive equilibrium will have similar qualitative properties when some resources can be shifted after the realization of uncertainty. Evidently, the same allocations obtain if decisions are made after the state of nature is observed: this we call anticipation. We dealt with a relatively simple framework, which allowed for a complete characterization of aggregate properties. The qualitative results can be sustained in more elaborate frameworks, where the timing of investment relative to private information is explicitly specified.

An important aspect of this analysis is that, as far as the paths of output and investment are concerned, this is observationally equivalent to an economy with a genuine aggregate shock. This holds as well for large economies, modulo the fact that the probability distribution of aggregate productivity cannot be entirely arbitrary.

Acknowledgments

This work was carried out while both authors were visiting the Department of Economics at the University of Bonn; it was supported by the Deutsche Forschungsgemeinschaft, SFB 303 and the Gottfried-Wilhelm-Leibnitz-Förderpreis during Bo Wo 89.

References

Azariades, C. 1981. "Self fulfilling prophecies." *Journal of Economic Theory* 25: 380–396.

Azariades, C., and R. Guesnerie (1987) "Sunspots and Cycles." *Review of Economic Studies* 53: 725–738.

Benhabib, J., and R. Day. 1982. "A characterization of erratic dynamics in the overlapping generations model." *Journal of Economic Dynamics and Control* 23: 37–58.

Cass, D., and K. Shell. 1983 "Do sunspots matter?" *Journal of Political Economy* 91: 193–227.

Diamond, P. A. 1967. "National debt in a neoclassical growth model." *American Economic Review* 55: 1126–1150.

Donaldson, J. B., and J. Dutta. 1989. Anticipations and the Aggregation of Sector Specific Risks. Discussion Paper 8929, C. O. R. E., Université Catholique de Louvain.

Dutta, J., and H. Polemarchakis. 1990. "Asset markets and equilibrium processes." *Review of Economic Studies* 56: 000–000.

Grandmont, J.-M. 1985. "Endogenous competitive business cycles." *Econometrica* 53: 995–1046.

Grandmont, J.-M., and W. Hildenbrand. 1974. "Stochastic processes of temporary equilibria." *Journal of Mathematical Economics* 1: 247–278.

Kydland, F., and E. Prescott. 1982 "Time to build and aggregate fluctuations." *Econometrica* 50: 1345–1371.

Malinvaud, E. 1972. "The allocation of small risks in large markets." *Journal of Economic Theory* 4: 312–328.

Malinvaud, E. 1973. "Markets for an exchange economy with individual risks." *Econometrica* 41: 383–412.

Scheinkman, J. A., and L. Weiss. 1986. "Borrowing constraints and aggregate economic activity." *Econometrica* 54: 23–47.

The Optimum Quantity of Money Revisited

Timothy J. Kehoe, David K. Levine, and Michael Woodford

The accepted wisdom on the optimum quantity of money was first expressed by Friedman (1953,1969): Real money balances represent a service to the economy provided by the government at no cost. The government should maximize the quantity of real balances it provides, since it is costless to do so. It can do this either by means of a deflationary monetary policy or by paying interest on nominal balances. Either policy reduces the cost of holding idle balances and increases the value of the money stock.

Hahn (1971, 1973) has objected to Friedman's analysis because it is not grounded in a fully specified model of an economy with money:

> The necessary conditions for Pareto efficiency in a world of uncertainty with intertemporal choice will in general be fulfilled by a market economy only if money plays no role. There are no grounds for supposing that the Friedman rule is either necessary or sufficient for Pareto efficiency since it is of the essence of an explanation for the existence of money that other conventional necessary conditions are violated. Even where money is held only for "transaction purposes," Pareto efficiency relative to a transactions technology is a different animal than the usual textbook one. (Hahn 1971, p. 70)

In this paper we study efficiency of monetary policies in an economy in which money plays an essential role.

Brock (1974) and Benhabib and Bull (1983) have shown that Friedman's intuition is correct in a model in which real balances enter directly into the utility functions of traders. This type of model is fully Walrasian except for the assumption that real balances affect utility; hence, a reduction of the shadow value of real balances to zero suffices to make an equilibrium Pareto efficient. However, such an analysis ignores Hahn's point that the role of money is intimately tied to restrictions on the way transactions can be carried out. Grandmont and Younes (1973) show that Friedman's intuition is also correct in a model where money is required to purchase goods because of the assumption of a cash-in-advance constraint. While this type of model is more explicit in relating the value of money balances to restrictions on the execution of transactions, it is still not responsive to Hahn's concerns: Requiring money to be held to carry out transactions seems no less artificial than having real balances enter the utility function directly and, indeed, is equivalent to a special case of the money-in-the-utility-function model (Lucas and Stokey 1983).

Money-in-the-utility-function and cash-in-advance models ignore the role of money in buffering transactions and smoothing short-term intertemporal variations in purchases and sales. In such models, money balances increase utility even though both the allocation of resources and the real money balances held by different households remain constant over time. As a result, redistributional consequences of monetary policy either are assumed away (in representative-consumer examples) or simply represent transfers to some types of consumers at the expense of others. The idea that monetary policy could substitute for inoperative insurance markets by systematically redistributing resources to households in certain circumstances cannot be analyzed in such models. It is this aspect of monetary policy that we examine here. Our analysis ignores direct utility effects of real money balances and cash-in-advance constraints to focus on the use of money to improve the intertemporal allocation of resources.

Bewley (1980, 1983) and Townsend (1980) have given examples showing that Friedman's intuition is sometimes valid in a model where money serves as a short-run store of value. An excellent summary of this work can be found in Sargent 1987. In these examples, perfectly anticipated changes in endowments (or preferences) give rise to intertemporal trade. Because of problems in collecting debts, currency is the only asset that can be used to carry out these intertemporal trades. In the Townsend interpretation, the difficulty in debt collection arises because of the changing locations of traders. A more general discussion of the way in which limited collectibility of unsecured debt can lead to a role for money can be found in Bryant 1980. Although this type of model is too stylized to represent a real economy, it does capture the idea that in the short run money is held as a buffer between periods in which a trader sells and periods in which he buys. As Friedman suggests, in this setup a steady contraction of the stock of currency reduces the cost of holding real balances, increases intertemporal trade, and makes all traders better off. Conversely, a steady expansion of the stock of currency reduces welfare.

An alternative possibility is discussed by Levine (1988), who argues that a steady expansion of the money supply can improve possibilities for trade. This is because real balances are redistributed from rich sellers to poor buyers. Scheinkman and Weiss (1986) offer a similar argument in favor of a one-time inflation. Here we investigate the strengths of this effect relative to that studied by Friedman, Bewley, and Townsend.

In the intertemporal framework, in contrast with Friedman's aggregative framework, the question of how money is injected into or withdrawn from the economy arises. For simplicity, we suppose that it takes place through lump-sum taxes or subsidies. If arbitrary lump-sum transfers are available as an instrument to the government, it can improve upon any monetary policy simply by calculating the intertemporal allocation of consumption that maximizes its welfare criterion and enforcing that plan by means of lump-sum transfers. In practice, however, the government cannot identify individuals and their preferences sufficiently accurately to carry out short-run trades on their behalf. As a result, it is sensible to impose on the analysis the additional restriction that the only feasible monetary policies give all agents equal lump-sum subsidies, or charge them all the same lump-sum taxes. In other words, the government cannot identify agents sufficiently well to give them differential treatment. Levine (1988) shows how a careful model of private information about preferences can lead to the formulation used by Bewley and Townsend, but with the additional proviso that only equal treatment is possible.

Limiting the way in which money can be injected into or withdrawn from the economy has significant consequences. If we modify the model to allow the possibility that traders cannot perfectly forecast their own future demand, a trader may occasionally find himself in a position where he wishes to buy from another trader who wishes to sell but does not have enough money on hand to make the purchase. An expansionary monetary policy that gives both traders equal amounts of currency effectively redistributes wealth from the relatively rich seller to the relatively poor buyer. This can make possible socially desirable trades that could not otherwise take place. Levine (1988) considers the extreme case in which in equilibrium sellers sell their entire endowment. This is the case, for example, if the marginal utility of buyers exceeds that of sellers throughout the range of socially feasible trades. Since sellers are at a corner, changing the price of money relative to goods does not in general change the amount of goods they trade, and, by virtue of Walras' law, does not change their holdings of real balances either. Friedman's original argument rests essentially on the idea that changing prices affects real balances. As a result, in the boundary case, the Friedman-Bewley-Townsend effect of inflation reducing trade is not present, and inflation, if it is feasible, leads to an unambiguous welfare improvement.

In Townsend's model and Bewley's model, there is no uncertainty and there are interior solutions to agents' optimization problems. In Levine's model, there is uncertainty and there are corner solutions. A model with uncertainty but interior solutions contains both effects; that is, inflation has both positive and negative consequences. Here we try to sort out the costs and benefits of inflation in such a world. The results are mixed: For a broad range of parameter values, deflation is clearly good. On the other hand, these parameter values do not reflect the short-run nature of the model very well. Sensible assumptions about short-term trading are that trade is frequent, that the gains to trade are large, and that the degree of unpredictability is small. Unfortunately, with these realistic parameter values it is less likely that there exist equilibria of the simple kind that we can compute. This is especially the case for parameter values that imply positive net benefits from inflation. That is, we can find sensible examples in which inflation is beneficial. If we push too far in this direction, however, we find that we can no longer use our simple methods of computing equilibria.

Our numerical computations lead to one other significant conclusion: In no case is welfare very sensitive to monetary policy. With reasonable parameter values, we find that if inflation increases by 1 percent this is equivalent to changing GNP by about 0.004 percent. It is conceivable that these numerical effects may be more significant in a model with many types of agents and many assets and in which money plays a more complex role in the economy. At the least, these calculations should serve as a warning against arguments that tell us how to improve upon existing policies but not whether the improvement is worth having.

1 The Model

We study a stylized economy in which agents randomly alternate between being buyers and sellers. There are two types of agents, $i = 1,2$, and two states of the world, $\eta = 1,2$. In state 1, type 1 agents are sellers (that is, have low marginal utility of consumption) and type 2 agents are buyers (that is, have high marginal utility of consumption); in state 2, type 2 are sellers and type 1 are buyers. In other words, the state is the same as the type that is a seller. The states themselves form a Markov chain, π being both the conditional probability in state 1 that the subsequent state is 2 and the conditional probability in state 2 that the subsequent state is 1. In short, π is the probability of *reversal*—that buyers and sellers switch roles.

The horizon is unbounded, and periods are $t = 1,2,\ldots$. The state at time t is η_t and is common knowledge among traders. At time $t = 0$, before the economy begins, each trader has an equal chance of beginning life in period 1 as a buyer or a seller.

There is a single composite consumption good, c, and a single asset called currency, M. Planned holdings by a representative agent of type i in period t are c_t^i and M_t^i. Agents' preferences are given by the expected present value

$$\mathrm{E}_0 \sum_{t=1}^{\infty} \delta^t u_i(c_t^i, \eta_t),$$

where $0 \leq \delta < 1$ is a common subjective discount factor and $u_i(c_t^i, \eta_t)$ is a period utility function that depends on consumption and on whether a trader is a buyer or a seller. In other words, $u_i(c_t^i, \eta_t) = u^{\mathrm{s}}(c_t^i)$ if $\eta_t = i$ so that agent i is a seller, and $u_i(c_t^i, \eta_t) = u^{\mathrm{b}}(c_t^i)$ if $\eta_t \neq \mathrm{i}$ so that agent i is a buyer. The function u^{s} and u^{b} are increasing, concave, smooth, and bounded above. The derivatives are denoted Du^{s} and Du^{b}.

Consumption must be non-negative. A representative seller is endowed with ω^{s} units of the consumption good, a buyer with $\omega^{\mathrm{b}} \leq \omega^{\mathrm{s}}$ units. To ensure that sellers want to sell and buyers to buy, we assume that buyers receive more marginal utility from their endowment than do sellers:

$$Du^{\mathrm{b}}(\omega^{\mathrm{b}}) > Du^{\mathrm{s}}(\omega^{\mathrm{s}}). \tag{1.1}$$

The consumption good is perishable, and there is no production. Social feasibility therefore requires that

$$c_t^1 + c_t^2 \leq \omega^{\mathrm{b}} + \omega^{\mathrm{s}}, \tag{1.2}$$

that is, that total consumption does not exceed the social endowment.

We assume that private debts are prohibitively expensive to collect. This means that currency is the only asset. We also assume that a single type of currency is issued by the government and cannot be forged. Consequently, individual holdings must be non-negative, $M_t^i \geq 0$. We denote the aggregate stock of money in period t by M_t. Social feasibility requires that

$$M_t^1 + M_t^2 \leq M_t. \tag{1.3}$$

To simplify calculations, we investigate only steady-state equilibria; we assume that initially money balances are distributed as they are in the steady state.

Unlike the consumption good, currency is durable. However, holdings of currency depend not only on past savings, but also on the amount of currency injected into the economy. The impact this has on the economy depends on how currency is injected. If each trader receives new currency in proportion to existing holdings, then each type's share of the total stock is not affected by the injection. This is a neutral policy. We assume, however, that the government cannot distinguish between buyers and sellers and cannot observe currency holdings. Consequently, currency must be injected into the economy in a lump-sum manner so that both buyers and sellers get equal amounts. Each type receives a grant equal to half of the total injection. If g is the rate of growth of currency (possibly negative), then, with an initial stock of M_{t-1}, each type receives $gM_{t-1}/2$ dollars. The total money stock at time t is

$$M_t = (1 + g)M_{t-1}. \tag{1.4}$$

The type of expansionary or contractionary policy being considered is a fiscal policy financed by a monetary expansion or contraction. This corresponds to the class of policies analyzed by Friedman. It is clear that the fiscal transfers involved in the policy are essential to its having the kinds of effects studied below; this type of model cannot, for example, shed light upon what the impact of open market operations between currency and other assets should be. Nonetheless, some insight may be gained into the effects of actual monetary policies insofar as such policies have a redistributive aspect. This is true if the injection of liquidity is not proportional to the existing distribution of liquid assets.

Let p_t denote the price of currency with consumption as the numeraire. In other words, p_t is the reciprocal of the price level. The budget constraint for a representative agent of type i in period t is given by

$$p_t[M_t^i - M_{t-1}^i - gM_{t-1}/2] + [c_t^i - \omega_t^i] \leq 0, \tag{1.5}$$

where ω_t^i equals ω^s or ω^b as i is either a seller or a buyer at time t, and where M_0^i is type i's initial holdings of money.

An *equilibrium* assigns prices, consumption plans, and asset holdings to each history of the states. It must be socially feasible (in other words, satisfy (1.2) and (1.3)), and each type must maximize utility subject to the budget constraint (1.5).

In common with many other monetary models, this model has an equilibrium in which money has no value, where $p_t = 0$: Autarky, where $c_t^i = \omega_t^i$, satisfies social feasibility. Since the budget constraint becomes $c_t^i \leq \omega_t^i$, it also maximizes utility subject to this constraint.

2 Two-State Markov Equilibria

We now introduce a special class of equilibria called *two-state Markov equilibria*. These equilibria have the property that what happens in each period is independent of history. Because these equilibria are relatively easy to compute, the impact of monetary growth can be explicitly studied.

If history is not to matter, then the distribution of currency between the buyers and the sellers at the end of each period must always be the same. There are three possibilities: First, if buyers hold all the currency at the end of each period, then they never consume more than ω^{b} units of the consumption good. This implies that the combined utility of both buyers and sellers is no more than it would be under autarky. Since each type can guarantee itself the autarkic utility level, buyers holding all the currency is possible only if the equilibrium is autarkic. Second, if buyers and sellers each hold a fixed positive amount of currency at the end of each period, then, throughout time, no trader's holding of currency falls below the smaller of these two amounts. We can argue that this cannot be an optimal policy for the trader: A trader should plan on holding very small amounts of currency under some circumstances. Consequently, equilibria of this sort do not exist. The third and final possibility is that the sellers hold all the currency at the end of each period. This is the only case in which currency can have value, and we now restrict our attention to this case.

If the sellers hold all the currency at the end of each period, then in each state there are only two possibilities: With probability π, a reversal occurs, and the traders holding the currency at the end of the previous period become buyers in the current period. In this case the buyers have the currency from the previous period, as well as their share of newly injected currency, to spend on the consumption good held by the sellers. On the other hand, with probability $1 - \pi$, a reversal fails to occur, and the agents holding the currency at the end of the previous period remain as sellers in the current period. In this case the buyers have only their share of newly injected currency to spend on the consumption good. Although the time periods here are too short to capture business cycles, it is useful to think of the case where buyers have most of the money as a boom and the case where sellers have most of the money as a recession. In a boom there tends to be a great deal of trade because buyers are wealthy; in a recession there tends to be relatively little because they are poor.

We assume that the initial distribution of currency is consistent with a two-state Markov equilibrium—that is, that the previous sellers hold all the money at the end of the previous period. A two-state Markov equilibrium is like a steady state, and this amounts to assuming that we begin at the steady state. It is not difficult to show that, for a wide range of initial money distributions, the steady state is reached after a single period (Levine 1989a). This means that in the welfare calculations below we are comparing different steady states and are ignoring the initial transitional period.

In addition to requiring that sellers hold all money at the end of each period, in a two-state Markov equilibrium we require that prices and trade in each period depend only on whether the economy is currently in a boom or a recession. To do so, we measure money holdings as a share of the social total, rather than in dollars (which obviously are not stationary if $g \neq 0$). We let $m_t^i = M_t^i/M_t$ be type i's share of the total money stock and let $\rho_t = p_t M_t$ be the real value of the money stock. The budget constraint (1.5) can then be rewritten as

$$\rho_t \left[m_t^i - \frac{m_{t-1}^i + g/2}{1 + g} \right] + [c_t^i - \omega_t^i] \leq 0. \tag{2.1}$$

The individual optimum can be characterized using the marginal utility of income μ_t^i, which measures the increased present value of an extra dollar. The marginal utility of a dollar must be at least the marginal utility of a dollar's worth of consumption,

$$\mu_t^i \geq Du_i(c_t^i, \eta_t). \tag{2.2}$$

Moreover, exact equality must hold if consumption is positive. In addition, since dollars are durable, the marginal utility of a dollar held today must be at least as great as the marginal utility of a dollar tomorrow. In utility terms, a current dollar depreciates by

$$\Delta = \frac{\delta}{1 + g} \tag{2.3}$$

as a result of subjective discounting and inflation. Consequently,

$$\rho_t \mu_t^i \geq \Delta \mathrm{E}_t \rho_{t+1} \mu_{t+1}^i. \tag{2.4}$$

Again, there must be exact equality if money holdings are positive.

In addition to the familiar first-order conditions (2.2) and (2.4), we require that the individual consumption-money holding plan satisfies the transversality condition that μ_t^i is uniformly bounded. (For details see Weitzman 1973 and Levine 1989b.) This requires that $\Delta \leq 1$. To simplify calculations, we assume that $\Delta < 1$. This allows us to consider rates of deflation arbitrarily close to, though not exactly equal to, the discount rate proposed by Friedman. As in money-in-the-utility-function models in which consumers always have positive marginal utility of money and demand infinitely large money balances when the deflation rate is equal to the discount rate, there are technical problems if $\Delta = 1$ (see also Bewley 1983). The restriction to $\Delta < 1$ still allows us to consider whether welfare increases as the money growth rate is lowered.

In a two-state Markov equilibrium, we use overbars to indicate the values variables take on in booms and underbars to indicate the values they take on in recessions. For example, the variable $\underline{\rho}$ denotes the value of the money stock in a recession. We also define $\bar{z}$ to be the amount of consumption purchased by buyers in a boom and $\underline{z}$ to be the amount purchased by the buyers in a recession. In addition, if i is a buyer, we write $i = b$; if a seller, $i = \mathrm{s}$. For example, $\bar{\mu}^{\mathrm{b}}$ denotes the marginal utility of income of a buyer in a boom. With this notation, the marginal conditions (2.2) and (2.4) for a boom are

$$\begin{aligned} &\bar{\mu}^{\mathrm{b}} = Du^{\mathrm{b}}(\omega^{\mathrm{b}} + \bar{z}), \\ &\bar{\rho}\bar{\mu}^{\mathrm{b}} \geq \Delta[(1-\pi)\underline{\rho}\underline{\mu}^{\mathrm{b}} + \pi\bar{\rho}\bar{\mu}^{\mathrm{s}}], \\ &\bar{\mu}^{\mathrm{s}} \geq Du^{\mathrm{s}}(\omega^{\mathrm{s}} - \bar{z}), \\ &\bar{\rho}\bar{\mu}^{\mathrm{s}} = \Delta[(1-\pi)\underline{\rho}\underline{\mu}^{\mathrm{s}} + \pi\bar{\rho}\bar{\mu}^{\mathrm{b}}]. \end{aligned} \tag{2.5}$$

For a recession they are

$$\begin{aligned} &\underline{\mu}^{\mathrm{b}} = Du^{\mathrm{b}}(\omega^{\mathrm{b}} + \underline{z}), \\ &\underline{\rho}\underline{\mu}^{\mathrm{b}} \geq \Delta[(1-\pi)\underline{\rho}\underline{\mu}^{\mathrm{b}} + \pi\bar{\rho}\bar{\mu}^{\mathrm{s}}], \\ &\underline{\mu}^{\mathrm{s}} \geq Du^{\mathrm{s}}(\omega^{\mathrm{s}} - \underline{z}), \\ &\underline{\rho}\underline{\mu}^{\mathrm{s}} = \Delta[(1-\pi)\underline{\rho}\underline{\mu}^{\mathrm{s}} + \pi\bar{\rho}\bar{\mu}^{\mathrm{b}}]. \end{aligned} \tag{2.6}$$

Because these conditions are stated in terms of net trades, social feasibility is automatically satisfied. By Walras' law, one budget constraint is redundant. The remaining equilibrium conditions are given by a single budget constraint for each state:

$$\bar{z} = \bar{\rho}[1 - g/2(1 + g)],$$
$$\underline{z} = \underline{\rho}[g/2(1 + g)]. \tag{2.7}$$

These must satisfy $\bar{z},\underline{z} \leq \omega^{s}$. In addition, in the deflationary case, $g < 0$, we require $\underline{z} \geq -\omega^{b}$. Notice that a two-state Markov equilibrium does not necessarily exist for all values of δ, π, and g.

3 Efficiency

There are two efficiency criteria we can consider. *Ex post* efficiency takes the realization of uncertainty in the first period, but not subsequent periods, as given. In other words, it takes the initial identification of the two types as buyers or sellers as given and asks if both types can be made better off. An *ex post* efficient allocation maximizes a weighted sum of utilities of the two initial types. *Ex ante* efficiency does not take the realization of any uncertainty as given. It recognizes that each type of agent is equally likely to begin life as a buyer or a seller. Following the mechanism-design literature (see, for example, Townsend 1982 and Green 1987), we consider *ex ante* efficiency because, given that agents are *a priori* identical, it provides an unambiguous ranking of any two equilibria even when neither is fully efficient.

No autarkic equilibrium is *ex ante* efficient unless $\pi = 0$. If $g = 0$ and $0 < \pi < 1$, then no monetary equilibrium is efficient in either sense. To see why, consider the case of linear utility, $u^{b}(c_t^i) = \min(\eta^{b}c_t^i,\bar{u}$ and $u^{b}(c_t^i) = \min(\eta^{b}c_t^i,\bar{u})$ where $\eta^{b} > \eta^{s}$, and equal endowments, $\omega^{b} = \omega^{s} = 1$. (Here $\bar{u} = \eta^{b}(2\omega^{b} + 2\omega^{s})$ serves only to bound utility from above.) Maximizing the sum of the two types' utilities shows that any efficient allocation gives all of the consumption (two units' worth) to the type with the higher marginal utility. Can such an allocation be achieved by a monetary equilibrium? Since it can be shown that the price of currency is bounded above, to purchase a single unit of consumption from the other sector requires a minimum expenditure of currency $m^* > 0$ (Levine 1988). This means that a sector cannot purchase the other sector's endowments more than $1/m^*$

times in a row before running out of currency. If, by a stroke of bad luck, the type that is supposed to receive all the consumption when it has the high value happens to have the high value more than $1/m^*$ times in a row, then it cannot purchase any consumption, even though Pareto efficiency requires it to. Notice how setting the rate of monetary expansion $g > 0$ can avoid this problem: By constantly redistributing currency, it ensures that neither type ever runs out.

This argument for inefficiency is closely related to the "classical corridor" property proposed by Leijonhufvud (1973). Leijonhufvud argues that money, or more generally liquidity, acts to cushion small shocks, allowing an economy to follow a classical efficient path. If shocks are too large or too prolonged, however, all liquidity is squeezed out of the system and the economy is stuck in a situation of Keynesian inefficiency. He refers to the range of shocks in which the economy behaves classically as the "classical corridor." In our economy, mutually beneficial trade can be sustained while both sectors have money. A persistent series of shocks can eventually cause one sector to draw its money down to zero, however, forcing it to stop trading. Mutually beneficial trade becomes impossible because money is in the wrong hands. This may be regarded as a recession. In contrast with Leijonhufvud's conception, however, in our model there is no particular tendency of the system to get stuck outside the corridor. Once outside, a reversal of agents' types can easily restore money to the right hands, moving the system back into the corridor.

Let us consider *ex ante* welfare in a two-state Markov equilibrium. Let $\bar{u}^{\mathrm{b}}$ be the momentary utility of a buyer in a boom, $\bar{u}^{\mathrm{s}}$ that of a seller in a boom, $\underline{u}^{\mathrm{b}}$ that of a buyer in a recession, and $\underline{u}^{\mathrm{s}}$ that of a seller in a recession. Let $\bar{V}^{\mathrm{s}}$, $\bar{V}^{\mathrm{b}}$, $\underline{V}^{\mathrm{b}}$, and $\underline{V}^{\mathrm{s}}$ be the corresponding present values. These can be calculated from the following equations:

$$\begin{aligned}
\bar{V}^{\mathrm{b}} &= \bar{u}^{\mathrm{b}} + \delta[(1-\pi)\underline{V}^{\mathrm{b}} + \pi\bar{V}^{\mathrm{s}}],\\
\bar{V}^{\mathrm{s}} &= \bar{u}^{\mathrm{s}} + \delta[(1-\pi)\underline{V}^{\mathrm{s}} + \pi\bar{V}^{\mathrm{b}}],\\
\underline{V}^{\mathrm{b}} &= \underline{u}^{\mathrm{b}} + \delta[(1-\pi)\underline{V}^{\mathrm{b}} + \pi\bar{V}^{\mathrm{s}}],\\
\underline{V}^{\mathrm{s}} &= \underline{u}^{\mathrm{s}} + \delta[(1-\pi)\underline{V}^{\mathrm{s}} + \pi\bar{V}^{\mathrm{b}}],
\end{aligned} \tag{3.1}$$

In period 1, the economy has probability $(1 - \pi)$ of beginning in a recession, in which case welfare is $\underline{V}^{\mathrm{b}} + \underline{V}^{\mathrm{s}}$, and probability π of beginning in a boom, in which case welfare is $\bar{V}^{\mathrm{b}} + \bar{V}^{\mathrm{s}}$. Consequently, *ex ante* welfare is

$$W = \pi(\overline{V}^{\mathrm{b}} + \overline{V}^{\mathrm{s}}) + (1 - \pi)(\underline{V}^{\mathrm{b}} + \underline{V}^{\mathrm{s}}). \tag{3.2}$$

We can solve (3.1) and (3.2) to find

$$W = (1 - \delta)^{-1}[\pi(\overline{u}^{\mathrm{b}} + \overline{u}^{\mathrm{s}}) + (1 - \pi)(\underline{u}^{\mathrm{b}} + \underline{u}^{\mathrm{s}})]. \tag{3.3}$$

4 Costs of Inflation: The Deterministic Case

We now suppose that $\pi = 1$, so that each trader switches back and forth deterministically between being a buyer and a seller. In this case there are no recessions. The only relevant equilibrium conditions are those for booms (equations 2.5), and equations 2.7 serve to define prices. Examining these conditions, we find either that

$$\Delta Du^{\mathrm{b}}(\omega^{\mathrm{b}} + \omega^{\mathrm{s}}) > Du^{\mathrm{s}}(0),$$

in which case $\overline{z} = \omega^{\mathrm{s}}$ and sellers sell all of their endowment to buyers, or that $\overline{z}$ is determined by

$$\Delta Du^{\mathrm{b}}(\omega^{\mathrm{b}} + \overline{z}) + Du^{\mathrm{s}}(\omega^{\mathrm{s}} - \overline{z}).$$

In the latter case, $\Delta Du^{\mathrm{b}}(\omega^{\mathrm{b}}) \geq Du^{\mathrm{s}}(\omega^{\mathrm{s}})$ must hold if a two-state Markov equilibrium is to exist.

Turning to welfare, we can simplify (3.3) to

$$W = (1 - \delta)^{-1}(\overline{u}^{\mathrm{b}} + \overline{u}^{\mathrm{s}}), \tag{4.1}$$

which implies that

$$\frac{dW}{dg} = (1 - \delta)^{-1}[Du^{\mathrm{b}}(\omega^{\mathrm{b}} + \overline{z}) - Du^{\mathrm{s}}(\omega^{\mathrm{s}} - \overline{z})]\frac{d\overline{z}}{dg}. \tag{4.2}$$

Since $\Delta Du^{\mathrm{b}}(\omega^{\mathrm{b}} + \overline{z}) \geq Du^{\mathrm{s}}(\omega^{\mathrm{s}} - \overline{z})$,

$$Du^{\mathrm{b}}(\omega^{\mathrm{b}} + \overline{z}) - Du^{\mathrm{s}}(\omega^{\mathrm{s}} - \overline{z}) > 0.$$

If $\overline{z} = \omega^{\mathrm{s}}$, then $d\overline{z}/dg = 0$ and inflation has no effect. If, on the other hand, $\overline{z} < \omega^{\mathrm{s}}$, then differentiating

$$\Delta Du^{\mathrm{b}}(\omega^{\mathrm{b}} + \overline{z}) = Du^{\mathrm{s}}(\omega^{\mathrm{s}} - \overline{z})$$

implies that $d\overline{z}/dg < 0$, which implies that $dW/dg < 0$. Consequently, inflation is bad or—if the seller sells his entire endowment—neutral. This is the Freidman-Bewley-Townsend perspective: Inflation lowers real balances and reduces trade.

5 Benefits of Inflation: The Linear Case

To study the benefits of inflation, we must allow for recessions, that is, $\pi < 1$. As an extreme case, let us suppose utility is linear. This ensures that the seller sells everything. In the deterministic case, therefore, inflation is neutral. Let us consider the stochastic case. Specifically, we suppose that $\omega^{\mathrm{b}} = \omega^{\mathrm{s}} = 1$, that $\mathrm{u}^{\mathrm{b}}(c_t^i) = \min(\eta^{\mathrm{b}} c_t^i, \bar{u})$, and that $\mathrm{u}^{\mathrm{s}}(c_t^i) = \min(\eta^{\mathrm{s}} c_t^i, \bar{u})$ where $\eta^{\mathrm{b}} > \eta^{\mathrm{s}}$. To aid in manipulating the Lagrangian conditions (2.5)–(2.7) we define the constants

$$\underline{\Delta} = \frac{\Delta\pi}{1 - \Delta(1-\pi)},$$
$$\overline{\Delta} = \frac{\Delta^2\pi(1-\pi)}{1 - \Delta(1-\pi) - \Delta^2\pi^2}. \tag{5.1}$$

Notice that $\underline{\Delta} < 1$ and that $\overline{\Delta} < 1$, provided that $\Delta < 1$. The constant $\underline{\Delta}$, for example, represents the present value in the low-valued state of a dollar received the next time a high-valued state occurs; it serves as an effective discount factor for the low-valued state. Finally, define

$$\gamma = g/(2 + g). \tag{5.2}$$

This variable ranges from -1 to 1 and is increasing in the rate of money growth, g. The Lagrangian conditions (2.5) and (2.6) become

$$\begin{aligned}
&\bar{\mu}^{\mathrm{b}} = \eta^{\mathrm{b}}, \quad \underline{\mu}^{\mathrm{b}} = \eta^{\mathrm{b}}\\
&\underline{\Delta}\bar{\rho} \geq \overline{\Delta}\underline{\rho}, \quad \underline{\rho} \geq \underline{\Delta}^2\bar{\rho}\\
&\underline{\Delta}\eta^{\mathrm{b}} \geq \eta^{\mathrm{s}}, \quad \bar{\rho}\underline{\Delta}\eta^{\mathrm{b}} \geq \underline{\rho}\eta^{\mathrm{s}}\\
&\bar{\mu}^{\mathrm{s}} = \underline{\Delta}\eta^{\mathrm{b}}, \quad \underline{\rho\mu}^{\mathrm{s}} = \overline{\rho\mu}^{\mathrm{s}}.
\end{aligned} \tag{5.3}$$

The remaining equilibrium conditions, (2.7), become

$$1 \geq \bar{z} = \bar{\rho}/(1 + \gamma), \quad 1 \geq \underline{z} = \underline{\rho}\gamma/(1 + \gamma) \geq -1. \tag{5.4}$$

To calculate equilibria, we observe that either an inequality in the third line of (5.3) holds with equality or the corresponding $\bar{z}$ or $\underline{z}$ equals 1. This means that there are always six equations to use in solving for two prices and four marginal utilities of income.

If $\underline{\Delta} < \eta^{\mathrm{s}}/\eta^{\mathrm{b}}$, then $\bar{z} = 1$. Even if $\underline{\Delta} = \eta^{\mathrm{s}}/\eta^{\mathrm{b}}$, we can argue that if there is a two-state Markov equilibrium there is one with $\bar{z} = 1$. There are, there-

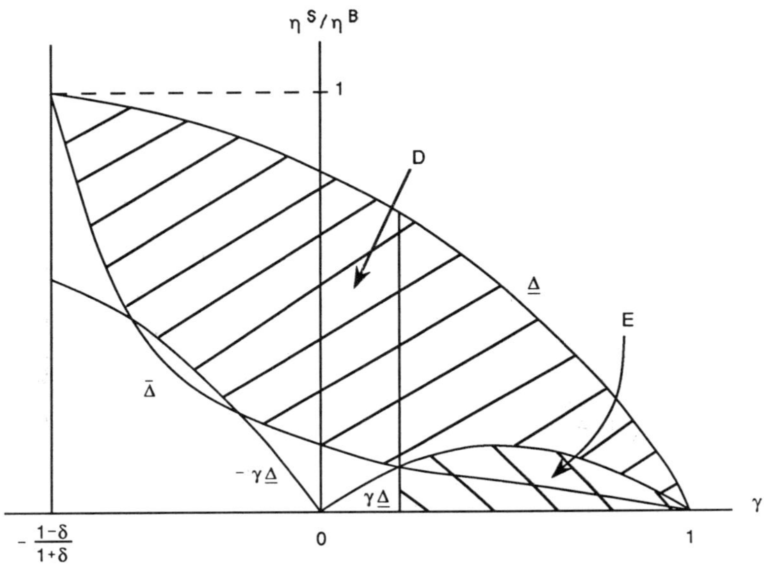

Figure 1

fore, two cases: $\underline{z} = 1$ and $\underline{z} < 1$. We refer to the former case as the *efficient case*: The buyers consume all of the consumption good in every state, resulting in an equilibrium which is *ex ante* efficient. The latter case, where $\underline{z} < 1$, represents an equilibrium that is Pareto dominated, although not necessarily by another equilibrium. We refer to this as the *inefficient case*.

The inequalities characterizing equilibria of the two types are illustrated in figure 1. Here we have used (2.3), (5.1), and (5.2) to calculate

$$\underline{\Delta} = \frac{\delta(1-\gamma)\pi}{1+\gamma-\delta(1-\gamma)(1-\pi)},$$
$$\overline{\Delta} = \frac{\delta^2(1-\gamma)^2\pi(1-\pi)}{(1+\gamma)^2-\delta(1-\gamma^2)(1-\pi)+\delta^2(1-\gamma)^2\pi^2}. \tag{5.5}$$

The inefficient equilibria lie in the region labeled D and the efficient equilibria in the region labeled E. For other values of η^{s}/η^{b} and γ there is no two-state Markov equilibrium. In the efficient region E, η^{s}/η^{b} lies below the curve $\gamma\underline{\Delta}$ and γ is such that $\overline{\Delta}$ curve lies below the $\gamma\underline{\Delta}$ curve. The inefficient region D lies above the $\gamma\underline{\Delta}$ curve for $\gamma > 0$ and above the $-\gamma\underline{\Delta}$ curve

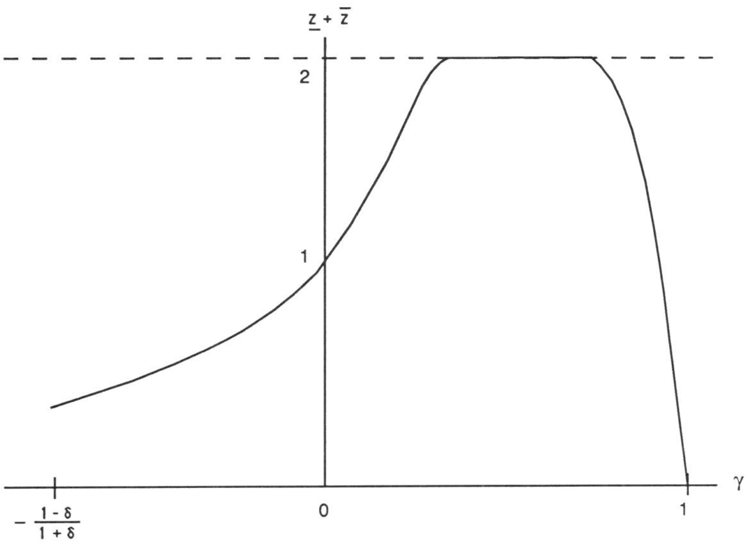

Figure 2

for $\gamma < 0$. It also lies below the $\underline{\Delta}$ curve and above the $\bar{\Delta}$ curve. General qualitative features of the diagrams are that the $\underline{\Delta}$ and $\bar{\Delta}$ curves are downward sloping with $\underline{\Delta} > \bar{\Delta}$, are both equal to zero at $\gamma = 1$, and are both equal to one at $\gamma = -(1 - \delta)/(1 + \delta)$. Finally, the $\bar{\Delta}$ and $\gamma\underline{\Delta}$ curves intersect at a unique point; the $\bar{\Delta}$ and $-\gamma\underline{\Delta}$ curves intersect at two points or not at all.

Within the region where $\eta^s/\eta^b \leq \underline{\Delta}$, it is not always true that a two-state Markov equilibrium exists. When $\eta^s/\eta^b < \bar{\Delta}$ or $\eta^s/\eta^b < -\gamma\underline{\Delta}$ and $\gamma\underline{\Delta} < \bar{\Delta}$; that is, in the lower left corner of figure 1 there is no two-state Markov equilibrium. If η^s/η^b is very small and g is small or negative, then the value of future trade is sufficiently great that the buyer wishes to hold money in the high-valued state. This in no way contradicts the existence of a monetary equilibrium. If the buyer holds money and the price of money is positive, however, the equilibrium cannot be two-state Markov.

It is useful to consider how total trade in both states depends on the rate of money growth. Figure 2 illustrates this dependence. To draw this figure, we use the fact that at an inefficient equilibrium $\underline{z} = \gamma\underline{\Delta}\eta^b/\eta^s$. In other words, the dependence of $\underline{z}$ on γ is proportional to the height of the curve

$\gamma\underline{\Delta}$. Unless money growth causes a collapse to autarky, the output in a boom is fixed at 1, so only the variation in $\underline{z}$ matters. Trade gradually rises as the inflation rate increases from $\gamma = -(1-\delta)/(1+\delta)$, where $g = -(1-\delta)$, and reaches a peak with $\gamma > 0$. The peak may or may not equal 2, depending on how great $\eta^{\mathrm{b}}/\eta^{\mathrm{s}}$ is. Then trade falls, gradually or suddenly, to zero as γ is increased further.

Interpretation of figure 2 would be most straightforward if the different equilibria were Pareto ordered, with larger values of $\underline{z}$ corresponding to more efficient equilibria. This is true with *ex ante* welfare criterion. Unfortunately, it is not true with the *ex post* welfare criterion. Calculating the expected present value of utility to each type shows that $\overline{V}^{\mathrm{b}}$, $\underline{V}^{\mathrm{b}}$, and $\overline{V}^{\mathrm{s}}$ are all increasing in $\underline{z}$. We can solve (3.1) to calculate

$$\frac{d\underline{V}^{\mathrm{s}}}{d\underline{z}} = \frac{(1-\delta+\delta\pi-\delta^2\pi^2)\eta^{\mathrm{s}} - \delta^2\pi(1-\pi)\eta^{\mathrm{b}}}{(1-\delta)(1-\delta+2\delta\pi)}$$

$$= \frac{(1-\delta+\delta\pi-\delta^2\pi^2)}{(1-\delta)(1-\delta+2\delta\pi)}[\eta^{\mathrm{s}} - \overline{\Delta}\eta^{\mathrm{b}}]. \tag{5.6}$$

Since the equilibrium conditions imply that $\overline{\Delta}\eta^{\mathrm{b}} \geq \eta^{\mathrm{s}}$, $\underline{V}^{\mathrm{s}}$ cannot be increasing in $\underline{z}$. During a boom, both types agree that more $\underline{z}$ is better. During a recession, however, the seller type, who loses immediate consumption if $\underline{z}$ is increased prefers smaller values of $\underline{z}$, while the buyer who stands to make an immediate gain prefers larger values of $\underline{z}$. In practice, it is to be expected that during a boom both types will agree that a policy leading to a higher value of $\underline{z}$ in the future is desirable. *Ex post*, after a recession occurs, there is disagreement. The buyer, who is the direct beneficiary of the policy, continues to want the policy to be implemented; the seller, who must give up current consumption, is opposed to the policy.

Using *ex ante* utility as a criterion, the vertical axis in Figure 2 may be interpreted as "efficiency." The optimal monetary policy can also be calculated. For small values of $\eta^{\mathrm{s}}/\eta^{\mathrm{b}}$ (large gains to trade), any level of money growth that leads to full efficiency is optimal. For intermediate values of $\eta^{\mathrm{s}}/\eta^{\mathrm{b}}$, the value of γ that maximizes $\gamma\underline{\Delta}$ should be chosen. For high values of $\eta^{\mathrm{s}}/\eta^{\mathrm{b}}$, the largest value of γ consistent with the existence of an equilibrium should be chosen.

The case in which the largest possible value of γ should be chosen points up a possible problem with an expansionary policy: The government flirts with disaster. A little extra expansion causes the economy to collapse. As γ

is gradually increased, welfare increases. Suddenly, however, there is a catastrophe and welfare drops radically. In this situation, taking into account the government's uncertainty about the nature of the parameters, it might be better to use a more conservative policy and keep the level of monetary expansion well away from the growth rate that would lead to collapse, even though a small increase may bring a small benefit.

The possibility of catastrophic collapse due to an overexpansionary monetary policy can be illustrated in the previous case where $\pi = 1$. If a two-state Markov monetary equilibrium exists, even with $g = 0$, recall that it is fully efficient. A two-state Markov equilibrium exists if and only if

$$(\underline{\Delta} =)\Delta \geq \frac{\eta^{\mathrm{s}}}{\eta^{\mathrm{b}}}. \tag{5.7}$$

It is instructive to consider what happens when (5.7) holds with exact equality. In this case, sellers are exactly indifferent between autarky and the monetary equilibrium. Buyers strictly prefer the monetary equilibrium, however; next period they are indifferent, but now they receive an extra η^{b} that they would not receive in autarky. If (5.7) is violated by a small amount, then sellers marginally prefer autarky, causing the monetary equilibrium to collapse. This marginal gain to sellers causes a substantial loss (of η^{b}) to the buyers. In this sense the collapse to autarky is catastrophic.

6 Inflation Tradeoffs: The Logarithmic Case

In the previous two sections we have studied extreme cases. In the deterministic model, inflation has unambiguously negative effects. In the linear model, it has unambiguously positive effects. We now study a model in which there are both costs and benefits to inflation. Suppose that

$$u^{\mathrm{s}}(c_t^i) = u^{\mathrm{b}}(c_t^i) = \min(\log c_t^i, \bar{u})$$

and that

$$\omega^{\mathrm{s}} > \omega^{\mathrm{b}}.$$

In this case consumption must always be positive, and conditions (2.5) and (2.6) become

$$\begin{aligned}
\bar{z} &= \frac{\underline{\Delta}\omega^{\mathrm{s}} - \omega^{\mathrm{b}}}{\underline{\Delta} + 1}, \\
\underline{z} &= \frac{g\omega^{\mathrm{s}}\bar{z}}{2\omega^{\mathrm{s}} + g\omega^{\mathrm{s}} - 2\bar{z}}, \\
\bar{\rho} &= \frac{\bar{z}(2 + 2g)}{2 + g}, \\
\underline{\rho} &= \frac{\underline{\Delta}\bar{\rho}(\omega^{\mathrm{s}} - \underline{z})}{\omega^{\mathrm{b}} + \bar{z}}.
\end{aligned} \tag{6.1}$$

Here $\underline{\Delta}$ is defined as in (5.5). To compute an equilibrium, we solve these four equations for $\bar{z}$, $\underline{z}$, $\bar{\rho}$, and $\underline{\rho}$. To be an equilibrium, the solution must further satisfy the following inequalities:

$$\begin{aligned}
&\frac{\bar{\rho}}{\omega^{\mathrm{b}} + \bar{z}} \geq \Delta\left[\frac{(1 - \pi)\underline{\rho}}{\omega^{\mathrm{b}} + \underline{z}} + \frac{\pi\bar{\rho}}{\omega^{\mathrm{s}} - \bar{z}}\right], \\
&\frac{\underline{\rho}}{\omega^{\mathrm{b}} + \underline{z}} \geq \Delta\left[\frac{(1 - \pi)\underline{\rho}}{\omega^{\mathrm{b}} + \underline{z}} + \frac{\pi\bar{\rho}}{\omega^{\mathrm{s}} - \bar{z}}\right], \\
&\bar{\rho} \geq 0, \\
&\underline{\rho} \geq 0, \\
&\frac{1 - \Delta\underline{\Delta}\pi}{\Delta\underline{\Delta}(1 - \pi)} \geq \frac{\omega^{\mathrm{s}} - \underline{z}}{\omega^{\mathrm{b}} + \underline{z}} \geq \frac{1}{\underline{\Delta}}.
\end{aligned} \tag{6.2}$$

Our goal is to analyze dW/dg at $g = 0$: Does welfare increase or decrease as the rate of growth of money is slightly increased from zero? Simple but tedious calculations using (3.1) and the equilibrium conditions (6.1) yield

$$\frac{\mathrm{dW}}{\mathrm{dg}} = \frac{1}{(1 - \delta)(1 - \delta + \delta\pi)} \times \left(-\frac{\pi(1 - \delta)}{1 - \delta + 2\delta\pi} + \frac{(1 - \pi)(\omega^{\mathrm{s}}/\omega^{\mathrm{b}} - 1)(\delta\pi\omega^{\mathrm{s}}/\omega^{\mathrm{b}} - 1 + \delta - \delta\pi)}{2(\omega^{\mathrm{s}}/\omega^{\mathrm{b}} + 1)}\right). \tag{6.3}$$

This expression has two terms, the first negative and the second positive. The first term corresponds to the derivative of welfare in a boom. Since we can show that $d\bar{z}/dg < 0$ and welfare is increasing in $\bar{z}$, increasing the growth rate of money increases the cost of holding money balances and consequently lowers their value. This reduces trade during a boom, $\bar{z}$, and reduces welfare. This is the Bewley-Townsend effect; in the deterministic case they consider, the economy is always in a boom. The second term is positive because $d\underline{z}/dg > 0$ and welfare is increasing in $\underline{z}$. In other words, the reduction in the value of real balances is more than offset by the redistribution of money to the low-endowment sector, making it possible for trade to take place and increasing welfare. This is the only effect in the linear case.

In addition to determining how dW/dg depends on values of the parameters, we must check that a two-state Markov equilibrium actually exists. The inequalities in (6.2) in the case where $g = 0$ reduce to

$$\frac{1 - \delta + \delta\pi - \delta^2\pi^2}{\delta^2\pi(1 - \pi)} \geq \frac{\omega^s}{\omega^b} \geq \frac{1 - \delta + \delta\pi}{\delta\pi}, \tag{6.4}$$

which is necessary and sufficient for a two-state Markov equilibrium to exist near $g = 0$ and to validate the use of (6.3) for welfare computations.

More interesting than dW/dg is $(1 - \delta)dW/dg$, the elasticity of welfare in consumption units with respect to the money supply. We compute this various parameter values in table 1. Notice that two-state Markov

Table 1

		$(1-\delta)\frac{dW}{dg}$ ω^s/ω^b		
		2	4	8
$\delta = \frac{1}{2}$	$\pi = \frac{1}{2}$	*	−0.2833	−0.0093
	$\pi = \frac{3}{4}$	*	−0.2893	−0.1067
	$\pi = \frac{7}{8}$	*	−0.3069	−0.2065
$\delta = \frac{3}{4}$	$\pi = \frac{1}{3}$	−0.1833	*	*
	$\pi = \frac{3}{4}$	−0.1518	−0.0351	*
	$\pi = \frac{7}{8}$	−0.1451	−0.0834	*
$\delta = \frac{7}{8}$	$\pi = \frac{1}{2}$	*	*	*
	$\pi = \frac{3}{4}$	−0.0514	*	*
	$\pi = \frac{7}{8}$	−0.0592	*	*

* No two-state Markov equilibrium exists.

equilibria often do not exist. Notice too that for a broad range of parameter values inflation decreases welfare. This is not to say that inflation always decreases welfare: At $\delta = \frac{1}{2}$, $\pi = \frac{1}{2}$ and $\omega^s/\omega^b = 10$, for example, $(1-\delta)dW/dg = 0.1439$.

It is evident from (6.3) that, for fixed δ and π, dW/dg is a monotonically increasing function of ω^s/ω^b: The greater the fluctuations in endowments (and hence the greater the need for intertemporal trade), the more likely that the optimal growth rate of currency is positive rather than negative. It can also be seen from (6.3) that when ω^s/ω^b takes the lowest value consistent with (6.4), that is, when $\omega^s/\omega^b = (1 - \delta + \delta\pi)/\delta\pi$, the second term is 0 while the first is negative. Consequently, $dW/dg < 0$. Furthermore, dW/dg would eventually become positive—indeed unboundedly large for ω^s/ω^b large enough—if a two-state Markov equilibrium continued to exist for such large values of ω^s/ω^b.

For fixed δ and π, it may or may not be possible to have $dW/dg > 0$ when ω^s/ω^b is in the interval specified by (6.4). Indeed, since dW/dg is increasing in ω^s/ω^b, this is possible if and only if it is true when ω^s/ω^b is chosen equal to the upper bound in (6.4). Substituting this value into (6.3) shows that $dW/dg > 0$ if and only if

$$(1-\delta)^2(1+\delta\pi) > 2\delta^2\pi(1-2\pi+\delta\pi). \tag{6.5}$$

This condition holds for some, but not all, choices of δ and π that satisfy $0 < \delta < 1$ and $0 < \pi < 1$. The region where it holds is shown in figure 3. Notice that, for fixed π, (6.5) is satisfied for δ small enough but is violated for δ close enough to 1. Since the case of δ close to 1 (where time periods are very short) is of great interest, this may make it seem unlikely that there are interesting parameter values for which a two-state Markov equilibrium exists and $dW/dg > 0$.

Nonetheless, if π approaches either 0 or 1 rapidly enough as δ approaches 1, the inequality (6.5) continues to hold. If $\pi = k(1-\delta)^2$, where $0 < k < \frac{1}{2}$, then (6.5) holds for all δ close enough to 1. Similarly, if $\pi = 1 - \theta(1-\delta)^k$, where $1 > \theta > 0$ and $k \geq 1$, then (6.5) holds for all δ close enough to 1. In either of these cases, it is possible for a two-state Markov equilibrium to exist and for dW/dg to be positive, even with δ arbitrarily close to 1.

In the case where $\pi = 1$, Bewley and Townsend conclude that $dW/dg < 0$ for all values of δ and ω^s/ω^b. How robust is this conclusion? Suppose that δ and ω^s/ω^b are fixed and that $\omega^s/\omega^b > 1/\delta$, so that a two-state Markov

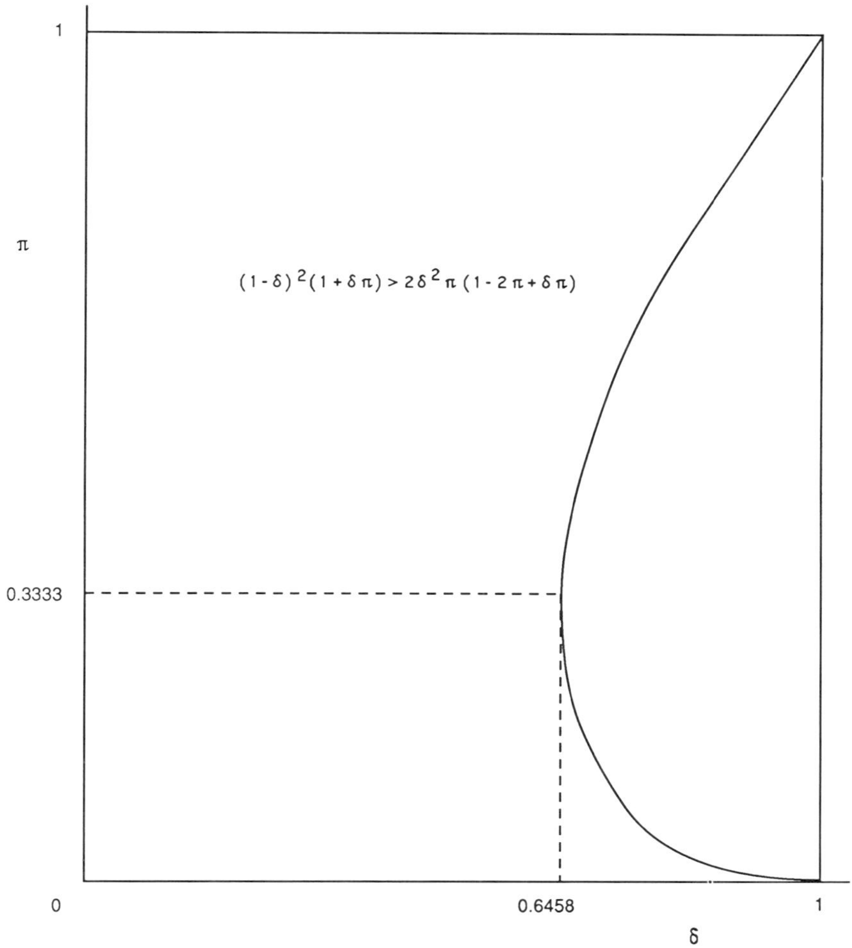
1
π
$(1-\delta)^2(1+\delta\pi) > 2\delta^2\pi(1-2\pi+\delta\pi)$
0.3333
0
0.6458
1
δ

Figure 3

Table 2

		$(1-\delta)\frac{dW}{dg}$ ω^s/ω^b		
		50	200	500
$\delta = 0.97$	$\pi = 0.999$	0.0076	*	*
	$\pi = 0.9999$	−0.0129	−0.0057	0.0089
	$\pi = 0.999999$	−0.0150	−0.0143	−0.0128
$\delta = 0.99$	$\pi = 0.999$	*	*	*
	$\pi = 0.9999$	−0.0027	0.0047	*
	$\pi = 0.999999$	−0.0048	−0.0041	−0.0026
$\delta = 0.999$	$\pi = 0.999$	*	*	*
	$\pi = 0.9999$	*	*	*
	$\pi = 0.999999$	−0.0003	0.0005	*

* No two-state Markov equilibrium exists.

equilibrium exists in the limit. This is also the case in which the monetary steady state studied by Townsend exists. As π approaches 1, the first term in (6.3) approaches $-1/(1+\delta)$, the second term approaches 0, and $dW/dg < 0$. On the other hand, the Bewley-Townsend welfare result is nonrobust in the sense that for π arbitrarily close to 1, there are values of ω^s/ω^b for which $dW/dg > 0$. This is established in the previous paragraph. Welfare elasticities for a range of cases of this type are displayed in table 2.

Thus far, we have considered only the possible benefits from a steady expansion. It is clear, however, that a policy that expands only in recessions would have the positive effects of the expansions considered here but would mitigate the negative incentive effects. This is an important rationale for a central bank or an international monetary system as a lender of last resort. By providing cash to liquidity-constrained individuals and organizations, such an institution provides socially desirable insurance.

7 Measuring the Costs and Benefits of Inflation

One problem with the discussion of the previous section is that when δ is near 1 the actual magnitude of the welfare loss or gain is very small. Some numerical examples bear out this point. Suppose that periods are a month long, and that the monthly real interest rate is 1 percent. Then $\delta = 0.99$.

Suppose also that $\omega^s/\omega^b = 200$ and that $\pi = 0.9999$. A two-state Markov equilibrium exists when $g = 0$. The welfare elasticity is $(1 - \delta)dW/dg = 0.0047$. Suppose that $g = 0.0020$, corresponding to a 2.4 percent annual growth rate of money. This results in a decline in W that is equivalent to reducing consumption forever and for sure by only 0.00067 percent—about what is predicted by $(1 - \delta)dW/dg$. As the annual growth rate of currency is increased above 5 percent, the welfare gain falls, and at a 10 percent annual rate welfare is roughly the same as at 0 percent. At a 400 percent annual inflation rate, there is a welfare loss equal to about 1 percent of consumption forever. An annual deflation of 0.12 percent leads to a minuscule welfare loss of 0.000048 percent of consumption. Higher rates of deflation are not consistent with the existence of a two-state Markov equilibrium. A simple calculation shows why the actual magnitude of welfare loss is so small when δ is near 1. If π equals 1 as δ approaches 1, dW/dg approaches $-\frac{1}{2}$. This is the Bewley-Townsend case. To convert welfare changes into units of consumption, we must multiply by $1 - \delta$; the elasticity of consumption lost due to inflation or deflation goes to 0.

These results suggest that the welfare costs and benefits of inflation are small. Unfortunately, the simple structure of our model and the restrictive nature of the equilibria we can analytically compute limit the force of our results. Nevertheless, our analysis points out some factors that any serious attempt to measure the costs and benefits of inflation should take into account.

The first framework developed for measuring the costs of inflation was that of Bailey (1956), who suggested computing the area of the triangle under the demand curve for money. Fischer (1981), using this approach, finds the welfare costs of 10 percent inflation to be 0.3 percent of GNP. Lucas (1981), using Ml rather than currency as the measure of the money supply, modifies this estimate to 0.45 percent. Cooley and Hansen (1989) impose a cash-in-advance constraint on a real business cycle model of the sort developed by Kydland and Prescott (1982). They find that the welfare cost of 10 percent inflation is 0.4 percent of GNP. It comes as no surprise that inflation is bad in the welfare triangle and the cash-in-advance approach. In each case the optimal monetary policy is to set $g = \delta - 1$ and deflate.

An interesting approach to measuring the costs of inflation, which uses a model similar in many respects to ours, is taken by Imrohoroglu (1988). In her model money is also held to self-insure. All risk is idiosyncratic, however; there is no aggregate uncertainty. Imrohoroglu finds that the welfare costs of inflation are substantially higher than do Bailey, Lucas, and Cooley and Hansen. In a model where the welfare costs of a 10 percent inflation would be 0.42 percent if measured using the welfare triangle approach, the correct measure of the cost is 1.09 percent.

Like the model of this paper, Imrohoroglu's model has a tradeoff between costs and benefits of inflation because seignorage revenues, which are redistributed in equal lump-sum transfers to agents, improve insurance possibilities. There are two possible explanations for the large disparity in results: First, as noted, Imrohoroglu's model has no aggregate uncertainty, whereas our model relies on it. Second, in her model the transition probability of going from a low-endowment state to a high-endowment state is much higher than that of going from a high-endowment state to a low-endowment state. This implies that the probability of being in a low-endowment state for two consecutive periods, where the insurance benefits of inflation are most valuable, is relatively insignificant. Since our model has only two types of agents, who are always in different states, these two probabilities need to be equal. To explore the differences and their consequences would require more powerful techniques for computing equilibria of this type model: Imrohoroglu's approach is heavily dependent on there being no aggregate uncertainty. Our approach is heavily dependent on there being only two types of uncertainty and on equilibria being two-state Markov. A more general approach to computing equilibria is provided by Kehoe and Levine (1985).

To measure the costs and benefits of inflation in a serious way, we would want to consider the whole range of alternative government policies for financing expenditures: money financing, bond financing, and distortionary taxation. Woodford (1990) provides a summary of much of the research in this area. Judd (1989) stresses the importance of the interactions among these alternatives. Simple calculations suggest, for example, that the effect of inflation on the economy through capital taxation because of nonindexation of capital depreciation allowances is far greater than those calculated in the traditional Friedman framework by Bailey (1956).

Acknowledgment

This paper benefited substantially from discussions with V. V. Chari, Patrick Kehoe, Robert Lucas, Joseph Ostroy, Edward Prescott, and Robert

Townsend. We are also grateful to Roger Guesnerie, Frank Hahn, Andreu Mas-Colell, Thomas Sargent, Jose Scheinkman, Guido Tabellini, and participants in seminars at Cal Tech, UCLA, UC San Diego, Universidad Autonoma de Barcelona, University of Chicago, and University of Minnesota. NSF grant SES 87-08616 provided financial support.

References

Bailey, M. J. 1956. "The welfare cost of inflationary finance." *Journal of Political Economy* 64: 93–110.

Benhabib, J., and C. Bull. 1983. "The optimal quantity of money: A formal treatment." *International Economic Review* 24: 101–111.

Bewley, T. 1980. "The optimum quantity of money." In *Models of Monetary Economies*, ed. J. H. Kareken and N. Wallace. Federal Reserve Bank of Minneapolis.

Bewley, T. 1983. "A difficulty with the optimum quantity of money." *Econometrica* 51: 1485–1504.

Brock, W. A. 1974. "Money and growth: The case of long run perfect foresight." *International Economic Review* 15: 750–777.

Bryant, J. (1980): "Transaction demand for money and moral hazard." In *Models of Monetary Economies*, ed. J. H. Kareken and N. Wallace. Federal Reserve Bank of Minneapolis.

Cooley, T. F., and G. D. Hansen. 1989. "The inflation tax in a real business cycle model." *American Economic Review* 79: 733–748.

Fischer, S. 1981. "Towards an understanding of the costs of inflation: II." In *Carnegie-Rochester Conference Series on Public Policy: The Costs and Consequences of Inflation*, ed. K. Brunner and A. H. Meltzer: North-Holland.

Friedman, M. 1953. *Essays in Positive Economics.* University of Chicago Press.

Friedman, M. 1969. *The Optimum Quantity of Money and Other Essays.* Aldine.

Grandmont, J.-M., and Y. Younes. 1973. "On the efficiency of a monetary equilibrium." *Review of Economic Studies* 40: 149–165.

Green, E. J. 1987. "Lending and the smoothing of uninsurable income." In *Contractual Arrangements for Intertemporal Trade*, ed. E. C. Prescott and N. Wallace. University of Minnesota.

Hahn, F. H. 1971. "Professor Friedman's views on money." *Economica* 38: 61–80.

Hahn, F. H. 1973. "On the foundations of monetary theory." In *Essays in Modern Economics*, ed. M. Parkin and A. R. Nobay. Longman.

Imrohoroglu, A. 1988. The Welfare Costs of Inflation. Unpublished manuscript, USC.

Judd, K. L. 1989. Optimal Taxation in Dynamic Stochastic Economies: Theory and Evidence. Unpublished manuscript, Hoover Institution, Stanford University.

Kehoe, T. J., and D. K. Levine. 1985. Approximate Markov Equilibria of Stationary Rational Expectations Models. Unpublished manuscript, UCLA.

Kydland, F. E., and E. C. Prescott. 1982. "Time to build and aggregate fluctuations," *Econometrica* 50: 1345–1370.

Leijonhufvud, A. 1973. "Effective demand failures." *Swedish Journal of Economics* 75: 27–48.

Levine, D. K. 1988. Asset Trading Mechanisms and Expansionary Policy. Research Department Working Paper 388, Federal Reserve Bank of Minneapolis.

Levine, D. K. 1989a. "Efficiency and the value of money." *Review of Economic Studies* 56: 77–88.

Levine, D. K. 1989b. "Infinite horizon equilibrium with incomplete markets." *Journal of Mathematical Economics* 18: 357–376.

Lucas, R. E., Jr. 1981. "Discussion of the Fischer paper." In *Carnegie-Rochester Conference Series on Public Policy: The Costs and Consequences of Inflation*, ed. K. Brunner and A. H. Meltzer. North-Holland.

Lucas, R. E., Jr., and N. L. Stokey. 1983. "Optimal fiscal and monetary policy in an economy without capital." *Journal of Monetary Economics* 12: 55–93.

Sargent, T. J. 1987. *Dynamic Macroeconomic Theory*. Harvard University Press.

Scheinkman, J. A., and L. Weiss. 1986. "Borrowing constraints and aggregate economic activity." *Econometrica* 54: 23–45.

Townsend, R. M. 1980. "Models of money with spatially separated agents." In *Models of Monetary Economies*, ed. J. H. Kareken and N. Wallace. Federal Reserve Bank of Minneapolis.

Townsend, R. M. 1982. "Optimal multiperiod contracts and the gain from enduring relationships under private information." *Journal of Political Economy* 90: 1166–1186.

Townsend, R. M. 1987. Optimal Activist Currency Rules. Unpublished manuscript, University of Chicago.

Weitzman, M. L. 1973. "Duality theory for infinite horizon convex models." *Management Science* 19: 783–789.

Woodford, M. 1990. "The optimum quantity of money." In *Handbook of Monetary Economics*, ed. B. Friedman and F. H. Hahn. North-Holland.

On the Impossibility of Perfect Capital Markets

Peter J. Hammond

Neither a borrower nor a lender be; For loan oft loses both itself and friend, And borrowing dulls the edge of husbandry.
—*Hamlet* (Act I, Scene 3, 75–77)

But where a system of borrowing and lending exists, by which I mean the granting of loans with a margin of real or personal security, a second type of risk is relevant which we may call the lender's risk. This may due either to moral hazard, i.e., voluntary default or other means of escape, possibly lawful, from the fulfilment of the obligation, or to the possible insufficiency of the margin of security, i.e., involuntary default due to the disappointment of expectation.
—Keynes 1936, p. 144

But contracts which encourage the dishonest select adversely.
—Hahn 1988, p. 970

A lot of money got put into people's pockets and they've rat-holed it somewhere. Some of it is in artwork, fancy homes, fancy airplanes and Rolls-Royces. Some of it went to Rolex watches, lizard shoes, hunting parties and yachts.
—*New York Times*, January 10, 1989 (quoted from a statment by H. Joe Selby, former chief regulator for the Federal Home Loan Bank of Dallas)

The general-equilibrium theory developed by Walras, Arrow, Debreu, Radner, and others, and expounded in Arrow and Hahn 1971, involves linear budget constraints and market-clearing prices. For intertemporal environments, this is what is required for "perfect" capital markets, in which agents are free to borrow and lend at the same market rate of interest for all loans of the same maturity, and the rates of interest adjust to match the plans of borrowers and lenders. This theory is for an economy of honorable agents who always satisfy their intertemporal budget constraints. Agents never expose themselves deliberately to the risk of default. With perfect foresight, no default would ever occur. Without perfect foresight, of course, some agents may be unable to avoid bankruptcy *ex post* (Green 1974; Bliss 1976). Yet in the theory of temporary equilibrium (Grandmont 1982, 1988) agents still arrange their affairs so that, according to their own expectations, they can fulfill their budget constraints with probability 1. As Milne (1980) has pointed out, this is consistent with two traders' making a contingent contract which each is sure that he himself can honor and yet is sure that the other cannot! By contrast, the world is full of less honorable agents who, to the extent that they find it profitable, will knowingly incur debts which they may find themselves unable to honor *ex post.*

Jaffee and Russell (1976) showed the need for nonlinear pricing of credit in a model where some borrowers would undertake investment projects leading to a risk of default on their loans while others would arrange always to honor their budget constraint, but where the two types were indistinguishable *ex ante.* Stiglitz and Weiss (1981, 1983) demonstrated the need, in a somewhat more elaborate model, not only for nonlinear pricing, but also for a ceiling on borrowing and also, in some cases, for asymmetric treatment of borrowers who are identical *ex ante.* Apart from being restricted to somewhat special economic environments, this work did not point out how what Keynes (1936, p. 144) called "moral hazard, i.e., voluntary default" affects even economies without uncertainty. Nor did it explain why some agents would choose to repay their loans, or why others would choose to expose themselves to the risk of becoming defaulters. Without drastic noneconomic penalties, some agents will gain by deliberately planning to violate their Walrasian budget constraints. There has been some recognition of this by Allen (1981, 1983) and by Eaton and Gersovitz (1981), yet their works include production, or international debt, in a way that may obscure somewhat the fact that enforcement is a problem even in the simplest of intertemporal-exchange economies.

In fact the essential difficulty in having perfect capital markets turns out to be the incredibility of an intertemporal Walrasian budget constraint. This actually places no limit whatsoever upon what an agent is allowed to borrow. In a two-period economy, an honorable agent will not borrow more than he anticipates being able to repay, with interest. But a dishonorable agent can borrow an arbitrarily large amount, and face the consequences of default later on. For some dishonorable consumers who do not care much about the future—perhaps because they are so ill that their survival is in doubt—no bankruptcy penalty will be able to deter them from deliberate default, so the Walrasian budget constraint fails completely to limit their borrowing.

Real economies may have few consumers with such preferences. Yet real economies do have firms whose owners enjoy limited liability, and legal restrictions are clearly needed to prevent the owners from having the firm borrow indefinite amounts which are then paid out as dividends to the owners, leaving the firm bankrupt. The usual Walrasian models typically presume honorable agents who, when they die, leave estates large enough to discharge any debts. Such budget constraints are especially impossible to enforce because agents have to die before they can be declared in default. One could have all liabilities as well as assets inherited by descendants (if there are any). But with perfect capital markets, the descendants themselves can borrow to discharge the debts they have just inherited, so this is no deterrent either. To put the matter at its simplest: budget constraints can be enforced only if there is a credit ceiling or a borrowing constraint at some date in the future, otherwise debts of any size can be rolled over and allowed to grow indefinitely. Such credit ceilings may appear to create imperfections in the capital market.

Credit ceilings may not, however, make capital markets imperfect by themselves. Suppose that we were in an Arrow-Debreu economy in which any information that becomes available to one agent becomes available to all simultaneously. Thus all information would be public, and there would be a publicly known event tree (see Debreu 1959). Then all agents would know what contingent contracts other agents could honor. In other words, at each event of the publicly known tree, it would be possible to limit each agent's total net short sales of Arrow contingent securities and/or Debreu contingent commodity contracts to what that agent was known to be able to repay for sure after that event has occurred. This form of credit rationing, mentioned by Foley and Hellwig (1975), makes the Arrow-Debreu budget constraint enforceable by replacing it with a sequence of short-selling constraints preventing the agent from becoming excessively indebted in any possible event. Yet any allocation which is achievable in Arrow-Debreu complete markets is still achievable with these "perfect" short-selling constraints. These constraints only prevent default—they do not prevent agents from making any short sales which can actually be honored for sure. Equilibrium allocations with such perfect constraints are *identical* to those in perfect capital markets, and no loss of efficiency or welfare will result.

The above discussion makes it clear then that credit rationing creates capital-market imperfections only when we move outside the standard Arrow-Debreu framework of a publicly known event tree. Even so, there are some forms of asymmetric information that still fail to create problems for Walras-Arrow-Debreu perfect capital-market allocations. For example, if there is a continuum economy with private information regarding only agents' preferences, then the results of Hammond (1979) for static continuum economies are easily integrated with those of Gale (1980, 1982),

Harris and Townsend (1981), and Harris (1987) for resource-allocation mechanisms in sequence economies. The point is that private information concerning preferences does not destroy the publicly known limits on what each agent in each event is able to borrow without any risk of later default.

Although the literature on incentive compatibility concentrates on the special case when only preferences are private information, this is, of course, very special. Real economic systems must deal with private information concerning labor skills (Mirrlees 1971; Dasgupta and Hammond 1980; Maskin 1980) or other endowments (Postlewaite 1979; Hurwicz, Maskin, and Postlewaite 1979; Maskin 1980; Postlewaite 1985). This work, however, assumes that individuals are allowed only to understate their true skill or to understate or perhaps even destroy their endowments. This is the kind of manipulation to which Walrasian equilibrium allocation mechanisms are often vulnerable. As Hurwicz, Maskin, and Postlewaite in particular have pointed out, if individuals can overstate their true endowments instead, and if their consumption sets are bounded below, then there will be a problem in ensuring that an allocation mechanism actually produces feasible outcomes.

In addition, Green (1987) has considered an infinite-horizon economy with a continuum of agents in which each individual's endowment stream is private information. But there is a single commodity, and utility is both additively separable and negative exponential. The possibility of an infeasible net trade vector never arises, because agents are modeled as being always able to repay any arbitrarily large sum they may have borrowed, even if this requires negative consumption in some periods. Of course, in Green's model it might well take a very long run of unluckily low endowments before a debtor was forced to suffer negative consumption. Nevertheless, the feasibility issue with which I shall specifically be concerned is not addressed.

My own past work (Hammond 1979, 1987a) and that of Gale (1980, 1982) concentrated on allocation mechanisms or game forms which determine net trade rather than consumption vectors. This implicitly allowed agents' endowments and feasible sets (consumption sets, together with any domestic production possibilities) to be private information. It did not really deal with the feasibility issue satisfactorily, however, because it assumed explicitly that agents in any game form would never choose strategies which could result in net trade vectors that are infeasible for them.

If the economy lasts for only a single period, this last assumption can often be justified by suitable monitoring of defaulters; if an agent in a game form plays a strategy that would result in an infeasible net trade vector, presumably this fact will be discovered before the allocation has been determined irreversibly. After all, even if consumption demand falls below subsistence, that is typically still feasible for an agent who is not supplying anything (Coles and Hammond 1986). So an infeasible net trade vector arises only, one may assume, when a "defaulting" agent fails to supply something that has been promised. Typically this will be detected, if only because some agent who was expecting to receive at least a part of this supply will be disappointed and can be relied upon to complain. Then, in a single-period economy, it is not too late to change the allocation by requiring the defaulting agent to amend his net trade vector to one that really is feasible. Indeed, it may be possible to monitor any defaulter's endowments, if necessary, and to confiscate enough of them to deter any such defaults.

In a sequence economy, however, the situation can be quite different. Suppose for simplicity that the economy lasts for just two periods. Then a consumer may be able to play the game form in a way which appears in the first period to ensure feasibility, but which involves commitments that cannot possibly be honored in the second period. More concretely, an agent may be able to consume excessively in the first period by acting in the economic system as would someone whose endowments were much larger—in effect, borrowing more than can ever be repaid. If the agent has been careful, this inability to repay will not manifest itself until the second period. By then it may be too late to make appropriate rearrangements to enforce an intertemporal allocation mechanism that is incentive compatible in the usual sense. It may even be too late to punish the defaulter severely enough to deter such default—the defaulter may have disappeared without trace, or even died. Excessive consumption of this kind, of course, is precisely what fraudulent borrowers achieve in actual economies. In real economies defaulters have the additional advantage of being able to seek the protection of bankruptcy laws. Such deliberate default may be criminally fraudulent, but it does occur.

In any case, potential fraud of this kind introduces a form of moral hazard to add to the obvious problems of adverse selection arising from private information about future endowments. The consequences of default really need to be specified within the game form. This was originally pointed out by Shubik (1973, 1974) in the context of a very specific trading game, but only with a finite number of players. Later, Shubik and Wilson (1977), as well as Dubey and Shubik (1979), did consider continuum economies, but they also introduced noneconomic penalties for bankruptcy. The question of whether there can ever be purely economic penalties strong enough to deter all default still needs to be carefully investigated within the framework of a game form. This paper attempts to fill the gap.

Section 1 below considers allocation mechanisms with monitoring in order to take this additional moral hazard into account. This is done with a simple two-period economy having just one consumption good. In the first period each agent has private information which tells him exactly what his second-period endowment will be. Only in the second period does default become apparent, however, and only then can monitoring be used to acquire public information about the second-period endowment. By the time the second period arrives it is too late to reduce a defaulting borrower to autarky, because the benefit from the loan taken out in the first period can no longer be taken away. Thus, in sequence economies it becomes necessary to consider additional incentive or "individual feasibility" constraints beyond those already considered by Hammond (1979, 1987a), Gale (1980, 1982), Harris and Townsend (1981), Prescott and Townsend (1984a,b), Harris (1987), and Townsend (1988), and to introduce credit rationing in a way that may well prevent attainment of an allocation which "perfect" capital markets would produce if only Arrow-Debreu budget constraints could somehow be enforced.

This may appear to contradict the results of Harris and Townsend (1981) and Harris (1987, pp. 121–131) on incentive constraints in sequence economies. They were careful to consider mechanisms as extensive-form games and to demonstrate the revelation principle for "perfect Bayesian equilibrium," closely related to Kreps and Wilson's (1982) concept of "sequential equilibrium." They proved that a sequential allocation mechanism is implementable in perfect Bayesian equilibrium strategies if and only if there is an equivalent direct mechanism in which each individual commits himself to a single strategy of direct revelation, and in which to do so truthfully is a Bayesian equilibrium (theorems 1 and 2, pp. 46–47 of Harris and Townsend 1981).

By contrast, in section 2 below the equivalent direct mechanism will be required to depend not merely on the first-period announcement of the second-period endowment, as would be the case for the kind of equivalent direct mechanism which Harris and Townsend construct. In addition, the need for monitoring implies that in the second-period the equivalent direct mechanism must also depend on what the second period endowment actually turns out to be, which will be different if a false announcement has been made in the first period. It is as though agents were allowed to revise their earlier announcements and to claim that they had previously misstated their true type. In Harris and Townsend's framework, this kind of claim is equivalent to no more than a different and inconsistent deceptive strategy in the original (indirect) game form, and never benefits the deceiver in equilibrium. But their framework incorporates the assumptions of a known common consumption possibility set (p. 40) and a known set of allocations which are "achievable" or feasible for each coalition of agents (p. 41). Since a coalition of size 1 can presumably achieve only its initial endowment, or some private production-possibility set, this specifically rules out the crucial assumption that agents are privately informed of their own endowments. Indeed, in Harris and Townsend's framework, private information never affects what is feasible—as Harris (1987, p. 121) indeed recognizes, but without being able to suggest any resolution. Accordingly, it should not be surprising that Harris and Townsend's results need some modification in sequence economies for which there is private information regarding endowments, consumption sets, or private production-possibility sets. When one constructs an equivalent direct mechanism in such a sequence economy, one cannot afford to ignore any non-null set of agents who claim that they previously misstated their types and now cannot supply what they are supposed to—some form of monitoring and modification of their net trade vectors seems inevitable if the allocation mechanism really is to be both physically feasible and implementable in dominant strategies. That is why both the announced and the true endowments feature in the equivalent direct mechanism of section 2. One can expect more complicated equivalent direct mechanisms to emerge when there are many periods in which monitoring may be triggered—and corresponding additional incentive constraints.

Section 1 will set out the basic assumptions of a continuum economy lasting for two periods with one good each period. It also describes the basic framework of extensive game forms in which endowment monitoring is used to ensure individual physical feasibility. Section 2 discusses implementation in dominant strategies, as well as the incentive and individual-feasibility constraints which this requires. It also describes the problem of finding incentive-constrained Pareto-efficient allocation mechanisms. Section 3 explores the conditions under which an allocation mechanism can be implemented without any monitoring occurring in equilibrium. Section 4 presents a particular example of a demand-revelation game form which generates an incentive-compatible allocation mechanism. An even more special example with just two possible second-period endowment levels, one of which is zero, is then considered. It is shown how, when the Walrasian equilibrium allocation cannot be sustained, there will be a non-Walrasian equilibrium with binding borrowing constraints for some individuals. Moreover, the borrowing rate of interest must exceed the lending rate, even though there are no defaults on any loans.

1 Two-Period Extensive Game Forms with Endowment Monitoring

A Continuum Economy

Consider a continuum economy with a nonatomic measure space of agents $(N, \mathscr{N}, v)$—in fact, one could assume that $N = [0,1] \subset \Re$, that $\mathscr{N}$ is the usual Borel σ algebra, and that v is the usual Lebesgue measure. For simplicity, suppose that all agents $i \in N$ have the same known utility function, $u: \Re^2_+ \mapsto \Re$, which is continuous and strictly increasing on the known common consumption set $\Re^2_+$. To keep the model simple, suppose also that all agents have the same known endowment of 1 in the first period, but that their different second-period endowments $e \in \Re_+$ remain as private information in the first period, and can be discovered only through monitoring in the second period. Assume too that there is a set $E \subset \Re_+$ of possible second-period endowments. Note that no trade is always possible for each consumer, even if it does not necessarily guarantee survival.

Random Endowments

Suppose that the allocation mechanism in this economy emerges from an extensive game form with the following sequence of events. At the first stage of the game, nature determines at random the measurable function, $e(\cdot): N \to \Re_+$, that specifies the endowment vector e_i of each agent $i \in N$.[1] This function determines the joint distribution $\lambda \in \Delta(N \times E)$ of agents' names and endowments given by

$$\lambda(K) = \nu(\{i \in N | (i,e_i) \in K\}) \tag{1}$$

for every Borel set $K \subset N \times E$. Obviously, λ induces the marginal distribution ν on N.

Agents $i \in N$ are supposed to be informed only of their own endowments e_i, and to remain uninformed about the endowments of others and even about the distribution λ.

Strategies

At the second stage of the game form, each agent has the same set A of possible strategies a. These can be interpreted as bargaining strategies, offers to borrow and lend, announcements of credit demand functions, or whatever. All agents $i \in N$ choose their strategy functions $a_i : E \to A$ specifying how their respective actions in the economic system depend on their endowments, which represent the differences in what they know. For simplicity it is assumed that the resulting function $a(\cdot) : N \times E \to A$ is measurable and so induces a well-defined joint distribution $\sigma \in \Delta(N \times E \times A)$ on the set of agents' names, endowments, and strategies which is given by

$$\begin{aligned}\sigma(K) &= \lambda(\{i,e) \in N \times E | (i,e,a_i(e)) \in K\}) \\ &= \nu(\{i \in N | (i,e_i,a_i(e_i)) \in K\})\end{aligned} \tag{2}$$

for every Borel set $K \subset N \times E \times A$. This distribution has appropriate marginals λ on $N \times E$ and so ν on N, of course.

Also, let $\alpha(\sigma) \in \Delta(N \times A)$ denote the resulting marginal joint distribution of agents' strategies and names in the game form, which is given by

$$\begin{aligned}\alpha(\sigma)(K) &= \lambda(\{i,e) \in N \times E | (i,a_i(e)) \in K\}) \\ &= \nu(\{i \in N | (i,a_i(e_i)) \in K\})\end{aligned} \tag{3}$$

for every Borel set $K \subset N \times A$. It will be assumed that all the relevant features of this distribution can be observed by all those individuals in the economy who are responsible for arranging net trades and any monitoring activities which are undertaken at later stages of the game form, to be described below.

The Provisional Allocation Mechanism

Suppose now that, at the third stage of the game form and still in the first period of the sequence economy's two periods, a *provisional allocation* of net trades

$$\xi_i^0(a,\alpha): N \times A \times \Delta(N \times A) \to \Re^2 \tag{4}$$

is determined for each agent i, as a jointly measurable function of i's name, i's strategy a in the game form, and the entire distribution of strategies α played by all the other agents. Notice that $\xi_i^0(\cdot)$ does not depend directly upon i's endowment e_i, so the allocation mechanism is not using private information.

It is presumed that the first-period part $\xi_{i1}^0(a,\alpha)$ of this provisional mechanism comes into immediate effect during this third stage of the game form, and that this is always possible because $\xi_{i1}^0(a,\alpha) + 1 \geq 0$ for all $i \in N$, all $a \in A$, and all $\alpha \in \Delta(N \times A)$. It is presumed in addition that the second-period part $\xi_{i2}^0(a,\alpha)$ will also come into effect unless there is some non-null set of agents who default in the second period by failing to repay what this provisional mechanism prescribes.

Endowment Monitoring

In the second period, the game form goes on to fourth and further stages. First it is assumed that agents are given the opportunity to make payments to each other voluntarily, in an effort to settle their debts if they want to. If these voluntary payments do in fact settle (almost) all debts, so that (almost) all agents $i \in N$ have their appropriate net expenditures $\xi_{i2}^0(a,\alpha)$, then the game stops and the provisional allocation becomes the actual one. Otherwise creditors pursue defaulting debtors and set in motion processes of monitoring and debt collection, as is the standard practice in bankruptcy proceedings. It is therefore natural to suppose that monitoring signals are affected by true endowments—indeed, in the extreme case of perfect monitoring, an agent's true second-period endowment will be discovered. Thus, the monitoring signal $m_i \in M$ for each monitored agent $i \in N$ is supposed to be a deterministic but possibly imperfect indicator of the true endowment e_i—obviously, randomness could be introduced into a more complicated model.

In fact, it will ease notation to suppose that all agents are monitored, but that for some of them the monitoring only produces a "null signal" m_0 which can be interpreted as meaning that no real monitoring has taken place. It is therefore assumed that there is a measurable *monitoring function*

$$m_i(e,a,\sigma): N \times E \times A \times \Delta(N \times E \times A) \to M. \tag{5}$$

The range of this function is taken to be the fixed set M of possible monitoring signals, which has the null signal m_0 as one of its members. For technical reasons, it will be necessary to assume that M can be given a topology and so also a Borel σ algebra of measurable sets. Of course, this is hardly a serious restriction.

Note that the monitoring signal is allowed to depend on the entire joint distribution $\sigma \in \Delta(N \times E \times A)$ of agents' names, endowments, and strategies, rather than just on the marginal distribution $\alpha(\sigma) \in \Delta(N \times A)$ of names and strategies. This is because, as discussed below, several rounds of monitoring will often be needed, with monitoring decisons at later stages depending on the results of previous monitoring.

Given the joint distribution $\sigma \in \Delta(N \times E \times A)$, this monitoring function induces a joint distribution $\mu(\sigma) \in \Delta(N \times A \times M)$ which is given by

$$\mu(\sigma)(K) := \sigma(\{(i,e,a) \in N \times E \times A \mid (i,a,m_i(e,a,\sigma)) \in K\}) \tag{6}$$

for every measurable subset $K \subset N \times A \times M$. This distribution summarizes whatever information about individuals' endowments is available to the economic system, and how those endowments are correlated with their behavior in that system. Let $\alpha(\mu) \in \Delta(N \times A)$ denote the corresponding marginal distribution on just names and strategies.

Notice how one can only have $m_i(e,a,\sigma) = m_0$ for almost all $i \in N$ when $\xi_{i2}^0(a,\alpha(\sigma)) + e \geq 0$ for almost all $i \in N$. Otherwise there will be a non-null set of agents who are bound to default in the second period when the economic system tries to implement the provisional allocation by calling upon them to repay their debts in full. If these defaulting agents were not monitored and punished in some way, no borrower would ever repay his debts, and the credit allocation mechanism would collapse to autarky. So nontrivial monitoring of defaulters is usually an essential part of any well-functioning credit-allocation system.

In addition, if there is a non-null set of agents for whom $\xi_{i2}^0(a,\alpha) + e < 0$, their unavoidable default and the consequent changes to the allocation mechanism may trigger defaults by other agents—a familiar problem in real economies when significant numbers of agents are in financial difficulties. That is why one cannot just assume, for each separate $i \in N$, that $\xi_{i2}^0(a,\alpha(\sigma)) + e \geq 0$ implies $m_i(e,a,\sigma) = m_0$. For the same reason, several rounds of monitoring may be necessary, and the ultimate monitoring signal $m_i(e,a,\sigma)$ may depend on actual endowments through the entire distribution $\sigma \in \Delta(N \times E \times A)$ of names, endowments, and actions, rather than just on the marginal distribution $\alpha(\sigma) \in \Delta(N \times A)$ of names and actions. This will be true for the special demand-revelation mechanism discussed in section 4, for instance.

The Final Second-Period Allocation Mechanism

Here, however, I shall consider only the final outcome after all necessary rounds of monitoring and recontracting have been completely carried out in order to ensure feasibility. So, in the very last stage of the game form, there will be a measurable *final second-period allocation function*

$$\xi_{i2}^{M}(a,m,\mu): N \times A \times M \times \Delta(N \times A \times M) \rightarrow \Re. \tag{7}$$

There is also an associated *direct second-period allocation function*, ξ_{i2} (a,e,σ), whose second argument is the individual's true endowment e rather than the monitoring signal m which was generated by e, and whose third argument is the joint distribution σ in the population of combinations (i,e,a). This measurable function,

$$\xi_{i2}: N \times A \times E \times \Delta(N \times E \times A) \rightarrow \Re,$$

is given by the composition

$$\xi_{i2}(a,e,\sigma) \equiv \xi_{i2}^{M}(a,m_i(e,a,\sigma),\mu(\sigma)) \tag{8}$$

of the above allocation and monitoring functions.

Ensuring Physical Feasibility

Since the whole purpose of monitoring is to ensure physical feasibility, it will be assumed that, for all

$$(i,e,a,\sigma) \in N \times E \times A \times \Delta(N \times E \times A),$$

the individual feasibility constraint

$$\xi_{i2}^{M}(a,m_i(e,a,\sigma),\mu(\sigma)) + e = \xi_{i2}(a,e,\sigma) + e \geq 0 \tag{9}$$

is satisfied. Note in particular how, for agents whose second-period allocation would be individually infeasible in the absence of monitoring, the inevitable default that follows must trigger active monitoring and lead to an adjustment of the allocation to something that is feasible given the true endowment e. The assumption (9) guarantees that a feasible allocation always results, even when individual consumers use disequilibrium strategies. This is an essential condition for an economic system to be able to function, which must always be satisfied somehow. Remember, after all, that I do *not* assume that feasibility entails survival.

To illustrate how (9) is actually quite plausible, consider first the following *perfect monitoring mechanism*. The monitoring signal space M is taken to be $\Re_+ \cup \{m_0\}$. The associated monitoring and second-period allocation functions are then

$$m_i(e,a,\sigma) = \begin{cases} m_0 & \text{if } \xi_{i2}^M(a,m_0,\mu(\sigma)) + e \geq 0 \\ e & \text{if } \xi_{i2}^M(a,m_0,\mu(\sigma)) + e < 0 \end{cases} \tag{10}$$

and

$$\xi_{i2}^M(a,m,\mu(\sigma)) = -m \Leftrightarrow m \neq m_0.$$

This evidently implies that

$$\xi_{i2}(a,e,\sigma) = \max\{\xi_{i2}^M(a,m_0,\mu(\sigma)), -e\} \tag{11}$$

and so (9) is indeed satisfied. Under this perfect monitoring mechanism, agents are monitored if and *only if* they would have to default otherwise. Also, monitoring detects all the endowment of any agent who is actively monitored. All this endowment is then confiscated, so consumption is forced down to zero in the second period. Because of our assumption that the consumption set is $\Re_+^2$, this guarantees individual feasibility. It will also deter default provided that the null monitoring consumption stream

$$(\xi_{i1}^0(a^*,\alpha(\sigma)) + 1, \xi_{i2}^M(a^*,m_0,\mu(\sigma)) + e)$$

for the best strategy a^* is always at least weakly preferred to

$$(\xi_{i1}^0(a,\alpha(\sigma)) + 1, 0)$$

for every alternative strategy $a \in A$.

Punishing defaulters by reducing their consumption to zero in the second period is obviously rather drastic, especially as there is no guarantee that the individual defaulter can then even survive. In addition, not all of an agent's endowment can always be detected through monitoring—and even if it can be, if may be too costly to do so. Thus, one may be forced to have "imperfect" monitoring mechanisms instead, with $m_i(e,a,\sigma) \leq e$ when $\xi_{i2}^M(a,m_0,\mu(\sigma)) + e < 0$, and $\xi_{i2}^M(a,m,\mu(\sigma)) \geq -m$ when $m \neq m_0$. Then (11) is replaced by the inequality

$$\xi_{i2}(a,e,\sigma) \geq \max\{\xi_{i2}^M(a,m_0,\mu(\sigma)), -e\},$$

and so (9) is still satisfied in this case. Such a mechanism does serve to show how individual feasibility might be guaranteed even out of equilibrium.

Resource Balance

Physical feasibility also requires aggregate resource balance constraints to be satisfied. In the second period, such constraints should reflect the resource costs of the monitoring that is required in order to bring about the specified monitoring function. Thus, a reasonable formulation of such constraints is

$$\begin{aligned} &\int_{N \times A} \xi_{i1}^{0}(a,\alpha)\alpha(di \times da) \leq y_1, \\ &\int_{N \times E \times A} \xi_{i2}(a,e,\sigma)\sigma(di \times de \times da) \leq y_2(y_1,\sigma) \end{aligned} \tag{12}$$

for every joint distribution $\sigma \in \Delta(N \times E \times A)$ with marginal $\alpha \in \Delta(N \times A)$. Here y_1 represents the mean level in the population of net expenditure (or excess of expenditure over saving) during the first period; then $y_2(y_1,\sigma)$ is an upper bound on the mean second-period net expenditure levels which are physically feasible. It reflects the nonmonitoring production possibilities of the economy. The dependence of y_2 on σ, however, is a general formulation recognizing that the process of producing monitoring signals according to the function $m_i(e,a,\alpha)$ must use up some real resources. These have to be diverted away from meeting the net demands in the nonmonitoring sector of the economy. Note that the costs of monitoring an agent's endowments are presumably always observable by the person doing the monitoring and so incurring the costs. For this reason they can be treated as part of the monitoring signal m, with a value of 0 when $m = m_0$, the null signal.

Aggregate feasibility constraints like (12) play no role, however, in determining the incentive constraints, which are our primary concern here. Thus, they will largely be ignored except when constrained Pareto-efficient allocation mechanisms are discussed in section 2.

That completes the basic description of the multi-stage extensive game form for determining net trades in the simple two-period sequence economy. Although its formulation may appear rather special at first sight, in fact it is hard to imagine any really different formulation of an economic system that allows trades to be consummated without any monitoring when all individuals are indeed honoring their obligations and that also provides for the necessary monitoring when there are defaulters.

2 Implementation in Dominant Strategies

Dominant Strategies

Suppose that each individual $i \in N$ in this game form has a dominant strategy function $a_i^*(e): E \to A$ at the second stage, and that this function depends upon i's own endowment e but not on the distribution α of strategies chosen by other individuals. Thus,

$$\begin{aligned} a_i^*(e) &\in \arg\max_a \{u(\xi_{i1}^0(a, \alpha(\sigma)) + 1, \xi_{i2}^M(a, m_i(a, e, \sigma), \mu(\sigma)) + e) | a \in A\} \\ &= \arg\max_a \{u(\xi_{i1}^0(a, \alpha(\sigma)) + 1, \xi_{i2}(a, e, \sigma) + e) | a \in A\}, \end{aligned} \tag{13}$$

which means that $a_i^*(e)$ is always a best response to any joint frequency distribution $\sigma \in \Delta(N \times E \times A)$ generated by the other agents' choices of strategies. Notice that there is no need to incorporate any feasibility constraint explicitly in the maximization problem (13) because of the earlier assumption (9). Finally, assume that the dominant strategy function $a_i^*(\cdot)$: $N \times E \to A$ is measurable and so, for each distribution $\lambda \in \Delta(N \times E)$ of names and endowments, induces the well-defined joint distribution

$$\sigma^*(\lambda)(K) := \lambda(\{(i,e) \in N \times E | (i, e, a_i^*(e)) \in K\}) \in \Delta(N \times E \times A) \tag{14}$$

for every measurable subset $K \subset N \times E \times A$, whose corresponding marginal distribution is given by

$$\alpha^*(\lambda)(K) := \lambda(\{(i,e) \in N \times E | (i, a_i^*(e)) \in K\}) \in \Delta(N \times A) \tag{15}$$

for every measurable subset $K \subset N \times A$. In addition, the monitoring functions $m_i(e, a, \alpha)$ then determine the joint distribution in $\Delta(N \times A \times M)$ given by

$$\mu^*(\lambda)(K) := \lambda(\{(i,e) \in N \times E | (i, a_i^*(e), m_i(e, a_i^*(e), \alpha^*(\lambda))) \in K\}) \tag{16}$$

for every measurable subset $K \subset N \times A \times M$.

An Equivalent Direct Mechanism

For each agent $i \in N$ there are now two equivalent direct mechanisms, one for each period, described by the measurable functions

$$f_{i1}(\lambda,e) := \xi^0_{i1}(a^*_i(e), \alpha^*(\lambda)) : \Delta(N \times E) \times E \to \Re$$

and (17)

$$f^M_{i2}(\lambda, e; m) := \xi^M_{i2}(a^*_i(e), m, \mu^*(\lambda)) : \Delta(N \times E) \times E \times M \to \Re.$$

But also, given the game form and the dominant strategy function specified above, each agent $i \in N$ has an equivalent *direct monitoring function*, defined by

$$g_i(\lambda, e'; e) := m_i(e, a^*_i(e'), \alpha^*(\lambda)) : \Delta(N \times E) \times E \times E \to M, \quad (18)$$

which is also measurable. Thus, $g_i(\lambda, e'; e)$ is the monitoring signal generated when agent i with true endowment e is deceptive, and acts as would agent i with endowment e', when the joint distribution of all agents' names and endowments appears to be λ. There is then an even more direct second-period mechanism, given by

$$\begin{aligned} f_{i2}(\lambda, e'; e) &:= \xi_{i2}(a^*_i(e'), e, \sigma^*(\lambda)) \\ &\equiv \xi^M_{i2}(a^*_i(e'), m_i(e, a^*_i(e'), \alpha^*(\lambda)), \mu^*(\lambda)) \\ &\equiv \xi^M_{i2}(a^*_i(e'), g_i(\lambda, e'; e), \mu^*(\lambda)) \\ &\equiv f^M_{i2}(\lambda, e'; g_i(\lambda, e'; e)), \end{aligned} \quad (19)$$

which is a measurable function

$$f_{i2}(\lambda, e'; e) : \Delta(N \times E) \times E \times E \to \Re.$$

Thus, $(f_{i1}(\lambda, e'), f_{i2}(\lambda, e'; e))$ is the net expenditure stream that results when agent i acts "deceptively," as if having second-period endowment e' when it is really e, and when the joint distribution of names and endowments appears to be λ.

Note how the first-period net borrowing $f_{i1}(\lambda,e')$ of somebody who acts as though his second-period endowment were e' must be independent of the true endowment e, because e is unable to influence the monitoring signal $m \in M$ until the second period, and so can affect only the second-period allocation. Of course, $f_{i2}(\lambda, e'; e)$ does depend, in general, not only upon the apparent value e' of the agent's endowment but also upon the true endowment e, since that ultimately influences the monitoring signal $m \in M$. But it must be independent of e for those true second-period endowments satisfying $g_i(\lambda, e'; e) = m_0$, because then no monitoring occurs even in the second period.

Incentive and Individual Feasibility Constraints

Because of our assumption (13) that $a_i^*(e)$ is always a dominant strategy for each agent $i \in N$, we have

$$u(\xi_{i1}^0(a_i^*(e'), \alpha^*(\lambda)) + 1, \xi_{i2}(a_i^*(e'), e, \sigma^*(\lambda)) + e)$$
$$\leq u(\xi_{i1}^0(a_i^*(e), \alpha^*(\lambda)) + 1, \xi_{i2}(a_i^*(e), e, \sigma^*(\lambda)) + e) \tag{20}$$

for all (λ, e', e). Then it follows immediately from (17) and (19) that

$$u(f_{i1}(\lambda, e') + 1, f_{i2}(\lambda, e'; e) + e) \leq u(f_{i1}(\lambda, e) + 1, f_{i2}(\lambda, e; e) + e) \tag{21}$$

for all (λ, e', e). These are precisely the *incentive constraints* needed for truth-telling to be a dominant strategy in the direct-revelation game form induced by the direct mechanism $(f_{i1}(\lambda, e'), f_{i2}(\lambda, e'; e))$.

Because of (9), it must also be true that

$$\xi_{i2}(a_i^*(e'), e, \sigma^*(\lambda)) + e \geq 0 \tag{22}$$

for all (λ, e', e). But then (19) implies that, for all (λ, e', e), the equivalent direct mechanism must satisfy the important additional *individual feasibility constraint*

$$f_{i2}(\lambda, e'; e) + e \geq 0. \tag{23}$$

In our simple sequence economy, *both* constraints (21) and (23) must be satisfied for all possible (λ, e', e) if a direct mechanism is to be implementable in dominant strategies. Satisfying the incentive constraints (21) alone is not enough.

Pareto-Efficient Mechanisms

Now that the physical feasibility and incentive constraints have all been specified, it is possible in principle to describe Pareto-efficient mechanisms that satisfy these constraints. The choice variables are the first-period allocation mechanism $f_{i1}(\lambda, e)$ and then, in the second period, the combination consisting of the space M of monitoring signals, the monitoring function $g_i(\lambda, e'; e)$, and the second-period allocation mechanism $f_{i2}^M(\lambda, e'; m)$ based on these monitoring signals. The latter allocation mechanism gives rise to the measurable function

$$f_{i2}(\lambda, e'; e) \equiv f_{i2}^M(\lambda, e'; g_i(\lambda, e'; e)).$$

For each possible distribution $\lambda \in \Delta(N \times E)$, a Pareto-efficient mechanism will usually maximize an objective which can be expressed as a utility integral,

$$W \equiv \int_{N \times E} \omega_i(\lambda,e)u(f_{i1}(\lambda,e) + 1, f_{i2}(\lambda, e; e) + e)\lambda(di \times de), \tag{24}$$

with welfare weights $\omega_i(\lambda,e)$. This should then be maximized subject to the individual feasibility constraints (23), the incentive constraints (21), and resource-balance constraints such as

$$\int_{N \times E} f_{i1}(\lambda,e)\lambda(di \times de) \leq y_1$$

and (25)

$$\int_{N \times E} f_{i2}(\lambda,e; e)\lambda(di \times de) \leq y_2(y_1) - \int_{N \times E} \gamma_i^M(\lambda, g_i(\lambda,e; e))\lambda(di \times de)$$

for each of the two periods. Here, the function

$$\gamma_i^M(\lambda,m) : \Delta(N \times E) \times M \rightarrow \Re_+$$

indicates the resource cost of monitoring, which can be assumed to satisfy the condition that $\gamma_i^M(\lambda,m_0) = 0$—i.e., the resource cost of the null signal is zero, as that monitoring should be avoided if possible. Nevertheless, it is quite possible that monitoring will occur for some agents even when they use their (truthful) dominant strategies. Indeed, monitoring of endowments could be part of an optimal solution even if there were no problem of default: it could simply be the most cost-effective incentive-compatible method of arranging the redistribution needed to achieve allocations that are both distributively just and fully Pareto efficient. After all, if monitoring of endowments were both perfect and costless, it could be used to bring about a first-best allocation in every possible economic environment. For instance, since land holdings are often quite easy to monitor, land reform is often advocated as a powerful tool for redistribution.

Although the problem of finding an incentive-constrained Pareto-efficient allocation mechanism has now been formulated in a fairly simple way, its solution seems to be very far from simple, even in very special cases such as when the set E of possible endowments has only two values. Thus the characterization of such solutions has had to be left for later work. No doubt this will build on important insights such as of Harris and Raviv (1979), Townsend (1979), and Gale and Hellwig (1985).

3 When Can Monitoring Be Avoided in Equilibrium?

Incentive Constraints without Monitoring

This section will examine the conditions under which there is (almost) no monitoring in the economy when (almost) all agents use their dominant strategies in the game form. After all, if monitoring is costly, and if the second-period resource-balance constraint is tight even in the absence of monitoring—as it presumably should be for an optimal mechanism—then there cannot be any monitoring at all if that mechanism is indeed to be physically feasible.

To this end, first define the function

$$f_{i2}^{0}(\lambda,e) := f_{i2}^{M}(\lambda, e; m_0) : \Delta(N \times E) \times E \to \mathfrak{R}. \tag{26}$$

This is the second-period allocation in the event of no monitoring. In terms of the equivalent direct mechanism, in which agents reveal their true endowments in equilibrium, there will be no monitoring in equilibrium provided that, for all $e \in E$,

$$g_i(\lambda, e; e) = m_0$$

and (27)

$$f_{i2}(\lambda, e; e) = f_{i2}^{M}(\lambda, e, m_0) = f_{i2}^{0}(\lambda,e).$$

Now suppose that a typical agent $i \in N$ acts as though he has endowment e' even though the true endowment is e. If agent i is not monitored in the second period either when his endowment is e or when it is e', this deception can never be detected because monitoring is the only way of noticing the difference between these two endowment levels. But because of (27), an agent whose endowment appears to be either e or e' will not be monitored in dominant strategy equilibrium when those endowments are the real ones, and when $\lambda \in \Delta(N \times E)$ is the real joint distribution of names and endowments. Thus, the only way in which this deception can ever be detected is if it triggers monitoring because it leads to default. In other words, if agent i acts as though his endowment were e' when it is really

e, there will be no monitoring unless $f_{i2}^{0}(\lambda,e') + e < 0$, which is precisely when agent i will have to default and so trigger monitoring. So (27) implies that

$$g_i(\lambda, e'; e) = m_0 \text{ and } f_{i2}(\lambda, e'; e) = f_{i2}^{M}(\lambda, e', m_0) = f_{i2}^{0}(\lambda,e') \Leftrightarrow f_{i2}^{0}(\lambda,e') + e \geq 0. \quad (28)$$

Thus, active monitoring occurs if and only if it is needed to ensure individual feasibility in the second period.

Notice how (28) implies that, if $f_{i2}^{0}(\lambda,e') + e \geq 0$ and the incentive constraints (21) are also satisfied, then

$$\begin{aligned} u(f_{i1}(\lambda,e') + 1, f_{i2}^{0}(\lambda,e') + e) &= u(f_{i1}(\lambda,e') + 1, f_{i2}(\lambda, e'; e) + e) \\ &\leq u(f_{i1}(\lambda,e) + 1, f_{i2}(\lambda,e; e) + e) = u(f_{i1}(\lambda,e) + 1, f_{i2}^{0}(\lambda, e) + e). \quad (29) \end{aligned}$$

In particular, this shows that the implication

$$f_{i2}^{0}(\lambda,e') + e \geq 0 \Rightarrow u(f_{i1}(\lambda,e') + 1, f_{i2}^{0}(\lambda,e') + e) \leq u(f_{i1}(\lambda,e) + 1, f_{i2}^{0}(\lambda, e) + e) \quad (30)$$

must be true for all pairs $e,e' \in E$. These are "restricted" incentive constraints in the sense that they need only be satisfied for those deviations e' that result in individually feasible net expenditure streams $(f_{i1}(\lambda,e'), f_{i2}^{0}(\lambda, e'))$. Incentive constraints involving deviations that lead to individually infeasible allocations are simply ignored. For the case of static economies, this corresponds precisely to the assumption made in Hammond 1979, 1987a, in Gale 1980, 1982, and apparently in Postlewaite and Schmeidler 1986, 1987 too.

It is therefore especially important to understand clearly the difference between (30) and the earlier combination of the incentive constraints (21) with the individual feasibility constraints (23). Because of the need to ensure individual feasibility (through monitoring if necessary), each individual's second-period net expenditure $f_{i2}(\lambda, e'; e)$ in (21) depends on both e' and e (as well as on λ, of course), and the incentive constraints are required to hold for *all* possible pairs e,e'. In contrast, (30) restricts attention to just those pairs e,e' for which the individual feasibility constraint $f_{i2}^{0}(\lambda,e') + e \geq 0$ is satisfied anyway, and does not need to make $f_{i2}^{0}(\lambda,e')$ depend on e as well as on e'.

Furthermore, when (27) holds, the incentive constraints (21) must implicitly include "deterrence constraints" ensuring that if agent i defaults in the second period, and so allows monitoring to be triggered, then allocating to i the net expenditure level $f_{i2}^M(\lambda, e'; m)$ with $m \neq m_0$ is an effective punishment ensuring that there are no benefits to default. So, if (27) could be made true, not only would truthful revelation always be a dominant strategy, but it would also follow that monitoring is never necessary when individuals reveal their true endowments.

Sufficient and Necessary Conditions

Second-period consumption $f_{i2}(\lambda, e'; e) + e$ must always be non-negative, however, even if all of a defaulter's endowment is monitored and then confiscated. Since utility is strictly increasing, combining (27) with the incentive constraints (21) implies that, for all pairs $e, e' \in E$,

$$\begin{aligned} u(f_{i1}(\lambda, e') + 1, 0) &\leq u(f_{i1}(\lambda, e') + 1, f_{i2}(\lambda, e'; e) + e) \\ &\leq u(f_{i1}(\lambda, e) + 1, f_{i2}(\lambda, e; e) + e) \\ &= u(f_{i1}(\lambda, e) + 1, f_{i2}^0(\lambda, e) + e) \end{aligned} \tag{31}$$

is a necessary condition for feasibility to be possible without any monitoring in equilibrium.

Some unnecessarily strong sufficient conditions for the key property (31) to hold are that $f_{i1}(\lambda, e) + 1 > 0$ and $f_{i2}^0(\lambda, e) + e > 0$ for all $e \in E$, and also that

$$u(c_1', 0) \leq u(c_1, c_2) \text{ whenever } c_1' \geq 0 \text{ and } c_1, c_2 > 0. \tag{32}$$

This will be true in particular when preferences are "smooth," implying that no indifference curve intersects the $c_2 = 0$ axis. When (32) is satisfied, (31), (21), and (23) can indeed all be made true provided that any defaulter's second-period consumption gets reduced to zero by means of a mechanism such as (10). In this special case, then, there will be no need for monitoring in equilibrium, when all agents use their dominant strategies.

On the other hand, if zero consumption (or whatever other lower bound is imposed on defaulters) is not too bad, perhaps because the defaulter is no longer in a position to care very much anyway, then the necessary condition (31) for deterring all default imposes an upper bound on $f_{i1}(\lambda, e')$. For the specific case when

$$u(c_1,c_2) \equiv \sqrt{c_1} + \sqrt{c_2}, \tag{33}$$

for instance, (31) obviously implies that

$$\sup_{e' \in E} \{f_{i1}(\lambda,e')\} \leq \inf_{e \in E} \{[\sqrt{f_{i1}(\lambda,e) + 1} + \sqrt{f_{i2}^0(\lambda,e) + e}]^2 - 1\} \tag{34}$$

for almost all $i \in N$. This necessary condition for the absence of default when agents use their dominant strategies need not be true even for the usual kind of Walrasian mechanism, with budget sets given by the familiar

$$c_1 + (1 + r)^{-1}c_2 \leq 1 + (1 + r)^{-1}e \tag{35}$$

for a suitable rate of interest r. For in a pure exchange economy with utility function given by (33), the appropriate unique Walrasian equilibrium is symmetric, with net expenditures and an interest rate which are easily calculated as being given by the functions

$$f_{i1}(\lambda,e) \equiv \frac{e - \bar{e}(\lambda)}{\bar{e}(\lambda) + \sqrt{\bar{e}(\lambda)}}, \quad f_{i2}^0(\lambda,e) \equiv \frac{\bar{e}(\lambda) - e}{\sqrt{\bar{e}(\lambda)} + 1}, \quad r(\lambda) \equiv \sqrt{\bar{e}(\lambda)} - 1. \tag{36}$$

Here $\bar{e}(\lambda)$ denotes the mean second-period endowment,

$$\int_{N \times E} e\, \lambda(di \times de).$$

In this case it is easy to check that (34) is satisfied if and only if

$$\frac{e^* + \sqrt{\bar{e}(\lambda)}}{e_* + \sqrt{\bar{e}(\lambda)}} \leq [\sqrt{\bar{e}(\lambda)} + 1]^2, \tag{37}$$

where e^* and e_* denote respectively the supremum and the infimum of the set E of possible second-period endowments which the allocation mechanism has to allow for. In particular, (37) is never satisfied if e is lognormally distributed.

Accordingly, it seems that one has to abandon the hypothesis that, even when individuals are privately informed about their endowments, there are always dominant-strategy incentive-compatible mechanisms in which all defaults can be prevented, without the need for any monitoring in equilibrium. Also, even if such mechanisms do exist, it may still be true that the incentive constraints (21) and the feasibility constraints (23) are together strictly stronger than just the restricted incentive constraints (30).

4 A Special Case

A Demand-Revelation Mechanism

A particular demand-revelation mechanism of some interest occurs when each individual $i \in N$ has a strategy space A consisting of all possible net expenditure demand correspondences

$$D(r,\bar{x}_1) : \mathfrak{R}_+ \times \mathfrak{R}_+ \twoheadrightarrow \mathfrak{R}^2$$

which have closed graphs and nonempty compact values, as well as satisfying the condition

$$D(r,\bar{x}_1) \subset \{(x_1,x_2) \in \mathfrak{R}^2 \mid -1 \leq x_1 \leq \bar{x}_1 \; \& \; x_1 + (1+r)^{-1}x_2 \leq 0\}. \tag{38}$$

The relevant parameters which determine the budget set on the right-hand side of (38) are an interest rate r and a first-period borrowing ceiling $\bar{x}_1$. The economy is supposed to be one of pure exchange. So there will exist functions $r(\alpha)$ and $\bar{x}_1(\alpha)$ of the distribution $\alpha \in \Delta(N \times A)$, together with selections $x_i^0(\alpha) \in D(r(\alpha), \bar{x}_1(\alpha))$, such that the resource balance constraints

$$\int_{N \times A} x_{it}^0(\alpha)\alpha(di \times da) \leq 0$$

are always satisfied for both periods $t = 1, 2$.

The monitoring signal space is taken to be $\mathfrak{R}_+$, the set of possible endowment levels. When some agents default in the second period, and have endowments which turn out to be too low to cover their debts, there will be an aggregate deficit. For simplicity it is assumed that this is financed by means of a proportional reduction in the return to lenders, while borrowers pay no more than their nominal obligations require. If this were not true, and borrowers were also expected to contribute to the deficit, one would have to consider which additional borrowers would be forced to default because of these extra payments, how much extra deficit arises, and so on—as in Green 1974. Thus, for each possible value of $\sigma \in \Delta(N \times E \times A)$, it is simply assumed that there exists some $\theta(\sigma) \in [0,1]$ with the following properties:

(i) In the absence of monitoring, each agent i's net expenditure level in period 2 is given by

$$\xi_{i2}^{M}(a, m_0, \mu(\sigma)) := \begin{cases} \theta(\sigma)\xi_{i2}^{0}(a,\alpha) & \text{if } \xi_{i2}^{0}(a,\alpha) > 0 \\ \xi_{i2}^{0}(a,\alpha) & \text{if } \xi_{i2}^{0}(a,\alpha) \le 0. \end{cases} \tag{39}$$

(ii) The monitoring function is given by (10).

(iii) The appropriate simplified form for an exchange economy of the second-period resource-balance constraint in (12), namely

$$\int_{N \times E \times A} \max\{\xi_{i2}^{M}(a, m_0, \mu(\sigma)), -e\}\sigma(di \times de \times da) \le y_2(\sigma), \tag{40}$$

is satisfied.

Then capital markets have just two "imperfections": first, those who want to borrow large amounts may find their credit being rationed; second, there may be some default, even though defaulters have their second-period consumption reduced to zero.

Demand Behavior

In this special case, the utility-maximizing first-period net demand correspondence of an agent whose true second-period endowment is e will be

$$D_1^*(r, \bar{x}_1; e) \equiv \arg\max_{x_1} \{u(x_1 + 1, \max\{0, e - (1 + r)x_1\}) | -1 \le x_1 \le \bar{x}_1\}. \tag{41}$$

Note that $D_1^*(r, \bar{x}_1; e)$ will be equal to $\{\bar{x}_1\}$, with the agent facing zero consumption in the second period, whenever both $e < (1 + r)\bar{x}_1$ (so that the credit rationing does not prevent the agent from ever borrowing more than can be repaid) and the default utility level $u(\bar{x}_1 + 1, 0)$ exceeds the usual indirect utility

$$V^W(r;e) := \max_{x_1} \{u(x_1 + 1, x_2 + e) | x_1 + (1 + r)^{-1}x_2 \le 0\} \tag{42}$$

from optimizing subject to the Walrasian budget constraint. Of course, those agents who are induced to borrow more than they can repay at the rate of interest r must be among those who have their credit rationed, since otherwise their demands for first-period consumption would be unlimited.

Some typical properties of the first-period net demand correspondence D_1^* can be illustrated by taking the specific utility function (33), for which

$$D_1^*(r, \bar{x}_1; e) \equiv \arg\max_{x_1} \{\sqrt{x_1 + 1} + \max\{0, \sqrt{e - (1 + r)x_1}\} | -1 \le x_1 \le \bar{x}_1\}. \tag{43}$$

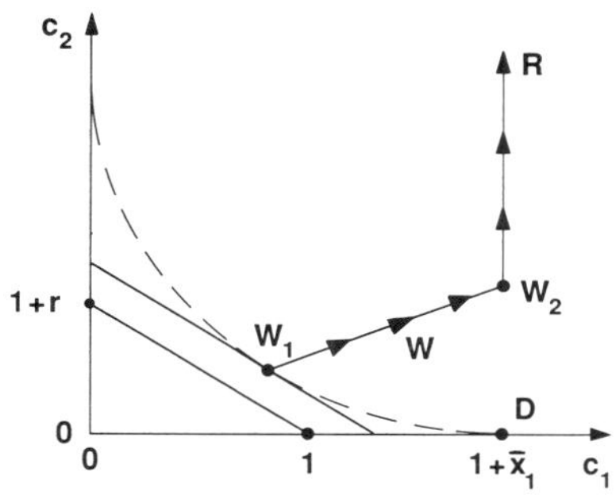

Figure 1
A typical wealth-expansion path.

Now, as the second-period endowment e increases, with the first-period endowment held fixed at the level 1, the consumer's wealth-expansion path takes a form like that illustrated in figure 1. There are three distinct cases to consider.

The first (case D) occurs for very low levels of e. Then the consumer borrows as much as possible—up to the credit ceiling $\bar{x}_1$—and later defaults, thus choosing the point D in figure 1 at which $D_1^*(r, \bar{x}_1; e) = \{\bar{x}_1\}$.

As e increases, this default option eventually becomes sufficiently unattractive that the individual switches discontinuously from borrowing to lending, and then starts moving up the line segment between W_1 and W_2. This is the usual Walrasian case W, in which the credit ceiling does not bind and the agent repays in full. Then $D_1^*(r, \bar{x}_1; e) = \{x_1^W\}$, where

$$x_1^W := \frac{e - (1 + r)^2}{(1 + r)(2 + r)} \leq \bar{x}_1. \tag{44}$$

So, once case W occurs, the consumer is a lender for values of e up to $(1 + r)^2$. But he switches back to being a borrower thereafter, as e becomes large enough to make it desirable to transfer some purchasing power from the future to the present even though (unlike in case D) the loan will be repaid.

The indirect utility function for case W is

$$V^W(r;e) := \sqrt{(2 + r)[1 + (1 + r)^{-1}e]}. \tag{45}$$

Accordingly, the borderline between cases D and W must occur when

$$e = (2 + r)^{-1}(1 + r)[\bar{x}_1 - (1 + r)], \tag{46}$$

because then the Walrasian indirect utility $V^W(r;e)$ given by (45) is just equal to the default utility $\sqrt{\bar{x}_1 + 1}$. Note how (46) implies that $e < (1+r)\bar{x}_1$, so that, for all e below this critical value, default is indeed bound to occur after the consumer has borrowed up to the limit $\bar{x}_1$ in the first period.

Ultimately, however, at the point W_2, the credit ceiling that was necessary to control the default behavior of those with very low values of e begins to bind even for those with very high values of e, who cannot be distinguished *ex ante*. This is true even though individuals with very high values of e have no intention of defaulting. This is the third case, R, in which the individual's credit is rationed but there is no default. Then $D_1^*(r, \bar{x}_1; e) = \{\bar{x}_1\}$ and $e - (1+r)\bar{x}_1 \geq 0$. This case occurs when

$$e > (1+r)^2 + (1+r)(2+r)\bar{x}_1, \tag{47}$$

because then (44) implies that the Walrasian net demand x_1^W exceeds the ceiling $\bar{x}_1$. Case R corresponds to the last part of the wealth-expansion path shown in figure 1, represented by the vertical line up from W_2.

The intermediate Walrasian case W will occur on a nontrivial interval of values of e whenever $\bar{x}_1 + 1 > 0$, because this is sufficient to ensure that the lower limit determined by (46) is less than the upper limit determined by (47).

A Two-Type Example

Let us now restrict this special example further by assuming that the set of possible second-period endowments E is just the pair $\{0, e^*\}$, and that $e^*(>0)$ is the endowment of a proportion π of the population, while a proportion $1 - \pi$ have a zero endowment. Then the mean second-period endowment is πe^*. So, according to (36), the unique Walrasian equilibrium for this distribution λ has the interest rate $r = \sqrt{\pi e^*} - 1$ and (in an obvious notation) the allocation

$$x_1(e^*) = \frac{e^* - \pi e^*}{\pi e^* + \sqrt{\pi e^*}}, \quad x_2(e^*) = \frac{\pi e^* - e^*}{\sqrt{\pi e^*} + 1},$$
$$x_1(0) = \frac{-\pi e^*}{\pi e^* + \sqrt{\pi e^*}}, \quad x_2(0) = \frac{\pi e^*}{\sqrt{\pi e^*} + 1}. \tag{48}$$

Thus, those with zero second-period endowment save by making loans to those with e^* so that both types of agent have positive consumption in both periods.

Also, according to (37), this unique Walrasian equilibrium is unsustainable in case

$$e^* + \sqrt{\pi e^*} > \sqrt{\pi e^*}(\sqrt{\pi e^*} + 1)^2$$

which is true iff $\pi^{-1} - 2 > \sqrt{\pi e^*}$ or iff $\pi < \frac{1}{2}$ and $e^* < (1 - 2\pi)^2\pi^{-3}$. Recall that the unsustainability arises because agents with zero second-period endowment prefer the consumption stream they can get by borrowing like an agent with e^* and then defaulting in the second period over the consumption stream they can get by being "honest."

When this Walrasian allocation is unsustainable, we shall look for an alternative allocation with a borrowing rate r_B which is typically higher than the lending rate r. There will also be a credit ceiling $\bar{x}_1$ imposed to prevent those with zero second-period endowment from borrowing with the intention to default. In addition, those agents who do not default in the second period will each receive a dividend d which is financed by the profits earned from the difference between the borrowing and lending rates of interest. Those with zero second-period endowment will still be lending to those with e^*. And even though the need to allow for default prevents attainment of the Walrasian allocation, there will actually be no default in the new equilibrium. The need for differential borrowing and lending rates will also be demonstrated, in the case when the Walrasian equilibrium is unsustainable.

Since individuals with $e = 0$ are lending, the credit ceiling does not affect them at all (except to deter borrowing with intent to default), and so their net borrowing is at the Walrasian level given by

$$x_1^W(r, d; 0) = \frac{d - (1 + r)^2}{(1 + r)(2 + r)} \tag{49}$$

after changing (44) to take account of the dividend d in the second period and then putting $e = 0$. To ensure that $x_1^W(r, d; 0) < 0$, of course, requires that $d < (1 + r)^2$. The net repayment of each such individual, in the event of no default, is

$$x_2^W(r, d; 0) = d - (1 + r)x_1^W(r, d; 0) = \frac{(d + 1 + r)(1 + r)}{2 + r}. \tag{50}$$

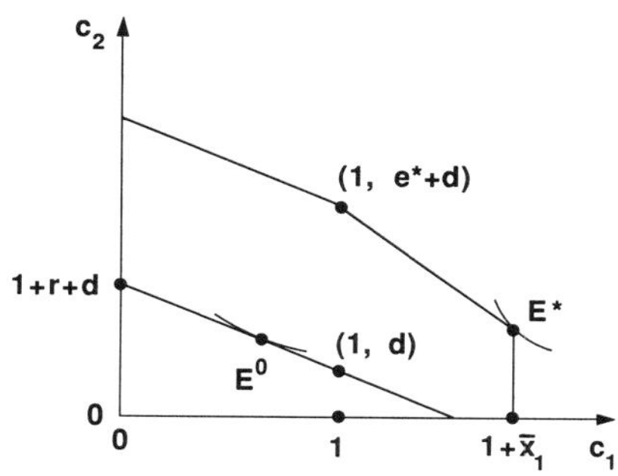

Figure 2
A non-Walrasian equilibrium.

Thus, these individuals are at the point E^0 in figure 2. The associated utility level is

$$u^W(0) = \sqrt{\frac{(d+1+r)(2+r)}{1+r}}. \tag{51}$$

On the other hand, in order to investigate whether there can be a non-Walrasian equilibrium even when the borrowing and lending rates of interest are equal, it will be assumed that individuals with second-period endowment e^* are credit constrained. So they must be at the point E^* in figure 2, with $x_1(e^*) = \bar{x}_1$ and $x_2(e^*) = \bar{x}_2 = d - (1 + r_B)\bar{x}_1$. Then the market-clearing conditions $\pi x_t(e^*) + (1 - \pi)x_t(0) = 0$ in each of the two periods $t = 1$ and $t = 2$ obviously require that

$$\bar{x}_t = -(1-\pi)x_t^W(r, d; 0)/\pi. \tag{52}$$

But then the borrowing rate of interest must be given by

$$1 + r_B = \frac{d - \bar{x}_2}{\bar{x}_1} = 1 + r + \frac{(1+r)(2+r)d}{(1-\pi)[(1+r)^2 - d]}, \tag{53}$$

as can be shown by routine manipulation. In particular, this shows that the borrowing rate exceeds the lending rate if and only if the dividend d is positive. Also, r_B must increase whenever d increases, because (as remarked above) it must be true that $d < (1 + r)^2$.

Default will be deterred if the (indirect) utility (51) of those with $e = 0$ does not fall below $\sqrt{\bar{x}_1 + 1}$. So we must have

$$d \geq \underline{d}(r) := \frac{(1+r)^2[1-\pi(3+r)]}{1+\pi(1+r)(3+r)} = \frac{(1+r)(2+r)}{1+\pi(1+r)(3+r)} - (1+r). \tag{54}$$

Note that $(1+r)^2 > \underline{d}(r)$ and so this is consistent with allowing $x_1^W(r, d; 0) < 0$.

In order to have a non-Walrasian equilibrium, it must also be true that agents with $e = e^*$ are borrowing no more than they wish. Thus, their marginal rate of substitution $(1 + \bar{x}_1)^{-1/2}/(e^* + \bar{x}_2)^{-1/2}$ at the consumption stream $(1 + \bar{x}_1, e^* + \bar{x}_2)$ cannot be less than the borrowing interest factor $1 + r_B$. This is true iff

$$e^* \geq (1 + r_B)^2(1 + \bar{x}_1) - \bar{x}_2 = (\bar{x}_1)^{-2}(d - \bar{x}_2)^2(1 + \bar{x}_1) - \bar{x}_2, \tag{55}$$

where the last equality follows from (53). Now consumption expenditure in each period is evidently a normal good, with $x_1^W(r, d; 0)$ and $x_2^W(r, d; 0)$ both increasing functions of d. Then (52) implies that $\bar{x}_1$ and $\bar{x}_2$ are both decreasing functions of d. As $\bar{x}_1 > 0$, it follows that the right-hand side of (55) is an increasing function of d. So this inequality serves to define an upper bound $\bar{d}(e^*,r)$ on allowable values of d. Of course, (55) also ensures that $e^* + \bar{x}_2 \geq 0$, thus guaranteeing individual feasibility.

So all non-Walrasian equilibrium allocations of this form are sustainable provided that d satisfies $\underline{d}(r) \leq d \leq \bar{d}(e^*,r)$ for the chosen lending rate r, and provided that the credit ceiling and the borrowing rate are then determined by (52) and (53) respectively. Some tedious calculation shows that, whenever the sufficient condition $\pi^4 e^* < 1 + \pi(1-\pi)^3$ is satisfied, such a non-Walrasian equilibrium exists, with

$$1 + r = \pi(1-\pi)\sqrt{\frac{e^*}{1+\pi(1-\pi)^3}} \; (<\pi^{-1} - 1)$$

and (56)

$$d = \frac{(1+r)^2[1-\pi(2+r)]}{1+\pi(1+r)(2+r)} \; (>\max\{0, \underline{d}(r)\}).$$

Moreover, the above sufficient condition *is* satisfied whenever e^* is too low to allow the Walrasian equilibrium to be sustained—i.e., whenever $\pi < \frac{1}{2}$ and $e^* < (1-2\pi)^2\pi^{-3}$.

It remains to be shown that, for any non-Walrasian equilibrium, the borrowing rate must exceed the lending rate in the case when the Walrasian equilibrium is unsustainable. Indeed, suppose it were true that

$d = 0$ and so $r_B = r$. Then (54) clearly implies that $0 \geq 1 - \pi(3 + r)$ or that $1 + r \geq \max\{0, \pi^{-1} - 2\}$. But when $d = 0$, (55) reduces to $\pi e^* \geq (1 + r)^2$, and so an equilibrium of this particular form exists for interest rates in the range satisfying

$$\max\{0, \pi^{-1} - 2\} \leq 1 + r \leq \sqrt{\pi e^*}. \tag{57}$$

When $\pi \geq \frac{1}{2}$, such equilibria exist for all positive values of e^*. But when $\pi < \frac{1}{2}$, such equilibria exist only if and only if $e^* \geq (1 - 2\pi)^2\pi^{-3}$, which is precisely the condition for Walrasian equilibrium to be sustainable anyway. This proves the assertion: when the Walrasian equilibrium is unsustainable, a non-Walrasian equilibrium with credit rationing of the kind considered here can be sustained only by means of a positive gap between the borrowing and lending rates of interest.

Conclusion: Perfect Capital Markets Are Generally Not Possible

This paper has considered borrowing and lending in the simplest of all possible models, in which capital markets have the best chance of performing perfectly because there is a continuum of agents. There are no jointly owned private producers and no uncertainty—just an exchange economy lasting for only two periods with a single consumption good, in which agents have the same utility function and the same known first-period endowment. It was also assumed that all agents know in the first period what their second-period endowment will be, but this is private information. Apart from the continuum of agents, none of these features of the model is important except insofar as they help us to concentrate on essentials.

Of much more significance is the assumption that (32) is violated. This requires that the consumers' common utility function $u(c_1,c_2)$ for two-period consumption streams satisfy the condition $u(c_1',0) > u(c_1,c_2)$ for some c_1' which is sufficiently large. So there must be some indifference curves meeting the c_1 axis. Then the threat of imposing zero second-period consumption may be ineffective. This is crucial to the specific simple model used here—but not really to the need for credit rationing, because the familiar lifetime budget constraints of more general models are clearly incredible. Indeed, even a lifetime budget constraint is just a particular borrowing constraint that purports to prohibit dying in debt.

So the model presented here illustrates rather starkly the fact that, when some information about individuals is private, "perfect capital markets" may be impossible. If agents have private information about their future endowments, then an allocation mechanism that always selects a "perfect" Walrasian equilibrium in every economic environment is generally manipulable by agents who plan deliberately to violate their Walrasian budget constraints. By contrast, in a static continuum economy, such a mechanism is not manipulable, provided only that default can be detected in time and defaulters punished by being reduced to autarky or with some other sufficient deterrent. Thus the inevitable "market failure" in these economic environments is due to the sequential nature of the economy rather than to private information *per se*.

It appears that Stigler's (1967) plea for a theory behind assumed capital-market imperfections can now be answered—or, if not, that our conception of what constitutes a perfect capital market should be changed drastically to allow incentive-constrained Pareto-efficient allocations which generally require credit rationing, nonlinear pricing, and regulated entry into and participation in credit markets. Indeed, in future work I would like to consider "perfected" capital markets, with option contracts somewhat similar to those introduced in Hammond 1989.

The model used here also has the virtue of bringing out the need to control fraud. It should be remembered that U.S. banks have been said to lose eighteen times as much from fraud as they do from robbery, and that the Federal Bureau of Investigation is reported to have fifty agents working on bank fraud cases in Los Angeles alone.[2]

Acknowledgments

This paper is a drastically revised version of Hammond 1987b, which was originally produced with the support of U.S. National Science Foundation Grant SES-85-20666 to the Institute for Mathematical Studies in the Social Sciences, Stanford University. It has evolved through presentations at C.O.R.E., at Western Ontario, Southern Methodist, Tulane, Stanford, Cambridge, Mannheim, Southampton, Oxford, and Bonn Universities, at the Ecole Normale Supérieure in Paris and the University of California at San Diego, and to the European Meeting of the Econometric Society in Budapest. My gratitude to all the participants for their encouragement, to Frank Hahn, Mordecai Kurz, and Joe Stiglitz for extensive discussions, and to an anonymous referee, Ed Green, and Oliver Hart for useful suggestions.

Notes

1. For simplicity it will be assumed that this and other functions of i are measurable. This is in common with almost all the rest of the literature on continuum economies and games with a continuum of players—e.g., Green 1984. Yet it is not entirely satisfactory, because, for instance, a continuum of random variables almost never produces a measurable function (Gale 1979; Feldman and Gilles 1985; Judd 1985). It fact one should probably consider distributions rather than functions—e.g., the distribution $\lambda \in \Delta(N \times E)$ described in this section—without necessarily assuming that there is a (measurable) function at all. To do so would complicate the notation even further, however.

2. This is based on my own notes from a television documentary on the crisis in banking which was shown on the Public Broadcasting Service station KQED in the San Francisco Bay area early in 1989.

References

Allen, F. 1981. "The prevention of default." *Journal of Finance* 36: 271–276.

Allen, F. 1983. "Credit rationing and payment incentives." *Review of Economic Studies* 50: 639–646.

Arrow, K. J., and F. H. Hahn. 1971. *General Competitive Analysis.* Holden-Day.

Bliss, C. J. 1976. "Capital theory in the short run." In *Essays in Modern Capital Theory*, ed. M. Brown, K. Sato, and P. Zarembka. North-Holland.

Coles, J. L. and P. J. Hammond. 1986. Walrasian Equilibrium without Survival: Existence, Efficiency, and Remedial Policy." Stanford University Institute of Mathematical Studies in the Social Sciences Economics Technical Report 483.

Dasgupta, P. S., and P. J. Hammond. 1980. "Fully progressive taxation." *Journal of Public Economics* 13: 141–154.

Debreu, G. 1959. *Theory of Value: An Axiomatic Analysis of Economic Equilibrium.* Wiley.

Dubey, P., and M. Shubik. 1979. "Bankruptcy and optimality in a closed trading mass economy modeled as a non-cooperative game." *Journal of Mathematical Economics* 6: 115–134.

Eaton, J., and M. Gersovitz. 1981. "Debt with potential repudiation: Theoretical and empirical analysis." *Review of Economic Studies* 48: 289–309.

Feldman, M., and C. Gilles. 1985. "An expository note on individual risk without aggregate uncertainty." *Journal of Economic Theory* 35: 26–32.

Foley, D. K., and M. F. Hellwig. 1975. "A note on the budget constraint in a model of borrowing." *Journal of Economic Theory* 11: 305–314.

Gale, D. M. 1979. "Large economies with trading uncertainty." *Review of Economic Studies* 46: 319–338.

Gale, D. M. 1980. "Money, information and equilibrium in large economies." *Journal of Economic Theory* 23: 28–65.

Gale, D. M. 1982. *Money: In Equilibrium.* James Nisbet.

Gale, D. M., and M. Hellwig. 1985. "Incentive-compatible debt contracts: The one-period problem." *Review of Economic Studies* 52: 647–663.

Grandmont, J.-M. 1982. "Temporary general equilibrium theory." In *Handbook of Mathematical Economics*, volume 2, ed. K. J. Arrow and M. D. Intriligator. North-Holland.

Grandmont, J.-M., ed. 1988. *Temporary Equilibrium: Selected Reading*. Academic Press.

Green, E. J. 1984. "Continuum and finite-player noncooperative models of competition." *Econometrica* 52: 975–993.

Green, E. J. 1987. "Lending and the smoothing of uninsurable income." In *Contractual Arrangements for Intertemporal Trade*, ed. E. C. Prescott and N. Wallace. University of Minnesota Press.

Green, J. R. 1974. "Pre-existing contracts and temporary general equilibrium." In *Essays on Economic Behavior under Uncertainty*, ed. M. S. Balch, D. L. McFadden, and S. Y. Wu. North-Holland.

Hahn, F. H. 1988. "On monetary theory." *Economic Journal* 98: 957–973.

Hammond, P. J. 1979. "Straightforward individual incentive compatibility in large economies." *Review of Economic Studies* 46: 263–282.

Hammond, P. J. 1987a. "Markets as constraints: Multilateral incentive compatibility in a continuum economy." *Review of Economic Studies* 54: 399–412.

Hammond, P. J. 1987b. On the Impossibility of Perfect Capital Markets. Stanford University Institute of Mathematical Studies in the Social Sciences Economics Technical Report 516.

Hammond, P. J. 1989. Perfected Option Markets in Economies with Adverse Selection. European University Institute Working Paper 89/426.

Harris, M. 1987. *Dynamic Economic Analysis*. Oxford University Press.

Harris, M., and A. Raviv. 1979. "Optimal incentive contracts with imperfect information." *Journal of Economic Theory* 20: 231–259.

Harris, M., and R. M. Townsend. 1981. "Resource allocation under asymmetric information." *Econometrica* 49: 33–64.

Hurwicz, L., E. Maskin, and A. Postlewaite. 1979. "Feasible implementation of social choice correspondences by Nash equilibrium." Paper presented to the Stanford University Institute of Mathematical Studies in the Social Sciences, Summer Workshop in Mathematical Economics.

Jaffee, D. M., and T. Russell. 1976. "Imperfect information and credit-rationing." *Quarterly Journal of Economics* 90: 651–666.

Judd, K. 1985. "The law of large numbers with a continuum of random variables." *Journal of Economic Theory* 35: 19–25.

Keynes, J. M. 1936. *The General Theory of Employment, Interest and Money*. Macmillan.

Kreps, D., and R. Wilson. 1982. "Sequential equilibria." *Econometrica* 50: 863–894.

Maskin, E. S. 1980. "On first-best taxation." In *Income Distribution: The Limits to Redistribution*, ed. D. Collard, R. Lecomber, and M. Slater. Wright.

Milne, F. 1980. "Short-selling, default risk and the existence of equilibrium in a securities model." *International Economic Review* 21: 225–267.

Mirrlees, J. A. 1971. "An exploration in the theory of optimum income taxation." *Review of Economic Studies* 38: 175–208.

Postlewaite, A. 1979. "Manipulation via endowments." *Review of Economic Studies* 46: 255–262.

Postlewaite, A. 1985. "Implementation via Nash equilibria in economic environments." In *Social Goals and Social Organization: Essays in Memory of Elisha Pazner*, ed. L. Hurwicz, D. Schmeidler, and H. Sonnenschein. Cambridge University Press.

Postlewaite, A., and D. Schmeidler. 1986. "Implementation in differential information economies." *Journal of Economic Theory* 39: 14–33.

Postlewaite, A., and D. Schmeidler. 1987. "Differential information and strategic behavior in economic environments: A general equilibrium approach." In *Information, Incentives, and Economic Mechanisms: Essays in Honor of Leonid Hurwicz*, ed. T. Groves, R. Radner, and S. Reiter. University of Minnesota Press.

Prescott, E. C., and R. M. Townsend. 1984a. "Pareto optima and competitive equilibria with adverse selection and moral hazard." *Econometrica* 52: 21–45.

Prescott, E. C., and R. M. Townsend. 1984b. "General competitive analysis in an economy with private information." *International Economic Review* 25: 1–20.

Shubik, M. 1973. "Commodity money, oligopoly, credit and bankruptcy in a general equilibrium model." *Western Economic Journal* 11: 24–38.

Shubik, M. 1974. "Money, trust and equilibrium points in games in extensive form." *Zeitschrift für Nationalökonomie* 34: 365–385.

Shubik, M., and C. Wilson. 1977. "The optimal bankruptcy rule in a trading economy using fiat money." *Zeitschrift für Nationalökonomie* 37: 337–354.

Stigler, G. 1967. "Imperfections in the capital market," *Journal of Political Economy* 85: 287–292.

Stiglitz, J. E., and A. Weiss. 1981. "Credit rationing in markets with imperfect information." *American Economic Review* 71: 393–410.

Stiglitz, J. E., and A. Weiss. 1983. "Incentive effects of terminations: Applications to the credit and labor markets." *American Economic Review* 73: 912–927.

Townsend, R. M. 1979. "Optimal contracts and competitive markets with costly state verification." *Journal of Economic Theory* 21: 265–293.

Townsend, R. M. 1988. "Information constrained insurance: The revelation principle extended." *Journal of Monetary Economics* 21: 411–450.

Optimal Taxation of Identical Consumers when Markets Are Incomplete

Peter A. Diamond and James A. Mirrlees

This paper examines the optimal form of taxation for a simple model of an economy with an incomplete set of markets. The reasons for absence of the missing markets are not explicit. Consumers are identical, and production is under the control of the government. The optimal policies have some striking features, which we believe may be inherited by more satisfactory models.

Many markets that one can conceive of do not exist. In particular, consumers cannot fully insure themselves against macroeconomic fluctuations. Various explanations for the lack of markets have been suggested. One of the simplest, and one of the most plausible, is that the costs of running markets, or the transactions costs, are sufficiently great that a large number of longer-term, contingent-payment markets do not operate. A model of markets that are costly to run was put forward by Foley (1970) and Hahn (1971). Simplifying somewhat, we can describe such an economy as one in which some markets are just not available, and in which, consequently, consumers have multiple budget constraints. If, for example, markets for contingent saving, or equivalent insurance markets, are not available, the level of a consumer's saving must be the same for all future states of nature. There is an intertemporal budget constraint for each state of nature.

Many of the reasons often suggested for the incompleteness of markets, such as asymmetric information or moral hazard, are ignored in the present paper. The set of absent markets is treated as given and as invariant to the policies analyzed.[1] On the whole, we doubt that the reasons ignored are important for the particular incompleteness of markets to be considered, where insurance for social risks is not available.

Another difficult issue in modeling economies with incomplete markets is the treatment of firms and their trade possibilities. We avoid that problem here by assuming that all production is controlled by the government. These production possibilities allow the transfer of resources between states of nature: it is possible to invest in ways that favor one or another future state. Associated with an optimal production plan there are shadow prices, which we shall call producer prices. With convex production possibilities, equilibrium production maximizes expected profit when producer prices for future contingent goods are interpreted as the discounted mathematical expectation of prices. But there is no particular reason why private producers should maximize expected profits. Nevertheless, we shall call the difference between consumer and producer prices taxes, and interpret equilibria as market equilibria with prices and taxes.

In an economy with identical consumers, there are no incentive-compatibility difficulties in the way of raising revenue a government requires by lump-sum taxation. We shall briefly discuss optimality when lump-sum taxation is allowed; however, most of the paper is devoted to the Ramsey problem, in which revenue has to be raised and can be raised only by commodity taxation. The justifications are the usual ones: the Ramsey problem is the easiest case of distortionary taxation, and can be expected to generate insights relevant to the more general case of many consumers; and it is an approximation to optimal linear taxation for an economy where the dispersion of preferences is not great, but there are some consumers so poor that it is not feasible to have a positive lump-sum tax.

We focus on the situation where there are no poolable individual risks, only social risks. We find that, in some cases, the structure of taxes and subsidies can completely compensate for the absence of markets. The precise sense in which taxation can compensate for incompleteness of markets is the following. Imagine an optimal allocation for a world with complete markets, but in which only commodity taxes are available as policy tools. That allocation is an equilibrium with complete markets. The same allocation might also be an equilibrium, even if some markets are not available, when appropriate taxes and subsidies are introduced in the markets that do operate. If so, we can say that taxation is a perfect substitute for the missing markets in this policy environment.

Taxation cannot always perfectly compensate for incomplete markets. When it cannot there are two possible types of optima. One is a local complete-market optimum which is not the global optimum. With the other, it is best to cancel past saving or dissaving in some state of nature. Cancellation of saving is introduced as a policy tool that is a natural extension of commodity taxation. In effect we find a reason for forgiveness of debt; though elimination of accumulated wealth is also a possible outcome.

It would be possible to set up the optimal-tax problem in the usual way, with taxes in all first-period and second-period markets, and to write out and attempt to interpret the first-order conditions for the optimum. That would hide the possibility of complete compensation by taxation, and the possiblity that in other cases there is no optimum, unless we also allowed the cancellation of savings as a further policy tool. We therefore attempt to discriminate directly between those cases where optimal taxation can fully compensate for the absence of markets and those where it cannot, and only then go into a more precise analysis of the optimal tax rules for the latter case. We begin by formulating the economic model with multiple budget constraints.

Complete and Incomplete Equilibria

The economy has two periods. In the second period there are two possible states. There are production possibilities, in the control of the government, allowing investment of goods in the first period for production in either or both of the states of the second period. There are no insurance markets for consumers. Consumers can save or dissave, but must do the same for both states. The model takes this form because a single private asset and two states of nature is the simplest case of asset-market incompleteness.

Assume that consumer preferences are convex and strictly monotonic. Consumers have utility $u(x, y, z)$ in terms of the period-1 consumption vector, x, and the period-2 consumption vectors, y in state 1 and z in state 2. When markets are incomplete, the consumer maximizes utility subject to multiple budget constraints,

$$p \cdot x + q \cdot y \leq a, \tag{1a}$$

$$p \cdot x + r \cdot z \leq b, \tag{1b}$$

where p are the prices faced by consumers in the first period, q are the present discounted consumer prices for goods bought in the second period when state 1 occurs, r are the present discounted consumer prices when state 2 occurs, and a and b are lump-sum incomes contingent upon each of the two states. In our Ramsey world, a and b are constrained to be zero. These constraints state, in effect, how consumption levels in the two states of period 2 are constrained by saving or dissaving in period 1.

Because preferences are monotonic, both constraints are binding. Since preferences are convex, there exists a scalar α, $0 < \alpha < 1$, such that, for this consumer, utility is maximized subject to the single budget constraint

$$p \cdot x + \alpha q \cdot y + (1 - \alpha) r \cdot z \leq \alpha a + (1 - \alpha) b. \tag{2}$$

This is defined by the hyperplane that separates the convex set of vectors (x, y, z) preferred by the consumer to his equilibrium vector from the convex set defined by the inequalities (1). The scalar α lies strictly between 0 and 1: if, for example, $\alpha = 0$, (3) is equivalent to (1a) alone, and (1b) would be violated. (Neither q nor r can be the zero vector, for then a finite consumption vector would not maximize utility.[2])

First, consider the first-best welfare problem: we maximize the utility of our consumers, subject to available production possibilities. We know from Hart 1975 that an equilibrium is not necessarily an optimum, and indeed the conditions for an equilibrium to be always Pareto-efficient are very stringent. But it is easier to arrange for an optimum to be an equilibrium. If there were complete markets, consumers would be subject to a single budget constraint,

$$p' \cdot x + q' \cdot y + r' \cdot z \leq c, \tag{3}$$

where p', q' and r' would be producer prices as well as consumer prices. Now suppose markets are incomplete. The first-best allocation might still be an equilibrium, if we can find budget constraints of the form (1) that have consumers choose the same consumption plan as in the first-best allocation. That requires that (3) be equivalent to (2), with a equal to the value of $p \cdot x + q \cdot y$ at the optimum and with b equal to the value of $p \cdot x + r \cdot z$ at the optimum. Clearly we should have $p = p'$, $\alpha q = q'$, and $(1 - \alpha) r = r'$. Any value of α between 0 and 1 will do. If q and r are interpreted as expected discounted prices, setting α equal to the probability of the first state means that the rate of interest is the same in the two states. For this implementation of the optimum, state-contingent lump-sum transfers a and b are required.

If it is required that a single lump-sum transfer be used (i.e., that $a = b$), it may not be possible for the first-best allocation to be an equilibrium, even if interest rates in the two states are allowed to be different. If $a = b$, we must have $q \cdot y = r \cdot z$ in equilibrium; i.e.,

$$\frac{1}{\alpha} q' \cdot y = \frac{1}{1 - \alpha} r' \cdot z.$$

This must hold with α and $1 - \alpha$ both positive. It can do so if and only if, in the equilibrium that implements the optimum, $q' \cdot y$ and $r' \cdot z$ have the same sign, in the strong sense that both are positive, both zero, or both negative. If that is not the case, it will be desirable to introduce commodity taxes into the equilibrium. The problem is then analogous to the Ramsey one. That is, if the first-best allocation involves saving from the first period for state 1 and dissaving from the first period for state 2, this pattern cannot be reproduced by private decisions with a single asset (with rates of return above -1 in both states).

In the problem to be addressed in the present paper, $a = b = 0$. We have established that utility maximization subject to (1) implies utility maximization subject to (2). That is, for any two-budget choice problem there is a one-budget choice problem that generates the same demands. That proposition has an important implication for the maximization of utility in the economy with incomplete markets. It shows that an equilibrium with zero lump-sum incomes and incomplete markets is also an equilibrium with zero lump-sum incomes and complete markets. A Ramsey optimum for incomplete markets is therefore a tax equilibrium with complete markets.

On the other hand, the Ramsey optimum for complete markets may not be a tax equilibrium with incomplete markets. It could very well involve insurance that amounts to a different rate of saving for the two second-period states. If this Ramsey optimum is an incomplete-market equilibrium, in the sense that the same real allocation can be obtained with suitable consumer prices when consumers have no access to insurance, then it is also the Ramsey optimum for incomplete markets, since, as argued above, the Ramsey optimum for incomplete markets is a feasible complete-market equilibrium. We shall need to see when the two optima coincide.

Denote the Ramsey optimum consumer prices for complete markets by p^*, q^*, r^*, so that the consumer faces a budget constraint

$$p^* \cdot x + q^* \cdot y + r^* \cdot z \leq 0. \tag{4}$$

We ask when the consumer's choices (x^*, y^*, z^*) could also have arisen as an equilibrium in the economy with incomplete markets. That is so when (4) takes the form (2) for prices p, q, r that satisfy (1) at the equilibrium (x^*, y^*, z^*). A necessary and sufficient condition is that $q^* \cdot y^*$ and $r^* \cdot z^*$ should both be positive, both negative, or both zero. To see this, notice first that it is immediate when $q^* \cdot y^* = r^* \cdot z^* = 0$. Suppose that neither is zero, and they have the same sign. We can then define

$$\alpha = \frac{q^* \cdot y^*}{q^* \cdot y^* + r^* \cdot z^*}, \tag{5}$$

which is a number between 0 and 1, and then define suitable prices

$$p = p^*, \quad q = \frac{1}{\alpha} q^*, \quad r = \frac{1}{1-\alpha} r^*. \tag{6}$$

This argument demonstrates that when the complete-market tax optimum has consumers provide positive saving for both future states, the same real allocation is the incomplete-market optimum. Then the incompleteness of markets imposes no welfare penalty. Whether this is the normal case depends on the range of possible future outcomes compared with the present state. With complete markets, it is possible for consumers to arrange to save for poor future states and dissave against exceptionally good ones. Incompleteness of markets prevents precisely that. If such arrangements were a feature of the optimum, that optimum would not be achievable as an incomplete-market equilibrium.

Incomplete-Market Optima

We turn now to an analysis of the optimum when the incompleteness of markets makes the complete-market optimum unattainable. That arises when, under the complete-market tax optimum, the consumer wants to save for the bad state and dissave for the good state. Because of incompleteness, he cannot do so, and the use of taxes cannot fully substitute for this loss. We first consider the nature of the optimization problem.

The incomplete-market equilibrium allocations are the complete-market allocations with the property that $q \cdot y$ and $r \cdot z$ have the same sign. But these allocations do not form a closed set. On consideration, that is because the multiple-budget-constraint way of representing incomplete markets excludes some perfectly reasonable equilibria. If we introduce an explicit scalar s for savings, and entertain the possibility that the rate of interest is different in the two states, then the budget set is described by

$$\begin{aligned} &p \cdot x + s \leq 0, \\ &q \cdot y \leq \alpha s, \\ &r \cdot z \leq \beta s, \end{aligned} \tag{7}$$

where the numbers α and β are 1 plus the interest rate in the two states of nature.

So long as α and β are positive, meaning that there is some return to saving, q and r can be adjusted proportionately so that $\alpha = \beta = 1$, and (7) is equivalent to the previous description of the budget set by (1) and (2). But either α or β might be zero in equilibrium; that amounts to confiscation of all savings, or forgiveness of all outstanding consumer debt. With savings or loans in nominal terms, putting matters loosely, equilibrium in a model with incomplete markets may involve hyperinflation in some state of nature. Our previous arguments suggest, furthermore, that in many cases such an equilibrium is optimal.

An equilibrium with $\alpha = 0$ could be brought about by taxation that includes the cancellation of savings or dissavings—in effect, a 100 percent tax on wealth in the first state of nature. This taxation is foreseen, but because it happens only in one state it does not eliminate saving or encourage infinite dissaving. If we did not allow government that policy tool, it might well want to introduce taxes at arbitrarily high rates in the second period, in one of the states, so as to make savings essentially worthless in that state.

If a consumer maximizes utility subject to a single budget constraint

$$p' \cdot x + q' \cdot y + r' \cdot z \leq 0, \tag{8}$$

and if (the maximizing choice being x',y',z') $q' \cdot y'$ and $r' \cdot z'$ have the same sign, in the weaker sense that either $q' \cdot y' \geq 0$ and $r' \cdot z' \geq 0$, or else $q' \cdot y' \leq 0$ and $r' \cdot z' \leq 0$, then the consumer maximizes utility subject to some set of constraints (7) with $\alpha \geq 0$ and $\beta \geq 0$. We have already seen the truth of this when $q' \cdot y'$ and $r' \cdot z'$ have the same sign in the stronger sense. Suppose now that $q' \cdot y' = 0$ and $r' \cdot z' > 0$. Then x',y',z' satisfy the constraints

$$\begin{aligned} &q' \cdot y \leq 0, \\ &p' \cdot x + r' \cdot z \leq 0, \end{aligned} \tag{9}$$

and since any x,y,z that satisfy (9) also satisfy (8), the consumer is maximizing utility subject to (9). The two constraints (9) are equivalent to (7) with $p = p'$, $q = q'$, $\alpha = 0$, $r = r'$, and $\beta = 1$. Other cases are handled in the same way.

We are now able to express the incomplete-market optimal-tax problem as the maximization of utility subject to the following constraints:

(i) the production constraint; which we take to be a linear production-possibility set, fully controlled by the government:

$$\pi \cdot x + \chi \cdot y + \rho \cdot z = -g, \tag{10}$$

where π, χ, and ρ are interpreted as producer prices and g as the public-expenditure requirement

(ii) the constraint that the consumer maximizes utility subject to a budget constraint,

$$p \cdot x + q \cdot y + r \cdot z \leq 0$$

(iii) the constraint that $q \cdot y \leq 0$ and $r \cdot z \leq 0$, or $q \cdot y \geq 0$ and $r \cdot z \geq 0$.

As we have seen, the solution to this problem may satisfy (iii) strictly; i.e., the third constraint may not bind. That is true when the incomplete-market optimum is the complete-market optimum. It may also be true when a local optimum for the complete-market case satisfies (iii) strictly and is the incomplete-market optimum. Otherwise, either $q \cdot y$ or $r \cdot z$ is zero at the optimum, and the budget constraints take the form (7) with α or β zero, meaning that there is 100 percent taxation of transfers between the first period and one of the states in the second period.

Zero-Expenditure States

We now analyze the optimum for cases in which the complete-market Ramsey optimum is unattainable. These are cases in which taxation does not fully compensate for incompleteness of markets, and in which the usual conditions for optimal taxation do not apply, requiring derivation of a new form for the optimal tax conditions.

Suppose that the complete-market optimum has $q \cdot y$ and $r \cdot z$ of opposite signs. To be more specific, suppose that $r \cdot z > 0 > q \cdot y$ in that optimum. The idea is that if markets were complete, consumers would save for state 2 and would dissave for state 1. In the absence of insurance, the same amount must be saved or dissaved for both states. Then it may be optimal to have saving, or to have dissaving. If saving, it is to be presumed that the constraint $q \cdot y \geq 0$ binds in the incomplete-market optimum. We first analyze the optimal tax rules assuming that the optimum has this structure. We then analyze a special case to study conditions for the choice between the two types of local optima.

Denote the consumer's expenditure function by $E(p, q, r, u)$. Constraint (ii) means that $E = 0$. The relevant part of constraint (iii) says that $q \cdot E_q \geq 0$. Then the derivatives of the Lagrangian

$$u - \lambda[\pi \cdot E_p + \chi \cdot E_q + \rho \cdot E_r + g] - \mu E(p, q, r, u) + vq \cdot E_q \tag{11}$$

with respect to p, q, r, and u should be zero (ignoring the possibility of zero consumer prices). Since we have taken it that $q \cdot E_q$ was constrained to be non-negative, $v \geq 0$. From this we get, differentiating with respect to p,

$$-\pi \cdot E_{pp} - \chi \cdot E_{qp} - \rho \cdot E_{rp} = \frac{\mu}{\lambda} E_p - \frac{v}{\lambda} q \cdot E_{qp}. \tag{12}$$

The other first-order conditions are

$$-\pi \cdot E_{pq} - \chi \cdot E_{qq} - \rho \cdot E_{rq} = \frac{\mu}{\lambda} E_q - \frac{v}{\lambda} q \cdot E_{qq} - \frac{v}{\lambda} E_q. \tag{13}$$

and

$$-\pi \cdot E_{pr} - \chi \cdot E_{qr} - \rho \cdot E_{rr} = \frac{\mu}{\lambda} E_r - \frac{v}{\lambda} q \cdot E_{qr}. \tag{14}$$

A Modified Ramsey Rule

Since the incomplete-market optimum is a complete-market equilibrium, the optimal quantities are identified if we describe the consumer prices that would induce the optimal levels of demand if there were complete markets. This solution gives the correct relative prices for each period and state. These prices are also equilibrium prices when markets are incomplete, and optimal taxes can be taken to be the differences between these consumer prices and producer prices. But since the consumer's budget constraints are $p \cdot x + r \cdot z = 0$ and $q \cdot y = 0$, consumer prices for period 2, state 1 could also be multiplied by any positive constant, and the implied tax rates would also be optimal. If that were done, the resulting consumer prices would no longer constitute a complete-market equilibrium.

In the usual way, we can interpret the second derivatives of E as compensated demand derivatives. But note carefully that they are derivatives of compensated demand functions for a consumer with a single budget constraint. We use the notation x_p^c for the compensated derivative of x with respect to p, equal to E_{pp}, and similarly for the other goods and prices. We denote optimal taxes for the economy with incomplete markets by t_x for period 1, t_y for period 2, state 1, and t_z for period 2, state 2. We then have the complete-market equilibrium consumer prices corresponding to the incomplete-market optimum

$$p = \pi + t_x,$$
$$q = T(\chi + t_y), \tag{15}$$
$$r = \rho + t_z,$$

where T is a scalar factor whose magnitude depends on the particular arbitrary normalization of prices in period 2, state 1.

Using the fact that

$$p \cdot E_{pp} + q \cdot E_{qp} + r \cdot E_{rp} = 0$$

by the homogeneity of the expenditure function, and using the definitions of tax rates, (15), we can write the first-order condition (12) as

$$x_p^c \cdot t_x + x_q^c \cdot \{[(1 + \nu/\lambda)T - 1]\chi + (1 + \nu/\lambda)Tt_y\} + x_r^c \cdot t_x = \frac{\mu}{\lambda} x. \tag{16}$$

If we now fix the normalization T so that

$$(1 + \nu/\lambda)T = 1, \tag{17}$$

equation (16) becomes

$$x_p^c \cdot t_x + x_q^c \cdot t_y + x_r^c \cdot t_z = \frac{\mu}{\lambda} x. \tag{18}$$

Similarly, we obtain from the other first-order conditions (13) and (14)

$$y_p^c \cdot t_x + y_q^c \cdot t_y + y_r^c \cdot t_z = \frac{\mu - \nu}{\lambda} y \tag{19}$$

and

$$z_p^c \cdot t_x + z_q^c \cdot t_y + z_r^c \cdot t_z = \frac{\mu}{\lambda} z. \tag{20}$$

These conditions may be regarded as a modified form of the Ramsey rule. With complete markets, when consumers are identical and lump-sum income is zero, public expenditure should be financed by taxes that reduce all compensated demands in approximately the same proportion. With incomplete markets, that rule might lead to prices for which $q \cdot y$ and $r \cdot z$ have opposite signs, and that is inconsistent with multiple budget constraints. Then the Ramsey rule should be modified in such a way that compensated demands in one of the two states, say the first, are reduced proportionately, but by a smaller amount than in period 1 and state 2 of period 2. These compensated demands are the complete-market demand functions at the consumer prices that would induce consumers to have zero net income in period 2, state 1.

Recollect that we are dealing with a case where the wishes to save for state 2 and to dissave from state 1 are in conflict. The incomplete-market optimum might have $q \cdot y < 0$ and the constraint $r \cdot z \leq 0$ binding, instead of $q \cdot y \geq 0$ binding and $r \cdot z > 0$ as we supposed. In that case, we would get similar results with reduction in the taxation of period 2, state 2.

One wants to be able to identify the state that is subjected to extra taxation in the way just described. It may seem plausible that it is the state that would, in the complete-market optimum, have had expenditures the same sign as period-1 expenditures. Suppose, for example, that, with insurance markets available, saving would have been positive (so that $p \cdot x$ would be negative), and furthermore that insurance would have been taken out in period 1 that would have paid compensation if state 2 occurred but not otherwise. In that case, one naturally thinks of state 2 as the "bad" state. One might expect that in the incomplete-market optimum it will be best to induce positive saving that will yield a return only in state 2, being canceled in state 1.

This line of thought assumes that, if $p \cdot x < 0$ in the complete-market optimum, the same is true in the incomplete-market optimum; but of course that need not be the case. If it is the case, the incomplete-market optimum has increased taxation of the "good" state. In the opposite case, with dissaving in period 1, there is reduced taxation of the "bad" state. In the example that follows, we explore the type of optimum that occurs as a function of the parameters of the example.

An Example

To see that the incomplete-market optimum can well be different from the complete-market optimum, and to get more insight into the problem, it is natural to consider a model with one good in each period and with additively separable preferences. Consumers save for a future that may be either relatively bad or relatively good. To avoid income effects, which complicate matters considerably, assume constant marginal utility of consumption in the first period. On the production side, an initial stock of goods can be consumed now, or can be invested in production for either of the two second-period states at constant rates of return.

To identify the optimum when there is cancellation of saving, it will be necessary to compare directly allocations that differ markedly, by having cancellation of saving in one or the other state. These allocations are not "near" each other, but in order to make comparisons it will be assumed that the rate at which goods in the two states are transformed into one another is constant. This production assumption is highly restrictive, unlike the use of the linear approximation to the production set in the calculation of the first-order conditions. The general features of the solution would no doubt be similar if a nonlinear production frontier were assumed, but one would also need to include the effects production-frontier curvature.

The consumer's utility is

$$x + u(y) + v(z), \tag{21}$$

where u and v (the utilities of the two states, multiplied by their probabilities) are increasing, strictly concave, twice continuously differentiable functions, with infinite derivatives at $-\eta$ and $-\zeta$, respectively, and zero derivatives at infinity. Take η and ζ to be positive numbers that can be interpreted as stocks of future consumer goods already in the hands of the consumer (and so not subject to a tax on transactions). Here x is net dissaving in period 1, consumption less the initial stock of goods; y and z are incomes in period 2, net of any endowment, such as fixed labor income. For convenience, and without loss of generality, we set $u(0) = 0$ and $v(0) = 0$.

The production constraint is linear:

$$x + \chi y + \rho z = -g, \tag{22}$$

where g is a government expenditure requirement. These production possibilities allow the government to transfer resources between the states of nature, at fixed terms.

The form (21) for utility implies that the consumer prices for future consumption relative to present consumption are $u'(y)$ and $v'(z)$. Since the consumer's budget has to be zero, we are constrained to have

$$x + yu'(y) + zv'(z) = 0.$$

Utility is to be maximized by choice of x, y, and z, subject to this constraint and (22).

Now eliminate x, and combine (22) and the zero-budget constraint to obtain

$$y[u'(y) - \chi] + z[v'(z) - \rho] = g. \tag{23}$$

Utility is also expressed as a function of y and z by means of (22):

$$u(y) - \chi y + v(z) - \rho z - g. \tag{24}$$

The government's optimization can now be expressed in a particularly convenient form. When complete markets are available, we are to maximize (24) subject to the single constraint (23). When markets are incomplete there is the further restriction that y and z have the same sign (in the weak sense).

It is useful to derive the first-order conditions that hold if there is a complete-market optimum. Using γ as the Lagrange multiplier on (23), the maximization of (24) requires

$$\begin{aligned} (1 + \gamma)[u'(y) - \chi] &= -\gamma y u''(y), \\ (1 + \gamma)[v'(z) - \rho] &= -\gamma z v''(z). \end{aligned} \tag{25}$$

With concave utility functions, $y[u'(y) - \chi]$ and $z[v'(z) - \rho]$ have the same sign at a complete-market optimum. From (23), the sign is positive. That is, in a complete-market optimum, revenue to cover government expenditures is raised from both goods.

It is not always possible to satisfy the constraint (23). If the government's revenue requirement is too great, there is no tax system that will yield sufficient real revenue to meet it. In the Ramsey problem, it is hard to raise much revenue if consumers would have little wish to trade even in the absence of taxes. To obtain a precise condition for the existence of an optimum, define M and N as the maximal revenues that can be collected from taxation of output in the two states, respectively:

$$\begin{aligned} M &= \operatorname*{Max}_{y > -\eta} y[u'(y) - \chi], \\ N &= \operatorname*{Max}_{z > -\xi} z[v'(z) - \rho]. \end{aligned} \tag{26}$$

With χ and ρ both positive and with $u'(y)$ and $v'(z)$ going to zero as y and z increase without limit, M and N are well defined.

PROPOSITION 1 Let $g > 0$. Provided that $M + N \geq g$, a complete-market optimum exists. If $u'(0) - \chi$ and $v'(0) - \rho$ have the same sign, this complete-market optimum is also the incomplete-market optimum.

Proof Our assumptions about the functions u and v imply that $y[u'(y) - \chi]$ tends to $-\infty$ as $y \to -\eta$, and similarly for $z[v'(z) - \rho]$ as $z \to -\xi$. Therefore, the assumption $M + N \geq g$ implies that (23) has a solution, and the set of solutions is compact. An optimum therefore exists. Suppose that $u'(0) > \chi$ and $v'(0) > \rho$. (The proof for the other case is exactly the same.) It is claimed that optimal y and z are both positive. The argument follows from the positivity of tax revenues $y[u'(y) - \chi]$ and $z[v'(z) - \rho]$, as noted above. If y were negative, $u'(y) > u'(0)$ by concavity of u. Since we are assuming $u'(0) > \chi$, tax revenue $y[u'(y) - \chi] < 0$. Therefore y must be positive. The same is true for z. Since y and z have the same sign, our general analysis shows that the complete-market optimum is also the incomplete-market optimum. ∎

The converse of proposition 1 holds: If $u'(0) - \chi$ and $v'(0) - \rho$ have opposite signs, the complete-market optimum is not an incomplete-market optimum. The precise result is stated in the next proposition. The condition for the existence of an incomplete-marke optimum is then much more stringent than that for a complete-market optimum. We also want to identify cases where $y = 0$ and cases where $z = 0$ at the optimum. In order to do that we must compare utility when $y = 0$ with utility when $z = 0$.

Recall that the resource constraint is (23):

$$y[u'(y) - \chi] + z[v'(z) - \rho] = g.$$

Since the first term on the left vanishes when $y = 0$, it is impossible to have $y = 0$ when N (the maximum value of the second term) is less than g. Similarly, we cannot have $z = 0$ when $M < g$. If $M \geq g$, and we do have $z = 0$, the value of utility is

$$\phi = \text{Max}[u(y) - \chi y] \tag{27a}$$

subject to

$$y[u'(y) - \chi] \geq g. \tag{27b}$$

Note that (27a) uses $u(0) = v(0) = 0$. The value of y satisfying (27b) with equality which has the largest absolute value is the relevant one, because, with $g > 0$, $u(y) - \chi y$ is increasing or decreasing in y as (27b) is satisfied with y positive or negative. Similarly, when $N \geq g$, define ψ as the optimal utility when $y = 0$. When $\phi > \psi$, it is better to have $z = 0$; in the opposite case, $y = 0$ is better. This line of argument gives us the following criteria:

PROPOSITION 2 Let $g > 0$. Suppose that $u'(0) - \chi$ and $v'(0) - \rho$ have opposite signs. An incomplete-market optimum exists if and only if

$$\mathrm{Max}(M,N) \geq g. \tag{28}$$

If $g \leq M$, and $g > N$ or $\phi > \psi$, the optimum has $z = 0$, and the sign of y is the sign of $u'(0) - \chi$. If $g \leq N$, and $g > M$ or $\psi < \phi$, the optimum has $y = 0$, and the sign of z is the sign of $v'(0) - \rho$.

Proof Suppose that $u'(0) > \chi$ and $v'(0) < \rho$. The opposite case is handled symmetrically. Tax equilibria with incomplete markets satisfy (23) and the additional requirement that y and z have the same sign. When y and z have the same sign, the two terms on the left-hand side of (23) cannot both be positive. Therefore, in any tax equilibrium, $\mathrm{Max}(M,N) \geq g$. Conversely, if $M \geq g$, we can have an equilibrium with $z = 0$, and y a solution to $y[u'(y) - \chi] = g$; and if $N \geq g$, we can have an equilibrium with $y = 0$, and z a solution to $z[v'(z) - \rho] = g$. This shows that (28) is a necessary and sufficient condition for existence of an optimum. Next we have to show that one of y and z vanishes. Consider first an equilibrium with $z > 0$ and ($y \geq 0$). We can do better than that by reducing z to 0, thereby increasing $z[v'(z) - \rho]$ to 0, and, as we maintain the constraint (23), increasing y and reducing $y[u'(y) - \chi]$ to g. Since $g > 0$, this allows $u(y) - \chi y$ to increase. Also, $v(z) - \rho z$ has been increased by reducing z to 0. Therefore we have an improvement. In a similar way, we can always do better than an equilibrium with $y < 0$. It follows that the optimum has $y = 0$ or $z = 0$. If $g > N$, there is no tax equilibrium with $y = 0$, for such equilibria do not cover the government's revenue requirements. Therefore $z = 0$. Similarly, $y = 0$ if $g > M$. The only cases remaining are those with $g \leq M,N$. When $y = 0$, we saw above that utility is ψ; and when $z = 0$, utility is ϕ. Comparing these two values, we have the result stated in the proposition. (When the two are equal, there are two optima.) ∎

The Pattern of Optima

It is instructive to see how the optimum varies as the producer prices χ and ρ vary. From (26), M is increasing in χ when y is negative and is decreasing in χ when y is positive. The same conclusions for ϕ can be drawn from (27). Thus, there exists a pair of values, χ_1 and χ_2, with $\chi_1 < u'(0) < \chi_2$, such that M is at least as large as g for $\chi < \chi_1$ and $\chi > \chi_2$. In exactly the same way, we see that there is a pair of values $\rho_1 < v'(0) < \rho_2$ such that N is at least as large as g for $\rho < \rho_1$ and $\rho > \rho_2$. These values are shown in figure 1. Figure 1 also shows that curve $M(\chi) + N(\rho) = g$. From proposition 1, we have a complete-market optimum outside this curve provided $u'(0) - \chi$ and $v'(0) - \rho$ have the same sign. These are the northeast and southwest regions of figure 1. From proposition 2, we have an incomplete-market optimum when $u'(0) - \chi$ and $v'(0) - \rho$ have opposite signs and Max(M,N)

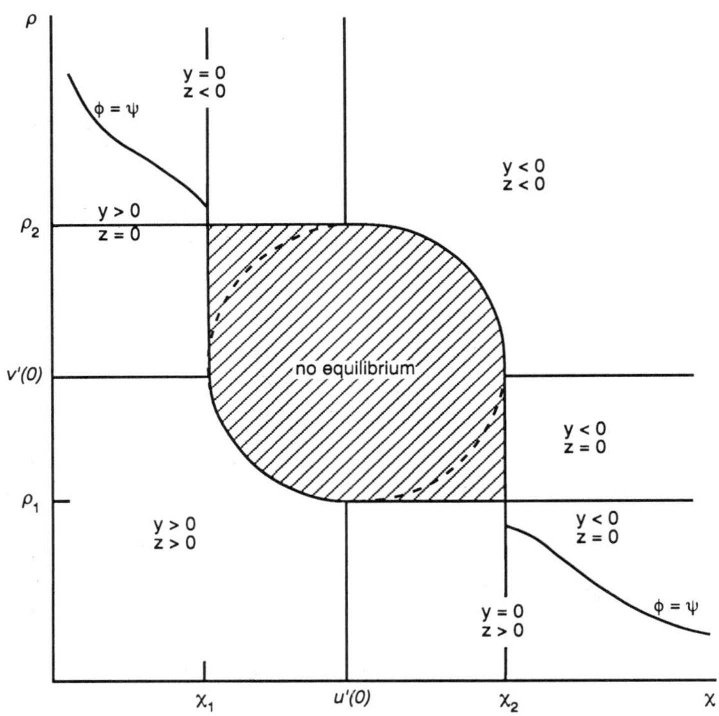

Figure 1

is at least as large as g. These are the southeast and northwest regions of figure 1. The curve $\phi = \psi$ separates the regions with the two different incomplete-market optima.

The curve $\phi = \psi$ is downward sloping because where $\chi < \chi_1$ and $\rho > \rho_2$, ϕ is a decreasing function of χ and ψ is an increasing function of ρ; and the opposite holds in the region with $\chi > \chi_2$ and $\rho < \rho_1$. (The curve could have vertical or horizontal sections, since ϕ and ψ need not be continuous functions of χ and ρ.) In general, the curve $\phi = \psi$ does not reach the point (χ_1, ρ_2) or (χ_2, ρ_1).

A Special Case

We examine a special case to see how the optima depend upon income levels η and ζ. Define the utility function by

$$u(y) = \theta \log \frac{y + \eta}{\eta}$$
$$v(z) = (1 - \theta) \log \frac{z + \zeta}{\zeta}, \tag{29}$$

where θ is a parameter, $0 < \theta < 1$. Because of the special forms chosen, the nature of the optimum depends only on two composite parameters, $\eta\chi$ and $\zeta\rho$. Consequently, the classification of optima we have just given for χ and ρ can be reinterpreted as a classification for η and ζ.

From (29), we deduce by routine calculations that

$$M = \operatorname*{Max}_{y > -\eta} \frac{\theta y}{y + \eta} - \chi y = \theta + \eta\chi - 2\sqrt{\theta\eta\chi} \tag{30}$$

with the maximizing y,

$$y_{\mathrm{M}} = \sqrt{\theta\eta/\chi} - \eta; \tag{31}$$

that

$$N = \operatorname*{Max}_{z > -\zeta} \frac{(1 - \theta)z}{z + \zeta} - \rho z = 1 - \theta + \zeta\rho - 2\sqrt{(1 - \theta)\zeta\rho} \tag{32}$$

with the maximizing $z_{\mathrm{N}} = \sqrt{(1 - \theta)\zeta/\rho}$; and that

$$u'(0) - \chi = \frac{\theta}{\eta} - \chi$$

and

$$v'(0) - \rho = \frac{1-\theta}{\zeta} - \rho.$$

The last two expressions show that $u'(0) - \chi$ is positive if and only if $\eta\chi < \theta$ and that $v'(0) - \rho$ is positive if and only if $\zeta\rho < 1 - \theta$. The equation $M = g$ gives the values χ_1 and χ_2, and $N = g$ gives ρ_1 and ρ_2. Explicitly, in the present case, we can classify optima using the following notation:

$$\begin{aligned} \theta_1 &= (\sqrt{\theta} - \sqrt{g})^2, \quad \theta_2 = (\sqrt{\theta} + \sqrt{g})^2 \\ \pi_1 &= (\sqrt{1-\theta} - \sqrt{g})^2, \quad \pi_2 = (\sqrt{1-\theta} + \sqrt{g})^2. \end{aligned} \tag{33}$$

The first pair come from setting M equal to g in (30), the second pair from N given in (32). In figure 2 we have redrawn figure 1 for this case, adding these values to the picture.

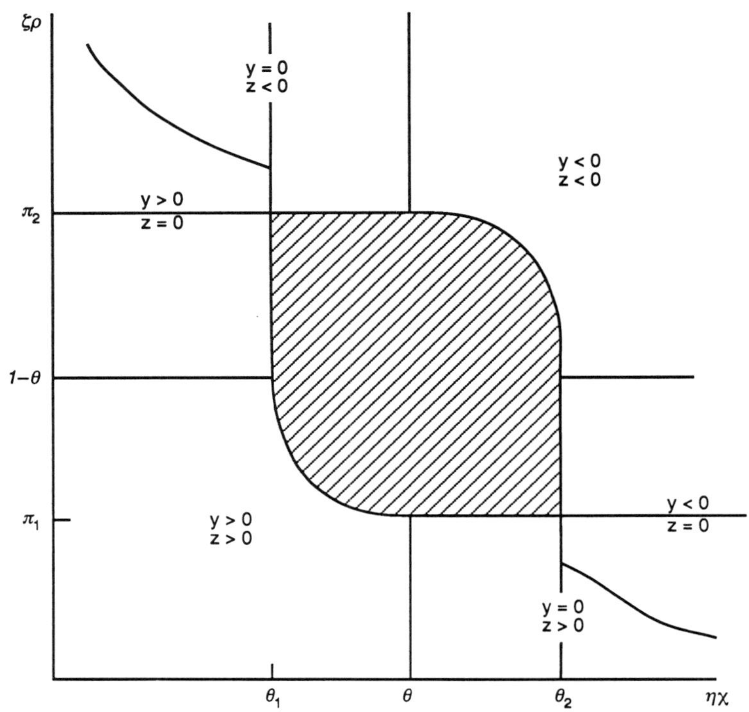

Figure 2

We have seen that the curve $\phi = \psi$ is downward sloping. This means, for example, that if $y > 0$ at the optimum for some particular (χ,ρ), then $y > 0$ at the optimum also for any smaller ρ (and the same χ). For this particular example, we now examine whether the $\phi = \psi$ curve cuts the vertical line, on which $y = 0$, as shown in figure 2, or the horizontal line, on which $z = 0$. We shall show that it always cuts the vertical line. Thus, it is somewhat more likely that there should be saving, sometimes fully taxed, than that there should be dissaving.

The location of the end of the curve $\phi = \psi$ is found by comparing ϕ and ψ at the points where $M = N = g$, i.e., at (θ_1,π_2) and at (θ_2,π_1). Consider (θ_1,π_2). If the optimum occurs at $(y_M,0)$ rather then at $(0,z_N)$, then

$$\phi = \theta \log \frac{y_M + \eta}{\eta} - \chi y_M = \theta \log\left(1 + \frac{y_M}{\eta}\right) - \theta_1 \cdot \frac{y_M}{\eta}. \tag{34}$$

Since y_M, θ, and θ_1 are related by

$$\sqrt{\theta} = \sqrt{\theta_1} + \sqrt{g}$$

(from the definition of θ_1 in (33)) and

$$1 + \frac{y_M}{\eta} = \frac{\sqrt{\theta}}{\sqrt{\theta_1}}$$

(from (31)), we have

$$\theta_1 = g\left(\frac{\eta}{y_M}\right)^2, \quad \theta = g\left(1 + \frac{\eta}{y_M}\right)^2.$$

Substituting in (34) yields

$$\phi = g\left(1 + \frac{\eta}{y_M}\right)^2 \log\left(1 + \frac{y_M}{\eta}\right) - g\frac{\eta}{y_M}. \tag{35}$$

This is at least $\frac{1}{2}g$, for it can be rewritten as

$$\phi = -\frac{g}{\alpha^2}\log(1 - \alpha) - \frac{g}{\alpha} + g, \quad \alpha = \frac{y_M}{\eta + y_M} > 0. \tag{36}$$

Similarly,

$$\psi = -\frac{g}{\alpha^2}\log(1 - \alpha) - \frac{g}{\alpha} + g, \quad \alpha = \frac{z_N}{\zeta + z_N} < 0. \tag{37}$$

This function of α is an increasing function (for $\alpha > -1$), by differentiation. Consequently, $\psi < \phi$, as claimed.

In the bottom right cell, we have to compare the possibilities $y < 0$ and $z > 0$. By the same argument, it is found that positive saving, $z > 0$, is better at (χ_2, ρ_1).

Essentially the same argument as the above applies to the more general case with utility functions

$$u = \theta[w(\eta + y) - w(\eta)],$$

$$v = (1 - \theta)[w(\zeta + z) - w(\zeta)]$$

provided that the function w has a non-negative third derivative. It is hard to tell just how strong is the preference of the optimum for saving rather than dissaving, but there is some bias in that direction.

Concluding Remarks

The example analyzed above lends itself to consideration of several extensions. It appears that it would be straightforward to go to many states of nature, preserving the assumption of a single good in each state. We expect that the set of states would be partitioned into two groups as it is desirable to save into or out of the states. One would consider optimal revenue raising and the welfare level achieved for the two groups. It would be more complicated to analyze the case of five goods, with two goods in each of the future states. It should also be straightforward to consider different production technologies for the government.

The Ramsey case is interesting mainly as a prelude to a many-person analysis. We expect that the possibilities of both achieving and not achieving the complete-market optimum would carry over to a many-person model with state-specific poll taxes as well as commodity taxes. Cancellation of saving in some states may be a feature of the optimum. This suggests that the Ramsey case will be a valuable stepping stone on the way to understanding optimal taxation for the realistic case of incomplete markets.

Acknowledgments

Support by the U.S. National Science Foundation is gratefully acknowledged Valuable comments were received at seminars at Cambridge, Oxford, the London School of Economics, Princeton, and the University of Florida at Gainesville, and from a referee.

Notes

1. The question of optimal policies when markets are incomplete has been studied in the context of commodity-price stabilization by Newbery and Stiglitz (1981) and in the context of tariff policy by Eaton and Grossman (1985). Eaton and Grossman showed (again for a model where markets are simply incomplete) that in an otherwise first-best world, positive taxation of trade is desirable. Dixit (1987, 1989) has explored the consequences for this argument of introducing moral hazard or adverse selection as an explicit explanation for the incompleteness of markets.

2. It might be helpful for one's intuition to consider the special case of a single good in each period-state. The budget constraints (1) then represent a line in three-dimensional consumption space. The constraint (2) is a plane containing the budget line and tangent to the indifference surface through the optimal consumption point.

References

Dixit, A. K. 1987. "Trade and insurance with moral hazard." *Journal of International Economics* 23: 201–220.

Dixit, A. K. 1989. "Trade and insurance with adverse selection." *Review of Economic Studies* 56 (2): 186, 235–247.

Eaton, J., and G. Grossman. 1985. "Tariffs as insurance: Optimal commercial policy when domestic markets are incomplete." *Canadian Journal of Economic* 101: 258–272.

Foley, D. K. 1970. "Economic equilibrium with costly marketing." *Journal of Economic Theory* 2: 276–291.

Hahn, F. H. 1971. "Equilibrium with transactions costs." *Econometrica* 39: 417–440.

Hart, O. D. 1975. "On the optimality of equilibrium when the market structure is incomplete." *Journal of Economic Theory* 11: 418–443.

Newbery, D. M. G., and J. E. Stiglitz. 1981. *The Theory of Commodity Price Stabilization: A Study in the Economics of Risk.* Clarendon.

IV MISCELLANY

Educating Our Masters

Terence Gorman

Preface (1991)

The sole[1] duty of the Hinkley Professor at Johns Hopkins University is to give a public lecture on law, and, if possible, British constitutional history. This was my attempt, in 1980. It is included here because it seems appropriate to Frank Hahn, and because the problem of how to educate our masters—now taken to be potential managers and/or entrepreneurs—is being discussed pell mell and without much informed thought in the UK now, just as was that of lawyers in the US years ago; because the resulting blend of special interests, political personalities, and mere chance may be equally important in forming other institutions, and should be taken into account by economists; because the neglect of the value of students' time in the recent reevaluations of the American law schools shows a mistake often made by academic administrators in high relief; because I suspect similar mistakes are common among their peers in government and in industry; but mainly as an illustration of one way to do economics economically: to discard our professional blinkers; find out what we can about a particular problem or subject from other experts and from practitioners; ask ourselves, "is there something here for professional economists to do?"; if so, to do it as professionals in the light of what we learned as amateurs.

I have included this informal lecture just as I gave it, to celebrate aspects of Frank's work not celebrated elsewhere: his spontaneity, quick interest in, and ability to bring economics to bear on, all sorts of subjects, engagement in other social sciences—all of which were particularly audible during the marvelous decade he and I spent in the Faculty of Commerce and Social Science in Birmingham.

Of course the lecture included many errors and absurd claims, as did conversation in these days. I have corrected the most obvious in the notes.

Introduction (1980)

This lecture commemorates Mr. John Hinkley, a noted Baltimore lawyer and a student of British constitutional history. As such, as I understand it, it is meant to deal with both these subjects, about which I am somewhat ignorant. Nevertheless I have ventured to try to cover them. I will accordingly talk a lot of nonsense, but may occasionally hit on something which scholars have missed in their more single-minded searches. May I appeal to Francis Bacon: "truth emerges more readily from error than confusion."[2] You will certainly find confusion here, but one of the errors may, I suppose, breed a pearl if it irritates someone enough.

When a student is confronted with a new subject, I commonly urge him to fill his head with it for some weeks, leave it, and return months later to see how it has come along on its own. The theory is that he should then set down what he finds there before seeking to verify or dispute it.

In my own case, I left myself far too little time for this last stage. This has proven less harmful than it might, because I decided to take quite a different tack from that on which I had originally embarked, and discuss constitutional history more, and the education of lawyers and its economics less, than I had intended. Much of what I am going to say will be wrong. In the circumstances debate is in order. Consider how to attack me.

The Hinkley Lecture (1980)

When the Liberals returned to power in 1880, Robert Lowe was old, blind, and unpopular, having been driven out of politics four years before for having slandered Queen Victoria. Yet Gladstone insisted that she should give him a viscountcy, "as a tribute to his former elevation, which, though short-lived, was due to a genuine power of mind. It seemed to me that a man who had once soared to those heights trodden by so few, ought not to be lost in the common ranks of official barons."

That glorious episode was his defeat of Gladstone's own Reform Bill in 1866. This he did in a series of speeches in Parliament, culminating in one which forms the core of a German *Study of Political Rhetoric*. In it Lowe argued that the function of Parliament was to govern the empire, and that of elections to provide *able* men in sufficient *variety* to do that well. Large constituencies were already expensive to fight. He gave figures suggesting that an election would have cost \$150–250 million (1980) had all constituencies been large and vigorously fought. Only the very rich would be able to enter politics were the bill to pass; and of them, those willing to pander to a largely illiterate electorate—not much chance of ability, variety or good government to be expected there!

Lowe defeated the bill, and with it the government of which he had recently been a member. He also aroused a considerable portion of the existing electorate to such fury by his attacks on the illiterate working classes that a fiercer reform became inevitable, and one was put through by the Tories under Disraeli in 1867. Fierce though it was by Lowe's standards, it was opportunistic and full of peculiarities. For that reason or some other, the Tories were decisively defeated in the 1867 elections, and the Liberals came in, with Lowe as their chancellor, strong enough to risk an Education Bill, dangerous though that was because of deep disagreement between Anglicans and Nonconformists about control of the schools and the role of religion in them. Despite earlier disagreements with its sponsor, Lowe backed him strongly, arguing that, having extended the franchise to the urban working classes, "we must now educate our masters."

He may have been wrong on both counts.

E. G. West has recently argued that education had spread rapidly among the urban workers during the previous thirty years, that they were politically very much alive, and that their schools would have done a better job if not shackled by Foster's Education Act; while they themselves were not to become the masters in British politics in any reasonable sense for many years, if ever.

Lowe was an academic, a lawyer, a Fellow of the Royal Society, and a Member of the Political Economy Club. However deficient he may have been in a sense of history, I believe that his analysis of government was right in at least three leading points. The education of our masters is an important matter, and it should be such as to provide a sufficient number of able men, in sufficient variety, to govern the country—variety, I might also add, not simply to represent varied interests, and bring different pieces of knowledge into the common stock, but above all in modes of thought, in instinctive reaction to a situation or problem.

Who are "our masters"?

In the United States, two-thirds of the presidents, of recent cabinet members, and of the current Senate were or are lawyers. As we go down the scale, the proportion of lawyers falls too; 56 percent of the state governors and 48 percent of the Representatives, though I would not be surprised were it to go up again among the state legislators, at least in the South and the East.

Now the proportion of lawyers is very high in the U.S.—twenty times as high as in Japan, for instance. Nevertheless, it is only about one-half of 1 percent, as against over 50 percent[3] of the leading politicians. "As you would expect", you may think. "Politics is about law and lawyers know about laws." Melbourne would not have agreed; to him the important thing was that the politicians should not lay down the law for ordinary people, the main argument against further reform being that, drunk in the glory of their popular election, they would do so far too often. One would not expect lawyers to follow his precept, and their practice shows us to be right: to a cobbler there is nothing like leather. Be that as it may, any group who fill half to two-thirds of the main political posts in the U.S. are strong candidates for the title of "our political masters."

Clearly many of the ablest people in American politics are lawyers. Whether it is the ablest lawyers that enter politics is another matter, which I will not debate here. Instead I will address myself to the question: Is the education of lawyers such as to provide a sufficient variety of points of view, information, and, above all, modes of thought among our political masters?

According to almost everything I have read or heard, the first year at law school is a traumatic intellectual and emotional experience. According to Packer and Ehrlich, who wrote the Carnegie Study *New Dimensions in Legal Education*, "The excitement and intellectual interest of the average well taught first year has to be seen to be believed. The learning curve for the first-year students is typically steeply pitched, and the élan of students going through their initiation in the first few months ... in full-time law schools has been truly extraordinary." Moreover, "Taking the run of national and regional full-time university connected law schools as a unit, a visitor could sit blindfold in, say, a first year torts class in any one of them with some assurance that he would not be able to tell whether he was at Harvard, Yale, Columbia, Stanford, or East Cupcake"—a view endorsed by teachers from Chicago and Yale, which are commonly thought to lean more heavily towards the social sciences than other leading schools. "It is not accident," they say, "that the cream of any faculty tend to teach first-year classes," though these teachers are "typically ham actors," according to David Riesman—as were Irving and Tree. The students I have talked to say that *The Paper Chase* was a fair representation of first year life.

All seem to agree that a year at a law school changes its acolytes fundamentally. Sonia Menshifkoff warned the wives of first-year students at Chicago, where she was a law professor, that "Your husbands are going to change. Their personalities are going to change in law school. They will get more aggressive, more hostile, more precise, more impatient."

The avowed aim of all this activity is to make the students "think like lawyers," and hence like each other; and it seems to be generally agreed that it works. That would not provide the variety of modes of thought which Lowe believed so important among our rulers.

Law courses run for three years. Possibly, once the fundamentals are agreed upon, each is successfully urged to follow his own path? Not so, according to my reading. Just as virtually everyone I have read praises the students' élan in the first year, "or at least in the first term," they bemoan the lassitude and boredom that follow. Such lassitude often follows a period of high intellectual and emotional excitement and as such must be accounted a cost of the method of teaching used in the first year, but that would hardly explain two years of increasing boredom. Packer and Ehrlich say that "the second and third years of law study still seem to most students as too often more of the same and a bore," and David Riesman—who elsewhere can be seen to love the law and law schools—says "law school was unbelievably boring, endless cases —this bombastic give and take of law school teaching which I did not like then and do not like now." Moreover, it seems to be generally agreed that students find the third year even duller than the second.

That is not the soil in which a hundred flowers bloom.

What about their experience later? Possibly it is sufficiently varied to generate the variety of approach after which Lowe hankered?

For the moment let us look at the abler students in the better schools—a very bright lot on any definition. It is generally agreed that their future is determined by their success in the first year. The top 10 percent, say, in the grades, "make Law Review," are interviewed by top firms in New York, Boston, or some regional capital such as Chicago; are given vacation jobs by them in the hope of securing their interest, and go on to future security and modest splendor. A few others make Law Review in the second year, commonly by writing good essays—their future is much the same. Of the very best, a few become clerks to Supreme Court justices and the like; I presume that rather more of them may go into politics, though possibly in the executive rather than the legislature—otherwise their picture is much the same. People somewhat further down the first-year ranking, or from less well-known schools, go into less prestigious firms, perhaps in smaller cities, but follow much the same path.[4]

It seems to be generally agreed that this is a relatively new phenomenon. One used to get known by what one did in the courtroom or in politics.

Robert Lowe, for instance, emigrated to New South Wales soon after being called to the bar in 1842. He did badly until he entered the colonial legislature, first as a nominated and then as an elected member. He spoke vigorously on financial and educational matters, denouncing the alienation of huge areas of public lands to a few rich squatters. "His prominence in public life," according to the British *Dictionary of National Biography*,[5] "had for many years brought him much practice in the law courts. But this means he amassed a considerable capital, which he judiciously invested in the purchase of real property in Sydney," so that he was enabled to return to England in 1850 and enter politics there, first as a leader writer for the *Times* and in 1852 as MP for Kidderminster. He had become rich enough to fight a smallish constituency and to live the life of a politician without a parliamentary salary—although he did soon achieve junior office.

In 1933 Adolph Berle wrote that "the law firm became virtually an annex of some group of financial promoters, manipulators or industrialists, and such firms have dominated the organised profession, although they have contributed little of thought, less of philosophy, and nothing at all of responsibility or idealism. What they have contributed, however, is the creation of a legal framework for the new economic system, built largely around the modern corporation, the division of ownership of industrial property from control and the increasing concentration of economic power in the industrial East in the hands of a few individuals"—a quotation which, I hasten to add, I have taken from a book sponsored by the American Bar Foundation, the research affiliate of the ABA. Those who wished to do something for the public had accordingly to become academics, judges, or, perhaps, politicians. However, "the forces of financial concentration needed political influence quite as much as legal ability," and a lawyer who was successful in public life was all the more valuable to them. The common result was that "after a relatively brief period of public office the lawyer returned to his profession with enhanced reputation and became a more effective servant of the evolving industrial scheme."

Others would judge the adaptation of law to economic reality as a more valuable activity than did Berle, writing at the bottom of the slump, and I quote him for the evidence he may give on the recruitment of lawyers into politics rather than for his own political judgments. On this evidence this would be just another route into the elite firms, possibly for those who did not do quite well enough to enter them directly, or (more likely, in my opinion) for those who had not attended the nationally famous law schools.

This last opinion arises from the strong local basis of American politics, which I personally believe to be one of its strengths. It is supported by some statistical evidence collected by Matthew Salomon.

Harvard dominates legal education both in prestige and in size. A fourth of all law professors were educated there, but so were 6 percent of all lawyers,[6] and, I would not be surprised to find, over 25 percent of the partners in really prestigious firms. Twenty-nine of the governors and federal legislators were educated there—that is, less than 10 percent of the lawyers among them and less than twice that in the profession at large. Next comes Virginia with 11, Georgetown with 10, Yale 7, and Columbia and Stanford 6 each. Moreover, lawyers commonly represent eastern and southern rather than central or western states, so that the dominance of Harvard among politicians is even less strong than the figure might at first suggest.

Were I in England, I would now say: What of the Civil Service, the real rulers[7] of the country? They are less certainly that here—but worth a glance nevertheless.

Who's Who in Government covers about 35,000 individuals, right down to sheriffs, fire chiefs and chief engineers to the local waterworks in quite small communities. I ran a brisk but tolerable sample yesterday. Of the 79 I chose, one in three were lawyers. Of course many of these were judges, district attorneys and the like. Remove them. Others were doctors in the National Institutes of Health, librarians in the Library of Congress. Nobel Prize winners on the Smithsonian Council, engineers running waterworks—remove them. Finally, very few of the women I turned up were lawyers; I imagine because there were very few to be had when the search was on for token women in government. Eliminate them too. Of the remainder, *one-half were lawyers.* Basically, then, if you leave out technical jobs, and allow for the peculiar position of women, about half of the *nonlegal* posts among the top 35,000 in government seem to be held by lawyers, and the legal jobs are important too. I would be surprised were the proportion not higher at the top, just as with the politicians.

What about Britain?

Robert Lowe took a strong interest in Civil Service reform. He was Secretary of the Board of Control when recruitment to the Indian Civil Service was thrown open to competitive examination in 1853, and was a strong supporter of Northcote and Trevelyan's report which proposed similar reforms in the Home Civil Service in 1854. Despite the setting up of a Civil Service Commission, this led to virtually no action until Lowe—by now chancellor, and as such head of one of the most prestigious departments—wrote to Gladstone in November 1869: "As I have so often tried in vain, will you bring the question of the Civil Service before the Cabinet today. Something must be decided. We cannot keep matters in this discreditable state of abeyance. If the Cabinet will not entertain this idea of open competition, might we not at any rate require a larger number of competitors for each vacancy, say seven or ten?"

Twelve days later Lowe suggested that his own department take the lead in making all appointments by open competition, and that other department heads might be asked to do the same. That proposal was approved by the cabinet on December 7th. On December 8, a Treasury Minute went out to all other departments. All but the Foreign Office (the most snobbish) and the Home Office (the most reactionary) agreed to follow suit.[8] Lowe then designed a system of examinations covering an English essay and history (1,000 points), the language, literature and history of Greece, Rome, France, Germany and Italy (750 each), mathematics (1,250), five branches of science and engineering (500 each), moral science (500), jurisprudence and political Economy (350 each), and additional subjects (500 in all).

Here again you see his zeal for variety. Nobody expected any individual to cover so much, though each might have a shot at as many papers as he wished within limits. It was variety of types he wanted.

As it happens, this great reform was, in my judgment, ultimately to prove one of the instruments of Britain's headlong decline. The reason is interesting.

In practice the Civil Service Commission managed effectively to restrict recruitment into the administrative grade to arts graduates from Oxford and Cambridge—with Oxford on the whole dominating the more prestigious departments while Cambridge graduates went into the Boards of Trade and Works and the like.[9]

The declared aim of American law schools—to teach its students to think like lawyers—is modest indeed beside Oxford's, which is to teach them to think. Moreover, the chosen method—the weekly or twice weekly tutorial essay—is arguably as effective as the law school's first year in forming the student's mind. When I taught at Oxford, in the 1960s, an average student reading "Modern Greats" in philosophy, politics, and economics went to three lectures a fortnight in his second year, and to no classes or seminars, but he wrote two essays each week and defended them before his tutors. All knowledge, then, is divided into two-day morsels and the student comes to believe that he can get up anything in that time. It makes marvelous journalists[10] and is one reason why the BBC still does some of the best TV, but it is in my judgment a disastrous training on its own for civil servants and managers, and it certainly does not yield the variety which Lowe wanted.

Notice too how closely this resembles the process whereby a lawyer gets up a case. Milton Pollak, a New York trial lawyer, said: "I have a bathtub memory. I can fill it up, and when it is over I pull the plug and all this stuff drains right out. In a matter of days." In this age of specialists, that may overstate the norm, but surely it approximates it. It is not one go well with deep thinking about policy.

"If you get someone from the American civil service," said Frances Wolff of the ILO, "seventy percent of the time you get a lawyer: from the British Civil Service seventy percent of the time it is someone from history or literature or classics."

History is often Ancient,[11] though Cambridge has provided some notably successful modern historians. Literature probably refers to foreign languages useful in those seconded to an international organization. Classics is Greats—the most prestigious Oxford subject by far, based on classics in high school and in the first year at university and on Oxford philosophy in the second and third. Oxford philosophy is largely linguistic philosophy and is a marvelous tool for making anyone who says anything in particular look a fool—the essence of English committeemanship. Is not law a little like that too?

Interestingly enough, Lowe was one of those who most wished to reform British university education. He was the first MP from London University, and a helpful adviser to those setting up universities after the German style in English provincial cities. But he was old, going blind, and declining in power. The Civil Service Commission went on forever; had done little to implement its brief between 1854 and 1869, and, I suspect, took care that matters did not get out of hand afterwards. In any case, Oxford and Cambridge dominate English university education a good deal less than Harvard Law School dominates American legal education—but dominate they do nevertheless, and increasingly so as the radical provincialism which gave birth to the municipal universities died down.

I imagine, then, that Lowe would have been quite as unhappy about the education of British Civil Service, as deeply as he had engaged himself in the matter, as he would have been about that of American politicians and bureaucrats—and for the same reason. Of course, British politicians tend to come from Oxford[12] and to a lesser extent Cambridge, and (like the bureaucrats) from the humanities rather than the sciences, so a stultifying uniformity of approach pervades both American and British politics as well as administration.

I thought at this stage to turn to an analysis of the economics of American legal education, but Alan and Paddy Walters have persuaded me that it would be at least as interesting to say how the present system came into being. It is an interesting study, both for what it says about lawyers and for what it says about the importance of chance and timing in forming institutions.

Charles Elliott was a great reforming president of Harvard. He was appointed in 1870 and immediately sought out a promising young practicing lawyer, Christopher Columbus Langdell, to be the first dean of law at Harvard or anywhere else. Within a year Langdell had thought out his whole strategy, based on the scientific method which was so influential at the time. Just as scientists experimented and dissected in the laboratory, isolating the basic principles on which their subjects were based, so fledgling lawyers would discuss cases—lawyer's pleadings and judgments—and isolate the legal principles which these illustrated. Within a year he had written his first case book, and soon after that he appointed a young lawyer with no experience of legal practice as his first colleague. This was James Barr Ames, who put Langdell's ideas quickly into practice.

Calvin Woodward claims that Langdell really cheated. He introduced torts into the curriculum for the first time, for instance, because it had been a major branch of Roman law. Civilians argued from principle to practice, and not vice versa, so Langdell had merely to uncover what they had been observed to put in.

Be that as it may, the cases are actual court cases. What they study is judges making law—common rather than statute law.[13]

Now the struggle for the common law as against royal fiat was one of the core elements in the Puritan revolution of the 1640s, to which the American Revolution seems to me to owe a lot. Coke, the Puritans' intellectual leader, had rebuffed James I when he said "was not 'law founded on reason', and that 'he and others had as good reason as the judges'?" by saying that "causes which concern the life or inheritance of goods, or fortune of his subjects *are not to be decided by natural reason, but by the artificial reason and judgment of law, which law is an art which requires long study and experience*, before man can attain the cognizance of it; and that the law was the golden met-wand and measure to try the cases of subjects; and *which protected his Majesty in safety and peace*; with which the King was greatly offended and said that then he would be under the law, 'which was treason to affirm', as he said; to which I said, that Bracton saith *quod Rex non debet sub homine, sed sub Deo et lege*."

Though the Inns of Court were already in decline, many of the gentry still spent a year or two there after the university, steeping themselves in common law and frequently having a high old time. The former was one of the things which made the Puritan gentry in particular such effective parliamentarians. It was the common law too, as adapted to eighteenth century needs by Mansfield, that Blackstone expounded in the *Commentaries*, which were, with the Bible and Paine's *Rights of Man*, the best sellers of late-eighteenth-century America.

Traditionally, common law has been the enemy of statute law. One might think that those brought up in that tradition would themselves be wary of new written law; but that is not my impression—except insofar as American judges are willing to overrule particular statutes in the light of the Constitution. In fact both Congress and the executive have generated more and more detailed law year by year.

That is, I think, another disadvantage in having lawyers as the main legislators and top executives. Just as a pair of lawyers will draw an agreement an inch thick to join two close friends in a business partnership, so, I imagine, their reaction to each new problem is to encircle it with legal barbed wire.

That there should be some people in the legislature and in each government department who react in this way is right and proper; that such should be the reaction of the majority seems to me dangerous indeed.

It is mitigated, I imagine, by the experience of hard, real life. Lawyers deal with people in trouble, or mad at each other. Part of their job in practice is presumably to calm and conciliate, so many of them may become natural compromisers. Unfortunately the compromises in question tend to be between active clients—a dangerous precedent for those whose main duty, according to Lowe at least, should be to look after common general interests. American lawyers, too, may be less given to conciliations than the solicitors whom English clients must first approach and who are said to find litigation notably less profitable than conveyancing and probate work.

Postscript (1980)

After the lecture, the questions turned on the practical problem: "Assuming you are right, what should be done?"

I think that quite a lot probably could be.

Faced with increasing boredom in the second and third years, teachers at some of the leading schools believe *on academic grounds* that the basic law course should be reduced by a year. The Carrington Committee of the American Association of Law Schools reflected this view, and went into the teaching costs involved. In doing so they neglected the value of the students' own time, and thus badly understated their case.

Take Harvard for instance. Suppose the starting salary of a newly fledged lawyer from there is half that of an average Harvard law teacher, or a quarter when the cost of supporting services is allowed for. Salary includes fringe benefits in both cases, but excludes consulting fees and the like in the teacher's. Assume that a student earns one-third of his starting salary in his final year from vacation work and research assistance. The remaining two-thirds would pay one-sixth, $= \frac{2}{3} \times \frac{1}{4}$, of the total cost of an extra teacher. There are more than 30 students per teacher at Harvard, so that each absorbs the services of less than a tenth of a teacher—or teacher-year, if you can bear the term—in his three year course. In other words, reducing the course by one year would save each student nearly twice the entire cost of teaching and supporting services in the existing three-year program!

These are startling figures.

Let us look at them in another way. Assume precisely 30 students per teacher and no dropouts. Were the school to take the entire savings in increased fees, it could support 8 teachers where it had three before; if it took 80 percent, 7; if 60 percent, 6; if 40 percent, 5; if 20 percent, 4. Remembering that the course would now be two years, there would be $7\frac{1}{2}$, $8\frac{1}{2}$, 10, 12, or 15 students per teacher instead of the 30 in the present three-year program, or the 20 which the Carrington Committee implicitly assumes, over two years.[14]

This is an embarrassingly oversimplified bit of economics, based on distantly inspired guesses. I would be surprised nevertheless were it to be proved seriously misleading,[15] and I think it may well err on the conservative side. The most important factor pointing in the opposite direction is my neglect of income tax. Suppose therefore that the school takes half the savings, leaving the other half for the student to share with his tax man. Each teacher would then have to look after about 11 students instead of more than 30. That would permit much more intensive teaching methods to be used. I think that these could be deployed so as to produce lawyers in greater variety than before without reducing general academic standards.

In the lecture I criticized both the Socratic method (as used in American law schools), and the tutorial (as used at Oxford) fiercely. That is a tribute to their effectiveness. The Socratic case-study approach appears to produce its effect by shock, followed by anticlimax, boredom, and inattention. If so, it should be used discriminatingly, and only where its comparative advantages are great; and something should be done to mitigate its after-effects. Since these are generally agreed to last throughout the course, I do not think that they can be ascribed completely to the aftermath of a traumatic shock. Remember that the first-year Socratic teachers are the cream of the faculty according to Packer and Ehrlich and "ham actors" according to Riesman. My guess is that their onslaught on the personalities of their students opens up a rift between teachers and taught which makes co-operation difficult later in the course, and that their dominance among the faculty leads others to model themselves on them, some possibly to rebel against them, both helping to keep the rift open.

Tutorials, on the other hand, tend to breed trust and easy relations between tutor and pupil.[16] As such I think they should be used as an antidote to the Socratic method from the beginning. Take it as a datum that the focus will remain on teaching students "to think like lawyers" in the first year. That would not seem to require each particular subject to be studied. To free their time for tutorials, the students might be required to go to fewer of the first year courses.

Tutorials are not just a social device, they are extremely flexible teaching instruments. I believe that they are at their most effective in pulling together the different courses in a program; and bringing in considerations, information, and strands of thought which are not formally taught at all. I used to do a good deal of tutoring in a social science faculty in which the students had gained a smattering of each others' subjects in the first year, but normally concentrated on two or three in their second and third. By mixing up my tutorial groups, and setting essays on history and current affairs, I was able to keep their wider interests awake and let them see for themselves how important it was to look at particular problems and episodes from a variety of points of view. So, too, here?

In my guess the second year should revolve around workshops, as the first revolves around the Socratic discussions. To be effective workshops have to be small, though I have found 25 to be just feasible. I believe that only one teacher should attend each—otherwise discussion among the teachers kills discussion among the students. Suppose each student takes part in one workship a week throughout the year. Then the varying styles and interests of their teachers will tend to generate variety among the students, as will the dynamics of the groups themselves. This will become a cumulative process as these students themselves become teachers. I believe that most workshops should require serious research from their members. They have to be prepared for that. Here again is a role for the tutorial. Suppose one normally meets one's pupils once a week in groups of two, one of whom presents a paper. Once a month, for instance, one can have two groups together in a two-hour session; choosing the subject well beforehand, with the presenter circulating his paper well in advance, and perhaps choosing a formal discussant, whose function is not to open the discussion but to be ready with things to say should others not. In such a way one can allow individual students to pursue their particular interests in an informal setting where they need not worry about making mistakes, incidentally preparing them for more thorough research to be presented in the more formidable atmosphere of a workshop.

I have little doubt that all this is economically feasible, despite the interference of the tax man, and that it is consistent with high academic standards. Is it socially feasible? There I have doubts, based on the key role which the Socratic first-year teachers now appear to play in the entire life of the law school. People call them prima donnas. Would a prima donna yield her dominant role without a fight? Even if they would, would their colleagues, used to living in their shade, be able to take up the crucial roles of tutor and workshop leader?

If it is feasible, I have argued, it would generate a more varied legal profession, more cheaply, even if all the schools remained as similar to each other as they are now. However, there really is no reason why they should. The present tight orthodoxy was bred in Langdell's mind in a single hectic year of preparation, and is deeply embedded in the crude scientism of 1870. It became universal through the need for rapid compromises between the law schools with competing interests just before a crucial ABA meeting in the early 1920s.[17] Given fundamental change, there is really no reason why they should settle into a single new orthodoxy next time—unless, that is, the American Association of Law Schools insists on it. At the moment I understand "standards" are maintained between different schools by the application of mechanical rules and ratios. If that were to continue, it might hem all the schools into the same area. If "standards" are to be maintained, it would have to be by more flexible methods—such as external examining. But should you aim at a common standard? I for one gravely doubt it, and agree with Reid, for instance, in arguing that there is such a variety of legal jobs to be done that different types of lawyers, some cheap, some dear, are needed to do them. Let some schools appropriate most of the savings generated by a shorter course and give an appropriately excellent and expensive education; while others leave most of it in the student's pocket, educating him on the cheap, commonly for a less rewarding career.

Interesting enough, I understand that the Carrington Report was turned down partly because the lesser law schools feared that Harvard and the like would be able to graduate many more new lawyers on a two-year program, leaving fewer for them; while the bar associations feared a flood of competitors at the outset of a slump. If so, it demonstrates the danger of having only one pattern of thought represented on governing bodies.

There would be one year in which two sorts of lawyers graduated—though that should presumably be staggered.[18] Ultimately, if my arguments are broadly right, a given number of teachers would graduate many fewer lawyers under a well-designed two-year program than a three, so that the lesser schools would have more students to choose from and the existing lawyers fewer competitors to fear. In the long run the number of law teachers would presumably increase a lot. Some savings would probably be left in the student's hands, so that the supply of applicants would probably increase, and probably the annual supply of young lawyers too—but not for a long time, and proportionally far less than the number of teachers, and possibly not at all if competition led to teachers being paid relatively more highly.

All of these increases and decreases would, of course, be relative to what would otherwise have taken place. The oversupply of lawyers in the 1970s, and the declining number of 22-year-olds in the 1980s, would presumably have led to a fall in the number of law students—though this would probably have been offset, at least in part, by an increase in the number of young women entering the profession. If so the effect of a two-year course might have been to replace a notable decline in the demand for teachers' services by a continuing, but manageable, increase.

Of course lawyers run law schools and academic administrators the universities to which they are affiliated. Lawyers have traditionally been notably guild-minded, and I could not find a single piece of evidence in my perusal of some score of Carnegie Studies that any of the administrators took intelligent account of the value of students' time in prescribing for the academic future of the country. Education, law, and the law schools are scarcely perfectly competitive industries.'

In such circumstances, an economist's predictions may be badly out, even when they fall well short of the competitive equilibrium.

Notes

1. I also gave a series of lectures on "Doing Economics Economically." That was a pleasure. I do not remember whether it was also a duty. (1988)

2. While I read rather widely when preparing for this lecture last winter, I referred to only half a dozen books while writing it—excluding statistical compilations, general reference books and the like. My debt to Martin Miller, from whose study of The *Lawyers* this quotation comes, like several others in this paper, is particularly great. I am also indebted to Matthew Salomon for all sorts of help. (1980)

As will be clear, I set the lecture down in a great hurry. Hence in particular the lack of clear references, and even of definitions and sources of the statistics quoted below. I am especially contrite about the latter. However they do seem to hang together tolerably well. (1988)

3. "About one-half of 1 per cent" of what? You may well ask, but I cannot now answer. Possibly male lawyers in total male employment; possibly all lawyers in total full-time employment. It does seem too large if part-timers are included in the denominator. (1988)

4. I believe more of them enter individual practice.

5. Against which I tested most of the claims I made about Robert Lowe in the text. (1988).

6. As Byron Shafer has recently pointed out to me, this looks high. On the other hand, Matthew Salomon, to whom I refer in the previous paragraph, is not a person to get such things wrong. Perhaps he reported Harvard lawyers as a percentage of all lawyers trained in full-time university-connected law schools. Byron has confirmed my belief that some large law schools are not so connected, and tells me that Harvard currently graduates about 600 new lawyers a year, corresponding to 10,000 in the universities as a whole—a figure which does not go badly with the "6 percent" mentioned in the text. (1991)

7. This is not to defy Marx. Think of them as the executive arm of the ruling class, if you prefer.

8. When the decision was put into effect by an Order in Council in the middle of the following year, the Home Office had already backed down, but the new Department of Education, *coming directly under that Council's aegis*, had managed to opt out completely. It lacked social prestige, so the Macdonnell Cornmission was able to whip it into line in 1913; the Diplomatic Service, as the most snobbish of all, escaped reform for some considerable time after that. I am grateful to Michael Brock, Warden of Nuffield, for referring me to the McDonnell Commission here and the Fulton Committee below. (1988)

9. Oxford still dominates, especially in the more prestigious departments, though Cambridge has come up a bit, and the present Permanent Secretary of the Treasury is a gifted economist from Sheffield. (1988)

10. Not reporters, for whom a developed professional ethic is important.

11. I suspect that this is nonsense, because very few people seem to read ancient history. This set me searching for statistics, which turned out to be available in the Report of the Fulton Committee, set up in 1966 by a Labour Government intent on widening the entry into the Administrative Grade. By 1965 the Civil Service Commission seems to have bowed to the inevitable, and allowed in more outsiders—notably three economists and sixteen in all from outside Oxford and Cambridge. Of the 55 entrants to that grade in 1964, 34 were Classicists or Historians from Oxford or Cambridge. Unfortunately the statistics do not discriminate between these two universities. I suspect Oxford was not more dominant in Classics (Greats) than in History. (1988) Greats includes Ancient History too. That may be what underlay the claim in the text which I have just been disowning (1991).

12. Seven of the nine British prime ministers since the war were educated in Oxford. The other two, Churchill and Callaghan, did not go to university. (1988) Major has now joined Churchill and Callaghan, leaving Oxford's monopoly among graduates unaffected. (1990)

13. Commonly they interpret statutes, or disallow them as being against the Constitution. In that sense they are making statute law, rather than common. The tradition which led to so much judge-made law is, I believe, that of the common lawyers, as illustrated by Coke's sturdy stand against King James. (1988)

14. I write from memory in Oxford. (1980) Their calculations seemed to me to be based on a constant number of teacher-years per graduate. (1988)

15, Two American law professors on whom I have tried the underlying assumptions say they are roughly right. One even tried to get his Law School to reopen the question of such a reform. (1988)

16. Perhaps an overromantic view. Fellows of Oxford Colleges sometimes give up in fits of boredom in their forties; pupils complain at the inattention generated by such boredom.

17. "In the early 1920s": I am not sure of that date now. It seems later than one would have expected. I believe the rest of the sentences to be accurate. (1988)

18. Clearly this switch would require careful planning. (1988)

Risk Tolerances, Distributive Inequality, and Track Bettors' Equilibrium

Paul A. Samuelson

At the 1950 World Mathematical Congress, Robert Bishop weighed the empirical and theoretical evidence bearing on the Friedman-Savage (1948, 1952) hypothesis that people act to maximize the expected value, $E\{U(W)\}$, of a utility that is a function of wealth with double inflection points at some intermediate level of W. Bishop raised doubts, not since dispelled, that researchers had ever been able to identify the critical W range that the Friedman-Savage theory calls for.

What struck me most was Bishop's demonstration that such an interval of increasing marginal utility, if it were to exist, would self-destruct in the sense that its inhabitants would be inveterate gamblers who would cause themselves to be propelled out of it and into the absorbing wealth levels below and above it, where the von Neumann $E\{U(W)\}$ criterion would forbid any gambling at fair odds.

One sage's *reductio ad absurdum* is another conquistador's *tour de force.* By the time of the famous 1962 Paris conference on risk—famous because Kenneth Arrow announced there his fundamental breakthrough concerning contingent markets for different outcomes of the state of nature—Milton Friedman had traced much of observed income and wealth inequality to the life-cycle choices of risk that we each have embraced. As I explained to John Hicks at Oxford on my way home from Paris, when he asked me what had gone on there: "Those unequal beds we all lie in are supposed to be beds we made for ourselves, as Rockefeller was lucky in his long-shot bets and Micawber was unlucky in his."[1]

Because the Bishop effect planted a seed in my mind that germinated only four decades later in a model of an ergodic wealth distribution, let me explicate this effect. Divide reality into three ranges, with the poor and the rich, who are risk averse, surrounding a middle range of risk relishers. Fair gambles can be contrived virtually costlessly. Neither the rich nor the poor are willing to engage in such zero-sum activities. But the risk relishers go at it with vigor. If all of them began deep in the middle, after a few turns of the roulette wheel the winners and losers will have moved toward the two extremes. It is a standard theorem in sequential analysis and gambler's ruin that, in enough time, with probability approaching 1, all the risk relishers will have disappeared into the absorbing barriers of the rich or the poor, where their itch will have been eliminated. (You may quibble that one orphan could be left stably in the middle range. However, by sweetening the odds a bit above fair odds, the orphan could coax from the risk averters above or below enough action that he will end up out of the middle. Alternatively, we can posit that Mother Nature throws up for him and anyone fair bets that by chance will either use up his principal or garner him a compensating profit. In either case the asymptotic state is an empty Friedman-Savage domain.)

The weight of the evidence suggests that in most societies, in *every* income range, some individuals will engage in recreational gambling: at the track, with the bookies, in periodic purchases of lottery tickets, over the bridge or poker table, down at Merrill Lynch, or hanging on the street corner waiting for a frog to lunge to the right or the left. Some people eschew (or minimize) such activities at every income level. Markowitz (1952b) sensibly suggested that hysteresis obtains, so that the Friedman-Savage inflection points recreate themselves for both winners and losers somewhere above *wherever* they subsequently land. (Again, at *any* W, they both buy insurance and back long shots.) The late Jimmie Savage, not one to take any old Yes for an answer, repudiated the Markowitz rescue line, saying that he would disown such a version of his own theory as uninteresting. My advice to Savage was to cut his losses and accept whatever scientific truth Nature doles out. We do want a handle on recreational gambling, and the Markowitz-Bishop twist of the Friedman-Savage effect can provide us with one—as I shall show in my later modeling of racetrack equilibrium. (Standing friction acts in real life just like the Markowitz construct: a rough block stays anywhere you place it on a rough inclined plane; its potential energy function has a V-bottom that follows it wherever it goes. Not elegant? Not economical in the sense of Mach? Too bad, Dr. Savage and Dr. Samuelson. Like Margaret Fuller, we must "accept the universe" and whatever ways the cookie crumbles.)

Risk Tolerance That Falls, Rises, and Falls

A major use of wavy total utility functions is to give us some handle on modeling recreational gambling. Many of my subsequent pages will be devoted to illustrating the general equilibrium for bettors in a parimutuel system. Before doing this, let me mention briefly how this generalized Friedman-Savage world is particularly lethal with respect to (mean, variance) approximations (discussed by Hicks (1935), Marschak and Makower (1938), Tobin (1958), Markowitz (1959), Latané (1959), Sharpe

(1964), Samuelson (1967, 1970, 1983, 1989) and many others) and how waviness in risk tolerances can generate models of ergodic income distribution that differ materially from those of the Pareto-Champernowne type. (See Champernowne 1953.)

The two parameters of mean money return and variance are known to be sufficient for decision making under the unrealistic and singular case where the utility function of wealth, $U(W)$, is quadratic; and/or under the case that violates limited liability, where securities have returns that obey a multi-variate Gaussian probability distribution. Except as a qualitative surrogate to describe general behavior of risk bearers, mean-variance analysis is understood to be primarily approximative. Samuelson (1970), in the context of the debates among Borch (1969), Feldstein (1969), and Tobin (1969) about mean-variance, defended these tools as giving limiting approximations when outcomes become more and more bunched by "compact probabilities." Fortunately, the Merton (1969, 1990) world of instantaneous Wiener-Ito probabilities offers a valuable paradigm in which the mean and the variance become exactly sufficient parameters for choice.

Generally, one does not sensibly cavil at a two-term Taylor expansion that provides approximating insight. But—as is developed below, and explicated in Samuelson 1990a, b—the recreational gamblers in a Friedman-Savage universe traverse small finite domains where things can get worse before they get better. There is an irreducible threeness (rather than twoness) involved in their decision making. "Why the heavy weather?" you will ask. "Use a three-term Taylor expansion, adjoining to the two moments of (mean, variance) a third moment of skewness." Alas, the derivatives at initial wealth, $[U'(W), U''(W), U'''(W)]$, cannot quite capture the requisite intricacies of the problem. That this is not a capricious consideration is exemplified by the laudable attempt of Quandt (1986) to *deduce* the observed relative unprofitability of bets on long shots by heuristic reasoning that reverses the role of variance from that of a "bad" for risk averters to that of a "good" for risk-relishers at the track.

As was mentioned above, Bishop (1950) and Friedman (1953) would have expected the wealth range around the double inflection points to empty themselves out as their inhabitants gambled out of them. More pedantically, one envisages an ergodic probability distribution with low but positive numbers in that wealth interval—this under the realistic proviso that Nature is constantly throwing up to everyone investment gambles that are favorable in money terms. Although the Friedman-Savage interval tends always to empty itself, it is always gaining some new entrants from those people above and below it who have been enticed into favorable investment bets that land them there.

Economists like Markowitz, Bishop, and me, who doubt that there exist identifiable wealth intervals where the average person loses risk aversion, are led to a different ergodic theory of income distribution by the considerations of the last paragraph.[2] In Samuelson 1989, I assume positive relative-risk aversion of the Arrow-Pratt type:

$$-WU''(W)/U'(W) = A(W) = A(W) > 0 \text{ for all } W.$$

If the very rich and the very poor have a high $A(W)$ while the intermediate class has a lower $A(W)$, then those in the middle will be more venturesome and will tend by chance to rise or fall out of their initial class. Realistic considerations of tax transfers, bequests, wage earnings, and consumption needs will complete the model and provide the reflecting barriers that keep the system's asymptotic ergodic probabilities positive in all ranges of W.

The Pareto-Champernowne distribution, by contrast, requires that *all* within the Pareto range face the *same* relative decision processes as those above them in the wealth scale. See, for example, Van der Wijk's well-known law of the exact Pareto distribution—which Chipman (1976) has traced to Bowley early in the century and to a long line of writers who preceded Van der Wijk (1939).

Sport of Kings: Recreational Gambling

Can models of wavy $U(W)$ that can rationalize recreational gambling generate exact models of bettors' equilibrium?

The crowd has a wisdom few members possess. The collective of consensus business-cycle forecasters usually outperforms in the end any one of the group—certainly any random member of it. Picking the winner at a horse race by tossing a fair coin in your own private cave is hardly optimal. Nor is going by euphony of name, in disregard of the horse's attributes, lineage. and past performances. Alas, when everyone is as free to study horses' haunches, pedigrees, and running records as you are, the profitability of such efforts can self-destruct.

At the parimutuel tracks, horse A will be regarded as more likely to win than horse B. When more bets are laid on A than on B in a two-horse race,

A becomes the favorite and *B* becomes the long shot. Statistics show that in real life favorites do win more often than long shots. That is the bottom line. (This doctrine of a Smithian invisible hand that leads the mob to wise forecasting will be developed below as law I, and will be modified in law II to a closer approximation.)

All this is to say that the "objective probabilities" in an *H*-horse race for each horse to win, $(p_1, \ldots, p_h, \ldots, p_H)$, tend to be correctly estimated by the observed fractions bet at the totalizer on the respective horses, $(y_1, \ldots, y_h, \ldots, y_H)$, where

$$y_h = b_h n_h \Big/ \sum_1^n b_j n_j, \tag{1}$$

$$n_h = \text{fraction of all betters who bet on horse } h, \tag{2}$$

$$b_h = \text{average dollar bet on } h, \tag{3}$$

$$1 = \sum_1^H y_j = \sum_1^H n_j = \sum_1^H p_j, \tag{4}$$

Rankings of $(p_1, \ldots, p_H)$ and $(y_1, \ldots, y_H)$ "tend to agree." (5)

Suppose races were handicapped so as to try to equalize the probability of winning for every horse, say—by having experts estimate how much extra weight the superior horse must carry. Under perfectionist handicapping, by definition, when there are *H* horses in the race each has a $1/H$ chance of coming in first. If people correctly believed in perfect handicapping, bets should tend to be made equally on all horses at the totalizer, so there would be no long shots and no favorites. In a two-horse race, *A* and *B* would promise the same odds; if that tended momentarily not to be so, independent of risk aversion and tolerance, rational hedonists would prefer to bet on the (spurious) long shot. Over many races, horses that were slight favorites by virtue of Brownian wobble alone would not show any tendency to win more often than the (spurious) long shots; and (5) would need modifying. A world with perfect handicappers might be a dull one for spectators.

Race betting under a totalizer system lets the bettors, all together, set the odds that each faces. Those of us who wisely bet on the horse that does win will receive all the money that is bet on all the horses—but subject to the fractional take by the track and the tax collector. Call this take factor *t*.

Ordinarily it is a fraction around $\frac{1}{5}$ or $\frac{1}{6}$. A negative t is rarely seen in real life, since it would involve an outright subsidy from some outsider. Even $t = 0$ would require someone to be an altruist.

The Complete Model of Bettor's Equilibrium: Premises

Suppose that H horses run a race, and a large number of spectators can bet on any one of them to win. Take as known the objective probability that horse h will win:

$$0 < (p_1, \ldots, p_h, \ldots, p_H), \text{ a specified vector.} \tag{6}$$

All bettors believe in these probabilities.

For simplicity, all bettors are to have the same tolerance for risk, each acting to maximize the expected value of his utility-of-wealth function, $U(W)$, which is the same function for all. Economists most often deal with risk-averse individuals, who display

$$U'(W) > 0 > U''(W), \quad W > 0 \tag{7}$$

and

$$U'(W) \to \infty \text{ as } W \to 0, \quad U'(W) \to 0 \text{ as } W \to \infty. \tag{8}$$

Recreational betting would stop in its tracks for such people until a research subsidy from the National Science Foundation made possible the negative t that would coax them into action.

To motivate bets of finite amount in the negative-sum game being run at the tracks, it suffices to posit a Friedman-Savage interval where $U'(W)$ rises for a range. Realism suggests that the Markowitz-Bishop version be assumed: Whatever the bettor's wealth just before his arrival at the track (call it $\overline{W}$), the same reversal of sign of $U''(W - \overline{W})$ recreates itself in $\overline{W}$'s neighborhood. It costs nothing to regard all spectators as starting with the same $\overline{W}$.

An elegant device to motivate a bettor's model, I have found, is to assume a *cusp* in the utility function at $\overline{W}$ itself: Below $\overline{W}$, U follows a strictly concave branch, $f(W)$; above $\overline{W}$, U follows a similar branch, $g(W)$; but $f'(\overline{W}-)$ is assumed to be below $g'(\overline{W}+)$, so that the essence of the Friedman-Savage and Markowitz-Bishop qualitative phenomena is contrived to be localized into a marginal-utility quantum up-jump at the point of initial wealth itself. Mathematically, cusped utility can be described as follows:

$$U(W - \overline{W}) = f(W - \overline{W}), \quad W \leq \overline{W} \tag{9a}$$

$$\quad\quad\quad\quad = g(W - \overline{W}), \quad W \geq \overline{W}; \quad f(\overline{W}) = g(\overline{W}) \tag{9b}$$

$$f'(W) > 0 > f''(W), \qquad g'(W) > 0 > g''(W). \tag{9c}$$

By dimension convention, we can stipulate a marginal utility of unity where W approaches $\overline{W}$ from below:

$$f'(\overline{W}-) = L = 1, \quad g'(\overline{W}+) = 1 + \Delta = R > 1, \tag{9d}$$

$$[-f''(\overline{W}-), -g''(\overline{W}+)] > 0 \text{ but otherwise arbitrary.} \tag{9e}$$

At the extremities of positive W, $f(W)$ and $g(W)$ obey (8). For total and marginal utility the pictures are  and .

For horses not too badly matched and the house's take factor large enough, all bets can be kept small enough so that the three parameters $[\Delta, -f''(\overline{W}-), -g''(\overline{W}+)]$ will essentially dominate the equilibrium solution's form—sophisticated "compact probabilities" for which m and σ^2 are *not* sufficient parameters!

All betting must be through the totalizer. I assume that one person bets on only one horse to win. For brevity I forbid bets on a horse to "place" or "show" (i.e., to come in at least second or third); I also forbid or ignore betting on more than one race per afternoon at the track, eliminating bets that require picking the winner in several races (e.g., daily doubles).

Recall that the totalizer gives the winners on horse h all that anyone has bet on any horse minus the track's fractional take of t times the total amount bet.

Mark Twain said that it is differences of opinion that make horse races. This is a one-third truth. Differences of risk tolerance can also motivate positive bets among persons with the same views about the probabilities. The present model abstracts from both of the above truths. (More exactly, I conceive of them as providing clustering approximations that wobble around the equilibrium points defined by this model.) What was understood by Twain, but not pithily enunciated, was that positive relish for risk taking can generate bets among people alike with respect to probability expectations and tolerances for risk. Cusped utility, or some other Markowitz-Bishop construct, formalizes the entailed equilibrium.

Preview of General Equilibrium's Properties

For broad domains of the specified parameters $(p_1, \ldots, p_H; t)$, it can be shown that a unique equilibrium will define itself, determining positive values for the $2H - 1$ independent unknowns comprising the $(\bar{b}_1 \ldots \bar{b}_H)$ positive bets and the $(y_1 \ldots y_H)$ fractions of total bets wagered on each horse. Of course, these solution values will be a functional of the $U(W - \overline{W})$ function specified; and they will be a function of the parameters $(p_1, \ldots, p_H; t)$:

$$0 < \bar{b}_h = B_h\{p_1, \ldots, p_H; t\}, \quad h = 1, \ldots, H \tag{10a}$$

$$0 < y_h = Y_h\{p_1, \ldots, p_H; t\}, \quad \sum_1^H Y_j\{p_1, \ldots, p_H; t\} \equiv 1. \tag{10b}$$

(Although it will be shown that each expression in (10a) can be written as $B\{p_h; t\}$ independent of h, where p_h is a scalar rather than a vector, a similar invariance will not hold for each $y_h\{p_1, \ldots, p_H, t\}$ function.)

If t were made so large as to seem confiscatory, there might be no bets made at all and an indeterminate Y vector would result. Also, were we to let $U(W)$ have multiple inflection points, there could well be a multiplicity of solutions. For $U''(\overline{W})$ positive and t not too large, all will be risk relishers motivated to bet. And if $U''(W)$ were assumed to be positive for W everywhere on $(-\infty, \infty)$—the case too many writers seem tacitly to accept—motivated bets would be *unbounded* in size and no proper equilibrium would seem definable.

The advantage of my proposed exact model is that it permits us to test conventional wisdoms:

Betting Law I The relative odds at the track tend to approximate the *ex post* probabilities of winning. If the vector of relative shares bet on the horses, $[y_1 \ldots y_H]$, agreed with *ex ante* and *ex post* probabilities, $[p_1 \ldots p_H]$, law I would be exact, a stronger version of equation (5):

$$P = (p_1, \ldots, p_H) = (y_1, \ldots, y_H) = Y. \tag{11}$$

Betting Law II Because of the house's take, bets on every horse tend to be unfavorable gambles. However, "long shots" with lowest p_h tend, statistics reveal, to have the worst relative odds; "favorites" with highest p_h tend to have the least unfavorable odds, and indeed runaway favorites can be worth betting on even to a canny risk averter. One weaker way to express law II would be this:

$$\text{If } p_1 \leq p_2 \leq \cdots \leq H^{-1} \leq \cdots \leq p_H,$$

$$y_1/p_1 \geq y_2/p_2 \geq \cdots \geq y_H/p_H. \tag{12}$$

Poincaré paraphrased a witty friend: "Everyone believes in the normal (Gaussian) law: theorists because they think it is a fact of experience; empiricists because they think it a valid deduction of mathematical theory." Today every schoolchild knows that many data depart from normality, and that well-founded axioms can entail systematic departures from normality. I must agree that most data do bear out law II's modification of law I; but I hope to show that Quandt (1986) cannot validly *deduce* that law II has to hold for risk relishers motivated to bet at the tracks.

Laws I and II: Bottom of the Bottom Line

To speak of the "true objective probabilities" for horses 1 and 2 to respectively win in a two-horse race smacks of metaphysics. Frank Ramsey, a logician and philosopher in the class of Frege and Russell, purported to define meaningful personal or subjective probabilities in terms of betabilities and not vice versa (see Ramsey 1930). Let me therefore try my hand at a revealed preference approach.

We can imagine the universe of all two-horse races. We have historical samples from it, with statistical records of the odds that obtained for each past race and data on what the odds were on the horse that won. For any past race, know $(y_1, y_2 = 1 - y_1)$. For each, $\text{Max}(y_1, 1 - y_1)$ provides the fractional bet on the favorite, y_f; $1 - y_f$ is the bet on the long shot. From past data on how often the favorite won, for each and every numerical value of y_f on the interval $(\frac{1}{2}, 1)$ we can compile the revealed frequency of victory; this gives the conditional probability distribution

$$\text{Prob}\{\text{favorite won} \,|\, y_f = x\} = \phi(x), \quad \tfrac{1}{2} \leq x \leq 1. \tag{13}$$

Mob wisdom would mean that $\phi(x)$ rises with x.

Law I can be phrased to express the strict hypothesis

$$\phi(x) \equiv x, \quad \tfrac{1}{2} \leq x \leq 1. \tag{14}$$

This would be Adam Smith's invisible hand of mob omniscience about chances.

Law II can be phrased to say

$$\phi(x) > x, \quad \tfrac{1}{2} < x < 1; \quad \phi(\tfrac{1}{2}) = \tfrac{1}{2}. \tag{15}$$

If you have no outside knowledge about the relative merits of the two horses, but know that the mob has picked a favorite and determined its y_f, then your knowledge of this $\phi(x)$ function and your belief that it applies will be valuable to you. As the putative "true p_f" for you to put in your $E\{U(W)\}$ maximand from which to calculate your best $\bar{b}_f$ bet, you will want to put in law II's $\phi(y_f)$ and not law I's y_f or the agnostic's $\frac{1}{2}$.

A Russell-Whitehead theory of types seems almost needed to resolve the circular iteration that this suggests. When bettors start out naive and generate an observable $\phi(x)$, some may become sophisticated; and in using the old $\phi(x)$ in the described fashion, they will alter their behavior and the frequency of different y_f values that clear the market. Law II will then partially self-destruct as more people see merit in betting on the favorite, thereby undermining its relatively favorable odds. The new $\phi(x)$ will be nearer to law I's x than the old one was. The iteration might well converge to a $\phi(x)^*$ function that is self- warranting and which leaves law I only an approximation to law II. Its shape must depend on what the sources are for relevant outside information. Because of the deadweight cost of arbitrage transactions, inherent when t is appreciable, the minority with better knowledge and better deductive capacity cannot generate the dominance relevant to the totals that we are led to expect will obtain in efficient security markets—as those who are most perspicacious accumulate ever more dollars and weighting votes.

Formal Conditions of Bettor Equilibrium: Bet Sizes

Begin with me, a typical individual deciding how much to bet on horse h, or indeed whether to bet anything on h. I feel too small to affect the posted $(y_1, \ldots, y_H)$ odds that I face.

If h loses, as will happen with probability $1 - p_h$, I will end with $\overline{W} - b_h$ when I bet b_h on h. With probability p_h I shall win, and then I receive my prorated share of all the dollars bet on any horse, minus the house's take of t times that total. As a winner who has bet b_h on h, I calculate to end up with

$$\overline{W} + b_h[(1 - t) - y_h]/y_h.$$

Therefore, my expected utility of $\mathrm{E}\{U(W)\}$ has to be written as

$$e(b_h \mid y_h; p_h, t) = (1 - p_h)U(\overline{W} - b_h) + p_h U(\overline{W} + b_h[1 - t - y_h]/y_h). \tag{16}$$

Note that $e(\mid)$ has no need for an h subscript: its expression is the same function for all horses—it being understood that the relevant p_h and y_h do carry their appropriate h subscript. (A subscript will be used in $e(b,y;p,t)$, as in $e_b(b \mid y;p,t)$, to denote $\partial e/\partial b$; likewise for $e_y(\quad)$, $e_p(\quad)$ and $e_{by}(\quad)$, and so on.

The optimal bet of $\bar{b}_h$ that I will make on horse h is generated as the solution to the Kuhn-Tucker programming problem

$$\begin{aligned} \bar{e}(y_h;p_h,t) &= \underset{b_h}{\mathrm{Max}}\ e(b_h \mid y_h;p_h,t) \quad \text{s.t. } b_h \geq 0 \\ &= e(\bar{b}_h \mid y_h;p_h,t), \end{aligned} \tag{17}$$

where $\bar{b}_h$ is a root for b_h of the Kuhn-Tucker relations

$$e_b(b_h \mid y_h;p_h,t) \leq 0, \tag{18a}$$

$$b_h e_b(b_h \mid y_h;p_h,t) = 0. \tag{18b}$$

Remark Negative bets are excluded because the totalizer will not permit them, being in the business of making commissions rather than giving them away.

If I am risk averse with a $U(W)$ that is everywhere strongly concave, (18) represents conditions both necessary and sufficient. The general Friedman-Savage $U(W)$ can, however, entail a b root for (18) that corresponds to a local minimum for $e(b\mid\ )$; and then, when $\partial e/\partial b$ is not a strictly concave function of b, we must choose, from (18)'s other pair of b roots, the $\bar{b}$ that corresponds to a *global* maximum.

If $U(W - \overline{W})$ is cusped as in (9), then (18) is also necessary and sufficient: e being a strictly concave function of b_h, $\bar{B}_h$ in (10a) will be a continuous function of its arguments both for concave and for cusped utility. If $U''(W)$ were positive for all W on $(-\infty, \infty)$, such a risk lover could find no finite $\bar{b}_h$ bet that would be optimal. If $U(W - \overline{W})$ has the Friedman-Savage property of possessing double inflection points for W above $\overline{W}$ and otherwise obeys the terminal properties of (8b), then (18) will almost always also define a unique and finite $\bar{b}_h$ even though the $B_h(\quad)$ function can have jumps. As mentioned, when $U''(W)$ changes sign on many intervals, the conditions of (18) are necessary conditions for each local maximum but by themselves do not suffice to determine the $\bar{b}_h$ that is (or are) maximum-maximorum.

Where (18) suffices to define a unique $\bar{b}_h$, write it as

$$\bar{b}_h = B\{y_h;p_h,t\}. \tag{19}$$

(Again, recall that B does not itself require an h subscript.)

Here are a few helpful examples. For risk averters facing $t = 0$ and $y_h = p_h$, the gamble is fair and zero is the optimal bet. *A fortiori*, for $0 < t < 1$, a risk averter calculates

$$e_b(0,p_h;p_h,t) = -t\,U'(\overline{W}) < 0, \quad \bar{b}_h = 0. \tag{20}$$

A risk relisher, with $U''(W)$ locally positive near $\overline{W}$, will eschew small unfavorable bets but still may select a finite positive $\bar{b}_h$ à la Friedman and Savage.

The equality variant of (18a) becomes necessary and sufficient when people are risk averse, t is slightly negative, and y_h is sufficiently near p_h. Then (18a)'s equality gives the condition

$$\frac{U'(\overline{W} + b_h[1 - t - y_h]/y_h)}{U'(\overline{W} - b_h)} = \frac{(1 - p_h)/(1 - y_h - t)}{p_h/y_h}. \tag{21}$$

For cusped utility (where the two Friedman-Savage inflection points are concentrated in a quantum up-jump of marginal utility at $\overline{W}$ itself), (18)'s first equality will similarly apply provided t is not too large a proper fraction and y_h is not too far from p_h. Then (21) becomes

$$\frac{g'(\overline{W} + b_h[1 - t - y_h]/y_h)}{f'(\overline{W} - b_h)} = \frac{(1 - p_h)/(1 - y_h - t)}{p_h/y_h}. \tag{22}$$

The comparative statics of the maximizing equilibrium is clear cut:

- $\bar{e}$ is if anything, raised by an increase in p_h, and hurt by an increase in t or y_h.
- A rise in p_h, if anything, induces a larger $\bar{b}_h$ bet.
- A fall in y_h or t, which sweetens the payoff odds on horse h, need not always raise $\bar{b}_h$ since there are opposing reactions (a bit like income and substitution effects). However, for t near enough to zero and y_h near enough to p_h, the $\bar{b}_h$ bet will be small and will be reduced in the naively intuitive way by rises in either t or y_h.

Final Market-Clearing Conditions

It is not enough that a bettor on h is required to make the $\bar{b}_h$ decided on be of optimal quantitative size. Since all are restricted to betting on but one horse to win, every horse will coax out some positive bets only if all the optimal bets $(\bar{b}_1,\ldots,\bar{b}_h,\ldots,\bar{b}_H)$ stand to yield equivalent $\mathrm{E}\{U(W)\}$ increments.

Therefore, to the optimum-size-bets conditions of (18) or (21) or (22), H in number, we must adjoin the following $H-1$ conditions ensuring *equality of ex ante utility of bets on all horses*: In terms of the $\bar{e}$'s of (17), we have

$$\bar{e}(y_1;p_1,t) = \cdots = \bar{e}(y_H;p_H,t). \tag{23}$$

This renders complete our formal model of general equilibrium for pari-mutuel bettors. Our $2H-1$ unknowns, $(\bar{b}_1,\ldots,\bar{b}_H;y_1,\ldots,y_H)$, are determined by the $2H-1$ relations of (18) and (23). Alternatively exposited, if the H $\bar{e}(y_n;p_n,t)$ functions are taken as known entailments of the H relations of (18), then they by themselves provide us in (23) the $H-1$ relations needed to determine the final $H-1$ independent unknowns:

$$y_h = Y_h\{p_1,\ldots,p_H;t\}, \quad h = 1,\ldots,H \tag{24}$$

$$\sum_1^H Y_h\{p_1,\ldots,p_H;t\} \equiv 1.$$

Notice that no vanishing of $\partial y_1/\partial p_H$ cross-terms can be expected in (23)–(24).

Mere counting of independent equations to ensure equality of their number with the number of endogenous unknowns was not really good enough for your dad—except of course in the exceptional case of linear relations. We must separately analyze the quality of the equations to decide whether there *exists at least one* positive and finite solution for $(\bar{b}_1,\ldots,\bar{b}_H;y_1,\ldots,y_H)$ and whether an existent solution is *unique*. Experience suggests that proof of uniqueness usually requires stronger hypotheses and more intricate argumentation, but I conjecture that existence proofs can be straightforwardly found.

For the special case of symmetric odds, t a negative number, and the customers all risk averse as in (8),

$$H^{-1} = p_1 = \cdots = p_H, \quad t < 0 \tag{25}$$

it is not hard to demonstrate that a solution exists in the symmetric form

$$H^{-1} = y_1 = \cdots = y_H. \tag{26}$$

This is a singular instance of law I (and of law II!).

For the odds still symmetric, where t is a small enough positive number and where the customers all have (9)'s cusped utility, the same symmetric Y vector is a solution.

By continuity arguments, we can let P be anywhere in a near neighborhood around (25)'s symmetry point and know that a solution for Y near (26)'s symmetry point will be ensured. Likewise for the cusped-utility case: when P is near the symmetry point, an almost-symmetric Y solution is ensured.

The reader can experiment with the tractable case of two-horse races, where (23) reduces to

$$\bar{e}(y_1;p_1,t) = \bar{e}(1 - y_1; 1 - p_1, t) \tag{27}$$

and a graphical examination of existence and uniqueness of equilibrium can be managed for the cusped-utility case.

Pitfalls in the Literature

The noted fact that these final functions in (24), or (10b), cannot be functions of the single scalar p_h, but must be functions of the whole vector, $P = (p_1, \ldots, p_H)$, has grave consequences for the existing horse-race literature. As seen, for $H > 2$ it is quite untrue that cross-terms such as $\partial y_i / \partial p_j$ will all vanish. At once we are alerted to blemishes in the published literature, where virtually all the authorities follow the pioneering lead of Weitzman (1965) and try to deduce a single relation between the probability of any horse winning (calculated *ex post* and now written as π) conditional on its observed payoff y, essentially a variant of (13) above:

$$\pi = \psi(y), \quad y = \psi^{-1}(\pi). \tag{28}$$

For $H > 2$, and even if all races were for the same number of horses, say $H = 8$, there simply is not such an invariant function. (Example: Let $H = 3$ and let p be the probability of some specified horse winning. The remaining probability, $1 - p$, might be divided up evenly between the two other horses if they happen to be well matched. Or one of them could be much more likely than the other to win. The same $\psi^{-1}\{p\}$ function could not be expected to apply to two such different cases—except, possibly, as some vague approximation. In real life, at best there could be in three-horse races a frequency distribution for the various *ex ante* probabilities (p_1,p_2,p_3). After (18) and (23) have converted each vector P into its entailed equilibrium Y, the record book would give us the empirical frequency of horse 1 winning conditional on each obserbed vector (y_1,y_2,y_3) Using π's to distinguish *ex post* winning frequencies from objective *ex ante* p's, a Weitzman would not be able to observe (28)'s expression for a $\psi(y_1) = \pi_1$; at best he would be able to observe expressions such as

$$\begin{aligned} \pi_1 &= \psi(y;y_2,y_3) = \psi(y_1;y_3,y_2), \\ n_2 &= \psi(y_2;y_1,y_3), \\ \pi_3 &= \psi(y_3;y_1,y_2). \end{aligned} \tag{29}$$

I must leave to a more leisurely occasion further elucidation of where the existing racetrack literature in the economic journals has taken shaky short cuts. See, for example, Ali 1977, Asch et al. 1984, and Ziemba and Hausch 1987.

Law I: Not a Correct Test of Prescience

Actually, even if it were miraculously to be the case that somehow the mob is omniscient in knowing the "true" $(p_1, \ldots, p_H)$, once their risk tolerances entered into the general-equilibrium solution of (24) we should *not* expect (28) or any one-variable correspondence to hold.

The realization of law I is not evidence for exact estimation by the mob.

The reader who has understood how peculiarities of risk tolerance in $U(W)$ result in a known P vector creating an observed equilibrium Y vector *different* from itself will realize that (generally) only when everyone incorrectly estimated the true P could the observed Y happen to equal that true P! (This is true even when all bets are "small" and the probabilities can be regarded as "compact.")

Law II: An Observed Regularity Not a Deducible Result

In Samuelson 1990b the Friedman-Savage geometry is used to generate an easy counterexample to the contention that risk relishers will, *as a matter of pure logic*, be prone to like betting on long shots so much as to penalize the relative odds offered by such bets. (They have to pay through the nose, so to speak for their kicks.) So goes the allegation. But when people start preponderantly above the Friedman-Savage top inflection point, they can be shown to reverse Quandt's rule.

Here I invite readers to create their own counterexamples, using cusped utility and assuming both t and Δ in (9) to be so small as to keep all $\bar{b}_h$'s small enough to permit us to regard $f(W - \overline{W})$ and $g(W - \overline{W})$ as simple quadratics. By specifying $-f''(\overline{W}-)$ in (9e) to be small relative to $-g''(\overline{W}+)$, the reader will verify that the reverse of Quandt's (1986) usual relation holds. That is, this case gives for $H = 2$,

$$\text{When } p_1 > \tfrac{1}{2} > p_2, y_1/p_1 > y_2/p_2. \tag{30}$$

As a by-product of this way of creating a counterexample, the reader will realize that even compact probabilities cannot justify (mean, variance) analysis, since at the very least the three parameters $[\Delta, -f''(0-), -g''(0+)]$ are involved in the quadratic approximation to $E\{U(W)\}$. In their neglected early classic on risk, Domar and Musgrave 1944 used cornered utility—where each dollar of loss is treated as more than each dollar of gain—to hint at the same point about the inadequacy of (mean, variance) analysis even locally. The present paper's corner is in $U'(W)$ whereas theirs was in $U(W)$.

Conclusion

Economic theory is a serious business not a game. The name of the game is understanding and testing observable reality. My first paper (Samuelson 1937) arose from a consideration that I considered too obvious even to mention:

> By observing how much more than my loss you must promise me as a gain in a 50-50 coin toss at each wealth level, your recorded
>
> Gain = f(Loss; Wealth)
>
> function can tell you: one, whether I am maximizing the expected value of *any* existent utility-of-wealth function; and two, how fast quantitatively its marginal utility declines with higher wealth levels.

The idea had come to me in my teens while listening to Professor Paul Douglas (later a Marine hero and a Senator) exposit at the University of

Chicago Bohm-Bawerkian notions of additive temporal utilities and alleged time-preference discounting, and my first paper later spelled it all out for testable life-cycle saving behavior.

In a sense I've not advanced far in 56 years from the ruts of revealed preference—or should I say "from the golden highways of empirical science"?

Frank Hahn, for whom this paper is a token of homage, is one of those rare minds of whom one can truly say, age does not stale his enthusiasm to insist upon adequate foundations for a proposed theory. Other scholars stay productive into their seventh, eighth, and ninth decades, but that is not quite the same thing. A Hicks stays true to his own star of originality; a Tinbergen stays faithful to his goal for human welfare. To me Hahn has seemed most like the late Jacob Marschak, whose love affair was with the science of economics itself. God bless!

Notes

1. When Hicks remarked "You don't suppose there is anything in that?" my reply was more frivolous than deep. Instead of saying "Actually, as I grow older and more successful, I find more and more merit in the notion," I should have said "Yes, some inequality is generated by differential tolerances for risk; and even more accumulates from differential ability to estimate real-world riskiness." See Friedman 1953 for a discussion of this matter. In particular, there used to be occasional references in the literature to an intermediate income range where fits of the Pareto distribution allegedly encountered a dearth of observations. Friedman adduced this as somewhat confirmatory of the Friedman-Savage phenomenon, employing precisely the Bishop line of reasoning. Before and since 1952, identifications of hollows in the income distribution have proved to be as elusive as the Scarlet Pimpernel. (One nice story involves Lord (Josiah) Stamp. When a tabulation of tax returns turned up a suspicious dearth in one interval, he asked his subordinates at the Inland Revenue Service to look into it. A misplaced packet of returns was conveniently found in a remote closet, clearing up the mystery. One wonders whether under different stopping rules other closets might be discovered, some adding to and others subtracting from Vilfredo Pareto's posthumous fame.)

2. See Keynes 1921 for the following misunderstanding of the mathematics of gambler's ruin:

> The true moral is this, that poor men should not gamble and that millionaires should do nothing else. But millionaires gain nothing by gambling with one another, and until the poor man departs from the path of prudence the millionaire does not find his opportunity. If it be replied that in fact most millionaries are men originally poor who departed from the path of prudence [shades of 1952 Friedman], it must be admitted that the poor man is not doomed with certainty. Thus the philosopher must draw what comfort he can from the conclusion with which his theory furnishes him, that millionaires are often fortunate fools who have thriven on unfortunate ones.[1]
>
> [1] From the social point of view, however, this moral against gambling may be drawn—that those who start with the largest initial fortunes are most likely to win, and that a given increment to the wealth of these benefits them, on the assumption of a diminishing marginal utility of money, less than it injures those from whom it is taken.
>
> (Keynes 1921, p. 320 and n. 1)

Any innuendo of the rich getting richer at the expense of the poor is ill-founded. To act so as to maximize your probability of winning—*à la* either Keynes or Latané, Kelly, and Breiman—can be a treacherous strategy. Actually, A and B with respective wealths of W_A and W_B, if risk averse, will never gamble with each other. Even when $W_A \gg W_B$, A will refuse to gamble, since for $U_A''(W) < 0$

$$\frac{W_B}{W_A + W_B} U_A(0) + \frac{W_A}{W_A + W_B} U_A(W_A + W_B) < U(W_A).$$

References

Ali, Mukhtar M. 1977. "Probability and utility estimates for racetrack bettors." *Journal of Political Economy* 85 (4): 803–815.

Asch, Peter, Burton G. Malkiel, and Richard E. Quandt. 1984. "Market efficiency in racetrack betting." *Journal of Business* 57 (2): 165–175.

Bishop, Robert L. 1950. Lecture on Expected Utility. World Mathematical Congress, Cambridge, Massachusetts.

Borch, Karl. 1969. "A note on uncertainty and indifference curves," *Review of Economic Studies* 36 (105): 1–4.

Champernowne, David. 1953. "A model of income distribution." *Economic Journal* 63: 318–351

Chipman, John S. 1976. "The Paretian heritage." *Revue Européene de Science Sociale and Cahiér of Vilfredo Pareto* 14 (37).

Domar, Evsey D., and R. A. Musgrave. 1944. "Proportional income taxation and risk-taking," *Quarterly Journal of Economics* 58: 388–422.

Feldstein, Martin. 1969. "Mean-variance analysis in the theory of liquidity preference and portfolio selection." *Review of Economic Studies* 36 (105): 5–12.

Friedman, Milton. 1953 "Choice, chance, and the personal distribution of income." *Journal of Political Economy* 61: 277–90.

Friedman, Milton, and L. J. Savage. 1948. "The utility analysis of choices involving risk." *Journal of Political Economy* 56: 279–304.

Friedman, Milton, and L. J. Savage. 1952. "The expected-utility hypothesis and the measurability of utility." *Journal of Political Economy* 60: 463–474.

Hicks, John. 1935. "A suggestion for simplifying the theory of money." *Economica* N.S. 2: 1–19.

Keynes, John Maynard. 1921. *A Treatise on Probability*. Macmillan.

Latané, Henry A. 1959. "Criteria for choice among risky ventures." *Journal of Political Economy* 67: 144–55.

Markowitz, Harry M. 1952a. "Portfolio selection." *Journal of Finance* 7: 77–91.

Markowitz, Harry M. 1952b. "The utility of wealth." *Journal of Political Economy* 60: 151–158.

Markowitz, Harry M. 1959. *Portfolio Selection*. Yale University Press.

Marschak, Jacob, and Helen Makower. 1938. "Assets, prices and monetary theory." *Economica* N.S. 5: 261–88.

Merton, Robert C. 1969. "Lifetime portfolio selection under uncertainty: The continuous-time Case" *Review of Economics and Statistics* 51: 247–257.

Merton, Robert C. 1990. *Continuous-Time Finance*. Blackwell.

Quandt, R. E. 1986. "Betting and equilibrium," *Quarterly Journal of Economics* 101: 201–207

Ramsey, Frank P. 1930. *The Foundations of Mathematics*. Routledge.

Rosett, Richard N. 1965. "Gambling and rationality." *Journal of Political Economy* 73: 595–607.

Samuelson, Paul A. 1937. "A note on measurement of utility." *Review of Economic Studies* 4: 155–61.

Samuelson, Paul A. 1967. "General proof that diversification pays," *Journal of Finance and Quantitative Analysis* 2: 1–13. Reprinted in *Collected Scientific Papers of Paul A. Samuelson*, Volume 2, ed. R. C. Merton. MIT Press, 1972.

Samuelson, Paul A. 1970. "The fundamental approximation theorem of portfolio analysis in terms of means, variances, and higher moments." *Review of Economic Studies* 37 (4): 537–542. Reprinted in *Collected Scientific Papers of Paul A. Samuelson*, Volume 3, ed. R. C. Merton. MIT Press.

Samuelson, Paul A. 1983. *Foundations of Economic Analysis*, enlarged edition. Harvard University Press.

Samuelson, Paul A. 1989. "The $\sqrt{N}$ law and repeated risktaking." In *Probability, Statistics, and Mathematics: Papers in Honor of Samuel Karlin*, ed. T. W. Anderson et al. Academic Press.

Samuelson, Paul A. 1990a. General Equilibrium Model for Parimutuel Track Odds. Working paper, MIT.

Samuelson, Paul A. 1990b. The Geometry of Friedman-Savage and Revealed Preference for Risk Taking. Working paper, MIT.

Sharpe, William F. 1964. "Capital asset prices: A theory of market equilibrium under conditions of risk." *Journal of Finance* 19: 425–442.

Tobin, James. 1958. "Liquidity preference as behavior towards risk." *Review of Economic Studies* 25: 65–86.

Tobin, James. 1969. "Comment on Borch and Feldstein." *Review of Economic Studies* 36 (105): 13–14.

Van der Wijk, J. 1939. *Inkomens- en vermogensverdeling*. De Erven F. Bohn N.V.

Weitzman, Martin. 1965. "Utility Analysis and Group Behavior: An Empirical Study." *Journal of Political Economy* 73: 18–26.

Ziemba, W. T., and D. B. Hausch. 1987. *Beat the Racetrack*. Wm. Morrow.

Poverty and Living Standards

Partha Dasgupta

General-equilibrium theory, to which Frank Hahn has made so many significant contributions, is a theory of interacting agents and agencies. At its broadest, it studies fundamental questions regarding the manner in which the fates of individuals and families are dependent upon the organization of society. The theory tends to assume background rights and privileges within whose rubric people pursue their own ends. Frank Hahn's most recent writings have often broached some of this wider motivation propelling general equilibrium theory. These writings reflect a clearly defined social-democratic political philosophy. What also stands out is that, in contrast with most other social scientists, Hahn's explorations in economics have had a strong influence on his political philosophy. The essay that follows is at the interface of economics and political philosophy. It is written in the spirit in which I imagine Frank Hahn would have written on the subject had he had the patience to study international data on living standards.

1 Plural Measures

Measures of well-being can take one of two forms: they can reflect the *constituents* of well-being, or they can be measures of the access that people have to the *determinants* of well-being. Indices of health, welfare, and freedom of choice (more specifically, basic liberties) are instances of the constituents of well-being; indices that reflect the availability of food, potable water, legal aid, education facilities, and health care, resources devoted to national security, and income in general are examples of the determinants.

There are strong analogies here with the way we think of the production and distribution of commodities and services. The constituents of well-being can be thought of as *outputs*, and the determinants of these constituents their *inputs*. If we know what we are after, then in principle a suitable measure of either on its own will be good enough. Thus, if we were to follow the first route, we would measure the constituents of well-being directly, and we would measure changes in well-being by studying changes in these constituents over time. If, on the other hand, we were to follow the second route, we would value all the goods and services that are determinants of well-being in terms of their social accounting prices, and we would arrive at an all-embracing measure of real national income. A great many of these accounting prices would be person-specific—since a great many of the goods would be *named goods*, to use Hahn's (1971)terminology—to account for differences in individual needs, household income, and so forth. Were the (relative) person-specific accounting prices to remain constant, increases in this ideal measure of real national income would reflect improvements in the quality of life. Put another way: When these ideal accounting prices are in use, economic growth—in other words, growth in net national product, is consonant with increased well-being.

All this is well known. In practice neither route on its own captures what we wish to see captured in any reasoned conception of the quality of life. For this reason, governments and international agencies take recourse to both, and it is today a commonplace to assess the standard of living in a country by studying a heterodox collection of socio-economic indicators. (See, for example, the annual *World Development Report* of the World Bank.)

This is not a new development. As early as 1954, a United Nations Expert Group (see United Nations 1954) recommended that, in addition to real per-capita income, use should be made of quantitative measures in the fields of health, education, employment, and housing for assessing the standard of living in a country. It has been a long journey since then, and if the cross-country socio-economic indicators in the annual *World Development Report* are any guide we may well be reaching a point where there is agreement on how the standard of living can effectively be measured. Quite obviously, some balance has to be struck between the claims of completeness and costs. But, all things considered, we now seem to be arriving at a consensus that, at a very aggregate level, real per-capita national income, life expectancy at birth, infant and child survival rates, and the adult literacy rate make up a comprehensive package of indices. To be sure, we would also be interested in the distribution of well-being along class. or caste, or gender, or regional lines. But it is the distribution of *these* indices we seem to seek today.

The rationale behind these measures isn't difficult to find. Life expectancy at birth, and, more generally, age-specific survival rates, reflect (albeit in a coarse way) the state of health. Now, health is an essential constituent of well-being; it not only affects welfare, it is an index of the inherent capacity of a person to be able to *do* things. The state of a person's health therefore provides us with an essential constitutive element of freedom.

Age-specific survival rates address life-and-death questions literally. It would be nice if we could include data that directly bear on *morbidity*, and not merely mortality. Unfortunately, morbidity data are unreliable indicators of actual health. Thus, for the most part such data have to be collected from questionnaires ("Have you been ill, or felt ill, over the past three days?") or from hospital records. Now, it is an interesting fact that, as actual health improves, morbidity rates based on such data often increase. This is because with growing wealth people's expectations about what good health consists of become more demanding. Illnesses which were not detected in earlier times are now acknowledged, the idea of "stress" gets amplified in the common culture, and so forth. This is not to say that morbidity rates and mortality rates must necessarily move together; it is merely to say that data on morbidity rates aren't at the moment reliable indicators of physical or mental health. More specifically, changes in morbidity data over time don't really reflect changes in the state of community health. For the moment, then, we will have to rely on mortality tables and their changes over time to get an idea the state of a community's health and its progress.

Measures of real income are different. They are indices of a person's command over goods and services. They can be seen as measures of welfare, and this is how they are usually treated in welfare economics. But they can also be seen as indices of the extent of choice, increases in real income denoting a widening of choice. And finally, the rate of adult literacy is almost invariably appealed to when the standard of living is discussed, because the literacy rate measures the extent of an ability that uniquely confers a wide variety of attendant advantages on people. The literature on human capital gives shape to the idea that formal education is a means to a widening of choice. Taken together, these four indices—per-capita national income, the infant survival rate, life expectancy at birth, and the adult literacy rate—would seem to make up a comprehensive package.

As one might expect, there are persistent and justifiable complaints against these indices—for example, that the informal sector does not get reflected in existing measures of real national income, or that a range of nonmarketed goods and services (such as a great deal of women's production in poor countries) don't get a look. But these are conceptual details. They are of profound importance, and their incorporation will require much work, but they don't involve any change of principle. It is only a matter of time before they find their way into national income figures.

The problems are compounded when we try to make international comparisons of living standards. Mercifully, this is not so for all the constituents of well-being. For example, infant survival rates, as rates, pose no problems for comparisons. Thus, the fact that India scores better on this count than, say, Pakistan (a richer country) is not in dispute. (See table 1.) There is also no dispute over how we should interpret this fact when we come to making a comparison of living standards in these two countries. The serious difficulties lie in international comparisons of national income.

In a pioneering research program undertaken by Irving Kravis and his associates, one aspect of the problem of making international comparisons has been attacked to great effect: namely, correcting for the fact that at official exchange rates domestic currencies differ in their purchasing powers. As it happens, the ranking of poor countries in terms of real national income per-capita is quite different when corrections are made for this fact. This is immediate if one compares the first column of figures in table 2 with the ranking of countries on the basis of per-capita national income in World Bank 1986. Nevertheless, the Kravis adjustments involve only better measurement; they do not involve any matter of fundamental principle.

What I want to argue in this article is something else. I want to argue that the current consensus on ways of measuring the quality of life is premature, because these measures are misleading. They neglect aspects of living of the most profound value to personhood. Later in this article we will try and see how some of these aspects can be included in measures of well-being, and I shall provide a preliminary ranking of the world's poorest countries on this wider basis. I shall also compare this new ranking with those based on customary measures of the living standard. Finally, I shall ask whether as a matter of fact poor countries are faced with cruel choices among competing constituents of well-being.

2 Environmental Degradation and Net National Product

Before coming to those neglected aspects of the quality of life, which later in this article I will be able to include in making international comparisons, I want to say something about an aspect that, for lack of data, I will be forced to ignore. It also involves a matter of principle. It concerns the attitude we ought to have toward the depreciation of capital assets.

For the most part, the figures for real national income that we see are for *gross* national income. If one digs deeper, one can obtain estimates of *net* national income. But as customarily measured, this only deducts the depreciation of manufactured capital. It does not recognize environmental capital assets and, more generally, stocks of natural resources. Real net national product, when correctly measured, is an index of sustainable consumption. As it is currently measured, ignoring as it does environmental degradation, net national product does not reflect sustainable consumption.

Now, this practice of ignoring environmental assets is not only odd, it is pernicious. Environmental resources, such as the atmosphere, underground and surface water, fisheries, bird and animal species, forests, soil, and soil cover, are all part of our capital assets. Some of them offer pure amenities, some are essential for the production of goods and services, and many offer both sorts of service. So too are exhaustible resources a part of our capital assets. Resources such as oil, natural gas, and minerals cannot, of course, be accused of offering us direct amenities, but they are vital in the production of goods and services, some of which *are* amenities. Indeed, *all* production and consumption are based ultimately on natural resources.

Stocks of environmental natural resources have to be measured in different ways, depending on the resource in question: in mass units (e.g. for soil cover and wood biomass), in quality indices (e.g. ambient air and water quality indices), in volume units (e.g. acre-feet for aquifers), and so on. A decline in their stock is a signal of a possible environmental problem. However, despite their importance, we have little quantitative feel for the extent of these stocks and the changes in these stocks brought in their wake by the passage of time, and by the activities of production and consumption. There are countries which suffer from an almost total paucity of information on the extent of their forest cover, rates of soil erosion, water supply, and so forth. As matters stand, estimates of net national product are based on the assumption that environmental natural resources *on site* are all free goods. Consequently, these estimates are biased, and they are biased upward. Moreover, it is also almost certainly the case that growth rates of net national product in poor countries, as customarily measured, are higher than what in truth they are. This is because there is overwhelming evidence that, in the aggregate, environmental resources are currently being depleted in poor countries—in quality, in quantity, or in both. Thus, for example, a 2 percent annual growth rate of per-capita gross national product for a country is no indication that net national product per-capita has not in fact declined. For the moment, however, such valuable documents as the *State of the Environment* reports issued by the Centre for Science and Environment in New Delhi and the World Resources Institute in Washington, D.C. (see CSE 1982, 1986; WRI/IIED 1987) fall on one end of the spectrum—there is no economic evaluation at all of environmental resources—and national income accounts fall on the other. The gap between the two remains unjustifiable.

3 Political and Civil Liberties

All this, important though it is, is not nearly enough. Well-being is a more complex concept. The quality of life involves much more. The indices I have referred to thus far, namely health, education, and income, are what are often called socio-economic indicators of well-being. They say nothing about the political and civil liberties people may or may not be enjoying. But to ignore them when we evaluate the quality of life is simply grotesque. It is also to live in an intellectual world disconnected from life. In the now-enormous literature on applied welfare and development economics (for example, Morris 1979; Sen 1981), there is practically nothing that looks at the quality of life in the way living and breathing people realize it.

This neglect of what are often given the more general label *human rights* is indefensible. Today, in the light of what has been happening in Eastern Europe and, in their contrasting ways, what was experienced in China in June 1989 and in India in November 1989, this neglect is also ironic. The international comparisons of living standards routinely published in the World Bank's *World Development Report*, which are the ones most frequently cited, are based solely on the socio-economic constituents of well-being. The consensus I spoke of earlier among development economists is, of course, a consensus on what is to be included in *this* set of constituents.

Consider as an example UNDP 1990, which ranks countries in terms of a human development index (HDI). Now, the HDI is a cardinal index and it is based on three ingredients: per-capita national income, life expectancy at birth, and adult literacy rate. But it is recognized in the document that suitable (increasing) transformations need to be applied to life expectancy at birth and to the adult literacy rate before they are entered into the aggregate index. The point is that an increase in life expectancy at birth from, say, 39 years to 40 years does not reflect the same achievement as an increase from 69 years to 70 years. The transformation which is applied to life expectancy at birth captures this fact. The same argument is made for the adult literacy rate.

But all this finessing is applied to the socio-economic indicators of well-being, and the HDI has nothing to say on what Berlin (1969) called *negative liberties*, or what in common parlance we call the protection and promotion of human rights. The HDI is rather like an air plane on the design of whose engine attention has been lavished, but which can't fly because it has no wings.

As it happens, there *are* internationally comparable indices of the extent to which citizens enjoy rights to political and civil liberties. There are several extant sets of indices. (See Dasgupta and Weale 1990 for an account.) They differ much the way national income estimates differ. As with any other index, there are subjective elements in their construction. Moreover, they are an incomplete list, for political and civil rights do not cover all negative rights. There are others, such as for example those which are all too frequently violated by political and economic discrimination founded upon ethnic, linguistic, religious, or regional identities. I don't know enough about quantitative measures in these spheres. So I am forced to ignore them. Despite this, the plural measure we will be looking at is a good deal better than measures of the standard of living currently offered in the literature.

I am interested here in the quality of life in poor countries. The criterion I will use for judging poverty is low per-capita income. For reasons which will become clearer later, we will consider countries which in 1970 enjoyed a per-capita national income less than $1,500 in 1980 international dollars. The year we want to study is 1979–1980. As it happens, comparable data on all the six constituents of well-being that I want to study here are available for only 48 of the more than 55 countries which should be on our list.

Table 1 summarizes the data. Countries are listed alphabetically. The first column provides estimates of per-capita national income for the year 1980. The second, third, and fourth columns present life expectancy at birth, infant mortality rates and adult literacy rates, respectively, for the year 1980. (See World Bank 1986, 1989.) They require no explanation.

The fifth and sixth columns represent indices of political and civil rights in our sample of countries for the year 1979. They have been taken from Taylor and Jodice 1983. Political rights are taken here to be the right on the part of citizens to play a part in determining who governs their country, and what the laws are and will be. Countries are coded with scores ranging from 1 (highest degree of liberty) to 7 (lowest degree of liberty).

Table 1
Living-standards indicators for 1980.

	Y	E	M	L	R1	R2
Bangladesh	540.0	48.0	140.0	26.0	4.0	4.0
Benin	534.0	47.0	124.0	28.0	7.0	7.0
Bolivia	1529.0	50.0	130.0	63.0	3.0	5.0
Botswana	1477.0	55.0	78.0	35.0	3.0	2.0
Burundi	333.0	46.0	126.0	25.0	6.0	7.0
C. A. R.	487.0	47.0	143.0	33.0	7.0	7.0
Chad	353.0	42.0	147.0	15.0	6.0	6.0
China	1619.0	67.0	41.0	69.0	6.0	6.0
Ecuador	2607.0	63.0	75.0	81.0	3.0	5.0
Egypt	995.0	58.0	108.0	44.0	5.0	5.0
Ethiopia	325.0	44.0	155.0	15.0	7.0	7.0
Gambia	556.0	40.0	159.0	15.0	2.0	2.0
Haiti	696.0	52.0	132.0	23.0	6.0	7.0
Honduras	1075.0	60.0	87.0	60.0	3.0	6.0
India	614.0	54.0	107.0	36.0	3.0	2.0
Indonesia	1063.0	53.0	105.0	62.0	5.0	5.0
Jordan	1885.0	62.0	58.0	70.0	6.0	6.0
Kenya	662.0	55.0	83.0	47.0	5.0	5.0
Korea	2369.0	67.0	32.0	93.0	5.0	5.0
Lesotho	694.0	52.0	116.0	52.0	4.0	5.0
Liberia	680.0	52.0	100.0	25.0	4.0	6.0
Madagascar	589.0	51.0	146.0	50.0	5.0	5.0
Malawi	417.0	44.0	169.0	25.0	6.0	6.0
Mali	356.0	44.0	184.0	10.0	7.0	7.0
Mauritania	576.0	43.0	142.0	17.0	6.0	6.0
Mauritius	1484.0	65.4	45.2	85.0	2.0	4.0
Morocco	1199.0	57.0	102.0	28.0	4.0	3.0
Nepal	490.0	45.1	142.2	19.0	6.0	5.0
Niger	441.0	42.0	150.0	10.0	6.0	7.0
Nigeria	824.0	48.0	118.0	34.0	3.0	5.0
Pakistan	989.0	49.0	124.0	24.0	5.0	6.0
Paraguay	1979.0	66.0	47.0	84.0	5.0	5.0
Philippines	1551.0	61.0	52.0	75.0	5.0	5.0
Rwanda	379.0	45.0	127.0	50.0	5.0	6.0
Senegal	744.0	45.0	147.0	10.0	3.0	4.0
Sierra L.	512.0	38.0	172.0	15.0	5.0	6.0
Somalia	415.0	44.0	147.0	60.0	7.0	7.0
Sri Lanka	1199.0	68.0	34.0	85.0	3.0	2.0
Sudan	724.4	46.0	123.0	32.0	5.0	5.0
Swaziland	1079.0	51.7	133.4	65.0	6.0	5.0
Tanzania	353.0	50.0	119.0	79.0	6.0	6.0
Thailand	1694.0	62.0	51.0	86.0	4.0	6.0
Tunisia	1845.0	60.4	91.8	62.0	6.0	5.0
Uganda	257.0	46.0	113.0	52.0	7.0	7.0
Yemen	957.0	42.9	163.7	21.0	7.0	7.0
Zaire	224.0	49.0	111.0	55.0	6.0	7.0
Zambia	716.0	50.1	90.4	44.0	5.0	5.0
Zimbabwe	930.0	55.0	82.4	69.0	5.0	5.0

Civil rights are, of course, quite different. They are rights the individual has *vis à vis* the state, consituting the right to justice. Thus, civil society is the sphere of autonomous institutions, protected by the rule of law, in which men and women may conduct their business freely and independently of the state. Of particular importance are freedom of the press and other media concerned with the dissemination of information, and the independence of the judiciary. The index we are interested in here measures the extent to which people, because they are protected by an independent press and judiciary, are openly able to express their opinions without fear of reprisal. Countries are coded with scores ranging from 1 (highest degree of liberty) to 7 (lowest degree of liberty).

A mere glance at these columns tells us that, for the most part, political and civil liberties are scarce goods in poor countries. Citizens of 33 nations in our sample of 48 countries suffer from systems that score 5 or more for political rights, and those of no fewer than 40 nations from systems that score 5 or more for civil rights. (A score of 5 for political rights amounts to a system in which elections are controlled closely or are limited, or in which election results have little significance. A score of 5 for civil rights amounts to a system in which civil rights are often denied, but in which there is no doctrine on which the denial is based. The media are often weak, controlled by the government, and censored.) There are exceptions, of course, most notably Botswana, Gambia, India, Mauritius, and Sri Lanka. But for the most part the columns make for dismal reading. And when they are combined with the columns that reflect income, education, and the state of health, the picture that emerges is chilling. There is nothing to commend the state of affairs in a large number of the countries in our sample.

Our international comparison of living standards will be based on these six indices. Patently, they reflect only a limited aspect of the idea of well-being. But as an approximation, they together are a good deal better than those currently offered in the empirical literature. Now, the quality of the data being what it is for a great many of the countries, it is unwise to rely on their cardinal magnitudes. In any event, the political and civil rights indicators do not have any cardinal significance. We will therefore base our comparison on an ordinal measure. But first, we need an ordinal aggregator. Of the many one may devise, the one best known and most studied is the Borda Rule. In what follows we will construct the Borda ranking of the countries in our sample.

The first six columns in table 2 present country rankings for the six constituents of the standard of living under study; seventh column presents their implied Borda ranking. Rankings for per-capita national income, life expectancy at birth, and the adult literacy rate go up from the worst (score of 1) to the best (score of 48). Rankings for infant mortality rate and political and civil rights go up from the best (score of 1) to the worst. The Borda ranking given in the seventh column is arranged from the worst-off country (score of 1) to the best (score of 48).

It is a useful exercise first of all to look at the best- and worst-off sets of countries. From the seventh column, we note that, in *ascending* order of the standard of living, the ten lowest-ranked countries in 1980 were Niger, Mali, Ethiopia, Yemen, Sierra Leone, Chad, Mauritania. Burundi, Malawi, and Benin. How does this list compare with the ranking of nations based exclusively on per-capita national income? To see this, merely note from the first column that, in ascending order, the ten poorest countries in our sample in 1980 were Zaire, Uganda, Ethiopia, Burundi, Chad and Tanzania (tied at 5), Mali, Rwanda, Somalia and Malawi. The lists aren't the same, but they are strikingly similar. All but one (Yemen) of the countries are in sub-Sahara Africa, and the lists contain five countries in common.

Turning next to the ten highest-ranked countries, we note first that in terms of living standard they are, in descending order, Sri Lanka, the Republic of Korea, Mauritius, Paraguay, Ecuador, the Philippines, Tunisia, Zimbabwe, Thailand and China. I don't know if this list should come as a surprise. As it happens, it is quite similar to the list of the ten most affluent countries in our sample, which are, in descending order, Ecuador, the Republic of Korea, Paraguay, Jordan, Tunisia, Thailand, China, the Philippines, Bolivia and Mauritius. There are eight countries in common. We conclude tentatively that, among the poorest of poor nations, rankings in terms of the standard of living are not too different from rankings based on per-capita income.

But this is a qualitative claim, and it will be informative to get a quantitative feel for the relationship between our Borda ranking and each of the rankings based on the six constituents of well-being. Statistically. how close *is* the Borda ranking to the other six? It transpires that the Spearman correlation coefficient between the Borda rankings and the others are 0.79 with national income per-capita, 0.91 with life expectancy at birth, 0.86 with the infant survival rate; 0.85 with the adult literacy rate, 0.52 with political rights, and 0.64 with civil rights. I wasn't expecting this. I had no

Table 2
Rankings of living-standards data.

	Y	E	M	L	R1	R2	BORDA
Bangladesh	16	19	34	16	11	6	23
Benin	15	17	27	17	42	38	10
Bolivia	40	23	31	36	3	9	31
Botswana	38	33	10	22	3	1	34
Burundi	4	14	29	13	29	38	8
C. A. R.	12	17	37	20	42	38	11
Chad	5	3	40	4	29	26	6
China	42	46	3	38	29	26	39
Ecuador	48	43	9	43	3	9	44
Egypt	32	37	20	24	16	9	33
Ethiopia	3	7	43	4	42	38	3
Gambia	17	2	44	4	1	1	14
Haiti	24	28	32	11	29	38	12
Honduras	34	38	13	32	3	26	27
India	20	32	19	23	3	1	35
Indonesia	33	31	18	34	16	9	38
Jordan	45	41	8	40	29	26	36
Kenya	21	33	12	26	16	9	32
Korea	47	46	1	48	16	9	47
Lesotho	23	28	23	29	11	9	29
Liberia	22	28	16	13	11	26	21
Madagascar	19	26	39	27	16	9	28
Malawi	10	7	46	13	29	26	9
Mali	7	7	48	1	42	38	2
Mauritania	18	6	35	8	29	26	7
Mauritius	39	44	4	45	1	6	46
Morocco	36	36	17	17	11	5	30
Nepal	13	13	36	9	29	9	19
Niger	11	3	42	1	29	38	1
Nigeria	28	19	24	21	3	9	24
Pakistan	31	21	27	12	16	26	17
Paraguay	46	45	5	44	16	9	45
Philippines	41	40	7	41	16	9	43
Rwanda	8	11	30	27	16	26	18
Senegal	27	11	40	1	3	6	16
Sierra L.	14	1	47	4	16	26	5
Somalia	9	7	38	32	42	38	13
Sri Lanka	36	48	2	45	3	1	48
Sudan	26	14	26	19	16	9	22
Swaziland	35	27	33	37	29	9	37
Tanzania	5	23	25	42	29	26	25
Thailand	43	41	6	47	11	26	40
Tunisia	44	39	15	34	29	9	42
Uganda	2	14	22	29	42	38	15
Yemen	30	5	45	10	42	38	4
Zaire	1	21	21	31	29	38	20
Zambia	25	25	14	24	16	9	26
Zimbabwe	29	33	11	38	16	9	41

reason for thinking that "health-related" indices would be the closest to our measure of the standard of living. If we had, therefore, to choose a single ordinal measure of living standard, life expectancy at birth would appear to be the best that is available. There must be a moral in this.

4 Are There Tradeoffs between the Socio-Economic Sphere and the Political and Civil Spheres of Citizenship?

International comparisons of well-being tell us something about the natures of differing societies. We have seen how we can determine whether those countries that were relatively prosperous in 1979–1980 were also the ones where political and civil liberties were least constrained. But a cross-section study at one date can't tell us anything about a matter all of us at some time or other have queried and argued about: Are civil and political liberties *conducive* to growth in the socio-economic constituents of the standard of living? Or, in euphemistic terms: Do "authoritarian" governments achieve better "economic" results? Or, to put it bluntly: Are civil and political liberties a "luxury" that poor countries can't afford, in that they act as a drag on economic growth?

It would be impertinent to suggest that this sort of question has an airtight answer. But cross-sectional data on countries can give us some hints. In what follows I shall summarize the results I have reported in Dasgupta 1990.

It will be noticed that the issue we are discussing now is quite different from an international comparison of living standards. What we want to do is to ask whether, over a given period of time, the countries that *on average* enjoyed greater political and civil liberties were also the ones that enjoyed the greatest *improvements* in the socio-economic constituents of well-being. On this, the most comprehensive set of data that I have been able to locate for the 48 countries in our sample are for the decade of the 1970s. The main conclusions that one can reach with the data are the following.

• Political and civil rights, averaged over the decade, were *positively* and *significantly* correlated with growth in national income per capita, with improvements in life expectancy at birth, and with improvements in infant survival rates. Thus, the countries that over the decade enjoyed on average greater political and civil liberties were also the ones that performed best in terms of growth in per-capita national income, improvements in life expectancy at birth, and infant survival rates.

• Increases in per-capita national income were positively and significantly correlated with improvements in longevity and infant survival.

• Political and civil rights, while not the same, were strongly and significantly correlated.

• Improvements in adult literacy weren't correlated significantly with per-capita national income, or with its growth, or with improvements in infant survival rates. But they were *negatively* and *significantly* correlated with political and civil liberties.

These conclusions suggest that literacy stands apart somewhat from other goods. Regimes that had bad records in political and civil rights were associated with good performance in the field of adult literacy. I have no compelling explanation for this.

Of course, correlation doesn't imply causation. But the exercise does suggest that the claim that restrictions in political and civil liberties are necessary for growth in the socio-economic constituents of well-being in poor countries is belied by data. To me, and quite plainly to Frank Hahn, this is reassuring.

Acknowledgment

I am most grateful to Martin Weale for many helpful discussions on the subject matter of this article. Section 3 is based on joint work by us (Dasgupta and Weale 1990).

References

Berlin, I. 1959. "Two concepts of liberty." In *Four Essays on Liberty*. Oxford University Press.

CSE. 1982, 1986. *The State of India's Environment*. New Delhi: Centre for Science and Development.

Dasgupta, P. 1990. "Well-being and the extent of its realization in poor countries." *Economic Journal* (supplement): 100.

Dasgupta, P., and M. Weale. 1990. On the Measurement of Well-Being. Mimeo, Stanford University.

Hahn, F. 1971. "Equilibrium with transaction costs." *Econometrica* 39.

Morris, M. D. 1979. *Measuring the Condition of the World's Poor: The Physical Quality of Life Index*. Pergamon.

Sen, A. 1981. "Public action and the quality of life in developing countries." *Oxford Bulletin of Economics and Statistics* 43.

Taylor, C. L. and D. A. Jodice. 1983. *World Handbook of Political and Social Indicators*, Vol. 1 Yale University Press.

United Nations. 1954. *International Definition and Measurement of Standards and Levels of Living.*

United Nations Environment Programme. 1990. *Human Development Report.*

World Bank. 1986. *World Development Report*. Oxford University Press.

WRI/IIED. 1987. *World Resources* 1987 Basic Books.

Contributors

Kenneth J. Arrow Stanford University
Anthony Barnes Atkinson London School of Economics
Robert J. Aumann Hebrew University of Jerusalem
Christopher Bliss Nuffield College, Oxford
Adam Brandenburger Harvard University
Pierre-André Chiappori DELTA, Paris
Partha Dasgupta Stanford University and University of Cambridge
Peter A. Diamond Massachusetts Institute of Technology
Pradeep Dubey State University of New York, Stony Brook
Jayasri Dutta Columbia University
Douglas Gale Boston University
John Geanakoplos Yale University
Terence Gorman Nuffield College, Oxford
Roger Guesnerie DELTA, Paris
Peter J. Hammond Stanford University
Oliver Hart Massachusetts Institute of Technology
Walter P. Heller University of California, San Diego
Timothy J. Kehoe University of Minnesota
David Kreps Stanford University
Mordecai Kurz Stanford University
David K. Levine University of California, Los Angles
Louis Makowski University of California, Davis
Andreu Mas-Colell Harvard University
Eric Maskin Harvard University
James A. Mirrlees Nuffield College, Oxford
David M. Newbery University of Cambridge
Joseph M. Ostroy University of California, Los Angeles
Heraklis Polemarchakis Université Catholique de Louvain
Roy Radner Bell Laboratories
Hamid Sabourian University of Cambridge
Paul A. Samuelson Massachusetts Institute of Technology
Robert M. Solow Massachusetts Institute of Technology
David A. Starrett Stanford University
Joseph E. Stiglitz Stanford University
Michael Woodford University of Chicago

Index